# Managerial Marketing for Industrial Firms

# Managerial Marketing for Industrial Firms

## B. CHARLES AMES
Chairman and CEO, ACME-Cleveland Corp.

## JAMES D. HLAVACEK
Weatherhead School of Management
Case Western Reserve University

RANDOM HOUSE
BUSINESS DIVISION    NEW YORK

*This book is dedicated to our understanding and supportive partners,*
*Jay Ames and Ursula Hlavacek.*

First Edition
987654321
Copyright © 1984 by Random House, Inc.

Library of Congress Cataloging in Publication Data

Ames, B. Charles.
    Managerial marketing for industrial firms.

    Includes index.
    1. Industrial marketing.    2. Marketing management.
I. Hlavacek, James D.    II. Title.
HF5415.A596    1984        658.8        83-15996
ISBN 0-394-33583-X

Manufactured in the United States of America

Design by Jennie Nichols/Levavi & Levavi

# Advisor's Foreword

Industrial marketing as a field of study in collegiate schools of business has been around for a long time. But in recent years the field has enjoyed dramatic growth, as more and more students have recognized the challenges and opportunities offered by careers in industrial marketing and business schools have responded with more and expanded course offerings in the field. Indeed, industrial marketing is now probably one of the fastest growing areas in the entire marketing curriculum in both business schools and executive development programs.

Yet, in spite of this renewed interest and growth in industrial marketing, something has been missing. Existing marketing texts have not kept up with the dramatic changes occurring in the world of industrial marketing, nor do they offer the kind of perspectives and up-to-date knowledge needed to meet these changes successfully.

*Managerial Marketing for Industrial Firms* by Ames and Hlavacek closes this gap in marketing management and industrial marketing. Ames, a leading practitioner with a broad range of experience in industrial marketing, and Hlavacek, a distinguished academic authority in the field, have collaborated to create a truly outstanding text. Ames' insights and depth of expertise gained from an insider's view of industrial marketing and Hlavacek's broad range of knowledge of the field are combined in a high-quality text that is both practical and academically sound.

Stressing a marketing management approach to industrial marketing, the authors show how modern marketing management concepts and methods can be applied in the realm of industrial marketing. All phases of industrial marketing are thoroughly covered within a strategic marketing management framework, and the authors illuminate the field with a coherent body of knowledge unrivaled by previous texts.

These innovations have not come at the cost of pedagogical strength. On the contrary, as an industry leader and leading academic, both authors recognize the importance of effective communication, and they have taken great care to make their text immediate and accessible. Throughout each chapter, carefully developed vignettes and interesting examples are used to show the kinds of problems and issues faced by managers, and thoroughly developed discussions are presented of the types of analyses, decisions, and actions that are required of managers to deal with these problems and issues. Chapter summaries, review questions, and a set of complete in-depth cases contribute further to making this text the best learning resource available for all serious students of marketing management and industrial marketing.

*Managerial Marketing for Industrial Firms* is an important contribution to the field of marketing and will have far-reaching effects on future thought and practice in the field. As the advisor in marketing for Random House, I am delighted and proud to be associated with this outstanding text.

Bert Rosenbloom
Drexel University

v

# Preface

The goal of *Managerial Marketing for Industrial Firms* is to provide a text on industrial or business-to-business marketing that is substantive, focused on the management requirements to make the marketing process pay off, and interesting to read. While a number of other books have been written about industrial marketing, some tend to be superficial, many are too process oriented, most indicate limited first-hand understanding of the managerial requirements, and, finally, most tend to be dull. *Managerial Marketing for Industrial Firms* overcomes these major deficiencies and fills a critical need in both the academic world and the field of life-long executive education.

This book is not intended as a primer for a beginning marketing course. Rather, it is a multilevel management book that describes what management must do to make marketing a more powerful force in the industrial or technically based firm. Its focus is on the understanding management must have of the industrial marketing process and the role management must play to make the company operate effectively around the marketing concept.

*Managerial Marketing for Industrial Firms* should be of interest and practical value to serious students who want to learn more about marketing in industrial or technically based firms where the majority of them will build their careers. It should also be of interest to any employee or practitioner who aspires to a career in general management and, therefore, needs to learn more about the requirements for effectively managing marketing activities. Finally, it should be of use to CEOs and senior managers who want to ensure that marketing is the powerful force it should be in their industrial or technically based businesses.

## ORGANIZATION

*Managerial Marketing for Industrial Firms* is structured around six parts that include 17 chapters and 15 case studies.

Part I provides the background information necessary to think and talk intelligently about industrial marketing. It defines the marketing concept in the industrial world, describes the differences between industrial and consumer markets, and explains how industrial organizations make their buying decisions.

Part II is designed to deepen the reader's understanding of how industrial markets are structured and how to determine the requirements for effectively serving these markets. It outlines the kind of knowledge that one must have about potential customers and competition and also explains the importance of segmenting industrial markets so that meaningful assessments of potential and opportunities can be developed.

Part III covers the key components of the industrial marketing mix: (1) product development, (2) pricing, (3) sales and distributor management, and (4) advertising and promotion. Each component is discussed in terms of the difficulties many firms encounter and the strategies and managerial actions required to overcome these problems.

Part IV outlines the procedure and management requirements for developing and evaluating sound marketing/business strategies and plans fully geared to achieve corporate objectives. The section also describes the important link between corporate and product-market strategies and operational plans and how to determine whether this link exists as plans are reviewed.

Part V discusses the organization alternatives that

might be employed to structure and integrate the marketing function with other disciplines and describes the key considerations that would lead to an election of one organization alternative over another. It also spells out in some detail when and how to use a product-market management approach effectively. Finally, it concludes with a summary of management principles that should be followed to ensure effective implementation not only in marketing, but in all business activities.

Obviously missing are discrete chapters on strategy development and international marketing. These subjects have been woven into material where they apply, rather than presented as abstract discussions in separate chapters.

Part VI includes 15 case studies for classroom or executive development use.

While there is logic to the sequence of chapters, each chapter is a freestanding module and informative on its own. This adds a great deal of flexibility to the way the book is read and used. For the reader who is new to the marketing scene, it probably makes sense to stick reasonably close to the chapter sequence, since the early chapters provide a foundation of understanding. For readers with marketing experience, the text may be regarded as a reference book, and chapters can be selected for reading according to particular interests or current needs.

## FEATURES

*Managerial Marketing for Industrial Firms* contains many exciting features and pedagogical aids.

### Vignettes

A brief vignette or mini-case outlines a real-life situation relating to the chapter that follows. The characters and companies involved in each vignette are disguised, but the situations are drawn from the authors' first-hand experiences. The purpose of the vignette is to show the reader the kinds of problems that occur daily in the business world and introduce the central theme of the chapter. The chapter itself discusses the issues raised by the vignette and prescribes the managerial actions required to correct and avoid such situations.

### Exhibits

Exhibits—consisting of schematics, flowcharts, business memoranda, and industrial marketing advertisements—appear frequently throughout the text to illustrate important concepts.

### Boxed Examples

Each chapter contains several extended examples of real-life successes, failures, and news-making trends in the industrial world, all relating to the principles under discussion. Because these examples are more in-depth than other examples appearing in the book, they have been extracted from the text and boxed to allow for easier use and to avoid interrupting the presentation of substantive material.

### Summaries

A summary of the chapter content appears at the end of each chapter to reinforce important points and to provide a valuable tool for study.

### Discussion Questions

Discussion questions also appear at the end of each chapter to stimulate class discussion and to signal students to the important concepts they should understand.

### Case Studies

Part VI is comprised of case studies that may be used to supplement the text. The cases, written by the authors and by other acknowledged experts in the field, are of varying length and have been carefully chosen to complement the text material and reinforce the general business philosophy presented in the text.

### Indices

*Managerial Marketing for Industrial Firms* contains two separate indices. The name index is comprised of the names of the many well-known executives, academics, and firms mentioned throughout the text and in source notes. The subject index that follows is a comprehensive compilation of the many topics covered in the text.

# Acknowledgments

While we are entirely responsible for writing this book, many people made some very helpful contributions.

First we owe a thank you to Ted Alfred, Dean of the Weatherhead School of Management at Case Western Reserve University, who served as a matchmaker in bringing us together. We are also very indebted to the hundreds of managers, from a wide range of industries, who influenced our thinking. These managers and their corporations served as our laboratories to observe good and bad marketing management practice.

There were a number of people who provided us with specific examples, materials, approaches, and constructive comments. They were: Igor Ansoff, Ray Corey, Bob Garda, Dick Grimm, George Havens, Dick Hill, Phil Hofmann, Cary Kizilbash, Joe Leonard, Don Manning, Mike Marvin, Tommy McCuistion, Roger More, Jim Narus, Derek Newton, Emory Orahood, Mohan Reddy, Stu Rich, Sara Roche, Paul Ruckman, Adrian Ryans, Ron Schill, Milt Shapiro, Don Sommers, Ralph Sorenson, John Thanopoulous, Ulrich Weichman, Bo Wennerbom, and Tim Wilson.

The writing and rewriting of chapters created an enormous typing task. We are grateful to Cheryl Guizzotti, Adrienne Koppenhaver, Anita Nuibe, and Debbie White for wading through our notations and deciphering our handwriting.

Special appreciation is due to the reviewers who helped us fine-tune our manuscript: Peter J. LaPlaca, *University of Connecticut—Storrs*; Lynn J. Loudenback, *Iowa State University*; Timothy L. Wilson, *Indiana University of Pennsylvania*.

We would also like to thank the following people for their contributions to the review process: Russell W. Belk, *University of Utah*; Harper Boyd, *University of Arkansas at Little Rock*; Timothy M. DeVinney, *Vanderbilt University*; Ben M. Enis, *University of Southern California*; Harold H. Kassarjian, *UCLA*; E. Laird Landon, *University of Houston*; H. Lee Mathews, *The Ohio State University*; John G. Myers, *University of California, Berkeley*; Francesco Nicosia, *University of California, Berkeley*; John K. Ryans, Jr., *Kent State University*; Hans B. Thorelli, *Indiana University*; David T. Wilson, *The Pennsylvania State University*.

Finally, we would like to thank our partners at Random House who have contributed so much to the text.

# Contents in Brief

**I**  ESTABLISHING THE FOUNDATIONS  1

1 The Substance of Industrial Marketing  2
2 Industrial and Consumer Markets  17
3 How Business Organizations Buy  33

**II**  EVALUATING THE MARKET ENVIRONMENT  65

4 Understanding Customers and Competition  66
5 Segmenting Business Markets  90
6 Assessing Business Markets  110

**III**  MANAGING THE MARKETING MIX  139

7 Product Development  140
8 Pricing for Profit  169
9 Competitive Bidding  186
10 Linking Sales to Marketing  203
11 Marketing with Distributor Partners  221
12 Advertising and Promotion  245

**IV**  DEVELOPING AND EVALUATING PLANS  269

13 Developing Strategies and Plans  270
14 Evaluating Strategies and Plans  299

**V**     **STRUCTURING AND MANAGING THE ORGANIZATION**     **315**

**15** Organization Alternatives     316
**16** Product-Market Management     337
**17** Guidelines for Effective Implementation     362

**VI**     **CASE STUDIES**     **375**

# Detailed Contents

INTRODUCTION   xvi

## I   ESTABLISHING THE FOUNDATIONS   1

### 1   THE SUBSTANCE OF INDUSTRIAL MARKETING   2
Where Marketing Fails   4
Understanding the Concepts: Key Dimensions   5
Commitment to Action   6
   Functional Cooperation   7
   Investing for the Long Term   8
   Facing Up to Deficiencies   9
Implementing the Concept   10
   Qualified People   11
   Reliable Information   12
   Strategic Planning   13
Summary   16
Review Questions   16

### 2   INDUSTRIAL AND CONSUMER MARKETS   17
Derived Demand   20
Narrower Customer Base   21
More Rational Buying Decisions   22
More Buying Influences and Locations   22
Different Basis for Segmentation   23
Greater Importance of Technology   23
Multinational Markets   23
Greater Interdepartmental Dependence   24
Customer Contact   28

Multiplicity of Markets and Channels   29
Less End-User Information   29
Product Management   30
Key Part of Long-Term Strategy   31
Summary   31
Review Questions   32

### 3   HOW BUSINESS ORGANIZATIONS BUY   33
Multiple Buying Influences   36
   The Purchasing Manager   37
   Engineering and Production   39
   The Buying Committee   39
Planning Material Needs   40
Economic-Based Buying   41
Value Analysis   42
   How Value Analysis Works   43
   Analyzing Prices and Costs   43
   Guiding Product Development   45
   Reverse Engineering   45
Standards and Specifications   47
   Why Have Specifications?   48
   Writing and Influencing Specifications   48
Sourcing Decisions   50
   Make or Buy Situations   50
   Customer Make Decision   52
   Selling to "Make-Buy" Customers   54
   Sole Sourcing   55
   Developing Sources of Supply   56
   Evaluating Suppliers   57
Maintaining the Relationship   59
Summary   61
Review Questions   61
Appendix: Government Buying   62

## II     EVALUATING THE MARKET ENVIRONMENT     65

**4  UNDERSTANDING CUSTOMERS AND COMPETITION     66**
Understanding Customers     68
  Customers' Operations and Products     68
  Customers' Costs     70
  End-User Cost-Benefit     75
Understanding Competitors     79
  Competitive Structure     79
  Competitor Economics     80
  Market Success Factors     81
Marketing Strategy Implications     87
Summary     89
Review Questions     89

**5  SEGMENTING BUSINESS MARKETS     90**
Foundations for Business Strategy     92
Errors in Segmenting the Market     93
  Thinking Too Broad     93
  Thinking Too Narrow     94
  Misusing the Consumer Goods Approach     96
Segmenting the Business     96
  Segmenting by OEM, User, and Aftermarkets     96
  Segmenting by SICs     98
  Segmenting by End-Use Application     101
  Segmenting by Common Buyer Factors     102
  Two Other Segmentation Approaches     103
Combining Segmentation Levels     103
  Too Few or Too Many Segments     104
Validating a Market Segment     105
Segmenting and Resegmenting     107
Responsibility for Segmentation     108
Summary     109
Review Questions     109

**6  ASSESSING BUSINESS MARKETS     110**
Assessing Current Market Position     112
  Internal Sales Analysis     113
  Pressure Point (Rate of Change) Curves     115
Estimating Market Potential     119
  Defining the Market     119

Historical Data     119
Derived Demand     122
Trade Association Sources     122
Conversion Factors     122
Conducting Market Studies     123
  Specifying Information Needed     124
  Secondary Market Studies     124
  Primary Market Studies     125
  Data Analysis     130
  New Product-Market Studies     130
Project Proposals     131
Frameworks for Evaluating Market Segments     134
Summary     137
Review Questions     137

## III     MANAGING THE MARKETING MIX     139

**7  PRODUCT DEVELOPMENT     140**
The Product Life Cycle     142
  Better Mousetraps     142
  New Technologies     145
Bettering the Chances: Principles of New Product Development     148
  Defining the Right Product-Market Focus     150
  Facing Up to Cost and Performance Deficiencies     150
  Pruning the Existing Line     152
  Linkage to the Business Plan     155
  Following a Disciplined Process     156
  Matching Future Products and Current Profits     159
  Organizing New Product Activities     164
  Going Outside for New Technology     166
Summary     168
Review Questions     168

**8  PRICING FOR PROFIT     169**
Management Deficiencies     171
  Inadequate Understanding of Market and Economics     172
  Overemphasis on Volume and Market Share     174
  The Impact of Inflation     174

Link to Business Strategy 177
Inadequate Administration 177
Management Solutions 178
Establish Growth and Profit
Targets 178
Determine Product Line Costs
and Profits 179
Develop and Enforce Pricing
Policy 180
Strengthen Ability to Compete 182
Standing Firm When the Market
Turns Soft 182
Summary 184
Review Questions 185

9 COMPETITIVE BIDDING 186
Some Commonsense Practices 189
Understand the Customer's
Requirements 189
Analyze Past Bids 190
Know Whether to Bid for the
Short or Long Term 191
Set Proper Pricing Terms 195
Make the Proposal—A Total
Business Plan 196
Negotiating Bid-Contract Situations 197
Large Customer Advantage 197
Price Gambits 198
Supply Contract Obligations 199
Bidding Guidelines 200
Summary 202
Review Questions 202

10 LINKING SALES TO MARKETING 203
Use Simple Economic Analysis to
Make Key Sales Decisions 206
Define and Articulate the Steps
Necessary for a Successful
Selling Job 209
Provide Capable, Full-Time
First-Level Supervision 210
Conflicting Demands 211
Inadequate Training 212
Excessive Paperwork 213
Use the Compensation Plan as a
Management Tool 214
Strive for a Sharp End-User Focus 217

Carve Out a Strong Marketing Role
for Sales Management 218
Summary 219
Review Questions 220

11 MARKETING WITH DISTRIBUTOR
PARTNERS 221
Producer-Distributor Relationships 225
Managing the Distribution Network 227
The Distribution Selling Decision 227
Recognizing Market Differences 228
Matching Distributors to
Segments 229
Assigning Distributor Territories 230
Developing Distributor Policies 231
Providing Training and Support 232
Turnover and Yearly ROI 235
Distributor Councils 236
Assigning Responsibility for
Distributor Development 237
Evaluating Distributor Performance 238
Selecting New Distributors 242
Multidivision Products 242
Summary 244
Review Questions 244

12 ADVERTISING AND PROMOTION 245
The Problem of Wasted Effort 247
The Money Involved 248
The Special Problems of
Industrial Advertising 250
The Industrial Promotional Mix 253
Some Effective Programs 256
Planning and Control 261
Budgets Versus Plans 261
The Policy Statement 265
The Plan 266
Review and Control 267
Summary 268
Review Questions 268

IV DEVELOPING AND
EVALUATING PLANS 269

13 DEVELOPING STRATEGIES AND
PLANS 270
Why Planning Is Important 272
Some Planning Pitfalls 273

Matching Concept and Context 273
Confusing Various Types of
   Planning 274
Overemphasizing the System 279
Lack of Alternatives 280
Some Successful Practices 281
   Good Direction 281
   Planning Based on Cold, Hard
      Facts 288
   Superior Programming 296
Summary 297
Review Questions 298

**14 EVALUATING STRATEGIES
AND PLANS 299**
Structural Considerations 301
   Strategy Statement 302
   Recommended Programs and
      Control 303
   Summary Projections 304
   Structure Overview 304
Credibility Issues 304
   Fact Base 304
   Sales, Cost, Profit Projections 305
   Key Performance Ratios 308
   Risk-Reward Ratio 310
   Allowances for Contingencies 312
Management Approach and Attitude 312
   Functional Integration 313
   Management Commitment 313
Summary 314
Review Questions 314

**V     STRUCTURING AND
         MANAGING THE
         ORGANIZATION 315**

**15 ORGANIZATION ALTERNATIVES 316**
Alternative Structures 320
   The Four Basic Structures 320
International Marketing 326
Selecting an Alternative 330
   Requirements for Competitive
      Success 330
   Marketing Strategies and Plans 330
   Realities of the Present Situation 331
   Management Philosophy 331

Principles of Organization 332
When to Make a Change 334
Summary 336
Review Questions 336

**16 PRODUCT-MARKET
MANAGEMENT 337**
When Should the Concept Be
   Employed? 339
Making the Concept Work 341
   Clear Responsibilities 342
   Proper Position in the
      Organization 346
   The Right Qualifications 348
   Adequate Training and
      Orientation 349
   Appropriate Performance
      Measures 351
When Both Product and Market
   Managers Are Required 352
   Examples 354
   Who Does What 355
   System Changes 357
Summary 360
Review Questions 360

**17 GUIDELINES FOR EFFECTIVE
IMPLEMENTATION 362**
Planning and Implementation 365
Organization and Staffing 368
People Development 371
Summary 374
Review Questions 374

**VI     CASE
          STUDIES 375**

CASE 1
WRT, Inc.: Engineered Products Division
   Creating a Market-Driven
      Orientation 376

CASE 2
Warwick Company
   Developing a New Electronic
      Component 386

**CASE 3**

Jones & Jones, Counselors at Law
  Procurement of Word Processing
    Equipment    390

**CASE 4**

Gulfcoast Chemical, Inc.
  Managing Supply Sources and
    Finished Goods Inventories    399

**CASE 5**

Raytronics Corporation
  Surveying Customers' Requirements    402

**CASE 6**

Industrial Consolidated Corporation
  Identifying and Evaluating Applications
    for a New Material Product    407

**CASE 7**

Trus Joist Corporation
  Developing a New Market for an
    Established Product    416

**CASE 8**

Cantro Corporation
  Marketing and Pricing Strategies for
    Multiple Product Lines    427

**CASE 9**

Hartman Elevator Corporation
  Competitive Bidding for a Parts-Service
    Contract    433

**CASE 10**

Pape Bros., Inc.
  Introducing a New Hydraulic Log
    Loader    446

**CASE 11**

S. C. Johnson and Son, Ltd.
  Marketing Direct and with
    Distributors    454

**CASE 12**

ROLM Corporation
  Developing a Market Entry Plan    469

**CASE 13**

Judson Industries, Inc.
  Evaluating a Market Reentry
    Situation    496

**CASE 14**

Gould, Inc. — Graphics Division
  Selecting a Product-Market Strategy    502

**CASE 15**

The Eagle Pump Company
  Evaluating and Revising Product-Market
    Strategies and Programs    518

**NAME INDEX**    545

**SUBJECT INDEX**    549

# Introduction

The case for stronger marketing can be made at almost any time for any company, but we believe it is especially timely now to ask what it takes to make marketing a more powerful force in industrial or technically based companies that sell their products or services to other business firms. The reason is clear. Most industrial or technically based companies will find themselves faced with a far more challenging business environment in the decade ahead than at any time in the past. In many respects, industrial companies are involved in an entirely new game—with new competitors, technologies, and customer requirements—and failing to understand how the new game is played can lead to disastrous consequences.

More and more industrial and technical firms all over the world are attempting to tap foreign markets, which means that worldwide expansion is intensifying competition on almost every front. Thus, companies are being forced to improve marketing skills to stay abreast of competitors with whom they have never had to contend before. In addition to fighting the inroads of competition, marketing skills will become increasingly important to keeping pace with and capitalizing on new technology. American industry has had more failures than successes in this area so far, and with the continuing acceleration of technological change, the job of moving profitably from the laboratory to the marketplace will become ever more difficult and risky.

Fundamental structural changes in many traditionally stable and productive industrial markets have occurred that greatly limit the opportunities for future sales growth. Substitute technologies are rapidly displacing products and processes that have been sources of sales and profit growth for decades, and our changing social and economic values have changed the demographics of many industrial nations and limited the ultimate demand for manufacturing products and services required to satisfy consumption patterns. Many traditional industrial markets have been sharply diminished by these changes and will probably never return to their former size and growth potential.

Finally, at least in the United States, added marketing strength will be needed to tap new sources of profit growth so as to reduce reliance on growth through acquisition and mergers. While acquisitions and mergers can undoubtedly contribute to a company's growth plans, history has shown that these activities alone are not the answer to sustained profit growth. Unless there is a dramatic shift in the thinking of various government groups, this avenue to growth, which has been so popular in recent years, is likely to be at least partially blocked in the years ahead. Moreover, even when acquisitions are made, experience shows that management must demonstrate a much higher degree of marketing skill to focus and profitably grow the acquired business.

Few will quarrel with these facts of business life, and certainly in this day and age no one quarrels with the marketing concept. In fact, it would be hard to get anyone to argue against the idea that gearing the business to be responsive to customer or user needs—which is a simple but meaningful description of what industrial marketing is all about—is not only sensible, but the only way to run the business. Top management increasingly stresses the importance of stepping up marketing effectiveness as a means of being more competitive and accelerating profit growth.

Yet, despite their conviction that marketing is important, many of these industrial executives are disappointed with their marketing efforts so far and are clearly perplexed about what they should do to achieve the improvement they want. One all-too-common problem is that many executives tend to regard marketing solely as an isolated function and reason that if the function is strengthened, the company's marketing should improve. Unfortunately, it doesn't work this way. Obviously, marketing is a function, but this definition is far too restrictive. To be effective, marketing must be defined as a way of life that is woven into the very fabric of every function or discipline involved in the business. Every business plan and decision must be based on an awareness and understanding of customer requirements and competitor positions in each market. Thinking this way is the only sound basis for the prudent allocation of the company's resources, which is management's most important responsibility.

B. Charles Ames
James D. Hlavacek

# I

# ESTABLISHING THE FOUNDATIONS

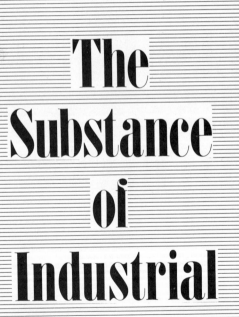

# 1

# The Substance of Industrial Marketing

Where Marketing Fails

Understanding the
Concepts: Key Dimensions

Commitment to Action
   Functional Cooperation
   Investing for the Long
   Term
   Facing Up to
   Deficiencies

Implementing the Concept
   Qualified People
   Reliable Information
   Strategic Planning

Summary

Review Questions

Ambex was a successful $25 million manufacturer of telecommunications equipment located on the West Coast, which had grown rapidly around a narrow line of technologically superior transmission devices. The company's president, who invented the products and founded the business in 1972, was convinced he had to do a better job of marketing to be competitive. He had personally recruited and hired Charles Bruce to do the job. Charles had majored in marketing and worked as a sales engineer and an area sales manager for a competing manufacturer for five years before returning to school for an MBA. He was pleased with his new assignment: The position of marketing manager was new to the company, and he wanted a chance to show how a strong marketing effort could pay off.

His enthusiasm, however, was short-lived. A week after he arrived on the job, the company's senior vice president of manufacturing made it clear what he and the other operations managers thought of the idea of marketing. He pointed out that his department had worked well with the company sales manager over the years, and it was hard for him to see what Charles was going to "bring to the ball game." But he did invite Charles to attend his next weekly staff meeting to explain to the manufacturing group what marketing was and how it could help the company.

Charles, anxious to have the opportunity to explain why marketing was so important to the future of Ambex, agreed. That night he sat down to plan his presentation. Charles was no fool; he knew full well how important this meeting was to his success at Ambex and ultimately to his career as a marketing executive.

Why did Charles get such a cold reception?

Why does he have to prove the value of marketing?

What are some things he should do to prepare for the meeting?

**O**nly in a very few industrial companies can executives honestly say they are happy with what marketing has done for them. More important, in even fewer can they support this belief with concrete evidence of improved results. The majority of executives in the industrial world talk about the concept, but it's hard to find examples where strong marketing has actually produced positive results. And in many companies, executives are downright discouraged with the results of their efforts. Very few of these executives have written the concept off; it is fundamentally too sound. But many of them are perplexed about what they need to do to get the results they want.

This chapter is designed to shed some light on the roadblocks that have prevented industrial companies from getting the payoff they should from marketing, as well as to present some ideas on how to clear these obstacles out of the way. It should serve as a useful introduction to later chapters, which will cover the key points made here in greater detail.

## WHERE MARKETING FAILS

Marketing in the industrial world has not measured up to expectations in many companies because management has concentrated on the trappings rather than the substance. When most executives talk about what their companies have done to become more marketing-oriented, they usually point to such things as:

> Declarations of support from top management in the form of speeches, annual reports, or talks to the investment community.

> Creation of a marketing organization, including appointment of a marketing head and product or market managers, transfer to marketing of the product development and service functions, establishment of a market research function, salespeople reassigned around markets, advertising function strengthened.

> Adoption of new administrative mechanisms, such as formal marketing planning approaches, more and better sales information, and revised information systems structured around markets rather than products.

> Increased marketing expenditures for staffing, training and development, advertising, marketing, research.

Our point is not that these moves are useless, but that by themselves they are no guarantee of marketing success. Effective industrial or business-to-business marketing requires a fundamental shift in attitude throughout the company so that everyone in every functional area places paramount importance on being responsive to market needs. This is why the steps taken in most companies are nothing but trappings: They fail to accomplish this shift in attitude. And without this shift in attitude, the most highly developed marketing operation cannot produce any real results.

Why have so few companies gone beyond the trappings and achieved the change in attitude that ensures substantive marketing? Experience suggests that frequently one or more of these situations exist:

In a surprising number of cases, management does not fully understand the marketing concept as it applies to industrial companies.

In many other cases, management understands the implications of the marketing concept but has not committed itself to the actions and decisions needed to reinforce it.

In almost every case, management has failed to install the administrative mechanisms necessary for effective implementation of the concept.

We'll discuss each of these situations in turn, illustrating the kinds of problems they can cause and pointing out the major steps required to build substance into the industrial or business-to-business marketing effort.

## UNDERSTANDING THE CONCEPT: KEY DIMENSIONS

When we say that in many cases management does not understand how the marketing concept applies to industrial companies, you may wonder how highly paid, presumably intelligent executives can fail to understand a concept that has been talked about and written about so extensively. But time and time again, we have found evidence that although most executives are quick to say that they understand and believe in the marketing concept, many of their actions and decisions show otherwise.

To prove our point, we need to define what marketing in the industrial world is not. It is not simply a departmental operation set up to handle advertising, promotion, merchandising, and selling, as might be the case in a consumer goods company. Nor does it necessarily mean striving for the greatest short-term profit contribution, going all out for volume, or seeking to serve everyone in the market. Rather, marketing in the industrial world is a total business philosophy aimed at improving profit performance by identifying the needs of each key customer group and then designing and producing a product or service package that will enable the company to serve selected customer groups or segments more effectively than its competition.

Marketing in the industrial world is much more a general management responsibility than it is in the consumer products field. In a consumer goods company, major changes in marketing strategy can be made and carried out within the marketing department through changes in advertising emphasis or weight, promotion emphasis or type, package design, and the like. In an industrial company, changes in marketing strategy are more likely to involve commitments for new equipment, shifts in product development activities, or departures from traditional engineering and manufacturing approaches, any one of which would have companywide implications. Marketing may identify the need for such departures, but general management must make the decision on the course the company will take to respond to the market. More important, it must see that this course is pursued in every functional area.

This definition reveals four key dimensions of business marketing: (1) aiming for improved profit performance; (2) identifying customer requirements; (3) selecting customer groups for which the company can develop a competitive edge; and (4) designing and producing the right product or service package or packages. Let's enlarge on each point.

1. *Aiming for improved profit performance.* Too many industrial companies talk a lot about a marketing and profit orientation, but a close look at how they make decisions reveals that volume is still the main consideration. Many of these companies would actually have a better profit picture if they gave a lower priority to volume, even if it meant scaling back the business.

2. *Identifying customer requirements.* There are still many equipment manufacturers who know all there is to know about their own technology and virtually nothing about how their customers really operate and make money. Many of these manufacturers spend millions developing labor-saving machinery for the least costly parts of their customers' production processes, or they design costly features without considering the value of such features to their customers. Then they wonder why their sales personnel are not able to sell the products.

3. *Selecting customer groups for emphasis.* We all know companies that strive to be all things to all customers. Companies that take a shotgun approach to the market inevitably end up with a warehouse of marginal product items and a long list of unproductive customers who generate a small fraction of sales and an even smaller fraction of profits. It is not surprising that more selective companies earn better profits, for they concentrate their limited resources on filling specialized product needs for customers who will pay for value.

4. *Designing the product or service package.* We have all heard horror stories about companies that failed in the marketplace because they tried to sell a Cadillac when the trade wanted a Model A Ford. Actually, a company does not have to be this far off the mark with its product or service package to be a marketing flop. The buying decision hinges on minor differences, and a company is in trouble whenever the competition has a package that matches the customer's needs just a little better.

Now that industrial or business marketing has been defined as a total business philosophy, it should be easy to distinguish those executives who understand the concept from those who do not. The president or general manager who consciously frames a total business strategy in response to market needs shows that he or she understands the marketing concept. The president or general manager who merely enlarges the marketing department, who continually spurs salespeople on to find new customers of any sort, or who indiscriminately adds more products to the line does not understand the concept in the industrial context.

## COMMITMENT TO ACTION

Understanding the marketing concept is one thing; following through with the commitment to make tough decisions is quite another. Many companies stumble badly here.

Companies with a superior marketing effort, on the other hand, repeatedly demonstrate their commitment to follow the marketing concept by their willingness to require cooperation from all functions, to invest for long-term goals, and to face up to deficiencies in product, price, or service.

## Functional Cooperation

A willingness to require—and force, if necessary—all functions to make the changes needed to be responsive to market needs is the first commitment top management must make. In many cases, doing this is more difficult than one might think. (See the box for an example that shows how hard it can be.)

Management often has had to overcome a long-standing preoccupation with objectives that cripple the marketing effort—objectives such as "get maximum engineering content into the units," "keep the plant loaded," "increase the value added," or "move maximum tonnage." Why these attitudes are so hard to overcome is understandable when you consider that in many industrial companies the product is the origin and chief reason for the past success of the enterprise. So people are naturally reluctant to abandon a concept that has proved itself superior. Remember too that marketing recommendations lack the precision of technical data. Typically, top management is confronted with hard numbers from manufacturing and engineering—material costs, production costs, installation costs, and so on. Marketing must make its case on the basis of forecasts and judgments. Of course these forecasts are quantified, but they can never be stated with as much precision as the performance data submitted by manufacturing and engineering. Finally, many general management executives have a technical background themselves and frequently tend to assess their products from a technical rather than a user point of view.

---

### THE RUGGED ENGINEERING TRAP

In a capital goods company, management had historically focused on selling the largest, highest-powered, most maintenance-free units possible, with the thought that this approach favored its manufacturing economics. However, user needs had shifted toward smaller, less costly units without the rugged engineering characteristics required for maintenance-free operation. Since this trend was clear, and the company was losing its market position, marketing had recommended a major redesign of the product line. The company's manufacturing and engineering executives, who were acknowledged industry experts, argued convincingly that the current product design was still superior to any competitor's, and all that was needed was a better selling effort.

Faced with these conflicting points of view, top management decided to stick with the original product and put pressure on the marketing group for a more aggressive selling effort. It was not until the company lost substantial market share and its entire profit structure was threatened that the president could bring himself to put aside the expert opinion of his engineering and manufacturing executives and force the redesign.

An article about Sperry dramatically illustrates this point.[1] The company obviously has a large and presumably sophisticated marketing department. It spends millions of dollars each year on advertising and promotion programs, product development, and marketing planning. Yet the perception among financial analysts is clearly that it is not in any sense a marketing-oriented company:

> Sperry's mainframe mentality has locked them into solving problems with big computers, while the market is now moving to small micro processors. Sperry's technically oriented executives continue to focus on building bigger computers when the trend is in the other direction.
>
> Along the way, Sperry has also acquired a reputation for lacking sensitivity to customers and marketing. Says McClellen of Salomon Brothers, "They have never been marketing-oriented, and office automation is a tough marketing game." Explains a former Sperry executive, "The problem there is that their big computers were more than competitively necessary; they were at the leading technology edge, but there is a lack of marketing. I don't think the executives at Sperry realize the need and reason for marketing. Marketing, of course, encompasses not only selling, but also the packaging of products and systems to meet the current marketplace demand. A perfect example is Sperry's failure to have the new smaller micro computer products [which] has severely hurt the company."
>
> Wall Street analysts also note that IBM, Burroughs, NCR and Control Data have elected to buy state of the art technology and equipment from small specialty manufacturers like Convergent Technologies and Altos Computer. Sperry, by contrast, has opted to design and assemble new systems on its own. Many analysts are leery of what they call Sperry's "not invented here" philosophy and attitude on the company's part that no one but its own engineers can design a good product. However, the technology is moving too fast for them to rely on their own capabilities for everything.

In short, the task of shifting a company that has been dominated by engineering and manufacturing considerations to one that is truly marketing-oriented is enormous. It takes a lot of effort on the part of marketing executives to ensure that their proposals are carefully thought through, solidly documented with market and economic facts, and show an understanding of their impact on operating functions. And it also requires top management's understanding, as well as active support with both actions and words, to make the transition successfully.

## Investing for the Long Term

Another commitment management must make is a willingness to invest to achieve long-term goals. The idea of investing to strengthen one's marketing position is accepted and practiced every day in consumer goods companies, even though these investments commonly have a relatively long payback period. For some reason, this idea does not seem to be acceptable or even considered in most industrial companies. Yet one could argue that an investment point of view is more critical in industrial companies than in consumer

[1]"Sperry's Mainframe Mentality," *Financial World*, March 15, 1983.

package goods companies because of the long time frame attached to the design, manufacture, and selling cycle for any new product. Designing performance or cost improvements for an already established product is a long, hard job. Developing the test or performance data to prove these advantages takes even more time. Finally, it is understandably difficult to get an industrial customer to even try a new or different piece of equipment that may cost thousands or even hundreds of thousands of dollars and, more important, affect an entire product process. So it can take years to gain full customer acceptance and build a solid market base for a product or service innovation in the industrial world.

Despite these considerations, management in many industrial companies is reluctant to look at increased expense for product development, testing, or launching as an investment, or to take any actions to build a stronger market position if those actions cut into short-term profits. One company, for example, had committed over a million dollars to the development of several new products to make its line more competitive. It had also invested heavily in manufacturing equipment to get the new products ready for the market. When plans for market introduction were being made, the marketing director requested a budget increase to set up a special sales group to work on these new products. He pointed out that although the added costs of a special sales group would not be recovered during the first year or so, by the end of two years the added volume would more than cover the cost of this group. The division manager at first balked at the budget increase, claiming it would cut too deeply into short-term profits. It took a lot of effort, but the marketing director finally convinced him this was shortsighted by saying: "If we don't get these products established this year, we will lose the slim lead time we have in the market—and the $2 million we sank into development and equipment will be down the drain."

Unhappily, only rarely does marketing succeed in getting the breathing room it needs to make a substantive contribution, as it did in this case. Usually, the overriding emphasis on the short term prevents new products from being developed or effectively launched when they are clearly needed. Division managers generally are reluctant to weed out marginal products or customers so the mix can be upgraded, even when this is clearly the right move. In all these cases, it is clear that the actions needed to respond to the market were blocked, without regard for the long-term impact, because they would have led to a temporary drop in profits.

Too few industrial executives are sympathetic to the idea of investing marketing dollars for a longer-term payoff, though they are perfectly willing to think in these terms when it comes to a capital proposal for new plant or equipment. There are executives who can be convinced that this approach can pay off. But until more of them start to think naturally in these terms, the marketing effort operates under a serious constraint.

## Facing Up to Deficiencies

Management must also demonstrate its commitment to the marketing concept with a willingness to face up to critical deficiencies in product, costs, price, or service. A critical deficiency is anything the customer or user perceives that causes a negative reaction. These disadvantages are tough to overcome in any business, but they are impossible to ignore in the industrial world. Deficiencies cannot be glossed over when some steely-

---

**THE TOP QUALITY PRODUCT THAT FAILED**

A company that makes electronic test equipment was losing considerable business because management would not face up to the fact that its product was inferior to its competitors' in terms of both price and performance characteristics. This was the situation:

The company had been losing its share of market in one of its major product lines for several years. During this period, three different product managers had made the point that competitor changes in product and price had made it impossible to compete with this line as currently designed and priced. They recommended a redesign program to take cost out of the line and to add certain product features. At the same time, they proposed a lower price structure to make the line more competitive.

Top executives, including the vice president of marketing, reacted negatively. They simply could not accept the fact that their product line, which had traditionally been the top quality product, was that far out of position. Instead, they blamed the product managers for not having a good grasp of the business and for not being imaginative in their recommendations to rebuild market share.

It was not until a new division general manager came on the scene that this position was reversed. He took a fresh, unprejudiced look at his company's product as compared with the competition. The conclusion that he reached was that the product managers had been right, and that no amount of "more aggressive selling," "creative merchandising," or any other so-called marketing activity could overcome the basic competitive disadvantages of this product.

---

eyed engineer or purchasing agent typically makes or controls the buying decision. Unlike the consumer, the industrial buyer is largely unaffected by the emotional appeals of advertising, packaging, and merchandising.

Many industrial managers have a natural tendency to view their products through rose-colored glasses and to conclude that any advantages claimed for competitors' products are exaggerated or insignificant, that the competition is "giving the business away," or that it has a "cheaply engineered" or "shoddily manufactured" line, which explains its lower price (see the box). Admittedly, facing up to critical deficiencies is difficult, but we are not suggesting that a company must always do things differently or always suffer a short-term profit loss in order to follow the marketing concept successfully. It is clear, however, that critical deficiencies must be acknowledged if that is what it takes to be responsive to the market. Management cannot allow emotional ties to what has been done in the past to overrule market considerations. Otherwise, as a marketing manager in one company said: "Management does a lot of talking about following the marketing concept, but in reality it's a joke."

## IMPLEMENTING THE CONCEPT

The third reason companies have not succeeded in getting positive results from marketing is ineffective implementation. The three key ingredients essential to proper implementation are (1) qualified people, (2) reliable market and economic information, and (3) planning to ensure the right strategic focus for the business. Many executives who are vitally interested in making marketing the cutting edge of the business are often frustrated in this attempt because of deficiencies in these areas. Let's examine each one individually to see where the difficulty lies.

## Qualified People

It takes superior knowledge of the market competition and the economics of the business, along with a healthy dose of good business judgment, to be an effective marketing executive in the industrial world. Without these characteristics, the marketing executive cannot command the respect of the other executives and get them to follow marketing's lead. Yet many companies have staffed key marketing positions (marketing director, product manager, market manager) with people who clearly do not have any of these qualities.

Where does management go wrong? In some cases, the problem stems from a tendency to equate marketing with aggressive selling and thus to look only to the sales department for people to move into these positions. Many sales people simply are not able to develop a total company perspective, and their sales or volume orientation tends to dominate their marketing recommendations and decisions. As you would expect, with this point of view, they quickly lose the respect of other functional and top management executives, and they have no chance to influence major decisions. In other cases, management turns to the outside in a search for candidates with skills that will make the company marketing-oriented overnight. But except in rare cases, these people perform well below expectations, for they typically come equipped with skills that are not really applicable. There is no accepted bag of skills in business marketing that is readily transferable from one situation to another as there is in consumer goods marketing, where basic advertising and promotion skills are applicable to a wide range of product and market situations.

The experience of an equipment supplier to the telecommunications field illustrates this point. Top management had decided that the company needed a stronger marketing effort and recruited a successful sales manager from an electrical products company. His background included three years as a product line marketing manager, so he appeared to be very well qualified. His performance, however, was dismal. He did not understand the underlying technology and was unable to shepherd the company's new product program against very stiff competition, particularly from abroad. He also failed to understand the intricacies of designing and selling complex communication systems and was frequently caught off base with proposals that did not meet customer requirements. After six months, both top management and the individual recognized that he had a great deal of learning to do before he could really contribute to the company's marketing effort, and there was a real question in everyone's mind as to whether or not he should remain in the job.

Success in business-to-business marketing depends on skills related to a specific situation. It requires a comprehensive understanding of the particular market and of the economic and operating characteristics of the customers or users that make up that market. It also requires mature business judgment to achieve a balance among functional considerations (product design, manufacturing cost, selling price alternatives) and between long- and short-term interests, and then to come up with sound recommendations for achieving maximum profit growth.

In effect, the industrial marketing executive must be an embryo general manager, and this is what the most successful companies look for in staffing their key marketing positions. There is no magic in the way they get these people. They have no special recruiting sources, no extraordinary training or development programs; they do not pay excessive salaries, though they make sure salaries are fully competitive. What these companies do is very basic. They are aware that marketing people are attracted to a company in which the marketing function receives top priority. They therefore make certain that marketing is set up in the organization as the lead function, and they see to it that everyone understands its role. This means the marketing department has the responsibility for identifying the changing needs of the market and the opportunities these represent for the company. It means also that the marketing department is expected to translate market requirements into the actions that must be taken by the other principal functions of the company (R&D, engineering, manufacturing, finance) to capitalize on these opportunities. When we refer to marketing as the lead function of the company, we do not mean that marketing is organizationally superior to the other functions. Its role is to show the way to the marketplace, and the role of the other functions is to follow this lead and get the company firmly established.

Successful companies are also careful not to overlook sources that might provide good candidates. They seek able people who have the necessary qualities—or the potential to develop them—without regard for their functional background. In many cases, people from the financial, engineering, or manufacturing ends of the business have developed into marketing executives fully as effective as those who came via the sales route. Finally, these companies recognize that there is no shortcut to developing marketing executives. Whether they are home-grown or imported, they must be given both the time and the opportunity to learn about the business. The importance of this broad understanding of the business cannot be overemphasized; it is the foundation that permits the good marketing executive to make the kind of balanced decisions and recommendations that will ensure for marketing its rightful role as the lead function of the business.

## Reliable Information

Even marketing people with the highest qualifications cannot operate effectively without reliable information. Yet many marketing executives complain that they simply do not have access to the kind of information necessary to make intelligent plans and decisions. Their complaints, which relate to both market data (market share, sales to end user segments) and cost and profit information, could be overcome with relative ease, for the raw data are almost always available somewhere in the company. The trouble is that information typically is not organized in a way that is useful to marketing executives. In the case of cost and profit data, accountants usually design the information for external reporting and for manufacturing and cost control. It is not geared to nailing down the profit consequences of selling individual items or various mixes to different customer groups or through different channels. And all too often, market data are fragmented and incomplete. For this marketing executives must shoulder most of the blame, for they simply have not defined the information they need and shown how it should be drawn together.

An example can show how important it is to have reliable market and economic data.

In one broad-line industrial products company, marketing management wanted to weed out some of the marginal items in the line to reduce inventory costs and free sales time for more profitable items. Exhibit 1-1 shows the picture the managers developed using the profit information available to them—gross margin. On the basis of this analysis, they decided to cut out several low-margin items, such as fiber B. Fortunately, before any items were dropped, a plant controller made a special analysis to determine the variable contribution per machine-hour that each item generated—that is, the profit each product contributed for the amount of plant capacity it used. His analysis, shown in Exhibit 1-1, revealed a different picture from the gross margin comparisons and caused everyone to wonder if they were on the right track. Then the division controller decided to look even deeper and made another special analysis to factor in the selling costs. As Exhibit 1-1 shows, once selling costs were considered, what initially were thought to be the low-profit items were actually the most profitable. Complete information resulted in a conclusion just the reverse of the original one. Now the company has completely recast its information structure so its marketing executives get this kind of information as a matter of course.

Many companies with successful marketing records have made similar revisions in their information structure. This does not mean they have stopped collecting the information necessary for external reporting or effective manufacturing control. Rather, they have added to their information structure data that enable their marketing executives to make fact-based decisions on products, channels, markets, and customers.

## Strategic Planning

Most industrial companies regard planning as a key ingredient in their marketing effort. Many of them are quick to admit, however, that their efforts to do a good job of planning are not nearly as effective as they should be, and they cite this shortcoming as one of the chief reasons the marketing concept has not really taken hold. In a high percentage of cases, they are right. Soundly conceived market-oriented plans are the framework that keeps all the company functions operating around the marketing concept.

Planning, of course, is a broad and complicated subject in itself, and we cover it in more detail in later chapters. It is clear, however, that the reason many companies have difficulty with planning is that they pattern their efforts after companies in the consumer goods field. They tend to regard marketing as a separate function, and they develop separate marketing plans. This approach makes sense in the consumer products field, where the key volume and profit-making activities are within the marketing department (advertising, merchandising, promotion). It does not make sense in an industrial company, where activities outside the marketing function (manufacturing, engineering, technical service) typically control success or failure in the marketplace.

Companies that do a superior job of marketing concentrate their planning efforts on making sure they have the right strategic focus for the business. Reviewing the strategic focus is time well spent in an industrial company. For one thing, it is all too easy to develop "marketing myopia"[2] and allow the need to "load the plant" or "increase engineering

[2]See Theodore Levitt, "Marketing Myopia," *Harvard Business Review*, July–August 1960, p. 45.

EXHIBIT
1-1

## THE CASE FOR GOOD INFORMATION

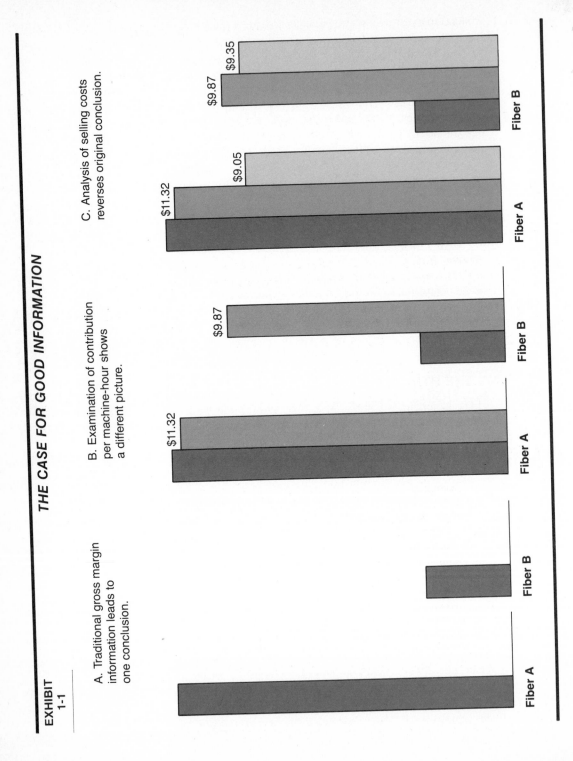

A. Traditional gross margin information leads to one conclusion.

B. Examination of contribution per machine-hour shows a different picture.

C. Analysis of selling costs reverses original conclusion.

content" to override indications that customer needs are changing or that additional needs exist. Because of this pitfall, in many companies the thinking of management is constrained by existing products and technology; opportunities to gain a competitive edge in present markets, develop new markets, or enter related markets go unnoticed. Moreover, the velocity of technological change and the consequent impact of this change on the competitive structure, on customer acceptance of existing products, and on new market opportunities can easily make obsolete a strategic focus that was once highly successful (see the box).

In companies that take the strategic approach to planning, the marketing department, of course, plays the lead role in defining needs and opportunities, as well as in determining what it takes to serve various markets or segments. From this point on, however, planning becomes a collaborative effort, with all the key functions contributing their points of view in a series of face-to-face discussions. These companies place much less emphasis on the planning system—that is, on such components as format, techniques, and lengthy memos. Naturally, the recommended plan gets the inputs and final stamp of approval from top management before it becomes an operating blueprint for the business. This approach—based on a continuous dialogue between key managers rather than on the completion of forms by function heads working in isolation—ensures the kind of balancing among functions, and between long- and short-term interests, that is required to make the marketing concept work.

## SHIFTING THE STRATEGIC FOCUS

The experience of a motor manufacturer shows how a shift in strategic focus can create vast differences in market potential and ultimately change the entire character of the business. Here is the picture:

The company had traditionally held a 25 percent to 30 percent share of a market that was worth about $400 million and was growing at about 5 percent a year. Recognizing that it would probably have to cut into its margins to capture a larger share from competitors, management took a hard look at how the market might be defined differently to expand the opportunity.

The first step was to include the drive linkage and systems that were powered directly from their motors. This more than doubled the potential market for this company and opened up a whole range of new product opportunities. Management then shifted its view of the market to include the whole field of automation. As management defined automation, this shift in focus gave the company a market of some $2 billion—eight to ten times the size of its original market opportunity. More important, the automation market is growing over 10 percent a year, or twice as fast as the motor market alone.

In recent months, the president of the company has said repeatedly: "It took us a long time to define our market in the right way, but once we did, the door was open for a whole stream of new product businesses that we wouldn't even consider before. Getting the right product and market focus has contributed to our accelerated growth and profits more than anything else."

## SUMMARY

There is nothing particularly sophisticated about the marketing concept as it applies to the industrial world. Nor is there anything conceptually difficult about what it takes to build substance into business-to-business marketing as opposed to simply having the trappings. What it takes is total company involvement—from top management to the shop floor—in the marketing effort, and management willingness to depart from traditional practices if this is what is required to be responsive to the market.

There are four key dimensions of the business marketing concept: (1) aiming for improved profit performance, (2) identifying customer requirements, (3) selecting customer groups, and (4) designing and producing the right product or services packages.

However, understanding the marketing concept is not enough. The marketing concept will not succeed without a strong commitment that involves functional cooperation, an investment in long-term goals, and facing up to company deficiencies.

In addition to commitment, successful implementation of the marketing concept is dependent on qualified people, reliable market and economic information, and planning to ensure the right strategic focus for the business.

Saying there is nothing particularly sophisticated about the marketing concept does not in any sense minimize the task of making an operations-oriented company into one that is market-oriented. It is a tough job. It takes time, probably several years, and a lot of training and development effort. Proof of the difficulty lies in the fact that only a few companies have done the job well. For those few that have been successful, however, the time and effort involved have been well spent. Their responsiveness to the market will give them a competitive advantage that is certain to accelerate their profit growth in the years ahead.

## REVIEW QUESTIONS

1. How does an emphasis on products, volume, and "ride the growth curve" cause industrial firms to ignore the market view of the business?

2. Why is marketing in the industrial world very much a responsibility of general management?

3. Why is cross-functional or interdepartmental cooperation necessary to implement the industrial marketing concept?

4. Why is it very difficult to change a firm that is traditionally dominated by engineering or manufacturing to one that is market driven?

5. How are capacity utilization and short-term profit goals often in direct conflict with a market orientation?

6. Why are many industrial salespeople not effective as marketing executives?

7. How should marketing be a lead activity for R&D, engineering, and production in the technical firm?

# 2

# Industrial and Consumer Markets

Derived Demand
Narrower Customer Base
More Rational Buying
Decisions
More Buying Influences
and Locations
Different Basis for
Segmentation
Greater Importance of
Technology
Multinational Markets
Greater Interdepartmental
Dependence
Customer Contact
Multiplicity of Markets and
Channels
Less End-User Information
Product Management
Key Part of Long-Term
Strategy
Summary
Review Questions

The chairman and CEO of a *Fortune* 100 diversified manufacturing corporation, who had spent parts of his career in both the consumer and the industrial sectors of the company, was concerned that the industrial sector did not have as much of a marketing emphasis as the consumer sector. The consumer goods sector of the corporation was known for its strong advertising and promotion support. So the CEO appointed a marketing executive from one of the consumer goods units to a new position as corporate vice president of marketing, with the primary responsibility of developing more marketing emphasis in the industrial units. The CEO told the new corporate vice president of marketing: "I would like to see a marketing renaissance in our industrial business units!"

After three months in the job, the new corporate vice president of marketing had come to four conclusions about what he saw as the trouble in the industrial business units. First, marketing in the industrial units was a self-contained operation, whereas in the consumer divisions marketing teams were also located at the group level. Second, advertising and promotion activities appeared to have relatively low priority. Third, the industrial marketing executives appeared to be more concerned about customer needs and their operations than about psychological appeals or the esthetics of their products. Finally, industrial marketing tended to address worldwide customer needs and downplayed cultural differences among countries.

Before making recommendations to the CEO to correct these problems, the corporate vice president discussed his observations with some industrial sector executives. To his surprise, they disagreed sharply—and they told him why: "There is a world of difference between consumer and industrial marketing. What works in their world usually doesn't work in ours. You should spend some time in our plants and with our customers to learn how and why we go to market as we do. Once you have a chance to do this, we'll all feel more comfortable about how you might be of help to us."

Was the CEO wrong? Was the VP wrong? Were the industrial executives just being defensive?

How are industrial customers different from household buyers?

Why would psychological appeals and media hype fail to sell an industrial product?

he characteristics of the industrial marketplace are very different from those of the consumer goods marketplace. It is the failure to recognize and understand these differences that is the root of so many misconceptions about marketing in so many industrial firms. Industrial or business markets exist at all steps in the production chain from the extraction of raw materials up to, but not including, wholesale and retail transactions, which are consumer activities. Sometimes, industrial distributors or facilitators operate between five value-added stages. Table 2.1 shows the value-added stages in the chain.

| TABLE 2.1 | STAGES IN THE PRODUCTION CHAIN | | | | | |
|---|---|---|---|---|---|---|
| | First Stage | Second Stage | Third Stage | Fourth Stage | Fifth Stage | → Consumption |
| | Raw materials extraction | Material processing | Manufacturing of parts and subassembly | Final assembly | Distribution and after-market | Wholesale and retail sale to household consumers |

At each stage, actions add value to the product. Generally, the greater the value added at each step, the larger the profit margin or spread between purchase costs and selling price. Many industrial firms provide products or services at more than one stage in the chain. The more stages an industrial firm participates in, the more linked or integrated the firm is. For example, in stage 1, a firm extracts a metal ore from open pit mines. In stage 2, manufacturing or processing, it separates the foreign material from the metal ore and in a chemical process produces nearly pure concentrate pellets. Also in stage 2, metal ingots are produced and then transformed into strips, coils, and bars. In stage 3, the material is made into electronic chip components that are sold to stage 4 manufacturers of computers and numerous electronic products.

Of the six stages in the production chain, industrial marketing dominates the first five stages. While it is difficult to be precise on this point, it is clear that the dollar value of industrial or business-to-business transactions is far greater than the value of transactions in the final stage—wholesale-retail household consumption. There are also many more people employed in the five industrial stages than there are in the manufacturing and marketing of household products. This is why one can argue persuasively that activities in our industrial markets impact our whole economy to a far greater extent than the manufacturing and retailing of consumer products.

One way to appreciate the stages, and the interrelationship of stages, in the production chain in the business marketplace is to examine the dynamics involved in the manufacture of a major industrial product. The Electromotive Division of General Motors produces diesel locomotives. Every working day, their main production facility completes 5.5 diesel locomotives that cost between $550,000 and $750,000 each. The only other American producer is General Electric. The domestic customer base consists of about eight railroads. Internationally, the customers are government-owned railroads that often have different track gauge specifications. The life cycle of industrial products is usually long; for locomotives, it is 30 years or longer. As a consequence, the maintenance and overhaul or replacement parts demand is great. Rebuilding and supplying replacement parts business exceeds the 900 new units per year purchased by the industry. As more locomotives are produced and put into service, the maintenance market demand increases geometrically. In 1980, GM had 27,000 locomotives in place that needed parts.

The General Motors division assembles the locomotive units at the third stage in the value-added chain. Thousands of industrial firms supply General Motors with crank cases, controls, wheels, components, and subassemblies for the horsepower specifications of each railroad in each country. This same complex supplier process takes on a different set of dynamics when General Motors tailors its basic diesel engine to fit specific end-user requirements for oil rigs or mobile power units or tugboat engines. Note the breadth and levels of business activity derived from the demand for the original product.

## DERIVED DEMAND

The demand for all industrial products can be traced to and is derived from consumption at the individual or household level, even though that demand may be very remote from the specific industrial product supplied. This is why changes in consumer spending patterns have such major repercussions for the entire economy. For example, when consumers started conserving electricity in response to the high electric bills that accompanied the energy crisis, demand for electricity slackened. As a consequence, utilities cut back orders for new generating equipment from suppliers of gas turbines. These suppliers in turn reduced their orders to component and subassembly manufacturers. And these firms reduced their orders for steel and specialty metals produced by companies that extract raw materials from the earth. Less extraction, in turn, reduced the need for heavy mining machinery, and so another web of suppliers saw their business reduced.

Some industrial or business markets depend on demand that is derived from both private and public sector spending, or a combination of both. Take construction equipment as an example. Private sector spending includes the building of private roads, private industrial and commercial buildings, and residential housing. Public sector spending includes the construction of roads, waterways, or projects such as bridges, public office buildings, or government housing. Both private and public sectors are important markets for products such as excavating machines, cranes, and other kinds of heavy construction equipment.

Since all industrial product demand is derived from consumer spending patterns, it is important for the industrial manufacturer to watch for major population trends and shifts in social patterns (such as later marriages, fewer household formations, lower birth rates) that will ultimately affect industries the company supplies now or might supply in the future. A major population trend in the United States and in other developed countries is that people are having fewer children and having them later. The implications of this trend are quite severe for many industrial manufacturers in the production chain. For example, the supplier of glass containers to the baby food industry most likely will be faced with a declining market. Conversely, related trends toward increased leisure time and activity and toward discretionary spending can favorably impact other manufacturers—such as the manufacturer of aircraft required to meet the increased demand for transportation and the manufacturer of restaurant equipment required to accommodate the increased demand for dining outside the home. The astute marketer identifies these trends and serves the industries that have a favorable derived demand for the long term, shifting the focus away from declining markets. Because the concept of derived demand is so fundamental, the industrial marketer should always look beyond immediate customers to analyze the causal factors of demand.

# NARROWER CUSTOMER BASE

Most consumer goods products are purchased by thousands or even millions of customers every day, month, or year. An industrial product has a much narrower customer base. An active base of 4,000 to 5,000 customers is considered very large for an industrial product. It is not unusual for 100 to 250 key or major customers from that base to account for well over half the sales volume. In some situations, a handful of customers represent 100 percent of a firm's customer base, and one or two other suppliers may be vying to serve this same small group of customers. The narrow industrial customer base is especially common when original equipment manufacturers (OEMs) supply a large customer like General Motors or Caterpillar with a component or subassembly. A manufacturer of large aircraft landing gear, for example, has a domestic customer base limited to Boeing, Lockheed, and McDonnell-Douglas. Similarly, the three jet engine marketers—United Technologies, General Electric, and Rolls Royce—have only a handful of commercial and military aircraft buyers.

The narrower the industrial customer base, the more control or influence the customer has over suppliers. This narrow customer base leads to a much closer relationship between buyer and seller than exists in consumer markets. No one household customer can exert this kind of purchasing power. As an industrial customer's quantity requirements grow, it can exert added pressure for concessions (lower prices, extended terms, consigned stocks, and so on). Industrial firms with a very narrow base of, say, two to four customers for a product line will often attempt to reduce their vulnerability to swings in their customers' business by broadening the base so no one customer is more than 10 percent of the demand for one product line.

There are many approaches to broadening a customer base. One involves marketing the same product to customers in new countries. Another approach is to seek new applications or new market uses for the same product. A third approach is to focus more on the maintenance and replacement aftermarket, which nearly always has a broader customer base than the original market for the product. If it is difficult to have a broader base of customer prospects, it is desirable to concentrate on the more rapid growth customers who are growing or maintaining a strong competitive position.

# MORE RATIONAL BUYING DECISIONS

Industrial products are not sold because someone really wants to buy them. Industrial or business customers have economic requirements, not wants. Unlike consumer products, industrial products do not make anyone look or feel better, and they generally do not have any significant esthetic value. Industrial products are bought only to help the user manufacture, distribute, or sell more effectively so that it can improve its economic and competitive position. This means industrial buyers require much more specific cost and performance information about the products they purchase. This information is essential so the buying organization can determine the economic value of the item to its operations or its customers. The industrial supplier has the burden of providing documented test data to support any cost or performance claims. This means there is no place for exaggeration or puffery in industrial advertising and promotional activities. Many industrial customers routinely check actual cost and performance against suppliers' claims and demand restitution in the event unfavorable variances occur.

Industrial firms emphasize price and quality checks and balances in procurement that are often nonexistent in household purchase situations. In addition, most industrial customers are well aware of their needs. As a consequence, customers often provide parameters and specification requirements that help guide product development or determine whether a product will function within their system. In contrast, household customers' needs and wants are often much less specific or even latent. Household customers' less defined needs often result in purchases they later realize they really do not need or want. In the industrial world there is personal and career risk for wrong purchase decisions. When an industrial item is purchased but never used, the purchaser has failed in its responsibility to employ the capital that has been invested in the business prudently. For example, a maintenance manager for a major oil producer came under fire from top management when, to save money, he replaced the original pump on an oil field gathering system with a much lower-priced one. The pumping application required a high pressure pump that could move high viscosity crude oil. The lower-priced pump was not designed to meet the rigorous requirements of this application and soon developed leaks and broke down completely on several occasions. Management's criticism of the maintenance manager's decision was understandable. The savings on the pump was a few hundred dollars; the downtime cost of each oil rig was $50,000 an hour.

# MORE BUYING INFLUENCES AND LOCATIONS

Nearly all household consumer decisions involve only one or two influences or decision makers—wife and husband or child. The industrial procurement decision typically revolves around engineering, manufacturing, and even sales considerations for the end product. This means that all these departments, in addition to the purchasing agent, have a voice in the buying decision. Engineers usually set the technical performance parameters or standards that a supplier's product must meet. The engineering and production personnel evaluate the quality of the supplier's shipped product. Purchasing personnel compare competitive prices and on-time shipment performance. To complicate matters, the engineer, production manager, and purchasing manager may be influencing the purchase decision from two or three different locations.

The industrial decision is even more complex when the product is formally purchased centrally but requirements are determined and ordered in multiple locations. The decentralized units may exert considerable influence on decision makers in the central purchasing location.

## DIFFERENT BASIS FOR SEGMENTATION

Household or individual customers are often segmented by psychological and sociological factors. For example, in addition to standard demographic data, a manufacturer of health and beauty aids or designer jeans might be very interested in life styles, dress codes, hair styles, and so on. Industrial firms and industrial customers are more likely to be concerned about industry characteristics, four-digit SICs, technical and functional requirements, applications, annual purchase quantities, cost and benefits, and any physical alteration to the product. (In Chapter 5 we will discuss the whole subject of market segmentation in the industrial world in much greater detail.)

## GREATER IMPORTANCE OF TECHNOLOGY

The products marketed by most industrial producers often have a significant impact on their customers' production processes. This means the manufacturer of industrial products must consider the tasks and functions that the customer needs to have performed. The industrial marketer must consider the capabilities of its products, components, or materials and the customer's or user's system. There is a much greater focus on a customer's production system and alternative technological solutions in the industrial buying and selling situation than in the household buying and selling situation. In consumer goods companies, a large amount of the marketing expenditure or budget is allocated to advertising, promotion, and merchandising, which form the central core of consumer goods marketing. In industrial firms, there is usually a heavy investment in technical field selling, technical support services, and engineering considerations. Marketing such products often means interaction between company technical and engineering personnel and customers.

Spending levels for technology and the risks of failure are generally much greater in the industrial world. It is not unusual for industrial success or failure to hinge on advances in either product, process, or materials technology. While product, process, and materials technology are important considerations in the consumer world, disadvantages can often be offset by creative advertising and/or strong brand loyalty.

## MULTINATIONAL MARKETS

Industrial firms, largely because of the uniqueness and benefits of their technology or products, tend to be more export-focused than consumer goods firms. Different preferences and social norms are less likely to affect the purchase and use of industrial products than consumer products because accepted worldwide standards ensure product specifications are met. For this reason, technological or performance advantages of superior industrial products generally override geographic or cultural differences. As a result, the major exporters of finished products in industrialized countries tend to be industrial firms rather than consumer goods firms. In a *Fortune* magazine listing of the 100 leading U.S. exporters, industrial firms dominated the list. The major firms included aircraft and aircraft component manufacturers. The exports of this group of aerospace companies amounted to more than a third of the total export sales of the top 50 U.S. exporters in 1979. These high-technology companies in turn are fed by parts and components suppliers in the United States and from foreign-based operations. Other large industrial exporters with major international businesses include DuPont, Union Carbide, and Monsanto in chemicals; and John Deere and GMC in industrial and farm equipment. Table 2.2 shows the top 25 U.S. exporters and their main product lines.

Another view of the worldwide marketplace for industrial products can be seen in an analysis of the machine tool industry. As shown in Table 2.3, the machine tool industry is truly international, with significant import and export trade among all the producing countries. For example, the United States is a major manufacturer or producer of machine cutting tools; however, in 1977 it imported or bought nearly as much as it produced. Exhibit 2-1 shows the world electronics market in 1980 and projected market shares for 1990. Table 2.4 shows market shares in Europe for integrated circuit supplies and the supplier's country of origin.

# GREATER INTERDEPARTMENTAL DEPENDENCE

Securing and maintaining a better market position for an industrial product is not simply a matter of changing the advertising campaign, changing the advertising agency, changing the package design, or changing the name of the product. Success with industrial products depends on being able to show performance advantages that result from engineering, production, or technological developments. The fact that these developments originate outside the marketing department creates an interdependence among marketing, R&D, engineering, and technology in the industrial firm. Industrial marketing and success depend largely on the activities of functions like engineering, manufacturing, and technical services (see the box, page 28). The closer the linkage, and the better the communication between marketing and R&D, the shorter the lead time to the marketplace and the more successfully customer requirements can be met. The process can make or break the company. One company, for example, took almost three years to develop an aircraft industry alloy product. By the time it was developed according to users' specifications, they no longer needed it in that type of aircraft.

Because of the functional interdependence in an industrial goods company, the role of an industrial product manager or marketing planner is significantly different from that of his or her counterpart in consumer goods firms. The industrial product manager cannot develop self-contained marketing plans and strategies, but must work closely with all operating functions.

**TABLE 2.2**

## THE LEADING EXPORTERS

| Rank 1979 | Company | Products | Exports ($000) | Fortune 500 Sales ($000) | Fortune 500 Rank | Exports as percent of sales % | Rank |
|---|---|---|---|---|---|---|---|
| 1 | Boeing (Seattle) | Aircraft | $3,967,900 | 8,131,000 | 29 | 48.80% | 1 |
| 2 | General Electric (Fairfield, Conn.) | Generating equipment, aircraft engines | 2,772,100 | 22,460,600 | 9 | 12.34 | 26 |
| 3 | Caterpillar Tractor (Peoria, Ill.) | Construction equipment, engines | 2,499,900 | 7,613,200 | 33 | 32.84 | 4 |
| 4 | McDonnell Douglas (St. Louis) | Aircraft | 1,788,425 | 5,278,531 | 54 | 33.88 | 3 |
| 5 | E.I. du Pont de Nemours (Wilmington, Del.) | Chemicals, fibers, plastics | 1,764,000 | 12,571,800 | 16 | 14.03 | 20 |
| 6 | United Technologies (Hartford) | Aircraft engines, helicopters | 1,417,257 | 9,053,358 | 26 | 15.65 | 17 |
| 7 | Weyerhaeuser (Tacoma, Wash.) | Pulp, logs, lumber, wood products | 978,000 | 4,422,653 | 26 | 22.11 | 10 |
| 8 | Lockheed (Burbank, Calif.) | Aircraft and related support services | 956,000 | 4,069,800 | 82 | 23.49 | 9 |
| 9 | Westinghouse Electric (Pittsburgh) | Generating equipment, defense systems | 879,840 | 7,332,000 | 37 | 12.00 | 27 |
| 10 | Raytheon (Lexington, Mass.) | Electronic equipment | 734,000 | 3,727,930 | 92 | 19.69 | 12 |
| 11 | Northrop (Los Angeles) | Aircraft and related support services | 701,577 | 1,582,477 | 204 | 44.33 | 2 |
| 12 | Union Carbide (New York) | Chemicals, plastics | 602,000 | 9,176,500 | 25 | 6.56 | 44 |
| 13 | Archer-Daniels-Midland (Decatur, Ill.) | Soybean meal and oil, wheat, corn | 564,808 | 2,297,838 | 153 | 24.58 | 8 |
| 14 | Signal Companies (Beverly Hills, Calif.) | Trucks, engines, chemicals | 544,700 | 4,241,200 | 75 | 12.84 | 24 |
| 15 | Rockwell International (Pittsburgh) | Electronic, automotive, and industrial equipment | 536,000 | 6,466,100 | 45 | 8.29 | 40 |
| 16 | Philip Morris (New York) | Tobacco products | 521,235 | 6,144,091 | 49 | 8.48 | 38 |
| 17 | Occidental Petroleum (Los Angeles) | Agricultural and chemical products, coal | 499,000 | 9,554,795 | 21 | 5.22 | 50 |
| 18 | Kaiser Aluminum & Chemical (Oakland, Calif.) | Aluminum | 496,800 | 2,926,500 | 113 | 16.98 | 14 |
| 19 | Textron (Providence) | Helicopters, chain saws, metal products | 489,000 | 3,392,974 | 100 | 14.41 | 19 |
| 20 | Deere (Moline, Ill.) | Farm equipment | 480,000 | 4,933,104 | 60 | 9.73 | 33 |
| 21 | R.J. Reynolds Industries (Winston-Salem, N.C.) | Tobacco products | 476,000 | 7,133,100 | 39 | 6.67 | 42 |
| 22 | FMC (Chicago) | Industrial and farm equipment | 462,398 | 3,307,484 | 102 | 13.98 | 21 |
| 23 | International Harvester (Chicago) | Farm equipment, trucks | 447,000 | 8,392,042 | 27 | 5.33 | 49 |
| 24 | Dresser Industries (Dallas) | Oil-field and industrial equipment | 435,500 | 3,457,400 | 98 | 12.60 | 25 |
| 25 | Monsanto (St. Louis) | Herbicides, textile fibers, specialty chemicals | 406,400 | 6,192,600 | 48 | 6.56 | 43 |

*Source: Fortune, September 22, 1980, p. 115.*

| TABLE 2.3 | WORLD MACHINE-TOOL PRODUCTION AND TRADE (Millions of U.S. dollars) |

| | 1981 | | | | |
| | Production | | | Trade | |
| Country | Total | Cutting | Forming | Export | Import |
|---|---|---|---|---|---|
| 1. Japan | $4798.1 | $3861.3 | $936.8 | $1692.9 | $215.8 |
| 2. United States | 5111.2 | 4046.9 | 1064.3 | 972.1 | 1437.0 |
| 3. FRG (West Germany) | 3953.5 | 2774.3 | 1179.2 | 2584.9 | 616.4 |
| 4. Soviet Union* | 2932.3 | 2268.5 | 663.8 | 242.4 | 951.9 |
| 5. Italy | 1513.0 | 1029.2 | 483.8 | 795.2 | 300.0 |
| 6. GDR (East Germany)* | 827.7 | 632.8 | 194.9 | 673.6 | 214.6 |
| 7. Switzerland | 845.7 | 803.4 | 42.3 | 740.3 | 188.9 |
| 8. United Kingdom | 932.9 | 797.0 | 135.9 | 537.4 | 432.0 |
| 9. France | 809.6 | 625.8 | 183.8 | 390.5 | 566.6 |
| 10. Rumania* | 624.9 | 578.7 | 46.2 | 133.1 | 311.5 |
| 11. PRC (China)* | 440.0$^u$ | 330.0$^u$ | 110.0$^u$ | 30.0$^u$ | 125.0$^u$ |
| 12. Czechoslovakia* | 357.8 | 311.5 | 46.3 | 310.4 | 168.2 |
| 13. Yugoslavia | 276.7 | 188.0 | 88.7 | 55.1 | 131.0 |
| 14. Spain | 319.6 | 219.3 | 100.3 | 206.8 | 141.9 |
| 15. Poland* | 310.0$^u$ | 270.0$^u$ | 40.0$^u$ | 170.0$^u$ | 200.0$^u$ |
| 16. Canada | 269.2 | 208.0 | 61.2 | 99.8 | 557.4 |
| 17. Sweden | 204.8 | 127.4 | 77.4 | 164.3 | 191.4 |
| 18. India | 209.0 | 173.2 | 35.8 | 23.1 | 103.9 |
| 19. Bulgaria* | 201.5 | 182.0$^c$ | 19.5$^c$ | 200.9 | 267.8 |
| 20. Brazil | 305.0 | 231.7 | 73.3 | 73.9 | 123.6 |
| 21. Korea* | 178.1 | 115.8 | 62.3 | 32.0 | 324.5 |
| 22. Taiwan | 249.4 | 237.2 | 12.2 | 182.6 | 99.2 |
| 23. Hungary* | 127.7 | 111.2 | 16.5 | 95.7 | 127.3 |
| 24. Austria | 107.8 | 74.1 | 33.7 | 107.8 | 290.2 |
| 25. Belgium | 103.3 | 33.1 | 70.2 | 119.2 | 139.5 |
| 26. Israel | 70.0$^c$ | 55.0$^c$ | 15.0$^c$ | 33.8 | 71.5 |
| 27. Australia | 68.9$^{cj}$ | 43.6$^{cj}$ | 25.3$^{cj}$ | 7.3$^j$ | 195.6$^j$ |
| 28. Netherlands | 60.5 | 31.7 | 28.8 | 74.2 | 110.6 |
| 29. Denmark | 41.6 | 16.9 | 24.7 | 31.9 | 28.2 |
| 30. Singapore | 43.5 | 38.8 | 4.7 | 27.0 | 114.4 |
| 31. Argentina | 35.3$^u$ | 18.8$^u$ | 16.5$^u$ | 19.5$^u$ | 70.0$^u$ |
| 32. South Africa | 36.8 | 14.7$^c$ | 22.0$^c$ | 5.0$^c$ | 250.0$^c$ |
| 33. Mexico* | 24.0$^u$ | 12.0$^u$ | 12.0$^u$ | 4.0$^u$ | 450.0$^u$ |
| 34. Portugal | 16.3$^u$ | 7.3$^u$ | 9.0$^u$ | 4.1 | 53.9 |
| 35. Hong Kong | 12.5$^c$ | 3.1$^c$ | 9.4$^c$ | 4.1 | 4.0 |
| Total | $26418.1 | $20472.3 | $5945.8 | $10844.9 | $9573.8 |

Source: *American Machinist*
Notes: Whenever possible, data include machine tools only; they do not include parts and attachments.
$^c$Rough estimate from fragmentary data.
$^j$Year ended June 30.
$^u$Unrevised.
*Country with controlled currency whose official rate may not represent real value.
Exchange rates: Controlled currencies have been converted as follows: Soviet Union at 80% of the official rate; GDR at 65% of the FRG rate; Czechoslovakia at the official rate; Bulgaria at 65% of the official rate. Poland and PRC (China) are based on estimates of the amount of production so no exchange rate is involved. Hungary, Korea, Mexico, and Rumania are all members of the IMF and though conversion is currently restricted were converted at IMF rates.

**EXHIBIT
2-1**

# THE WORLD ELECTRONICS MARKET
## (Billions of 1979 U.S. dollars)

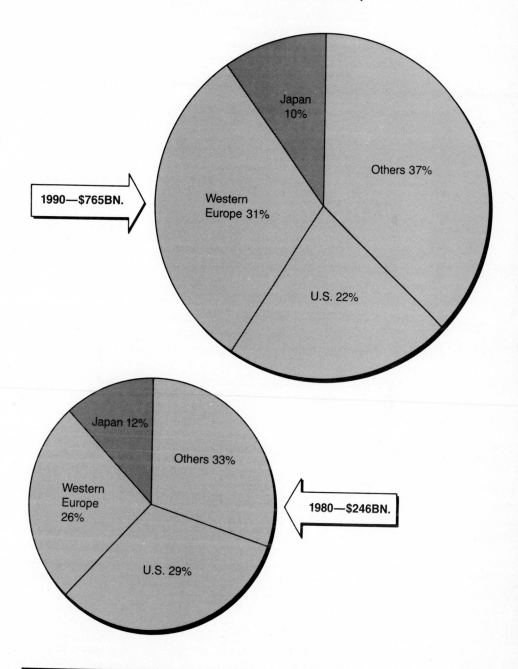

1990—$765BN.

Japan 10%

Others 37%

Western Europe 31%

U.S. 22%

Japan 12%

Others 33%

Western Europe 26%

U.S. 29%

1980—$246BN.

*Source:* Mackintosh Consultants

| TABLE 2.4 | INTEGRATED CIRCUITS: EUROPEAN MARKET SHARES, 1979 |
|---|---|

| | |
|---|---|
| 1. Texas Instruments (U.S.) | 15.9% |
| 2. Phillips (Netherlands) | 14.7 |
| 3. Intel (U.S.) | 8.0 |
| 4. Motorola (U.S.) | 8.0 |
| 5. Siemens (Germany) | 7.5 |
| 6. National (U.S.) | 7.0 |
| 7. Fairchild (U.S.) | 4.7 |
| 8. ITT (U.S.) | 4.2 |
| 9. SGS-ATES (France) | 3.7 |
| 10. NEC (Japan) | 3.1 |
| Others | 23.2 |

## CUSTOMER CONTACT

In a typical consumer goods company, product managers spend about 75 percent of their time on packaging, advertising, and couponing, since these factors, more than any others, control the growth and profitability of the business. In a large, broad-based industrial electronics company, in contrast, product managers spend much of their time working with their counterparts in engineering to evaluate bid opportunities to determine the focus of product development, and to coordinate and participate in technical discussions with major customer groups or user segments. These activities are what make a product a success.

Since most industrial products are bought during or after face-to-face technical selling, experience in the field with engineering, production, and purchasing personnel provides

### INTERDEPENDENCE IN A CHEMICAL COMPANY

A field salesman for a chemical company perceived a need for a liquid that could be used in a customer's cooling system. He communicated this need through the organization to the R&D people. After some research, R&D determined that mercury was the best liquid for the application. However, marketing soon discovered that mercury could not be used, as the application required a low-cost fluid of low toxicity. Marketing then provided R&D with better technical parameters and more specific customer requirements.

An application engineering team went to work developing a liquid that fit the customer's technical performance requirements. After six months of work and meetings between the supplier's and the buyer's technical personnel, a satisfactory product was developed. Manufacturing and cost personnel then determined the feasibility and economics of manufacturing in various quantities. Finally an agreement was negotiated with the customer that led to a firm purchase order.

a valuable base for developing business marketing programs and making product and market decisions. Top executives of the more successful industrial goods companies spend considerable amounts of time with ultimate customers in the marketplace, unlike their counterparts in consumer goods firms whose contacts in the marketplace are limited to wholesalers and retailers that distribute their products. Top managers at IBM and Digital Equipment, for example, spend approximately 30 days a year meeting with key customers. Such firms believe there is no substitute for meeting periodically with customers to keep abreast of the market.

## MULTIPLICITY OF MARKETS AND CHANNELS

Another major distinguishing characteristic between consumer and business markets is the multiplicity of markets and channels with which the industrial firm must deal. A consumer goods company typically markets its brands through one or two channels; a multiproduct industrial firm is likely to sell in many different markets through a variety of channels. One equipment company promotes *one* of its product lines to 20 distinct markets that are reached through different distribution channels. No company can market to such a complex combination of markets and channels with a single marketing strategy or plan; what is needed is a number of different marketing plans. Although essentially the same product is sold to all markets, different customer applications result in different ways of purchasing the product. The delivery systems (distribution channels) must be selected to meet each distinct purchase and user situation. The implication for the industrial product manager is that he or she must understand how the product is made and used, and what happens when design or manufacturing changes are introduced. For example, the Parker Hannifin Corporation is the world's largest manufacturer of O-Rings, which are used in fluid and air connections to seal against leaks. Various sizes and forms of O-Rings are used in literally hundreds of applications ranging from aircraft landing gear to cigarette lighters. Different sales and distribution channels are obviously required to effectively serve each identified market segment. Some of these products are standard catalog items; others are custom designed. Some are sold direct to OEMs and end users; others are sold through different types of distributors. Some markets buy primarily on price and delivery; others place a premium on application engineering and technical superiority. To meet the unique requirements of these different markets, Parker Hannifin has set up a number of full-fledged divisions that operate almost as totally separate businesses. They may share technical and selling information, but the responsibility for serving assigned markets has been clearly designated to different division managers.

## LESS END-USER INFORMATION

Consumer goods producers can readily purchase bi-monthly market data (based on a valid sample of retail outlets) that show inventory movement, relative market share, out of stock occurrences, and competitive prices. The A. C. Nielsen Company and the Market Research Corporation of America regularly provide consumer goods companies with this vital set of market facts. No industrial firm we know has access to anything close to this kind of data. At best they get annual aggregate shipment data from a trade association from which they might be able to determine their relative market share position. Often, however, this information is outdated by the time they get it, or it is unreliable, as many industrial firms refuse to participate in trade association surveys or will report inaccurate information. Since many industrial customers sell products to other industrial firms, an item often becomes a component of another firm's finished product, which creates a major information problem for the original producer of the item; it is very difficult for the industrial producer to know where and in what final applications its product is being used. Many industrial customers and distributors are reluctant or unwilling to keep track of information that will tell their suppliers who their customers are. As a result, many industrial firms do not know where and how major portions of their output are being used, and they must go to extraordinary lengths to develop meaningful information about the ultimate users of their products.

# PRODUCT MANAGEMENT

The differences between business marketing and consumer goods marketing can also be seen in their product manager systems. In business marketing, product managers are typically older and have spent some time in the business. Many industrial product managers have a technical background and generally remain within the industry or in a closely allied group of industries. The need to understand how the product is made and used, and what happens when design or manufacturing changes are introduced, is crucial to the successful industrial product manager.

It is rare indeed for an industrial product manager to have spent a major part of his or her career in an advertising agency as an account executive. In the consumer goods industry, however, it is common for product managers to move between advertising agencies and manufacturing firms. The reason is that the advertising agency's role and activities are a major part of the consumer goods marketing and product management responsibility.

The need for industrial firms to be in close face-to-face contact with their customers causes many industrial firms to be more sales-oriented. A sales orientation, rather than a market focus, can result in shorter-range goals and a lack of concentrated efforts. This shorter time horizon often fails to group customers with like problem needs together for later sales emphasis. Some of the factors that distinguish an industrial marketing focus from an industrial sales focus are shown below:

| *Marketing-Focused Industrial Company* | *Sales-Focused Industrial Company* |
|---|---|
| Long-term planning to serve markets | Short-range planning to achieve sales goals |
| Define and segment total market and identify specific requirements | Profile the market by account potential |
| Select segments and customers to serve | Sell products to anyone who will buy |
| Products and technology vary with market needs | Products and technology are fixed |

# KEY PART OF LONG-TERM CORPORATE STRATEGY

Business-to-business marketing strategy is often indistinguishable from corporate strategy. Business market strategy involves general management in making the decision on which course the company will take as it responds to market needs, and it requires top management or division general management involvement to provide the follow-up to ensure that the strategy is pursued in every functional area of the business unit.

Ideally, industrial product organizations should view all strategic marketing decisions as long-term investments because of the long time frames needed to design, make, and ultimately market and sell an industrial product. In consumer goods, product "changes" are usually quicker to perform and often involve only packaging, promotion, or advertising campaign changes. An industrial product improvement, such as designing performance or cost improvements into an already proven product, can take months and typically years and considerable capital expense before test and performance data are generated to prove the advantages over competitive or substitute products. It may take just as long for an industrial customer to try a new component or piece of equipment that may cost thousands of dollars or ultimately affect its entire production plan. In many cases, it takes three to six years for an industry to openly purchase and use a product improvement.

## SUMMARY

Because business and consumer markets are very different, the marketing effort for each needs to reflect and take into account these differences.

The demand for industrial products is derived, not direct; there are often several levels of customer between the industrial producer and the ultimate consumer. Industrial products are bought rationally and primarily for economic reasons; many people participate in the buying decision, not just the members of a household. And careers can depend on the quality of the decisions.

An industrial producer may have a large segment of the total market and still have only three or four customers because the customer base is generally very narrow. And in industrial products, technology is not just a gimmick, it is vital. Technology makes the marketing of industrial products a worldwide operation, since these products carry no cultural "freight" and are needed for the development of industry. Technology also means a close working relationship between producer and buyer; products must be matched to the changing requirements of the user, and often a sale is made only after in-depth, face-to-face consultations and visits to manufacturing or producing sites. All this is far different from repackaging a household product, mounting a new advertising campaign, and conveniently purchasing bi-monthly reports containing market data that reflect the success or failure of the new packaging and advertising campaign.

## REVIEW QUESTIONS

1. How do changes in demand at the household level provide early warning signals of vulnerability or opportunities for the astute industrial marketer?

2. Why is the industrial buyer usually more rational than household consumers?

3. Why are there usually attractive international markets for highly effective industrial products?

4. What is meant by this statement: "Many industrial marketers have nonmarketing titles"?

5. How do the job responsibilities of an industrial product manager differ from the job responsibilities of a consumer goods product manager?

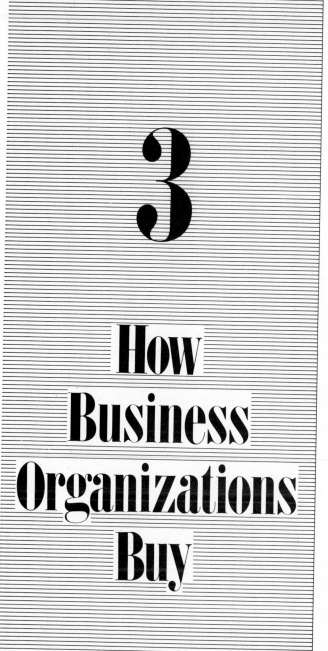

**3**

# How Business Organizations Buy

Multiple Buying Influences
    The Purchasing Manager
    Engineering and
    Production
    The Buying Committee
Planning Material Needs
Economic-Based Buying
Value Analysis
    How Value Analysis
    Works
    Analyzing Prices and
    Costs
    Guiding Product
    Development
    Reverse Engineering
Standards and
Specifications
    Why Have
    Specifications?
    Writing and Influencing
    Specifications
Sourcing Decisions
    Make or Buy Situations
    Customer Make Decision
    Selling to "Make-Buy"
    Customers
    Multiple or Sole Sourcing
    Developing Sources of
    Supply
    Evaluating Suppliers
Maintaining the
Relationship
Summary
Review Questions
Appendix: Government
Buying

Jim Rodgers, a recent college graduate, had been recruited by Worldwide Electric to join its sales training program. Worldwide was known for having one of the finest training programs in the industry. The in-house phase of the program took six months and covered the company's products, markets, and selling requirements. It emphasized the increasingly more sophisticated customer evaluations of competitive offerings and supplier capabilities.

The second phase of the program consisted of on-the-job training with senior salespeople. Every new salesperson was required to work with two to three senior staff over a three-month period. The trainee worked with the senior salespeople to prepare and make sales calls and was expected to work out the strategy and purpose of each call.

Jim was impressed with the in-house training program, which emphasized analytical and comprehensive account evaluations to determine how and why each company buys from a given supplier. When he began phase two of his training, he set out to analyze each account to determine his company's past history and competitive position with the account, to learn who made or influenced the buying decision, and to find out what caused the account to buy from the company. On the second day in the field, the first senior salesman he traveled with said: "You'll only get paralysis from all that analysis. Let's go and call on the accounts in this town, where I'm close friends with the buying people."

Why does the senior salesman place so much emphasis on personal relationships?

Is the senior salesman being practical or is he living in the past?

Should Jim follow his advice?

Why did the company program stress analysis and planning?

**S**ound procurement practices can favorably affect a firm's profitability. For the long term, they result in securing the better suppliers. In the shorter term, a 2 percent procurement savings will favorably affect the profit and loss statement or provide the firm with a competitive cost advantage that could be passed on to customers. The high cost of inventories and the many longer-term negative effects of poor quality put a great deal of pressure on procurement. Furthermore, when a company faces limited market growth prospects with mature products, there is certainly more pressure for internal efficiencies to improve earnings.

Materials planning and procurement have received more time and attention in recent years as enlightened management has become aware of the importance these activities can have on the ability to serve the marketplace. A quote from Reliance Electric's procurement policy statement brings this point into sharp focus.

> Suppliers play a vital role in Reliance's commitments to provide our customers with maximum total value to help them achieve superior financial results. Reliance, in turn, seeks to buy from suppliers who provide us with maximum total value.
>
> The elements of total value include more than quality, delivery, and price. Technological innovations, assured supply during shortages, cost reduction aid, and engineering, managerial, or process assistance are some of the vendor contributions Reliance considers in determining total value.
>
> Reliance believes the best way to achieve maximum total value received from its purchases is to establish business partnerships with suppliers. In a supplier/customer partnership both parties coordinate and combine their actions to produce mutually profitable, superior results.

With more and more industrial firms thinking this way about procurement, it is critically important for industrial marketers and sales personnel to thoroughly understand the industrial buying process and the major considerations that impact the buying decision. This understanding is fundamental to the development of sound product-market and account strategies, as well as to the actual sales implementation.

Today's industrial buyers often know more about the value of a supplier's product and the competitive substitutes than the supplier knows. Armed with product performance information and driven by economic-based buying, the progressive industrial buying organization identifies, evaluates, selects, and switches to the supplier(s) providing the greatest value. The same buyers are evaluating more worldwide sources of supply. When NCR needed a new 5,000-line telephone system for its headquarters, it rejected American and Canadian manufacturers in favor of Japan's Nippon Electric Company. An NCR company spokesman stated:

> In the past we always did business with the local telephone company, but this time we looked around and found the Japanese had the best equipment for the money. It really wasn't much of a contest.[1]

---

[1]"Japanese Now Target Communications Gear as a Growth Industry," *The Wall Street Journal*, January 13, 1983, p. 1.

Business-to-business marketing is not merely attracting more customers. It always involves serving and maintaining the customers after they agree to buy. The relationship, in many respects, begins only after the formal sale is made. The customer determines the long-term requirements and service level necessary to maintain and keep its business. When a large customer has its own competitive problems, it nearly always seeks help from existing or new suppliers. For example, the Xerox Corporation realized in 1980 that it was not cost- or quality-competitive in the small copier market, the fastest growing market segment. In order to reposition itself more competitively in that segment, Xerox examined its supplier situation. First, it had many parts redesigned so that assembly would be less labor-intensive. It standardized more parts across many machine models and decided to buy more items rather than continue to make them. Xerox reduced its parts inventory to one month from the previous three months. It awarded more business to suppliers that had lower rejection rates and could also meet the new "just-in-time" delivery requirement. The move to make Xerox more competitive from 1980 to 1982 resulted in reducing the number of its suppliers from 2,200 to 1,400.

A thorough understanding of industrial procurement practices is necessary for a firm to be and remain a successful supplier. Industrial salespeople who are not tuned into sound organizational buying practices will serve fewer accounts and enjoy less of each customer's business. Many industrial salespeople do not appreciate the need to understand the buying process for each of their products and market segments. The following comments are often heard from unresponsive sales executives:

"There are too many people involved."

"It varies greatly by each company."

"The right price is all that counts."

These comments are often nothing more than an excuse for superficial thinking. The people speaking probably do not know their customers' procurement requirements. A lack of awareness of competitive suppliers' practices may also exist. These comments are most often heard from salespeople who achieved some success by riding an industry growth curve when procurement was not very sophisticated and when social visits and friendships generated many purchase orders. Today, things have changed. With the increased use of sophisticated buying methods like value analysis, supplier rating systems, formal buying committees, and worldwide competition, only the astute suppliers will succeed. (Since government buying is somewhat different from the process and relationship between for-profit suppliers and buyers, it has been placed in an appendix to this chapter.)

## MULTIPLE BUYING INFLUENCES

It is rare, except in very small organizations,[2] for one person to be solely responsible for the industrial buying decision. In industrial organizations, the buying decision for most items is usually shared by several people. These multiple influencers have been called

[2]Hugh P. Buckner, *How Industry Buys* (London: Hutchinson, 1966); and John H. Platten, Jr., *How Industry Buys* (New York: Scientific American, 1955).

"the buying center" or the decision-making unit.[3] Whatever terms are used to identify the decision makers, it is the task of the industrial marketer to determine who initiates, who specifies, who ultimately controls, and who can reject the decision to purchase a particular product or service. Locating the decision makers is not as quick and easy as interviewing the members of an identifiable household or conducting random interviews at a shopping center. Organizational titles are often misleading in terms of a person's buying responsibility or influence role. The people involved in an industrial buying decision are often at different geographic locations. Specifications may be written at one location, annual volume requirements determined at another. Still another centralized location may make the final choice of supplier. Therefore, phrases like "buying center" or "decision-making unit" may be interesting academic terms, but operationally they are not very helpful in analyzing the actual decision that the industrial salesperson must effectively influence.

## The Purchasing Manager

The multiple purchase influences in industrial buying typically involve engineers, production people, purchasing agents, middle management, and sometimes top management. The professional industrial salesperson needs to know the buying role influence and the procedure or process firms use to purchase a product. The salesperson usually enters the organizational buying network through the purchasing department, even if that department does not actually make the purchase decision for the item. The protocol is first to register with the purchasing department before identifying and seeing other people in the organization. As a consequence, purchasing personnel can open many doors to the actual network or they can hinder the salesperson in seeing the other appropriate influencers in the organization.

The purchasing function has gained significant status since the mid-1970s. When material shortages and price fluctuations were as great as they were in the 1974–75 energy crisis, the procurement function suddenly was seen as vital. Today purchasing managers are using more analytical tools and techniques, including economic order quantity (EOQ), value analysis, and supplier rating systems. Many purchasing departments are making greater use of their internal engineering capability to evaluate supplier products. It is not unusual for purchased materials to account for as much as 50 percent of total manufacturing costs. So a 1 or 2 percent improvement on the procurement side of the operation can immediately and dramatically affect the economics and profit of the business. Firms are realizing that it would take a considerable amount of additional sales revenue to equal the incremental profit increase obtained from more prudent procurement. In times of limited economic growth, the internal efficiencies provided by better procurement practices can help sustain the attractiveness of the business (see the box).

Industrial procurement managers are increasingly involved in decisions beyond the traditional purchasing of inventory and negotiating supplier contracts. The purchasing manager has more knowledge of price trends for purchasing products and materials than any

[3]See Patrick J. Robinson, Charles W. Faris, and Yoram Wind, *Industrial Buying and Creative Marketing* (Boston: Allyn and Bacon, 1967); Frederick E. Webster and Yoram Wind, *Organizational Buying Behavior* (Englewood Cliffs, N.J.: Prentice-Hall, 1972); and Jagdish Sheth and Arch Woodside, *Consumer and Industrial Buying Behavior* (New York: Elsevier North-Holland, 1978).

## MODERN PROCUREMENT PRACTICE

An increasingly sophisticated approach to procurement is seen in the changing buyer-seller relationships between U.S. automakers and their steel suppliers.

According to an ARMCO salesman, "GM's steel buying had become automatic process. At the beginning of each year a supplier would be awarded a fixed percentage of GM's needs for specific types of steels at each plant. We did the same thing the same way every year in Detroit, and we'd get our share of the pie."

In the past, an automaker who wanted steel made to certain specifications was apt to be told that he would have to accept the standards and tolerances of the American Iron and Steel Institute. As *Fortune* magazine states, "Neither buyers nor suppliers paid much attention to quality. Thousands of tons of rejected steel piled up at many auto plants. Banking on the consumer's willingness to absorb price increases, the suppliers and buyers chose to pass costs on rather than disrupt the comforts of doing business as usual."

Because of declining sales over the last several years, automakers have had to introduce new procurement practices in order to increase efficiency and reduce costs. GM cut the number of mills supplying its plants from 341 to 272. Ford now offers larger orders and longer-term contracts to suppliers who meet higher standards. Suppliers now receive a detailed list of over 5,000 parts made at 53 plants on which they can quote. More important, GM suppliers are now given advance notice of GM's production plans to help their own planning – something suppliers never got before. GM is gaining lower rejection rates, lower inventories, and manufacturing efficiencies from the greater reliability of material from suppliers.

The changes in steel buying practices have made things more difficult for suppliers. Suppliers have been forced to rationalize their operations, sharpen their marketing and selling skills, and look at their own production costs. Most important, suppliers have had to reconsider the mix of products they sell. Bethlehem invested $60 million in a continuous heat treating line, and Jones and Laughlin is building a $160 million slab caster mainly dedicated to auto steel.

With the changes in procurement practices has come increased cooperation between buyers and suppliers. ARMCO presented GM with a study showing that GM could reduce the number of steel sizes it orders by 50 percent by combining different sizes of products whose gauges (thicknesses) are within .05 millimeters of each other or whose widths were within a range of 2 percent. Such standardization benefits both buyers and suppliers by improving quality, lowering material costs, and reducing inventories. ARMCO also showed GM how it could substitute lower priced steel for some it was already buying from ARMCO, saving about $10 per ton on steel averaging $500 per ton without compromising quality.

*Source:* Steven Flax, "How Detroit Is Reforming the Steelmakers," *Fortune,* May 16, 1983.

other executive. In firms where 50 percent of all costs of manufacturing is accounted for by material purchases, the purchasing manager's predictions on material costs have a major impact on marketing and overall business strategy. And research, development, and engineering staffs are now realizing that purchasing can facilitate their new product programs by identifying qualified vendors with special product, process, or some other know-how that supports their efforts.

## Engineering and Production

After the purchasing agent, the other two major influences in most industrial manufacturing purchases involve engineering and production. Engineering and sometimes production are involved in setting specifications and quality standards. With multiplant locations and the repurchase of standardized items in quantity, there is more and more centralized procurement. This has implications for the marketer, who in many cases must exert influence and market to both the decentralized locations and the centralized formal purchasing points. In large corporations, more procurement is being done at the corporate level for the more uniform or standardized products used across many operating divisions. For example, the B. F. Goodrich Company found 60 separate orders being placed each year with six different producers for 120 lift trucks. Each lift truck costs about $18,000, and many of Goodrich's orders were placed with local distributors. Now all such orders are placed through Goodrich's corporate purchasing department. The saving to Goodrich on this item was about $400,000 a year,[4] after it was bid and placed directly with two suppliers. Furthermore, 62 percent of the sales dollars at Goodrich is spent for supplies and services; as one of their executives stated: "No one area touches as much of the corporation's money as purchasing." Centralized buying of 350,000 items at Goodrich saved the company about $18.2 million in 1980, nearly one-third of its 1980 earnings of $61.8 million.[5] The trend of more organizational buyers to place more orders centrally has forced some suppliers to realign their pricing and sales force activities.

## The Buying Committee

Central purchases are usually reviewed and approved by a buying committee. These committees are typically composed of an engineer and representatives from various technical groups, production supervisors, buyers, and often specialists such as methods people or internal auditors. As an example, one equipment manufacturer has an electrical components committee that includes electrical engineers, the production supervisor of the electrical assembly section, a specialist, and a buyer. The committee meets once every two weeks. The members discuss changes, design specifications, order quantities, particular components or materials, and price-quantity stability for key items. Such buying committees are often very slow in evaluating alternatives and making a decision. In response to the increase in buying committees, one large supply division general manager stated: "When the customer's dust settles in choosing a supplier(s) for an item, it is still the design engineer who is responsible for quality, the shop or production foreman who is responsible for output, and the buyer who is responsible for contract negotiations and the fulfillment of that contract." Yet, many believe that committee procurement activities will grow in importance as the materials management concept increases and greater cooperation, coordination, and cost savings are sought between departments.

Setting product specifications and placing the actual purchase orders with a specific supplier can create authority and power conflicts.[6] The supplier can be caught between

---

[4]"New Status for Purchasing," *The New York Times*, June 2, 1981, p. 25.
[5]*The New York Times*, ibid.
[6]George Strauss, "Work/Flow Frictions, Interfunctional Rivalry, and Professionalism: A Case Study of Purchasing Agents," *Human Organization*, 23, 2 (1964), 137–49.

the desires of purchasing agents and the engineers who have control over specifications. Purchasing agents tend to stress price; engineers generally stress quality. It is much easier for engineers to specify by brand rather than develop precise technical specifications. Purchasing managers dislike brand specification because it biases the purchase to the supplier of the named brand. If a brand is specified, the purchasing department may attempt to have technical specifications written or have the engineers add the words "or equivalent." These changes allow the purchasing agent more influence and negotiating leverage in making the buy. In most confrontations between engineers and purchasing in selecting suppliers, the engineers usually prevail. As one production engineering manager stated: "Some engineers become purchasing agents, but no purchasing agents become engineers." Due to the close working relationships and interdependence between production and procurement activities, some companies have regrouped or combined the production scheduling function with procurement and called the combined function "materials requirement planning." This is also an attempt to gain greater coordination and cooperation between suppliers and users.

## PLANNING MATERIAL NEEDS

The materials requirement planning (MRP) concept brings together production, engineering, scheduling, and value analysis. It is a focused organizational unit that analyzes and manages industrial buying practices—specifications, design, annual requirements, sources, quality, and price. A materials management staff is a unit as important as a financial or market analysis staff. The existence of a multidisciplinary materials management operation can be an advantage to the astute supplier salesperson for two reasons. First, it is easier to identify the buying influencers when such an organization exists. Second, it is easier to get a sympathetic ear for the idea of developing long-range material plans.

Materials requirements planning is a technique of working backward from the scheduled quantities and need dates for end items specified in a master production schedule.[7] An MRP computer program is run periodically, usually once a week, to incorporate new production plans and information about the scheduled receipt of components and materials. The inventory status file is updated each time the MRP program is run to reflect the scheduled usage, the balance on hand, the quantities on order, and when they are scheduled to be received.[8]

In a company where the performance and cost of materials are a major part of its success, there should be greater emphasis on the materials management function. A materials management program can help a producer achieve a lower-cost position in the marketplace. The materials management unit in some organizations has installed computers to order and keep track of suppliers. When a unit's inventory is down to a programmed reorder point, the computer returns a card that shows who the existing vendor(s) is (are), and an automatic reorder occurs. As a consequence, new firms marketing

---

[7]James B. Dilworth, *Production and Operations Management*, 2d ed. (New York: Random House, 1983), p. 239.
[8]Ibid., p. 240.

to such a firm will have difficulty if they are not programmed on the computer. But once the supplier manages to get a product onto the computer reorder system, it is equally difficult for a competitor to remove it.

For MRP to work effectively, buyers must inform suppliers well in advance of their production schedules and supply requirements. In return, the buyer can carry less inventory. To better link directly into a customer's production needs, some producers and suppliers have linked computers to exchange supply and delivery information. Dana supplies drive shafts to Ford with such a computer linkage. Dana delivers to Ford daily, and it knows four days in advance exactly what each Ford factory needs. It is not a system to push inventory back up the pipeline; it is a system that keeps both producer and buyer happy and inventory down. Weak suppliers are rapidly weeded out. Too many irregularities and defective items will disrupt the entire system.

This approach is very similar to the Japanese "just-in-time" (JIT) or *kanban* system. The Japanese system is characterized by more frequent deliveries in smaller quantities, longer-term supply contracts, fewer suppliers, and a very close relationship between suppliers' and buyers' people. Some of the benefits of the JIT system are lower inventory carrying costs, quicker detection of defects, less need for inspection, and a faster response to engineering changes. The benefits of JIT buying are greatest in the case of materials used every production day.[9]

## ECONOMIC-BASED BUYING

An understanding of organizational buying and subsequent marketing strategy development must focus on the economic need underlying industrial purchases. Industrial firms buy a product or service for only one purpose: to fulfill an economic need. The economic function is basic; the type of product or service that performs the function is secondary. Industrial firms are very much influenced in their purchasing behavior by the same profit-making motive that influences the sellers or suppliers who market to them. The profit-making motive of the industrial buyer creates a strong desire for cost-benefit value. Key needs motivating industrial buyers to purchase a certain product include energy consumption, energy costs, productivity, material costs, capacity utilization, OSHA, and on-time delivery. These are also economic needs. As the vice president of marketing at IBM states: "Every proposal should be overwhelmingly cost-justifiable from the customer's standpoint."[10] An ex-IBMer states: "An IBM salesman always sells the cheapest product that will get the job done," adding that he wishes the same could be said of his present company.[11] IBM has also stated that it is in the business of solving customer information problems rather than merely selling computers.[12] The economic basis of industrial buying can be seen in the cost-benefit value of purchasing an industrial robot (see the box).

Problem recognition does not always originate with the industrial buyer. The industrial

[9]Richard J. Schonberger, *Japanese Manufacturing Techniques* (New York: Free Press, 1982), p. 163.
[10]Thomas J. Peters and Robert H. Waterman, *In Search of Excellence: Lessons from America's Best Run Companies* (New York: Harper & Row, 1982), p. 161.
[11]Ibid.
[12]J. W. Cannon, *Business Strategy and Policy* (New York: Harcourt Brace Jovanovich, 1968), p. 15.

## INDUSTRIAL ROBOTS

Industrial robots are typically used to perform the more routine, unskilled, or semi-skilled tasks. The more advanced robots are able to sense, touch, grasp, hold, and place items. Specific applications now include spot and arc welding, spray painting, machine tool loading, press loading and unloading, heat treating, metal part deburring, and assembly. The increasing reliability and cost-benefit value of robots provide high potential for improved manufacturing productivity.

The most obvious benefits of introducing robots are in terms of reducing labor costs. Up to 1981, 45 percent of all robots were installed to cut the expense of labor. As wages and fringe benefits increase each year, robots become more attractive. In 1983, each factory robot typically costs $50,000. Each robot has a six- to seven-year life and replaces one worker per shift whose average annual wage-benefit cost is about $21,000. When the robot is operated in two shifts daily, it pays for itself in just over a year. If there are three shifts, the payback is less than one year. The use of robots in continuous shifts favorably affects breakeven points and offers significant improvements in productivity. Robots are also more flexible than less automated machines. This feature allows for shorter production runs. In some applications, a robot is more efficient than humans. A robot used for painting uses 20 to 30 percent less paint than the worker it replaces. Robots do not require air conditioning, lighting, or special protection. By taking humans out of hot, dirty, or dangerous situations, the organization can improve industrial safety without increasing costs. Robots also offer a benefit or insurance against a shortage of skilled labor, especially in rural areas where plants are often located. In larger industrial cities, an aging and smaller skilled manufacturing work force can be supplemented with robots.

supplier with a new and better product must often show the problem area to the customer and explain the resulting cost and benefits of the new solution. Plant managers and manufacturing executives had to be shown in detail the significant cost-benefits of robots before trial machines were allowed in their plants. Due to the new technology of many new industrial products, the supplier must often take the initiative and educate users as to how new products will better solve a problem or need.

# VALUE ANALYSIS

Value analysis is a key analytical tool used systematically to study the cost-benefits of a material, component, or machine. There are many names for this procedure, including value engineering, purchasing research, and product research. Some companies make a distinction between value analysis and value engineering. In those firms, value analysis is directed toward existing products and is primarily concerned with cost reduction. Value engineering focuses more on products and proposals that are in the development stages. In the following discussion, we use the term value analysis in the inclusive sense, for both proposed and existing products.[13]

[13]Gary J. Zenz, *Purchasing and the Management of Materials* (New York: Wiley, 1981), p. 389.

## How Value Analysis Works

Value analysis begins by asking the question: "What function does the item perform?" For example, the function of a fastener is to join two or more parts. Every item has a primary function and may also have a secondary function. In defining a function, it is best to be as brief as possible: "It measures temperature," or "It connects two pieces." Value analysis then examines the value of the function performed by the material, part, or machine. It also examines the value of the identified function in terms of alternative methods such as welding, taping, stapling, or glueing in a specific application. The best product to purchase is the one that will satisfactorily perform the identified function(s) at the lowest costs without degradation of quality.[14] The lowest cost for the function performed involves the use of cost and price analysis for the alternative solutions or products. Maximum value is achieved when the essential function(s) are achieved for minimum costs, as shown in the following equation:

$$\frac{\text{Function desired}}{\text{Minimum cost}} = \text{Maximum value}$$

Value analysis causes organizations to pay greater attention to substitutability, consolidating, eliminating, simplification, and standardization. A value analysis buying orientation results in a continuous search for new materials, processes, and products to perform a function better and/or at a lower cost. The value analysis approach often includes a checklist that asks questions about the item or component.

Value analysis personnel of a major farm equipment manufacturer assist suppliers with specifications and with finding substitute parts or materials by providing present and potential suppliers with the value analysis checklist shown in Exhibit 3-1.

## Analyzing Prices and Costs

When procurement managers receive price increases for major or critical items, the search intensifies for functional alternatives, alternative suppliers, or cost reductions by suppliers. If the price is too high, or even if it isn't, the buyer will frequently go over the prices in detail. One of the buyer's objectives is to see where the highest costs and profits are for the supplier. The buyer may even bend the minimal specifications in such a way as to reduce the supplier's cost and price. Many buying organizations conduct an intensive price-cost analysis as a separate part of the value analysis procedure. The buyer's question is essentially: "What is the cost to the supplier for the item we purchase, and how much should we pay for the item?" Supplier costs are questioned in relation to efficiency, age of equipment, and reasonable return on investment. Buyers often visit existing and competitive suppliers' facilities to help answer these questions.

If the conclusion is that all the suppliers' prices are too high for the item, the customer may decide to make the item rather than buy it. In many situations, the customer will make specific recommendations to the supplier on how to reduce or contain costs. The search for alternative, multiple, or new suppliers is often fueled by the customer's desire

---

[14]Fred Asbudnick, "Value Engineering—A Form of Industrial Engineering," *Journal of Industrial Engineering,* 15 (July–August 1964), p. 184.

**EXHIBIT
3-1**

## SUPPLIER VALUE ANALYSIS CHECKLIST

Name and number _____

Buyer _____

In order to assure the functional usefulness of the above part, we solicit your help through answers to the following questions:

| QUESTIONS | CHECK Yes | No | SUGGESTIONS |
|---|---|---|---|
| 1. Do you understand part function? | | | |
| 2. Could costs be reduced by relaxing requirements:<br>Tolerances?<br>Finishes?<br>Testing?<br>By how much? _____ | | | |
| 3. Could costs be reduced thru changes in:<br>Material?<br>Ordering quantities?<br>The use of castings, forgings, stampings, etc.?<br>By how much? _____ | | | |
| 4. Can you suggest any other changes that would:<br>Reduce weight?<br>Simplify the part?<br>Reduce overall costs?<br>By how much? _____ | | | |
| 5. Do you feel that any of the specifications are too stringent? | | | |
| 6. How can we help alleviate your greatest element of cost in supplying this part? | | | |
| 7. Do you have a standard item that could be substituted for this part? | | | What is it? _____<br>What does it cost? _____ |
| 8. Other suggestions? | | | |

SUPPLIER: _____    ADDRESS: _____

SIGNATURE _____    TITLE _____    DATE _____

*If "No," functional information can be obtained from Buyer involved.

to reduce prices on certain items. Exhibit 3-2 gives examples of how a customer value analysis study reduced costs for three items. The value analysis approach can result in the substitution of lower-priced materials or components without a reduction of quality. The total costs of an air shutoff valve disk used in sewage aeration tanks was reduced by 88 percent by switching from cast bronze to molded plastic.[15] The molded parts cost 97 cents each, as compared to a unit cost of $5.66 for the cast bronze parts. In addition, the eliminated machining cost per unit on the part was $2.30. A yearly savings of approximately $14,000 was obtained by applying value analysis to this small part.[16] The molded plastic supplier was not the same firm that supplied the cast bronze valve disk.

## Guiding Product Development

The functional approach to value analysis helps product development and manufacturing engineering objectively assess each product and its relation to components. A value analysis team composed of engineering, marketing, and accounting personnel would examine each of the subassemblies in relation to each other and to the total end product. The result could be a new material, possible elimination of the item, or a different method of manufacturing.

The Xerox Corporation involves vendors in value analysis in the predesign stage. Their early supplier involvement program is staffed by 11 senior buyers who do no actual buying. Instead, they work with the best of Xerox's vendors, taken from a list of approximately 100 "consulting suppliers," who may be called in for advice at the concept stage or during the predesign idea stage. These suppliers can be called in by the value analysis team to brainstorm new approaches. Together they work on new ideas before drawings are produced or use sketches in order to get production started prior to a bill-of-material release. As a result of supplier involvement at an early stage, a machine frame that had previously been roll-formed with secondary piercing is now press-formed and pierced in progressive dies. Cost per machine has been reduced from $36 to $14. And Xerox projects manufacturing savings of $60 million since the program started near the end of 1977.[17]

## Reverse Engineering

Reverse engineering is a value analysis approach that is critical to value improvement and new product development efforts. Reverse engineering is a process in which companies take apart their competitors' products to find out how they work and determine the cost of performing the functions. Reverse engineering is a universal practice, especially in industries where technological change is rapid.[18] Makers of automobiles, cameras, appliances, and business machines routinely strip down competitors' products. The Ford Motor Company has a "tear-down room" where competitive components are compared

---

[15]"Shift to Plastic Saves Machining," *Purchasing,* March 29, 1978, p. 163.
[16]Ibid., p. 163.
[17]Zenz, *Purchasing and the Management of Materials,* p. 395.
[18]"Reverse Engineering of Microchips Is Slow, Costly and Universal," *The Wall Street Journal,* August 5, 1982, p. 1.

EXHIBIT
3-2

## HOW VALUE ANALYSIS REDUCES COSTS

This insulating washer was made from laminated phenolic resin and fiber. Machined from individual pieces of material, it cost $1.23. A supplier with specialty equipment now fly-cuts the parts, nesting them on full sheets, at 24¢ each.

Standard nipple and elbow required special machining to fit a totally enclosed motor. Casting a special street "L" with a lug eliminated machining and a special assembly jig. The cost dropped from 63¢ to 38¢.

An insulator costing $4.56 was originally porcelain, leaded extra heavy. Now molded from polyester and glass, it is lighter and virtually indestructible. New cost: $3.25.

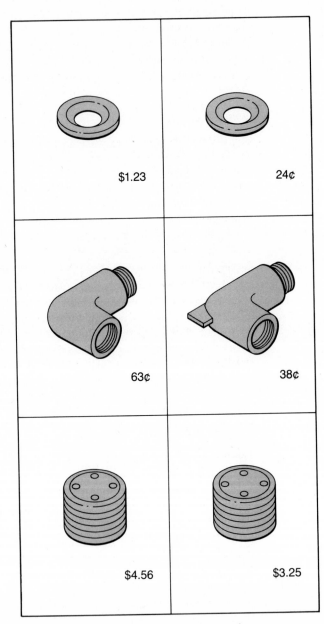

$1.23          24¢

63¢          38¢

$4.56          $3.25

part by part for quality and design cost differences. One result was that Ford saved 45 cents in the redesign of a master brake cylinder and thereby saved $1.5 million in less than two years on this one item.

Reverse engineering per se is not illegal or immoral. Buying, analyzing, and testing competitive products is good competitive behavior. Copying that infringes on a patent, copyright, or trademark is illegal if the item has such legal protection, but many products do not have such protection. In the rapidly changing electronics industry there is considerable "technological borrowing," or learning from one another's products. There are engineering firms whose sole business is to provide reverse engineering studies and reports to clients. Many industrial firms find that their original product development efforts are complemented by reverse engineering studies of competitive products. They can build on the strengths and improve the weaknesses of competitive products in their own new product. However, a reverse engineering effort does not reveal the skill and art necessary to produce a product.

Value analysis creates threats for high-cost suppliers and opportunities for other suppliers who can accomplish the desired function for less cost. The industrial marketer should convert the initial obstacles created by customer value analysis into opportunities by updating product designs and making improvements more in tune with customers' functional needs. One producer instructs its salespeople to attempt to determine which products its customers are reviewing on a value analysis program. Often they are displayed on company schedule boards, and the customer usually does not mind if a supplier's salespeople review the projects. One customer's materials management department periodically holds sessions for all suppliers to show what kinds of problems they are currently reviewing in their value analysis program. This allows suppliers to see how and where their existing and new products might be better used or modified. The mere fact that a supplier knows a product will be reviewed in a value analysis engineering procedure should cause that firm to reevaluate its product's costs and functions with an eye toward improving performance.[19]

## STANDARDS AND SPECIFICATIONS

The use of value analysis increases the use of standardization and buying by technical specifications. The setting of a so-called standard is the process of obtaining an agreement on quality, design, and composition for a material, component, or machine. Some standards are developed by governmental agencies, including the U.S. Department of Commerce, the National Bureau of Standards, and all branches of the armed forces. Trade associations and professional associations are also frequently involved in developing nationwide standards. Trade associations active in developing industrial standards include the American Society of Mechanical Engineers, the Society of Automotive Engineers, and the Underwriters Laboratory. The International Standards Association and agencies of the United Nations also seek cooperation on common standards across countries.

[19]Vincent G. Ruter, "The Success Story of Value Analysis/Value Engineering," *Journal of Purchasing,* May 1968, pp. 52–69.

Industry standards provide a sorting process to reduce the number of possible items used and thus simplify the buying decision. The existence of a standard allows a buyer to describe an item without the use of a drawing or blueprint. However, commercial or industrywide standards are often so broad that the customer must develop product specifications to meet the requirements. Such specifications are a detailed description of the desired characteristics of the specific item. Military specifications, in addition to describing technical characteristics, also often describe the method of manufacturing to be used.

## Why Have Specifications?

There are a number of advantages and disadvantages for customers and suppliers when procurement is guided by specifications written by the buying organization. Developing and writing specifications require the customer to carefully review functional requirements. The process of value analysis guides the writing of specifications. When specifications are written, more suppliers will tend to bid on the business. This opens the customer's business to more vendors and may result in more price competition. With written specifications, the customer is more assured of uniformity if multiple sources of supply are selected.

If a selected supplier's product meets the customer's specifications but does not perform satisfactorily, the customer is responsible for the malfunction. However, industrial buyers generally do not like to assume such a responsibility. Once a customer writes a specification, it is difficult to change. This situation reduces the chances for different products to be considered from existing or new suppliers. For example, the aircraft industry was using a leather hide substance to seal fluid connections. The leather hides were difficult to work with and had to be soaked in oil and then stretched into a piston groove. The procedure was difficult and time-consuming, but the specifications were written for the leather substance. When another manufacturer developed a superior new Teflon composition sealing ring, it was repeatedly informed that it had to meet the existing leather hide specifications. The Teflon sealing producer had to mount a long-term and costly effort to change the existing specifications.

Whereas U.S. engineers tend to specify and develop very specific tolerances and requirements, which purchasing people pass on to suppliers, the Japanese rely more on performance specifications and less on design specifications. In the Japanese system of industrial buying, performance-focused specification might consist of a blueprint with only the critical dimensions. Kawasaki buyers ask suppliers for recommendations rather than force rigid specifications.[20]

## Writing and Influencing Specifications

It is important for the marketer to know who writes the specifications for the product area so the supplier can protect, influence, or change the specifications. Manufacturing, quality control, and engineering are usually involved in developing and writing specifications. It is sometimes done in a committee, but an engineer usually has the specific

[20]Richard J. Schonberger, *Japanese Manufacturing Techniques* (New York: Free Press, 1982), p. 165.

responsibility for writing the technical product specifications and quality standards. Sometimes the specification writer inserts a brand name instead of technical specifications. The actual wording, for example, would state "Teflon or equivalent." This allows the brand name to be the standard. Specifications can also be written in such a way that only one supplier's product will meet the specifications even though there are equivalent competitive substitutes. Such a situation presents a difficult challenge for another supplier who wants to obtain that customer's business.

When a large system or turnkey operation is being built, those writing specifications are often at different geographic locations. A supplier of pressure gauges, for example, was attempting to get its product specified into a new chemical plant Exxon was building (see Exhibit 3-3). The actual writing of the technical specifications was done collectively by Exxon engineers located in New Jersey and Baton Rouge, with assistance from the construction firm's engineers in California. The supplier of pressure gauges called on the key engineers at all three locations to show the economic benefits of its new gauges and then tried to influence the specifications they were in the process of writing. The gauge supplier knew that, if it were not specified in the design and construction stage, it would be virtually locked out of the more lucrative and long-term replacement market business. For this item, the plant managers nearly always bought replacements that were specified in the OEM stage and that were earlier tested and qualified by corporate and construction engineers.

When multiple influences are involved in the buying decision, all the bases have to be covered. This often requires sales calls on different buying locations, which sometimes are located in different states and countries and generally are located beyond any traditional

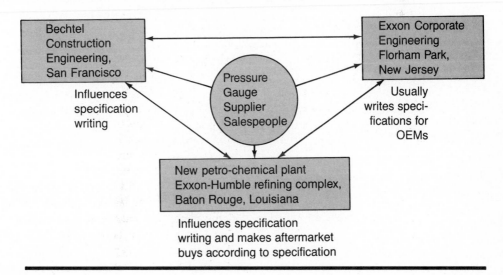

**EXHIBIT 3-3**

## *GEOGRAPHIC SPREAD OF BUYING INFLUENCES COMPOUNDS SERVING TASK*

Bechtel Construction Engineering, San Francisco

Influences specification writing

Pressure Gauge Supplier Salespeople

Exxon Corporate Engineering Florham Park, New Jersey

Usually writes specifications for OEMs

New petro-chemical plant Exxon-Humble refining complex, Baton Rouge, Louisiana

Influences specification writing and makes aftermarket buys according to specification sales territory boundaries. In these situations, sales specialists or team assignments are essential to ensure coordination and open communication among all the parties involved.

Another way suppliers influence specifications is to play an active role in setting industrywide standards. At the industry level, this involves having a person from the producer's company on the appropriate association or government standards writing committee. Since a supplier's market success is often dependent on or threatened by standards and specifications, this responsibility should not be delegated to a junior person. This task is the responsibility of middle or top management or both. Specification writing by the customer is time-consuming and costly. For small-lot purchases, it may be prohibitive to prepare technical specifications. In such a situation, a supplier may literally write the specifications for the customer. An "industry standard" can also be established by a supplier providing technical information in a problem area where the product is used. In fact, a well prepared customer-user manual that provides technical assistance can actually help establish a company and its products as the "standard." This approach was employed by the Johnson & Johnson Company when it developed the first manual on sterile operating procedures for hospitals in the late 1800s. The manual was used in teaching antiseptic procedures to medical schools. Although Johnson & Johnson surgical products were mentioned only occasionally, the manual promoted Johnson & Johnson as an ethical or "antiseptic" supplier of medical products to hospitals. Interns and doctors adopted the antiseptic procedures and Johnson & Johnson products for their hospitals and office practices. Today, new editions of the manual are used as textbooks by medical and nursing students—the people who are tomorrow's buyers and specifiers.

## SOURCING DECISIONS

In the business world it is imprudent to rely on a single source of supply for almost anything. A sole source supplier has too much of an advantage in the negotiating process, and too many things can go wrong. For this reason, most business organizations identify and evaluate alternative sources of supply to meet their procurement needs.[21] If alternative sources do not exist, the smart buyer will develop additional sources either externally or internally. Once a supply source is selected or developed, the buying organization usually formally evaluates the supplier's product and service performance. The supplier's performance determines whether the relationship is maintained, decreased, or terminated. But before outside suppliers are considered, many industrial manufacturing firms ask this question: "Should we make or buy the item?"

### Make or Buy Situations

Customers who manufacture or have the potential to manufacture internally as well as buy externally are common in many industrial markets. The mental processes of

---

[21]Richard M. Cyert, Herbert A. Simon, and Donald B. Trow, "Observations of a Business Decision," *Journal of Business,* October 1956, pp. 237–48.

customers who are deciding whether to make or buy have many marketing implications for suppliers.

That the industrial buyer frequently has the option, incentive, and ability to make a product rather than buy it from an outside supply source is one of the major differences between household buying and industrial buying. The household buyer does not have this option. It is neither practical nor economical for a household buyer to even think about producing a water faucet. But for an industrial firm that manufactures sinks and bathtubs for builders and architects, it might be economically favorable, technically quite feasible, and competitively advantageous to make faucets rather than buy them from outside suppliers. If a customer decides to make rather than buy all or a portion of its annual requirements for an item, it represents a form of backward integration. Any manufacturer who buys a substantial volume of parts, components, subsystems, or assemblies is a prime candidate to begin producing the component and therefore to begin withdrawing its business from the open marketplace.

In many cases, straightforward cost or economic considerations swing the decision to internal production. Management simply determines that it would be economically advantageous to make an item rather than to continue to buy it from outside sources. In other situations, demanding requirements for quality and/or delivery are the factors that lead to the commitment to produce internally. For example, for many years General Electric purchased nearly all integrated circuits from outside. The company then decided to make rather than buy a larger percentage of the integrated circuits needed because an increasing number of its products required customized electronic components that were not readily available. Management is frequently faced with a make or buy decision whenever a component item becomes a large proportion of the manufacturer's costs for the product or a critically important part in the manufacturing process (if the producer cannot ship the final item if the component is not "on hand" or does not meet quality standards). Volume is always a consideration, but not always the deciding one. General Electric continues to produce customized integrated circuits internally, but buys the long-run standard items outside.

The decision to make rather than buy is not at all uncommon and is frequently reported in the news media. The NCR Corporation announced it would be spending nearly $200 million over four years to expand its internal capacity to develop and manufacture semiconductor parts, which are used as components in its computer systems and computer terminals. Previous to this, the company was manufacturing 40 percent of its needs internally. The added internal capacity will enable the company to produce 60 percent of its annual requirements. This action will significantly reduce the market for outside suppliers. NCR found it desirable from a performance and cost standpoint to enlarge its in-house capabilities. The firm also believes that greater in-house component capability will enable it to control quality, respond more quickly to the market, and "protect its supply of components in times of shortages."[22]

Many business markets consist of both captive producers and external sellers of the same item. The captive producers usually also buy part of their annual requirements from outside suppliers. When demand slows, the outside suppliers are usually the first to

[22] *The Wall Street Journal,* July 18, 1980, p. 5.

experience reduced orders. Exhibit 3-4 shows the major captive and noncaptive U.S. chipmakers. In 1982, the captives accounted for about 37 percent of the total market. As a result, the captive or make-buy customer is usually also a competitor.

In recent years, many backward integration situations have been prompted by extreme shortages of critical components. In addition to semiconductors, castings, forgings, and high-quality printed circuit boards have been in sufficiently short supply to prompt many manufacturers to consider internal production. Reliance Electric Company bought two small foundries to ensure a continued source of supply for an important part of its motor line. The company's president stated that he did not really want to be in the foundry business, but he recognized that environmental restrictions had forced many foundries out of business and jeopardized the company's supply lines for this critical component.

Although it is less common, industrial companies sometimes give up their make capability and turn to outside suppliers. When this occurs, it is usually because the company's make capability has become obsolete and it is too costly to bring up to date. For example, Tenneco Chemical Company discovered that it was less costly to buy a vinyl chloride monomer than it was to produce the product internally with its old and inefficient production process. In such situations, when a company does not update or reinvest in more current and efficient production processes, it may revert from being an internal producer to buying outside, as happened at Tenneco. In such situations, the supplier should analyze which internal captive sources are not updating production or processes and which may therefore become buying customers.

## Customer Make Decision

There are essentially two ways a manufacturer can achieve a make position once the decision to do so has been made. One alternative is to start from scratch and make the investment necessary to get into the manufacture of the desired component or part. Another alternative is to acquire a supplier company.

The start-up alternative is generally preferable when the technology of manufacture is not complex and investment requirements are not excessive. For example, many companies have started to manufacture their requirements for standard fasteners because the manufacturing process is not a difficult one to master and the machinery can easily be obtained. Sometimes a customer is forced into a startup program when none of the suppliers are realistic acquisition candidates because of size, ownership structure, or financial condition. On the other hand, many companies have successfully implemented a make decision by acquiring one or more suppliers. For example, NCR Corporation bought a company called American Digital Data Systems. NCR was the company's largest customer, buying about 42 percent of the firm's $50 million annual output.

The decision to acquire a supplier, particularly a large one, is generally a major strategic move. Such a decision often adds significantly to the investment and fixed cost base and makes the company more vulnerable to downturns in the economy. It also frequently takes the company into new markets, since the acquired source should maintain a free market position with customers other than the parent company. This is essential to maintain a competitive position that could easily erode if all the business were captive.

EXHIBIT
3-4

## THE LEADING U.S. CHIPMAKERS

| Merchants | | | Captives | | |
|---|---|---|---|---|---|
| Percent change from 1980 | | | Estimated IC production (Equivalent sales value in millions) | | |
| Estimated 1981 IC production (millions) | | | | | |
| Company | | | Company | | |
| 1981 rank | | | 1981 rank | 1981 | 1982 |
| 1. Texas Instruments | 1012 | +16 | 1. IBM | 1860 | 2580 |
| 2. Motorola | 795 | +16 | 2. Western Electric | 350 | 385 |
| 3. National Semiconductor | 683 | +5 | 3. Delco | 180 | 185 |
| 4. Intel | 544 | −12 | 4. Hewlett-Packard | 140 | 160 |
| 5. Fairchild | 375 | +7 | 5. Honeywell | 70 | 80 |
| 6. Signetics | 344 | −7 | 6. NCR | 60 | 70 |
| 7. Mostek | 304 | +10 | 7. Digital Equipment | 50 | 60 |
| 8. Advanced Micro Devices | 295 | +3 | 8. Burroughs | 40 | 40 |
| | | | 9. Data General | 25 | 35 |
| 9. RCA | 240 | −3 | 10. Tektronix | 20 | 25 |
| 10. Harris | 150 | −19 | | | |
| 11. General Instruments | 50 | +25 | | | |

Source: Integrated Circuit Engineering Corp.

## Selling to "Make-Buy" Customers

Selling to an existing or potential make customer is a difficult situation for any industrial marketer. In an existing make situation, where the customer buys outside as well as produces part of its requirements, the supplier is always faced with a high degree of risk. Any time business softens or turns down, the make customer will more than likely reduce or stop outside purchases to keep the captive producing facilities fully utilized.

The potential make customer is also difficult and risky to serve, especially as its annual requirements grow to a significant level. Large and growing volume requirements often trigger a make decision and leave the supplier with a costly gap in sales volume and capacity utilization. Also, the ever-present threat of making internally gives the buying organization negotiating leverage that puts downward pressure on the supplier's prices and margins. A key ingredient in selling effectively to existing or potential make customers is a comprehensive understanding of the customer's costs of producing the product. Said another way, it is essential to know whether:

1. The customer production cost is *more* than the supplier's production cost and desired profit margin price.
2. The customer's production cost is *about equal* to the supplier's production cost and desired profit margin price.
3. The customer's production cost is *less* than the supplier's production cost and desired profit margin price.

In situations 1 and 2 above, it is easier for a supplier to obtain a major portion of the business, but always with a continuing threat of losing the business if the customer's costs or situation changes. Situation 3 is a much more difficult marketing problem that can be overcome only by demonstrating noncost advantages that outweigh the straight cost comparison.

It is important for the market manager, market researcher, or industrial salesperson to identify and then determine the validity of a customer's stated reasons for making rather than buying a particular item. The respondent will typically say the company has decided to make rather than buy because the price is too high. Often further inquiry[23] will show that even though cost considerations are important, the decision to make rather than buy is based on multiple reasons rather than cost alone. As a consequence, it is important for the industrial salesperson to be aware of both the direct cost comparisons and the indirect costs or risks the customer incurs when it shifts to a make position. This requires the salesperson to have an understanding of some basic cost accounting concepts so that he or she can be sure that all indirect costs are fairly considered in the make-buy comparison. Factory or overhead costs and opportunity costs should always be considered, along with the risks that are always present when a customer moves into any new manufacturing operation.

In addition to clarifying cost comparisons, the industrial supplier should stress other considerations that need to be taken into account by the customer. For example, if the

[23]Vearl A. Williams, "Should You Make or Buy?" *Production Magazine*, June 1972, p. 79.

supplier has multiple factory locations, the salesperson can point out that they are less vulnerable to labor problems that could cripple the customer's production capability. It might also be pointed out that lack of technical experience, knowhow, and learning costs invariably inflate the estimated costs of any new production activity. In higher-technology areas, the risk associated with technological obsolescence and old inventories can be emphasized. In short, the supplier should stress any valid points it can to show the advantages of avoiding the risks and uncertainties of moving into a make position, even though there may be an apparent direct cost saving.

The unanticipated loss of a big account can have a major effect on total industry demand as well as a dramatic effect on the supplier to that firm. In many cases, the entire profit structure of the business can be unfavorably altered as suppliers with excess capacity cut their prices to compete for a smaller noncaptive market.

If the supplying firm does not continually monitor key customers who are in a position to make rather than buy, it can be in for some very unpleasant surprises. Often, the customers that choose to make are the largest in the industry and critically important to the supplier. One of the largest customers for hydraulic systems and hose connecting devices is the Caterpillar Tractor Company. Both its major suppliers were stunned when Caterpillar decided to manufacture about 90 percent of its annual hydraulic hose requirements rather than buy outside. Actually, Caterpillar's move was not surprising. These items represented a major annual purchase for final assembly of its earth-moving machines. Furthermore, these items had an annual aftermarket requirement several times larger than the original equipment requirement. When one considered both markets, it was logical to anticipate that Caterpillar Tractor would enter the manufacture of hydraulic hoses.

In one company that buys a large number of components for making its capital equipment, the materials management department created three categories of purchased parts. Category 1 lists the items they believe the company must make and reasons why it must make them. Category 2 are products and components the company has an option to make or buy along with the pluses and minuses of making versus buying each item. The third category is items the company feels it must buy outside, with the reasons for buying. Over time, and with increases in price, materials, and unit costs, the firm has found that components will sometimes move between the must-make, can-make-or-buy, or must-buy categories.

## Multiple or Sole Sourcing

Multiple supply sources create a more competitive environment among suppliers. It is common for the large U.S. buyer to have its annual purchasing requirements spread among two or more suppliers and to provide enough business for each supplier to keep all of them interested. When a buyer divides business among too many suppliers, it often is not sufficiently attractive for any supplier to perform the way it should. The insightful salesperson will stress this point in seeking additional business for his or her company.

Being a second or even third source with a similar item can sometimes be as profitable as being the primary source. To be a second source usually requires less capital, less technical capability, and less risk than that faced by the primary source. One supplier sees many of its second source customer relationships as "quick cash crops."

The importance buyers attach to multiple sources cannot be overemphasized. Buyers have been known to insist that a supplier of a proprietary item (even with demonstrable advantages) license or somehow help set up a second supply source before the product is adopted. This situation can create a major roadblock for the industrial salesperson who is unable to secure large buy commitments until such arrangements are made.

Only when a product is a relatively small proportion of the total cost or price, or is not a critical item, is there a tendency for buyers to have a sole or single source. For example, in the construction of a new chemical plant that may cost $10 to $15 million, there is approximately $100,000 to $125,000 worth of small precision fittings needed for each plant. With the cost of these fittings being such a small fraction of the total construction costs, there is little economic incentive for the design engineer or procurement people to use multiple sources. They may develop functional specifications and solicit bids from vendors, but they will typically award such business to one source.

A single supply situation is also common in the introductory stage of a customer's new product, since second sources may not exist or annual volume may not yet warrant two sources. A supplier may also enjoy a single source relationship because of production know-how, a patent position, or a proprietary process. However, any of these advantages are likely to be eroded as volume requirements for any customer become larger and the smart buyer exercises its leverage to insist on a second source.

Japanese manufacturers generally do not follow the U.S. procurement practice of frequently having multiple sources for an item. The Japanese believe that multiple sources and frequent rebidding and switching of suppliers fail to build supplier loyalty and tend to emphasize price. Frequent rebidding can sometimes open the door to suppliers who buy in low for the short term and then fail to perform satisfactorily. The rule of thumb of U.S. purchasing agents is "Always have at least two sources of supply for every item." Japanese companies, in contrast, prefer to buy a given item from one supplier and preferably one that does little or no business with competitors. The Japanese also tend to buy from the same few suppliers each year so that the suppliers thoroughly understand and respond to the service and quality needs of the buying organization.[24]

## Developing Sources of Supply

Industrial procurement managers are responsible for finding good suppliers. This task sometimes involves extensive research and field work by the buying organization to establish one or more suppliers as reliable sources. In some large firms procurement specialists do extensive research, including tracing the availability of an item all the way back to its origins.

A number of buyers have identified strategic components or raw materials in their manufacturing process or final products and have established long-term purchasing programs to support them. In some cases, either stockpiling or contractually securing longer-term sources of supply of the strategic item occurs. Rolls Royce in England is a major manufacturer of jet engines. The gas turbines within the jet engines need a high-temperature alloy. Rolls Royce found that two countries, Zaïre and Zambia, were pro-

[24]Schonberger, *Japanese Manufacturing Techniques,* p. 175.

viding 70 percent of the free world supply of cobalt, which was a critical metal in its gas turbines. Rolls Royce first began a major stockpiling program of the critical raw material and ultimately proceeded to buy an interest in one of the cobalt-producing mines. Similarly, backward integration through the acquisition of a critical raw material was done by a major machine tool company to establish a secure source of vanadium, which is an essential ingredient in making machine tool alloys. The ultimate goal of long-term source procurement programs is to protect stable sources of supply from economic, political, and labor instability. In some countries, the government identifies critical raw material source problems. In West Germany, the Bundesbank has provided low-cost loans to help West German corporations develop long-term sources of supply for critical key materials.

In an attempt to develop long-term sources of supply, a number of manufacturing firms have formal supplier development programs. In the development of secure and stable sources of supply, some buying organizations have spelled out their criteria for a source development program. In one company these criteria included the following:

1. Evidence of strong supplier fundamentals:
   a. On-time delivery.
   b. Low rejection rates in present work.
   c. Technical problem-solving capabilities.
   d. A good labor relations history or record.
   e. Compliance with OSHA and EEO and EPA regulations.
2. The capability to upgrade to specific requirements with minimal models or no additional capital investment.
3. An identifiable core or key group of supplier personnel who can develop production specification and documentation skills that may be required for close tolerances, such as industry or military specifications.

In supplier development programs, the buying organization may help the supplier to buy equipment; and help in job setup, quality control, raw material selection, job scheduling techniques, bid preparation, and cost accounting procedures. To have effective supplier development "reachout" programs, the buying organization should spell out the specific capabilities it is seeking. This helps the organization identify and select likely new sources of supply (see the box).

The development of new sources of supply usually takes many months and often years when there is no crisis. It requires close synchronization with the buying organization's requirements and the supplier's capabilities. Supplier and buyer staffs must work as a team to develop the supply relationship. Numerous visits to one another's plants occur before and during the startup period to achieve product features, to reduce defects, and to meet quality standards.

## Evaluating Suppliers

The continuing objective of a good supplier-buyer relationship is to achieve maximum value for both parties as they coordinate and combine their actions to produce mutually profitable results. The relationship requires suppliers to make a wide range of com-

## HOW TWO SUPPLIER DEVELOPMENT PROGRAMS WORKED

Proctor and Gamble is a large manufacturer of packaged household items for which it has virtually hundreds of suppliers that provide manufactured materials and containers. In such a situation, smaller suppliers often do not have the resources to develop equipment to manufacture an end product that may have a very short life cycle. For example, a bottle of antiperspirant spray has plastic extruded parts. The product may only have a market life of one or two years. To encourage firms to be suppliers in such situations, it is often necessary for Proctor and Gamble to provide financial resources to put the ingredient, component, or packaging supplier in business. In cases where special machinery or special tooling is required, it is not uncommon for the buyer to purchase or finance a large amount of the specialized tooling cost. Rather than develop these external sources, the larger buyer may choose to manufacture all or a portion of its annual needs.

The Tylenol capsule crisis caused Johnson & Johnson to look to its suppliers for a new packaging approach. A team of key suppliers worked nonstop for four months to develop and produce tamper-resistant packaging after the first victim died of Tylenol laced with cyanide on September 30, 1982. The director of materials management at the J. J. McNeil Division stated:

> We immediately called our suppliers on September 30, 1982, to consider alternatives. Gilbreth International provided the new sealing material, and Doboy Packaging Machinery provided the equipment for sealing the packages. Carton suppliers were very involved. 3M provided a cap with an inner seal. Lastly, special equipment was needed to attach the new seal-cap to the bottle. We scrambled, and all worked round the clock seven days a week to get out eight million new bottles in the tamper-resistant packages.[25]

mitments and buyers to explain the basis of their purchasing policies and practices. In maintaining stable and steady sources of supply, the purchasing department is usually responsible for performance evaluation of all supply sources. Materials, components, or products delivered late will disrupt most customers' manufacturing cycles, will cause delays that require production rescheduling, and in some cases can have a dramatic effect on a firm's profitability for that product or on an entire smaller corporation. Late deliveries inhibit an industrial customer from meeting commitments to its customers and can reduce its profitability and ultimately jeopardize reputations with customers.

Products or materials shipped to the buyer too early foster costly and abnormally high inventory levels that directly affect a manufacturing facility's space and cash flow. As a consequence, on-time—neither too early nor too late—supplier delivery is critical to the productivity and functioning of most manufacturing facilities. In most progressive procurement departments, on-time delivery is measured. Many buyers have developed delivery performance analysis systems that focus on the delivery times for a supplier on a monthly or yearly basis. Such evaluation systems compare promised delivery dates to actual dates of receipt by the customer. The rating systems award points the closer the

[25]"Drug Repackaging Is a Team Triumph," *The New York Times*, February 14, 1983.

actual delivery is to the promised date. Conversely, the later the delivery is from the promised or acknowledged date, the fewer points the supplier receives.

To avoid too much slack, many buyers will allow anywhere between one to two weeks early and up to one week late as "on-time" delivery. The Japanese "just-in-time" system usually has a much shorter time frame for "on time." A specific point system or weight that relates to how early, how late, or on-time the shipment is is preferable to systems using adjectives that say whether a supplier's delivery was unpredictable, excellent, bad, or good. A quantitative or analytical rating system also allows the buyer to rate a vendor's delivery performance against the buyer's standard and against any competitive vendors who are striving for a greater portion of the buyer's business. A delivery rating system should also factor in partial shipments that are on time compared to full shipments that are on time. Total on-time delivery should be defined as the receipt of 100 percent of the ordered quantity within the allotted early and late time period for on-time arrival. One company's delivery evaluation system for vendors is shown in Table 3.1. Industrial buyers increasingly provide all suppliers with monthly or quarterly computer printout delivery rating reports. These reports show, for each location shipped to, the number of units shipped on time, the percentage shipped early and late, and rejection rates. Some buyers seek a 95 percent "pieces on time" for each supplier to each location shipped. Supplier delivery performance rating reports are typically the first item of discussion when the supplier's salesperson calls on the account.

This emphasis on delivery performance obviously places any supplier at a disadvantage if its production scheduling system is weak or sloppy. In a situation like this the salesperson is bound to make delivery promises that are "guesstimates" based largely on what he or she thinks is required to get the order.

## MAINTAINING THE RELATIONSHIP

Most industrial buying situations hinge on several buying factors. The key decision to buy from one supplier and not from another typically turns on three or four of the seven factors described below:

**TABLE 3.1**

### DELIVERY EVALUATION SYSTEM

| Time Frame | Points |
|---|---|
| More than two weeks early | 8 |
| On time | 12 |
| 8–14 days late | 6 |
| 15–24 days late | 4 |
| 22–28 days late | 2 |
| More than 28 days late | 0 |

1. The unique or special capabilities performed by any one competitive product (performance).
2. Consistent quality equal to or better than the standards or specifications (quality).
3. The helpfulness of the relationship between an industrial customer and the sales or technical people that serve the account (service).
4. The promised or expected delivery date (delivery).
5. The historical experience, favorable or unfavorable, the buying organization has had with the producer (past experience).
6. Delivered per-unit price (price).
7. The cost-benefit value of alternative products performing the same or similar functions (competitive value).

How well the industrial supplier and its products serve the buyer according to these factors determines whether a relationship will occur or be terminated. A healthy supplier-buyer relationship is not adversarial or arm's-length; long-term supplier-buyer relationships are mutually dependent and beneficial.

Caterpillar Tractor, for example, has outlined the steps and basis for establishing and maintaining a supplier relationship with it. For any product, part, or subassembly, the company has outlined the following sequence of events it uses to select, evaluate, maintain, and terminate suppliers.

*Stage 1. Evaluate suppliers' quality capabilities.* Quality control performs a detailed examination of potential suppliers' control over the materials received from their suppliers. Potential suppliers are expected to show the specification requirements of *their* suppliers; an approved supplier list; a method of inspection or their supplier field auditing; and the presence of appropriately trained personnel for raw material and finished goods quality control. Any deficiencies will be improved or corrected through mutual agreement with Caterpillar and the supplier. Caterpillar quality control periodically conducts follow-up quality audit visits.

*Stage 2. Communicate quality requirements.* After a supplier has been selected, the buyer communicates the technical specifications and requirements to the supplier. Caterpillar maintains a series of manufacturing practices seminars and a manual that serves as a basis for assisting suppliers to fulfill its requirements.

*Stage 3. Preproduction sample approval.* Suppliers provide samples according to the agreed-upon sampling procedures for the item. Full-scale production does not commence until the samples are approved by the company. Preproduction sample approval does not relieve the supplier from sampling full production runs.

*Stage 4. Production shipments.* Any supplier's materials and components will be subject to dimensional, metallurgical, and functional inspection at the company. Inspection rates will be decreased as a good history is developed with suppliers and maintained or increased until a good history is developed. The company will also provide all suppliers with monthly or quarterly computerized delivery reports. These reports show the number of pieces or units shipped on time to each location, the percentage shipped early and late, and the rejection rate.

When a supplier's sales representative or executive calls on the company, these reports, whether favorable or not, are always an item of discussion.

*Stage 5. Measuring supplier performance.* Caterpillar continually reviews each supplier's history relating to shipments in stage 4, rejections, and any other nonconformance. Based on historical data, a status rating is assigned to each supplier. A less favorable status results in increased inspection and a decision to reduce the use of the source. Those suppliers who have continued excessive nonconformance are identified, and a program for improvement is established. Lack of response will result in reduced or terminated business. In this situation, Caterpillar will identify new potential suppliers and begin the process in stage 1.

## SUMMARY

A knowledge of how organizations buy will help the alert industrial supplier in many ways. First and most important, a thorough awareness of what a customer buys, how it buys, and who buys is at the heart of the concept of industrial marketing. Such a total procurement orientation helps the supplier better serve those who are buying for others.

Second, the business-to-business marketer should take the value analysis buying tool and use it as an analytical marketing, product development, and selling tool. Value analysis concepts help to satisfy the economic need of for-profit buying organizations. Value analysis helps to provide the cost-benefit reasons for maintaining an existing customer and converting the new prospects.

The industrial supplier should never assume it will be a sole or dominant supplier forever with existing customers. It should continually work at improving and thus maintaining existing favorable supplier-buyer relationships. Similarly, the industrial supplier should be persistent in attempting to understand and better serve a potential customer that is currently being served by a competitor. By learning what, how, and who buys, a competitive edge can often be developed that will turn a prospect into a profitable customer.

## REVIEW QUESTIONS

1. How does organizational buying differ from individual or household buying?
2. Since the organizational buying process is usually influenced by several people, what implications does this have for sales efforts?
3. What are the key areas buying organizations consider when evaluating suppliers?
4. What causes a customer to make a product rather than buy it?
5. How is value analysis a powerful tool for both buyer and seller?
6. What are some benefits to producers from reverse engineering?
7. Why do many customers have technical purchase specifications?
8. Why do companies typically maintain dual or multiple sources for an item?
9. Why is it sometimes necessary for the buying organization to develop a source of supply?

# APPENDIX

## Government Buying

Municipal, state, and federal governmental agencies and many nonprofit organizations do much of their purchasing through a bidding system. Each year, governmental agencies purchase billions of dollars worth of office equipment, cars, trucks, computers, medical supplies, and a wide range of other products. The majority of some corporations' or an entire division's business may come from government business as prime or subcontractors. Some industrial firms began as government suppliers and then later became OEM suppliers. Marketing to a government or defense market is somewhat similar to marketing to a very large OEM manufacturer. Industrial marketing occurs in government defense contracting with prime defense contractors, but it is the subcontractors to the 50 to 100 prime defense contractors that provide most of the tooling, machinery, equipment, and finished products. Government buying is basically a specification-delivery-price buying situation, and often a winner-take-all situation with no "market shares."

The for-profit buying organization is interested in value added, lower unit cost, or whatever affects the profitability of its end products. The profit motive or return on investment are not factors in government procurement. The price paid or cost of some government contracts is based on technical requirements and the amount of government appropriations. Within those parameters, profits are distributed to the major contractors and the subcontractors to develop an "effective" system or product. Federal appropriations determine the size of the system and subsequent contracts.

A cartoon that appeared in a popular magazine showed two astronauts in a space ship ready to blast off from Cape Canaveral, with one saying to the other: "Frank, was every product in this space ship built by the lowest price bidder?" In reality this is not usually the case. Government organizations often buy less on a cost-benefit dimension than for-profit corporations. Many government contracts never are bid. If the public or government agency is a municipality or even state agency, it will tend to favor suppliers within the country, political party, town, region, or state. United States senators and representatives aggressively try to obtain contracts for corporations with manufacturing facilities in their constituents' geographic regions.

Most of the U.S. government's procurement is done by the air force, army, and navy through the Department of Defense (DOD). The General Services Administration purchases for many other agencies. The agencies or departments develop standards for most of the items purchased so they can be assured of minimum quality levels. Government agencies set specifications and then evaluate or qualify potential suppliers against these specifications. In order to become qualified, it is necessary to meet procedural standards often set forth in quality control manuals that cover each step of a manufacturing process and quality control sampling. These regulations are usually enforced by the government agency's inspectors. In many instances, the government agency continually evaluates a supplier or contractor by maintaining a resident government inspector at the supplier's production site. The inspector may be full time or may maintain an office at the site that he or she visits periodically.

Commercial firms refer to buying as "purchasing" or "procurement," but the Department of Defense refers to it as "acquisition" or "acquisition programs." The acquisition

**EXHIBIT
3A-1**

### DEFENSE ACQUISITION CONTRACTING CYCLES

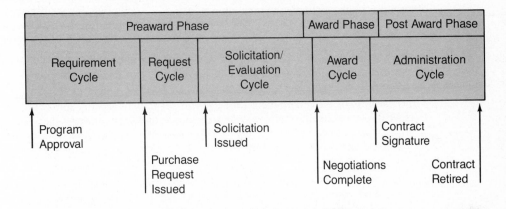

| Preaward Phase | | | Award Phase | Post Award Phase |
|---|---|---|---|---|
| Requirement Cycle | Request Cycle | Solicitation/ Evaluation Cycle | Award Cycle | Administration Cycle |

Program Approval

Purchase Request Issued

Solicitation Issued

Negotiations Complete

Contract Signature

Contract Retired

programs of the military buy a specific function that is specified by a military need. The military or "market" need is first established in an agency like the Strategic Air Command in the U.S. Air Force. These are, in essence, problems based on defense threats for which suppliers are to provide solutions. The need is budgeted by Congress and then contracts are let to suppliers to provide the products and services. Alternative suppliers are considered, and one or possibly two suppliers are then chosen. Exhibit 3A-1 illustrates a flow path for the defense acquisition process.[1] It is divided into the preaward, award, and postaward phases.

The requirements cycle and request cycle consists of the submission and approval of the mission need statement, and the solution and evaluation cycle consists of the concept formulation stage. The preaward phase "product" is a paper product, rather than hardware. In the award phase, hardware is developed—physical, tangible products. This consists of both prototypes (development) and production items (final products). The postaward phase is the contract administration stage where progress on the production contracts is monitored and delivery and testing occurs. At the end of this phase the contract is retired. . . . New systems evolve through four design states—conceptual design, preliminary design (narrowed-down concepts), engineering design (based on engineering development), and production design (ready to go to the presses and foundries).[2]

The Department of Defense procurement or acquisition process is all initiated by, monitored by, pursued by, and approved by the buyer rather than the supplier. The suppliers rarely risk their resources. The need and supplier selection are similar to for-profit procurement, but source loyalty is less prevalent.

[1]Ronald L. Shill, "Buying Process in the U.S. Department of Defense," *Industrial Marketing Management,* 9 (1980), pp. 291–298.
[2]Ibid., p. 293.

The *Commerce Business Daily* is the traditional place the federal government uses to inform potential suppliers of forthcoming bids. Any federal order over $5,000 by law must be listed in that publication. But the astute supplier is aware of the buying need long before it is published in the newspaper. The earlier a supplier can know of a need and influence the process, the greater chance it will have to get the business.

Contrary to public opinion, many government buyers prefer a sole source. The sales manager of a large medical instrument company stated the following after receiving a large order from a U.S. government health agency:

> Regardless of the government procurement regulations against sole sourcing, the Lab directors usually find a way to sole source on whatever items they only want from one source. Before the bid is advertised or published, the chosen supplier often has the order all but signed.

Government agencies often like sole sources because they can choose a known supplier and avoid the risk of having a low-bid supplier that later cannot deliver on time or meet quality specifications. The smaller the per unit or annual purchase amount, the more likely the government agency will not put it out for a competitive bid. Furthermore, if the need is immediate, as it usually is in an aftermarket situation, it will not wait for competitive bids. Government competitive bids that specify a brand name "or equivalent" force the second source supplier to prove equivalency. The proof requires that the salespeople or proposal must often have technical product test information to show the performance of the product compared to that of the specified brand name.

High-level agency officials are usually not aware of all the sole sourcing and noncompetitive buying that occurs. Protests to high government levels can get a second source or competitive bid situation activated. It is also easier to become a second source in a nonprofit organization when it is one to three months away from the end of its fiscal year and if the budget funds are not expended by the end of the year. One major electric typewriter company instructs all salespeople to learn each nonprofit organization's fiscal year period and to make more frequent calls in the six- to ten-week period before it ends. If a budget surplus exists, the organization may also be more willing to experiment with new or different products.

# EVALUATING THE MARKET ENVIRONMENT

# 4

# Understanding Customers and Competition

Understanding Customers
  Customers' Operations
  and Products
  Customers' Costs
  End-User Cost-Benefit
Understanding Competitors
  Competitive Structure
  Competitor Economics
  Market Success Factors
Marketing Strategy
Implications
Summary
Review Questions

At the monthly staff meeting, the general manager of the specialty chemical division of Dumont Chemical Corporation expressed concern about the downward sales trend and declining margins in the division's bread and butter product line. Sales were not only far off the plan for this year, but had dropped below last year's level for the same period. The general manager received several different responses. Said the sales manager: "We are being out-priced." With a better price discount structure, he felt he could restore the volume level. The division controller pointed out that a 5 percent reduction in price would require much higher volume to recapture the lost margin income. The controller also pointed out that there had been a long-term decline in unit sales growth for the past four years and that the numerous price increases had tended to obscure this fact. The manufacturing manager maintained there was no way to reduce costs further without affecting product quality and the service level.

After three hours, they were getting nowhere. Frustrated, the division general manager finally snapped: "Who knows what is really going on in the marketplace? Is the total market off? How are our competitors doing? I have a strong suspicion that a fundamental change has occurred in the way our product is being used or in the way competitors are serving these markets. A trend like this doesn't occur overnight, and we probably can't correct the problem with a short-term fix like cutting price. We need to have a very clear understanding of what is happening at the customer level and what our competitors are doing. Something fundamental is obviously affecting this product."

What is likely to happen if Dumont attempts a short-term fix?

What are the effects of the problem?

What are the real causes of the problem?

**M**any industrial producers often focus only on the products they produce and pay little attention to their customers' operations or to competitors who seek the same customer dollar. This is what is meant by a "product-driven" company. A product-driven industrial company is a sharp contrast to a truly market-oriented industrial company. Business-to-business marketing is too often a one-way flow of product communication to customers. But this is only part of the marketing job, since effective marketing depends on a flow of information about customer needs and competitors' actions. Vital information about customers and competition helps the industrial producer recognize, assess, and seize opportunities and counter threats. The industrial company whose products, strategies, and programs flow from analysis of customer requirements is a market-driven firm.

## UNDERSTANDING CUSTOMERS

Most industrial managers know who their major customers are and generally what these customers do. However, far too few managers really have the depth of understanding they should about how their customers operate and make their money. Even worse, most fail to understand the importance of this point or do not show the interest they should in developing this understanding. Peter Drucker wrote 30 years ago: "A business is not determined by the producer but by the customer."[1] Learning everything possible about the customer's business is the very essence of business marketing. It is the foundation for designing a product and service package that will offer the customer economic value, which is the basis of business marketing. It then allows the business marketer to segment markets and to determine which customers to pursue more, less, or to avoid entirely. It is this thought process that distinguishes effective marketing from simply trying to sell more products.

### Customers' Operations and Products

Each group of customers has, as the heart of its business, a unique set of functions to perform. Exhibit 4-1 shows the major functions involved in a metal production and rough machining process. Similar schematics can be developed to identify the critical functions performed by any customer group. Understanding the critical functions is the first step toward understanding the customer's operations and products. A much deeper study and analysis are required to achieve the depth of understanding that will enable the business marketer to consider ways in which its products can really help the customer become more cost effective. Many of the best business marketing companies have developed substantial banks of industry skills that help to provide this knowledge of customer operations. With this kind of knowledge, it is much easier to develop marketing strategies and sales proposals that contribute real value to the customer and are difficult for uninformed competitors to match.

[1]Peter Drucker, *The Practice of Management* (New York: Harper & Row, 1954).

**EXHIBIT
4-1**

# *METAL PRODUCTION AND FABRICATION*

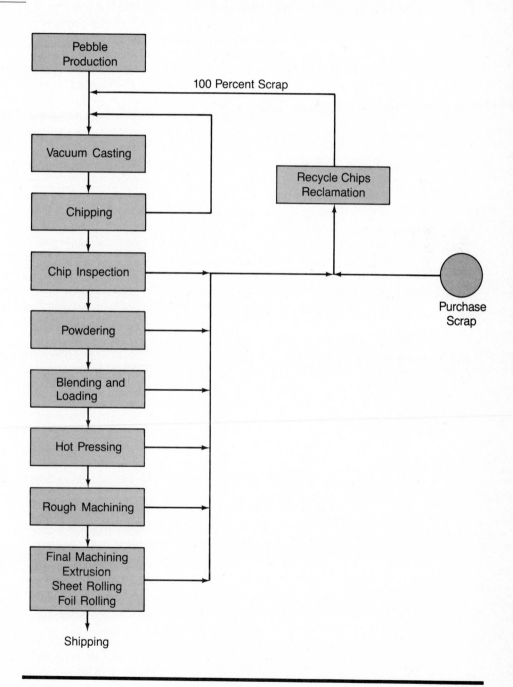

Exhibit 4-1 was helpful to a supplier in thinking through how a toxic dust and fume collection system should be designed to meet OSHA requirements. Its understanding of each function in the flow led to a system design that was more effective and less costly than those submitted by competitors. In another situation, a scale supplier sold a system that reduced waste at several points during the conversion of raw potatoes to chips. Again, the supplier's intimate knowledge of the customer's operations helped it design a system that concentrated on the areas of maximum payoff for the least investment in weighing equipment. In both examples, the supplier, rather than merely seeking an order, was able to help the customer improve performance.

Progressive manufacturers of almost anything are continually searching for ways to streamline their manufacturing processes or utilize new, more cost-effective approaches or materials. Unless the supplier keeps pace with the customer's thinking and ideas for altering the way it operates, it can easily find that new methods or materials have made its product obsolete. For example, automotive oil was packaged and distributed in metal cans for many years. The principal can supplier was unaware that oil companies were experimenting with cardboard containers that cost and weighed less and would not corrode during storage. Because these advantages were so significant, the oil producers abruptly shifted to cardboard containers and completely eliminated the metal can supplier from the picture. There may not have been any way the can supplier could have prevented this shift, but had it been aware of what was going on, it might have decided that the container business was sufficiently large to invest in equipment to manufacture cardboard containers itself, since the customer was first buying a function and then the best product to perform the function.

Learning and knowing the customer's functions and the products available to perform those functions enable the supplier to think, talk, and perform around the customer's needs. For example, the Office Products Division of IBM, which primarily manufactures and markets typewriters and word processing equipment, developed a functional approach to analyze word processing in an office. The three functions are (1) word origin, (2) production (typing), and (3) distribution and storage. This functional view of office word processing (Exhibit 4-2) allows IBM to improve products in each function and to consider combining functions in a product. A good example is IBM's memory typewriter, which now performs both production (typing) and storage functions.

Still another example points up the need to evaluate the customer's flow of work as a system to gain a better understanding of its requirements. The Pitney Bowes Corporation analyzed its customers' mailroom and mailing activities as a production system. It partitioned the mailroom "production system" of customers into identifiable functions and from this has developed a line of products beyond postage meter machines that now includes mail sealers, mail openers, folders, inserters, collators, counters, weight scales, and mailroom furniture as part of the functional system.

## Customers' Costs

Once the customer's functions and production stages are identified, the supplier can develop a much clearer picture of where and how the customer incurs costs to perform the functions and where there are opportunities to improve an existing cost structure. The

**EXHIBIT
4-2**

## OFFICE WORD PROCESSING

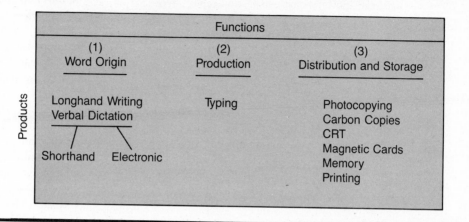

customer costs that need to be identified fall into two categories. What costs does the customer incur by buying or using a product and what costs does it recover or avoid? Although these sound like obvious questions, the answers are not so simple. Cost-benefit advantages and comparisons are not always readily apparent or clear-cut, especially when the full range of costs is considered. The range of costs to consider includes the initial purchase cost, installation costs, operating costs, and life cycle costs.

INITIAL PURCHASE COST.   The initial purchase or first cost is the amount the customer pays up front. In addition to the list or quoted price of the product, there are charges for financing, freight, insurance, installation, technical assistance at startup, warranty, and/or service. It is essential to be certain that all these costs are considered in making competitive comparisons. Failing to do so can easily lead to the wrong economic decision even though the chosen supplier appears to offer the lowest price. Customers that base their buying decision primarily on initial purchase cost are a prime target for the low-cost producer that can gear its whole marketing strategy to providing the best value on this initial cost comparison.

INSTALLATION AND STARTUP COSTS.   Installation costs may involve space alterations, connections to power sources, facilities for ensuring proper temperature and ventilating conditions, and arrangements for handling noise, waste materials, scrap, and so on. Startup costs typically occur after installation and involve all the activities required to ensure that the product or system actually performs to specification or the producer's claims. Both of these are typically nonrecurring, but nevertheless substantial, costs. In many cases, highly skilled individuals or teams of supplier personnel actually operate the product or system on the user's site and make the final adjustments necessary to ensure performance.

OPERATING COSTS.   Operating costs are the ongoing costs of utilizing a particular product or system. They include most of the standard accounting charges like labor, material, power, maintenance and repair, depreciation, and interest charges on the purchased item or inventory. Short-term differences in these costs are typically minimal, but they often become significant when calculated over the longer term. Table 4.1 shows how an annual savings of $1,125 could be achieved by using an energy-efficient 150-horsepower motor. Although this motor would undoubtedly cost more initially, the return could be very attractive, particularly when these savings are extended for the estimated useful life of the motor and a reasonable allowance is made for rising energy costs. Similar analyses can be made for any operating costs that are reduced as a result of a higher investment in the initial purchase price.

Exhibit 4-3 shows the operating cost savings or payback for a new commercial light bulb. The initial purchase price of $10 for an electronic bulb is cost-effective when compared to an incandescent bulb over a two-year period. The more rational industrial buyer thinks in terms of operating costs after the purchase much more than the average consumer does. As a consequence, operating cost considerations often weigh heavily in industrial purchase decisions.

SWITCHING COSTS.   Beyond the traditional user costs defined above, one final set of costs must sometimes be considered. These are the costs of switching from one supplier's product to another's. For example, the cost of switching from IBM equipment to another

| TABLE 4.1 | | ANNUAL ENERGY SAVINGS* | | |
|---|---|---|---|---|
| *Horsepower* | *XE Eff.* | *Ind. Avg. Eff.* | *Watts Saved* | *Money Saved* |
| 3 | 88.5 | 81.3 | 224 | $   64 |
| 5 | 88.5 | 83.6 | 252 | $   72 |
| 7-½ | 90.2 | 84.6 | 410 | $  118 |
| 10 | 90.2 | 85.7 | 434 | $  125 |
| 15 | 91.7 | 86.7 | 704 | $  203 |
| 20 | 93.0 | 87.8 | 950 | $  274 |
| 25 | 93.0 | 88.3 | 1,067 | $  307 |
| 30 | 93.0 | 89.5 | 941 | $  271 |
| 40 | 93.0 | 89.8 | 1,143 | $  329 |
| 50 | 94.1 | 90.5 | 1,577 | $  454 |
| 60 | 94.1 | 90.7 | 1,783 | $  513 |
| 75 | 95.0 | 91.3 | 2,387 | $  687 |
| 100 | 95.0 | 92.0 | 2,561 | $  737 |
| 125 | 95.0 | 92.1 | 3,091 | $  890 |
| 150 | 95.8 | 92.7 | 3,906 | $1,125 |

*Based on typical utility rates of $.04 per kilowatt hour and 7,200 hours per year of motor operation.

**EXHIBIT
4-3**

## HOW A $10 LIGHT BULB PAYS FOR ITSELF

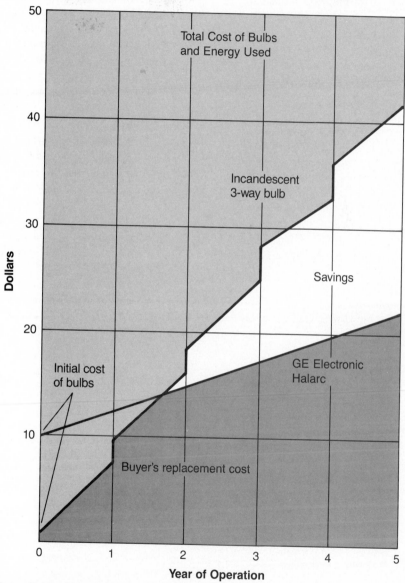

Total Cost of Bulbs
and Energy Used

Incandescent
3-way bulb

Savings

Initial cost
of bulbs

GE Electronic
Halarc

Buyer's replacement cost

**Dollars**

**Year of Operation**

Data: General Electric Co. (assumes electricity cost of 4.6¢ per kw
and use of 1,000 hours a year)

*Source: Business Week,* May 19, 1980, p. 124.

manufacturer's equipment is significant because in-house personnel must be retrained to operate the new equipment. Similarly, changing suppliers that provide consignment stocks can involve substantial costs unless careful plans are made to gradually phase out of one supplier's remaining stock into the other. Switching costs can be both tangible and intangible. Tangible costs include costs like those in the examples just cited. They are real and can be calculated or measured. Often equally important, however, are the intangible or penalty costs that can be incurred whenever a new supplier is brought on stream; there is always a risk that a new supplier will fail to provide consistent quality, on-time delivery, or proper service support. Although these costs cannot be calculated in advance, they can certainly be significant if the new supplier fails to perform.

LIFE CYCLE COSTS.   These costs are important to consider whenever the estimated useful life of one product differs from another. In addition to all the costs described so far, they include any residual or salvage value as well as replacement costs when the original equipment has completed its useful life. Evaluating life cycle costs has assumed an added importance during the past decade because inflationary forces have greatly increased the residual or salvage value of many items and caused replacement prices to rise much faster than they had in the past. Table 4.2 shows how life cycle costing was used to compare the economics of a solar and a conventional heating system over a 20-year life. Even though the initial purchase cost of the solar system is 40 percent greater than the

| TABLE 4.2 | LIFE CYCLE COSTING: A 20-YEAR COMPARATIVE ANALYSIS* | | |
|---|---|---|---|
| | Type of Energy System | Combined Solar/ Standard System | Conventional System Only |
| P = | Initial investment costs | $20,000 | $12,000 |
| | Salvage | 0 | ($4,000) 20th yr |
| S = | Present value of salvage | 0 | $596 |
| | Maintenance and repair costs | 0 | (0) |
| M = | Present value of maintenance and repair | 0 | 0 |
| | Replacement costs | 0 | ($6,000) 15th yr |
| R = | Present value of replacement costs | 0 | $1,434 |
| | Base-year energy costs | ($500) | ($2,000) |
| E = | Present value of energy costs | $6,359 | $25,436 |
| LCC = | Present value of total costs | $26,359 | $38,274 |

Formula: LCC = P − S + M + R + E

Combined solar/standard system: LCC = $20,000 − 0 + 0 + 0 + $6,359 = $26,359

Standard system only: LCC = $12,000 − $596 + 0 + $1,434 + $25,436 = $38,274

*Only present values are used in the LCC formula, and numbers in parens cannot be inserted directly into the formula.

conventional system, the costs over the full life cycle are approximately 30 percent less. The salvage and replacement costs, as well as the operating savings, are the major plus factors that offset the higher initial investment costs. If products performing the same function have different useful life periods or wear-out rates, the concept of life cycle cost can provide a favorable advantage to a supplier. Exhibit 4-4 shows the life cycle costs involved in owning a lift truck; it deemphasizes the initial purchase price and stresses the life cycle costs of owning and operating the unit. The Caterpillar advertisement in Exhibit 4-5 emphasizes the real costs a customer incurs when purchasing a machine. Caterpillar stresses that the total customer cost for its machines may be less than that of the competition, which should mean higher profit or lower cost for the Caterpillar owner.

## End-User Cost-Benefit

Once cost components are quantified, it is possible to determine the cost-benefit for the end user. The cost-benefit analysis helps in determining the economic value-in-use of a producer's product in a customer's particular application. Table 4.3 shows how an end-user cost-benefit analysis was used to (1) determine the costs of activities to perform the function, and (2) compare competitors A and B on the cost components and total value.

Table 4.3 is a general framework for identifying a customer's costs for purchasing a part, machine, or materials. Some of the cost components will not be applicable for every product situation. The industrial supplier should select those costs that are applicable to the specific product and market situation. In many situations, the economic cost terms will have to be modified to the language and units of analysis of that particular industry. For example, Table 4.4 is a similar cost analysis for a finger implant for arthritic patients. It shows that although the initial purchase price is higher, the total cost to the end user (customer or patient) is lower. Since this analysis shows that end user's total costs are *significantly* lower for producer B's product, it raises a question of whether or not producer B has set its initial purchase price high enough.

| TABLE 4.3 | END-USER COST-BENEFIT COMPARISON | |
|---|---|---|

|  | End-Use Segment | |
|---|---|---|
| Cost Components | Competitor A | Competitor B |
| 1. Initial purchase cost | | |
| 2. Installation and startup | | |
| 3. Operating cost | | |
|     Yearly | | |
|     Product life | | |
| 4. Switching costs | | |
| 5. Salvage value | | |
| 6. Average product life | | |
| Total cost | | |

*Source:* Clark Industrial Truck

EXHIBIT
4-5

## REAL COSTS OF OWNERSHIP

# Profit conscious buyers know total machine cost

**Total Cost Evaluation is the profitable way to examine machine costs.** Buyers purchasing based only on initial price overlook very important costs that affect potential profit.

That's because true machine cost goes far beyond initial price. You must add operating and maintenance costs to your repair and downtime costs. Then subtract depreciation and resale value to get Total Cost.

And, Total Cost Evaluation demands a search for machines having high resale values and low operating, maintenance, repair and downtime costs. Lower costs mean higher profits.

**Total Cost Evaluation is the objective way to select new machines.** Your Caterpillar Dealer stands ready to help set up Total Cost record systems. Such professional assistance is only one of many CAT PLUS services available from Caterpillar Dealers.

**CATERPILLAR**

Caterpillar, Cat and ⊞ are Trademarks of Caterpillar Tractor Co.

INITIAL
PRICE

**PLUS**
Operating & Maintenance Cost

**PLUS**
Repair & Downtime Cost

**MINUS**
Depreciation & Resale Value
**EQUALS**
TOTAL COST

*Source:* Caterpillar Tractor Company

**TABLE**
**4.4**

## COST-BENEFIT FINGER IMPLANT COMPARISON

| Cost Components | Competitive Products | |
| --- | --- | --- |
| | A | B |
| 1. Initial purchase price for four: | | |
| 4 × 82    (A) | $ 328 | — |
| 4 × 275  (B) | — | $1,100 |
| 2. Preoperative evaluation | 28 | 28 |
| 3. Surgical procedure (installation) | 1,100 | 1,100 |
| 4. Splints | 65 | 40 |
| 5. Hospital stay: | | |
| 12 days × $300/day   (A) | 3,600 | — |
| 4 days × $300/day   (B) | — | 1,200 |
| 6. Hospital occupational therapy | 280 | 0 |
| 7. Follow-up outpatient treatment | 0 | 40 |
| 8. Follow-up outpatient visit | 120 | 120 |
| Total cost | $5,521 | $3,628 |

The major cost benefits are not necessarily found with the immediate customer. For example, a high-temperature heat-resistant hydraulic hose that is installed on commercial bakery oven doors has a safety and downtime value to bakeries but offers little or no "cost savings" to the bakery oven manufacturers. If the major benefits are beyond the supplier's customer (in this case the OEM), the producer's selling effort must be directed at the end user to get it to specify or request the supplier's product.

**EXHIBIT**
**4-6**

## PUSH OR PULL VALUE-IN-USE

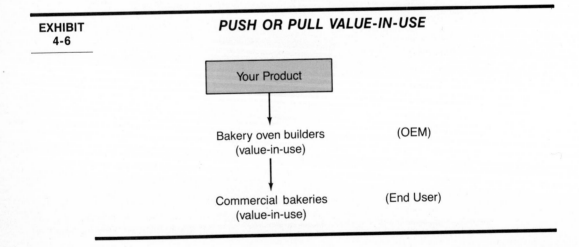

It is often necessary to develop in-depth case studies with a few customers to identify and calculate the cost-benefit value by application or market segment. This is especially necessary when the customer has not kept good cost-benefit information.

# UNDERSTANDING COMPETITORS

After the business marketer knows the customer's operations and need for the product, it is necessary to examine the competitors that provide a product that performs the same function(s). A competitor may not supply an exact "pin-for-pin" product or one made of the same material, but if in the customer's eyes the competitive product fulfills the same function, it is a competitive product and therefore a competitor to analyze. An analysis of competitors is an analysis of businesses that compete for the same customer's sales dollars.

An assessment of the competition is always important—whether the company is protecting, improving, or entering a new market situation. Competitive assessment entails a knowledge of who present and potential competitors are; an analysis of how well each competitor meets the requirements of a segment; and an analysis of competitors' plans and likely reactions. Since there is usually a different set of competitors in each product or market segment, any meaningful form of assessment should be conducted for *each* product or market segment.

## Competitive Structure

It is important to know the number and market share of the competitors supplying each market segment, since these factors greatly influence all marketing plans and decisions. Fragmented markets, characterized by a large number of competitors, each with a small market share, tend to be more unstable and unpredictable. Conversely, when a small number (e.g., two to four) of competitors account for 70 to 80 percent of the market, competitive behavior is more stable and predictable. Generally, the more capital intensive industries have fewer producers, whereas industries that are relatively easy to enter and leave are usually much more highly fragmented.

The existence of a captive or internal supply source is a competitor even though that source may not be selling to other customers. Some captive competitors also buy a percentage of their requirements from outside suppliers. A thorough competitive analysis should identify the total market served by those with and without captive sources. When a large or increasing percentage of a segment is supplied by captive sources, market economics are generally less attractive.

The major sources of present and potential competition to consider in conducting a competitive analysis can be classified as follows:

1. Present competitors supplying a directly competing product or a functional substitute to current and potential customers in the geographic areas the firm now serves.
2. Competitors supplying a directly competing product or a functional substitute to cus-

tomers in geographic areas the firm does not serve. This is often a foreign producer supplying customers outside the domestic market.

3. Captive sources that determine what percentage of the total market is available to outside suppliers. The make-buy customer can also compete directly by selling the captive product to outside customers.

4. Suppliers that integrate forward to earn greater profits. If the market size, market growth, and profitability of a segment are attractive, suppliers who know the business may move forward and compete with their customers.

5. Employees leaving to go to competitors or go it alone. The hiring of these employees by a current noncompetitor may signal a new competitive entrant. If these employees start their own business to compete, they frequently "cherry pick" key products and accounts.

6. Surprise sources. New competitors, especially those with a unique technology advantage, often come from outside the existing competitors or industry. The diesel locomotive was introduced by a firm that had never before made steam locomotives. Plastic beverage bottles were developed and introduced by chemical firms, not glass or metal bottle manufacturers.

## Competitor Economics

Companies within the same industry can have very different cost structures, which can be due to a number of factors, including these:

1. The age and condition of their physical plant
2. The effectiveness and efficiency of their machines
3. The productivity of their labor force
4. The degree of forward or backward integration
5. Size and market share

How competitive a firm is in the marketplace often depends on the cost and productivity of its workforce and manufacturing process. This is especially true in mature industries where one must be a lower-cost producer to be an effective competitor. Many different manufacturing strategies are being employed to reduce labor costs and improve productivity and manufacturing efficiency. Many companies have abandoned their huge centralized manufacturing facilities in favor of smaller decentralized plants that typically employ 200 to 500 people. Overhead costs can be reduced in these smaller facilities, they are easier to manage and control, and the lines of communication to the workforce are much easier to maintain. Many other companies have invested heavily in robotics or other automation devices and systems in an effort to eliminate high-cost labor and build greater cost efficiency into their manufacturing process. Still other companies have migrated to other countries, particularly for high-labor content assembly operations, to take advantage of the much lower labor costs.

Some producers have a lower-cost advantage because they have integrated backward to a material source. For example, many chemical companies have become "basic" in one or more of their key ingredients in an effort to become a lower-cost producer. A firm may also become a lower-cost producer by integrating forward and acquiring a customer's products or operations, which can then be combined with its own in a cost-effective way. Still other producers have achieved significant cost advantages by setting up their operations in close proximity to a critical material source. For example, Montreal's Alcan Aluminum Ltd. has about 60 percent of its primary smelter capacity in Canada. Plentiful hydroelectric power keeps Alcan's average cost to about $.05 per pound of aluminum[2] while the major U.S. competitors, Alcoa, Reynolds, and Kaiser, spend over $.15 per pound. This cost advantage allows Alcan to compete profitably even when shipping near its competitors' plants. If the cost of electricity in petroleum-fed aluminum mills increases, the less costly hydroelectric facilities will provide even greater competitive advantage for Alcan.

Being the biggest or having a dominant market share does not assure any firm of being the low-cost producer. For example, the electromotive division of General Motors, with 1980 sales of $1.2 billion, had approximately a 75 percent market share of the U.S. locomotive market. The only significant competitor, the General Electric Transportation Systems Division, had the remaining 25 percent of the U.S. market but a lower manufacturing cost structure. General Motors' overwhelming volume and market share did not give it a cost advantage because of its very high labor costs: General Motors United Auto Workers were paid $3 to $4 dollars an hour more than GE's United Electrical and Radio Machine workers. This cost disadvantage persisted despite the fact that General Motors' electromotive division had been in the business of making diesel locomotives approximately 20 years before General Electric entered the business in 1960.[3] In short, the popular belief in experience curves and lower cost per unit of volume is refuted by such "real world" factors as labor rate differentials.

Because experience curve costs are frequently misused or misunderstood, an explanatory comment is worthwhile. The experience curve concept holds that the "costs of value added to a product decline approximately 20 to 30 percent in real terms each time the manufacturing experience is doubled." Supporters of this concept contend, therefore, that the producer with the highest market share will generally have the lowest cost because of its perceived economies of scale and greater manufacturing experience. In many cases these supporters are mistaken. They have not differentiated the degree of cost improvement that can be achieved in a mature business from that that can be achieved in a new or rapidly growing business where there is still plenty of room for manufacturing improvements.

The experience curve should not be confused with the learning curve, which was discovered over 50 years ago. The learning curve is very real for new, growing businesses and in situations where true productivity gains are achieved by working smarter. However, the opportunities for cost efficiencies diminish over the long term as manufacturing methods become routine and producers' facilities and equipment reach state-of-the-art.

## Market Success Factors

Before a supplier can compete in any industrial product or market situation, there are a number of capabilities it must have in place. These market entry factors vary by market

---

[2]"The Sign of the Water Bearer," *Forbes,* March 2, 1981, p. 50.
[3]*Business Week,* June 8, 1981.

served, but often include having a minimum level of quality, proven manufacturing capability, technical know-how, service capability, and possibly an extensive distributor network. However, simply having the necessary capabilities does not ensure success in a competitive marketplace.

When industrial producers ask "How are we doing compared to competition?" they should look beyond sales volume or market share figures. The more appropriate question to ask might be this: "What factors cause a customer to choose one supplier over another?" One could call the "causes" the key success factors for serving the identified market. They are the vital factors on which the buying decision turns. Customers' explanations of why they buy or do not buy from a particular supplier are often different from what suppliers think. Astute suppliers recognize this point and go to their customers to find out firsthand what factors swing the buying decision.

The worksheet shown in Table 4.5 can be used to conduct a competitive analysis of the key success factors for serving a given market. Since successful business marketing involves the supplier's production, engineering, and marketing personnel, it is helpful to have the inputs of all these people.

CONDUCTING A COMPETITIVE ANALYSIS.   The steps involved in conducting such a competitive analysis are straightforward:

1. List the success factors that control or influence the buying decision for a product in a defined market segment. Three to six factors are usually sufficient.
2. Rank order the competitive success factors that were listed in step 1.
3. Weigh each ranked success factor. For example, success factor 1 might have a weight of 35 percent. All the success factors must total 100 percent (see "Weights" column of Table 4.5).
4. List the major competitors that account for 80 to 90 percent of the defined market segment.
5. On a scale of 1 to 10 (10 = most favorable, 1 = least favorable), rate the competitors on each success factor.
6. On a scale of 1 to 10 (10 = most favorable, 1 = least favorable), rate your firm on each success factor.
7. Multiply each competitor and your firm's 1 to 10 rating number times the success factor weight. For example, in Table 4.5, multiply sealing capabilities (.35) times competitor 1's rating of 9: .35 × 9 = 3.15.
8. Total each competitor's total in the row labeled "competitive position." The competitive position scores should compare closely to current market share. If the competitive position scores do not compare closely to known current market shares, the key success factors, ranks, or weights are inaccurate. If market shares are not known, competitive position scores can serve as a surrogate market share estimate.

A quantitative competitive analysis can be very useful when developing product or market strategies to enter a market, to protect an established position, or to improve an existing position. The analysis helps one see which competitors are strong and weak and what success factors account for their strong or weak positions. It helps a company focus

**TABLE 4.5**

## COMPETITIVE ANALYSIS WORKSHEET

Product/Market Segment

| Key Competitive Success Factors | | Major Competitors | | | | | | Self-Analysis | |
|---|---|---|---|---|---|---|---|---|---|
| | | 1 (Rockgood) | | 2 (Best-Warner) | | 3 (Tokyo Products) | | (ARW) | |
| Factors | Weights | 1–10 | | 1–10 | | 1–10 | | 1–10 | |
| 1. Sealing capabilities | .35 | 9 | 3.15 | 5 | 1.75 | 8 | ? | 9 | 3.15 |
| 2. On-time delivery | .25 | 9 | 2.25 | 6 | 1.50 | ? | | 2 | .50 |
| 3. Technical assistance | .20 | 8 | 1.60 | 3 | .60 | | | 5 | 1.00 |
| 4. Price | .20 | 6 | 1.20 | 7 | 1.40 | | | 8 | 1.60 |
| 5. | | | | | | | | | |
| Competitive position | 1.00 or 100% | | 8.20 | | 5.05 | | | | 6.25 |
| Current market segment share | | 42% | | 19% | | | | 32% | |

on the factors it needs to improve. In one case, a company thought a price reduction would help its position. However, the competitive analysis done by interviewing customers revealed that customers were much more sensitive to rapid delivery service. It used less money than the price reduction would have cost to improve delivery and showed a significant market improvement over the next two years.

For longer-range planning and strategy development, the industrial producer should utilize a competitive analysis by asking the following future-based questions:

1. How might the success factors change in ranking and weight in the next two to three years?
2. Which existing competitors are likely to improve their competitive position?
3. Which existing competitors are likely to decline in position or exit from this market?
4. What new competitors might appear or enter the business?

Asking these questions often provides an "early alert" to competitive changes by helping the firm anticipate threats and opportunities.

GATHERING COMPETITIVE INTELLIGENCE.   Gathering competitive intelligence is an ongoing process. Even the smallest suppliers can and should gather information about competitors. Competitive intelligence tends to come in fragments from many sources and often is not "hard" information. Nevertheless, it can provide very useful insights that can help formulate strategies and plans.

Competitive intelligence gathering should seek information from:

1. Product comparisons
2. Pricing
3. Expansion plans and plant closings
4. Promotional strategy
5. R&D expenditures
6. Manufacturing processes
7. Patents filed
8. Labor contract expiration dates, wages, and strikes
9. Profit and loss statements
10. Number of employees per unit or division
11. New product announcements
12. Changes in personnel
13. Interviews with competitors' personnel
14. Analysis of past bidding situations
15. An incident of very high bidding
16. Common suppliers
17. Trade shows
18. Local newspapers
19. Technical standards committees
20. Other divisions that buy from or sell to the competitor

There are many monitoring techniques a company can use to keep tabs on present and potential competitors. One technique is to buy competitors' products and evaluate them for performance and, if possible, take them apart piece by piece. This approach enabled one component supplier to market an item for less than its competitors by substituting plastic for many metal parts. A major photocopy machine producer has a full-time staff analyzing all U.S. and foreign-made copiers for performance, benefits, and features. The analysis is used for product development improvements, sales training, and product literature comparisons.

The industrial sales force is sometimes considered a biased and poor source of comprehensive information. This is sometimes true, but the problem is that the receivers and users of the information have not been properly trained. The industrial salesperson's role in understanding end-use markets is critical. The intelligence he or she develops about end users' needs, business patterns, and competition can be the lifeblood of future product-market plans and strategies. Field sales personnel should be required to obtain and should be rewarded for providing feedback on the activities of customers, distributors, and competitors. Because of paperwork and commission pressures, this approach is often not very productive. One company's division top management meets periodically with all salespeople to discuss competitive matters. At another firm, the product managers frequently travel with different salespeople to gather information.

A periodic review of patent dockets can also reveal key product features. Patent searches have revealed so much information to competitors that some firms deemphasize the filing of any patents and stress the need to guard trade secrets. Engineers and technical professionals attend the same professional society meetings where they interact with their competitive counterparts. In this situation, competitive information is often exchanged freely, especially when loyalty to one's technical discipline is stronger than loyalty to the current employer. Some of these same technical people are the company's representatives on industry standards committees. When one company desires to change a standard, it usually provides clues and sometimes technical data on a new product or material it plans to market.

Bidding situations also offer the opportunity to learn about competitors. One supplier follows a practice of submitting ridiculously high bids when it just wants to learn about the competition. A lost bid analysis in serious bidding situations helps it learn the reasons why one firm got the business and the other firms lost it. And when a customer requests a second bid from all suppliers, it often allows bidding suppliers to analyze the competitive proposals.

Common suppliers are one of the most valuable sources of competitive information. A major pump manufacturer had a buying relationship with a machine tool company salesman. The same machine tool company salesman sold equipment to the pump manufacturer's largest competitor. The salesman told the pump manufacturer the competitor's floor space, current production schedules, age and type of machines, labor costs, and explained the reasons why the competitor had purchased some new equipment.

Other divisions within a large corporation can often provide competitive information. The sister division may be supplying the competition with products, or it might be buying an item from the same competition. When sister divisions or subsidiaries are highly autonomous and geographically separated, this source of competitive intelligence is often untapped.

Top management of the division and corporate headquarters management should spend a number of days a year talking to customers in the field. This is an excellent way to gather intelligence, and the top executive will then understand comments from customers about competitors' actions. The chairman and CEO of NCR, William Anderson, believes it is a critical part of his job to keep abreast of the marketplace and therefore spends a number of weeks per year in the field gaining competitive intelligence.

Trade shows are a source of competitive intelligence and a place to leak your company's proprietary information. Salespeople, who are often extroverted and like to talk, will often tell too much about their company and products at trade shows. In one instance, a salesperson attending a trade show told "prospects" in the booth the company's profit margins on a number of products. The salesperson was not aware that he was giving proprietary information to "prospects" who were actually competitors. However, a trade show is an excellent place to learn about competition, especially about the small or private company, since this is frequently the only time its staff is accessible. A smaller company's strategy and approaches can sometimes be observed at trade shows. Some competitors disguise their trade show badge affiliation so they can learn more by visiting other competitors' booths. Other firms will hire consultants to visit competitive booths. One major office product company that always sends technical and marketing teams to visit trade shows repeatedly obtains product improvement ideas and sources of acquisitions this way.

An analysis of competitors' advertising in trade magazines and direct mail pieces usually reveals the product benefits and features the producer is emphasizing in general or to a specific segment. These advertisements should be considered when evaluating overall strategies and conducting sales meetings. Trade advertising, like trade shows, is again when the small, privately held competitor becomes more public.

A subscription to a clipping service that scans local newspapers, financial publications, and trade publications for competitive information can be an excellent investment at minimal cost.[4] After retaining a news clipping service for a nominal amount, a plastics manufacturer learned that one of its stronger competitors had had a severe fire in one of its major plants. The aggressive manufacturer knew this would disrupt deliveries, so its salespeople were advised to emphasize the risk of relying on a supplier with such a severe problem. In still another situation, a clipping service found a help wanted ad placed by its client's competitor that showed the competitor was designing a new technical capability into an old product line. It is also possible to learn an enormous amount about competitors and their intentions when interviewing competitors' personnel for job openings.

The *Wall Street Transcript* covers corporate presentations to security analysts and brokerage house assessments. The CEO of a machinery manufacturer once described the two-year marketing plan of a new machine to security analysts. After reading the speech reproduced verbatim, a competitor altered many parts of its strategies and plans for the product. The purchase of a few shares of a competitor's stock will bring quarterly earn-

---

[4]Robert Hershy, "Commercial Intelligence on a Shoestring," *Harvard Business Review*, September–October 1980.

ings reports, prospectuses, 10 Ks, and sometimes press releases and new product announcements. One company has managed to get on nearly all of its competitors' mailing lists.

Competitive intelligence should be maintained and kept as close as possible to the *user* of the information—that is, the one who makes product or market strategy decisions. A product manager is an obvious candidate. In one business, the VP of marketing has an assistant who works full time keeping competitor files. Assembling competitive or commercial intelligence is like putting a puzzle together, but it is one of the lowest-cost and most useful forms of market information. However, it is the customer that is frequently the best source of information about competitors. The customer's evaluations and perceptions of every competitor's practices and products is where the sale is made or lost.

Unfortunately, the notion of gathering competitive intelligence frequently connotes actions that are devious or underhanded. When we talk about gathering competitive intelligence, we mean being imaginative and resourceful in gathering and piecing together bits of competitor information that help one to assess competitor strengths, weaknesses, strategies, and plans. We are not in any sense referring to "competitive espionage" or any type of cloak and dagger activity. Useful competitive intelligence can be gathered in completely ethical ways. Over the years, Reliance Electric has done an outstanding job of gathering competitive intelligence as a foundation for developing and selecting many of its strategic moves. Like many companies, Reliance adheres to well-defined standards of ethical conduct. The following paragraph, taken from the company's statement of operating philosophy, illustrates this point very well.

> We know that solid profit growth can only come from providing customers with genuine value in a more effective way than competition and by controlling our costs. It should never come from taking unfair advantage of any supplier, employee, customer, user, business partner, or competitor. If we can't win by these rules, we don't deserve to win. And we don't want anyone on our team who doesn't want to play the game fairly.

As one can see, major emphasis is placed on never taking unfair advantage of any group, including competitors. By being smart, and in no way unfair, marketing managers in this company have traditionally done an outstanding job of gathering the necessary information about competitors to determine how and where they can gain a competitive advantage.

# MARKETING STRATEGY IMPLICATIONS

Understanding a customer's costs and a competitor's situation provides a sound basis for developing better product and market strategies. Here are several specific ways that knowing customer cost and competitors can assist the industrial marketer.

REDUCES SURPRISES. Having a deep and current understanding of customers and competition can help a supplier avoid the penalties of getting "caught off base" and be more responsive to changing market conditions.

## IDENTIFYING OPPORTUNITIES

The Tremco Company developed a mastic compound that was a functional substitute for putty used in glazing glass windows. Because of the higher initial price of the Tremco product, glazing contractors were hesitant to buy it because they felt the higher price would make it difficult for them to bid successfully on glazing contracts. An end-user application study discovered that wherever windows were glazed with either putty or the new glazing compound, the windows were always painted *after* the glazing was done. Special care while painting was needed to prevent smearing the window glass. This type of painting, known as "cutting-in" in the trade, was a very high labor cost. Existing putty manufacturers required the paint coating as a protection from the weather. But the Tremco mastic did not require a protective paint coating. Windows could be painted before they were glazed and then glazed with this mastic, using a colored material to blend the mastic with the color of the painted window. The study of the production work in process for the material showed it actually lowered the cost of painting contracts. The initially higher-priced Tremco glazing material actually resulted in overall lower costs per job.

IDENTIFIES NEW MARKET SEGMENTS.   End-user analysis can provide hard economic facts and help identify new customer segments or market requirements. As the boxed example shows, economic analysis of a product application in a customer's operations can sometimes identify a new approach to segmenting a marketplace.

FOCUSES PRODUCT DESIGN AND DEVELOPMENT.   Product design efforts can be better focused after a thorough analysis of product applications in various customer groups. For example, a product can be designed to be less costly on initial purchase than competitive products. It can be designed smaller so that installation and startup are easier and less costly. It can be designed to operate more efficiently (use less power, generate less scrap, produce at a faster rate) or to have a longer useful life. Or it can be designed to be fully compatible and easily interchangeable with competitive products. What it probably cannot be is all of the above, because tradeoffs and compromises are generally involved. If the product is designed to last longer, operate at a faster rate, or use less power, it probably requires added labor and material costs as it is manufactured, thus adding to the initial purchase price. If the product is designed around the lowest possible manufacturing costs, it probably will not have the same performance characteristics as more costly products. This is why it is so important to select the target customers and market segments to be served and then to design the product that will offer the greatest economic advantage to the users that make up those markets.

AIDS DEVELOPMENT OF PRICING STRATEGIES.   Once the product is designed to enhance the operating performance and economics of a particular set of customers, pricing strategies can be developed based on value received rather than a straight writeup on costs. Obviously, this pricing for value received approach cannot be carried to an extreme, since industrial customers often have a good idea of what a product costs to manufacture and will not permit the producer to realize exorbitant profits. End-user customer cost analysis tends to cause the producer to price closer to what the market will bear, rather than using a cost-plus approach that might be below the customer's value-in-use and willingness to pay. If the competitive products are not as cost effective, competitive prices are not as relevant.

SHARPENS SALES FORCE TRAINING.   The alert marketer should educate its sales force to sell its product on the strength of real economic advantages to the user. This is a difficult task, since most selling organizations tend to shy away from the costs and economics of their customer's business and dwell instead on the virtues of their product. However, the training effort required is worthwhile because it puts the salesperson in the position of being a professional genuinely interested in helping the customer improve its position rather than merely being someone who pitches the company's products.

IMPROVES ADVERTISING EFFECTIVENESS.   Product benefits that are derived from a careful evaluation of customer needs and operations should be emphasized in business advertising headlines and copy. Advertising with this focus creates higher awareness and recall. Such advertising will also be more effective as a direct mail piece or as visual aids for salespeople.

## SUMMARY

A close knowledge of customers' needs coupled with ongoing competitive intelligence gathering will help the alert industrial producer achieve and maintain a differential advantage. The closer a supplier stays abreast of customers' operations and changing requirements, the more market-focused the supplier will be. An intimate knowledge of how and where the customer uses the product provides information for developing competitive products and competitive product and market plans. Such close customer contact and a continuous awareness of the competitive situation help the industrial producer match the right product capabilities to the appropriate market segment. This approach also helps to avoid producing "me too" products that have no real demonstrable advantage.

## REVIEW QUESTIONS

1. What are the benefits to the industrial firm that thoroughly understands its customers' products and operations?
2. What are five different kinds of costs that help analyze the value of a supplier's product within the customer's operation?
3. Why do customer's costs sometimes vary between customers or between market segments?
4. What should we know about the competitive structure and competitive economics?
5. Why should a competitive key success factor analysis be done for *each* market segment?
6. What are some of the more common legal sources of competitive information?

# 5

# Segmenting Business Markets

Foundations for Business Strategy

Errors in Segmenting the Market
  Thinking Too Broad
  Thinking Too Narrow
  Misusing the Consumer Goods Approach

Segmenting the Business
  Segmenting by OEM, User, and Aftermarkets
  Segmenting by SICs
  Segmenting by End-Use Application
  Segmenting by Common Buying Factors
  Two Other Segmentation Approaches

Combining Segmentation Levels
  Too Few or Too Many Segments

Validating a Market Segment

Segmenting and Resegmenting

Responsibility for Segmentation

Summary

Review Questions

Ken Roy, general manager of the industrial machinery division of a *Fortune* 100 company, was surprised to find a note from the company president calling off the review session that had been set up to go over a strategic plan to enter the "flexible manufacturing system" field. Ken had given the president a draft of the plan to read for the meeting. The president had returned it along with a short note that said it was a waste of time to do a review until the market they wanted to serve was much better defined.

Ken Roy immediately called his staff together. All the members of his team were dismayed, because they had put a lot of effort into the draft. The national sales manager was particularly discouraged because he saw flexible manufacturing as a growth market the company had to enter. The director of engineering believed he had superior in-house capabilities to rapidly develop a wide range of flexible manufacturing systems that would leave competitors far behind. After two hours of discussion, it became clear that the division team did not know what the corporate president meant when he said, "We need a much better definition of the market."

Ken arranged to meet the next day with the president to discuss the problem. When the president met with Ken and his staff, he expressed a point of view that caused them to think somewhat differently about the plan:

As I see it, flexible manufacturing is not a market. Rather, it is a product or general concept that is adapted to and then sold into various markets. We are a little late in entering this business. This means we need to identify and concentrate on selected market segments where we can secure a unique competitive advantage. Otherwise, we will be following others with a "me too" product. There are a lot of different ways to segment an industrial market. We might begin by selecting certain growth industries like electronic components or medical equipment and then identify subsections of these industries that have similar requirements. Or we might begin by examining the requirements of various sizes and kinds of machine shops that have not been automated in any appreciable way. I can't tell you specifically how to segment the market, but I can tell you it is essential to segment first before we commit a lot of time and money to an area as competitive as this one.

What was the division team's elementary mistake?

What are the strong points of the president's argument?

What are some obvious problems that would result if the company were to follow the director of engineering's advice and "rapidly develop a wide range of flexible manufacturing systems"?

**M**arket segmentation as a business practice has long been recognized and accepted in the consumer goods sector, but among industrial or technically based manufacturing businesses, there has been no corresponding level of interest and rigor. Yet, the identification and selection of market segments is the most strategic decision facing the industrial firm. Segmenting an industrial marketplace is the starting point for all strategic planning and decision making. The selection of segments determines the business units that management will plan around. They may be defined by SIC codes, end use or application, by common buying factors, by geographic boundaries, or by size of customer. Sometimes a combination of these considerations is used to define the segments. Whatever factors are used to segment a business, the objective is always to define a market niche that can be focused on in a way that provides a distinct competitive advantage. Examples of sales, market share, and profit gains from careful segmentation are legion.

Deere, the large farm equipment manufacturer, identified a market trend to fewer but larger farms that required large horsepower tractors and equipment. Deere designed and manufactured large horsepower machinery and subsequently captured a market opportunity. The existing market leader, International Harvester, was late to recognize and pursue the new and growing market segment and lost substantial market share as a result.

Xerox, the pioneer of photocopy machines, emphasized the high-speed segment for very large customers. The Japanese competitors were the first to identify and develop a desktop plain paper copier for businesses' low-speed needs. It rapidly became the fastest growing copier market segment. The president of Canon U.S.A. stated, "It has been our strategy to identify a market demand and then create a product to fill that demand."[1] Xerox failed to resegment the marketplace and by so doing allowed Canon and other Japanese competitors to do it for them.

Both General Electric and RCA withdrew from the computer industry after unsuccessfully attempting to compete with IBM. The most successful entrants in the computer business concentrated their R&D, manufacturing, and marketing on one or a few select market segments. The chairman of Control Data stated, "We avoided going head-on with IBM but rather focused in on the largest computers, where IBM was not as strong."[2] Similar examples of successful computer market segmentation are NCR in retail systems, Burroughs in banking, and Honeywell in manufacturing and process controls.

## FOUNDATIONS FOR BUSINESS STRATEGY

Over the past two decades, a number of industrial companies have rediscovered Demosthenes' idea: "Small opportunities are often the beginning of great enterprises." Unable to compete broadly against entrenched competitors, they have adopted a successful niche, or "divide and conquer," strategy: They identify a market need, then focus their resources and energies on meeting that need better than anyone else.

[1] "Copiers Still A Growth Industry," *High Technology,* May 1983, p. 54.
[2] Joel Ross and Michael Kami, *Corporate Management in Crisis: Why the Mighty Fail* (Englewood Cliffs, N.J.: Prentice-Hall, Inc., 1973), p. 80.

92

The identification and selection of market segments determines the producer's customer mix, what business it is in, and who the competition is. The identification and selection of industrial segment(s) to concentrate on will significantly affect all the functional areas of the firm. As Corey states:

> All else follows. Choice of market is a choice of the customer and of the competitive, technical, political, and social environments in which one elects to compete. It is not an easily reversed decision; having made the choice, the company develops skills and resources around the markets it has elected to serve. It builds a set of relationships with customers that are at once a major source of strength and a major commitment. The commitment carries with it the responsibility to serve customers well, to stay in the technical and product-development race, and to grow in pace with growing market demand. Such choices are not made in a vacuum. They are influenced by the company's background; by its marketing, manufacturing, and technical strengths; by the fabric of its relations with existing customers, the scientific community, and competitors.[3]

# ERRORS IN SEGMENTING THE MARKET

How an industrial producer defines a market segment determines the boundaries of the business it is in. When the competitors' segment definitions are the same, industrial market share measurement is clear and straightforward. However, market segments are not always easily defined. The difficulty of determining market boundaries and resulting market shares can be seen in the antitrust controversy. Whether or not a firm is dominating or restraining competition depends on how one segments and defines the market. For example, IBM was accused by the U.S. Justice Department of "dominating the computer market." However, in 1981 IBM did not have a leadership position in the fastest-growing segment—minicomputers. The identification of various market segments, and an analysis of IBM's strength in each, helped dismiss the case.

Firms that consistently fail to identify meaningful market segments usually do so for one of two reasons. Many product-driven firms simply don't think enough about their markets or are not willing to commit the time or money to do the job. Instead, they concentrate only on selling their products. Others that try to think in terms of segments lack the understanding to do the job correctly.

## Thinking Too Broad

An *industry* is a wide group of manufacturers producing and selling products, whereas a *market* is a much more distinct group of customers or users that have similar requirements. Sales-focused industrial firms often do not attempt to make a distinction between the two. For example, one component manufacturer stated: "We serve the computer market with solid state connectors." This kind of a statement is useless since there are many

[3] E Raymond Corey, "Key Options in Market Selection and Product Planning," *Harvard Business Review,* 53 (September–October 1975), p. 120.

distinct market segments within the computer industry, and each segment has specific customer requirements. It might have been more useful to say: "We primarily serve mainframe computer firms and some microprocessor computer builders." In still another situation, an industrial firm's division charter states: "The division is a supplier of hydraulic pumps and hoses to machinery markets." The division is again defining a general industry, not market segments. A further analysis revealed that the division was primarily supplying certain types of farm equipment manufacturers, three kinds of construction machinery producers, and heavy-duty truck makers. To avoid this kind of thinking, the president of one company told his marketing team that they were not segmenting properly if their total market was more than a hundred million dollars.

Some of these firms classify current customers by annual sales, as shown in Table 5.1. While this approach highlights the key accounts and defines them by sales volume as As, Bs, or Cs, it does not begin to be a useful form of market segmentation. This kind of a list, especially when grouped geographically, can be useful for aligning territories or making sales assignments, but is not particularly useful in making product-market decisions.

The limitation of key account or sales classification is that such classification does not reveal any differences or similarities in customer characteristics or requirements. For example, a further analysis of the customers in Table 5.1 revealed that:

1. The key customer list consisted of six end-use market segments.
   a. Construction equipment
   b. Heavy-duty highway trucks
   c. Off the road vehicles
   d. Farm equipment
   e. Materials-handling equipment
   f. Mining equipment
2. There were major differences among each of the identified six segments in annual purchase potential, growth rates, and long-term prospects.
3. The cost-benefit value of the producer's high-performance component was the greatest in two market segments where the producer had little market penetration.
4. In some segments, it was competing with different materials or technologies. In one low-performance segment, its quality was far above what was required.
5. There were different competitors in three of the six identified segments.

## Thinking Too Narrow

At the other extreme, some sales-focused firms do not think beyond the needs of one or a few customers that dominate their business. One manufacturer of machining systems developed a $150 million business with the three major auto manufacturers in Detroit. This total involvement with just three firms in one industry led to myopic thinking that prevented the manufacturer from even considering other situations or groups of customers (e.g., farm implement, aerospace, oil field equipment) that had similar requirements.

Other manufacturers often think too restrictively about their markets because they are constrained by their existing products and technologies. They tend to think of expansion

| TABLE 5.1 | ANNUAL DOLLAR SALES—HYDRAULIC HOSE | |
|---|---|---|

| | | Dollars (000) |
|---|---|---|
| As | Caterpillar | $17,000 |
| | Detroit Diesel-Allison | 5,050 |
| | J.I. Case | 2,000 |
| | John Deere | 2,500 |
| Bs | Allis Chalmers | 1,200 |
| | Clark Equipment | 600 |
| | Ford Tractor | 975 |
| | Hyster Company | 588 |
| | New Holland | 610 |
| | Rockford Clutch | 1,063 |
| | Saab Scania | 675 |
| | Twin Disc | 1,000 |
| | U.S. Government | 1,576 |
| | Warner Gear | 500 |
| Cs | Caterpillar—Mexico | 250 |
| | Clearing Division, U.S. Industries | 170 |
| | Fiat Allis | 357 |
| | Franklin Equipment | 181 |
| | Funk Manufacturing | 150 |
| | International Harvester | 400 |
| | Jeffrey Mining | 268 |
| | Joy Manufacturing | 127 |
| | Marathon LeTourneau | 188 |
| | Massey Ferguson | 409 |
| | Mine Machinery | 80 |
| | Pacific Car | 201 |
| | White Farm Equipment | 12 |
| Others | | 1,345 |
| Total | | 39,475 |

only in terms of extending their product line. They do not think about what other products or services beyond their existing capabilities could help them strengthen their position or develop more attractive markets. For example, a switch producer sold chiefly to nuclear plants where its line had been qualified and approved by the appropriate agencies. This narrow focus on a slow growth market greatly limited sales potential. Management ultimately redefined its business as one that served additional hazardous environments and, by both acquisition and internal development, added several complementary products.

## Misusing the Consumer Goods Approach

Some industrial firms have been misled by advertising agencies or consumer goods marketers that eloquently tout the sophisticated segmentation approaches that work well in the consumer goods world. However, segmentation for consumer and industrial markets is as different as potato chips and integrated circuit chips. Household consumer buying can be segmented on the basis of demographic factors and sociopsychological considerations. Moreover, new consumer segments can often be defined in terms of different packaging, brand names, or advertising appeals. In contrast, industrial market segmentation must be based on common economic, application, or usage considerations, and any talk about demographic factors or sociopsychological considerations is pure nonsense. Despite the differences between consumer and industrial market segmentation, much of the literature discusses industrial market segmentation as though it could be accomplished by using consumer goods techniques.

# SEGMENTING THE BUSINESS

There is no one right way for an industrial or a technically based company to segment an industrial market. Successful segmentation is both creative and judgmental. What will be an effective and profitable way to segment one market may not be a good method to segment another. However, there are a number of basic approaches to segmenting industrial markets that have proved successful.

What is most important is that the firm distinguish between the industries it sells into and the discrete markets that lie within these industries. Segmenting can be done by OEM and aftermarket, by four-digit SICs, by end use, by common buying factors, and by buyer size.

## Segmenting by OEM, User, and Aftermarkets

One approach to industrial market segmentation is to classify present or potential customers as original equipment manufacturers (OEM), end users, or aftermarket customers. Aftermarket is sometimes called the maintenance, repair, and overhaul market (MRO). For farm tractors, Deere would be an original equipment manufacturer, and the individual farmer would be the end user. The repair parts bought by the farm implement dealer or the farmer would constitute the aftermarket.

All industrial products can be classified into one of three categories.

1. *Components or subassemblies.* These are parts or items used to build and repair machinery and equipment, which includes items such as switches, integrated circuits, machine tool parts, connectors, and pistons, and are often required for both the OEM and aftermarkets.
2. *Machinery and equipment.* These are end products used by the industrial users, such as machine tools, bulldozers, computers, laboratory instruments, and trucks. They require repair parts (components) as aftermarket items.

**EXHIBIT
5-1**

## OEM-AFTERMARKET SEGMENTATION

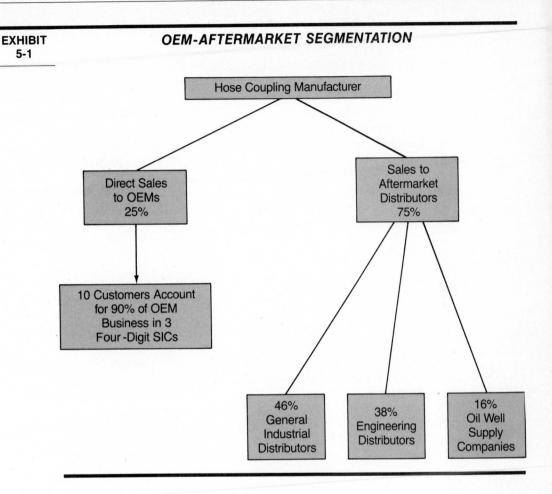

3. *Materials.* Materials are consumed in the end user's production process or components and include such items as chemicals, coolants, metals, herbicides, and adhesives. They do not usually have an aftermarket.

Materials, machinery, and equipment are typically sold only in the OEM and end-user segments. Components and subassemblies, on the other hand, are sold in the aftermarket segment, as well as in the OEM and end-user segments.

OEM, end-user, and aftermarket segmentation generally cannot be done from existing sales records as sales records do not usually show any information about the product beyond the customer or distributor. Sales personnel can be helpful in developing some of the necessary information, but they are often limited in their knowlege of end-user and aftermarket customers, especially when distributors are involved. Exhibit 5-1 shows how easy it is for a supplier to lose track of its products once they move beyond the customer or distributor level. In some cases the problem is further complicated by intermediate resellers or subdistributors that are integral links in the customers' sales chain.

Unfortunately, the OEM-aftermarket classification is far too often the beginning and end of segmentation in many industrial firms. Such companies are flying blind. This lack of knowledge of who the real customers are is especially common when producers sell primarily to industrial distributors who in turn serve other OEMs or aftermarket customers. A major manufacturer of hose couplings found segmentation beyond the OEM-aftermarket level very revealing. The manufacturer had always known that 25 percent of the coupling business was direct to OEMs and the remaining 75 percent went through independent distributors. However, until the manufacturer segmented the market further, as shown in Exhibit 5-1, it did not know that some of its products were being bought by the oil industry. A product-market plan targeted to the oil patch customers resulted in a 39 percent increase in unit sales in one year.

## Segmenting by SICs

A second approach to segmentation involves the use of Standard Industrial Classification (SIC) codes, which are published by the U.S. government. This publication classifies all business firms by the main product or service provided. It then classifies all like manufacturers under broad industry groups and assigns a numerical code that indicates the basic industry and the type of product and service.

To explain how to segment by SIC codes, let's use the example of a producer of industrial brakes that wants to identify specific types of OEM prospects that make heavy construction equipment. Since the construction equipment builders are manufacturing firms, they will be within the 20–39 range of two-digit basic industry groups, as shown in Table 5.2. The next step is to look through the manufacturing subdivisions, shown in Table 5.3, to identify the manufacturing groups that represent potential users for industrial brakes. Assuming we identify Group 35, "machinery except electrical," as the most likely prospects, we would then turn to page 167 where we find the two-digit classification expanded to four digits, as shown in Table 5.4. Here we must exercise judgment to identify the four-digit area(s) where brake products will most likely fit. Each four-digit category has an extensive listing of the machinery produced in that four-digit SIC, as also shown in Table 5.4. Once this extensive list is available, it is then possible to determine what manufacturers make what products by going to one of four sources:

1. *Duns' Market Identifiers (DMI)*—computer-based records of 3 million United States and Canadian business establishments by four-digit SIC.
2. *Metalworking Directory*—a comprehensive list of metalworking plants with 20 or more employees, as well as metal distributors by four-digit SIC.
3. *Thomas Register of American Manufacturers*—a directory of manufacturers, classified by products, enabling the researcher to identify most or all of the manufacturers of any given product.
4. *Survey of Industrial Purchasing Power*—an annual survey of manufacturing activity in the United States by geographic areas and four-digit SIC industry groups; reports the number of plants with 20 or more and 100 or more employees, as well as total shipment value.

**TABLE 5.2**

## CATEGORIES OF THE U.S. ECONOMY

| Basic Industries | First Two Digits |
|---|---|
| 1. Agriculture | 01–09 |
| 2. Mining | 10–14 |
| 3. Construction | 15–17 |
| 4. Manufacturing | 20–39 |
| 5. Transportation | 40–49 |
| 6. Wholesale and retail | 50–59 |
| 7. Finance | 60–67 |
| 8. Services | 70–89 |
| 9. Public administration | 91–97 |
| 10. Nonclassifiable | 99 |

*Source: Standard Industrial Classification Manual, 1972* (Washington, D.C.: U.S. Government Printing Office).

**TABLE 5.3**

## MANUFACTURING SIC SUBDIVISIONS

| Group | Description | Page |
|---|---|---|
| Major Group 20. | Food and kindred products | 59 |
| Major Group 21. | Tobacco manufactures | 70 |
| Major Group 22. | Textile mill products | 71 |
| Major Group 23. | Apparel and other finished products made from fabrics and similar materials | 82 |
| Major Group 24. | Lumber and wood products, except furniture | 90 |
| Major Group 25. | Furniture and fixtures | 96 |
| Major Group 26. | Paper and allied products | 100 |
| Major Group 27. | Printing, publishing, and allied industries | 106 |
| Major Group 28. | Chemicals and allied products | 111 |
| Major Group 29. | Petroleum refining and related industries | 127 |
| Major Group 30. | Rubber and miscellaneous plastics products | 129 |
| Major Group 31. | Leather and leather products | 133 |
| Major Group 32. | Stone, clay, glass, and concrete products | 136 |
| Major Group 33. | Primary metal industries | 145 |
| Major Group 34. | Fabricated metal products, except machinery and transportation equipment | 153 |
| Major Group 35. | Machinery, except electrical | 167 |
| Major Group 36. | Electrical and electronic machinery, equipment, and supplies | 184 |
| Major Group 37. | Transportation equipment | 196 |
| Major Group 38. | Measuring, analyzing, and controlling instruments; photographic, medical, and optical goods; watches and clocks | 202 |
| Major Group 39. | Miscellaneous manufacturing industries | 211 |

*Source: Standard Industrial Classification Manual, 1972* (Washington, D.C.: U.S. Government Printing Office).

**TABLE 5.4**

## MAJOR INDUSTRY GROUP 35—SUBDIVISION (MACHINERY, EXCEPT ELECTRICAL)

| Four-Digit SIC | Specific Industry |
|---|---|
| 3511 | Steam, gas, and hydraulic turbines |
| 3519 | Internal combustion engines |
| 3523 | Farm and garden machinery |
| 3524 | Garden tractors and lawn equipment |
| 3531 | Construction machinery and equipment |

↓

3531   Construction Machinery and Equipment

Establishments primarily engaged in manufacturing heavy machinery and equipment used by the construction industries, such as bulldozers; concrete mixers; cranes, except industrial plant type; dredging machinery; pavers; and power shovels. Establishments primarily engaged in manufacturing mining equipment are classified in Industry 3532, and well drilling machinery in Industry 3533.

Aggregate spreaders
Airport construction machinery
Asphalt plants, including travel-mix type
Backfillers, self-propelled
Backhoes
Ballast distributors
Batching plants, bituminous
Batching plants, for aggregate concrete and bulk cement
Blades for graders, scrapers, dozers, and snow plows
Breakers, paving
Buckets: clamshell, concrete, dragline, drag scraper, shovel, etc.
Bulldozers (construction machinery)
Capstans, ship
Carriers, crane
Chip spreaders, self-propelled
Cleaners, catch basin
Compactors, soil: vibratory-pan and vibratory-roller types
Concrete buggies, powered
Concrete grouting equipment
Concrete gunning equipment
Concrete plants
Construction machinery, except mining
Cranes, except industrial plant
Cranes, locomotive
Cranes, ship
Crushers, portable
Derricks, except oil and gas field
Derricks, ship
Distributors (construction machinery)
Ditchers, ladder: vertical boom or wheel
Dozers, tractor mounted: material moving
Draglines, powered

Drags, road (construction and road maintenance equipment)
Dredging machinery
Entrenching machines
Excavators: cable, clamshell, crane, derrick, dragline, power shovel, etc.
Extractors, piling
Finishers and spreaders (construction equipment)
Finishers, concrete and bituminous: powered
Grader attachments, elevating
Graders, road (construction machinery)
Grapples: rock, wood, etc.
Grinders, stone: portable
Hammer mills (rock and ore crushing machines), portable
Hammers, pile driving
Line markers, self-propelled
Loaders, shovel: self-propelled
Locomotive cranes
Logging equipment
Mixers: concrete, ore, sand, slag, plaster, mortar, and bituminous
Mortar mixers
Mud jacks
Pavers
Pile drivers (construction machinery)
Planers, bituminous
Plaster mixers
Plows, earth: heavy duty
Power cranes, draglines, and shovels
Pulverizers, stone: portable
Railway track equipment: rail layers, ballast distributors, etc.

Rakes, land clearing: mechanical
Road construction and maintenance machinery
Rock crushing machinery, portable
Rollers, road: steam or other power
Rollers, sheepsfoot and vibratory
Sand mixers
Scarifiers, road
Scrapers (construction machinery)
Screeds and screeding machines
Screeners, portable
Ship cranes and derricks
Ship winches
Shovel loaders, wheel tractor
Shovels, power
Silos, cement (batch plant)
Slag mixers
Snow plow attachments
Soil compactors: vibratory-pan and vibratory-roller types
Spreaders and finishers (construction equipment)
Subgraders, construction equipment
Subsoiler attachments, tractor mounted
Surfacers, concrete grinding
Tampers, powered
Tamping equipment, rail
Teeth, bucket and scarifier
Tractors, contractors' off highway
Tractors, crawler
Tractors, tracklaying
Trucks, off-highway: heavy duty motor
Vibrators for concrete construction
Wellpoint systems
Winches, all types

*Source: Standard Industrial Classification Manual, 1972* (Washington, D.C.: U.S. Government Printing Office).

An allied source for identifying and estimating the size of industrial markets is *County Business Patterns*. This annual publication reports the number of employees and the value of shipments by the same four-digit SICs.

Segmentation by OEM and aftermarket and then four-digit SIC should always be done by the producer of industrial products. In addition, however, some very successful industrial producers have creatively segmented one or two levels beyond OEM-aftermarket and SIC levels by studying end-use application and common buying factors.

## Segmenting by End-Use Application

Industrial products are used differently by different customers, and segmenting by end-use application simply means determining how the product is used in various situations. It is important to understand these differences since the cost-benefit relationship is likely to vary by end-use application. For example, a front-end equipment loader will have greater value to a customer who uses it eight hours a day in a mining operation than to a customer who uses it two to three hours a day on a construction site. Cost-benefit analysis for each identified end-use application helps to determine the economic value of the product for each segment. When conducting a cost-benefit analysis by end use, the producer must ask: "What function(s) does the customer want performed with this product?" Three steps are involved in determining which end-use market segments have the greatest cost-benefit advantages.

1. Making field visits and conducting customer studies to determine how products are used.
2. Identifying and evaluating cost-benefit relationships in different applications.
3. Verifying variables that underly different cost-benefit relationships.

Here is an example of how one company used this approach to achieve a distinct competitive advantage. A manufacturer of electric motors discovered that its customers operated at different speeds and costs and that a new, lower-priced machine introduced by a competitor wore out quickly when used in high- and medium-speed applications. Armed with this user insight from extensive field visits, it then developed segment strategies as shown in Exhibit 5-2. For customers who needed primarily medium- and high-speed use, it doubled its sales effort, stressing the superiority of its product. For users in the low-speed segment, the manufacturer launched a program to develop a competitively priced product with an added maintenance advantage, meanwhile altering the short-term sales strategy to emphasize the life-cycle cost advantage offered by its existing machines.[4]

The identification of needs by end use should include a consideration of substitute or potential substitute products that can perform the function. For example, Continental Can has found it necessary to consider the customer value of containers made of many different materials (metal, glass, fiber, plastic) for each end use. This consideration helps Continental segment markets for its products creatively when the end user is currently using a different material than Continental produces. The evaluation of functional substitutes

[4]Robert A. Garda, "How to Carve Niches for Growth in Industrial Markets," *Management Review*, August 1981, p. 16.

EXHIBIT
5-2

## SEGMENTATION BY END-USE APPLICATION

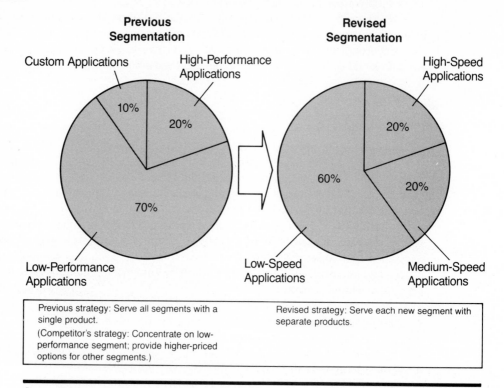

**Previous Segmentation**

Custom Applications — 10%

High-Performance Applications — 20%

Low-Performance Applications — 70%

**Revised Segmentation**

High-Speed Applications — 20%

Low-Speed Applications — 60%

Medium-Speed Applications — 20%

Previous strategy: Serve all segments with a single product.

(Competitor's strategy: Concentrate on low-performance segment; provide higher-priced options for other segments.)

Revised strategy: Serve each new segment with separate products.

*Source:* Robert A. Garda, "How to Carve a Niche for Growth in Industrial Markets," *Management Review,* August 1981, p. 17.

helps producers identify end-use markets where their products have greater customer value. Many product-focused companies have difficulty breaking out of the pattern of only comparing their products to end-use segments using a very similar product. From the customer viewpoint, a product or technology is only one solution to a problem.

## Segmenting by Common Buying Factors

Some industrial companies have successfully defined market segments by identifying groups of customers that attach importance to the same buying factors. Most industrial buying situations hinge on five buying factors: (1) performance, (2) quality, (3) service, (4) delivery, and (5) price. It is often difficult to define segments by common buying factors because they are not readily apparent. They often change with customer priorities, and they can vary dramatically among customers in the same business. Nevertheless, it is often worth the effort to segment this way as it can lead to significant marketing advantages, as shown in the boxed example on pages 104–105.

## Two Other Segmentation Approaches

Segmentation based on geographic considerations or account size are two other alternatives that are often used in industries, particularly when the business is based on commodity type products that flow into a multiplicity of markets through a complex series of channels. Certainly the first attempt should be to segment along the lines described previously to see if discrete and meaningful markets can be defined. However, if this turns out to be impractical for whatever reasons, there are generally advantages to be gained by segmenting around geographic boundaries and/or account size.

Sales managers are accustomed to grouping customers by geography or size for planning purposes, but until recently few top managers had thought to try developing niche strategies on this basis. Yet the opportunity often exists.

An example of ingenious geographic SMS is the case of a Midwestern commodity construction materials firm that found itself faced with overcapacity and unable to take share away from its competition in its 200-mile trading area without starting a price war. Industry folklore maintained that because of high transportation, no producer could ship more than 300 miles from plant to customer and make money. This was true on an all-in cost basis; yet, as this company discovered, the fixed costs included in its all-in costs were so high that sales to customers as much as 700 miles away would still contribute to overhead (Exhibit 5-3). The result of its analysis was three strategic market segments: core markets (up to 200 miles distant); secondary markets (200 to 400 miles); and fringe markets (400 to 700 miles). For each of these segments, the firm developed different pricing strategies. In the core market, the strategy was business as usual; in the secondary markets, prices were cut to take a few selected bids away from competitors, but not enough to provoke retaliation; in the fringe market, prices were reduced in order to fill the plants—but again, not frequently enough or severely enough to provoke retaliation. With this strategy, the company tripled its volume in the first year. Although much of the added volume was from marginal business, its profits doubled—and the industry price structure remained intact.

Another example relates to segmenting by account size. An electrical equipment manufacturer isolated 187 key accounts, accounting for 60 percent of the market, each of which bought direct and selected suppliers on the basis of price and sales coverage. These large accounts made up one strategic market segment. A second segment consisted of medium-sized OEM accounts that bought through distributors; a third comprised maintenance, repair, and operating supply accounts that required distributor servicing. Having identified these three strategic market segments, the company was able to develop programs (product pricing, distribution channels, and service policies) tailored to each.

# COMBINING SEGMENTATION LEVELS

In reviewing and choosing approaches to industrial market segmentation, it is helpful to think in terms of combining approaches, as shown in Table 5.5. The first three approaches, OEM end-user aftermarket, four-digit SIC, and end-use applications, should

## ADVANTAGES OF SEGMENTING BY COMMON BUYING FACTORS

In order to combat increasing price competition, an electrical components manufacturer had spent two years trying to develop detailed segment strategies for its 22 SIC markets. The breakthrough came when it discovered that the customers could be grouped or aggregated into four strategic market segments based on common buying characteristics. Segment A consisted of large-lot buyers that were extremely price sensitive (because the component was a significant portion of their product cost), did their own applications engineering, required dedicated capacity to meet their demand for a standard product, demanded only a very basic quality standard, and cared little for features. At the other end of the spectrum, segment D comprised a host of small-lot buyers, mostly makers of specialty products, that insisted on high quality and special features, relied on the supplier for applications engineering, and because they lacked buying clout, were not noticeably price sensitive. Having redefined these market segments for the total market, the manufacturer was able to develop strategies for each segment. Top management chose to price itself "up or out" of segment D by raising prices 25 percent. As anticipated, the price increase stuck; none of the competitors wanted the specialty business. Next, top management launched a facilities study that found the company could meet the low price and dedicated capacity requirements for the high-volume business in segment A.

*Source:* Robert A. Garda, "How to Carve Niches for Growth in Industrial Markets," *Management Review,* August 1981, p. 19.

usually be done in sequential steps. Segmentation by common buying factors, geography, and buyer size does not necessarily follow in any particular sequence, but it should always be preceded by one of the other steps.

### Too Few or Too Many Segments

After conducting a segmentation analysis, many industrial firms experience one of two extreme situations. First, they may not have identified enough market segments. If too few segments have been defined, a competitor may zero in on a segment and gain a major part of the business. Large corporations frequently segment the market into too few and therefore too broad market segments. What is small to a billion-dollar company might be large to a 40 to 100 million-dollar company or division. However, if large companies do not segment small enough, competition will often do it for them. Smaller industrial firms are usually more able to think in terms of small growing segments and to position themselves within them to gain real competitive advantages.

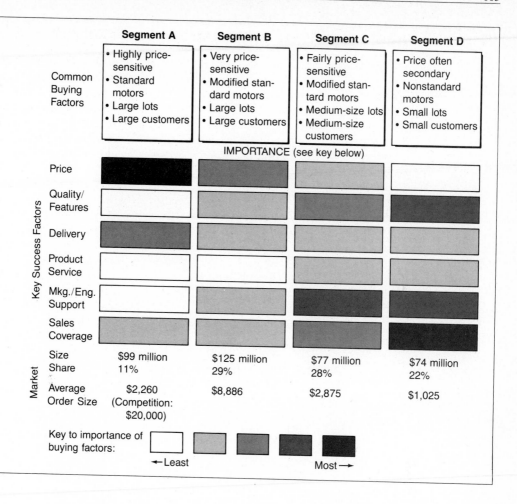

At the other extreme, some industrial companies define too many market segments. After investing in a seven month segmentation study that produced mountains of data, a division general manager stated:

> They have segmented our market into 18 segments. I've got a sneaking suspicion that's about one dozen too many. Even if it isn't, there's no way we can develop useful competitive strategies for each one in less than five years, and we haven't got five years.

## VALIDATING A MARKET SEGMENT

To avoid having too few or too many market segments, there are some qualifying criteria to consider. If any one of the following six criteria is not met, the segment should be discounted. The six validation criteria are these:

| EXHIBIT 5-3 | HOW GEOGRAPHIC SEGMENTATION ENLARGED A MARKET |
|---|---|

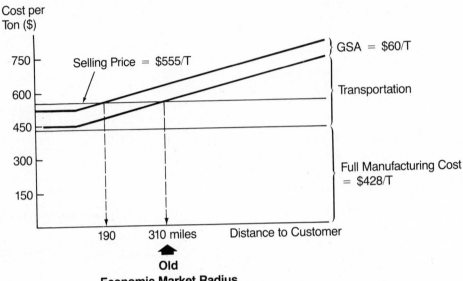

**Old**
**Economic Market Radius**

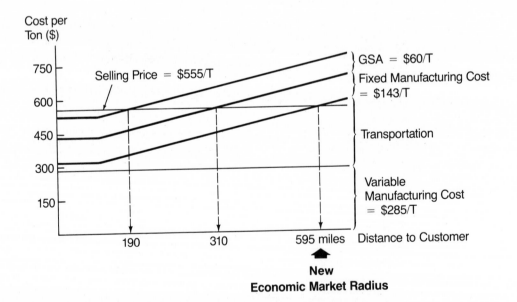

**New**
**Economic Market Radius**

*Source:* Robert A. Garda, "How to Curve Niches for Growth in Industrial Markets," *Management Review,* August 1981, p. 19.

| TABLE 5.5 | BUSINESS SEGMENTATION APPROACHES |
|---|---|

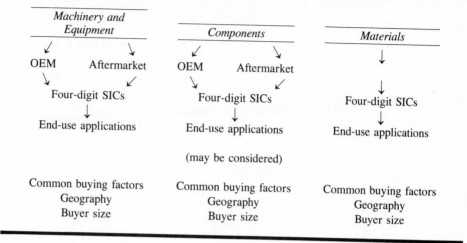

| Machinery and Equipment | Components | Materials |
|---|---|---|
| OEM ↓ ↓ Aftermarket | OEM ↓ ↓ Aftermarket | ↓ |
| Four-digit SICs | Four-digit SICs | Four-digit SICs |
| End-use applications | End-use applications (may be considered) | End-use applications |
| Common buying factors<br>Geography<br>Buyer size | Common buying factors<br>Geography<br>Buyer size | Common buying factors<br>Geography<br>Buyer size |

1. Each identified segment should be characterized by a set of common user requirements.
2. Each identified segment should have measurable characteristics (e.g., customer size, growth rate, and location) per year.
3. Each identified segment should have identifiable competitors.
4. Each identified segment should be served by common sales or distribution channels.
5. Each identified segment should be "large enough" so that it represents a significant business opportunity.
6. Each identified segment should be "small enough" to protect a position against competition.

These criteria are by no means exhaustive or inclusive. However, they do help to determine if a segment does exist and whether it is attractive enough to consider further.

# SEGMENTING AND RESEGMENTING

Industrial market segments are dynamic. Competitive activity, technological changes, swings in the business cycle, acquisitions, and make-buy decisions can dramatically change the boundaries and attractiveness of segments. Therefore, it is necessary to periodically evaluate existing segmentation and consider new or different approaches. Business history is replete with cases in which an existing competitor saw market segment boundaries as static or did not identify new, emerging segments and so lost out. The X-ray film market provides an example of just how dynamic a market can be. Although Kodak is the broadest line supplier of photographic film to most market segments, DuPont concentrated on the X-ray film segment and achieved a large market share. Now, developments in nuclear magnetic resonance technology promise to replace X-rays in some applications with a process that develops the "picture" electrically and displays it on a computer screen. As the X-ray market shrinks, DuPont must redefine and resegment the market if it is to hold on to its gains.

Look at the computer market for another example. With increased competition and new electronic capabilities, the computer market must be periodically resegmented with new approaches. One small computer manufacturer noticed there was a type of customer that required high reliability. This market segment included banks and other businesses where interrupted data response meant an immediate loss of customer revenue. To ensure reliability, these companies had to have backup computers or redundant systems that lay idle unless the on-line system failed. The manufacturer was able to design a fail-safe computer that would not lose any data, as the other systems did, if any part of the system went down. As a consequence, the producer was allowed three years of excellent growth and considerable lead time before it had any real competitors in its newly defined market segment.

In short, segmenting industrial markets is a creative process; management should not allow ties to how markets were previously segmented to strangle new ways to segment. In markets where there is rapid technological change, there is a need to resegment more frequently because new technologies blur segment boundaries.

# RESPONSIBILITY FOR SEGMENTATION

While many product-market managers and business planners are aware of the need to do a better job of segmenting the market, their enthusiasm or ability to do so is often blunted because of short-term sales and profit pressures. Far too many general managers still regard volume gains and relationships with key accounts as the most important factors in their business. Segmentation is some kind of a theoretical exercise that is not worth much time and money, especially if it interferes with "bringing in or running the business." As this chapter suggests, segmentation requires a good deal of careful thought and creativity, and it is the primary responsibility of general management to make the money and resources available to ensure that it is done. Segmentation is not a theoretical exercise, and any general manager that skips over or shortcuts the need to define the discrete markets to be served is making a bad mistake. To ensure that the business is properly segmented, every general manager should be satisfied with the answers to the following questions:

1. How do we now segment the business?
2. Have we segmented enough?
3. Have we defined the segments in the best way possible?
4. Which segments are most attractive?
5. Is there any evidence that competitors, especially small ones, have achieved an advantage by segmenting differently?

If for any reason these questions are difficult to answer or cannot be answered at all, the chances are good that the business has not been properly segmented and that general management has fallen down on its job.

## SUMMARY

Unable to compete broadly against entrenched competitors, threshold companies and those entering markets new to them have repeatedly adopted a "divide and conquer" or market segmentation strategy. Precise definition of a target market can lead to innovative product, price, distribution, and service strategies. Selective market segmentation allows a company to marshal its R&D and engineering efforts toward specific areas rather than spread a little across a wider range of vulnerable marketplaces. At the same time, market segmentation and the selection of specific segments provide direction to the business unit as to which capabilities it must develop to serve the identified market segment effectively. Knowing how to segment a marketplace is therefore one of the most important skills an industrial marketer must possess. Segmentation defines what businesses the firm is in, guides strategy development, and determines the programs necessary in cross-functional areas of the firm. Since industrial market selection is clearly a longer-term strategic decision that cannot be easily reversed, it is important that the general marketplace be first segmented into viable targets before any market selection and investment decisions are made.

## REVIEW QUESTIONS

1. Why is segmenting industrial or business markets the starting point for strategic management?
2. Why is market segmentation often not practiced in many industrial firms?
3. Why is segmentation by OEM and after-market usually not sufficient?
4. Why is segmentation by four-digit SIC and end use so useful?
5. What are ten criteria to follow to determine if a viable segment exists?
6. Why is it necessary periodically to resegment?
7. Why do small or emerging high-technology firms often succeed with a creative segmentation approach?

# 6

# Assessing Business Markets

Assessing Current Market Position
  Internal Sales Analysis
  Pressure Point Curves
Estimating Market Potential
  Defining the Market
  Historical Data
  Derived Demand
  Trade Association Sources
  Conversion Factors
Conducting Market Studies
  Specifying Information Needed
  Secondary Market Studies
  Primary Market Studies
  Data Analysis
  New Product Market Studies
Project Proposals
Frameworks for Evaluating Market Segments
Summary
Review Questions

The general manager of the electronic instrumentation division asked Joyce Eichhorn, a recent MBA with a marketing background, to help him appraise the potential acquisition of a product line. The company had an opportunity to acquire a product line that many believed would be complementary to the division's business. But the division general manager wanted to know a number of things about the product and its markets before making a decision:

1. What are the present and potential market segments in which this product line is sold, and what are the key customer accounts in each?
2. What are the future growth prospects in each segment?
3. Who are the major competitors in each segment?
4. How does the product line compare to the competition in manufacturing costs and key success factors?
5. What could favorably or unfavorably affect future derived demand for this product line?

The general manager told Joyce the decision had to be made in two weeks. Joyce spent the next few days talking to friends inside and outside the company about how to get this information. One friend suggested she rely on relevant government statistics. Another suggested she locate and buy a published industry forecast. Still another told her she would not find published material that was specific enough. That friend advised doing a custom-tailored study to obtain the facts. Joyce was not sure which one or combination of these approaches she should use. But she knew she had to work out her plan soon, because she couldn't afford to waste a lot of time getting started.

What are the advantages of using government statistics and an industry forecast?

What are the advantages and disadvantages of doing a custom-tailored study?

What should Joyce do before deciding which approach or combination of approaches is most appropriate in this case?

Is the general manager's two-week deadline realistic?

**F**ar too many industrial firms have not realized the strategic and tactical value of fact-based market information. Many industrial firms do not even have a market research unit. When an in-house marketing research staff does exist, it is typically one of the most underpaid and underappreciated units in the firm. Often it is staffed with castoffs from other departments who do not have the requisite professional skills to do a competent job of market assessment. These situations occur because top management does not appreciate the value of professional market assessment and relies instead on trade or secondary information, or "seat of the pants" estimates. As a result, the company tends to fly half blind and therefore misses opportunities, gets caught off-base by unexpected product or market developments, and is continuously vulnerable to competitors with a better base of market information.

Industrial marketers need to know the present size, potential, and competitor market shares for any market segment of interest. This includes markets the company is presently serving as well as those it is considering for entry. It needs this information to help select and then gear its operations to the most attractive market segments. The information also helps companies decide which products, markets, and individual customers to deemphasize or move away from entirely. The approach for evaluating both present and potential markets is essentially the same. The difference, of course, is that more historical sales and performance data and firsthand knowledge of the marketplace are available for the markets presently served. However, many of the market facts needed to assess either present or potential business markets are typically unavailable from existing sources. Therefore, special market analysis or study is usually needed to accurately assess market positions, potentials, preferences, and competition.

The balance of this chapter examines ways to assess the current position and outlook for markets where the company has a presence; it then goes on to describe how to estimate sales and profit potential for any market of interest. Finally, it outlines specific approaches to conducting market studies that will help determine the relative attractiveness of various markets.

## ASSESSING CURRENT MARKET POSITION

Every company must have a sound understanding of where its dollar sales and unit sales come from and how its profits are generated. This statement may appear straightforward and relatively easy to follow. However, most companies report sales only by product line. Very few have regular sales reports by market segment. Even fewer have any kind of profit information by either product or market segment. The following series of exhibits shows how sales and profit data are typically reported in terms of aggregate dollar sales, unit sales, yearly profit, and ROI. Certainly one can see how the product has performed in aggregate terms and what patterns have developed in the company's business. However, these data do not provide answers to several fundamental questions.

## Internal Sales Analysis

Let's look first at dollar sales (Exhibit 6-1):

1. Why was there a sudden jump in sales between 1977 and 1978?
2. Why have sales plateaued in the last three years?
3. Are there product-market segments that have different patterns than the aggregate?

Now let's turn to unit sales (Exhibit 6-2):

1. Why have unit sales declined over the past three years?
2. Is this an industry or market trend, or is the decline unique to us?

Finally, look at the profit data (Exhibits 6-3 and 6-4):

1. Why do profit and sales trends differ?
2. Which products within the line are more or less profitable?
3. Why has investment increased so sharply in a flat to declining business?

In most cases the sales account records do not identify what markets customers are in, what the customers' total purchases are, or which competitors have what share of the business. It is frequently necessary to survey existing customers to develop the necessary information required. Table 6.1 shows the data required to conduct a proper sales analysis. Table 6.2 shows how one company reclassified its major accounts under market seg-

**EXHIBIT 6-1**

### A FITTING-DOLLAR SALES (1976–1980)

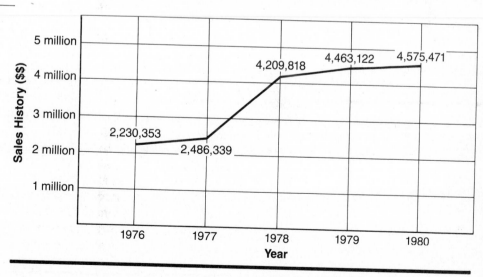

**EXHIBIT
6-2**

**A FITTING-UNIT SALES (1976–1980)**

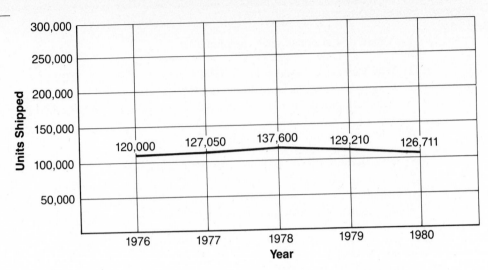

ments, which was a much more meaningful basis for developing product-market sales than the previous listing of accounts by annual purchases. Exhibit 6-5 shows how another company analyzed its sales by major accounts, market segments, customers, and geographic areas over a five-year period and saw that major shifts had occurred. This analysis led to important changes in its sales and product-market strategy.

**EXHIBIT
6-3**

**A FITTING-ANNUAL PROFIT (1976–1980)**

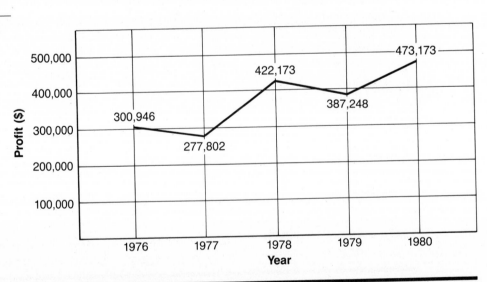

## A FITTING-YEARLY ROI (1976–1980)

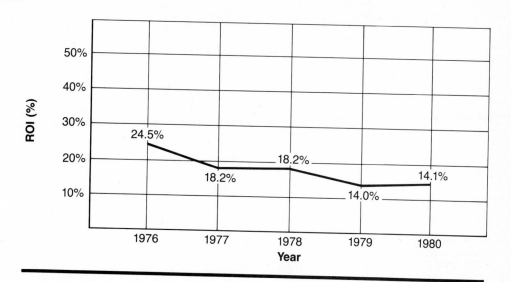

## Pressure Point (Rate of Change) Curves

Probably the most important tool for management in assessing the short-term outlook for any market is the pressure point analysis or curve, which helps to predict the direction of the product or market cycle. The pressure point curve or analysis works this way. Sales orders are posted and tracked to develop either a three-month or twelve-month moving average. Each current three-month and twelve-month average is then divided among corresponding averages for the same period of the prior year. The quotient is a numerical point that can be plotted, and when enough points are plotted the result is a pressure curve. Plotting these points shows the rate of change as sales orders move up or down and provides an early warning of trend changes that are not evident from the absolute sales data.

Exhibit 6-6 shows how pressure point curves can help management make critical decisions. The second chart in the exhibit simply tracks orders booked on a quarterly basis. Note how orders appear to be trending upward from June 1975 through December 1978. Looking at these data alone, one would conclude that the market and business outlook is attractive.

Now look at the three-month and twelve-month pressure curves. While orders moved up during the period, the three-month curve peaked in June 1976, and the rate of change started to decline. The twelve-month curve peaked six months later in December, before it too started to decline. To anyone tracking the data, this shift in the rate of change should have been an indicator that the order rate itself would start to decline, which it did in March 1978. Just think of the advantage to be gained if management can use this tool to plan ahead for changes in the order trend that are likely to occur several months ahead.

Obviously, pressure curves are more revealing if they are developed for discrete

| TABLE 6.1 | **DATA REQUIRED FOR CONDUCTING A SALES ANALYSIS** |
|---|---|

*Sales, Costs, Profit Analysis*
1. Annual sales—dollars and units
2. Annual net profits and ROI
3. Distribution channels and costs
4. Direct selling expenses
5. Seasonal, cyclical, irregular sales
6. Gross margin trends

*Customer Sales Analysis*
1. Major customers
2. End-use customer segments
3. SIC of customers
4. New versus old customers
5. Size of customer's annual purchases
6. Our market share penetration
7. Frequency of purchase
8. Purchases by types of products

*Geographical Sales Analysis*
1. States, cities, etc.
2. Sales territory
3. Individual salespeople
4. Types of customers
5. Product types

*Product Sales Analysis*
1. Classes of products
2. Product lines to customers
3. Product lines to market segments
4. Product lines to four-digit SIC

product or market segments instead of aggregate sales. Whether or not this can be done, however, depends on the way a company maintains or structures its sales records.

The pressure curve is a crucial tool for management because it enables timely actions to be taken that will reduce a company's exposure as the product or market cycle turns down, and it puts the company into a position such that it can capitalize on opportunities as the cycle turns upward. In October of 1976, a large electrical equipment manufacturer reported record bookings. Sales management was euphoric because bookings had increased steadily for several months. They were dumbfounded when top management ordered a major reduction in inventory and workforce. The sales managers did not recognize that the *rate* of sales growth had declined sharply and that top management had a clear indication that rough times were ahead. Because of top management's actions, the company was able to significantly reduce its costs and was actually able to improve profits during the following year, which turned out to be a severe recession period.

| TABLE 6.2 | **SALES – ORIGINAL EQUIPMENT CUSTOMERS (PRODUCT H)** |  |
|---|---|---|

|   |   | 1981 Dollars (000) |   |
|---|---|---|---|
| A | Caterpillar | $17,000 | |
|   | Detroit Diesel-Allison | 5,050 | |
|   | J.I. Case | 2,000 | |
|   | John Deere | 2,500 | |
| B | Allis Chalmers | 1,200 | |
|   | Clark Equipment | 600 | |
|   | Ford Tractor | 975 | |
|   | Hyster Company | 588 | |
|   | New Holland | 610 | |
|   | Rockford Clutch | 1,063 | |
|   | Saab Scania | 675 | |
|   | Twin Disc | 1,000 | |
|   | U.S. Government | 1,575 | Reclassified by four segments |
|   | Warner Gear | 500 | 1. Mining |
| C | Caterpillar – Mexico | 250 | 2. Agriculture |
|   | Clearing Division, U.S. Industries | 170 | 3. Construction |
|   | Fiat Allis | 357 | 4. Industrial lift trucks |
|   | Franklin Equipment | 181 | |
|   | Funk Manufacturing | 150 | |
|   | International Harvester | 400 | |
|   | Jeffrey Mining | 268 | |
|   | Joy Manufacturing | 127 | |
|   | Marathon LeTourneau | 188 | |
|   | Massey Ferguson | 409 | |
|   | Mine Machinery | 80 | |
|   | Pacific Car | 201 | |
|   | White Farm Equipment | 12 | |
| Others |   | 1,345 | |
| Total |   | 39,475 | |

The key to achieving value from this curve or analysis is not in plotting the data, but in using the curve as a decision-making tool. This data is often carefully plotted in companies by someone in the marketing or economic research groups. While the exercise may provide intellectual satisfaction to those doing the plotting, little real value accrues to the company until top management recognizes its importance and makes it an integral part of the decision-making process.

EXHIBIT
6-5

# SALES ANALYSIS PLANNING
## (PAST, PRESENT, AND FUTURE)

**Sales Analysis by Major Accounts**

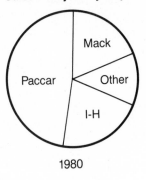

1980

1982

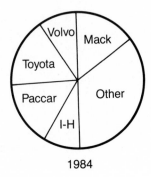

1984

**Market Segments**

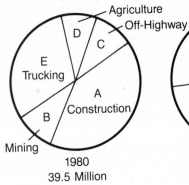

1980
39.5 Million

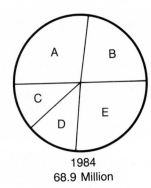

1982
48.7 Million

1984
68.9 Million

**Sales/Distribution Channel Analysis**

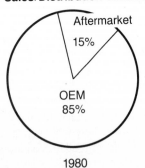

1980

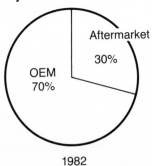

1982

1984

**EXHIBIT
6-5**

*(cont'd)*

**Geographic Sales Analysis**

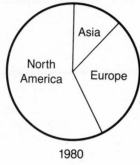
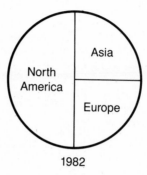
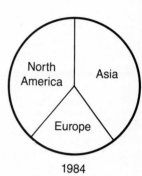

1980          1982          1984

# ESTIMATING MARKET POTENTIAL

In addition to assessing the company's current market position and near-term sales outlook, management is also faced with the task of estimating market potential for both existing and new markets. There are a number of ways market potential can be estimated, and how it is done depends chiefly on the sources and availability of data. However, before estimating market potentials, it is essential to carefully define the market segments.

## Defining the Market

As we saw in the previous chapter, there are many different ways to define a market. As a result, confusion often abounds in discussions of market potential because those involved have not reached common agreement on the parameters of the market in question. Many times potential estimates are discussed in terms of total industry sales. Other times they are discussed in terms of certain classes of accounts. However, these estimates of market potential are of little value to anyone trying to evaluate target markets for strategic planning and decision making. To be useful, any discussion of market potential should address a specific product or a defined customer or customer group as outlined in the previous chapter on segmenting business markets.

## Historical Data

Assuming the market has been properly defined, the first step in forecasting any market is to search for and examine any historical data that might be available. A translation of

**EXHIBIT 6-6**

## ELECTRONIC COMPONENTS—TOTAL REGULAR ORDERS

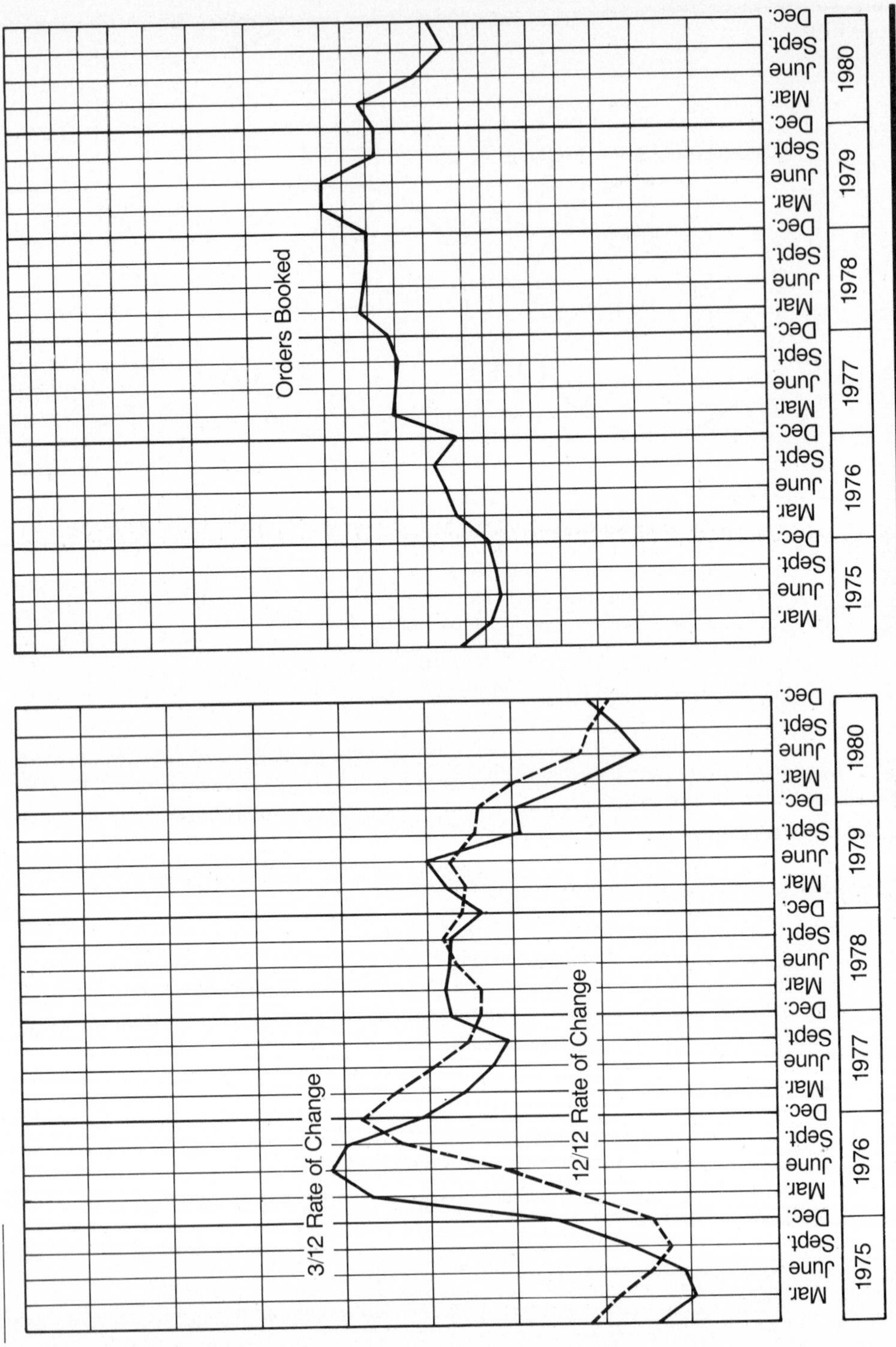

3/12 Rate of Change
12/12 Rate of Change
Orders Booked
Mar. June Sept. Dec.
1975 1976 1977 1978 1979 1980

**EXHIBIT
6-7**

## THE BUSINESS CYCLE

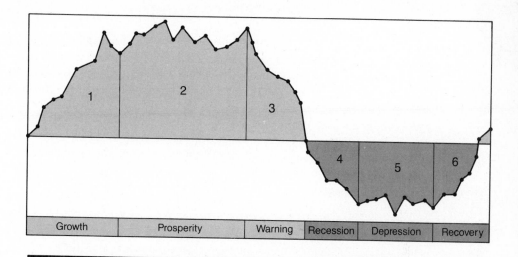

| Growth | Prosperity | Warning | Recession | Depression | Recovery |

the Latin phrase on the Archives Building cornerstone in Washington, D.C., reads, "What is past is prologue." There is a good deal of truth to this phrase in business where sales into markets tend to move in repetitive cycles, as shown in Exhibit 6-7. The duration of business cycles in the United States ranges from one to nine years, with the average length about three years.[1] Thus, a historical perspective of sales trends is a useful starting point for predicting the future. It must be remembered that this is only a starting point, and any simple-minded attempt to make a straight-line extrapolation of the past into the future is likely to be a mistake, especially in our increasingly dynamic and turbulent world.

Given this caveat, it is still helpful to look for cycles or patterns in historical data that will help in predicting the future. It is also useful to determine whether there is any valid correlation between the product or market cycle and general business cycles, like capital expenditures, capacity utilization, or some other measure of business activity that is regularly plotted and forecasted in published sources.[2]

GNP or the total index of industrial activity may be useful indicators for commodity items that are consumed across all or most markets. However, these indicators are of little use to the industrial marketer struggling to estimate potential for a particular product or market. The indices are simply too broad and too hard to relate to total product or market businesses. Nevertheless, management in many companies spends a lot of money for expert opinion and wastes a lot of time developing very detailed projections or input/output

[1]James A. Estey, *Business Cycles,* 3rd ed. (Englewood Cliffs, N.J.: Prentice-Hall, 1970).
[2]Elmer Lotshaw, "All the Economics You Need for Industrial Market Planning—and No More," *Industrial Marketing Management,* 7 (1970), p. 4.

analysis for our total economy. As we see it, this is more of a theoretical exercise and is simply too far removed from the product-market segment to be of practical use.

## Derived Demand

For component products or materials that are used in the production of other products, estimating market potential takes on an added dimension of complexity. Here it is essential to estimate the potential for each customer's markets, which may exist at various levels of the consumption chain described in Chapter 2. For example, a producer of ball bearings must examine a wide range of OEM and aftermarket segments where machines with bearings are used. Doing this requires the bearing producer to work closely with its customers in an effort to forecast the growth rate of each of their markets. This is the only way the bearing producer can estimate future demand for its products.

## Trade Association Sources

Many trade associations forecast total industry demand for their member companies. These forecasts usually show the annual total market size and sometimes indicate competitor shares. Exhibit 6-8 shows the aggregate worldwide market for jet aircraft turbine airfoils and the respective sales by U.S., foreign, and captive suppliers. This typical industry forecast does not show the demand by market segments within the total industry, which in the case of turbine airfoils includes military, commercial, and business jets. Each of these market segments has different growth rates, different requirements, and different sets of competitors and suppliers. In short, industry associations can serve as a useful source for aggregate industry data and trends, but further refinements are required before the data can be used to estimate product-market potential.

## Conversion Factors

Conversion factors can also be used to help estimate potential in some markets. A conversion factor can be used when there is a high correlation for demand in the product-market segment with consumption patterns or plans in other markets that are more visible and predictable. For example, in the biomedical industry, the type of hospital (general, teaching, specialty), the number of beds, and the occupancy rate are used to determine a weighted conversion factor by the type and size of hospital in each county. The demand for oil field pumps and parts is related to a composite conversion factor developed around the number of pumping wells, parts per type of machine, and number of barrels produced. The forecasts for new elevator systems can be related to new building permits for high-rise starts and renovation projects.

Extreme care must be used in selecting a conversion factor, even where a high statistical correlation exists, since there are many random correlations that are not based on a direct cause/effect relationship. If the wrong conversion factor is chosen, major strategic or technical errors can result. A major strategic error would be to select markets that consume considerably less than the conversion factor indicated. Tactical errors could result in the wrong alignment of sales territories, location of distribution centers, or sales

**EXHIBIT
6-8**

## TOTAL MARKET FOR JET AIRCRAFT TURBINE AIRFOILS
### (1982 Forecast)

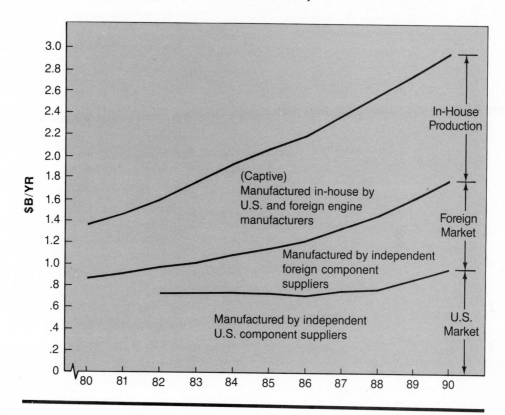

quotas. A common mistake is to regard the number of employees at various plant locations as an indicator of consumption for an industrial product. The number of employees at a plant can often be misleading as a conversion factor, especially with the increased use of automation, which reduces the employee head count. This could lead to a significant overstatement or understatement of demand estimates in geographical areas where there are heavy concentrations of new or old plants.

## CONDUCTING MARKET STUDIES

The complete range of information required to assess any business market is seldom available from internal sales records or trade association data. To obtain the more precise information required, it is usually necessary to conduct some kind of a market study that involves existing customers, prospective customers, and distributors. Market studies of this type can provide firsthand information about:

Market size and growth rates        Annual purchases, needs, and trends
Buying influences                   Competitive evaluations
Supply sources                      New product needs
Supplier performance                Product performance
Technical requirements              Technological trends
Product, brand, or company image

## Specifying Information Needed

The most important step before embarking on a search for market information is to define the problem and specify what kind of information is needed. A clearly and accurately stated marketing problem is often well on its way to being solved.[3] The definition provides the direction and control for the entire information-gathering process. If the marketing problem is not properly defined, time, effort, and money will be wasted — no matter how well the project is carried out. Who needs the right answer to the wrong question?

Defining marketing and business problems is frequently a complex process. In order to locate and define problems, a written list of all the pertinent areas to be considered should be prepared. Secondary research (research done and published by others) may help to define and develop a more specific checklist of information required before primary research is undertaken.

## Secondary Market Studies

Secondary research is the search for previously published material that can provide more background information and a closer focus on the problem. Sometimes called "desk research," secondary research utilizes internal data, including sales records, salespersons' call reports, and a reanalysis of previously conducted studies. Sales analysis is a form of internal secondary research.

External sources of market information include trade associations, technical journals, government agencies, and industrial directories. The *Census of Manufacturers* and *County Business Patterns* are secondary sources explained in Chapter 5. Another source, *Thomas's Register of American Manufacturers,* classifies all manufacturers by products produced, assets, state, and city. It is used by many purchasing departments to identify suppliers and producers. Each industry or profession usually has at least one trade association. Some trade associations are little more than a public relations office; others keep close track of industry sales and trends. The name, location, and major activities performed by all U.S. associations are contained in the *Encyclopedia of Associations,* a reference that is in most libraries and should be in the industrial firm. Some of the larger trade associations have their own full-time market assessment staff. However, trade associations often do not provide member market share data, and most trade associations do not provide much information to nonmembers.

[3]Howard L. Balsley and Vernon T. Clover, *Business Research Methods,* 2d ed. (Columbus, Ohio: Grid Publishing, Inc., 1979), p. 35.

As a general rule, no market study should be undertaken before a search of secondary sources has been completed. It can sometimes solve the problem without any primary research. The cost is much less than a primary investigation, and at the least, such a search will establish a higher plateau from which a primary study can be launched. Secondary sources will often help to refocus the original problem. Secondary research is not as exciting as primary research for both the analyst and user, but because of its exploratory nature, it can establish patterns of careful, thoughtful analysis that will carry over to any subsequent primary market assessment studies.

## Primary Market Studies

The quality of the data obtained from a primary market study depends on the quality and validity of the sample, asking the right questions, and employing qualified interviewers.

SELECTING THE SAMPLE.   Samples for industrial marketing studies are nearly always much smaller than those used for consumer goods marketing studies because of the concentrated nature of many industrial markets. For example, a manufacturer of specialty chemicals identified a total of 20 potential users for a new high-performance chemical. The producer was able to visit personally 6 users and to conduct telephone interviews with the remaining 14 in the total market. One hundred percent "sampling" of the entire universe is not uncommon in some industrial market segments. If larger customer bases are involved, it is often best to stratify the sample by size or type of customer. The actual selecting of individual samples in industrial markets is usually based more on a judgment of which companies or personnel are most knowledgeable than on statistical models or random probability methods.

SURVEY METHODS.   Survey information can be obtained through person-to-person interviews, telephone interviews, or mailed questionnaires. Person-to-person interviews allow the interviewer to see a customer's production process or system and ask some specific questions about how the supplier's product might be used. For example, one manufacturer developed a new insulating material for greenhouses that would reduce energy costs. There was no substitute for conducting person-to-person interviews in a good cross-section of greenhouses in the defined market segment. The field interviews helped the producer make a cost-benefit analysis of the energy-saving material in large, medium, and small greenhouses in each climate zone.[4] Energy costs and technical requirements were also obtained for each type of greenhouse. The person-to-person interviews also revealed some potential application problems. In other cases, a small number of interviews with customers can stop a supplier from providing an expensive function the customer does not need or want. For example, a major farm tractor manufacturer learned from farmers that a side power unit to raise and lower implements was not needed. The final engineering and manufacturing costs for the unit would have been nearly $1 million, and it would have added an unnecessary 5 to 6 percent to the purchase price of

[4]See also Chapter 4, "Understanding Customers and Competition," pp. 68–79.

the tractor. The probing nature of person-to-person interviews is excellent for learning how customers use and buy products.

Person-to-person industrial interviews typically involve small numbers. Sample sizes of ten to one hundred are far more common than the hundreds or thousands so typical in the consumer goods world.

Each business interview can last one to three hours, considerably longer than is practical for telephone or mail interviews. Person-to-person interviews are costly, especially if extensive travel is required, and may be ineffective if interviewers are not properly trained or indoctrinated. The cost of person-to-person interviews can be reduced by using focus groups. An industrial focus group consists of a small number of individuals with a common occupation. One machine tool manufacturer usually discusses a product with, and shows a prototype to, focus groups of machinists to obtain their reactions. A hospital equipment manufacturer conducts group interviews with nurses to obtain responses to its and competitors' machines. In still another situation, an electrical producer sometimes conducts group interviews with distributors at regional meetings to obtain competitive intelligence.

Focus group interviews are a relatively inexpensive and fast way to gather market information. The combined group effect often produces a wide range of information and insights, but the results are sometimes hard to interpret and quantify. The stronger personalities in the group can influence the more passive members. The tendency to seek consensus may also dampen the responses of some members. But if resources are limited, the focus group may be the best alternative to no interviews at all.

SEEKING EXPERT OPINION.   Sometimes the opinions of experts on a subject are far more important than the results of any other kind of study. For example, a manufacturer of surgical hip joints wanted to determine whether hip implants made of titanium would eventually be selected by physicians over the current implants made of aluminum. Expert opinions from leading orthopedic surgeons were obtained at a national orthopedic surgeons convention. After obtaining a preregistration list of physicians, the supplier was able to schedule interviews with 30 surgeons by offering $500 to each for participation. The supplier was able to gauge the physicians' initial reactions to the use of titanium and identify sources of resistance to the new product. The expert opinion interviews were a very efficient and rapid way to obtain information for final product development, market entry strategy, and competitive promotional plans.

Expert opinions are frequently sought in high technology industries like medicine, pharmaceuticals, and aerospace. Interviewers visit key people at universities and corporations who are recognized as the innovators or leaders in the profession. The whole approach depends on knowing how to identify the real experts. True experts are recognized by colleagues and peers as nationally and internationally knowledgeable about the topic. Good interviews with true experts usually reduce the need for additional interviews with more people. It is a mistake to think that expert opinion is inferior to more scientific approaches to gathering market information. In some industrial market situations, it can be far superior to large sample information.[5] However, a small sample of experts is usually better than a single expert.

[5]Philip Kotler, "A Guide to Gathering Expert Estimates," *Business Horizons,* October 1970, pp. 79–85.

MAIL OR TELEPHONE.   In situations where the cost of person-to-person interviews—either individual or group—is too high, the marketer can choose the mail or telephone approach. It is also not uncommon first to conduct a few person-to-person interviews and then complete the study with the mail or telephone approach. Telephone interviews, like the person-to-person approach to gathering market assessment information, allow marketers to reach the appropriate people and ask probing questions. A telephone interview of up to a half hour is a relatively low-cost approach. Like person-to-person interviews, it requires interviewers trained in the product or technology. Of course, complex technical questions that require seeing the respondent's situation or using visual aids are not feasible with the telephone approach. Telephone market assessment is limited to rather simple questions about annual purchases, current supply sources, and image perceptions.

Mail interviews are usually low in cost and do not require the training and supervision of interviewers. They are especially good when surveying a wide customer base with many segments about relatively few items. For example, a manufacturer of agricultural chemicals periodically surveys about 2,000 farmers to learn of different trends and purchase preferences for different chemicals. The producer supplements the periodic survey with person-to-person interviews at agricultural cooperatives and county fairs. The shorter the questionnaire, the better. Low response rates may create a strong response bias, and there is often little control over when the response is returned and who provides the information.

COMMON FORECASTING METHODS.   In summary, there are a number of forecasting methods to consider when estimating or evaluating a product or market situation. The more common methods of forecasting are shown in Table 6.3. A description of each method, along with the advantages and disadvantages of each approach, is also shown in Table 6.3, and other published sources provide still more information about these approaches.[6,7,8]

One of the major advantages of personal and telephone interviews is the ability to control who the respondent is. There is little such control with mail questionnaires. A response from the wrong users, specifiers, and buyers can be harmful. Skilled interviewers take great care to be sure they are talking to the key decision maker(s) in the purchase of the item being studied.

All these approaches to conducting primary market assessment studies should be considered when a problem is to be studied. Each of the approaches is a compromise of some form. The manager or user of the market information must weigh the cost, time, and value of the project when choosing one or a combination of approaches.

ASKING THE RIGHT QUESTIONS.   Once the correct respondents are identified and interview method chosen, the next problem is asking the questions in the right way. Poor wording can result in misleading and inaccurate studies. Questions that ask for ways to improve a product or "what would you like improved" will get more in-depth responses than questions that simply ask what the user likes and dislikes about an existing or new

[6]Steven C. Wheelwright and Spyros Makridakis, *Forecasting Methods for Management,* 2nd ed. (New York: Wiley, 1977).
[7]Harry D. Wolfe, *Business Forecasting Methods* (New York: Holt, Rinehart, and Winston, 1966).
[8]Richard D. Crisp, *Sales Planning and Control* (New York: McGraw-Hill, 1968), p. 42.

**TABLE 6.3**    *COMMON FORECASTING METHODS FOR PRODUCT-MARKET SEGMENTS*

| Method | Description | Advantages | Disadvantages |
|---|---|---|---|
| 1. Survey | Widely used technique—mail surveys, person-to-person, or telephone approach to determine potential by segments. Helps estimate annual purchases by bridge factor in each segment. | Current. Geographic concentrations. Major accounts. Helps detect purchase trends. Can provide competitive information. Provides sales leads. | Time-consuming—1 to 3 months. Cost may be $3,000 to $40,000+. |
| 2. Trend projection | Past trends are projected into the future, fitting curves to historical data. | Objective. Simple and quick. | Assumes the future is a direct extension of the past. Historical data are usually inadequate for new products. |
| 3. Expert opinion | Obtaining opinions of a representative sample or from knowledgeable experts in the area and building projections from consensus or composite of estimates. Also used to predict technological changes. | Basis for estimating uncertainties. Provides a "ballpark feel." Provides a focus on more specific segments and for new products. | Highly subjective. Determining experts. |
| 4. Substitution demand | Demand assumed to be related to another product. The selection of a conversion or bridge factor is a form of substitution demand analysis. | Allows rational extrapolation of limited data. | Subjective. Assumes same outside factors as for substitute product. |
| 5. Correlation analysis | Demand related to one or more independent variables can also be shown with a regression equation. | Objective if consistent correlations are identified. Requires choice of major factors affecting demand and statement of assumptions. | Truly independent variables are sometimes difficult to identify. Other variables must first be forecast themselves. Complexity increases with more variables. High correlation does not always mean cause-effect. |
| 6. Mathematical models | Equations developed to express interrelationships among several variables. Equations are solved to get values of dependent demand. | Same as correlation analysis. Forces "systematic" organization of data. | Same as correlation analysis. Precision likely to be confused with accuracy. |

product. Here are ten guidelines to consider when constructing a questionnaire and selecting words:

1. All questions should relate directly to the research objectives.
2. Avoid examples, because they may divert the response from the research objectives.
3. If you wish to extract many thoughts on the topic, add a probing question that goes deeper into the topic.
4. Use as few and as simple words as possible in each question.
5. Make questions specific without being elaborate.
6. Avoid wording that causes ambiguous responses.
7. Use trade jargon only if all the respondents know and use it.
8. Even if it is an open-ended question, consider providing categories or precoded check boxes for the answers. This is especially helpful when asking for amounts or figures.
9. Instead of asking "how much?" indicate the units for which you desire answers— pounds, dollars, gallons, yards, percentages, or whatever.
10. Provide for "don't know" responses rather than force a guess.

SELECTING THE RIGHT INTERVIEWERS.   Accurate business interviews depend on asking the right questions to the appropriate people and then listening with educated ears. Since person-to-person and telephone interviews are central for many market assessment projects, the person asking the questions and receiving the verbal responses plays a key role. The interviewer should know the industry and how the product is used and bought. Without such background knowledge, the interviewer cannot ask probing questions and will probably miss key words from the respondent. It usually takes extensive briefing and indoctrination into the industry, the technology, substitute products, and the competition to get less knowledgeable interviewers up to an acceptable level. The vice-president of marketing in a major industrial firm evaluates market studies by outside suppliers by the kind and type of briefing they do of their field interviewers. Often he personally inter-views one of the field interviewers to see how well they were briefed and made aware of the problem and concerns of the study.

The business respondent's time is usually important. Therefore, the interviewer must gain as much useful information as possible within a limited time. As a consequence, in-dustrial market research field interviewers must state questions clearly, attempt to trigger the memory, and listen very carefully. If more time and skill are invested in training in-dustrial interviewers, smaller sample sizes may be used to yield the same amount of in-formation in considerably less time and at a reduced cost.

One manufacturer of electronic testing equipment always sends a team of R&D and marketing people to conduct person-to-person interviews for product development. The team method allows for better questioning, note taking, and insights to better couple product development to customer requirements. R&D–marketing team interviews can also help in creative market analysis immediately following the interviews. In one case, a small number of R&D and marketing team personal interviews with customers helped to refocus product development.

The need to have expert interviewers knowledgeable in the technical language and users' needs is usually best addressed by in-house marketing research personnel. They need less timely and costly indoctrination. In a larger firm, an in-house marketing research staff is a necessary and usually cost-effective alternative to having outside firms plan market studies and conduct personal interviews.

SALES FORCE OPINIONS.   The industrial sales force is sometimes considered a biased and poor source of market information. This is sometimes true, but an industrial sales representative can also be a prime source of market information. The intelligence the industrial sales representative develops about end users' needs, business patterns, and competition can serve as the foundation for future product and market plans and tactics. It is impractical for most industrial companies to structure market tests as consumer goods companies do to evaluate the needs, likes, and dislikes of market segments. The industrial marketer must gear the sales force to provide this information or in many cases do without it. One major part of the market planning and research function of any company should be to develop and provide intelligent, continual feedback from the marketplace. Industrial firms should spend considerable effort and emphasize the importance of developing market assessment information from the field sales force. Salespeople usually have well-developed interpersonal skills, are familiar with customers' operations, and speak customers' language.

## Data Analysis

Most analysis of business research consists of drawing conclusions from statements made by knowledgeable people about their operations, applications, requirements, purchase plans, and buying considerations. When the results of the research are quantitative, graphs should generally be used to show trends, segments, or changing relationships. Graphs are generally limited to showing the relationship between two variables. The graph should show the manager if there is any relationship and also whether the relationship is up (direct) or down (inverse), or whether some type of curve best shows the relationship. Graphs show relationships that do not appear in various kinds of statistical analyses. Graphs help managers to make generalizations and predictions by looking beyond the data. There is limited need for the use of sophisticated statistical techniques driven by computers, and management should challenge any proposal that hinges on the utilization of these methods. There is a high probability that proposals of this type are made by people who are more interested in the technique than providing useful results.

## New Product Market Studies

New product market studies, like new product development, is difficult and risky. Usually the newer the industrial product or service, the less accurate or reliable will be the prospect's responses. If the product or service is fairly revolutionary or requires a different way of using the product, evaluations tend to be more negative. In cases where the product is radically different or performs the same function but in a different way, it is often difficult for customers to visualize the value-in-use. Revolutionary products also tend to be rejected as "crazy" or strange. New products often have more credibility and understandability if they come from a well-known producer. But since most innovations come from small companies who are not well known, new product market research for these producers is often difficult.

Two independent market studies done for the then new Xerox Corporation in 1959 concluded that there was a limited market for its later successful Model 914. The studies concluded that there was no market for a large, free-standing general document copying machine. In retrospect, Xerox executives contend that those interviewed applied the criteria of the existing methods of copying or reproduction, whereas they were interested in respondents evaluating the attributes of an entirely new technology. The product the studies said nobody wanted became a product everybody wanted. New product industrial market research must carefully examine the existing production systems of potential in-use customers and the cost-benefit value and be cautious about prospective customers' negative opinions.

It is also frequently difficult to obtain accurate market size and growth information for innovative industrial products. For example, the Smith Kline Corporation found it extremely difficult to anticipate the potential success and market size of the ulcer treatment drug Tagamet, which after four years had yearly sales of about $600 million. The initial market research for this product concluded that revenues would eventually attain $100 million a year for the drug and that ultimately it could attain revenues of $250 million when it was a mature product, six to eight years later. What confounded the market researchers was the absence of statistics on ulcer sufferers. Those who were being treated by a physician showed up in the public health records, but there was no way to be sure how many others were treating themselves with diets and various nonprescription antacids. A similar problem faced Merck Pharmaceutical Company when it was attempting to obtain market information on the size of the U.S. dog worm medicine market. Incomplete statistics and lack of information about the magnitude of the problem resulted in an inability to estimate the size and growth of what was thought to be a large market.

## PROJECT PROPOSALS

A sound project proposal is the framework and roadmap for conducting a professional market assessment study. All proposals should be developed with the managerial users of the information. These same managers should "sign off" on every proposal before it is implemented or before the data is gathered.

To assist the marketers in designing and implementing a market assessment study, we have provided two project proposals. The first, Exhibit 6-9, is an industrial valve study. This product has a wide potential customer base that buys primarily through local distributors. By explicitly stating the objectives of the study in the form of eight precise information needs, the problem and the specific information required are well defined.

EXHIBIT
6-9

# BALL VALVE PRODUCT-MARKET STUDY

## I. OBJECTIVES OF THE STUDY

The specific objectives of this marketing study are to:

1. Define the channels of distribution being used for each market segment studied.
2. Develop a list of distributors for each of the major manufacturers of ball valves.
3. Identify the major ball valve product attributes considered important buying factors.
4. Rank the product attributes in terms of important buying factors overall and market segment.
5. Rank the product attributes in terms of important buying factors by size (employment) of manufacturing plant.
6. Identify the major ball valve manufacturers' competitive strengths and weaknesses in terms of the product attributes.
7. Define the dollar market demand for brass ball valves by the market segments selected to be studied.
8. Provide a prospect list of qualified users of brass ball valves, including a dollar estimate of buying potential. This prospect list will be arranged by trading area and will include plants with more than 25 employees.

## II. MARKET ASSESSMENT METHODS

1. **Literature Search** All known literature indexes and directories will be searched to gather the names of firms operating in the identified OEM markets. Examples of literature sources include state industrial directories, *Iron Age,* and major periodicals.

2. **Mail Survey** A mail survey will be used to gather the quantitative and qualitative data to measure the perceived buying factor importance ranking and the types of distributors being used to serve the various market segments. A sampling of approximately 4,500 plants is planned.

3. **Field Interviews** This marketing research technique will be used to frame and pretest the mail questionnaire and gather qualitative information concerning the major buying factors and channels of distribution.

4. **Telephone Interviews** Telephone interviews will be conducted to verify and supplement data gathered through the mail survey and field interviews.

## III. METHOD OF PREPARATION

A mail questionnaire will be used as the primary research method for gathering the data. Field interviews will be conducted to pretest the questionnaire and identify the major product attributes in terms of important buying influences.

**A. OEM Markets** The OEM markets included in this study are as follows:

| SIC | Market Description |
|-----|--------------------|
| 3433 | Heating equipment |
| 3443 | Boiler shops |
| 3551 | Food products machinery |
| 3552 | Textile machinery |
| 3553 | Woodworking machinery |
| 3554 | Paper industry machinery |
| 3555 | Printing machinery |
| 3561 | Pumps and pumping equipment |
| 3563 | Air and gas compressors |
| 3564 | Blowers, exhaust, and ventilation fans |
| 3582 | Commercial laundry, dry cleaning, and pressing machines |

**B. Aftermarkets** The MRO/aftermarkets included in this study are as follows:

| SIC | Market Description |
|-----|--------------------|
| 1711 | Mechanical contractors |
| 2421 | Saw mills and planing mills |
| 2611 | Pulp mills |
| 2869 | Organic chemicals |
| 3069 | Fabricated rubber products |
| 3229 | Glass products |
| 3312 | Steel mills |
| 3441 | Fabricated metal products |
| 3523 | Farm and garden machinery |
| 3621 | Electrical motors and generators |
| 3728˙ | Aircraft parts and equipment |

**EXHIBIT**
**6-10**

*JET ENGINE PARTS STUDY*

## I. OBJECTIVES OF THE STUDY

The objectives of this study are to:

1. Identify the major buying influences for purchasing agents, maintenance engineers, and chief engineers that affect the decision to buy fuel injection and metering devices (fuel manifolds, spraybars, valves) and fuel nozzles.
2. Rank the major buying influences for purchasing agents, maintenance engineers, and chief engineers and their perceptions of the major suppliers.

   A. Engine Prime Contractors
      1. Pratt & Whitney, Florida
      2. General Electric, Evendale, and Lynn, Massachusetts
      3. Detroit Diesel Allison Division, Indianapolis

   B. Private Engine Rework Facilities (to be identified and sampled)

   C. Research & Development Facilities
      1. NASA Lewis Research Centers
      2. Naval Air Propulsion Test Center (Trenton, N.J.)
      3. Jet Propulsion Laboratory (California)
      4. Arnold Engineering Development Center

   D. USAF and USN Engine Rework Facilities
      1. USAF Bases
         a. San Antonio, Texas
         b. Oklahoma City, Oklahoma
         c. Wright-Patterson, Ohio
      2. USN Rework Facilities
         a. Alameda, California
         b. San Diego, California (North Island)
         c. Cherry Point, North Carolina
         d. Jacksonville, Florida
         e. Pensacola, Florida
         f. Norfolk, Virginia

   E. Aircraft Prime Contractors
      1. McDonnell Douglas
      2. Boeing
      3. Lockheed

   F. Major Commercial Airlines
      1. American
      2. Braniff
      3. Eastern
      4. Northwest
      5. TWA
      6. United
      7. Delta
      8. US Air

## II. METHODS OF ASSESSMENT

**Field Interviews** Based on the small number of facilities comprising the various market segments, it is estimated that approximately 12 personal interviews will be conducted.

**Telephone Interviews** This research method will be used for contacting the identified private engine rework facilities and performing all follow-up work that may be required.

**Mail Survey** In order to cut down on travel expenses and time, a mail questionnaire will be designed and sent to all facilities not personally visited. It is estimated that approximately 100 questionnaires will be sent.

## III. COMPLETION SCHEDULE

This research project will require approximately 12 calendar weeks to complete, starting the day of proposal approval. The actual marketing research time allocation will be for only four man-hour weeks.

The second study (Exhibit 6-10) is for jet engine fuel nozzles. The customer base is very small, less than 25 customers, and each customer provides a significant amount of business. The products are technically complex and are used in commercial business and military jet engines. Personal interviews were the primary method for gathering information; interviews were followed up with mail questionnaires.

# FRAMEWORKS FOR EVALUATING MARKET SEGMENTS ———

Because so many data are involved, the industrial marketer should have a framework to organize the relevant market potential information in a meaningful way. The worksheet shown in Table 6.4 illustrates such a framework. It provides the basis for presenting historical size and growth patterns, as well as estimated size and growth potential. It also provides for listing the major competitors and their market share positions along with major customers and their annual purchases. Obviously, simply filling out this form is not an end in itself. It is designed to help management evaluate and crosscheck a variety of data for various market segments into tradeoffs that must be considered before deciding which segments are most attractive.

Before a final selection of market segments is made, it is often useful to factor profit potential into the decision. In markets where a company does not have a presence, profit potential is generally not readily available. Nevertheless, profit estimates can usually be developed through published financial data, interviews with investment analysts who follow particular industries and companies, and competitor intelligence, as described in Chapter 4. Table 6.5 shows how estimated size, growth rate, and profit potential for a market can be combined to determine the relative value of a share point (1/100th of a market) on both a current and projected basis. The current value of a share point is determined by multiplying 1/100th of the market by the current profit percentage. For example, in market segment A, 1/100th of the market is $1 million. Multiplying $1 million by a 12 percent profit rate results in a current profit value per share point of $120,000. Looking ahead, the projected market size is determined by multiplying the size of the current market by the estimated growth rate. For example, market segment A, which is currently worth $100 million, is expected to grow at 15 percent each year, so the projected market five years out is $240 million. The profit percentage is expected to remain the same, and the projected profit value for each share point also doubles to $240,000.

From this table, you can see that the changes of the three key variables—size, growth rate, and EBT percentage over a five-year period—can often lead to different conclusions than market data alone might suggest. For example, compare the current and projected value per share point for market segment D. It actually shows a significant decline because of an expected deterioration in EBT percentage. And market segment E, which is currently the smallest segment, has such a high profit potential and growth rate that it becomes one of the more attractive markets five years out. Very few managers ever consider profit potential as they access various market segments. More should, however, because variations in profit opportunities can have a major impact on the relative attractiveness of market alternatives.

**TABLE 6.4**

## PRODUCT AND MARKET SEGMENT FORECASTS

| Industry Group | Identified Market Segments | Segment Size Today (In units/ dollars) | Segment Annual Growth Rates (In % for last four years) | Forecast Market Size (In units/dollars) 1 Yr | 3 Yr | 5 Yr | Present Competitors and Market Shares 3–5 Competitors | Market Share | Major Customers and Annual Purchase |
|---|---|---|---|---|---|---|---|---|---|
| Industrial | Medical instrumentation | | | | | | 1. | | |
| | Process controls | | | | | | 2. | | |
| | Test equipment | | | | | | 3. | | |
| Computers | Mainframe | | | | | | 4. | | |
| | Microprocessors | | | | | | 5. | | |
| | Calculators | | | | | | | | |

**TABLE 6.5**

## PROJECTING THE PROFIT POTENTIAL OF A SHARE POINT CURRENT AND FIVE YEARS OUT

| Market Segments | Current Size (Millions) | Current Profit (Percent) | Current Profit Value Per Share Point (Thousands) | Estimated Growth Rate (Percent) | Projected Market Size | Estimated Profit (Percent) | Projected Profit Value Per Share Point |
|---|---|---|---|---|---|---|---|
| A | 100 | 12 | 120 | 15 | 240 | 12 | 240 |
| B | 350 | 9 | 315 | 7 | 458 | 10 | 458 |
| C | 200 | 14 | 280 | 8 | 371 | 10 | 271 |
| D | 400 | 15 | 600 | 5 | 510 | 8 | 408 |
| E | 60 | 20 | 120 | 20 | 144 | 20 | 288 |

## SUMMARY

The day-to-day pressures of business tend to focus attention on the immediate situation. But a more systematic study and fact gathering of market trends, potentials, cyclical turns, and profitability will result in more active professional management and less defensive reaction. The time and cost required to conduct market studies that result in better direction should be considered a priority investment. The cost and risks of not having the necessary market facts can be high without such data. Wrong and irre- versible strategic commitments can be made to serve markets that are rapidly declining. With slow or no growth situations and rapid technical changes in many business markets, sound market facts are even more important. When market assessment is a key input in all strategic and tactical product and market thinking, strategy, and programs, the industrial firm will have the appropriate basis for sound decision making.

## REVIEW QUESTIONS

1. What information do managers need to know about each market segment?
2. How are four-digit SICs and yearly purchases per employee used to determine market potentials?
3. How can an internal sales analysis assess a firm's market and profit position?
4. What are some guidelines to consider when constructing an industrial market research questionnaire?
5. When is it best to use person-to-person in- terviews, telephone interviews, and mail questionnaires?
6. Why are industrial new product market studies difficult to obtain accurate information from?
7. Why does most business market analysis consist of frequency counts and cross-tabulations?
8. What specific types of information would be helpful in evaluating market segments?

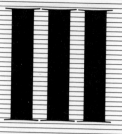

# MANAGING THE MARKETING MIX

# 7

# Product Development

The Product Life Cycle
  Better Mousetraps
  New Technologies
Bettering the Chances:
Principles of New Product
Development
  Defining the Right
  Product-Market Focus
  Facing Up to Cost and
  Performance
  Deficiencies
  Pruning the Existing
  Line
  Linkage to the Business
  Plan
  Following a Disciplined
  Process
  Matching Future
  Products and Current
  Profits
  Organizing New Product
  Activities
  Going Outside for New
  Technology
Summary
Review Questions

In the fall of 1974, top management of a large machine tool company made a major strategic decision. All new product development personnel and projects were pulled away from the four major divisions of the company and centralized in a new center under the direction of a corporate vice president of engineering. The technical center had cost $5 million to build and equip and was to be a showplace. Senior management was convinced that this move would put the company in a position to lead the industry in product development. Division managers were assessed 1.5 percent of sales for development projects on their products. They were also encouraged to forward their ideas for projects, but the vice president of engineering was authorized to commit funds in the best interests of the corporation.

After the recession in 1975 and 1976, the company's market and profit position deteriorated badly. The company also lost market share because it had not moved into electronic controls as rapidly as competitors. At a committee management meeting, the president complained about the lost market share and the company's poor position in electronic controls: "I can't understand it. We have the best R&D facility, the most engineers, and the highest ratio of R&D expense to sales. Why are we behind?"

In response, the vice president of engineering explained: "Things are not as bad as they seem. We are currently testing two prototype control systems that appear very attractive. We should have them ready to turn over to marketing within the next three to four months. Once these new systems are ready, our sales and marketing group should be able to regain our market share and then some." The vice president of marketing took quite a different tack: "I don't want to be the fall guy here. We are at least two years late with a competitive control system and we haven't had enough input to the systems currently on test. I don't know whether they will be competitive, and even if they are, we are going to have one hell of a job trying to recapture market share, particularly in this weak market."

The president exploded: "It's the same old story. Both of you have your own ax to grind and neither of you will accept responsibility for the problem. I don't know how good our new control system will be. I don't know how tough it will be to get back some of the business we have lost. All I know is that you two have not worked together, and our product development activities have suffered because of your failure to cooperate."

Is the president right?

What is the marketing vice president really saying?

What happens if the new products that are so attractive to engineering are not attractive to customers?

Is pouring money into R&D the key to succeeding with new products? What are some problems that could result from this action?

**D**eveloping new products that cost less or perform better has historically been a crucial activity for most industrial companies. Now, it is more important than ever, as industry girds itself to meet foreign competitors that have cut sharply into domestic markets. Product innovations that result in superior performance or cost advantages are the best means of protecting a strong market position or of taking entrenched customers away from competition without sacrificing profit margins. For this reason, new product development is typically regarded as the lifeblood of most industrial businesses. Exhibit 7-1, which is taken from a recent Booz, Allen & Hamilton study, shows that new products have contributed importantly to profits in every industry listed. Making any allowances you want for the inaccuracies that can exist in this kind of a table, one can still see that new products make a vital contribution to sales and profit growth in most industries. What is more important, the figure indicates that profit contribution from new products is expected to increase in the years ahead.

# THE PRODUCT LIFE CYCLE

The importance of new product development stems from a fundamental fact of business life: Every product moves through a life cycle that eventually leads to obsolescence (Exhibit 7-2). When a successful new product is introduced to the market, it typically enjoys a period of rapid growth as it gains acceptance with more customers and replaces those products made obsolete by its presence. But this period of growth does not last forever. As competitors match or improve on the new product, it moves from its growth phase into maturity and eventually into obsolescence. When this occurs, sales volume flattens and then trends downward, prices and margins typically decline below acceptable levels, and the product is ultimately squeezed out or deteriorates into profitless price competition. The life cycle period may be relatively short (two to three years), as it is in the electronics field, where technology leaps ahead almost every day and product life cycles are often discussed in terms of months rather than years. Or it may span a decade or more, as it has for many standard mechanical products and components (screw machines, standard fasteners, or gears). But sooner or later, every product yields to new technology and is preempted by another with better cost and/or performance characteristics.

## Better Mousetraps

No matter how superior a product might appear to be or how dynamic its growth has been, its leadership position is always tenuous. Modern technology is a powerful force and full of surprises; it is a serious mistake to assume that any product ever has a lock on any market. Any product can be pushed from the growth phase of its life cycle to a mature or obsolescent position very quickly by some new product or process that offers significant cost or performance advantages. Whenever a successful product enjoys a strong

**EXHIBIT
7-1**

# CONTRIBUTION OF NEW PRODUCTS TO PROFIT
## BY INDUSTRY

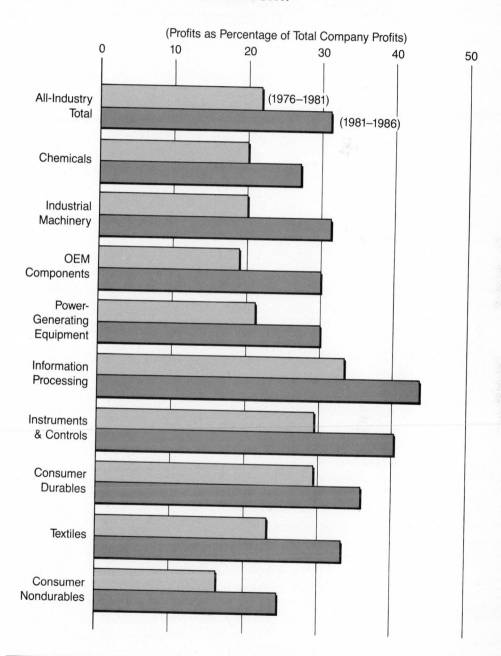

(Profits as Percentage of Total Company Profits)

All-Industry Total — (1976–1981) / (1981–1986)
Chemicals
Industrial Machinery
OEM Components
Power-Generating Equipment
Information Processing
Instruments & Controls
Consumer Durables
Textiles
Consumer Nondurables

*Source:* Booz, Allen & Hamilton Inc.

EXHIBIT
7-2

**PRODUCT LIFE CYCLE CURVE**

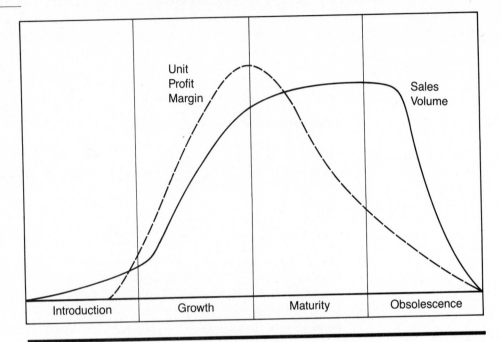

commercial position in an attractive market, management is foolish if it becomes complacent. For not a day goes by that someone, somewhere, is not working to come up with a "better mousetrap" that will weaken or possibly destroy the product's competitive advantage.

History is replete with examples of companies that have lost their competitive advantage and even their business because some competitor came into the market with a product that had superior cost or performance characteristics. This fate is not limited to small or weak competitors; even industrial giants like IBM, General Electric, and Western Electric have seen certain of their markets eroded by competition that surprised them with a distinctly superior product. IBM, despite its dominant position in the computer market, lost position in the late 1970s to several smaller companies that were first to develop powerful minicomputers to replace the large mainframe computers that were the cornerstone of IBM's business. The dramatic shift in market positions among the producers of CAT-scanning equipment in the medical equipment field is also a good example of how product innovation can pay off. Here, General Electric, which was a late entry in the field, gained significant market share over a three-year period at the expense of the companies that developed the market, but failed to keep pace with General Electric's technological advancements.

## New Technologies

Management must also be aware that products can be made obsolete by new technologies as well as improved products. Technological substitution is becoming more frequent and more dramatic. New technologies create opportunities for some firms and major threats for others. With new technologies, new industries and often new competitors emerge (see the box, page 146). New technologies cause industrial firms to redefine what business they are in or should be in. For example, the market boundaries between the data processing, office equipment, and communications industries are blurring. The two rapidly changing fields of electronics and chemistry clearly show the impact of technology on industrial products and markets.

Let's look first at the electronics field. Electronics encompasses subtechnologies that affect everything from television and microwave ovens to computer and missile systems. Electronics is rapidly reshaping the world's manufacturing industries. It often results in the use of new technology in older or mature industries. What one can do for a farm combine, a tractor, a truck, or a car with a little electronics is dramatic. It enhances quality, increases productivity, reduces costs, and may permit more sophisticated designs. It also usually saves on material and labor because it requires fewer workers and typically involves substituting low-cost electronics for high-cost labor.

Factory automation has very quantifiable cost-benefits for the customer. Robots can be shown to have many applications that provide an attractive payback to the purchaser. This usually involves replacing assembly workers and semi-skilled personnel with automation. The cost savings, and the competitive impact, can be so extraordinary that suppliers and buyers may have no choice but to adopt a new technology if they want to survive. The alternative to not adopting is often a decision to not be competitive in what is rapidly becoming a worldwide marketplace.

Now let's consider the chemical field. Chemical and biochemical technologies are another example of how a new technology affects traditional industrial products and markets. A single plastic part can replace several metal parts because plastic is much easier to mold into complex shapes. A metal component would have to be divided into several simpler pieces. Super-strong engineered plastics can outperform steel and brass in many applications. A metal piston must be molded and then finished on a lathe, whereas a plastic piston can be molded very precisely to "near net shape" in one step. By rearranging the molecular chains that determine a plastic's properties, producers can tailor end-use products to specific applications. Black & Decker's cordless surgical drill uses a specialty plastic for both internal components and housing. A medical equipment manufacturer now uses the same plastic material to replace brass connectors and valves in its resuscitators.

The substitution of plastic bottles for glass is a classic example of one technology replacing another. In 1955, high-density polyethylene plastic (PVC) was introduced as a direct competitive substitute for glass containers. It could be made rigid, impact-resistant, and crystal clear. Its lightness and unbreakability were features of significant value to bottlers. Plastic bottles were several times lighter than glass bottles of equal size, which reduced shipping costs and allowed bottlers to economize by using larger-capacity bottles. As a result of these advantages, the changeover from glass to plastic bottles occurred

## THE IMPACT OF ELECTRONICS

Changes in products and markets because of electronics have been dramatic. The old Frieden office calculator had hundreds of parts and sold for about $600. Its electronic version has 50 parts and sells for $80. One microprocessor replaced 350 parts in a Singer industrial sewing machine. A few dozen microchips replaced 80 pounds of switches and wiring in a vending machine. The impact of electronics on service firms can be equally dramatic. When Foremost-McKesson computerized its drug distributors and regional warehouse, it cut its warehouse personnel from 140 to 12. Operating costs were cut from 11.4 percent of sales to 8.3 percent. Inventory turns increased from 6 times a year to 7.5 times, and inventory costs were reduced accordingly.

The switch from mechanical to electronic technology in the commercial scale business substantially changed the outlook and character of that entire industry. Until the mid-1960s, most weighing in industry was done by mechanical scales and weighing systems. Some were more sophisticated than others, but all were mechanically based. The market was mature. Growth was essentially limited to replacement requirements, and the competitive structure was well established with companies like Toledo Scale, Howe Richardson, and Fairbanks Morse the major factors in the market. Then electronic technology entered the picture. It was immediately apparent that electronic scales offered major advantages. They were much more accurate, they could be programmed to compute and collect data, and they could be easily integrated into manufacturing and process control systems. Because these advantages were so significant, users replaced their existing mechanical scales, and sales of electronic units grew rapidly. The combination of more rapid replacement and higher unit price for electronic scales greatly increased the annual revenue generated and made the market for scales much more attractive.

As they attempted to convert from mechanical to electronic technology, traditional manufacturers faced many problems. Mechanical manufacturing had to be maintained at the same time the company moved into electronic manufacturing. Dual inventories had to be carried. Sales and service people had to be retrained.

At the same time new competitors entered the picture. Several smaller electronic firms saw an opportunity to capitalize on their skills and enter a market they perceived as growing away from the traditional manufacturers. Some of the larger electronic manufacturers, like IBM and NCR, recognized the need for systems integration and started to draw on their vast technical resources to move toward the scale producers' traditional business.

*Source:* "The Molting of America," *Forbes,* November 22, 1982, p. 165.

as shown in Exhibit 7-3. Although the substitution occurred over a 30-year period, it was steady and dramatic, and any bottle manufacturer that stayed with glass in specific applications had to lose market share. This is not an isolated case. The makeup of the textile industry changed dramatically as man-made fibers were found to have superior characteristics to wool and cotton. The increasing use of plastic or composite materials has had and will continue to have a major impact on the makeup and position of suppliers to the automotive and aircraft industries.

**EXHIBIT
7-3**

*TOTAL MARKET SHARES FOR GLASS AND PLASTIC BOTTLES:
THE SUBSTITUTION OF ONE TECHNOLOGY FOR ANOTHER*

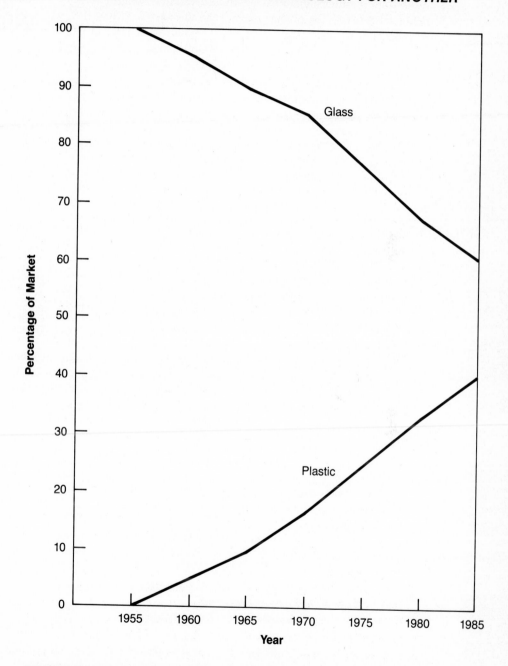

Most industrial managers recognize the importance of new product development. Billions of dollars a year are committed to this activity, but success does not automatically result from spending a lot of money. In fact, very few companies are ever really satisfied with their R&D or new product efforts. The ad shown in Exhibit 7-4, which appeared in several national publications, illustrates the point. Although cast in a humorous vein, it indicates the kinds of headaches that are all too common in most companies. If anything, the success ratio is understated. Many knowledgeable managers say that the odds are not 3 to 1 as implied, but actually closer to 100 to 1 against a product concept or idea being developed into a commercial prototype, and something like 1000 to 1 against its being a commercial success. In short, new product development is much like a gigantic crap game. The stakes are extremely high, and cost of failure by not getting into the game at all or by launching unsuccessful products is astronomical. Yet the profits to be earned by successful new products are almost without limit.

# BETTERING THE CHANCES: PRINCIPLES OF NEW PRODUCT DEVELOPMENT

Even though very few companies are completely satisfied with their new product efforts, it is clear that some companies do a much better job than others—and the results show in their growth rate, market share, and profit picture. Just look at industry leaders like General Electric, DuPont, and IBM. All have a record of new product introduction that has contributed much to their success. Why are they able to achieve better results with new products than their competitors? How do they work around, or at least minimize, the risks and pitfalls in new product development that plague most companies? Each of these companies has its own set of development priorities and needs, but they all follow the same fundamental principles:

1. They think through their product-market focus to provide maximum commercial opportunity.
2. They face up to fundamental cost and performance deficiencies.
3. They rigorously prune marginal products from the existing line.
4. They ensure that all development efforts are directly linked to corporate and product-market strategies.
5. They follow an organized and disciplined process to minimize risk.
6. They strike the right balance between investing in future products and generating current profits.
7. They ensure that marketing management and field sales personnel play an important role in planning new product activities.
8. They are willing to go outside for new technology.

Let's look more closely at each of these principles to see more clearly what is involved.

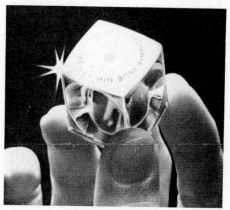
*Source:* General Telephone & Electronics

## Defining the Right Product-Market Focus

In most industrial situations, a product-market business can be defined in different ways. And there are vast differences in the size and potential of any market, depending on how it is defined. It can be defined narrowly to focus on a particular product-market niche or much more broadly to include a range of products flowing into a large industrial market like textiles, oil field supply, food processing, or office equipment. Any company's business strategy and the scope and flow of its new product activities are greatly influenced by how the product-market business is defined. As a general rule, the business definition should focus on the customer's or user's economic or functional objective—what the customer or user is trying to gain or achieve after purchasing the product or service from a supplier. Philip B. Hofmann, a former chairman and CEO of Johnson & Johnson, frequently stated to personnel in all the J&J operating companies, "Only develop and market new products that are demonstrably better for the customer or user." This is important: No one in the industrial world buys products or services because they want or enjoy them for themselves. Business products or services are purchased only to perform a specific function that directly or indirectly improves the customer's or user's business. It is essential to understand the economic or functional objective of the customer or user and to keep this point foremost in mind so that functional substitutes do not erode the supplier's market without its knowledge and thus lose the opportunity for counter action.

Consider the case of an old line company that is a market leader in industrial drilling and cutting tools. Its management and engineers have traditionally seen themselves as being in the business of simply making and selling more and better drilling and cutting tools. But it is obvious, when you think about it, that nobody really wants to buy drilling or cutting tools. What the customer or user wants to buy is the ability to make holes or fabricate parts in the most efficient way possible. In fact, from the user's point of view, drills or cutting tools are far from the final answer. They are costly and they break or wear out, and in that sense they actually interfere with the manufacturing process. If the company had defined its business objective as helping its customers or users make holes or fabricate certain parts more effectively, instead of making and selling more and better drilling and cutting tools, it would be on much sounder strategic footing. Instead of confining themselves solely to improving or expanding its line of drilling and cutting tools, its engineers would be looking for different methods of drilling holes or cutting materials, including such new approaches as the use of lasers, electron beams, and ultrasonic waves. It would also be aware of the increasing use of materials that are easier to cut and drill with these new and unconventional methods. If the company had pursued this broader business objective, it would have been better able to respond to equipment manufacturers that introduced laser, electron beam, and ultrasonic machines to drill holes or cut material far more efficiently in many situations. The example of Reliance Electric illustrates the importance of defining a product-market focus or business objective in a way that provides the maximum business advantage (see the box, page 151).

## Facing Up to Cost and Performance Deficiencies

If any statement about business or industrial marketing is axiomatic, it is the following: To be a strong competitor, a company must either be a low cost producer so it can sell

## RELIANCE ELECTRIC MOVES WITH THE TIMES

In the mid-1960s Reliance Electric had between 25 and 30 percent of its defined electric motor market, which had total annual sales of about $800 million. Since both the market and the line of motor products were relatively mature, it was very difficult for competitors to leapfrog ahead with significant product innovations. Instead, they tended to concentrate on manufacturing cost improvements and looked to price competition as the major competitive weapon. Sales growth was limited, and the situation obviously created downward pressure on margins and profit results. Not satisfied with this situation, Reliance management took a fresh look at how its market might be defined to see if opportunities could be expanded. The first step was to redefine the market to include the mechanical drive linkage and systems that connected the motor to a machine. This more than doubled the potential market and opened the door to a whole range of combined electrical-mechanical developments that eliminated many of the interface problems and costs that occurred when the products were designed by different manufacturers. Reliance management further enlarged its view of the market to include a broad range of automation products and services. This shift in focus gave the company an opportunity to work with a market of some $8 billion—eight to ten times the size of its original market—and paved the way for significant growth for the next decade. Commenting on his company's success after Reliance had become a recognized success in the automation field, the chairman said: "It took us a long time to define our market in the right way, but once we did, the door was open for a whole stream of new electrical/mechanical products that we wouldn't even consider before. Getting the right market focus has contributed to our accelerated growth and profits more than anything else."

effectively to price buyers or offer a superior product to customers that will pay a higher price for the perceived value. While this point might appear to be obvious, a surprising number of industrial companies are trying to compete today with industrial products that have not improved in any way over the past several years. Product performance is the same now as it was when the products were introduced, and in many cases the cost of manufacturing and delivering the products is higher. In the meantime, competitors, particularly from abroad, have introduced new products with superior performance characteristics or adopted new manufacturing methods that enable them to sell from a lower cost base. Large areas of American industry producing many commonly used industrial items—like fasteners, standard machine and cutting tools, electrical components, castings and forgings—have been rocked back on their heels and seen their business dwindle away to virtually nothing for this reason. It is one thing if management makes a conscious decision to do nothing and recognizes that they will eventually go out of the business as a result. It is quite another if a situation like this just happens. How can this occur? How can management in any company that knows the importance of staying competitive allow their products to drift into a noncompetitive position?

First of all, many companies fail to evaluate objectively their products against competitive offerings in the rigorous way they should. If they do go through some kind of an evaluation process, it is often superficial or biased and leads to a continuation of "business as usual" rather than the dramatic cost or performance improvements that are needed. In some cases, management is not presented with the real facts because it is easier not to "rock the boat." In other cases, management may see the facts but not accept or face them squarely, since it is not easy to admit that a "bellcow" product or product line is no longer competitive. As a result, a surprising number of companies continue to rely on tired, old products long after competitors have come into the picture with better offerings.

Second, not enough importance is attached to the need to be fully cost competitive, particularly with mature products. When products like those cited previously reach the mature stage in their life cycle, it becomes increasingly difficult to come up with product improvements that distinguish them from competitive offerings. Manufacturing cost improvements, then, become the key competitive weapon, and the low cost producer generally picks up the lion's share of the market. Despite the logic of this point, a great many producers of mature products are saddled with unimproved plants and equipment, and higher-than-average labor costs. And they don't seem to have a program for making the necessary improvements. The management team in these companies may be populated with the most innovative and brilliant sales and marketing executives in the world, and they can pursue the most ingenious sales and marketing strategies one can imagine, but if they are not cost competitive, they have virtually no possibility of winning against lower cost competition over the longer term.

We are not suggesting that all old products or product businesses be scrapped any more than we suggest that all old plants be scrapped. We are saying, however, that one cannot expect a business to grow if it is built around old-fashioned products manufactured in old-fashioned plants with old-fashioned equipment. And given the accelerating rate of technological change, the possibility of simply maintaining such a business is diminishing rapidly.

While these facts may be difficult for some to accept, they represent the harsh reality of today's competitive environment. Management in the companies that are most successful in building their business through product innovations and manufacturing cost improvements recognize them very clearly. And they are perfectly willing to squarely face product cost and performance problems as they occur and do whatever they have to do to make sure these deficiencies are corrected.

## Pruning the Existing Line

Product-market strategies in many industrial companies address only new products and sales growth; too little consideration is given to improving or deleting marginal or obsolete products. An objective assessment of the product lines of any ten companies would reveal a lot of tired or outdated products in nine of them. In many of these companies, management fails to recognize that its product lines are cluttered with obsolete and/or nonproductive items. In others, they may recognize the problem but fail to take the actions necessary to get rid of them. Not surprisingly, new product development efforts frequently tend to be too little or too late in these companies. They always seem to be struggling to catch up with competition and seldom achieve the advantage that a leader with new products enjoys.

The reasons for pruning a product line should be fairly clear. For one thing, when the product line is cluttered with products that have reached or are approaching obsolescence, costs tend to be high because of short manufacturing runs and excessive inventories, and sufficient money is simply not available for new product development. Moreover, it is difficult to get the kind of sales support required to launch new products effectively, since any sales force can absorb only so much product knowledge.

PRODUCT LINE ANALYSIS.   Some simple analyses can quickly show whether the product line is basically competitive or whether some products need to be improved or dropped. One analysis points up which products generate what percentage of a business unit's sales and profits. As shown in Exhibit 7-5, it is not unusual to find a pattern approximating the commonly referred to "80–20" rule. As you can see from the chart, 15 percent of the products generate 75 percent of the sales and 90 percent of the profits. Of the 240 items in the total line, a large number would appear to be deadwood, or at least marginal contributors. This does not automatically mean that all these items should be dropped from the line, but their continued presence without planned improvements should certainly be challenged.

The product life cycle concept also provides a framework for evaluating a business unit's products. Exhibit 7-6 shows how the product life cycle and competitive standing of each product can be plotted to provide an overview of growth opportunities or limitations. As you can see, marketing plans for products 1 and 2 need to concentrate on improving their competitive position. Products 3 and 4 appear to be deletion candidates. Admittedly, there is always room for argument on where or how products or product

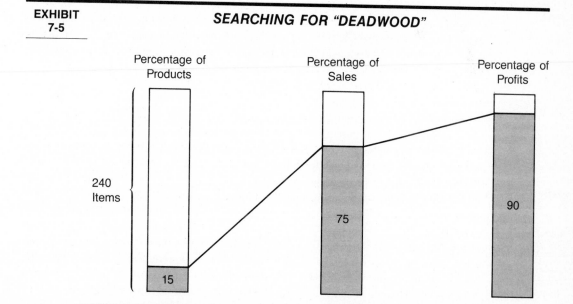

**EXHIBIT 7-5**

## SEARCHING FOR "DEADWOOD"

Percentage of Products

Percentage of Sales

Percentage of Profits

240 Items

15

75

90

EXHIBIT
7-6

## *PRODUCT/TECHNOLOGY LIFE CYCLE ANALYSIS*

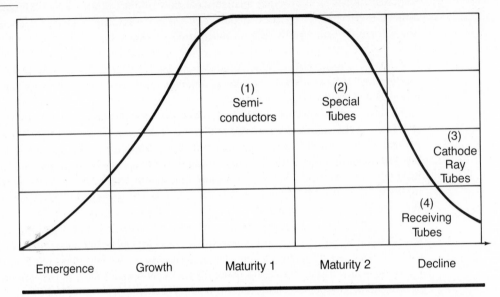

lines are positioned on this chart or where competitors' products should be positioned. However, it is a fairly simple matter to determine whether a product is in its introductory, growth, mature, or obsolete phase, and that's all you need to know. Precision is not a requirement to make an initial management judgment on the commercial health or viability of a product or product line. All you need is a reasonable perspective as to whether a company's products are positioned on the flat or downside stage of their life cycle or whether there is still plenty of room for growth.

INTERIM ACTIONS.   Before a final decision to delete a product is made, a number of interim actions could extend the product's useful life. For one thing, a mature product often has a niche in the marketplace that cannot be filled by another supplier or a substitute product. When this situation exists, the product's selling price should be raised significantly. A price hike in this situation will not affect demand, and therefore will greatly enhance the product's profit contribution.

A number of other steps can be taken to improve a mature product's profitability. Reduction or elimination of costly technical support and service activities should be tested to determine if the product can survive without the associated expense. Advertising is another cost that can be removed if no new product features exist. Finally, the minimum order size can be increased to reduce handling and shipping costs and to minimize finished goods inventory requirements. Although these seem to be mundane considerations, significant savings can usually be made as a result of taking steps like these. They are frequently sufficient to bring old products up to acceptable profit levels for a considerable period of time.

Further investment in product improvement and R&D efforts should always be considered very cautiously. When a product is in its mature or declining stage, total market prospects are clearly declining, and the R&D catchup cost and risk is often greater than the potential reward. As a general rule, R&D efforts on products in the mature or declining stage of a life cycle should be approved only if there is an opportunity to make sufficient improvements in cost or performance to move the product back to the growth stage. If this is not possible, and often it is not, management should concentrate on manufacturing or material cost improvements that will enable the product to compete more effectively in a mature market.

One final point is worth emphasizing. Marginal products are often retained too long because of emotional arguments that really do not hold up under careful scrutiny. For example, the sales group frequently argues that it needs a "full line" and that the line will not be competitive if certain products are dropped. Alternatively, someone or some group almost inevitably argues that deleting certain products will increase the overhead allocation to the remaining products in the line and in turn make them less cost competitive. It is when these arguments surface that management needs to be tough-minded. A "full line" may be necessary in some cases, but not nearly as often as salespeople claim. There may be added overhead to be absorbed if certain products are dropped, but in many cases it can be eliminated if management takes a hard-line approach. It is essential for management to determine factually when the "full line" or overhead claims are real and when they are simply hollow arguments to avoid a break with the past.

More specifically, the following cost-profit considerations should be addressed:

1. What is the product's new profit contribution (after all allocated costs are considered) at current and projected sales levels?
2. What allocated or shared costs would have to be absorbed by other products if the product in question were dropped?
3. What amount of capital could be recovered if the product in question were dropped?
4. Taking the answers to the preceding questions into account, what is the net cost-profit and capital impact of dropping the product?

When a decision is made to drop a product or product line, a carefully planned exit is essential. Even though the decision is logical and correct, it is almost certain to cause some disruption in the sales force and among certain distributors, customers, or users. Sales and manufacturing activities must be coordinated to ensure minimal exposure to excess or obsolete inventory costs. There is nothing complex about a product or product line exit as long as proper steps are taken to minimize disruption and ensure an orderly transition to any new offering that is ready for the market.

## Linkage to the Business Plan

Companies that have excellent records of successful new product introduction are more likely to ensure that all their new product programs flow from and are controlled by an agreed-upon business plan. This makes sense, since it is the best way to avoid the kinds of "dumbbell" mistakes described in the General Telephone & Electronics ad in Exhibit 7-4. Although this ad is obviously "tongue in cheek," it accurately reflects the kinds of results that occur in many industrial companies. From our own experience, we can cite several multimillion-dollar product development programs that resulted in products like the following:

- A high-speed printer that was three times as expensive as any competitive offering and far exceeded the requirements of any identified customer group.

- A twelve-axis screw machine that worked perfectly once set up, but only a handful of people in industry have the skill to do the setup work.

- A space-age robot designed to move material and parts to scheduled positions on the factory floor but insufficiently controlled so that it would run into or over anything that got in its way.

Many other equally ludicrous examples could be cited, but these should be sufficient to make the point. Unless product development efforts are linked to a carefully conceived product-market strategy for building the business, technical management will often assign the wrong priorities to development efforts or be led into products and markets that do not have real commercial value. Literally hundreds of millions of dollars are wasted each year because technical efforts are poured into products that are out of phase with market needs and opportunities. This is the chief reason the success ratio on new product development efforts is so low in so many companies. The plain truth is that left on their own, product development engineers will spend a lot of money developing something they are interested in or that they think is right. They will not just sit still waiting for direction. It is management's responsibility to provide sufficient direction through its business plan to avoid products that are not based on commercial reality.

Many executives will argue with this point, claiming that the idea of linking every new project to a business strategy or plan is impractical and too restrictive. We remain adamant. The only exception would be where senior management has made a conscious decision to spend money on basic or exploratory research to see what develops. This is an expensive process, however, and any company that follows this route had better have plenty of money to support "interesting" research that may not lead anywhere.

## Following a Disciplined Process

Most industrial companies have had some experience with product innovations that are technological triumphs but commercial flops. The products fail to meet stated performance requirements, are too costly or difficult to manufacture, or simply miss the market. Commercial flops can never be eliminated, since product development activities often involve advancing technology or breaking new ground in terms of manufacturing know-how or market development. However, a lot of time and money can be saved by recognizing product failures before the process is too far along and before too much time and money has been committed. Although it is essential to avoid discouraging new product ideas, the risk of wasting too much time and money on ideas that have no chance of success is substantial. This risk can be reduced or controlled by defining distinct stages of development for each project and establishing stringent criteria for advancing or terminating the project at the end of each successive stage.

**EXHIBIT
7-7**

## NEW PRODUCT FUNNEL

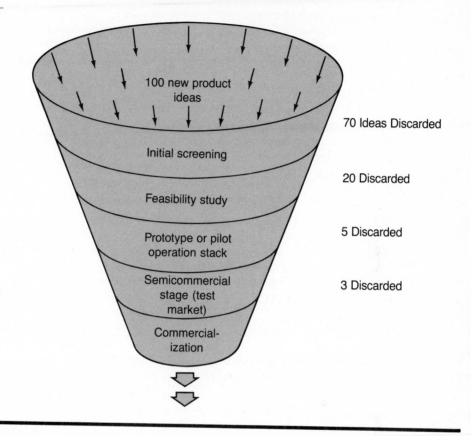

100 new product
ideas

70 Ideas Discarded

Initial screening

20 Discarded

Feasibility study

Prototype or pilot
operation stack

5 Discarded

Semicommercial
stage (test
market)

3 Discarded

Commercial-
ization

One way to think of the development process is in terms of a funnel. Exhibit 7-7 shows the typical stages of the development process in this funnel and also shows that there is always a large fallout of new product ideas between conception and commercialization. As you can see, the inputs to the funnel are ideas for new products that can come from a variety of sources. The sales force should be an excellent source of new product ideas, especially if sales personnel are trained to determine user problems and needs. Manufacturing personnel can also be excellent sources of ideas for product improvement that will improve the manufacturability and hence the costs of a particular product. First-line factory or service workers actually involved in building or assembling the product should be regarded as a part of the manufacturing group, since they often can see firsthand how minor changes in product design can improve the product itself or the way it is manufactured. Design engineers are trained to conceptualize new product ideas and to come up with functional as well as cost improvements for existing products.

All of these are traditional internal sources of new product or product improvement ideas. In addition, good ideas are frequently introduced by outside inventors or vendors who have, through research or experience, come up with something that is potentially useful. All these sources should be encouraged, since no one can predict with any degree of certainty where the best ideas will come from. The trick is to use a screening process that quickly identifies and filters out the ideas that are not technically and commercially feasible without spending an inordinate amount of time or money on the discards. The precise nature of the filtering process depends on the product. For example, the prototype stage may actually be a pilot plant operation if the product is some new chemical formulation instead of a "breadboard" model or prototype. The objective is to define the criteria that must be met before a project is allowed to go to the next stage to reduce the time and money wasted on projects that should not reach the commercial stage. These criteria will obviously vary by industry and even by company. However, they should always be developed around a few fundamental considerations that will help bring the degree of technical and market risk into focus.

### Technical considerations:
1. What new technical concepts are being utilized, and what cost or performance advantages do they offer? If successful, where are we positioned on the technology life cycle curve?
2. Where does the competition stand on any new technical concepts being considered? Have successful competitors pursued other technologies that are significantly different?
3. Has the concept been commercially utilized in other products or processes, or is it a groundbreaking effort?
4. Assuming the new technical concept proves to be successful, how much of a commercial advantage does it offer, and how can you substantiate this point?

### Market considerations:
1. Is the product concept basically new, or is it simply an improvement in performance or cost over an existing product?
2. Which end-use markets or market applications can be tapped most readily, and which will require further development?
3. Under what conditions (volume, price, costs) are the economics of the proposed product attractive?
4. Does the cost-profit structure of the new product match or exceed company objectives?
5. How much has the company already committed to this project, and how much time will it take to generate sufficient profits to cover total exposure?

If management does not seek specific answers to questions like these in a formal manner, you can be sure the company does not have a well-organized procedure for advancing ideas through the development process. And it would be a safe bet that whatever the company is doing about new product activities is not cost-effective and does not minimize risk.

## Matching Future Products and Current Profits

In companies known for their new product success, management has mastered the ability to strike the right balance between investing[1] in future products and generating current profits. This point raises some obvious questions. How much should you invest? How much is too little? How much is too much? There are no easy answers; it is a judgment call in each situation, the kind of judgment management gets paid to make and that will haunt management for a long time if it is made incorrectly.

THE COST OF ERROR. The penalties are severe if a mistake is made either way. A company can get by and may even prosper in the short term by spending too little, because anything not spent obviously increases short-term profits. It is not uncommon for managers, under pressure to meet certain profit goals, to take this tack in an effort to make their results look good. However, such an approach is shortsighted and foolish. If the market is attractive, enlightened competitors will introduce new and improved products that will quickly erode the company's market position and cut into its future earnings stream. By the same token, many managers tend to overspend for new products without sufficient regard for the need to achieve satisfactory near-term profits. These managers are so enamored of the promise of tomorrow that they spend a disproportionate amount of money on new product efforts that will ultimately undermine the financial health of the company. Managers in rapidly changing high-technology industries face the added problem of deciding which technology to invest in as well as when to invest. By investing too early in a new technology, the industrial firm faces the risks of premature entry before the market is ready. By reacting or investing too late in a new technology, a company may fall behind its competitors and lose market position that is tough to recapture once a new technology is established. And by failing to invest at all in a new technology, a company runs the very real risk of seeing its products become obsolete in a short period of time.

Computers, medical electronics, and pharmaceuticals are good illustrations of industries in which technological change is frequent and rapid. Each product cycle often has multiple and overlapping technology life cycles, as shown in Exhibit 7-8, where $T_1$ to $T_5$ are the cycles. In these situations, it is crucial to invest in the right technology at the right time. The medical CAT-scan business has had five distinct technology life cycles over the past ten years. When the early leaders in CAT equipment chose not to invest in the latest technology, they limited their participation in the market to the cycle patterns shown as $T_1$, $T_2$, $T_3$, or $T_4$ and in effect opted out of the business when the technology shown as $T_5$ made all the earlier products obsolete. This pattern, which is predictable in many high technology businesses, should be a warning for any management that plans to participate. It requires a different mentality to manage in this high-risk environment. The high level of R&D expenditures makes it impossible to manage with a short-term profit orientation. Moreover, a high tolerance for stress is essential to withstand the pressures that are an integral part of any volatile business. It also takes significant financial strength to fund the development activities required to maintain a competitive line of products as

---

[1]The cost of product development, except for capital items that might be involved, is expensed for tax purposes. Nevertheless, the expense is literally an investment of a company's profits for future gain.

**EXHIBIT
7-8**

## *TECHNOLOGY LIFE CYCLES*

**Cumulative Number of CAT Scanners Installed**

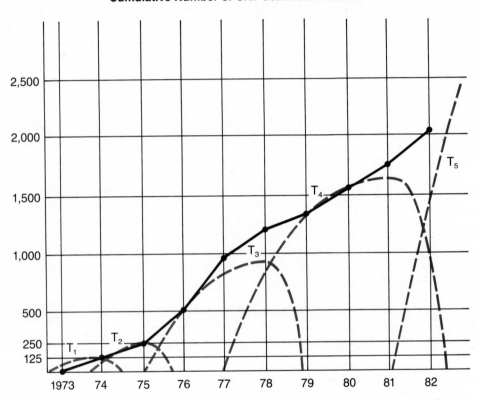

Sequence of New Technologies

1973; $T_1$—scan of head, 5 minutes
1974; $T_2$—scan of entire body, 2 minutes
1975; $T_3$—scan of entire body, 18 seconds
1977; $T_4$—scan of entire body, 2 seconds
1982; $T_5$—nuclear magnetic resonance replaces
radiation and instantly identifies
molecular structure of tissues

*Source:* U.S. Office of Technology Assessment

new technologies come into the picture. This is the reason so many smaller companies fail after taking an early lead in the marketplace with a new product. Even though they recognize that a new technology is clearly superior to the one they used to get their businesses started, they simply do not have the financial resources to move into a new technology (see the box).

SPENDING GUIDELINES. There is always published information available that indicates the appropriate level of spending for a particular industry. Table 7.1 shows data from a recent publication that contrast spending levels for new product activities in the information processing and farm and construction machinery industries. Although data like these are never perfect, they provide a general idea of the R&D level required in various industries. Note the difference in the composite percentage of sales in the two industries. Note also the range of ratios in each industry. The data would seem to suggest that to be competitive in the farm and construction machinery business, somewhere between 2 and 4 percent of sales should be committed to R&D activities. By contrast, 5 to 10 percent of sales appears to be the going rate of spending for R&D in the much more dynamic computer area. As you can see, the variation between the high and the low in each industry group is significant. Variances of this magnitude would be typical in any set of industry comparisons, since accounting methods for reporting R&D costs vary widely among companies, and the level of R&D expenditures for any particular company depends on its particular business strategy.

## COMPETING IN HIGH TECH MARKETS

When it was introduced to the medical diagnostic field, the CAT scanner was immediately recognized as the most significant development in the field since the discovery of X-rays nearly 50 years before. In 1970 Technicare, the first U.S. CAT scanner company, was founded by two former employees of Harris Corporation with funding from a venture capital firm in Cleveland.

Between 1975 and 1981 Technicare experienced tremendous growth, with sales multiplying from $20 million to $200 million. The number of its employees grew from 200 to more than 3,000 in the same period. The CAT scanning market went through several variations or technological innovations, each of which obsoleted products less than a year old. The company managed to anticipate each step of technology. The rapid obsolescence of technology, coupled with the rapid growth of sales, fueled the company's need for cash, which nearly spelled disaster for the company.

In 1981 Johnson & Johnson Company, whose sales total more than $4 billion, acquired Technicare. Without Johnson & Johnson's acquisition and infusion of cash, most believe Technicare would have gone bankrupt within a short period of time. Reflecting on the rapid developments in this business Richard Grimm, former Chairman of Technicare, made this comment: "The way this technology moved is unbelievable. There were four major developments in three years that basically obsoleted all prior CAT scanning devices. We were smaller than some of the other competitors and if we were not quick on our feet in terms of product development we could have been out of the picture overnight."

**TABLE
7.1**

# SPENDING FOR NEW PRODUCT DEVELOPMENT

| | Sales, 1980 ($ millions) | R&D Expense, 1980 ($ millions) | Percentage of sales | |
|---|---|---|---|---|
| **Information Processing** | | | | |
| American Management Systems | $ 59 | $ 4.1 | 7.1% | |
| Anderson Jacobson | 41 | 3.9 | 9.3 | |
| Applied Magnetics | 93 | 3.6 | 3.8 | |
| Auto-Trol Technology | 51 | 6.1 | 12.1 | High |
| Bell & Howell | 640 | 30.3 | 4.7 | |
| Centronics Data Computer | 128 | 4.9 | 3.8 | |
| Computer & Communication Technology | 46 | 3.8 | 8.2 | |
| Computer Consoles | 44 | 4.6 | 10.5 | |
| Computervision | 224 | 22.1 | 9.9 | |
| Comshare | 78 | 4.9 | 6.3 | |
| Data Card | 66 | 1.7 | 2.6 | |
| Data Terminal Systems | 118 | 6.0 | 5.1 | |
| Datapoint | 319 | 27.9 | 8.7 | |
| Dataproducts | 180 | 13.9 | 7.7 | |
| Decision Data Computer | 44 | 1.2 | 2.8 | |
| Electronic Memories & Magnetics | 99 | 6.1 | 6.2 | |
| Four-Phase Systems | 197 | 15.9 | 8.1 | |
| MSI Data | 45 | 2.1 | 4.7 | |
| Memorex | 769 | 34.6 | 4.5 | |
| Mohawk Data Sciences | 212 | 10.0 | 4.7 | |
| National Computer Systems | 39 | 1.8 | 4.6 | |
| National Data | 60 | 0.9 | 1.5 | |
| Recognition Equipment | 113 | 8.4 | 7.4 | |
| Scope | 71 | 2.9 | 4.1 | |
| Shared Medical Systems | 106 | 8.2 | 7.8 | |
| Storage Technology | 604 | 39.3 | 6.5 | |
| System Development | 168 | 2.5 | 1.5 | Low |
| System Industries | 38 | 1.9 | 5.0 | |
| Telex | 157 | 8.9 | 5.7 | |
| Triad Systems | 57 | 3.8 | 6.6 | |
| Tymshare | 235 | 12.2 | 5.2 | |
| Verbatim | 50 | 2.9 | 5.8 | |
| **Farm and Construction Machinery** | | | | |
| Allis-Chalmers | 2064 | 49.4 | 2.4 | |
| American Hoist & Derrick | 539 | 3.3 | 0.6 | Low |
| Barber-Greene | 227 | 2.9 | 1.3 | |
| Bucyrus-Erie | 511 | 19.1 | 3.7 | |
| CMI | 115 | 2.2 | 2.0 | |
| Caterpillar Tractor | 8598 | 200.2 | 2.3 | |
| Clark Equipment | 1534 | 26.9 | 1.8 | |
| Deere | 5470 | 231.2 | 4.2 | High |
| FMC | 3482 | 97.5 | 2.8 | |
| Hesston | 241 | 3.6 | 1.5 | |
| Pengo Industries | 78 | 1.5 | 1.9 | |
| Penn Virginia | 50 | 1.3 | 2.7 | |
| Portec | 251 | 2.7 | 1.1 | |
| Raymond | 113 | 4.1 | 3.6 | |
| Roper | 428 | 9.4 | 2.2 | |
| Steiger Tractor | 121 | 1.9 | 1.6 | |
| Toro | 402 | 9.1 | 2.3 | |
| Valmont Industries | 152 | 2.0 | 1.3 | |

Source: "Annual Survey of R&D Expenditures," *Business Week*, July 6, 1981, pp. 67, 71.

Many companies account for some of their product development costs by conducting the final stages of development in the customer's environment and charging some portion to sales engineering expense. This is a smart approach, since it moves the product out of the laboratory and permits the final bugs to be worked out in a real-life field situation. Other companies are often successful in getting their customers to share new product development costs for certain products, which is obviously an advantageous approach. The point of all this is simply that it is important to determine what real and total R&D costs are before concluding that a company is spending at a certain level for this activity.

Another explanation for the variation is that companies in the same industry can and do follow quite different strategies to enter or secure a position in a market. Three basic strategies would call for quite different expenditure levels for R&D activities. The strategies and the requirements for each are listed below:

1. **Pioneer innovator strategy**
   Outstanding technical people
   Research-intensive
   Large development investment
   Target is dominant "niche" position
   Always ahead on "next generation" product

2. **Follow the leader strategy**
   Excellent competitive intelligence
   Technically perceptive salespeople and engineers
   Superior application know-how
   Lower R&D costs
   Good imitator; rapid product development response time

3. **Low-cost strategy**
   No R&D activity or investment
   Major emphasis on material and process cost savings
   Strong manufacturing and delivery performance
   Marketing aimed at price-sensitive segments
   Price chief competitive weapon

Any one of these strategies can be followed successfully. However, it is essential that management fully understand the need to pursue a business strategy that is fully integrated across functions and cohesively developed around the requirements listed under each strategy. As a general rule, the company that seeks to be first in the market with new products will spend more on product development because of the inherent costs and risks that always exist when one tries to keep up with technology. This fact of life has caused many successful companies to pursue a strategy that knowingly allows competitors to be first in the market with new products. For example:

Going back to its early days, IBM has seldom put products on the market that are right in the forefront of new technology. UNIVAC and others have all showed the way; IBM has learned from others' mistakes. It was rarely the first to take a new technical step, but it wasn't far behind. And time after time, its new lines were better designed and more effectively sold and serviced than those of competitors.[2]

Even in the world of less arcane technology, we find the same phenomenon. Caterpillar is rarely the first to come up with a new offering in its markets. But being on the leading edge has never been one of the company's goals. It has built its reputation by letting other companies go through the trial and error process of introducing new products. Caterpillar later jumps in with the most trouble-free product on the market. Indeed, Caterpillar products do not usually sport the lowest price tag. The company relies, instead, on quality and reliable service to woo customers.[3]

Hewlett-Packard is seldom first into the market with its new products—Xerox and IBM, for example, were first with high-priced laser printers. The company's marketing strategy is normally that of a counterpuncher. A competitor's new product comes on the market and HP engineers, when making service calls on HP equipment, ask their customers what they like or dislike about the new product, what features the customer would like to have. . . . And pretty soon HP salesmen are calling on customers again with a new product that answers their needs and wants. The result: happy and loyal customers.[4]

As you can see, these are first-class companies that could afford to be first in the market if they wanted to. However, they firmly believe they can better serve their customers and reduce their product development expenditures by following a carefully planned "second in the market" strategy.

Although a company's spending level for R&D or product development may vary from time to time, there is not as much flexibility here as you might think. The problem is that you cannot simply turn an R&D or product development effort on and off like a water tap. You can obviously cut a program back by reducing or stopping the technical effort. However, stepping up an effort requires finding and recruiting the right technical talent, which is often much easier said than done. For this reason, most well-managed companies tend to select a reasonable spending level for R&D or product development activities consistent with their strategy and competitive requirements, and then stick pretty close to that level as a percentage of sales unless something very unusual occurs in the marketplace.

## Organizing New Product Activities

Clearly, there are different approaches to managing new product development activities. But although the approach may vary, the more successful companies ensure that their product development activities are directed by marketing and/or general management. This does not mean that the organization is structured so that new product or R&D personnel report directly to marketing or general management. It does mean, however, that the organization functions in a way which ensures that marketing and/or general managers have the final say on project priorities and evaluation. Some would argue with this

[2]"What Ails IBM," *Financial World,* May 15, 1981, p. 17.
[3]"Caterpillar Is Rarely First," *Business Week,* May 4, 1981, p. 77.
[4]"The One to Watch," *Forbes,* March 2, 1981, p. 60.

# 8

# Pricing for Profit

Management Deficiencies
    Inadequate
    Understanding of Market
    and Economics
    Overemphasis on
    Volume and Market
    Share
    The Impact of Inflation
    Link to Business
    Strategy
    Inadequate
    Administration
Management Solutions
    Establish Growth and
    Profit Targets
    Determine Product Line
    Costs and Profits
    Develop and Enforce
    Pricing Policy
    Strengthen Ability to
    Compete
    Stand Firm When the
    Market Turns Soft
Summary
Review Questions

When Mark Little, product manager for small motors of the Hercules Electric Company, answered the phone and found Roger Calkins, area sales manager for the company, on the line, he knew he was in for a tough session. For the past several months, Calkins had been criticizing the company's pricing policy for small motors, claiming he had lost significant market position as a result. Mark had responsibility for setting and policing the company's pricing policy and could agree to exceptions if he thought they were in the best interest of the business. Mark had raised prices on several items in the line four months ago, which Calkins claimed had made them noncompetitive in the marketplace.

Calkins started the conversation by saying: "Mark, I have the same problem now that I talked to you about before. I'm not competitive in the marketplace on your line, and we're losing a lot of business with key accounts. It's stupid for us not to lower our prices so we can take some of the business that is here." Calkins went on to explain that several companies were offering discounts from a list price that was already 5 percent lower than Hercules. He also said he had invoice copies his sales representatives had picked up to prove these lower prices were real. Mark had received similar calls from sales managers located in other parts of the country, but none of them seemed to have the same competitive problems. He didn't want to lower the company's prices across the board, since margins on his line were already below profit objectives. On the other hand, he knew Calkins was not "crying wolf" and wanted to help him get back into the market without retreating from a pricing policy he knew was sound.

What is Mark Little's best move?

Should he make an exception in this case? Why or why not?

Does he need marketing information to make a decision?

What kind of information does he need?

point of view, however, claiming that a centralized R&D function is more efficient. In some cases this may be true, particularly when the business is based on one or two products or a single technology. Some well-known companies like General Electric have centralized R&D activities that serve separate divisions and firmly believe this is the best approach. In most multiproduct industrial companies, however, centralized R&D is not a good idea. The arrangement gives division managers an excuse when their product technology falls behind, since they can claim they are not responsible. And centralized R&D activities directed and controlled by an independent division or corporate vice president generally tend to drift into a situation where technological considerations or interests prevail at a time when marketing or commercial considerations are actually much more important.

Any function suffers when there is an absence of commercial accountability, and this is especially true for an R&D function. One could argue that R&D management can be held accountable for both technical and commercial performance, but it simply does not work this way. Most R&D managers, quite correctly, tend to focus on achieving excellent technical results, without sufficient regard for commercial considerations. Unless some provision is made to ensure that someone with profit and loss responsibility has the final say on how much money will be spent on development efforts for what projects, the chances for poor commercial results are greatly enhanced. One president who shifted away from an arrangement under which R&D controlled the new product activity to one under which product managers were held responsible for R&D spending levels and priorities for their products explained why he made the change: "There are two types of product development activities—those that have a 'market in' focus and those that have a 'design out' focus. Something like 80 percent of our efforts have had a 'design out' focus, and I think this has caused us to be out of phase with market needs way too frequently. Now we are seeking to reverse this picture to ensure that the bulk of our new product activity has a 'market in' focus, which I think is essential if we are going to make it pay off."

One other point on organizing new product activities is worth emphasizing. Managements in many companies completely overlook the contribution the selling organization can and should make to new product development. They are overlooking an invaluable resource. Who in the organization is closer to the customer than the salesperson? Who knows more about the customer's business? Who has a better opportunity to know what product changes or features are really important to the customer or user? No one. The sales force should be the most reliable source of product-market information available to any industrial company. Obviously, however, every salesperson's comments about product-market requirements cannot be accepted at face value. Because a salesperson is a salesperson, there is always a natural tendency to sell the ideas that will help most with his or her particular customers, who may or may not represent the total market. For this reason, all the ideas emanating from the sales force need to be filtered and interpreted so that intelligent product judgments or decisions can be made. How do you structure or direct the sales force to ensure that this is done?

First, it is essential to ensure that sales assignments are not so broad in terms of products, markets, or customers that representatives do not have time to get to know their customers' operations in depth. When sales assignments are too broad, the salesperson becomes an order taker. He or she has little opportunity to carry out the professional sales role and cannot be counted on for any useful feedback. Next, salespeople need comprehensive training in the company's products, training that goes well beyond the typical product explanations which are a part of most introductory sales training programs. They need to have a deep understanding of the rationale behind the design, construction, cost, and performance characteristics of the company's products so that they can talk more intelligently with the customer or user about the product and its applications. It is these in-depth product discussions with customers that often lead to ideas on how the product can be improved or what new products could be developed to fill customer needs.

A formal procedure must be established to collect and distill the ideas developed by salespeople and to make sure this information is factored into new product plans. To reinforce the idea that the sales force is a valued source of input for new product ideas, all new products should be reviewed with a small but representative group of salespeople so they can react and recommend modifications before new products are released for commercial production. Finally, the company's value system must be tailored to recognize and reward those salespeople who contribute significantly to new product activities. Some kind of formal recognition, rather than monetary reward, of the salespeople or sales groups that have made a useful contribution in new product planning is generally the fairest approach and the best way to encourage others to make a similar contribution. However, the sales compensation plan must be designed to pay off for the effort required to launch new products successfully, since this usually uses up a large chunk of time that could be otherwise devoted to selling established products.

In short, well-managed companies recognize that nothing could be a greater waste of money than to invest heavily in technical skills for new product development without providing the right kind of headquarters and field marketing support to ensure that these technical skills are properly focused on meeting actual market needs.

## Going Outside for New Technology

In most industrial companies, particularly when their products are developed around different disciplines (electronic, mechanical, electrical), it is virtually impossible to stay abreast of all the technological developments that can impact the business. Recognizing this, enlightened management continuously monitors and searches for ways to capitalize on technological achievements outside the company as a means of sustaining or improving their product-market position. While this seems only logical, many companies do not do this, generally because their management has a self-centered or arrogant attitude that leads them to think that anything "not invented here" (often called the NIH factor) can't be very good. An attitude like this doesn't have much virtue in any situation, and in today's constantly changing world, it can easily trip a company into a position where its products or technology are suddenly and unexpectedly obsolete.

There is no mystery in the way management can keep up with outside developments. One way is to tie into any of the many fine university programs that exist. Most major universities throughout the world that have technical departments are involved in a variety of research activities and programs on the forefront of technology. As a general rule, they welcome and actively seek arrangements with companies that will support their efforts, and they in turn provide the company with a window into their developments. More industrial companies should follow the lead of many bio-medical companies who have built entire new businesses around their close relationships with leading scientists in medical and engineering schools.

Another way to gain technology is to participate either as a sub or prime contractor in government-funded projects that focus on or require advanced technological development. Many companies have been very successful in using this approach to capture technology for their own commercial use. Harris, Raytheon, and Motorola are good examples of companies that have concentrated on government-funded contracts that provide technological advances for the commercial side of their businesses. Technical personnel in these companies are routinely transferred from government projects to commercial business units as a means of ensuring the effective transfer of technology.

Licensing is still another way to gain new technology. Many inventors do not have the financial resources or the interest to commercialize their developments and can realize an attractive return without risk by entering a license agreement with a manufacturer that has the necessary capabilities. Many such developments exist in university research laboratories where those doing the research are more interested in advancing the state of the art than commercial accomplishments. The key here is to follow an organized approach that covers the sources where new ideas are likely to develop and ensures the early identification of developments with promising commercial potential.

Finally, new product technology can be gained through outright acquisition or through the formation of a joint venture with another company. Acquisition is probably the preferred route because any business is easier to manage when it is owned by a single entity. A joint venture is an alternate to an outright acquisition when acquisition is not feasible for any of a variety of reasons. The company with the technology may not want to be acquired; or it may be too big or too expensive, or the technology may be such a small part of the whole that acquisition doesn't make sense.[5] Whatever the reason, a joint venture that provides the basis for coupling technology with a commercial base is a very feasible alternative.[6] For example, Sundstrand Corporation, a manufacturer of machine tools and systems, developed a heavy duty automatic transmission as a result of work they had done on a government contract for Army tanks. Sundstrand management saw a potential application for this transmission in the heavy duty truck market, but did not have the marketing, manufacturing, or service capability to readily enter this market. Accordingly, they set up a joint venture with Cummins Engine, a major engine producer who had a strong position in the worldwide OEM and aftermarket for heavy duty trucks.

The most successful companies pursue some combination or all of these avenues to technological superiority. They recognize that no one has a monopoly on technological ideas or developments and constantly search the world over for opportunities to strengthen their competitive position and ability to serve their target markets.

[5]James D. Hlavacek, Brian H. Douey, and John J. Biondo, "Tie Small Business Technology to Marketing Power," *Harvard Business Review,* January–February 1977, p. 107.
[6]Lee Adler and James D. Hlavacek, "Joint Ventures for Product Innovation," AMACOM, American Management Association, p. 15.

## SUMMARY

Developing new products is a chancy, difficult process under the best of circumstances, but it is vital to the long-term success of the firm, especially in a time of rapidly changing technology and worldwide competition. There are some steps firms can take to better the chances for their products: They can think through their product-market focus carefully to zero in on real opportunities; they can face up to cost and performance deficiencies in their product line; they can prune marginal products from the existing line; they can ensure that all development efforts are coordinated with corporate strategies; they can follow an organized and disciplined process to minimize risk and ensure that marketing management and sales personnel play an important role in planning; they can work to strike the proper balance between investing in the future and generating current profits; and they can look outside the company for new technology.

All this means great and continued attention to new product development on the part of marketing and of top management to be sure that the products developed fit specific market segments and are tailored to the needs of actual users, rather than being bright ideas from R&D that are not really commercial, or expensive miscalculations. New product development is a gamble, but the odds need not be suicidal.

## REVIEW QUESTIONS

1. What is the link between the product life cycle curve and product development activities?
2. What causes one technology to be substituted for or to replace an existing technology?
3. How does market segmentation help guide product development efforts?
4. What are the key technical and market considerations in industrial new product development?
5. What factors determine the size of the yearly R&D budget?
6. Why and how should an industrial sales force be an active participant in new product development?
7. What are some alternatives to internal product development, and why are they sometimes pursued for new products?

**F**ew will argue with the notion that pricing policy is an important ingredient in the marketing mix for any product or company. In the industrial world, where buying decisions are typically more rational and less influenced by promotion and advertising appeals, it is crucial. Despite its importance, not very much has been written that is useful to management in thinking through alternative pricing policies or actions. Most text material and articles on industrial pricing deal with economic theory relating to price and demand curves, and the relative elasticity of demand for various products. Although interesting from an academic point of view, this information does not offer much practical help to the manager faced with the need to make day-to-day pricing decisions that can make or break the business. What is especially unfortunate is that management too often takes decisions and actions that literally destroy long- and short-run profit performance. Examples to support this contention are not hard to find (see the box, page 172). Examples of questionable pricing policy are all too common. Pricing policies are a chief cause of poor profit performance in industrial companies all over the world. What causes these situations? Why are examples of poor pricing decisions so common?

Management's explanations for what seem to be naive pricing actions do not vary much from one situation to another: "We lowered our prices to gain market share." "The market leader hasn't raised prices, and we have to wait for him." "We needed the volume to keep our plant loaded." "Our competitors are cutting prices, and we have to stay competitive." "We can't pass on all of our added costs and still maintain market position." However, these all too common explanations are not the real reasons at all. Rather, they are symptoms of and are related to fundamental deficiencies in management thinking that lead many companies into pricing problems and poor profit results.

In the balance of this chapter we'll examine these deficiencies in some detail and then suggest actions management should take to avoid or correct them. We do not attempt to recommend pricing policies or actions for any specific situation. Rather, we outline fundamental points that should be considered in thinking through and implementing a pricing policy for any industrial or business product.

## MANAGEMENT DEFICIENCIES

For purposes of clarity, we have structured our discussion of management deficiencies into five parts:

1. Inadequate understanding of the market and business economics
2. Overemphasis on volume and market share
3. Failure to comprehend the impact of inflation
4. Failure to ensure that pricing policy is linked to total business strategy
5. Inadequate administration of pricing policy

Let's examine each in some detail.

## DOING YOURSELF IN WITH PRICES: THREE CASES

Case 1: A company adopted the recommendations of its consultants to sharply cut prices on many items as a means of adding to market share. Not surprisingly, since the products were relatively mature and market demand was relatively inelastic, competitors with excess capacity counteracted with even lower prices as a means of protecting *their* market share. Although the company that initiated the price cutting achieved a pickup in volume, it was not profitable and the company's overall profit structure was severely damaged. Equally important, the company did not achieve a lasting gain in its market share position, and a vicious cycle of price competition was introduced that ultimately weakened the profit structure of the entire industry.

Case 2: A large company with a leadership position in its industry watched a small competitor cut steadily into its business with lower prices for competing products. Management's analysis of competitive product offerings indicated that material content, quality, performance characteristics, and presumably costs were essentially the same. Management concluded that the competitor was simply willing to operate at little or no profit and that ultimately this policy would lead the competitor to financial disaster. Unfortunately, this did not occur. In fact, the competitor flourished at the leader company's expense, and when it went public, management was surprised to see how profitable it really was. The leader company could not figure out how such high margins were generated with such low prices. What it had completely overlooked was its own bloated overhead costs.

Case 3: A product manager was reluctant to raise prices in his product area even though labor and material costs had increased dramatically. His major competitor, which was historically the price leader, had not raised prices, and he was concerned about losing volume and share position. As you would expect, profit margins declined. His response was to eliminate some of the product features that added to cost. Once this was done, some key customers turned to competitors to get the products they wanted, and volume as well as profit margins declined. Faced with another round of labor and material cost increases, the product manager concluded that the situation was hopeless and recommended to top management that the line be dropped.

## Inadequate Understanding of Market and Economics

Many managers simply fail to develop the deep understanding of their market and how and where the business generates profit to the extent required to make intelligent pricing decisions. There is nothing complicated about the information that is needed; it simply takes some digging and tough-minded thinking to put it together. For example, these kinds of questions about the market require specific answers:

1. How is the market segmented? What factors (such as performance, price, delivery, service) control or influence the buying decision in each segment? Which specific segments or customer groups are you seeking to serve and why? What is the value of the product or service to the customer or user?

2. What is the competitive structure in each segment? What is the relative market position of each major competitor? How do competitors match up on the factors that control or influence the buying decision?
3. How does industry capacity compare with total market demand? What significant changes in capacity are likely? Why? How does the changed capacity outlook compare with estimated demand for the future? How have industry or company pricing practices shifted in the past with changes in capacity or demand relationships?
4. To what extent does market demand vary with price? What underlying factors cause the relative elasticity or inelasticity of the demand curve (such as commodity product, unique product advantage)?

All these questions about customers, product demand and usage, competitors, industry capacity, historical patterns, and relationships provide the background essential to making intelligent judgments on how various pricing policies or changes in pricing policies will be received in the marketplace.

Now let's look at the questions about the company's profit economics that need definitive answers.

1. How much profit contribution and absolute profit (after all allocations) is generated by each product?
2. How does the cost and profit structure for each product vary with changes in volume?
3. How and where in the overall make and sell cycle are significant costs and value added?
4. How many dollars of assets are committed where, and what return is being earned on each major chunk of investment?
5. How sensitive are profits to changes in key variables, such as price, mix, costs?
6. What are true idle plant costs for abandoned or underutilized capacity?

As you can see, these questions are designed to generate the information about the cost and profit structure necessary to quantify the effect of pursuing one pricing policy versus another.

Without being able to answer these kinds of questions, it is impossible to make intelligent pricing decisions. For example, will a reduced price actually generate incremental volume? How much incremental volume is required to offset a lower price that reduces unit margins? Are competitors likely to react to a pricing action in a way that will damage the overall profit structure of the business? None of these questions can be answered without a deep understanding of the fundamental market and economic characteristics of the business. Managers typically rationalize their inability to answer these questions by claiming that their market research and accounting systems do not provide this information. To some extent this is true; most traditional information systems do not automatically generate the data necessary to answer these questions. But this deficiency is not a valid excuse for not knowing the answers. The data do not have to be 100 percent accurate or complete. In the vast majority of cases, the information can be developed simply by reordering existing data or even by making estimates that allow intelligent judgments to be made. Blaming the system is simply an excuse for the kind of sloppy thinking that inevitably leads to faulty pricing decisions.

## Overemphasis on Volume and Market Share

Recent emphasis by professional consultants and planners on the importance of volume and market share to profit performance and the experience curve to cost performance has led a lot of managers on a volume chase that does not make sense. These experts claim that the producer with the highest market share will have the lowest cost and greatest profit because of economies of scale. Their reasoning is based on the theory that the costs of value added to a product decline approximately 20 to 30 percent in real terms each time accumulated manufacturing experience is doubled. Believers in the theory advocate pricing below competition and sacrificing current margins as a means of gaining volume and market share. They argue that the higher profits achievable as volume grows and manufacturing experience is gained will more than offset the profit shortfall from lower prices.

There may be isolated cases where this strategy pays off in the industrial world, but it is an impractical approach in the vast majority of cases. Although it is quite reasonable to expect and plan for 20 to 30 percent cost improvement during the early stages of manufacture of a new product (or even of an old product in a new manufacturing facility), the picture is quite different for almost any established or mature product. As Exhibit 8-1 shows, there is a learning curve in these situations, and costs should improve dramatically as workers and management gain experience with a new manufacturing process. However, the curve is a curve, and the potential for further gains through additional manufacturing experience diminishes rapidly after the process reaches maturity. This does not mean that manufacturing costs cannot be reduced by 20 to 30 percent after the initial learning period, but it will not happen automatically when manufacturing experience doubles and certainly not without major investment and a specific plan for achieving this kind of improvement.

A lot of companies have fallen into the trap of cutting prices with the expectation that increased volume or "tonnage" alone will automatically lower manufacturing costs sufficiently to offset lower margins and add to profits. The results have been disastrous. Nothing is more painful to senior management than listening to some marketing manager try to explain why profits are down even though volume is far above plan. Anything the marketing manager might say about gaining market share through aggressive pricing or counting on some kind of experience curve to improve future profits does not go over very well with senior managers who know better from experience.

## The Impact of Inflation

It is essential to understand the impact inflationary pressures have or should have on pricing policy. Failure to recognize just how important this inflation factor is and how to adjust pricing policy to take it into account have triggered serious profit problems in many companies.

Nobody has to look very far to find examples of companies that have been seriously hurt because of management's inability to operate effectively in an inflationary environment. On standard products with short delivery cycles, there are myriad cases where

EXHIBIT
8-1

# THE EFFECT OF THE LEARNING CURVE

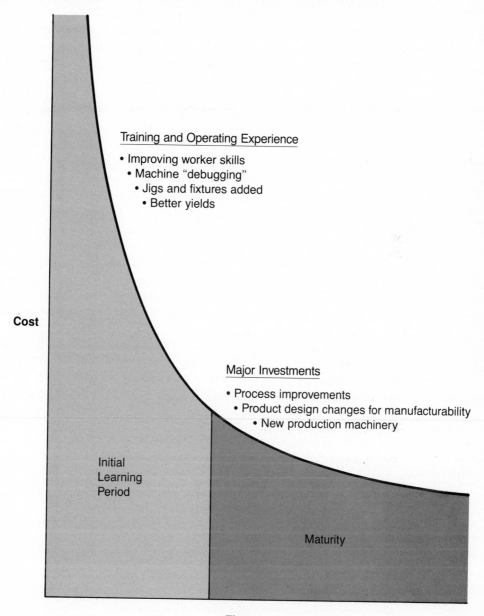

Cost

Training and Operating Experience
• Improving worker skills
• Machine "debugging"
• Jigs and fixtures added
• Better yields

Major Investments
• Process improvements
• Product design changes for manufacturability
• New production machinery

Initial
Learning
Period

Maturity

Time

costs escalated ahead of prices and profit margins showed a steady decline, frequently on greater volume. On longer-cycle products or systems sold on contracts that might call for delivery one or two years ahead, there are just as many cases where anticipated profits suddenly turned into red ink because inadequate allowance was made for cost escalation during the manufacturing cycle. The pattern of profit decline may vary somewhat in different situations, but the cause is basically the same. Stated simply, management does not anticipate or react effectively to the inflation spiral that quickly and inexorably pushes labor, material, and overhead costs higher and higher.

Business managers and governments in countries like Brazil, which has lived for years with an annual inflation rate of 40 to 50 percent, have a better grasp of the problems caused by high inflation and have adopted economic and pricing policies to protect profits and assets against its impact. Wages, rent, contract prices, assets, and other values that are affected by inflation are frequently and automatically indexed by government data, and managers move aggressively to adjust any values that are not indexed so that parity is preserved. But most managers in countries where high rates of inflation are a new phenomenon have not adjusted their thinking to the realities and tend to lag or fall short in their reactions. To start with, they don't understand the extent to which inflation affects profit requirements. Higher inflation demands higher returns just to stay even. Although this may sound like an amazing discovery of the obvious, far too many managers have not as yet adjusted their thinking to the realities of inflation economics. They are content with profit returns that are way too slim when the impact of inflation is taken into account. As a result, the company's return on capital and even its capital base can actually erode while management thinks the company is turning a satisfactory profit. Also, most managers are far too slow to react, and price adjustments tend to lag farther and farther behind increasing cost curves. Profit margins deteriorate and the business gets caught in a cost-profit squeeze. In some cases, managers simply don't move quickly enough or simply don't understand what is happening. In others, they are afraid the market won't accept a price increase and don't want to lose volume. Whatever the reason, profit results are severely penalized and never seem to catch up as costs move relentlessly ahead.

Making price adjustments to track inflation is unquestionably a high-risk exercise with high stakes. The precise inflation rate can never be known in advance because it is an approximation of the weighted average price shift of a "market basket" of values. It doesn't take much insight to see that there is a penalty for changing price too soon, too late, too much, or too little. However, the heaviest penalties are inflicted on those who do not adjust prices to inflation at all. Since it is a good bet that we will be plagued with inflation problems for many years, it is essential that managers start to think logically about the futility of chasing volume while costs continue to rise. Otherwise, as economists point out,[1] we will see a continuing erosion of industrial profits and capital that will lead ultimately to the liquidation of many important companies.

[1]George Terborgh, *Inflation and Profits*, Machinery and Allied Products Institute, October 1976 (5th printing).

## Link to Business Strategy

Few generalizations are useful in industrial management. However, one that is deals with the importance of ensuring that all parts of the business are linked together in a cohesive strategy geared to the fundamental characteristics and requirements of the market being served. Otherwise, impact in the marketplace will be diffused and profit results will not be satisfactory. This general principle applies especially to a company's pricing policy. For example, if the business strategy is aimed at participating in a mature, price-sensitive segment of the market, the business is likely to be structured around a narrow line of "bread and butter" products, high-volume–low-cost manufacturing operations, minimal engineering and redesign capabilities, and a selling effort targeted at price-oriented accounts. In this kind of situation, a pricing policy designed to achieve high-volume goals even at the expense of some unit margin probably makes sense. But this same pricing policy would make no sense at all if the business strategy were focused on a segment of the market where custom product design and superior performance features were the key factors in the buying decision. Here a more logical policy would be to price at a premium and be willing to sacrifice volume to preserve unit margins and a reputation for superior performance.

Differences in product design, manufacturing operations, or selling approaches obviously lead to substantially different cost structures for what may appear to be similar products. For example, a plant structured to produce a narrow range of products will generally have more automated equipment, lower direct labor costs per unit, higher fixed and indirect manufacturing costs, and a higher breakeven point than one set up to manufacture a similar product for a custom market in small quantities. However, when the business comes under tough competitive pressure or the market softens, these fundamental differences in economic structure are often forgotten and pricing policies or actions are implemented that are totally at odds with the profit-making strategy management originally set out to follow.

During the past few years, Cleveland Twist Drill, a broad-line manufacturer of high speed cutting tools, found that smaller specialty producers were cutting into its business by selling below cost on certain lines with selected high volume users. To preserve its position with these accounts, Cleveland Twist Drill matched the lower prices, but did not intend to lower prices across the board. There are few secrets in the marketplace, however, and once the lower price was granted to certain customers, other customers heard about it and demanded the same treatment. As a result, the price eventually dropped across the line and margins deteriorated. The narrow line producers then retaliated with an even lower price and again started taking market share from Cleveland Twist Drill. Discussions with vendors indicated that, even with the lower prices, at least three of the four specialty producers could still make satisfactory profits.

## Inadequate Administration

Once a pricing policy is defined, you might think that everyone will automatically follow it. Unfortunately, this isn't the way it works in the real world. Unless management takes positive steps to ensure that the policy is explicitly followed throughout the company, exceptions will occur at a phenomenal rate. A few exceptions to any policy are to be expected, but too many exceptions and the policy becomes nonexistent.

One might wonder how this happens, but it is easy to explain. There is almost always pressure from some quarter for a lower price. Salespeople the world over can always find persuasive reasons why prices below policy are required to be competitive, or to "crack a new account." A plant manager sees a costly gap in a near-term production plan and calls on the sales force to help him fill it by taking some short-cycle business (short period from sale to delivery) at reduced prices. A product or sales manager sticks to the list price, but offers the buyer some form of price concession through extended terms, a longer warranty period, a break on return goods, prepaid freight, or some other advantage that costs money. A systems marketing manager accepts an order within current price policy, but for delivery 12 months from now with no escalation clause to adjust the price at delivery for inflation. In short, any salesperson, market, product, or plant manager worth his or her salt can always find a hundred reasons and ways to deviate from stated price policy. Unless top management exercises tight control, the company's pricing policy will become a joke or, at best, simply the starting point for price negotiations. Most companies think they have the tight control necessary to avoid these situations, but they really don't. It takes a lot of top management attention and discipline in an organization of any size to make sure that unauthorized price concessions or policy deviations do not occur. And the plain truth is that management in many companies simply does not exercise the kind of tough-minded discipline required to make a pricing policy stick.

# MANAGEMENT SOLUTIONS

Let's turn now to the actions management can take to prevent or correct these problems. There are no easy answers or pat solutions. Preventive or corrective actions should be designed to keep a strong focus on bottom-line profits and the impact that changes in a product's cost structure and alternative pricing actions will have on these results. All these actions revolve around basic management requirements that are essential to success in any industrial operation.

## Establish Growth and Profit Targets

The first requirement is to define and communicate an explicit set of growth and profit targets. To be meaningful, the targets must be balanced to cover the expected return on sales and capital as well as a profit growth objective. To be worthwhile, they need to represent a level of performance that yields an attractive return on capital and provides the means to create an attractive work environment for employees. For example, an after-tax return of 7 percent on sales, 20 percent on capital employed, and a 15 percent growth rate would represent a satisfactorily explicit and balanced set of targets. These target numbers are precise and require balanced performance. They cannot be achieved by concentrating on sales growth alone without regard for the investment in working capital required. Nor can they be achieved by sacrificing growth and scaling back investment and costs to improve returns. Conversely, some vague statement about earning attractive profits or achieving large sales gains would not be worthwhile. The emphasis must be on profits and profit growth to counteract the strong volume orientation that commonly exists in most industrial companies.

Given the dynamic nature of our business environment, these targets (like interest rates) should be reviewed regularly and adjusted for changing inflation rates and economic conditions. It is clear that profit returns, like interest rates, require upward adjustment with the rate of inflation. In other words, if management expected to earn a 10 percent after-tax return on its capital with inflation at 3 to 4 percent, it makes no sense at all to settle for the same return when the inflation rate doubles. In the mid-1970s, many companies determined that their growth and profit targets had to be adjusted when the annual inflation rate jumped to double-digit numbers. Although they may not know it, those managers who failed to recognize this need actually suffered an erosion in their capital base when inflation rates exceeded profit returns.

A different set of targets needs to be developed for international operations. International targets must take into account differing inflation and tax rates, as well as the inherent economic and political risks in each country. For example, it simply doesn't make sense to settle for the same profit returns in a soft-currency country like Mexico or Brazil, where high inflation erodes half or more of the monetary value each year, and a hard-currency country like Switzerland, where inflation appears to be under control. Nor does it make sense to overlook the volatile political climates in some countries that greatly increase the risks of getting a payout on invested capital. Obviously, high-risk situations demand a higher return and a shorter payout period.

As important as defining these targets is the need to make sure they are communicated throughout the organization and that everyone understands the business strategy and basic pricing policies designed to achieve them. Special emphasis should be given to explaining these targets to the sales force and relating them to the company's sales and marketing plans and pricing policies. Communication with the sales force is crucial, since the sales organization is where most of the pressure for volume and deviations from pricing policy starts. Getting the sales force to understand how the company's pricing policies relate to achieving overall growth and profit targets and the importance of adhering to these policies will put a cap on a lot of this pressure.

## Determine Product Line Costs and Profits

A second requirement is to have an accurate picture of the cost and profit structure for each product line. Management in most companies has some means of knowing the relative profitability of its key business segments. Some rely on statements that show gross margin dollars and percentage of gross margin to sales; others use contribution dollars (sales dollars less "out of pocket" costs equal contribution to overhead and profit). These data can lead management to wrong pricing decisions because they do not include all the costs of doing business and thus do not fully reflect the true cost and profit picture. Unfortunately, even so-called fixed costs tend to increase steadily when inflation rates are high. As a result, what are traditionally regarded as relatively stable overhead costs (insurance, taxes, supervision) can escalate unexpectedly and dramatically affect any cost and profit structure. Relying on profit statements that do not take all these costs into account can easily lead to pricing decisions that generate more gross margin or contribution dollars but less bottom-line profits.

To keep the true profit picture in focus, net profitability statements need to be developed on a regular basis for each major product line. This is not an easy task, but neither is it impossible. Most accounting systems identify the direct costs (labor, material, direct overhead) for each major product line. Allocations of indirect costs, including corporate charges, can be assigned to each product line on some kind of rational basis. There will be plenty of arguments by those responsible for the profitability of one product line or another about the fairness of these allocations, and undoubtedly periodic adjustments will have to be made. However, all indirect and overhead costs must be completely allocated. None of them is going to go away, and they must be assigned somehow to specific product lines to reflect a true profit picture. The allocation process should not be arbitrary or left entirely to the accounting side of the business. Getting the managers with profit and loss responsibility involved is a good way to improve their understanding of the economics of their business and will help gain agreement on the fairness of allocation methods.

Once developed, these net profitability statements should serve as a starting point for regular review sessions to bring necessary management actions into focus. Estimated cost increases for labor, material, and overhead should be made frequently so that management can see how each product line statement will be affected. Doing this should highlight the need for management action to reduce material or labor costs, cut back overhead spending, defer major programs, or initiate price increases. Management needs to use these statements aggressively. They should be reviewed regularly as a formal part of the management process so that problems can be pinpointed quickly. Once problems are identified, strong action to raise prices or reduce costs should be initiated to ensure that target profits for each product line are achieved. Finally, management must take a hard line on product lines that do not meet profit objectives and be willing to drop them if necessary unless realistic plans to achieve satisfactory profits are presented. The whole idea is to get a regular and all-inclusive look at the cost and profit structure for each product line so that appropriate action can be taken to achieve satisfactory profits for the total business.

## Develop and Enforce Pricing Policy

A final requirement calls for top or general management to define and articulate the pricing policy and then provide strong follow-through to ensure that it is effectively administered. Although it sounds difficult, defining pricing policy is not the toughest part of the job. To begin with, there are only a limited number of pricing policies to choose from for any market segment. You can price low to build volume and market position. You can price high to hold or improve margins. You can tie price to the customer's perceived value. You can match or price off certain competitor prices. You can be a price leader or a follower. There are not many other alternatives.

The key is to determine which of these policies is most appropriate for each market segment of interest to the company. Exhibit 8-2 shows the network of interrelated considerations that need to be evaluated as a basis for selecting a pricing strategy for any busi-

EXHIBIT
8-2

## DEVELOPING PRICING STRATEGY

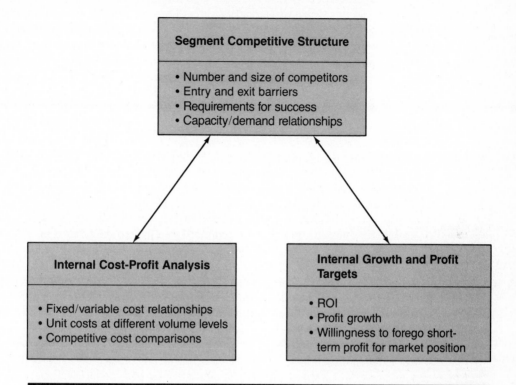

**Segment Competitive Structure**

- Number and size of competitors
- Entry and exit barriers
- Requirements for success
- Capacity/demand relationships

**Internal Cost-Profit Analysis**

- Fixed/variable cost relationships
- Unit costs at different volume levels
- Competitive cost comparisons

**Internal Growth and Profit Targets**

- ROI
- Profit growth
- Willingness to forego short-term profit for market position

ness. Exhibit 8-2 illustrates the need to have *both* market and economic facts on which to base pricing decisions. It also shows that pricing strategy decisions are in effect investment decisions, which commit the resources of the firm and which therefore must be directly linked to the company's overall business strategy. It is not necessary to define pricing policy in a way that covers every conceivable situation or set of circumstances. Broad but definitive statements, like "We intend to adhere to our standard list or discount structure and will make no special deals with anyone," or "We intend to price in a way that achieves our margin objectives on each sales transaction," or "We want to price at a 5 percent premium over certain competitors," are totally adequate pricing policy directives.

The most difficult part of management's job is to take the actions required to show that the policy is not just words. To start with, someone with an eye for profits has to be given the responsibility for monitoring individual pricing actions to ensure that unauthorized deviations do not occur. In some cases, the general manager may want to maintain this responsibility. In others, especially where multiple product-market businesses are involved, general management may delegate the responsibility to a product or market manager. In still other situations, the general manager may decide to give this responsibility to the controller as part of the overall accounting-control assignment.

Whoever has this responsibility must clearly play the role of enforcer. Carrying out the job will not win any popularity contests, for it involves such things as making sure any orders taken that do deviate from policy without appropriate authorization are turned back and the responsible party ordered to explain the situation to the customer, seeing to it that those who try to slide around established price policy in some clever way get their wrists slapped and everyone knows about it. Admittedly, actions like these are tough medicine, but they are essential to let everyone know that top managers really mean it when they say: "This is our pricing policy, and we intend to make it stick."

## Strengthen Ability to Compete

Beyond actions designed to ensure tight control over pricing, other management actions are required to make it practical to stick to a firm pricing policy in the face of competitors that may not. Continued or even increased investment is required in product development activities that can build greater proprietary value into the product or service offering. It is essential to put the salesperson in a position where he or she can emphasize new product features, shorter delivery cycles, quality assurance and reliability programs, product training, or any other conceivable advantage that provides genuine value to the customer. Arming salespeople with advantages like these enables them to sell in a way that takes the emphasis off price and encourages the customer to think about total value instead of which product is the cheapest.

Management must also place constant and heavy emphasis on cost reduction to help offset inflation-driven increases in material, labor, and other product costs that are certain to occur. Successful programs that take costs out of a product without penalizing its quality or performance are essential to preserve profit margins without passing every increase on to the customer. When inflation is running at a double-digit rate, however, it is unlikely that even the most successful cost reduction programs can completely offset spiraling cost increases, so timely price adjustments must be implemented along with the appropriate customer explanation. Timely means planned well in advance, and not waiting until accounting records show that profit margins have declined. This is not as difficult as it might sound. Most cost increases are predictable, and operating plans should include schedules that show both the cost reduction programs and the pricing actions that will be taken to preserve or enhance profit margins.

## Stand Firm When the Market Turns Soft

The acid test of management's determination to stick with a firm pricing policy comes when the market turns soft and a struggle develops to achieve volume goals. When this occurs, management can expect to see proposals to lower price as a means of picking up incremental volume or marginal contribution to help absorb overhead. On the surface, these proposals have a lot of appeal. Why not lower price to pick up volume you would not get otherwise? Why not take your price down even below full cost to pick up added volume that will help absorb a fixed amount of overhead that you have to pay anyway? There may well be times when it is smart to lower price to achieve objectives like these, but in most cases the proposals are ill-conceived notions that represent a snare and a delusion.

Think about what happens if competition matches or goes below a lower price and as a result captures some of your established business or customers. Consider how effectively you can compete if your action to lower price triggers an all-out price war among competitors who also have idle capacity and would like to have incremental volume to fill it. Or assume you are able to pick up low price volume that absorbs overhead without competitive retaliation. Have you really achieved an economic gain? Is there a real advantage in wearing out machines and people just to gain contribution dollars instead of scaling back capacity so that underutilized capital can be redeployed?

Pricing actions like these are never made in a vacuum. Aggressive competitor reactions should be anticipated, particularly in mature market situations where demand is relatively inelastic and competitor share positions are relatively stable. This does not mean that such pricing actions should never be taken. It does mean, however, that management must be judicious and consider probable competitor responses and the ultimate economics of such actions after all factors have been taken into account.

When it looks as though the market is turning soft, management needs to move quickly to cut back costs; otherwise, the fears of those arguing for lower prices will prove valid and lower volume will create an intolerable profit pattern. If management is on top of the business, it should be able to anticipate soft market conditions so that actions to reduce inventories, staff levels, and indirect costs can be initiated prior to the actual volume decline. Waiting until the condition actually reflects itself in the profit and loss statement is at least several months too late and often leads to panic reactions that penalize the firm over the longer term.

In most make and sell situations, the economic structure of the business is not totally dependent on volume, and market declines tend to be cyclical rather than permanent. Given these characteristics, it is surprising how well profit margins and even absolute profits can be preserved if management moves quickly and aggressively to scale back costs in anticipation of lower volume. As a general rule, a volume shortfall from plan of up to 5 percent—and in some cases up to 10 percent—should be absorbed without penalizing planned profits if the plan is soundly conceived and management moves quickly enough to make appropriate changes in its cost structure. If the volume shortfall is deeper than 10 percent, cost reduction efforts should be targeted at reshaping the cost structure so that planned profit margins are achieved on a much lower volume base.

Admittedly, these are demanding objectives that cannot be achieved with a "kid glove" approach to cost reduction. But it is clear that they can be achieved. History has recorded plenty of examples of businesses that actually generated the profit dollars and margins necessary to achieve these objectives on lower volume as those businesses grew through various stages to their present size. During the 1975–76 recession, one of Reliance Electric's plants operated at about 35 percent of its rated capacity and still broke even. It was able to do this for two reasons. First, the plant was basically an assembly operation, and the fixed cost base and breakeven point were relatively low. Equally important, operating management anticipated the decline in business and moved quickly to reduce both its direct and indirect costs. The direct workforce was cut from 700 to 200, and the ratio of indirect (supervisors and support personnel) to direct was improved from 1:3 to 1:5. When the economic cycle turned upward, the plant achieved higher profit levels than it had in prior years because management was able to return to former volume levels with fewer direct workers and with the stronger indirect to direct ratio developed during the recession period.

With proper management, a business can generate the same profit dollars and margins as volume slides down. To be successful, management must understand that discretionary costs tend to be regarded as variable when volume increases and fixed as volume goes down. These discretionary costs are the ones that must be attacked and scaled back to ensure a cost configuration that will yield satisfactory profit margins and profits on a lower than planned volume base. Belt tightening is always tough, but it is a necessary course of action for management when the market turns soft. And it is the only way to build real integrity and believability into a company's pricing policy.

Of course, if the economic structure of the business is volume-sensitive, as it is in many industries that operate with an unusually high percentage of fixed costs, there may be no alternative to lowering prices. And if at some point the total market really dries up, prices may have to be lowered and lower margins accepted in any business just to keep the doors open, since some contribution to overhead and profit is better than no contribution at all. However, unless the business is extremely sensitive to volume, cutting prices should be a last resort and seriously weighed against the alternative of scaling back or going out of the business so capital can be redeployed in areas where profit opportunities are more attractive.

## SUMMARY

Pricing policies are a vital part of the marketing mix for any company, and they need management attention if they are to foster the long-term success of the firm. Panicky decisions under market pressure, naive decisions made without proper marketing information, and chasing short-term gain at the expense of long-term success are common in industrial firms, although they need not be.

Most of the trouble stems from management deficiencies—not understanding the market and the economics of the business; overemphasizing volume and market share; failing to keep a step ahead of inflation; failing to link pricing to the total business strategy; and failing to administer a pricing policy consistently and carefully. All these mistakes can cost the company profits and even its existence.

Certain procedures can take the mystery and the danger out of pricing. One is to establish growth and profit targets and make sure they are communicated throughout the company; another is to determine actual product line costs and profits. One of the most important is to define and enforce a pricing policy, and to stand firm when the market turns soft. A management with a clear idea of where the company is going and a good grasp of economics can make and administer a firm, consistent pricing policy that will work to the company's advantage.

## REVIEW QUESTIONS

1. What questions about the market must be answered before a pricing decision is considered?
2. What information about the economics of each product line should be known before a pricing decision is considered?
3. Why do many industrial firms place too much emphasis on volume and market share?
4. What is the link between an overall business strategy and pricing policy?
5. Why are growth and profit targets necessary to develop and guide pricing policies?
6. Why is the enforcement of a pricing policy often difficult?
7. How might a company clearly define and enforce a pricing policy?

# 9

# Competitive Bidding

Some Commonsense
Practices
  Understand the
  Customer's
  Requirements
  Analyze Past Bids
  Know Whether to Bid for
  the Short or Long Term
  Set Proper Pricing
  Terms
  Make the Proposal—A
  Total Business Plan
Negotiating Bid-Contract
Situations
  Large Customer
  Advantage
  Price Gambits
Supply Contract
Obligations
Bidding Guidelines
Summary
Review Questions

Jerry Potter, senior sales engineer for Custom Machinery Company, was excited about the verbal agreement he had just received from the purchasing and engineering groups at U.S. Can Company, an account that could give him his largest single order. Jerry had worked closely with U.S. Can for several months to develop the parameters and design concept for a new machine that offered potential cost and performance advantages over the machines U.S. Can currently had in place. He had been assured verbally by an engineer at U.S. Can that he stood to get an order for another 35 machines if the first one met cost and performance specifications. At approximately $300,000 per machine, the total order could amount to over $10 million.

Jerry forwarded all the necessary information to the home office to enable it to prepare a firm quote and proposal. Several weeks passed with no response. Worried, Jerry called Fred James, the national sales manager, to see what was going on. Jerry opened the conversation by saying: "Fred, we'll lose this sale if we don't get the proposal in to U.S. Can. I promised it within a few weeks, and six weeks have already passed." Said James: "We've got a problem, Jerry. I think it's a heck of an opportunity, but the boss has a lot of concerns, and I have not been able to convince him that we should go ahead with the bid." "How can he have any concerns when such a huge piece of business is staring us in the face?" Jerry asked, astonished. "I agree with you," Fred said, "but let me read you the comments the boss made on your transmittal memo."

Even though this might be an attractive piece of business, it looks very risky to me.

1. We have no proven position or record with U.S. Can as a supplier. What is to stop U.S. Can from just picking our brains and sharing the ideas with their traditional suppliers?
2. We have no experience in making a machine that matches these specifications. How do we know we can build a machine that will perform at this cost?
3. What assurance do we have that there will definitely be follow-on business or that we will get any of it if it does develop?
4. As I see it, it would cost us $60,000 to $80,000 to prepare a definitive proposal. That's a lot of up-front money with these risks, especially compared to other opportunities we have with customers we know well.

Jerry, dismayed, answered: "I don't know how we will ever get new business with this kind of potential if we aren't willing to take some risks."

What else can Jerry do to prove his point?

Should he come back with more facts and more arguments? What kind of facts would he need?

What might be done to prevent this situation from happening again?

**G**ood procurement practice dictates the need to seek competitive bids on most purchases of any consequence. The buying need may be a one-time capital equipment purchase, or it may involve long-term repeat purchases over many months or years for a material, manufactured component, or service. If the customer needs a long-term steady and stable source for a critical item, a competitive long-term supply contract is often sought.

Products that require a long manufacturing cycle of many months are typically conducted on a competitive bid and supply contract basis. Most job-shop manufacturers secure business on a bid-contract basis. Major OEMs with large annual requirements for an item will seek competitive bids before selecting one or two long-term supply sources. Large corporate headquarters purchasing units, sometimes called national accounts, frequently buy centrally on a competitive bid and supply contract basis. For example, IBM now offers contracts for most products that include a "volume procurement amendment," which grants customers a discount for agreeing to buy a set number of units by a given date. These discounts and contracts appeal mainly to large customers. Once an end user signs an 18-month contract to buy IBM products, which is common in a volume deal, competitors find themselves locked out.[1] Finally, most municipal, state, and federal government purchases are conducted by requesting competitive bids and then awarding a contract. In most of these situations, large sums of money are involved.

If a bidding situation is not properly thought through, there can be significant long-term risks for the supplier. The most common areas of risk are these:

1. Not thoroughly understanding the customer's requirements.
2. Making wrong assumptions about the future and the competition.
3. Making wrong estimations of costs, purchase quantities, and expected profits.

Competitive bidding situations are like military warfare. The prudent supplier must select bid situations or "battles" that fit its capabilities and provide attractive profits. The technical challenge or "interesting project" has caused many suppliers to pursue bids for which they did not have the capabilities or resources. Technical or engineering driven bids without a close customer-market orientation can result in a lot of unprofitable "won" bids and lawsuits for failure to deliver. So can the pushing of a sales manager who says: "This could be a 'showcase account' that will result in a lot of follow-on business from the customer." This form of wishful thinking is usually nothing more than a desire to grab any business for the sake of volume. A statement like "Everyone else is submitting bids" is also not a valid reason to bid. In one company, the sales manager influenced the division president to sign bid proposals to fill a plant that was running at less than 50 percent capacity. The company bid low for one larger OEM's component needs and was locked into three years of shipments in which increases in labor and material costs nearly bankrupted the division.

[1]Peter D. Petre, "Meet the Lean, Mean New IBM," *Fortune,* June 13, 1983, p. 74.

# SOME COMMONSENSE PRACTICES

There are a number of sound business practices to follow *before* pursuing a competitive bid situation. These practices will help an industrial marketer decide how to bid, and equally important, when *not* to bid.

## Understand the Customer's Requirements

When examining any bidding situation, it is important to consider each customer or buyer individually. The astute marketer or salesperson will first identify the people who write the requirements and product specifications. This requires close contact with technical and purchasing personnel, and often top management. Every step in a government or private customer review process is a marketing opportunity to influence specifications or conditions so that the company becomes or remains a qualified supplier. But the first step is to identify the network of line and staff influences in the procurement process for the item.

Identification of the decision makers and the requirements of the account usually require numerous visits to the potential customer's organization. This interaction helps the supplier to discover the customer's real needs and lessens the chance of the supplier becoming preoccupied with a technology or a preconceived solution to a situation that may not exist. Repeated on-site visits, questions, and cross-questioning help a supplier better understand the customer's requirements. It is also helpful to verify with the customer what you believe its requirements are. This approach helps avoid misunderstandings that could misdirect a proposal. A team of marketing and engineering personnel listening to the customer is most helpful. Often random customer statements and information help get to the real requirements. In-depth discussions with one large potential customer, for example, revealed that it expected the chosen supplier to invest in special quality-control equipment, which would have had a very negative impact on the supplier's profits. In another situation, a thorough understanding of customer requirements revealed that, on smaller production runs, the customer would provide or pay for the costly injection molds. Armed with this information, the supplier bid only on that portion of the business.

The supplier considering entering a bidding position is usually putting a lot of eggs in one basket for a considerable time period. For this reason, there is a great need to learn as much as possible about the customer's requirements before deciding whether or not to bid and how to bid if the decision is yes (see the box, page 190).

When company or division top management teams are really customer oriented, they will have plenty of firsthand data on customers' requirements and competitive offers. Staying close to the customer also helps the supplier learn about a new technology or application. The result is a tailored product with a lot of value for the customer. This focus is contrary to the typical sales orientation that stresses a large number of calls per day. In short, the field people should be problem solvers rather than salespeople with a canned pitch.

Once the customer's requirements are understood, it is important that the potential customer understand the solution you have for his or her problem or requirements. Since there is rarely one person who influences the choice of supplier, it is important to get the solution to all the decision-making parties. In some situations, the supplier can know what the customer's requirements are before they issue the request for a quote (RFQ).

## STAYING CLOSE TO CUSTOMERS

Boeing designs and assembles jet aircraft for each customer's specifications. In its metamorphosis from a military to a commercial company, Boeing states:

> We built teams that were customer and not technology oriented. We came to a realization that if we were going to succeed in the commercial business, the important ingredients were the immediate customer and his customer's needs. . . . It took us a long time to recognize the customer's problems. Now this point of view percolates throughout our entire organization.

An accountant at a major specialty chemical company was at first surprised when, after two months on the job, he was asked to spend more time accompanying a salesman making calls. The accountant, who later became the division comptroller, commented afterward:

> If you don't understand how the customers use and buy an item, you won't understand the business and how to submit bids. All of our contract administrators spend time in the field with each customer before we decide to bid.

Much of IBM's data processing computer equipment is sold on a proposal-bid-service contract basis. The corporate vice president of marketing at IBM stated:

> Every proposal to a customer should be overwhelmingly cost-justifiable from the customer's standpoint. Such an orientation requires in-depth knowledge of what each customer can do with the machine. We want our salesmen to act as if they were on the customer's payroll. IBM is customer driven, not technology driven.

When Hewlett-Packard engineers make service calls, they ask customers what they like and dislike about the existing product. They also ask customers what specific new features they would like. The computer system division general manager at Hewlett-Packard stated:

> If we don't stay close to our customers, the Japanese or another competitor will leapfrog our position. As the division general manager, I still spend 1 week per month in the field, visiting installations, talking with customers and attending sales meetings. This helps us learn from others' mistakes, and it helps to avoid designing systems that are technically interesting but don't provide enough customer value.

*Source:* Thomas J. Peters and Robert H. Waterman, *In Search of Excellence: Lessons from America's Best-Run Corporations* (New York: Harper & Row, 1982), p. 169; and a personal conversation with R. (Buck) Rodgers, IBM Corporation, Armonk, New York.

## Analyze Past Bids

Armed with an exhaustive knowledge of the present or potential customer's requirements, the supplier should conduct a bid-history analysis whenever possible. A *bid-history analysis* is a systematic consideration of why bids were won or lost. Some executives are reluctant to conduct such analyses because they are a review after the fact. However, projections and decisions based on 20/20 hindsight are one of the most reliable forecasting tools available to management. Objective after-the-fact examinations can be most revealing and promote better account planning, better price determination, and the development of sales tactics that take advantage of patterns of customer requirements and competitive behavior.

Historical bid and contract award analysis should be conducted with both internal data and firsthand information from buyers. Internal data sources include salesperson call reports and past correspondence with potential and existing customers. The analysis should consider the economic, technical, competitive, and political reasons a contract was won or lost.[2]

The industrial supplier might initially analyze just those bids that were lost. Purchasing departments, buyers, and key customer executives are some of the best and most accurate sources for analyzing lost bid situations. Some purchasing departments have a policy of explaining to the losing bidders why they were not awarded the business. This practice helps the buyer develop better supplier relations and often increases competition for the buyer's business. An analysis of the customer's reason for lost business frequently refutes the salesperson's common reason of "price-buying" as the umbrella explanation for all lost business. Lost bid analysis may instead reveal that a technical proposal was unsound or that delivery dates were unacceptable. The specific reasons for the loss of business will usually focus on one or more of the following: quality, delivery, service, long-term availability, supplier's technical assistance, and price. IBM, for example, conducts monthly "lost account reviews" with its branch and regional people to discuss why business was lost and what needs to be done.

Lost bid reviews should also be done in face-to-face meetings with the customers. Often customers will not only explain why the business was lost, but suggest ways that near misses can be turned into hits. In one case, such a visit revealed that the quoted delivery of 12 weeks was the weak factor; the winner's delivery quote was 5 weeks. Bid-history analysis ultimately allows a supplier to profile both customers and competitors and better anticipate customer requirements and predict competitor responses.

## Know Whether to Bid for the Short or Long Term

In many industries, suppliers encounter situations in which the firm winning the initial contract has an advantage in obtaining the longer-term follow-on business. This situation typically results in suppliers "buying in" by offering low initial prices or other inducements to tie customers to them for long periods. This practice is often referred to as "getting well" on the "follow-on" business.[3] The initial sale is often made at less than desirable profits or possibly at a loss in anticipation of the more lucrative subsequent sales of the same or related products and services. For example, Goodyear bid $1 for the initial Boeing 757 order for the landing gear and wheel assembly. The aftermarket unit sales in

[2]Paul L. Smith and Lawrence G. Regau, "Before You Bid, Know Your Competition," *Aerospace Management,* March 1963, pp. 24–28.
[3]Robert E. Weigand, "Buying into a Market," *Harvard Business Review,* November–December 1980, pp. 141–49.

that situation are hundreds of times larger than the initial OEM sale. By winning the original order for $1 Goodyear is assured of the replacement part business because it is unlikely that another supplier will be qualified on the original equipment.

A basic issue in bidding and pricing for follow-on business is to ask: How likely or probable is it that the firm will obtain the follow-on business? The link between the initial buy-in business and the follow-on sales must be strong if this approach is to be profitable. If the link between the two is not strong, the supplier has probably obtained a low-profit or money-losing contract. Here are five ways to build strong links for more follow-on business:

1. Patents and proprietary products help build the link between initial and follow-on sales. However, other firms can sometimes "reverse engineer" around the proprietary product if there is not a strong patent position.
2. Noninterchangeable machines or parts tie the customer to additional purchases of your system, parts, or service. This type of customer dependence is commonly practiced in the computer and word processing and photocopy machine businesses.
3. Customers usually want to keep the number of parts, spares, and inventory to an economic minimum and therefore will often provide follow-up business to one supplier. Airlines are a good example. They will specify a jet airplane engine from one supplier and buy replacement engines and carry spare parts only from that supplier. In situations where multiple follow-on supply sources are sought, the link is less effective.
4. The cost of retraining employees can also keep customers loyal. Many manufacturers will provide full training to a customer's employees to ensure proper use of the product and to create high retraining or switching costs if the customer does not buy the follow-on products. For example, Airbus Industrie, the European airplane consortium, encountered difficulty in selling jet aircraft to flight and maintenance personnel who had been exclusively trained on U.S. equipment. To overcome this link to U.S. producers, Airbus invested in the training of hundreds of airline flight and maintenance personnel in how to operate and repair their airplanes.[4]
5. By influencing the specifications in the initial order, a producer can be presented as the only one with the performance capabilities for that application. One firm was able to influence the braking system specifications of two major truck manufacturers in such a way that there were not any available functional substitutes. The aftermarket repair manuals carried the same specification and referred to the sole supplier's brand name.

Without some of these links between initial and subsequent sales, producers should not price low or seek lower ROIs for the initial sales. If a supplier does not have enough current capacity or the funds to increase capacity to satisfy the follow-on business, it should not pursue the initial buy-in. Suppliers who have made this mistake have only primed the follow-on market for other suppliers.

Bidding or buying-in low for higher prices and better profits later is often limited to medium or large firms that have strong capital bases. A small one-product company or

---

[4]Ibid., p. 143.

a highly leveraged one often does not have the financial base or staying power to buy into long-term situations. In larger firms, with interdivisional buying, selling, and transfer pricing, a division may be asked to reduce its profits to allow another division to buy in with low prices. Top management must resolve this conflict by deciding where it wants to take the profit.

If there is a high probability of winning the follow-on contract with some strong links, the supplier must then determine what combination of bid prices on the initial purchase order and follow-on business will lead to an acceptable overall rate of return. Exhibit 9-1 shows how a series of purchase orders over time improves the supplier's ROI as additional profits accrue and original investment costs are amortized. The time intervals between orders and the quantities of subsequent buys are key pricing strategy considerations.

In complex follow-on business situations that require the supplier to think through the initial competitive bid prices, the probability of follow-on or subsequent business, and the ultimate profit payoff, it is helpful to sketch out the possibilities. A decision tree analysis with pricing alternatives, business volumes over time, and ROIs is a means to think through the alternative "what ifs." A decision tree analysis also helps to model competitive situation and potential profitability levels.[5,6] Exhibit 9-2 shows three possible bid prices considered by a supplier and the probability of profit payoff from different levels of follow-on business. As you can see, it probably makes sense to consider the $510 unit price since the probability of a large follow-on business is attractive. The required investment and additional operating cost can also be added to a decision tree framework to analyze more accurately a competitive bidding cost situation with successive orders, volumes, and resulting profits.

---

**EXHIBIT 9-1**                 *BIDDING FOR FOLLOW-ON BUSINESS*

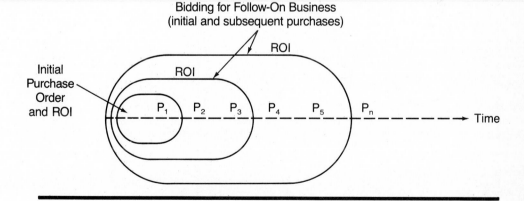

[5]John F. Magee, "Decision Trees for Decision Making," *Harvard Business Review,* July–August 1964, pp. 126–38.
[6]Jacob W. Ulvia and Rex Brown, "Decision Analysis Comes of Age," *Harvard Business Review,* September–October 1982, pp. 130–41.

# EVALUATING INITIAL PRICE VERSUS FOLLOW-ON

EXHIBIT
9-2

| Year 1 Initial Contract $260,000 | Year 2 Follow-On Contract $850,000 | Profit Payoff of Each Alternative |
|---|---|---|

Possible Competitive Bid Prices

A = $620 per unit

B = $510 per unit

C = $450 per unit

Probability of substantial follow-on

Probability of average follow-on

Probability of modest follow-on

Probability of substantial follow-on

Probability of average follow-on

Probability of modest follow-on

Probability of substantial follow-on

Probability of average follow-on

Probability of modest follow-on

## Set Proper Pricing Terms

Once a business strategy is chosen for the customer or account, the supplier must determine what pricing terms to put in the proposal. There are essentially four different ways bid or contract pricing terms can be structured: fixed price, fixed price with escalator, cost-plus, and PETS.

FIXED-PRICE BID.    In this system, the producer and buyer agree on a firm price and delivery dates. When cost increases are predictable, the producer bears less risk with this type of quotation. Since costs invariably increase with time, fixed-price bids are typically for less than one year. In high inflationary periods and over time periods of more than one year, a fixed-price contract substantially increases the producer's risk. For example, in 1972, a manufacturer of electrical products significantly underestimated the rate of material inflation for switchgear assemblies to be delivered in 1974. Table 9.1 shows the anticipated and actual percentage increases in labor and material. The higher actual material costs resulted in losses for each unit shipped. Producers can guard against these types of losses by employing either escalator or cost-plus clauses.

FIXED-PRICE BID WITH ESCALATORS.    When a supplier is not confident that major costs will remain stable during the contract period, a fixed-price bid with allowances for price escalation should be considered. The producer still assumes the risk of performance on all costs except those indexed according to escalator clauses. Escalator clauses result in a contingency pricing approach that usually moves more risk to the buyer. Producers should not quote fixed prices without escalators for any delivery dates more than a year ahead. Escalator clauses that typically cover increases in labor and material are usually tied to government statistical indexes for the appropriate industry.

COST-PLUS BID.    Cost-plus contracts were commonly used by government agencies during the late 1950s and early 1960s to purchase sophisticated weapon systems from suppliers who did not have the necessary experience base to submit fixed cost quotations. Profit targets ranging from 10 to 15 percent were negotiated before bids were awarded. These cost-plus contracts were highly criticized—and for good reason. Under the terms of these contracts there was absolutely no incentive for the supplier to control costs. In fact,

| TABLE 9.1 | SWITCHGEAR ASSEMBLY COST-PRICE STRUCTURE | | | |
|---|---|---|---|---|
| Cost Component | Price (%) | Anticipated Annual Increase | Actual Annual Increase |
|---|---|---|---|
| Material | 35% | 6% | 22% |
| Labor | 55% | 6% | 7% |
| Profit | 10% | – | – |

in some cases where fees were negotiated as a percentage of costs, it was to the supplier's advantage to build up the cost base as high as possible. Cost-plus contracts were largely to blame for many of the huge overruns that occurred on major defense programs. A cliché commonly heard in defense marketing circles stated that "an elephant is really a mouse designed to produce the military specifications under a cost-plus contract."

PRICE IN EFFECT AT TIME OF SHIPMENT (PETS). PETS bids allow for posting price increases to all buyers before shipment. PETS are desired escalation clauses when the producer must buy from a volatile supply market. General Electric uses PETS bids to market steam turbine generators, but with the limitation that the increase will not exceed 10 percent if delivery is taken within one year, 20 percent if within two years, and 30 percent if within three years.[7] PETS are also suitable in foreign export-import situations where currency rates often fluctuate widely.

Progress payments may be a part of any of these pricing approaches. General Electric and Westinghouse bid on all power generation systems for utility customers with progress payment in the bid. The generation systems require up to two years to deliver from the awarding of the bid. With such long manufacturing cycles, the supplier should always receive monthly progress payments. Progress payments are especially important to the supplier because they help its cash flow. If an entire company is essentially a job shop, progress payments may be a key to the producer's financial stability. McDonnell Douglas lost a $3 billion order for 60 jets from Delta Airlines because of a disagreement on progress payments.[8] Delta actually preferred the DC-11 to the Boeing 757 jet, but McDonnell Douglas wanted progress payments as each phase moved through production.

## Make the Proposal—A Total Business Plan

Understanding the customer's requirements, analyzing past bids, the potential for follow-on business, and pricing strategy are all combined in the preparation of a proposal. The development of a proposal is essentially the writing of a total business and marketing plan. Proposal and bid preparation is a costly activity. In the high-technology aerospace industry, a component supplier estimates it costs more than $100,000 to prepare and submit one proposal. Some companies maintain a substantial budget item called "new business development" that is primarily a pool of money to support proposal writing. In some situations, the customer will fund proposal submission by three to five potential suppliers before selecting one or two for the business. Bid preparation funds should be prudently allocated. Bid preparation or proposal expenses should be closely controlled and allocated only after a "to bid" situation is decided on by senior management. Otherwise, a lot of money will likely be wasted on proposal writing where there is little chance for success.

Bid and proposal preparation is a multifunctional effort. But if the effort is dominated by engineers, it may be doomed to failure. Good marketing people know what the customer needs or requires. If this concept is kept clearly in mind, the industrial marketer should never lose an argument to the engineer on what the customer needs. A careful

[7]R. G. M. Sultan, *Pricing in the Electrical Oligopoly* (Cambridge, Mass.: Harvard University Press, 1974).
[8]"The Big Deal McDonnell Douglas Turned Down," *Business Week,* December 1, 1980, pp. 81–82.

review must also be made of the supplier's technical and manufacturing capabilities and the customer's requirements. Accurate and successful proposal preparation requires a close working relationship between sales, marketing, engineering, accounting, and estimating personnel. On large projects or for large customers, it is common to have project teams submitting sections of the proposal from each functional area. If such teams are led by marketing, they will produce proposals that show closer understanding of a customer's needs and more accurate cost estimates of the requirements.

In the development of the proposal, which is also a marketing plan, it is important to anticipate the likely competitive responses. It is common to see five or six firms bidding on a large contract worth millions of dollars. Probably two or three are serious contenders for the contract. One should ask, "Why are these other firms submitting a bid?" The reasons are as many as there are firms. The contract may be related to the bidder's pet technology interest. It might be a bid from a desperate firm or a desire to fill in when business is slow. Someone's ego may be the driving force at another competitor. A firm should prepare a proposal and bid only when there is a good chance of winning against the known competition.

# NEGOTIATING BID-CONTRACT SITUATIONS

Most competitive bidding situations can be categorized as serious bids or courtesy bids. Courtesy bids are situations in which a buyer would like another bid for his or her management and to enhance his or her negotiating position. Some friendly suppliers will submit extremely high courtesy bids with little supporting documentation to earn other business. It is important for the serious supplier to know whether courtesy bids have been submitted. In a serious bidding situation, a supplier should first consider whether there will be a ritualistic first-round submission with the real decision in a second round, or whether the first bid of each supplier will be the final or last bid. The possible bids of identified competitors that have been profiled in the analysis stage should help to anticipate their pricing strategies. The more differentiated the product or service, the more that seller has control over price. Also, the closer a supplier is to full capacity and large backlogs, the more likely its bids will be on the high side. One division president stated: "We price low only when we're hungry for the business." Bids of survival-crisis firms or marginal divisions are often "low ball" prices.

## Large Customer Advantage

Most competitive bidding opportunities are characterized by one or two large customers and relatively few potential suppliers. Any one customer's business can represent 20 to 100 percent of the annual total market requirements. A typical supplier-buyer bidding business with few suppliers and few customers is shown in Table 9.2. This typical situation results in very large and concentrated purchasing power by the customers. Their purchasing power often results in customers' playing one supplier against the other in negotiating the final bid and terms. The larger customer will frequently use its size as an advantage or to leverage the relationship. For example, in June 1980, the Ford Motor

| TABLE 9.2 | SUPPLIERS AND USERS FOR JET ENGINE TURBINES | |
|---|---|---|

| Number of Suppliers | Number of Customers |
|---|---|
| 1. TRW (U.S.) | 1. Pratt & Whitney |
| 2. Howmet (France) | 2. General Electric |
| 3. Walbar (U.S.) | 3. Rolls Royce |

Company sent letters to 1,600 suppliers asking them to reduce their prices by 1.5 percent to ensure Ford as a customer. The letter stated: "Without this support and cooperation, the future market for our vehicles and in turn your products may be in jeopardy." Ford, in 1980, was having a profitless year; and 1.5 percent off its material cost would favorably affect its profit situation.

In heavy fixed-cost industries, capacity utilization may have to be running at 75 to 80 percent just to break even. This can be a bargaining chip for big customers in negotiating bids with suppliers. For example, when General Motors purchases commodity steel, it is aware that most steel companies need a minimum of 80 percent capacity utilization to break even. Such large customers can promise extra business, which steel producers may desperately need in times of falling demand, in return for holding the line on price increases. Smaller customers have considerably less or no effect on suppliers because of their smaller annual purchase requirements.

Large customers often also use the threat of future or more self-manufacture as a bargaining tool. When a large customer's purchases are a major portion of the supplier's business, the supplier frequently will concede to the large customer's desires. In situations where the supplier has a dedicated production line exclusively for the large customer, the supplier is even more dependent and vulnerable. The highly dependent contract industrial supplier is usually left stranded when the business from one customer is lost or reduced. These suppliers typically have a narrow product, little or no developed marketing capability, and little or no image among other potential users.

It is important for the supplier to avoid becoming dependent on a narrow customer base. To reduce this vulnerability, some OEM suppliers try not to have any one customer account for more than 7 to 10 percent of its business. One supplier of machine components, for example, has successfully sought out and bid on fragmented segments in which each customer is quite small. By doing this, the machine component supplier substantially broadened its customer base and per-unit profit margin.

## Price Gambits

The large purchasing power of some customers allows them to exert considerable influence on the pricing terms. Large customers with prudent procurement departments will learn as much as possible from potential suppliers before selecting sources. In situations where customers also have an internal supply source, they will usually have more cost information than buyers that do not have an internal self-manufacturing source. The more a large customer knows about a supplier's costs, the more negotiating leverage it has. The more prudent procurement organizations often seek comparative supplier information on cost, quality, performance, and delivery dates. In an attempt to obtain the best supplier information, some buyers request very specific line item bidder quote information. For example,[9] IBM's centralized procurement personnel are responsible for purchasing office furniture for all sales offices. IBM requested bid quotes from each supplier in the following form:

1. Separate price quotes for five major furniture items
2. Separate price quotes for one and two years' annual purchasing requirements
3. Separate price quotes for each of three shipping zones

This type of supply request allows purchasing managers to examine and compare supplier prices precisely. It provides the buyer with information to portion business out to one or multiple suppliers for each item. When buyers seek such specific information, there is often great emphasis on price and less on product quality and delivery capabilities.

The lowest price does not necessarily always get the contract. If supplier A's bid was not as low as supplier B's bid, the higher bidder might successfully challenge the lower bidder's capability to perform and deliver—especially if the lower bidder is a much smaller company. Furthermore, if the buyer is convinced that one firm is buying in low for the follow-up at much higher prices, the higher-bid firm might be chosen. The slightest deviation in the bid from customer specifications and requirements can also swing the award to another supplier. In addition, buyers and production personnel want secure and stable supply sources, especially for items that are key to their product or service offering.

## SUPPLY CONTRACT OBLIGATIONS

The pricing terms and supplier obligations in a competitive bid are usually formalized in a contract between supplier and customer. A basic question in most supply agreements is this: How will risks be assigned or shared by the two parties? The key areas of risk are inflationary cost increase factors and the risk of a buyer's earlier stated volume requirements fluctuating downward. If the stated volume amounts are firm, the buyer is obligated to purchase that volume at an agreed price, or pay penalties. However, large customers will often attempt to renegotiate in such a situation. Some supply contracts will have cancellation charges if cutbacks do occur. If the supplier had to incur considerable investment, there may be cancellation payments required of the buyer to cover all or part of the supplier's costs. This is an especially important clause if the supplier cannot sell the product elsewhere at the agreed-upon price.

Suppliers have firm legal obligations in contracts with customers. In the takeover battle

[9]Raymond R. Corey, *Procurement Management: Strategy, Organization and Decision Making* (Boston: CBI Publishing, 1978), pp. 212–30.

between Bendix, Martin Marietta, and Allied Corporation, Martin Marietta borrowed $900 million to keep its independence. In searching for ways to reduce its large debt, Martin Marietta was considering selling some of its divisions. Martin Marietta is in the aerospace, chemical, cement, and aluminum businesses. All these businesses have supply contracts with major customers. In light of the debt, the need for cash, and the existing supply contracts, Martin Marietta's options were greatly reduced. Their president and CEO stated: "We have long-term contracts with important customers. We just can't vacate the scene willy-nilly."[10]

Air Products and Chemicals received $50 million in a litigation settlement from Tenneco for failure to supply Air Products with contracted natural gas.[11] Air Products claimed it was forced to buy more expensive natural gas on the open market. The risk of delivery at agreed-upon prices nearly always falls on the supplier.[12, 13]

Relief from cost increases is not usually granted if such contingencies were not anticipated and written into the contract. Rolls Royce, a major jet engine builder, got locked into export supply contracts that were written principally in dollars. Rolls Royce's costs were mainly incurred in British pounds. As the pound strengthened and the dollar fell, the company's expenses soared to nearly $66 million.[14] The currency fluctuation helped plunge the division operations into the red for the year.

Purchasing departments often prefer long-term contracts at relatively fixed prices for major items. Continued inflation, increased labor and maintenance costs, and foreign currency fluctuations create an even greater desire to have more stable supply sources and prices. Furthermore, in market situations where there are relatively few producers and relatively large buying organizations, bids and supply contracts may increase in use. The major municipal, state, and federal government markets will continue to buy on a bid-quote basis. The legally bound but prudent supplier must systematically decide whether it wants to participate in each particular situation. In all such situations, industrial suppliers should attempt to share more of the risk with buyers. They should proceed cautiously before committing themselves to an agreement. Thorough preparation and caution are the watchwords.

## BIDDING GUIDELINES

All competitive bidding situations should be considered in terms of both potential risks and potential rewards. There are a number of guidelines or questions to ask before submitting a proposal or entering into a supply contract with a customer.

1. Knowledge of all the customer's requirements. The technical parameters are just the beginning of the customer's total business requirements.

[10]"Martin Marietta Looks for Ways to Reduce Its Large Debt, But Shuns a Fire Sale of Assets," *The Wall Street Journal*, January 12, 1983, p. 1.
[11]"Air Products Settles Tenneco Litigation," *The Wall Street Journal*, June 10, 1981, p. 32.
[12]K. S. Rosenn, "Protecting Contracts from Inflation," *Business Lawyer*, 1978, pp. 729–49.
[13]T. R. Hurst, "Drafting Contracts in an Inflationary Era," *University of Florida Law Review*, Summer 1976, pp. 879–903.
[14]*Business Week*, October 29, 1979, p. 65.

2. Our capabilities. Can we meet the customer requirements with existing capabilities? How difficult would it be to develop or acquire the additional capabilities? Are our firm's capabilities and past performance thoroughly known by all key people at the customer? Has any past poor record or problem been improved and made known to them?

3. Bid history. On what basis were past bids lost or won at the particular customer? Will these factors be the same or different in this situation?

4. Costs. Do we really know our costs to make this item or meet the requirements? Can we secure appropriate escalator clauses in the more volatile or unknown material and labor cost components? Do competitors have lower or more favorable cost structures?

5. Plant capacity. A supplier operating at 95 percent of capacity will not be eager to receive a bid that would add 20 percent more business. Conversely, a firm operating at 50 percent capacity would be eager to obtain the bid or long-term contract. The supplier's backlog also affects capacity utilization. A shrinking backlog may create a need to bid more aggressively.

6. Follow-up opportunities. Winning an initial contract or bid may yield much greater repeat orders. The concept of buying-in should be considered only if there are strong links to the follow-on business.

7. Quantity requested. The quantities the customer desires must be evaluated against plant capacity and production economics for various levels of orders.

8. Delivery requirements. Does the customer want periodic shipments or a "one-shot" shipment? The ability to meet customer delivery dates may determine whether or not to consider the business.

9. Competition. Who will be the likely or known competitors? How and what will they bid? Wherever competitive bid histories are known, they should be analyzed. Does one competitor have a strong inside position? What is the backlog of each likely competitor?

10. Special requirements. Are there specific qualification tests that only one supplier has equipment or ability to perform?

11. Wired bid. Is the bid wired to favor a specific supplier? Are the specifications written to fit only a favored source? Are there specifications directly from a supplier's product information? Are there short deadlines to favor an existing or favored supplier?

12. Customer information bid. Some customers request bids to help them decide whether to make or buy the product. Potential suppliers often help them by providing the comparative cost-price information needed. Sometimes the RFQ is written so that outside suppliers cannot perform as well as the customer's inside source.

13. Profit prospects. The contract or price should meet the supplier's rate of return objectives. If the initial price is a buy-in price, the secure repeat business prices should recoup the supplier's rate of return objectives over the time period. If the profit prospects are not attractive in either the short or the long term, the business should not be pursued.

## SUMMARY

Central to good competitive bidding by suppliers is practice of the industrial marketing concept. First, thoroughly understand the potential customer's requirements before deciding to pursue or not pursue the business. An attractive profit in the short term or a protected longer-term buy-in must be coupled to the industrial marketing concept. The customer and profit criteria will help guard against commitments to technically challenging and high-risk business with low profit rewards. The decision to bid or not to bid is as important as or more important than the decision to bid on many situations. A high bid-win ratio goal should never override a desired profit goal. The prudent industrial supplier should never gear up its operation for a large customer until it thoroughly understands the customer's requirements and its own costs, and truly believes it can earn an attractive profit if the business is won.

## REVIEW QUESTIONS

1. For what reasons do buyers put business out for competitive bids?
2. Why do suppliers often enter into a bid they should not have pursued?
3. How can suppliers better understand customer requirements before deciding to bid?
4. How can a supplier build links to better ensure the follow-on business?
5. How can decision trees help in analyzing a complex bidding situation?
6. How can a supplier structure bid pricing terms to reduce or share the risk with the customer?
7. How do some customers leverage suppliers in the negotiations and in setting pricing terms?
8. What criteria should a supplier consider in deciding to bid or not to bid?
9. What are the legal obligations of suppliers in a supply contract?

# 10

# Linking Sales to Marketing

Use Simple Economic
Analysis to Make Key
Sales Decisions

Define and Articulate the
Steps Necessary for a
Successful Selling Job

Provide Capable, Full-Time
First-Level Supervision
  Conflicting Demands
  Inadequate Training
  Excessive Paperwork

Use the Compensation
Plan as a Management
Tool

Strive for a Sharp End-
User Focus

Carve Out a Strong
Marketing Role for Sales
Management

Summary

Review Questions

Charles Wilson, vice president of sales for a large specialty steel company, was called into the president's office to discuss several major sales problems. Total industry prospects had declined, and the company's sales had dropped by 25 percent from the same period last year. The president started the discussion by saying: "I've just been going over our P&L projections, and we've got a real mess on our hands. With volume down as it is, your sales costs are way out of line. They've never been more than 8 percent of sales as long as I've been with the company, and they're now running closer to 12 percent. As I see it, you have to get rid of at least 25 salespeople and streamline your management structure to get costs back in line."

Charles was aware sales costs were a little high as a percentage of sales. He had added eight new salespeople last year in anticipation of increasing industry sales, and travel costs had moved up sharply with inflation. But even though industry sales had declined, Charles was reluctant to cut back; he knew the decline was temporary and believed the company should just ride it out. "I know our sales costs are a little high, but we have the best sales force in the industry. We have more sales experience and better customer relations than any of our competitors. It would be a mistake to get rid of anyone now when what we need more than anything are a lot of people who can get purchase orders."

The president listened while Charles made his arguments, but they didn't change his mind: "Charles, I have heard all this before, and I don't buy what you are saying. To avoid wasting any more time, I'm giving you a direct order to reduce the size and costs of your sales force by at least 25 percent. We have to weed out our marginal order takers and get rid of a lot of unnecessary management structure. You should also think about replacing some of our narrow-focused, product-oriented people with representatives who have a broader ability to evaluate, understand, and serve customer requirements effectively. Our long-term strategy is to focus on target markets with a broader and more complex range of products. A lot of your old-time product people simply can't do this job."

Charles left knowing it was impossible to change the president's mind. From Charles' point of view, the president, who had come up through the engineering side of the business, simply didn't understand what it took to sell effectively in today's market.

Who is actually more up to date?

What are the major requirements for successful selling in industrial markets?

What is the president's order designed to do? Where does he think the company is going?

In the industrial world, sales force performance has always been a very important contributor to marketing success. Other elements of the marketing mix—advertising, promotion, and merchandising—simply cannot have the same impact in industry as they do in consumer goods. There are very few situations in industry where the buying decision is made impulsively or clinched by some especially creative advertising or promotion appeal. Of course, advertising, promotion, and merchandising activities are important for communicating the company's image and product or service capability, and thus breaking the ground for the sales contact. But by themselves, these elements never close a sale and seldom even provide a competitive advantage, no matter how costly they are or how brilliantly conceived. Only the salesperson can carry out the lengthy transaction that characterizes industrial selling and finally gets the commitment to buy. Three forces are certain to make the role of the industrial salesperson even more important to marketing success:

1. Purchasing practices all over the world are becoming sharper and more sophisticated as more companies recognize the tremendous profit potential of building economic and value analysis into all major purchasing decisions.
2. The technical complexity and sophistication of products, systems, and applications are continuing to increase.
3. Competition from foreign producers will remain intense and even increase for many products.

The first two considerations will place a much greater premium on intelligent selling to help customers and users perceive their needs and to demonstrate the economic worth of the product in meeting these needs. The third consideration means that many companies will have to rely on a creative selling effort to overcome cost—and even technological—disadvantages. For these reasons, most industrial executives are quick to agree to the importance of having an outstanding selling force. As a general rule, industrial management supports this position by paying somewhat higher compensation to sales personnel than companies in the consumer products field. Despite their conviction and willingness to pay more for outstanding performance, however, only a few companies are fully satisfied with the quality and productivity of their selling organizations. Although executives in these companies voice their concerns in different ways, the concerns are all traceable to one root cause. Stated simply, the sales force in many industrial companies does not function according to the marketing concept, which holds that every business activity in the company should be responsive to market conditions and requirements in a way that generates maximum profits. More specifically, their industrial selling operations fall short of this objective in these critical ways:

1. They do not identify creative ways to establish a proprietary edge with customers or to take pressure off price as the key buying consideration.
2. They do not search for the new markets or applications necessary to achieve maximum growth and do not provide a flow of market intelligence to aid management in planning new product offerings.

3. They do not balance their efforts between long- and short-term selling needs to achieve marketing objectives.
4. They do not maintain the level of productivity necessary to keep abreast of constantly increasing costs of selling.

In short, the sales force in many industrial companies functions more as a collection of independent sales and distribution agents than as the integrated marketing arm it should be.

Why is this the case? Why, when its importance is generally recognized, is the sales force often relatively ineffective? We submit that the problem can be traced to failure to follow one or more of six principles that lead the sales force to function as a marketing arm. We'll discuss each of these principles in turn.

# USE SIMPLE ECONOMIC ANALYSIS TO MAKE KEY SALES DECISIONS

Total selling costs—that is, those costs recorded in the typical general selling and administration account—are not only the largest chunk of marketing expense, but also in many cases one of the largest annual expenditures an industrial company incurs during the normal course of business. When one looks at a compensation scale, and makes reasonable allowances for travel and entertainment expenses, benefits, supervision, and other overhead, it is very easy to come up with a cost of $60,000 to $80,000 for each salesperson in the field. When this figure is multiplied by, say, 50 salespeople, the annual cost can quickly amount to several million dollars for the smaller sales organization; multiplied by a few hundred, the selling costs can total $10 and even $20 million for companies with large-scale organizations.

With these huge amounts at stake, all sales decisions must be made very carefully. Yet in company after company, sales management is permitted to make decisions that have a significant cost and profit impact without really thinking through the market and economic consequences. Here are several examples of the kinds of decisions that are frequently made without sufficient thought being given to the economic implications:

Whether and where to add a new salesperson or a new sales or branch office.

Whether to engage in a greater or lesser degree of sales specialization.

Whether to sell directly or through agents, dealers, or distributors.

Whether a price concession should be granted to get more volume.

Whether certain customer demands (quick delivery, small orders, and customization) should be met.

Whether certain sales calls are productive.

Whether certain accounts are most or least profitable.

These considerations and others like them clearly have major cost and profit implications. For example, adding people or sales branch offices without ensuring an economic

## WHEN IS A SALES FORCE TOO LARGE?

In the late 1960s, Addressograph-Multigraph Corporation was a supplier of office equipment and charge card impressors. The company's sales organization of several hundred representatives was structured around more than 60 district sales offices throughout the United States. A routine economic analysis of the company's sales costs and productivity revealed several important factors.

Addressograph-Multigraph had at least 20 more district sales offices than its major competitors.

The average sales revenue generated by each salesperson was significantly lower than its competitors.

The total cost of the sales force as a percentage of sales was 2 to 3 percent higher than its competitors.

Over 200 salespeople did not appear to be generating sufficient revenue to cover the cost of maintaining them in the field.

When made aware of these facts, management replied that the sales force had always been a major strength of Addressograph-Multigraph and it would be criminal to think in terms of scaling it back. Shortly thereafter, the company encountered serious financial difficulty, and financial analysts who followed the company attributed many of its problems to higher selling and administrative costs.

payoff from incremental volume can easily lead to sales costs that are way out of line (see the box). Similarly, acceding to customer demands for unusual delivery schedules, small-order lots, or custom work without a clear fix on the economics can easily chew into the profit structure of the business. Deciding to grant some kind of price concession to pick up "plus business" without really evaluating the cost-revenue tradeoff can quickly lead to an untenable profit structure.

We are not suggesting that sales management decisions like these can be made by numbers alone. In today's fast-moving, competitive environment, none of these issues has one sure answer. Nor are we suggesting that sales executives be financial experts. However, all these considerations can be brought into much sharper focus through a few fundamental economic analyses that any controller's staff can make very easily. For example, Exhibit 10-1 shows simple economic analyses that were used in one company to determine the net contribution required to support the acceptance of an order and the relative profitability of accounts. Making these analyses helped management see the economic impact of accepting small orders and calling on marginal accounts. Once these facts became clear, management quickly decided to raise the minimum order level and to stop calling on unproductive accounts. Some volume loss occurred, but this was more than offset by the cost savings from dropping marginal accounts. More important, the move freed a lot of sales time that could then be focused on developing more profitable business.

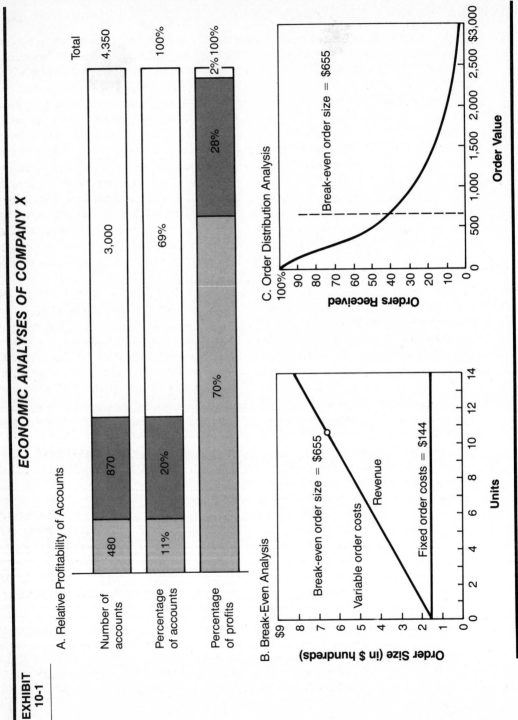

EXHIBIT
10-1

ECONOMIC ANALYSES OF COMPANY X

A. Relative Profitability of Accounts

|  | | | Total |
|---|---|---|---|
| Number of accounts | 480 | 870 | 3,000 | 4,350 |
| Percentage of accounts | 11% | 20% | 69% | 100% |
| Percentage of profits | 70% | 28% | 2% | 100% |

B. Break-Even Analysis

Order Size (in $ hundreds)

Break-even order size = $655
Variable order costs
Revenue
Fixed order costs = $144

Units

C. Order Distribution Analysis

Orders Received

Break-even order size = $655

Order Value

Source: B. Charles Ames, "Marketing Planning for Industrial Products," Harvard Business Review, September–October 1968.

Some sales managers say that although these calculations can of course be made, differences in the mix of sales from salesperson to salesperson or changes in the mix or margins over time render them useless as a measuring device. Others say they have too many products or too many accounts to even think about attempting to deal with them in terms of their individual profitability. The contention that the account list or product line is too long to permit analysis for relative profitability is easily refuted. If many products or accounts are involved, they can always be grouped according to their profitability and dealt with as classes of accounts or products instead of on an individual basis. The argument on differences or changes in mix or margins has some validity, since variation does add complications. But when one thinks of the amount of profit that can be dissipated if the economics are not clear, it makes no sense not to commit the time and effort required to work around the complications.

Still others argue that even though these kinds of economic analysis might be made, they really cannot be put to use. They maintain that most salespeople and many sales managers are not responsible enough to handle this information with discretion, and that they might unwittingly let it get into competitors' hands. This argument is nothing more than an excuse. If management does not want the salespeople to know actual cost and profit figures, it can easily have them coded in a way that gives a general picture of the margin structure on different items, yet preserves the confidentiality of the information. The salesperson still has a much better basis for concentrating on business that will generate the most profit dollars than if he or she is flying blind.

The key in making and using economic analyses is to recognize their limitations. They should be regarded neither as substitutes for managerial judgment nor as hard-and-fast rules that crank out answers. Rather, they are guidelines that provide sales management with a much better basis for making many fundamental decisions that affect the ability of the sales force to be productive, to compete effectively in the marketplace, and to serve as the marketing arm it should be. If sales management, in making its case for adding staff or seeking a "low ball" price to get a certain piece of business, is allowed to "fire from the hip" instead of relying on solid economic calculations, an insidious process is started that eventually undermines its image and effectiveness. When this kind of image is developed, it is virtually impossible for the sales staff, or any members of the sales organization, to make a contribution to the marketing effort.

# DEFINE AND ARTICULATE THE STEPS NECESSARY FOR A SUCCESSFUL SELLING JOB

In today's industrial climate, the sales job is a great deal more complex than simply selling the product. Management expects the salespeople to build a proprietary position with key customers, to provide market feedback, and to bolster profits by enriching the sales mix.

Rarely, however, does management give salespeople any explicit instructions on how they should accomplish these objectives. Usually, salespeople are given a quota, along with a pep talk, and told to "get out there and sell." This is not very helpful to the typical salesperson, who is constantly faced with a choice of how to allocate time among various products, customers, users, or other contacts that could influence the sale. Nor does it help the person to plan the specific actions he or she should take when the priorities have been decided.

Many sales executives are likely to take comfort in the thought that their training programs are designed to tell salespeople all they need to know to do their jobs. But most programs focus almost entirely on fundamental selling approaches, such as how to tell the product story, combat customer objections, refute competitor claims, pique customer interest, and close the sale. This kind of training is useful, of course; every salesperson must know the basics before he or she can make an effective sales call. But such knowledge alone is not sufficient in most cases to help salespeople do an outstanding job. To be in a position to accomplish that, they must have guidelines to help them decide such things as these:

> Which activities (identifying potential applications, telling the product story, generating or following up on bid inquiries, preparing proposals) are the key to selling success, and the standards of performance in each of these activities.

> What selling strategy (emphasis on cost savings, product reliability, product performance features, ease of operation) to use with various customers and products to take the emphasis off price as the dominant buying consideration.

> How to divide their time between servicing existing accounts and prospecting for new ones.

> How much emphasis to place on new product introduction, and which applications represent the best targets.

One could argue that any salesperson worth his or her salt should be able to figure these things out. But a recent confidential survey on sales effectiveness shows that only about a third of the typical sales force has demonstrated the capability to do this, and two-thirds flounder badly without adequate management direction. Thus, we submit that any management failing to provide the kind of training and selling guidelines that give salespeople the answers to the kinds of questions we have raised cuts sharply into the competitive effectiveness and productivity of its sales force (see the box, page 211). Defining the salesperson's job is not as easy as it might seem; however, if the job is not defined, management may find that its people are wasting their time or—even worse—working at cross-purposes with the company's marketing objectives. To avoid this possibility, the job for any sales force—regardless of its size or the complexity of its product line—should be defined with sufficient specificity so that any representative has a guideline to point him or her in the right direction in any given situation. This is a crucial step in forging the link that ties the sales force directly into the marketing effort.

## PROVIDE CAPABLE, FULL-TIME FIRST-LEVEL SUPERVISION

Most sales executives agree that strong first-line sales supervision is a key ingredient in building an outstanding selling organization. The reason for this is clear. The sales force is typically made up of a collection of people with widely diverse backgrounds, experience

## HOW NOT TO USE A SALES STAFF: THREE CASES

As you can see, failing to provide specific direction to a sales force is analogous to a quarterback's giving mixed signals to his team.

Case 1: Management knew that selling a certain mix was essential to the company's profit structure, but the salespeople were not advised specifically about how much of each product they should sell to help optimize the mix. As a result, many salespeople had the frustrating experience of not being able to get reasonable delivery commitments on orders they had worked hard to get because manufacturing was locked into a production plan that did not have room for the products they had sold.

Case 2: Although management knew that opening new accounts was more profitable than servicing existing ones, no one had bothered to tell the salespeople how much of their time was to be spent on new account development. Since breaking new ground is always a more difficult task than staying in friendly territory, most of them spent very little time on this activity.

Case 3: Management decided (as many companies in many industries are doing today) that the salespeople should try to sell a total system in certain situations, rather than individual components. The idea was fine, but management made no effort to define the situations where systems selling was appropriate, or to provide training for this more complex selling job. Not surprisingly, many of the sales representatives never even tried to sell systems; and when management made its disappointment clear by suggesting that the salespeople lacked the basic intelligence to do the job, turnover increased sharply and morale took a nosedive.

levels, and perceptions, and often they are separated from headquarters by thousands of miles. The first-line supervisor is the only manager physically close enough to them to direct their day-to-day efforts, coach them in the company's sales approach for various products and markets, and help them resolve problems in light of the company's marketing objectives and local market conditions. But although most sales executives agree with the idea that providing strong first-level supervision in the field is essential, many have not taken steps to ensure that it exists in actual practice. All too frequently, the people they are relying on to provide first-level supervision simply do not or cannot perform as they should. Let's see why.

## Conflicting Demands

In some cases, the performance of first-line supervisors falls short because their job is structured so that they have a supervisory title in name only. They are really supersalespeople or bureaucratic administrators, with the bulk of their effort focused on direct selling activities or paperwork. One company, for example, relied on its branch sales managers to handle the first-level supervisory role. Each manager was expected not only to watch over three or four salespeople, but to take on a sales territory of his or her own as well. The results were not at all what management expected. The branch managers spent the great bulk of their time in selling and developing their own territories, and thus provided little real supervision for their salespeople. Although their individual sales records were satisfactory, overall sales were below management's expectations. This should not have been surprising, for whenever salespeople must choose between doing the sales job that is second nature to them and carrying out the difficult tasks inherent in any managerial role, they tend to take the easiest path. Our experience shows that most people who have this combined sales-supervisory role quite naturally and honestly get so deeply involved in their own direct selling activities that they have little time for the coaching, training, and follow-up responsibilities that are the heart of the supervisor's job.

This dual-role approach to the first-line supervisory job may well be a practical necessity in outlying areas where a full-time supervisor cannot be economically justified. But in far too many cases the approach is followed throughout the sales organization. This is dead wrong. We are not suggesting that it is totally inappropriate for a sales manager to have any direct sales or account responsibility; we are saying that this responsibility must be strictly limited. Whenever a first-line supervisor has a direct sales responsibility that places major demands on his or her time, the odds are stacked against the organization having truly effective first-level supervision.

## Inadequate Training

In other cases, first-line supervisors fail to perform well because they do not know what the supervisory role is or how it should be carried out. In fairness, this is frequently not their fault, for surprisingly few companies provide any kind of training program to help new supervisors learn how to carry out their responsibilities. Most first-line supervisors are in their first managerial position, which they have typically earned by doing a superior selling job. Shifting their sights from managing their own time to managing the time and coaching the selling efforts of others represents a quantum jump in responsibility few people can accomplish without help. Most need assistance in learning how to carry out the sales management process that represents the heart of their job. In particular, they need to be shown:

How to determine which people or sales problems deserve the most time and attention.

How to make territory and/or market analyses, and how to determine market potential.

How to help salespeople plan their time and selling activities so they can be most productive.

How to evaluate the performance of their salespeople and to identify training and development needs.

How to carry out the on-the-job training and coaching activities necessary to improve selling performance.

Unless most first-line supervisors are taught how to do these things, they will drift into a pattern of operation that keeps them busy—but not on the right things. As a result, they never really provide the quality of supervision they should. In some cases, former star salespeople who can never make the transition to manager, no matter how much training is provided, are allowed to stay in supervisory positions far too long. Management often finds it difficult to face up to the fact that this situation exists, or to take the necessary corrective action once it is recognized.

Discussions with a number of sales and marketing executives indicate that this situation is more common than one would think. The consequences, of course, go beyond the reduced effectiveness of the sales force. Eventually, the management career path becomes clogged with people who are going nowhere. Understandably, this frustrates outstanding younger salespeople who are looking for an early promotion and leads to a high turnover of people who should not be lost. This situation starts a vicious circle that results in mediocrity at the supervisory level and ineffective training and direction for the sales force.

## Excessive Paperwork

A further problem that cuts into the effectiveness of first-level supervisors is the improper use of daily call reports. In many companies, the daily call report is sacred because it gives management a feeling that it knows what is going on. More likely, all management has is a massive paper flow that generates phony data. These are harsh words, but they are true. We know of company after company that looked to its call reporting system as a reliable means of control. In actual fact, however, the salespeople were simply going through the motions in "filling out their forms" and doing as they pleased in terms of the way they spent their time. Sales personnel for a large rubber company used to joke about the fact that they would meet at a local tavern late every Friday afternoon to fill out their call and trip reports. When anyone was stuck on what to put down to cover a block of time, others were quick to pass on ideas. The joke was that the ideas for fictitious calls or trips often became outlandish after a couple rounds of beer. It didn't really make any difference what the salespeople put on the reports, however, since no one in management followed up; in fact, most of the reports were not even read.

Clearly, some form of planning and control system is essential in every sales organization, but it should be designed around a weekly or monthly cycle to minimize the paperwork involved. And it should not be so form-oriented that it creates a burden for either the salesperson or the supervisor. Moreover, the supervisor must be taught to use this system as a tool for working with and providing active direction for salespeople. Whatever form this system takes, management must not allow it to degenerate into a paper-shuffling exercise that encourages the supervisor to function as a desk-top administrator.

Four ingredients are required to ensure strong first-level supervision:

1. The sales organization must be structured so that a capable, full-time supervisor exists for every eight to twelve salespeople. There may be exceptions to this ratio, but it is a good general rule to follow. Going much beyond twelve people starts to stretch the span of control; moving below eight pushes the supervisory costs out of line and, more important, creates a make-work situation for the supervisor.

2. Provision must be made to ensure that each supervisor has the proper training and tools to do the job.
3. Each supervisor should spend the bulk (75 percent or more) of his or her time in face-to-face work with salespeople to provide the on-the-job coaching and direction that is needed.
4. Senior sales management must be very tough-minded in evaluating supervisory performance and in weeding out supervisors who perform below expectations or who lack the capability to take on additional management responsibility.

## USE THE COMPENSATION PLAN AS A MANAGEMENT TOOL

No matter how strong or effective sales supervision is, all salespeople are on their own most of the time in deciding which accounts to call on, which products or applications to emphasize, or even whether or not to make another call. So it is essential to design and administer the sales compensation plan to motivate them to concentrate on activities that will contribute most to the achievement of marketing objectives. This sounds so fundamental the reader may wonder why it is included in this discussion. Obviously, no one can expect the sales force to function as a marketing arm unless the compensation system is designed and administered in a way that motivates people toward the accomplishment of marketing objectives. Nevertheless, in a great many cases the system is actually in conflict with marketing objectives.

In some cases, the levels of compensation are simply too low to attract and retain the caliber of people and to build the kind of sales force essential for marketing success. Exhibit 10-2, which shows the compensation opportunities in two sales organizations that competed head to head in the marketplace, brings this point sharply into focus. Comparison of the salary levels for various sales positions and the average time required to reach these positions shows clearly that company B offers a much more attractive career opportunity. Little wonder that company A's force was regarded as substantially inferior by many major customers. And since these major customers accounted for the bulk of the business, it is clear that company A had very little chance of doing the job it should in the marketplace.

As a matter of fact, many incentive arrangements actually work at cross-purposes to what management is trying to do. For example, many companies still pay salespeople strictly on the basis of volume, even though selling a certain product mix, or opening new accounts, or developing certain end-use markets is an equally or even more important objective in terms of ultimate success in the marketplace. Just think of this arrangement for a moment. Who in his or her right mind would spend time on longer-term sales development activities when the payoff is for orders written today? Some commission arrangements encourage salespeople to "skim the cream" from the market by concentrating on quick volume from smaller accounts, when the emphasis should be on developing the potential in larger accounts. Several salespeople from one company that sold powered hand tools freely admitted they set a daily volume quota for themselves that would yield

EXHIBIT
10-2

## AVERAGE COMPENSATION LEVELS OF TWO COMPETING SALES ORGANIZATIONS

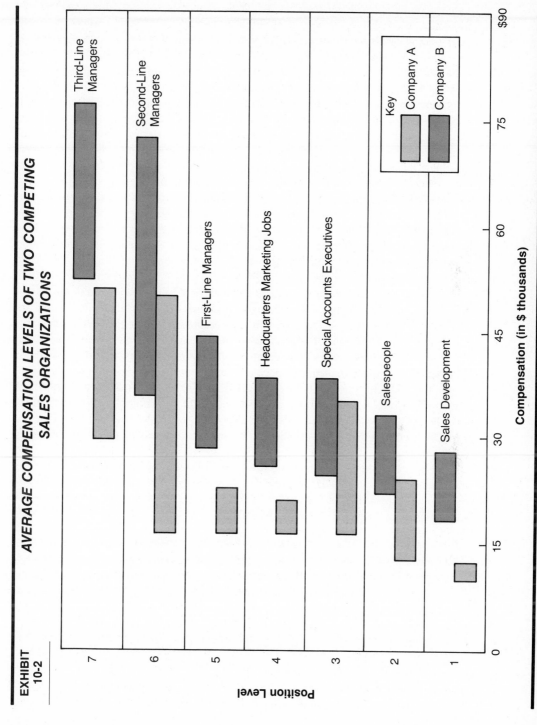

*Source:* B. Charles Ames, "Marketing Planning for Industrial Marketing," *Harvard Business Review,* September–October 1968.

enough commission to meet their needs. They frequently bypassed high-potential accounts that required development in preference to small, "sure thing" orders.

Other compensation systems are designed in such a way that they reward seniority rather than performance. This arrangement has a double-barreled effect; senior people tend to relax their efforts, and young, aggressive people are frustrated. One company that sold in the electrical equipment market was a classic example of this situation. Incentive payments were made out of a group bonus pot, and each person's award was based on a percentage of his or her salary. Since no adjustment was made to reflect individual performance and since senior people tended to have higher salaries, many hard-working younger people became discouraged and left. Equally important, when management looked into the situation, it found that many of the senior salespeople were relying on the younger people to build up the pot and thus were not pulling their own weight.

It is hard to see how any company could allow situations like these to develop, but they are all too common. Generally, one of the following reasons is at the heart of the problem. In many cases, sales executives are so concerned with the idea of keeping their compensation plan simple they fail to take into account key variables that affect performance. It is not at all uncommon to hear executives say something like this: "We know that our sales compensation plan is not right, but it is simple, and we don't have any difficulty getting the salespeople to understand and believe it." This holdover attitude that the sales force is a collection of not-too-intelligent drummers is not justifiable in this day and age. The typical industrial salesperson in today's complex technological environment has a college degree or the equivalent, and many have advanced degrees. Certainly, people of this caliber can cope with a compensation system that involves several variables. In still other cases, executives feel that once a system is in place, it should not be changed because the staff will become confused or suspicious. Of course, making any midstream changes that would be unfair to the salespeople should be avoided at all costs. But the fact is that marketing objectives do change frequently, and unless the compensation system is adjusted to reflect these changes, it is certain to drift out of phase with the company's goals.

As we have indicated, the paramount need is to tailor the compensation system to meet the particular requirements of the situation at a given point in time. There is no way to prescribe a compensation plan that is right for everyone. However, every compensation system should be designed and administered to:

Ensure a balanced selling job by paying off for new account openings, new applications, new product introductions, and other sales development activities essential to strengthen the company's short- and long-term market position.

Provide an attractive entry level for new people so there is adequate raw material to build the kind of organization necessary to achieve marketing objectives.

Provide an especially attractive earnings opportunity for career salespeople so there is a cadre of highly skilled, trained, and motivated people to serve as the cutting edge of the marketing effort.

Draw a sharp distinction in the rewards for average and outstanding salespeople, and penalize below-average performers severely.

The successful compensation plan is one designed and administered to help management achieve these four objectives. If these objectives are not accomplished, the plan is of little value, no matter how complex or sophisticated it might be.

# STRIVE FOR A SHARP END-USER FOCUS

Industrial products are typically sold to a number of user groups, each of which has particular application requirements. This diversity means that the requirements of each market or user segment must be understood and dealt with individually to ensure a successful sales and marketing effort. All-purpose products or buckshot approaches to the marketplace simply will not work in a world of increasing specialization. Industrial companies do not have access to market information sources like Nielsen, SAMI, and others that are available to guide product and market planning efforts in consumer goods. And it is not practical for most industrial companies to structure market tests as consumer goods companies do to evaluate the needs, likes, and dislikes of different user groups. Industrial management must gear its salespeople to provide this kind of information or do without.

Achieving this end-user understanding is, in many respects, the most important activity the industrial salesperson performs. The intelligence he or she develops about the end user's needs, business patterns, economics, and so on, are the foundation of future product and market plans. To carry out this activity, the sales force must be set up and trained to provide organized feedback on such questions as these:

How does the product fit into the end user's operation, fill a need, and compare with competitive offerings?

What features of the product are really important in the end user's mind?

What current or potential developments in the end user's business could change the product's cost or design requirements?

What changes in the end user's operation or the competitive environment could affect the customer's business, and how could these changes, in turn, affect selling requirements or demand for the product?

Management must do more than simply insist that the salespeople provide end-user feedback information; it must take three important actions.

First, organize the sales force to give each person a chance to achieve an understanding of what is going on at the end-user level. Typically, some degree of specialization by market or application is required so the person has a chance to learn about specific end uses in depth. Just how much specialization is required boils down to an economic trade-off between the added costs of specialization and the payoff anticipated. Achieving the appropriate degree of specialization may require restructuring the entire force around end-use markets or applications. Frequently, however, the economics prohibit this kind of a move. In these situations, a selected group of salespeople may be assigned as full- or part-time specialists to cover the most important user and application segments.

Second, install a formal system for distilling and interpreting the information received from salespeople so it can make intelligent judgments. Time after time we have heard salespeople say: "I send the market information in to headquarters, but nobody ever listens to me or believes what I say." This does not have to happen very often or very long before the person concludes, "Why bother?" Companies that do, in fact, regard and use the sales force as their eyes and ears in the marketplace have designed their planning process so that the collection and distillation of field sales intelligence is an important part of it. This not only ensures that plans are developed in the light of real-life market conditions, but also has the positive effect of showing the salespeople just how important their feedback is. With this encouragement, their natural inclination will be to try to do an even better job of sharpening their end-user focus.

Third, ensure that the company's value system reflects the importance management places on a clear perspective on end-user needs. This may be manifested in a compensation structure that pays a premium for developing business in certain end-user groups or for certain applications. Then again, it may simply show up in the way management compliments those who do a good job—or, more important, chastises those who do not. How it is done is an individual matter, and no one approach is necessarily better than another. Whatever the approach, however, management must support its point of view with actions as well as words, or the salespeople will never be convinced that they should make any extra effort to understand what is really going on at the end-user level.

# CARVE OUT A STRONG MARKETING ROLE FOR SALES MANAGEMENT

The top sales management of any industrial company—that is, the national sales chief and subordinates who typically have responsibility for sales performance in the largest geographic divisions—have an important role in the marketing-planning process. Their participation is essential to ensure that the company's product and market plans reflect customers' changing needs. It is also essential to gain the wholehearted commitment of sales management to the successful execution of the company's product-market plan. If the salespeople are enthusiastic about the plan and genuinely believe they can sell the volume and mix that is expected, they will do a good job. If they feel the expectations are unrealistic, or that unfair sales goals have been imposed on them, the plan will not be successful, no matter how brilliant it may be. It is not unusual for salespeople and field supervisors to charge: "Our sales quotas have nothing to do with rhyme, reason, or the marketplace. They are just 10 to 15 percent higher than last year." With this feeling, how can they be expected to do all the hard work that is necessary to achieve demanding sales targets?

Considering the importance of sales performance to the success of product-market plans, it is only logical to give top sales managers a voice in their development. What they should be doing is this:

Closing the feedback loop from the field by distilling and interpreting information on local market conditions and competitor moves.

## TURNING A BAD SITUATION AROUND

Top executives of a large company serving the building products field were concerned over a general deterioration in the company's marketing effectiveness. Share position in traditional markets was slipping badly, and important new markets were emerging in which the company had no position at all. The company's product edge had been lost, and new products were not coming along as they should. Finally, sales costs were increasing steadily while productivity (average sales per salesperson) was trending downward. In short, the current marketing situation was bad, and the outlook worse.

In recognition of the gravity of the situation, the marketing vice president called in his product managers and key sales managers for an emergency planning session. Including sales management in the planning session was more of an afterthought than anything else, since planning had traditionally been a headquarters marketing function, while sales had responsibility for execution. To the marketing executive's surprise, the most imaginative and effective ideas came from the sales managers. They recommended product modifications that could be made quickly, well before new products could become available to meet important needs in emerging markets. In addition, they suggested dropping a collection of low-volume products so that the sales force could be cut back, territories enlarged, and overall productivity increased. And they proposed a volume discount plan that would provide the basis for recapturing business which had been lost with large customers while still preserving the integrity of the company's pricing structure. The marketing vice president and the product managers were so impressed with the contributions made by the sales managers that they made it a regular practice to include them in planning sessions from that point on.

Participating in discussions with other functional managers about various strategic options for building the business.

Helping to select the most promising options, and considering the commitments and programs necessary for each alternative.

Agreeing on realistic volume and share of market targets under various options, and helping to decide which options are most attractive.

By having its top sales executives function in this way, a company can ensure that the sales force does in fact serve as a marketing arm, instead of as an independent sales and distribution system. The box above gives a good example.

## SUMMARY

Clearly, a host of things needs to be done to build an outstanding sales organization. Here, we have emphasized six principles that cause the sales force to function as a strong marketing arm.

Basing sales decisions on economic analysis

is necessary to ensure that sales productivity keeps pace with increasing selling costs. Defining essential selling activities gives the salesperson the platform of understanding he or she needs to view the job as more than simply selling the product at any price. Providing appropriate supervision and compensation are the mechanisms for ensuring the sales capability and focus necessary to accomplish marketing objectives, and for adjusting that focus as priorities change. Linking the planning and execution arms of the marketing department and ensuring that a firsthand understanding of market needs and opportunities is factored into product-market planning make it possible to achieve overall company objectives.

None of these principles is difficult, but in many cases implementation requires overcoming traditional ideas and methods, reeducation of managers and salespeople, and possibly even personnel changes. And it always requires a great deal of management thought and attention. However, all this effort is clearly worthwhile, for failure to manage the sales force according to these principles can cost any company a fortune in excessive selling costs and lost market opportunities. Many successful industrial companies have taken a hard look at their selling effort and made the changes necessary to build these six principles into their sales operation. In doing so, they converted a volume-conscious sales force into a team that followed a cost- and profit-conscious approach to developing the company's sales position in every present and potential market. This, in turn, has given these companies clout in the marketplace that has significantly strengthened their competitive position and ultimately accelerated profit growth.

## REVIEW QUESTIONS

1. Why is an outstanding sales force critical for industrial marketing success?
2. What factors help in considering the sales force as a for-profit business unit?
3. What customer or market-based facts should be an essential part of sales training?
4. Why is the first level of sales management so important?
5. How should sales compensation be a top management tool in the industrial firm?
6. How does the concept of market segmentation direct sales efforts and provide a focus on feedback from customer groups?
7. How can sales managers make contributions to short- and medium-range business plans?

# 11

# Marketing with Distributor Partners

Producer-Distributor
Relationships
Managing the Distribution
Network
  The Distribution Selling
  Decision
  Recognizing Market
  Differences
  Matching Distributors to
  Segments
  Assigning Distributor
  Territories
  Developing Distributor
  Policies
  Providing Training and
  Support
  Turnover and Yearly ROI
  Distributor Councils
  Assigning Responsibility
  for Distributor
  Development
Evaluating Distributor
Performance
Selecting New Distributors
Multidivision Products
Summary
Review Questions

John Rogers was the newest and youngest district sales manager for one of the country's largest standard and special purpose fastener companies. He had joined the company four years earlier as a distributor sales representative on the West Coast. Because he had done an exceptional job of helping his distributor accounts to build their business, he was promoted to a district manager job much earlier in his career than most of his counterparts.

After spending a few weeks evaluating his district's sales and distributor operations, he prepared a report to his boss, one of four regional sales managers, and sent a copy to the manager of distributor development at the headquarters office. The thrust of his report featured three points:

1. There are too many weak or poor-performing distributors in this district. Many of them have been with us for years, and the principals are good friends with many of our senior managers. Nevertheless, we need to cut back on the number of distributors we have and make sure those that remain have both the financial strength and the ambition to do the job we want.
2. Our policy of selling only through distribution is killing us with our major accounts. We are losing a lot of business to our competitors, who are willing to sell direct at a price much closer to our distributors' cost. These are big-volume accounts, and they simply do not want to pay a price that includes a distributor profit.
3. We need to set up some arrangement that enables our most aggressive distributors to earn price breaks on large-volume orders. It doesn't make sense for a distributor that buys in truckload quantities to pay the same price for a product as distributors that buy in broken lot quantities to fill particular orders. The smart distributors know this and won't work with us unless we come up with some kind of volume break program that makes sense.

The regional manager found the memo very disturbing. He had worked with the distributors in that district for nearly 30 years. He knew some of them were not as aggressive as they should be, but they were loyal to the company and they had made a real contribution during the company's initial years. He was even more disturbed about the idea of selling direct. The company's policy had always been to sell exclusively through distribution. He couldn't imagine trying to explain a shift in this policy to the distributors. He thought, however, that the last point had some merit. He and other senior sales managers had talked many times about the advisability of developing a pricing structure that allowed a better price for large quantity orders, but again they were concerned about offending some of the smaller old-time distributors that were not large enough to take advantage of quantity offerings.

As he picked up the telephone to talk to John about the memo, the manager couldn't help but remember that he had been opposed to appointing anyone to a district manager's job with such limited experience. He had found it was much easier to work with people who had been around for awhile and better understood the company's business.

Is the problem really the "new broom" syndrome?

What positive results may come from taking the proposal seriously, even though the proposal is ultimately rejected?

What are some obvious advantages of using distributors?

What are some alternative ways to reward old distributors' loyalty?

A significant and growing[1] percentage of the GNP every year is marketed through independent distributors or dealers. Industrial giants, including 3M, Caterpillar, Pfizer, and Mead Paper, market a major portion of their yearly sales volume through this channel. To counter competition from Japanese photocopy machine manufacturers, both IBM and Xerox named independent distributors to market lower-priced copiers and typewriters.[2] The distributor selling any industrial product, whether it is a machine, a pharmaceutical, a chemical, or a repair part, is a major avenue through which large, medium-size, and smaller producers serve key markets. The reasons are clear. The cost to the producer of making direct calls frequently becomes prohibitive in relation to the price of the product the customers buy. Furthermore, if customers reorder or repair the item, they often want rapid delivery, which is usually best provided by a local distributor or dealer that buys and maintains a local stock of products to sell to customers.

In the aftermarket or MRO market, the industrial distributor is often a vital link between producer and user. When a bearing or a hydraulic cylinder needs to be repaired, the user usually wants the product in a hurry. Availability and rapid service are critical and are usually best provided by a local distributor with the appropriate inventory (see the box). For more technically complex customer needs, the industrial distributor will be

---

## WHY CATERPILLAR USES DISTRIBUTORS

Due to the importance of rapid repair, parts delivery, and field services in the construction equipment industry, Caterpillar believes local distributors can best serve key customers. Caterpillar is not just selling machinery; it sees itself as marketing equipment and a parts-service package. The local distributor provides the basis for achieving maximum uptime or minimum downtime for very expensive machines. When a $200,000 machine is down because of a $50 part, every hour represents a significant loss of money to the user. To minimize downtime and the resulting financial loss to customers, local Caterpillar distributors carry parts for all Caterpillar equipment—including parts for equipment Caterpillar hasn't manufactured for the last 30 years.

When a Caterpillar road grader was an integral part of a road resurfacing crew in the Arizona desert, the breakdown of the grader idled four other pieces of road building equipment, seven asphalt trucks, and twenty workers. The local Caterpillar dealer sent a radio dispatched repair unit to the field with the appropriate parts for that model road grader. The 2.5 hour downtime could have been days had there not been a local distributor with the right parts in its inventory ready to provide prompt service.

---

[1]"36th Annual Survey of Distributor Operations," *Industrial Distribution,* July 1982, p. 37.
[2]"IBM Expands Outside Its Sales Channels, Names Concerns to Distribute Two Products," *The Wall Street Journal,* October 7, 1981, p. 2.

called to help solve specific problems or to install an item. Technical service, or "engineering in the field," is vital to repeat purchases for many industrial products. These service levels are sometimes quite intangible in the short term, but they often pay big long-term dividends. Exhibit 11-1 shows the important intermediate role between producers and users played by industrial distributors. Marketing through a distributor can save the user time and money in the item's purchase price. Industrial distributors can reduce the producer's selling cost and thereby reduce the selling price of the product to users. So paying the distributor a profit is not the same as paying a "double profit." If the functions performed by the distributor are shifted, they must be performed and paid for by the producer or the user. When distributors perform these functions effectively and customers benefit, the distributors are entitled to a profit for their efforts.

**EXHIBIT
11-1**

### LINKING PRODUCERS TO USERS

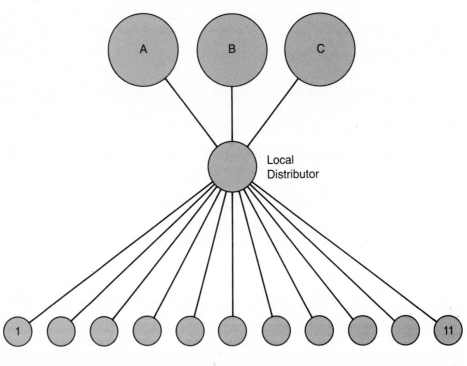

# PRODUCER-DISTRIBUTOR RELATIONSHIPS

Most industrial producers use distributors to achieve some of their sales and marketing objectives. But the marketing of products through distributors is frequently badly done, and the results are often poor for both producers and distributors. Far too many industrial firms see the distributor as merely an intermediary for pushing products through and are continually disappointed with this means of serving customers. The following statement by a marketing manager with a major chemical company captures the essence of this all too common problem:

> Since I've taken over this job, I've experienced a lot of difficulty in putting together an acceptable distribution system. Traditionally, our products have been sold direct to end users. This worked well when all of our customers were large volume purchasers. Within the last ten years, there's been a dramatic increase in the number of small accounts using the product, causing our firm to alter its strategy and sell through distributors. Sure, the prospects of added sales are fantastic, but listen to some of the problems we face: The discount system is falling apart because distributors are "giving away" portions of their discounts in the form of lower prices to gain business. Unfortunately, some distributors are even being forced into bankruptcy; our distributors on the West Coast are not pushing the products; in the Cleveland area, distributors are not utilizing our co-op funds properly; although we have five distributors in Chicago, their sales are far below a market potential prediction; perhaps more distributors are needed there; and our distributor in northern New Jersey won't tell us who he's selling our products to. Top management of our division feels that these difficulties can be eliminated through a return to aggressive direct sales. I'm not so sure we can make any money that way with these smaller accounts.[3]

Many industrial producers treat their distributors as stepchildren and fail to get the cooperation they need to capitalize on the distributors' sales and profit potential when large amounts of business are at stake. The same producers often use bullying or brinksmanship tactics to achieve their goals without regard for the distributor's needs. The result is a "relationship" that is far from a partnership. Other producers go to the other extreme and become totally dependent on what distributors do or don't do in the marketplace. This inevitably results in little or no knowledge of end-use customers and their changing requirements, and frequently places the producer at a serious competitive disadvantage.

Many distributor networks have been put together on a random basis that results in poor or no coverage in some markets and overlapping coverage in others. In both situations there are nearly always too many marginal distributors. The comment of a progressive cutting tool distributor in southern California shows the problems that can result from this kind of approach:

[3]James A. Narus, "The development of a marketing channel selection process model and its demonstration in an industrial chemicals business and in an electronic components business," unpublished doctoral dissertation, Syracuse University, 1981.

They signed up anybody and anywhere in Los Angeles for so long that we all felt they were not really serious about distributors. I get slow inventory turns from their line and if the large margin wasn't there, I'd drop them tomorrow.

One of the largest U.S. industrial corporations surveyed its marketing and sales executives to identify the most common problems encountered with their distributors. The survey was completed by 188 marketing and sales personnel in the firm's 24 operating divisions. The 14 most frequently reported problems with distributors are shown in Table 11.1. A key reason for all these problems is that the independent distributor is generally a small entrepreneur. The independent industrial distributor will work *with* a producer and follow its lead if properly coached. However, the distributor will never work *for* the producer in a subordinate relationship. The industrial distributor is not typically an "organization person." In fact, the personality and independence of the distributor is often in direct contrast to the producer's tendency to be more bureaucratic.

It is useful to examine the question of the distributor's independence more carefully, since it is such an important factor in the producer-distributor relationship. Although producers and distributors would seem to have the same objectives in terms of achieving sales and market share, their priorities are often different and even incompatible. To start with, the distributor is typically dealing with its own money and incurs all the risk, whereas the producer has stockholders, so the risk is syndicated. The cost-profit structures of producers and distributors are typically quite different. The producer generally has a relatively high capital and fixed-cost base and a longer-term business horizon. It is interested in building volume, even at lower margins, to gain profit leverage after covering its fixed costs. The distributor's operation, however, is totally different. The distributor operates a buy-sell business with low fixed capital cost and is interested in maximizing profit on each dollar of sales over as short a time period as possible. These economic

| TABLE 11.1 | *PROBLEMS WITH DISTRIBUTORS* |
|---|---|

1. Want all customers to come to them.
2. Don't provide us with information about who and where "their" customers are.
3. Are not good at problem solving—assistance with customers and our products.
4. Don't effectively use our factory personnel or territory managers.
5. Don't emphasize our lines enough.
6. Don't follow our suggested pricing.
7. Primarily sell on price, not the product's value.
8. Don't carry appropriate inventory levels to serve customers rapidly.
9. Don't stress our brand name.
10. Don't utilize promotional materials.
11. Have no succession plans.
12. Are very independent business people.
13. Can't or won't meet our territory goals.
14. Have objectives different from ours.

differences help explain the different business orientation and value system that make the whole concept of working with distributor partners a lot easier to talk about than accomplish.

The successful distributor can afford to be independent. He or she can probably secure a competitive line if he or she is threatened or sees the possibility of a better relationship with another producer. But their independence notwithstanding, distributor activities must be managed like any other marketing function. To develop, improve, and continually refine an effective distributor network always involves hard and uncomfortable work, and many sales and marketing executives do not have the will or the personality to do this job. Let's see what it entails.

# MANAGING THE DISTRIBUTION NETWORK

Attention to a few fundamentals is the key to developing and managing an effective distribution network. None of these fundamentals would be difficult to follow in a start-up situation. However, they are very difficult to implement in an established business with a distributor network already in place. Traditional relationships, values, and commitments to ways of doing things are serious roadblocks to thinking through and carrying out the required corrective steps. But because marketing with distributors is so necessary for many industrial firms, all levels of management must be concerned with building and maintaining an effective network. Lack of interest by any level of management and especially by senior management generally means the job will not be done the way it should. The first step, in any case, is to decide whether or not the product should be sold through distributors.

## The Distribution Selling Decision

The industrial producer must decide whether or which of its products fit logically into a distribution channel. Several considerations[4] need to be examined. If any one of the following criteria are not characteristics of the customer or market being served, the product should probably be sold directly by the producer.

RAPID DELIVERY AND SERVICE.   Probably the most important criterion is the need for rapid service, which is often stated in hours rather than weeks or months. If the product is needed immediately due to equipment breakdown or operating supply shortage, the customer needs the item as fast as possible. The driving force behind rapid delivery is also how practical it is to plan the purchase. The cost of downtime for an oil drilling rig is over $100 a minute; the downtime on an automotive engine assembly line is over $100,000 an hour. Minutes can be a matter of life and death when a hospital operating room needs a small piece of surgical tubing or parts for a life-support machine. In all these situations, the greater the downtime, the more costly the situation and the greater the need for prompt delivery and possibly technical service by a local distributor.

[4]James D. Hlavacek and Tommy J. McCuistion, "Industrial Distributors—When, Who and How?" *Harvard Business Review,* March–April 1983, p. 97.

LARGE POTENTIAL CUSTOMER BASE.   If only a handful of customers will ever buy the product, it is unlikely that a distributor will do as satisfactory a job as the direct sales to user approach. Producers often allow custom-tailored products to become distributor items. For example, one company's special gasket products designed for customers' unique requirements were given to distributors to sell. Virtually no new accounts were created. After several years, it became clear that the distributors received repeat orders only from the few customers originally obtained by the producer's salespeople. The broader the customer base with standard requirements, the greater the need for a distributor network.

STOCKABLE PARTS.   Most customer-designed parts, chemicals, or machinery, which are made to order, are easily eliminated as possibilities for distributors. Most of the product line should be able to be stocked and serviced locally. This implies catalog or standard items manufactured in large quantities and sold locally off-the-shelf a few at a time.

QUANTITY OF PURCHASE.   Items selling for a few dollars are the most likely distributor products to be sold off-the-shelf. If the yearly purchase volume of OEMs is large, they are usually not served through a distributor. On the other hand, maintenance, repair, and overhaul replacement parts for the same item are often best sold by the local distributor. For example, bearings are used in tractors, motors, and machines. When they wear out, they need to be replaced in the aftermarket. The small unit value purchase rule also applies to heavy equipment items like construction machinery and trucks. The customer buys one or a few at a time, and is often buying on the basis of later service and parts availability. Repair parts for the original equipment are nearly always of smaller unit value. Frequently the distributor or dealer in machinery and equipment has the larger items on consignment from the manufacturer or has one demonstrator and then orders for each customer from the producer.

CUSTOMER BUYING LEVEL.   The lower in the organization an item is bought, the more likely it will be sold through a distributor. The producer often does not consider at what organization level the large customer will buy the product. The flat organizational structure of an owner-operator business has little or no buying specialization, and therefore buys most frequently from a distributor. Some products, such as aircraft landing gear, are bought directly from the producer by very high levels within the airframe manufacturer; such items seldom become products bought through a distributor network. When designing and producing landing gear for a specific airplane, the supplier needs highly skilled engineering interaction with the customer's design engineers and procurement people. However, other products sold to that same airplane builder, such as o-ring seals or fasteners, are bought through distributors at lower levels in the organization. Here off-the-shelf service is important and the products are standardized. In this situation, the distributor's salespeople may need to know only the size and specification for the item.

## Recognizing Market Differences

Once the producer's target market segments are identified, management must determine the size, growth potential, and requirements for each segment and decide whether to serve that market with distributors or with its own direct sales force. Two producers successfully serving the same market segment with similar products will usually use the same selling approach. If one producer emphasizes the OEM market segment for the product, it will usually sell directly to users. If another producer of a similar product emphasizes the aftermarket segment, it will sell primarily through distributors. Many industrial or technical product producers think first in terms of geographic coverage and then of distinct markets or customer segments. Thinking this way can result in the wrong selling approach and limited sales. The marine and forest product industries, for example, are both located in the Pacific Northwest. But these two market segments generally buy the same product from different types of distributors in the same geographic area. The marine customer buys mostly from a marine supply distributor which stocks special products for customers' needs, speaks their language, and knows marine applications. For example, it is often necessary to have products with technical U.S. Coast Guard approvals for salt-water corrosion resistance. The wood products customers in the same geographic area often require many of the same products as marine customers, but they buy from a distributor that serves the forest products industry. Due to differences in marine and wood products customer needs and the trade languages that are so much a part of each business, customers and distributors in one market in many cases do not know the other exists. There are numerous end-use markets in each major industrial area (mining, railroad, trucking, oil well drilling), and they must be served by distributors set up to talk their language and meet their special needs. Deere, for example, employs different distributors to serve its agriculture and construction equipment market segments. Caterpillar frequently uses different sets of distributors to serve the construction equipment, lift truck, and diesel truck engine markets in the same geographic territory.

The specialized distributor serves and stocks the special needs of these respective markets, whereas a general distributor may not be as effective. If a producer's existing distributors are not able to penetrate the different market segments in the same geographic area, management would be wise to consider different types of distributors to serve different or specialized market segments. If one producer is already successfully penetrating the identified market segment, the second or third producer coming into that market segment should carefully examine what type of distributor the successful first entrant chose.

## Matching Distributors to Segments

There are different types of distributors for reaching and serving distinct market segments. In order to reach and penetrate multiple market segments effectively, it is often necessary for the producer to market through multiple channels. Exhibit 11-2 shows a producer of diesel engines that markets to three general types of markets: governments and municipalities; OEMs; and MRO-replacement markets. The government market (federal, state, and municipality) is often a direct sale because of the buying practices of these organizations. The OEM and MRO aftermarkets require distinctly different channels to serve the respective ultimate users. However, OEM and MRO channels are not always totally separate. As Exhibit 11-2 shows, MRO engine distributors may sell to OEM dealers, ultimate users, and engine rebuilders. As a consequence, the OEM and MRO channels compete.

EXHIBIT
11-2

## MULTIPLE DISTRIBUTION CHANNELS

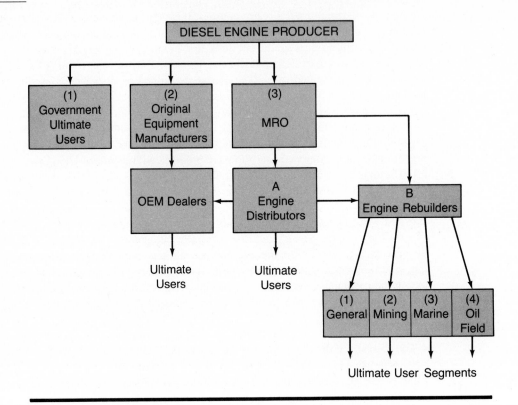

This particular diesel engine producer has further divided MRO engine rebuilders into four segments with distinct distribution channels: (1) general, (2) mining, (3) marine, and (4) oil field. Different marketing programs and distributors might be used to reach each of these subsegments of the aftermarket. In situations where there are multiple and complex channels and competition among a producer's channel members, special care must be exercised when developing strategies and prices for each channel. For analysis and strategy development, it is helpful to develop a scheme like that in Exhibit 11-2. Such schemes also help to isolate competitors, specifiers, and buying patterns in each segment.

### Assigning Distributor Territories

A distributor's suggested territory may range from part of a large city like Chicago to three or four counties in a state. If a distributor's business is based essentially on product lines from one producer, the distributor will typically ask for some protection from other distributors selling in the same area. Some distributors selling more technical products that must be specified or "designed in" will usually want some kind of protection to prevent another distributor in the same geographic area from getting the business after he or she has done all the work. Many distributors will simply not carry a producer's item unless some specific territory is assigned to them. Their investment in space, inventories, and time is simply too great if they do not have the assurance that they will be credited for sales in their area.

Producers, however, should be careful not to assign "exclusive" or "protected" territories in which the distributor is compensated for all sales irrespective of whether it participates in the transactions or contributes to the selling effort. Generally designated territories can be assigned to specific distributors. But the producer should not be trapped into paying a distributor commissions on direct sales to accounts that have the buying power to demand direct sales. Nor should the producer be obliged to pay a double commission on occasional sales made in one distributor's territory by another distributor that has aggressively pursued the business across designated distributor lines.

## Developing Distributor Policies

To avoid problems in working with distributors, all producers should define how they plan to work with those distributors before a distributor agreement is signed. It is essential to state clearly what products the producer wants the distributor to sell, what market segments or customer groups to focus on, and what geographic territory the distributor is expected to penetrate and serve. These ground rules should also spell out inventory requirements and what sales volume of the items the producer expects over time. If these conditions are not spelled out and understood by potential and existing distributors, a lot of time and effort will be wasted, and a lot of profit lost to competitors.

It is important to think through the common areas of potential producer-distributor conflict and then set down in writing specific policies for dealing with these situations that are fair to both parties. These policies should be discussed with all existing and prospective distributors. At a minimum, specific policies should be developed to address the areas of pricing, inventories and returns, sales to large accounts, market coverage, market volume penetration, and ultimate user information. For example, industrial manufacturers should have clearly defined pricing policies that encourage adequate distributor inventory levels. In many cases, the bulk of a distributor's capital is committed to producers' inventories. The supplying producer's pricing practices can enhance, protect, or penalize the market value and profit margins on these inventories. Some enlightened manufacturers have a policy of paying salespeople who call on distributors only for what the distributor sells, and not for what he or she buys. This reduces the tendency to overload the distributor with inventory.

Producers should also develop policies defining how large OEMs and end-use accounts will be served. Will large accounts that have been developed by a distributor ever be taken away from the distributor and sold on a direct basis? If so, when and under what circumstances? Some producers leave the distributor-developed account with the distributor as long as the distributor delivers an acceptable share of the account's business and can profitably serve the account with its normal price structure. This is admittedly a touchy subject, but specific written policies must be developed. Being completely open is the only way to minimize potential conflict and misunderstanding. There should also be specific written policies on the kind of sales information the producer requires from a distributor. Without information from distributors that shows who their customers or users are, or who is buying how much, the producer will not know what amount of penetration, if any, exists in a particular market or account. One successful producer has a policy, which is a condition of being a distributor, that calls for all distributors to report sales to every ultimate user by part number, customer, SIC, where shipped, and where billed. Another producer requires warranty cards to be completed and returned so it can track this same information. This kind of information enables the producer to evaluate distributor performance, set distributor quotas, and provide market direction by market segments.

In considering such policies, one caveat is worth emphasizing. Industrial distribution channels are outside the company, and therefore policies cannot be developed and implemented by issuing directives. This means that the industrial producer must carefully develop policies that are fair and consistent with the idea of the producer and distributors working together as partners to serve common customers.

Once the key areas and responsibilities of distributors are developed and written, they should be communicated to the producer's salespeople and to all present and potential distributors. A sound producer-distributor relationship should be regarded as a long-term partnership for profit, so the need to establish a solid foundation for that partnership is important. Exhibit 11-3 shows how the NAMCO Controls Division of Acme-Cleveland has defined its distributor policies. Exhibit 11-4 shows the same company's guiding "Distributor Partnership Philosophy."

Sales management in many companies often resists developing written policies like these. They argue that being so specific often creates hard feelings among distributors and reduces their flexibility to deal with distributor problems. We don't believe this is the case at all. As long as the policies are fair and responsive to market needs, they will be welcomed by distributors. And where there are honest differences of opinion, it is much better to get those into the open so they can be resolved. Allowing them to smolder under the surface will only lead to problems that will ultimately strain or destroy the relationship.

## Providing Training and Support

Often the distributor's sales force is undertrained and undersupported by the producer. This is commonly called "franchise 'em and forget 'em." Training a distributor sales representative to sell a new product takes many hours of instruction. The producer must demonstrate the product features, advantages, and benefits for many different user situations or applications. The more technical the product or "art" required to use or apply it, the more time necessary for training. Sometimes such training must be done by the producer for both the distributor and the first customers who use the product. Product literature must be supplemented with trade magazine advertising to generate inquiries and new sales leads for the distributor. The producer, in turn, must promptly channel inquiries to the appropriate distributor to have a local sales call made.

Improving the effectiveness of industrial distributors can be approached in many ways.

| EXHIBIT 11-3 | PRODUCER AND DISTRIBUTOR RESPONSIBILITIES |

## NAMCO's RESPONSIBILITY

NAMCO agrees to make products, which are included within the product line for which Distributor is authorized, available to Distributor for purchase on the same terms and conditions of sale which such products are made available to authorized NAMCO distributors generally. Additionally, NAMCO will:

— Make available its staff and facilities to provide adequate training for Distributor employees and for technical and marketing liaison with them.

— Provide Distributor with a reasonable number of its catalogs and other advertising matter for use by Distributor for display or other marketing purposes.

— Attempt to maintain an inventory of the most commonly purchased items based on overall demand. NAMCO shall not be liable to the Distributor for direct, consequential or exemplary damages arising out of NAMCO's failure to have any NAMCO products in inventory or of NAMCO's failure to meet a delivery commitment.

— Refer orders or inquiries from non-authorized customers to the Authorized Distributors in an area of primary responsibility.

— Provide Distributor with all technical information available for NAMCO products.

## DISTRIBUTOR'S RESPONSIBILITIES

While an authorized NAMCO distributor, Distributor shall:

— Maintain adequate stocks of NAMCO products for which Distributor is authorized, to service the needs of its customers, to allow NAMCO representatives to perform monthly stock reviews, and at least once each year participate in a business review with NAMCO.

— Actively promote all of NAMCO's products, for which Distributor is authorized, to its customers and aggressively solicit business for the products within the Distributor's areas of primary responsibility.

— Maintain a place of business with all necessary services and sales functions to service its customers and promote goodwill for NAMCO.

— Promote NAMCO products by inclusion in Distributor's advertisements and displays.

— Make its personnel available to NAMCO for training programs.

— Distributor specifically agrees to keep confidential all technical information made available to it or its employees except materials designed for promotional purposes such as specification sheets.

*Source:* NAMCO Controls Division, Acme-Cleveland Corporation

For example, a producer can open regional warehouses or depots to provide the means for the smaller but growing distributor to expand its volume for the line or item. Sometimes a good cooperative advertising program that provides leads and inquiries will help get new accounts. In dealing with larger customers, specialized sales support may greatly strengthen a distributor's performance. Under extreme circumstances, it may be necessary to give financial aid in the form of inventory, equipment, or accounts receivable financing.

When a distributor needs technical field assistance for a potential key account, the producer should ensure that such support is provided. Most producers have regional sales representatives who can accompany distributor salespeople on calls and provide the first

**EXHIBIT
11-4**

*DISTRIBUTOR PARTNERSHIP PHILOSOPHY*

Distributors play a vital role in helping NAMCO reach its market penetration and sales coverage objectives. Whenever and wherever practical, NAMCO will go to market with our Distributor Partners. Since we do consider our distributors as business partners, we intend to have clearly defined policies designed to make this partnership concept equitable and beneficial to both of us. We will have only authorized stocking distributors.

We want to work with distributors who are financially strong and who are geared to service our end user markets. These distributors will be willing and able to grow in strength and market coverage, with increasing capabilities of servicing our customers. These distributors will provide a positive contribution in sales to our joint customers, and, in return, they should expect to earn a satisfactory profit. It is NAMCO's responsibility to provide quality products, product and application training, promotional support, market guidance and prices which allow these distributors to maintain a competitive position in the market. In turn, these business partners are obligated to represent NAMCO in a business-like manner, to aggressively promote sales of our products, to carry inventories of NAMCO products adequate to service local customer needs.

A Distributor Agreement will be of interest to our distributors only if there is sufficient profit potential to support their sales effort. NAMCO will follow a selective distribution policy, authorizing only the number and type of distributors necessary to meet our marketing objectives in a geographical territory. NAMCO's first priority will be to authorize distributors who will market all of NAMCO's products within their trading area. Our second priority will be to authorize distributors for a portion of our products where they service specific market segments. A single distributor cannot always provide total market coverage, particularly within a large trading area. We will continually monitor each trading area to provide balanced coverage. We are willing to review our analysis with distributors at any time, and will advise current distributors if we plan any additional distributors in their trading area. NAMCO will drop ship to end user or OEM customers within a trading area only, for distributors authorized within that trading area. We will maintain recommended trade discounts for various classes of end

user and OEM customers, to provide a pricing structure that protects our authorized distributor partners' investment in inventory.

NAMCO may sell direct to User and OEM accounts, but only when technical or other special conditions warrant direct sale. We will advise our distributors who will be sold direct and the reasons why. Our field sales employees and representatives will call on major User and OEM customers to gain approval and specification for NAMCO products. We will endeavor to direct the resulting business through our distributors.

We do not expect to compete with our distributors for any NAMCO business. Any distributor that develops an account, no matter what the volume, as long as they can service the account satisfactorily at normal distributor pricing will continue to service the account. However, we expect our distributors to call us in if customer needs or competitive direct selling jeopardizes the business. We will discuss with our distributors any situation where it appears we are competing with our distributor for NAMCO business.

When it becomes evident that a distributor's goals and objectives are significantly different from NAMCO's market objectives, we will discuss this with the distributor and recommend appropriate action. If that distributor does not act on our recommendations within a reasonable time, we will seek a replacement distributor whose objectives more nearly match ours.

To document this philosophy and to assure equal treatment of all distributors, we will have a signed agreement with each distributor. A standard policy, including terms of sale, will also be provided. Any differences from standard policy will be granted only where special market needs and conditions or specific performance logically and legally justify such action.

This is a statement of our philosophy of doing business with our distributor partners. We will make every effort to follow it. If changing conditions dictate changes in these policies, we will make them. And, we will always welcome constructive comments from our distributor partners.

*Note:* This particular philosophy was developed by E. G. Orahood of Reliance Electric and later adopted and modified by Jon Slaybaugh of NAMCO Controls.
*Source:* NAMCO Controls Division, Acme-Cleveland Corporation

level of technical backup. Although some might regard this as an inordinate cost or a luxury the producer cannot afford, it is often a smart investment. The producer's sales rep, with his or her greater product and technical know-how, can help analyze an account's needs and get a product specified, which in turn will build volume six months to a year later. It is usually a mistake to assume that distributors will get the producer's product specified. If a product requires some specification work and that work is not done by the producer, the distributor will generate little or no business in that territory. In the health care market, drug company salespeople or detail people (who explain the technical details of the drug to the physicians) must first influence physicians to specify or prescribe one drug brand over another before the local drugstore or distributor can fill and possibly deliver the order to the ultimate user. Similarly, architects must be encouraged to specify one producer's product, or the local building material distributor will not get the business from the local user account.

Sometimes a product is technically specified in one geographic area but is bought in another. For example, General Motors in Michigan specifies what make of valve it wants on machine tools it is having built by a machine tool builder in Ohio for a production line in California. In order to sell to the machine tool builder who is selling an automated production line to General Motors, it is first necessary to meet the specification and get approval by General Motors' corporate office. Without General Motors' corporate approval, the Ohio distributor cannot serve the Ohio machine tool builder. It frequently pays big dividends for producers to have a person who does nothing but get their products specified or qualified at OEMs, government agencies, automotive companies, and railroads.

Manuals or handbooks that help people to design or use a product or solve technical problems have proved to be excellent "silent salespeople" that help get a producer's products specified and then ordered from a local distributor. Well-known examples exist in many industries. The *Merck Manual,* which first appeared in 1899, was written to meet the needs of physicians in selecting medications. It stated that "memory is treacherous and that even the most thoroughly informed physician needs a reminder to enable him to prescribe exactly what is needed for the patient."[5] In 1983, the *Merck Manual* was in its 14th edition, with 2500 pages covering disorders (problems) and suggested therapy (solutions). The *O-Ring Handbook* by Parker Hannifin Corporation helps a design engineer design a product or specify a solution to prevent leakage in an oil or air system. Ingersoll-Rand produced the *Drill Doctor's Book* for drillers to select the bit, speed, and setup in various rock and coal mining situations. All these manuals are designed to support the distributor in its efforts to sell a complete array of technical products and services.

## Turnover and Yearly ROI

It should be obvious that an independent entrepreneurial distributor is motivated primarily by profit margins and financial incentives. For this reason, distributors will typically emphasize the higher-margin lines and often carry lower-margin items as complementary

---

[5] *The Merck Manual,* published by Merck, Sharp & Dome Research Laboratories, Division of Merck & Co., Inc., Rahway, New Jersey, 1983.

fill-ins. Many distributors and industrial marketers do not fully understand the dynamics of inventory turnover as they affect yearly ROI. For example, if one manufacturer's product has a gross margin on an item of 20 percent and the inventory turns two times per year, the yearly gross margin is 40 percent. However, if the number of inventory turns for a similar competitive product also with a 20 percent margin is four times per year, the distributor receives a yearly gross margin of 80 percent. So there is more pricing flexibility on high-turnover items.

Many industrial producers have found it worthwhile to explain turnover to their distributors to help them improve their businesses. The price-turnover relationship is shown in Table 11.2. For this situation, we can assume a distributor desires a 120 percent gross margin of profit per year for the sales, investment, and working capital being used to cover all overhead and receive a 7 percent profit on sales per year after taxes. A distributor that receives a lower *unit* gross margin on a higher *yearly* turnover item will receive greater yearly returns.

## Distributor Councils

As we emphasized, industrial producers should view the distributor as a business partner with a common customer. The end-use customer is not considered to "belong" to the distributor; the distributor serves the customer with the producer's product. The producer

| | | | | | | | | | | |
|---|---|---|---|---|---|---|---|---|---|---|
| **TABLE 11.2** | | | | ***PRICE-TURNOVER RELATIONSHIP*** | | | | | | |

% gross margin per year

| Turnover per Year | Gross Margin on Sales | | | | | | | | | |
| | *10%* | *20%* | *30%* | *40%* | *50%* | *60%* | *70%* | *80%* | *90%* | *100%* |
|---|---|---|---|---|---|---|---|---|---|---|
| 0.5 | 5 | 10 | 15 | 20 | 25 | 30 | 35 | 40 | 45 | 50 |
| 1.0 | 10 | 20 | 30 | 40 | 50 | 60 | 70 | 80 | 90 | 100 |
| 1.5 | 15 | 30 | 45 | 60 | 75 | 90 | 105 | 120 | 135 | 150 |
| 2.0 | 20 | 40 | 60 | 80 | 100 | 120 | 140 | 160 | 180 | 200 |
| 2.5 | 25 | 50 | 75 | 100 | 125 | 150 | 175 | 200 | 225 | 250 |
| 3.0 | 30 | 60 | 90 | 120 | 150 | 180 | 210 | 240 | 270 | 300 |
| 3.5 | 35 | 70 | 105 | 140 | 175 | 210 | 245 | 280 | 315 | 350 |
| 4.0 | 40 | 80 | 120 | 160 | 200 | 240 | 280 | 320 | 360 | 400 |
| 6.0 | 60 | 120 | 180 | 240 | 300 | 360 | 420 | 480 | 540 | 600 |
| 8.0 | 80 | 160 | 240 | 320 | 400 | 480 | 560 | 640 | 720 | 800 |
| 10.0 | 100 | 200 | 300 | 400 | 500 | 600 | 700 | 800 | 900 | 1,000 |
| 12.0 | 120 | 240 | 360 | 480 | 600 | 720 | 840 | 960 | 1,080 | 1,200 |
| 24.0 | 240 | 480 | 720 | 960 | 1,200 | 1,440 | 1,680 | 1,920 | 2,160 | 2,400 |
| 52.1 | 521 | 1,042 | 1,563 | 2,084 | 2,605 | 3,126 | 3,647 | 4,168 | 4,689 | 5,210 |
| 365.0 | 3,650 | 7,300 | 10,950 | 14,600 | 18,250 | 21,900 | 25,550 | 29,200 | 32,850 | 36,500 |

assists in the promotion and specifications process. As an aid to maintaining closer distributor relationships and ensuring good feedback on markets, customer needs, and competition, some leading producers have formed very effective distributor councils.

A distributor advisory council should consist of six to twelve members that represent other distributors in their respective geographic regions. Each member serves for a maximum period, such as three years, and every year a specific number of members go off and new ones come on the council. The rotating membership keeps distributor councils from becoming just social gatherings of old friends. The full council might meet twice a year. Council members sometimes have regional meetings with the distributors they represent to raise and discuss common concerns. Minutes should be kept at meetings of the national distributor advisory council and then distributed to all distributors as well as to the appropriate producer personnel. The distributor meetings are conducted at a high level and address issues that include the producer's policies, the competition, sales, technical and promotion support, and needed products. Other topics might include return goods policies, a quality problem with a particular product, the need for new catalogs, new industry standards, a product line gap, or the training of inside salespeople to handle distributor problems. General economic trends and business conditions are also useful discussion topics for council meetings, as long as they are tied to specific actions the distributor and/or producer should take.

Properly directed, a meeting of a distributor council is an opportunity for the producer to capitalize on the distributors' direct contacts with hundreds of end-use customers. The council can provide reliable feedback on common problems that need attention from the appropriate division or from top management. The points of view expressed by council members can be very helpful to a division marketing manager or product manager attempting to think through a new program or policy.

## Assigning Responsibility for Distributor Development

In many manufacturing firms, no one person has responsibility for distributor development. In theory, the top marketing or sales executive bears this responsibility, but in practice it is often fragmented or even neglected. Merely writing the responsibility into sales representatives' job descriptions is seldom enough to ensure that the job is done properly. To most salespeople, loyalty to long-time distributors, the pressures of meeting the current quota, and earning bigger bonuses are usually more important considerations than the tedious assignment of keeping tabs on all the distributors in his or her group. Unless this duty becomes a real part of a salesperson's job performance standards, it will almost surely be neglected. Moreover, sales managers struggling to meet current quotas are unlikely to make distribution changes that might hurt the current quarter's sales. Finally, marketing executives usually have more exciting and seemingly more profitable projects to think about—such as new product introductions, sales promotion campaigns, and strategic planning needs. Not having the time or staff to spare, they will seldom be inclined to invest the necessary time and effort required to strengthen the distribution network. Some leading companies have established a position that is responsible for distributor development. However, the job really belongs to the marketing management executives, and they need to make sure it is done.

At Caterpillar, for example, the support and development of distributors is a concern that permeates the entire corporation. The Caterpillar chairman states: "We all approach our distributors as partners in the enterprise and not as agents or middlemen to pass products through. We worry as much about their performance as they do themselves."[6] Caterpillar dealers are effusive in their praise of relations with Caterpillar: "They have consistently supplied us with superior products and a high-quality program of parts and product information."[7] Every year, Caterpillar conducts dozens of intensive training programs for distributors and product demonstrations for end-use customers. Field demonstrations are common to show the distributor the competitive advantages of Caterpillar's track-type tractors, front-end loaders, graders, and other excavating equipment. The company even conducts a course at corporate headquarters in Peoria to encourage and show distributor families how the business can be passed on to the next generation. The average Caterpillar distributor tenure is 35 years, and most stay within the family for generations. Caterpillar's loyal distributor relationships are quite possibly the greatest barrier to its competition.

# EVALUATING DISTRIBUTOR PERFORMANCE

The starting point for evaluating distributor performance is a thorough knowledge of the market potential in each distributor's territory. To be meaningful, total potential should be established for each product-market segment in the territory. The marketing research staff should be able to determine the market segment or territory potentials to a county and major account level. No industry or marketplace is static: New uses are usually found for existing products. New products displace older ones. New market segment opportunities emerge, and other markets stagnate or shrink. As a result, end-use markets change in size and importance and producers' and distributors' market shares typically increase or decrease over time. Therefore, it is extremely important continually to survey and track market segment changes in size, growth, and buying locations. Market facts provide the base information necessary to determine where stronger, more, or new distribution coverage is needed.

Exhibit 11-5 illustrates the importance of this point. A nationwide market study revealed that a major gasket manufacturer had weak sales through distributors that served the two fastest-growing market segments, instrumentation and oil fields. Exhibit 11-5 also shows low market penetration in the fluid power market segment. These lost opportunities, and areas needing additional marketing emphasis from distributors, would be missed unless the producer first assessed what was happening in each key market segment. Once market share data have been developed, distributor quotas should be established. The distributor's initial quota should be established from these market facts and then adjusted by sales and marketing management to reflect the producer's marketing objectives and the realities of the competitive situation.

The next step is to track distribution sales in each product-market segment. Many com-

[6]"Caterpillar: Sticking to Basics to Stay Competitive," *Business Week,* May 21, 1981, p. 77.
[7]Ibid.

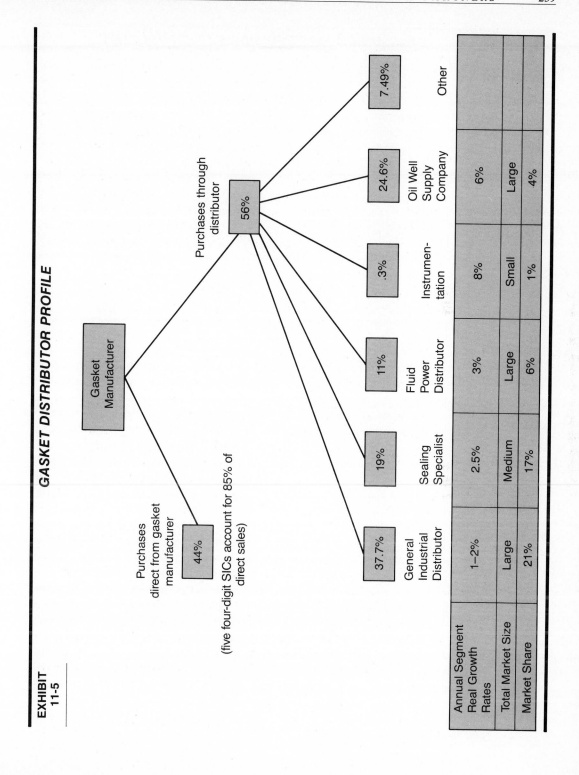

EXHIBIT
11-5

GASKET DISTRIBUTOR PROFILE

Gasket Manufacturer

Purchases direct from gasket manufacturer

44%

Purchases through distributor

56%

(five four-digit SICs account for 85% of direct sales)

| | General Industrial Distributor | Sealing Specialist | Fluid Power Distributor | Instrumen-tation | Oil Well Supply Company | Other |
|---|---|---|---|---|---|---|
| | 37.7% | 19% | 11% | .3% | 24.6% | 7.49% |
| Annual Segment Real Growth Rates | 1–2% | 2.5% | 3% | 8% | 6% | |
| Total Market Size | Large | Medium | Large | Small | Large | |
| Market Share | 21% | 17% | 6% | 1% | 4% | |

EXHIBIT
11-6

## CLASSIFYING DISTRIBUTORS BY PERFORMANCE

| | Low ——————— Market Share ——————— High | |
|---|---|---|
| **High** Segment Size or Growth Rate **Low** | Major problems | Generally satisfactory |
| | Generally insignificant | Generally an indication of weakness |

panies have no idea where their product goes after it leaves the distributor's shipping department. As a result, they lose touch with their ultimate customers and do not have a sound basis for evaluating distributor performance. Many sales personnel will argue that this kind of information is not available. This is not true. It is available and can be obtained with the distributor's cooperation. If a distributor is unwilling to cooperate or does not keep appropriate sales records, he or she shouldn't be allowed to carry the producer's line. As we mentioned earlier, some producers require each distributor to submit monthly sales information to them by product, customer name, and location as a condition of carrying their lines. When a motor, machine, or large piece of equipment is sold with a warranty, customer information is much easier to develop. Most of the ultimate customers fill in and return the warranty card directly to the producer. This means the producer should be able to track sales to the ultimate user without any distributor involvement. However developed, a system that reports sales to ultimate customers provides invaluable information for a wide range of distributor and marketing management decisions.

Another step in analyzing distributor performance is to determine which distributors are performing well or poorly in high- and low-value market segments. The matrix in Exhibit 11-6 shows an approach that is helpful in classifying distributors into these categories. This analysis can be developed for each distributor to determine how it has performed for each of the manufacturer's products. Or it can be used to compare the relative performance of all distributors in the producer's network. A common pattern to watch for is strong market share positions in the smaller or lower-value markets that are usually less competitive, coupled with a weak market share in the higher-value markets where competition is more intense. This reflects a serious weakness in the distribution network and results in a lower than average market share overall.

Once unsatisfactory or "problem" distributors have been identified, the person responsible for the territory should study the distributor's operation in more detail. Here factors like the following should be examined.

Annual inventory turns

Adequacy of business experience as reflected in quality of customer service

Coverage of assigned area and time available to seek new accounts

Distributor's competence in managing the business (sales management, financial control, recordkeeping, warehousing, and inventory control)

Historical trend of volume as measured against performance requirements established by the producer's regional sales manager

Share of market or penetration in assigned area

Willingness to carry a full line of products to service all customer needs

Condition of equipment and warehouse facilities

Financial position (accounts receivable, cash position, debts, inventories, fixed assets, and payment record)

Ability to grow in the assigned area

Almost every manufacturer periodically faces the task of getting much more effort out of certain distributors. To accomplish this successfully, management must be able to grade the performance and potential of its existing distributors and concentrate its support programs on those distributors that can generate the most sales and profit dollars by achieving realistic goals. For example, bringing the distributors in the top 20 markets up to the average market share performance levels of the entire group would seem to be a reasonable goal and can often generate significant sales dollars.

Complete and periodic distributor evaluations require considerable time and diplomacy. When distributors have interests or goals that are not consistent with the manufacturer's market objectives in the defined market and geographic trading area, producers should first try to explain what must be done and the payoffs for such efforts. If a distributor has not achieved satisfactory penetration or growth in a key market, the producer should establish an improvement plan with target dates. If no real improvement occurs after a reasonable time and appropriate producer assistance, a decision must be made. It is crucial to face up to the task of replacing distributors who will not or cannot upgrade. The producer's determination to improve a distributor network has proved to be the key to more than one outstanding marketing success story. For example, in 1974 Ray Snyder, Manager of Distributor Sales at Reliance Electric, made an analysis of distributor sales and found that the proverbial "80/20 rule" was in effect. Twenty percent of the company's 1,200 distributors accounted for a little more than 80 percent of total distributor sales. Faced with the obvious question of why carry a lot of nonproductive distributors, he launched into a program to upgrade the distributor group. Within 24 months, the number of distributors had been reduced by nearly 50 percent, average sales per distributor increased by 20 percent, and total distributor sales were up sharply.

## SELECTING NEW DISTRIBUTORS

After concluding that new or more distributors are needed to serve the market, a careful selection process must be followed so that the problem is not compounded. Many producers frequently choose additional distributors who are already overloaded with products. The successful distributor is usually courted by numerous producers and is frequently carrying as many product lines as it can effectively handle with existing sales and service capabilities. Producers also frequently make the mistake of choosing the more mature distributor with a successful history who has forgotten how to be aggressive. Admittedly, the credit rating on the newer, more aggressive distributor will rarely be something that excites the home office financial people. However, the producer often errs by not attempting to find a way to help finance or support a newer distributor who could do a good job with the right kind of assistance.

Distributors are never very happy when they are told that they are being canceled or that an additional distributor is being franchised in what had been their exclusive territory. Many producers are reluctant to take this step because they are unwilling to upset the longstanding personal relationship with the low-performing distributor. However, when the decision is made forcefully and objectively on a base of solid market facts and the distributor's lack of performance, the producer's market position inevitably improves. Conversely, procrastination or rationalization typically leads to further market deterioration.

Identifying and adding the specific distributors is generally a local or regional decision. Regional sales managers should be the first people to do an exhaustive search for new candidates. Since it is a regional decision, the search is frequently narrowed down to one or two key cities in the region. Trade directories and local Yellow Pages are typically used as sources for existing distributor candidates. Sometimes the number two person in an existing or competitive distributorship becomes a candidate to start a new distributorship. In some situations, the existing distributor may be interested in opening a new branch to provide the necessary coverage and is aware that if he or she doesn't, the producer probably will find a new distributor for the area. As a last resort, some producers will consider opening a company store on a temporary basis with one of its salespeople managing the distributorship. Often producers continue the person's salary, finance the new inventories, and provide management assistance to help get the operation running in the black. At this point, the company employee is often given the opportunity to arrange his or her own financing to buy out the producer's assets and become an independent business that will remain and develop accounts in that territory.

## MULTIDIVISION PRODUCTS

In many corporations, several different divisions often manufacture related products that are sold to common customers. In these situations, it is advantageous for the manufacturer to sell through a common distributor network. This enables the distributor to become a single-source shopping place where a customer can buy all related requirements. This common distributor concept has provided a focus to some producers' acquisition and product development activities as they sought complementary products or product

EXHIBIT
11-7

## MULTIDIVISIONAL OR GROUP DISTRIBUTION

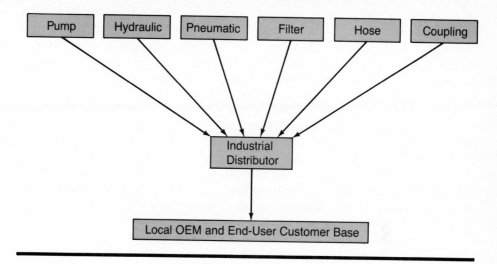

lines that fit with their established common existing distributor network. Exhibit 11-7 shows how complementary products from six separate divisions flow through a common distributor network to local customers.

Although this arrangement offers many advantages, it adds to the complexity of the management task. This is particularly true when the divisions involved were acquired rather than internally developed and have successful sales histories based on quite different distribution policies and practices. In these situations, buying terms and conditions, stocking requirements, returns and allowances, and credit evaluation are most likely to be different and often in conflict. On the surface, it would seem that problems like these are easily corrected. In practice, however, they are not. First, the divisions are generally autonomous and typically have a vested interest in distributor policies and practices that have proved successful in the past. Distributors will also want to preserve the policies and practices from each division that are best for them and will argue strongly against any change that is not in their best interest. This arrangement also can create difficult operating problems, particularly if division performance is uneven. Even though the manufacturer's divisions are separate operating entities, distributors will tend to evaluate the performance of all the divisions as a group. As a result, all divisions end up with a tarnished image if one division falls short with missed delivery dates or quality defects.

Given these concerns, the best management approach is to work toward a common set of distributor policies and practices acceptable to all parties. This will take careful thought and time as well as skillful negotiation, but it is do-able. At the same time, it is essential to preserve the individuality of each division and the brand name of the division's products. If this can be accomplished, it will provide the manufacturer with the leverage that results from being a major source to each distributor, while still permitting each division to stand on its own performance.

## SUMMARY

Experience shows that all too few sales managers understand how to market products with distributors successfully. Industrial producers with strong and loyal distributor relationships usually perceive distributors as business partners and not just as vehicles to pass products through. Such producers see that distributors must earn satisfactory margins and profits while serving their joint customers. These same producers cement the distributor partnership with market guidance, training, and technical and promotional support. By avoiding mistakes in distribution and taking care of the essentials in evaluating, selecting, and developing distributors, they substantially increase their chances of market success.

An effective distributor network is often a key to market leadership and overall business success for many manufacturing companies. It takes many years and continuous attention to develop and maintain a strong distributor organization. The time and cost required to develop a sound producer-distributor network is often a major barrier to new or foreign competitors. The manufacturer that wants to enter or better penetrate markets served primarily by distributors but has no developed network can be leveraged to provide a major competitive advantage with greater market penetration and attractive profits for both producers and distributors.

## REVIEW QUESTIONS

1. Why is an industrial distributor often the most effective way to serve a market segment?
2. Why is it important to have written producer-distributor policies? What areas should be covered?
3. In what situations do producers often sell direct rather than through distributors?
4. What five criteria are helpful to qualify a product for marketing with distributors?
5. How does market segmentation guide the use and selection of industrial distributors?
6. Why is distributor sales reporting by customer and location necessary for the producer?
7. How should producers periodically evaluate existing distributors?
8. How can a producer identify and develop new distributors?
9. How can the producer salespeople often help the distributor obtain new business?
10. How do producer's manuals and handbooks help bring business to distributors?
11. How can distributor councils be employed to build better producer-distributor partnerships?

# 12

# Advertising and Promotion

The Problem of Wasted Effort
    The Money Involved
    The Special Problems of Industrial Advertising
The Industrial Promotional Mix
Some Effective Programs
Planning and Control
    Budgets Versus Plans
    The Policy Statement
    The Plan
    Review and Control
Summary
Review Questions

Ursula Hartmann, advertising manager, Peter Fraser, marketing services manager, and Bill Lewis, the new controller for a large Midwestern materials handling company, were reviewing the results of their recent participation in an industry trade show. Ursula was particularly pleased with the show: "We had the best display by far. We showed more bells and whistles and had better attendance than anyone else in the industry. At least 200 people attended our reception." Peter was equally happy: "This is the tenth year we have been in this show, and this was the best ever. No one else even came close to us." With a typical controller's perspective, Bill raised a question that led to the following discussion.

*Bill:* How much does a show like this cost?

*Ursula:* About $250,000.

*Bill:* Is that the total cost?

*Ursula:* Sure. My budget was $218,000, and we had a few thousand dollar overrun.

*Bill:* Does the $250,000 amount include travel and living costs for everybody from our company who attended the show?

*Ursula:* No, that's a sales expense.

*Bill:* Do you know how much was involved for travel and other associated costs?

*Ursula:* No, it's not my cost.

*Bill:* Do you know how many of our salespeople attended the show?

*Ursula:* I don't know that either, but we usually try to have enough sales representation so customers can be handled properly.

After the meeting, Bill talked with Gordon Jones, a product manager for a major segment of the business. Gordon didn't have much more information, but said he knew that travel and other costs were significant because a big chunk of the total costs were allocated against his product line. He also said that he wasn't very happy about this charge and questioned what benefits his product or even the company got for all the money that was spent. "It's just a big ego trip for the advertising and sales guys" was his parting comment.

Bill did some research and found that the travel costs involved amounted to $121,000. Despite the glowing comments of the advertising and marketing services managers, Bill had real misgivings about the value received for the total amount of money spent on the show. He wrote a brief memo outlining his concerns to the vice president of finance and sent a copy to Ursula and Peter. Ursula reacted angrily: "This guy's only been here three weeks and already he's stuck his nose into an area that is none of his business." As she started toward Bill's office, Ursula thought about the effort she put into the trade show and wondered if Bill had any idea how important this activity was to the company.

If this isn't Bill's business, whose is it?

What are the criteria to use in judging how well promotion money is spent?

Who should decide how promotion money is spent?

Are there any hidden benefits of participating in trade shows?

Does the controller have the right to ask the questions he did?

**P**roperly planned and controlled, advertising and promotional activities are useful recognition and volume-building tools in the industrial world. They can introduce a new product or service to established or new markets in a cost-effective way. They can explain cost benefits to a much wider potential customer base than the typical industrial sales force can possibly reach. They can effectively turn up sales prospects or leads that help make the time of the sales force more productive. However, in reviewing advertising and promotion activities, it is important to keep this statement made by a cost-conscious businessman foremost in mind: "I know that 50 percent of the money we spend for advertising and promotion is wasted; I just don't know which half." There is a good deal of truth to this point in any advertising situation, and it is particularly true in the industrial world, where advertising and promotion expenditures are sizable.

## THE PROBLEM OF WASTED EFFORT

Responses to criticism about waste from those involved in business-to-business advertising and promotion activities can be anticipated: "You have to keep your product and name in front of the customers." "We must keep building the company's image." "Giveaways are a constant reminder of our product." "We lose face if we don't continue to make major commitments in our trade shows." As we see it, none of these responses are valid. In fact, they represent the kind of superficial thinking that is the root cause of much of the waste in industrial advertising and promotion. Our point of view is not simply an unsupported bias; there is plenty of evidence that is consistent with our thinking. For example, L. W. Rodger makes these comments about industrial advertising expenditures:

> The advertising budget probably represents the largest amount of money disbursed by manufacturers with no precise measure of what it can be expected to achieve. The spending of large sums of money on advertising without some system of accountability can be compared to conducting a business without a bookkeeping or accounting department. Advertising accountability has lagged far behind general management accountability in that the latter is held responsible for accomplishing certain specific and usually measurable results in relation to money spent.[1]

A recent *Wall Street Journal* article[2] reported that Edward MacEwen, director of advertising at General Telephone & Electronics, says: "All that most corporate slogans do is waste space. Such slogans rarely are remembered and even less frequently identified with the proper corporation." To prove his point, MacEwen developed a brief quiz that called for participants to match the advertiser with the appropriate slogan. Included in the list of companies that had spent millions of dollars on their corporate image were such well-known names as ITT, Bendix, W. R. Grace, Monsanto, 3M, U.S. Steel, LTV, Allied,

---

[1] Leslie Rodger, "Marketing in a Competitive Economy," *International Industries,* 1971, p. 110.
[2] *The Wall Street Journal,* December 9, 1982.

and others of equal stature. When MacEwen gave this quiz to about 250 advertising executives, only 6 entrants could correctly identify more than 10 of 31 slogans. The winner matched 19.

Trade shows are an advertising/promotion activity that is certainly subject to question. Some recent publications include these quotes:

> It is strange to find that so little is known about the usefulness of exhibitions (trade shows), that they are so often an expression of faith rather than fact, with such factors as size of stand (display) and budget determined intuitively by some senior executive. Evidence of this is to be found by discussing the matter with exhibitors and is confirmed by the random way in which in one year a company invests in a substantial stand, next year pulls out altogether, then later comes back with an even larger display.[3]

> Trade shows are terribly expensive and of limited value for the business you do versus the dollars spent. Once we did cut out a show, but there was such buyers' remorse that we were forced to reinstate it. Everyone wondered if we were having some financial difficulties and couldn't afford to participate! For us, trade shows are a self-perpetuating problem. If I could just throw that money into operating profit each year, I'd be a superstar. But we go, we go.[4]

> Everything nowadays is done for the show management, not for the exhibitors. The only other ones to get anything out of trade shows are the hotels and the prostitutes.[5]

All these negative comments do not mean that money should never be spent for advertising and promotion. Rather, they mean that careful consideration must be given to determining the role advertising and promotion can realistically play in the particular industrial marketing situation. When it is determined that these activities can make a useful contribution, they must be carefully planned and controlled. One must always remember, however, that the industrial buying decision typically swings on more important components of the marketing mix, like product performance, price, delivery capabilities, and service. Even the most creative or ingenious advertising and promotion will never offset deficiencies in these areas (see the box, page 249).

## The Money Involved

Although far from perfect, there are data which show that most industrial companies spend money on advertising and promotion, and that the sums involved are substantial. In a recent survey of 483 industrial companies of varying sizes, 93.1 percent responded positively to the question, "Does your company advertise?"[6] Although one can always find deficiencies in survey data, our experience with a wide range of industrial compa-

[3]Norman A. Hart, *Industrial Advertising and Publicity* (New York: Halsted Press, 1978), p. 17.
[4]Thomas Bonoma, "Get More Out of Your Trade Shows," *Harvard Business Review,* January–February, 1983.
[5]Ibid.
[6]"Highlights of Sales Management and Marketing Survey on Industrial Advertising," *Sales and Marketing,* June 8, 1981, p. 53.

## THROWING MONEY AWAY

It doesn't require any particular genius to see a lot of wasted dollars spent on advertising and promotion in the advertising world. Some common examples:

- Repeated pictures in trade journals of old, mature, or "me too" products that don't talk about or offer new benefits to anyone.
- Myriad giveaway items (golf balls, tee shirts, bottle openers, paperweights) and other promotional gimmicks that have no relationship to the company's products or capabilities.
- Countless TV and radio spots, as well as newspaper and magazine ads, devoted to so-called corporate image building developed around some catchy slogan designed to express the company's business purpose or accomplishments.
- Costly trade show participation that is more of a social get-together for competing sales personnel than a forum for showing and selling new products and technology.

nies suggests that this ratio is certainly realistic. And although the amount of money spent for business-to-business advertising and promotion is far less than that spent by consumer goods companies, the amount is still significant. Table 12.1, prepared from these same survey data, shows 47 percent of the companies had annual expenditures over $100,000, 13 percent over $500,000, and several companies had budgets running into the millions.

Like most other business expenditures, ad budgets continue to spiral upward. Table 12.2, again from the same survey, shows that most advertising budgets in the sample companies call for significant planned increases in 1981 over what was actually spent in 1980. Given the hundreds of thousands of industrial companies, it is safe to conclude that if aggregate data on their advertising expenditures were available, it would be expressed

**TABLE 12.1**

### INDUSTRIAL ADVERTISING BUDGETS, 1980

| Amount | Percentage of Companies |
|---|---|
| Less than $100,000 | 49.1% |
| $100,000–$499,999 | 34.4 |
| $500,000–$999,999 | 6.4 |
| $1 million–$2,999,999 | 5.6 |
| $3 million–$4,999,999 | 0.8 |
| $5 million or more | 0.4 |

TABLE
12.2

## INDUSTRIAL ADVERTISING INCREASES, 1980–1981

| Comparison | Percentage of Companies |
|---|---|
| Up 9% or less | 21.1% |
| Up 10%–19% | 27.7 |
| Up 20%–29% | 8.3 |
| Up 30% or more | 8.3 |
| Same | 21.3 |
| Down | 7.7 |

in hundreds of millions or possibly even billions of dollars. And as we have seen, the trend in spending is definitely upward. These numbers relate only to print, TV, and radio advertising; they do not include money spent for all the other activities generally considered to be a part of an industrial advertising and promotion budget, such as trade shows, catalogs, product literature, price lists, business cards, company signs, sales ads, giveaway items, slide shows, films, video presentations, direct mail, and product seminars. Obviously, the costs and importance of these activities vary widely by company, but as a general rule they typically match the amount spent for print, TV, and radio advertising.

## The Special Problems of Industrial Advertising

The difficulty of avoiding waste in advertising and promotion is certainly not limited to industrial companies. Anyone who advertises or promotes anything to any market is always concerned about this point, since the money spent is lost unless it ultimately generates sufficient additional volume and profit to cover the cost. Business-to-business advertising, however, is more susceptible to waste for several reasons. To start with, it is harder to do well and to quantify the results. The chairman of one of the largest and most successful advertising agencies expressed this point very well when he said: "Industrial advertising is tougher to create than consumer advertising. There are more facts required and less puffery. You have to convince a better informed and more knowledgeable audience. Emotional appeals are not particularly useful, since the benefits one communicates must be in dollars and cents and not emotions or dreams."

This comment accurately reflects three points that are facts of life in the industrial world. First, industrial customers tend to be fewer in number and make less frequent and higher-volume purchases of any particular product than customers for consumer items. Moreover, the lag between the time an impression is made through some advertisement or promotional offering and the time of need or purchase is generally much longer for industrial products. Finally, the industrial buying decision is generally more rational, and those making the decision are less likely to be swayed by advertising appeals, claims, or promotional offerings. For these reasons, it is far more difficult to test and measure the effectiveness of advertising or promotion activities in the industrial world and thus far easier to spend a lot of money on these activities without knowing whether the investment is paying off.

A revealing piece of research work from McGraw-Hill's *Special Report on Buying and Selling Techniques Used in the British Engineering Industry* supports this point.[7] Among other things, the research showed various methods of arriving at the advertising and promotion budget, as Table 12.3 shows. Although this survey reflects the practice in British industry, our experience suggests it is not far off the mark from what we would find in the United States if a similar survey were conducted. Making any allowance you want for greater marketing sophistication in the United States, the results still reflect the fundamental problem. Far too few industrial companies develop and carry out their advertising and promotion activities as an integrated part of their marketing and business plan. Budgets for these activities are frequently established independently or on an ad hoc basis that is difficult to track. Even when the budgets and programs are included in the plan, they are generally not subjected to the same rigorous challenge and review as other elements of the marketing mix, such as product development, pricing, inventory levels, and direct or distributor sales costs.

Contrast this situation with what occurs in consumer marketing. Here, the success of the product and even the company often depends on how effectively advertising and promotion funds are spent or invested. In fact, these activities are so important and the expenditures so large that consumer marketing is frequently referred to as "the science of spending" for these activities. To enhance their chances for success, consumer goods marketers routinely evaluate and measure the effectiveness of alternative advertising and promotion programs and spending levels in test markets before major recommendations or commitments are made. Moreover, any advertising or promotion program of consequence is presented as a vital and an integrated part of a marketing or business plan with quantifiable objectives designed to provide a basis for measuring actual performance against each planned expenditure. Management then monitors sales and profit results

| TABLE 12.3 | BASIS OF ADVERTISING BUDGETS | |
|---|---|---|

| Basis | Percentage of Respondents |
|---|---|
| Percentage of last year's sales turnover | 7% |
| Percentage of this year's expected turnover | 17 |
| Percentage of last year's actual and this year's estimate | 4 |
| A fixed figure without specific reference to sales | 39 |
| No known basis | 29 |
| Other | 4 |

[7]Hart, *Industrial Advertising and Publicity*, p. 132.

against advertising and promotion costs and makes appropriate adjustments in spending levels to improve the chances of an attractive payoff. This approach obviously increases the opportunity to base advertising and promotion decisions on profit economics rather than intuition, individual preference, or historical patterns.

There is one more contributing factor that needs to be pointed out. Many advertising agencies are not particularly well suited to working effectively on industrial advertising and promotion. Agency personnel are certainly knowledgeable about advertising and promotion techniques, but most agencies find it difficult to attract and retain personnel with the technical knowledge and understanding required to market industrial products effectively. Of course there are exceptions, especially in agencies geared primarily to serving industrial companies, but as a general rule this point holds true. A recent survey[8] highlights the deficiencies many industrial companies see in their advertising agencies. Responses were given to this open-ended question: "What added strengths should your agency develop to serve your company more effectively?" The answers were coded as follows:

A    A significant number of answers along these lines, and therefore a key factor.

B    This view was repeated a number of times, and some attention should be paid to it.

C    Mentioned only once or at most four times; much less significant.

Here were the responses:

| | |
|---|---|
| 1. Need for greater technical and product knowledge | A |
| 2. Improvement in creativity in all senses | B |
| 3. More comprehensive promotional planning | B |
| 4. Knowledge of technical media | B |
| 5. Complete involvement in clients' business | B |
| 6. Market orientation | C |
| 7. Less staff turnover | C |
| 8. Better production efficiency | C |
| 9. Greater use of free-lance talent | C |
| 10. Higher caliber of personnel | C |
| 11. Initiative | C |

The results of this survey are not surprising, since it is difficult for an outsider to develop the deep understanding of a company's technology, products, customers, and competition when it takes the company's full-time employees many years to learn the business. The business skills required to develop more technical or product knowledge to contribute to marketing plans or even to manage the sums of money involved prudently are simply not there. Of course there are many exceptions to this generalization, but it contributes to the waste that occurs in many industrial advertising and promotion programs.

Despite these problems and negative comments, advertising and promotion can be very cost-effective tools for the industrial marketer.

[8]Ibid., p. 133.

# THE INDUSTRIAL PROMOTIONAL MIX

Exhibit 12-1 shows a typical pattern of cost effectiveness for various industrial advertising and promotion activities. This illustration obviously reflects a generalization; variables, such as the type of product, stage in the life cycle, market-customer makeup, and competitive structure, would alter the picture in any particular situation. Nevertheless, it clearly shows the range of costs per contract for various promotional approaches that can be used to reach the customer. Obviously, each of these approaches has its advantages and disadvantages and is more or less effective in varying situations. Let's take a closer look.

Catalogs are next best to the salesperson for giving a customer what it needs to make a buying decision. Catalogs reach more people than the individual salesperson and are there with a product message when the prospect is ready to buy. Design, printing, and

**EXHIBIT
12-1**

### THE INDUSTRIAL PROMOTIONAL MIX

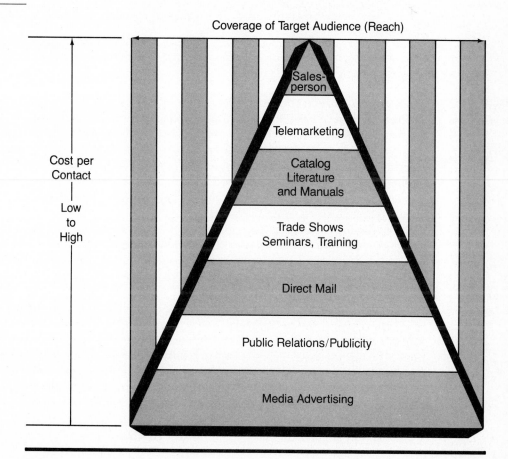

Coverage of Target Audience (Reach)

Cost per
Contact

Low
to
High

Sales-
person

Telemarketing

Catalog
Literature
and Manuals

Trade Shows
Seminars, Training

Direct Mail

Public Relations/Publicity

Media Advertising

## THREE USES OF TELEMARKETING

The B. F. Goodrich Chemical Group uses a telemarketing center for order taking, customer service, and information dissemination purposes. When customers call, a center specialist brings up the customer's file on a data terminal screen, records the order, checks inventory, and, when necessary, talks with production and shipping to schedule the shipment. Field sales personnel are also supported by being provided current inventory data and estimated arrival times. High volume accounts are scheduled for field visits, thereby increasing the number and quality of contacts between B. F. Goodrich and its best customers.

The 3M Company relies on a telemarketing center to assist customers with equipment trouble. After calling 3M's 800 number, the customer describes the problem to a skilled technician with access to an on-line computer system. On more than 30 percent of the calls, 3M finds that the equipment difficulty can be solved in minutes without having to dispatch a service technician. This has improved customer service activities and provided a valuable service at a very reasonable cost to 3M.

The Parker Hannifin Corporation utilizes telemarketing to sell to marginal accounts and keep closer contact with distributors. Telemarketing helps both Parker's and its distributor salespeople "call" on customers that would not be reached. Finally, new product features are quickly explained and questions answered for distributors and end users by telemarketing.

*Source:* Roy Voorhees and John Coppett, "Telemarketing in Distribution Channels," *Industrial Marketing Management,* 12, 2(April 1983), 106.

distribution, however, can be costly. Telemarketing is a form of marketing communication that utilizes telephone technology (WATTS lines, 800 numbers, and so on) to make sales "calls" and receive information from markets. Telemarketing is effectively used to generate sales leads, qualify customers, receive sales and service inquiries, and finally to substitute periodically for person-to-person sales calls (see the box).

Trade shows, seminars, and training are the only industrial communications vehicles through which prospects come to learn more about a product or service offering. Having made the effort to come, attendees represent a select target for some direct selling opportunity. An alternative to trade show participation (or a possible next step following an expression of interest) is scheduled plant visits that show the potential customer how the product is designed, manufactured, and serviced, and how it performs under various conditions.

Direct mail is the only mass medium that can be directed toward target groups or prospects. The message may be highly personalized and can also be designed as an effective market research tool. But rising postage rates make this an increasingly costly method to reach potential prospects. Public relations publicity has believability through perceived public endorsement and wide coverage of target audience. However, it is impossible to control the timing or content of the message. Media advertising is the only mass communication vehicle that can be controlled completely. You control what you want to say, when you want to say it, and to whom. It is the least effective in terms of actually closing a sale, but can be the most effective in low-cost coverage of an entire target audience with a controlled message. It is often difficult to use media advertising effectively because it is often hard to define a message or appeal that is truly meaningful to a sizable cross-section of potential customers.

The direct sales contact is clearly the most effective means of closing a sale, but far and away the most costly. As Exhibit 12-2 shows, the average cost of each industrial sales call has risen dramatically over the past 15 years and is probably well over $200 at the present time. Driven by inflation, direct sales costs will continue to rise and increase

**EXHIBIT 12-2**

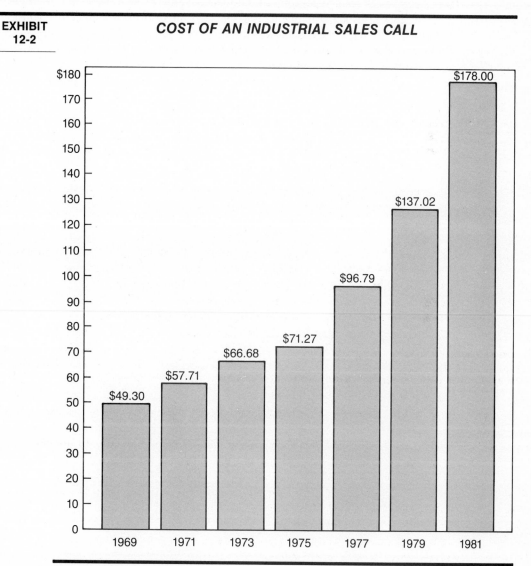

## COST OF AN INDUSTRIAL SALES CALL

*Source:* McGraw-Hill Research

the need for productivity improvement in most industrial selling organizations. For this reason, it should be clear that if advertising and promotion activities can be used to make the sales representative's calls more productive, they can provide a real economic benefit to the company.

## SOME EFFECTIVE PROGRAMS

Many companies have successfully used their advertising and promotion programs to generate sales leads and improve the salesperson's hit ratio. For example, the ad shown in Exhibit 12-3 for a wind deflector, a totally new product designed to improve fuel efficiency for long-haul truckers, appeared in many leading trade journals and other national publications. As you can see, the ad clearly shows how the deflector is mounted and how it works. More important, it specifically describes how much efficiency can be

**EXHIBIT 12-3**    *THE KENWORTH VARASHIELDS™ AD*

*Source:* Paccar

achieved and the kind of economic gain that results from investment in this device. Finally, the reader is told how and where to contact a local dealer for additional information. The response to this ad and others in the series provided the salespeople with a large number of leads and put them in a much stronger position to close a sale than when they simply made cold calls. Effective media advertising like this can be very useful in generating sales leads and contributing to the success of the new product or a product with distinctly new features.

Another good example is a series of General Electric ads that featured its new line of energy-saving motors. The ads shown in Exhibit 12-4 illustrate how the company used two different approaches to promote energy-saving motors across all industries and in selected market segments. The first ad appeared in broad-based purchasing and production-engineering magazines. The second ad for the same product was designed specifically for pulp and paper mill customers and appeared only in trade publications reaching that market. Both ads emphasize the savings potential from the motor, but the first describes the savings in general terms, and the second describes savings potential in terms related specifically to mill usage.

Many other companies have booked a substantial volume of new orders by participating in trade shows with the right kind of product exhibit. One independent manufacturer of telecommunications equipment regularly planned new product introductions to tie into the schedule of key industry trade shows and developed a very aggressive promotion and sales solicitation program to make sure potential customers were in attendance at these shows. Sales and marketing management were able to predict with a high degree of accuracy how successful the product would be by initial customer reaction at the trade show. Manufacturing and sales plans could then be realistically geared to high-probability volume estimates. This approach enabled the company to get a running start on new product sales that it would not have achieved if it had relied solely on the sales force to do the job.

Another group of companies has developed a strong position with customers by providing them with problem-solving handbooks that are of genuine value to potential users or specifiers of the company's products. Although some advertising experts may not think of these handbooks as a form of advertising, they are often the most effective promotional vehicle in the company's entire communications program. One reason advertising personnel are often less than enthusiastic about handbooks as a communication vehicle is that they have a limited role in their development. The handbook is generally organized around common customer problems that require technical data for solution, and there is simply no place for advertising puffery. Parker Hannifin's *O-Ring Handbook* is a prime example. It is in its 12th printing and is used by engineers the world over to help solve hydraulic sealing problems that may be encountered in any operation where fluid must be contained. Tommy McCuistion, a former vice president of marketing at Parker Hannifin, referred to the *O-Ring Handbook* as "a silent salesman that is always there when a customer needs help to solve a problem." Another very effective handbook was developed by the Crawford Fitting Company for the SWAGELOK tube fitting line. Exhibit 12-5 shows the contents page. As you can see, the book has been designed to help the engineer trouble-shoot and map out the connection and fitting requirements for many machines and applications.

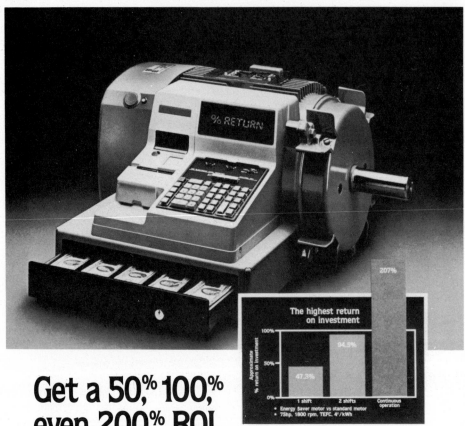
*Source:* General Electric Company

**EXHIBIT 12-4 (b)**

## GENERAL ELECTRIC'S AD FOR PULP AND PAPER MILL CUSTOMERS

Temperature effect on lubricant and insulation life

Energy $aver motors double bearing lubricant life and increase insulation life up to four times

# Turn a profit in your mill year after year with Energy $aver™ motors.

Downtime costs American industry millions of dollars in lost profits every year. But a simple switch to reliable Energy $aver ac motors from General Electric can help you cut this profit-draining downtime in your pulp or paper mill. Because Energy $aver motor insulation lasts up to four times longer than that of standard motors, GE motors can help you avoid expensive replacement and rewinding.

The reason? Energy $aver motors run much cooler under load. As the chart shows, the addition of more magnetizing steel and more copper results in a motor that runs 20 to 30 degrees cooler than normal-efficiency motors. And Energy $aver motors' superior aluminum-alloy frame and endshield efficiently transfer heat — up to three times faster than cast iron.

In addition, Energy $aver motors are far more energy-efficient than standard motors. Just one 125hp Energy $aver motor can save you $1,277* in the first year of operation in your pulp or paper mill. And $11,283 in just seven years.

So insist on Energy $aver motors from GE — the ones whose longer life and energy savings add up to lower life-cycle costs in your pulp or paper mill. For a free copy of our booklet, "How Energy $aver motors can help you turn a profit year after year," write today to: General Electric Company, Section 295-35, Schenectady, NY 12345.

TM — Trademark of General Electric Company
*4¢/kWh initial power cost, 10% annual increase

On Reader Service Card **Circle 114**

**GENERAL ⓖ ELECTRIC**

*Source:* General Electric Company

| **EXHIBIT** | |
| **12-5** | |

## THE SWAGELOK™ TUBE FITTING AND INSTALLATION MANUAL

### CONTENTS

| | Page |
|---|---|
| Preface | iii |
| Glossary of Terms | 1 |

CHAPTER I
| Using SWAGELOK Tube Fittings | 9 |

CHAPTER II
| Tubing | 25 |

CHAPTER III
| Tubing Installation | 48 |

CHAPTER IV
| Special Applications: | |
| 1. Steam Tracing | 79 |
| 2. Dowtherm "A" | 87 |
| 3. Dowtherm "E" | 87 |
| 4. Liquid Sodium | 87 |
| 5. Vacuum Systems | 88 |

CHAPTER V
| Trouble Shooting | 113 |

CHAPTER VI
| Types of Fittings and Type Numbers | 121 |
| 1. SWAGELOK Tube Fittings | 122 |
| 2. Quick Connects | 147 |
| 3. Valves | 163 |
| 4. Pipe Fittings | 166 |
| 5. Weld Fittings | 180 |
| 6. High Pressure Tube Fittings | 189 |
| 7. Metric Tube Fittings | 215 |

APPENDIX

SECTION I
| Determining Inside Diameter of Tubing | 225 |

SECTION II
| Tubing Calculations and Pressure Tables | 244 |

SECTION III
| Corrosion Charts | 253 |

SECTION IV
| General Information | 260 |

SECTION V
| Trademark Credits | 276 |

iv

*Source:* Crawford Fitting Company. SWAGELOK is a registered trademark of the Crawford Fitting Company. Reprinted with permission.

Many industrial companies have successfully employed some form of corporate advertising to help open the door for their salespeople. The ad from a Reliance Electric series shown in Exhibit 12-6 is a good example of this kind of an effort. As you can see, it clearly shows a broad range of capabilities in one of the company's target industries and emphasizes the company's growth record and financial strength. This ad and others directed toward other target markets were featured in *The Wall Street Journal, Fortune,* and other financial publications to present a successful picture to the investment community. They were also featured in appropriate trade publications to help promote the company's capabilities in the marketplace. The ads made a very favorable impression on potential customers, and Reliance salespeople were able to use them very effectively in their sales presentations.

The money spent in all these efforts contributed importantly to the sales performance of the companies involved and represented attractive investments. With proper marketing management and control, there is no reason why the great bulk of the money spent on advertising and promotion activities cannot yield the same kind of result.

# PLANNING AND CONTROL

To achieve this benefit and make these activities pay off requires the same kind of tough-minded management attention that prevails in any other aspect of business. And one principle of good business management must be rigorously applied to ensure that advertising and promotion activities are cost effective: Never spend any money without a plan, and never waste time planning anything that cannot be controlled.

Stating this principle is a lot easier than actually following it. As a general rule, advertising and promotion managers in the industrial world do not tend to be tough-minded themselves. Moreover, many senior managers find it difficult to "ride herd" on these activities in an effective way because they are generally unfamiliar with the jargon and techniques commonly employed by advertising and promotion managers. When review sessions are conducted, they more often than not degenerate into a discussion of the merits or demerits of a particular ad or promotion and seldom get into the managerial considerations that really count, like target groups, specific marketing objectives, and the basis for measurement. As a result, very few senior managers know how the total budget for advertising and promotion was established, what cost-benefit expectations were planned, and how actual results measure up against original objectives.

## Budgets Versus Plans

As we have stressed, the key to managing these activities is to ensure they are planned and controlled, with the emphasis on *planned.* What are often passed off as advertising and promotion plans in far too many industrial companies are actually only budgets established by calculating some percentage of sales, matching competitive expenditures, or plusing last year's expenditures by some amount. This sets up a budgeted amount of money for spending, but it is not a plan and does not establish an adequate basis for

**EXHIBIT 12-6 (a)**

## THE RELIANCE ELECTRIC SERIES

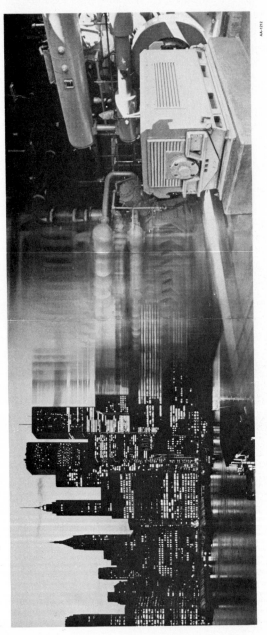

### Reliance Electric interaction helps turn a city on.

The job of putting "juice" into a city's power lines gets more challenging every year. But through successful interaction of technologies, products, and services, we help utility companies operate more efficiently to meet that challenge.

**Reliance Electric** has valuable firsthand experience in meeting the unique needs of nuclear power plants, including the requirements for software and drawings, seismic analysis, and radiation-resistant materials.

For fossil-fuel plants, Reliance V★S* Drives power limestone slurry pumps in SO2 removal systems.

Throughout the industry, Reliance supplies a broad line of Duty Master® A-C motors to power fans, pumps, and auxiliary equipment. And in the control room, Reliance control panels and consoles monitor complex operations and systems.

**Successful Reliance Electric businesses** interact in other important areas.

Dodge pulleys, clutches, and couplings are an integral part of handling systems that move coal from hopper cars, barges, and stockpiles.

Master gearmotors and speed reducers and Reeves variable speed drives provide precise power to control the motion of auxiliary systems handling coal, ash, and limestone.

Toledo Scale equipment weighs and identifies — in motion — loaded railroad cars that deliver coal and oil. And Toledo Weighveyors® measure the flow of coal on moving belts, automatically.

These complex, automated systems receive instructions and sequencing from AutoMate® programmable controllers that replace maintenance-prone relay panels.

Lorain Products provides inverter systems for power-failure protection of computerized grid control networks and for critical instrumentation and controls throughout the power plant.

Haughton elevators provide fast vertical transportation for people and equipment within multilevel generating plants.

Reliance Electric is also people. More than 20,000 people interacting around the world, including application engineers and industry managers concerned with the immediate and future needs of utility companies. They offer industrial and commercial automation components, systems, and services that no other company can match. And they're backed by networks of distribution and service centers to maintain the equipment they supply.

For fiscal 1974, our policy of disciplined acquisitions and interaction paid off with record sales of $580 million and record earnings of $2.10 per share, fully diluted. Records achieved by sales to the commercial, industrial, service, and international markets.

This multinational interaction is outlined in our new corporate profile. For a copy, write B. C. Ames, President, Reliance Electric Company, 29325 Chagrin Blvd., P. O. Box 22280, Cleveland OH 44122.

**Successful businesses interacting.**

## RELIANCE ELECTRIC ⌐

AA-1212

*Source:* Reliance Electric Co.

**EXHIBIT 12-6 (b)**

## THE RELIANCE ELECTRIC SERIES

### Reliance Electric interaction...automates beef from way out to weigh-in.

Putting meat on America's tables is no simple process. But through successful interaction of technologies, products, and services, we help cattle feeders, food processors, and supermarkets reduce the costs and speed the distribution of meat products.

**Toledo Scale is Reliance Electric,** supplying feeders with automated batching systems that carefully measure, weigh, and blend ingredients and supplements for livestock rations. Supplying automatic equipment to help packers weigh dressed sides — in motion — and keep track of inventories. Then, in retail supermarkets, Toledo automated wrapping machines, scales and checkout systems package, weigh, price, label, and count the items that appear, ready-to-buy, on today's meat counters.

**Successful Reliance Electric businesses** play other important roles in our interaction story. Reliance electric motors power pumps and refrigeration equipment. Reliance electrical V•S® drives control conveyors that move perishable meat products quickly and reliably through packing and processing lines.

Dodge bearings, screw conveyor drives, pulleys, couplings, and fixed speed drives are essential to material handling systems that move feed to fatten cattle for market.

Master gearmotors, speed reducers and Reeves variable speed drives provide precise power to control the motion of processing and packaging machinery.

Haughton elevators and escalators provide vertical transportation for people and materials in processing plants and shopping centers.

Lorain Products provides Uninterruptible Power Systems to protect the accuracy of computer inventory and distribution controls activated by entries from electronic point-of-sale cash register terminals.

Reliance Electric is more than 20,000 people interacting around the world, including application engineers and industry managers concerned with the needs of the food processing industry. They offer industrial and commercial automation components, systems, and services that no other company can match. And they're backed by distribution and service centers to maintain the equipment they supply.

For 1973, our policy of disciplined acquisitions and interaction paid off with a record $484 million in sales and a 51 percent increase in earnings. Sales to the commercial, industrial, service, and international markets in the first half of 1974 were a record $271 million, and earnings were up 37 percent over the same period in 1973.

This multinational interaction is outlined in our new corporate profile. For a copy, write B. C. Ames, President, Reliance Electric Company, 24701 Euclid Avenue, Cleveland, Ohio 44117.

**Successful businesses interacting.**

RELIANCE ELECTRIC COMPANY

This advertisement appears in
BUSINESS WEEK, July 20. FORTUNE, July. INSTITUTIONAL INVESTOR, August. MEAT PROCESSING, June. NEWSWEEK, August 12, 1974.
M&F Advertising / 5-7122

*Source:* Reliance Electric Co.

**EXHIBIT
12-6 (c)**

*THE RELIANCE ELECTRIC SERIES*

Photo courtesy American Airlines    AA-1181A

## Reliance Electric interaction makes connections at the world's largest airport.

Passengers making connections at the spectacular new Dallas–Ft. Worth Airport get lots of help from Reliance Electric. Our successful interaction of technologies, products, and services helps keep people, baggage and freight on schedule.

**Lorain Products is Reliance Electric,** totally involved in telecommunications through a complete telephone exchange built right on the airport grounds. A broad range of Lorain telecom power and line treatment devices helps assure dependable phone service throughout the sprawling flight complex, from a routine time check to an emergency phone alert in the world's largest control tower.

Even the unique "people movers" that make connections within and between airline terminals and the hotel are controlled by a computer system that receives non-stop power from a network of

Lorain Uninterruptible Power Systems (UPS). At airports across the land, Lorain UPS helps make connections by providing continuous power to computerized hotel and airline reservation systems.

**Successful Reliance Electric businesses** help make connections in other important ways. Toledo Scale equipment quickly weighs baggage and freight for incoming passengers and records the totals for conformance with load-limit requirements. Haughton elevators and escalators whisk passengers from ticket counters to check-in gates. Haughton service specialists maintain all types of transportation and handling equipment in vast and busy terminals.

Reliance electrical drives control conveyors on X-ray and inspection equipment to speed passengers through security areas.

Master gearmotors driven by Reliance electrical V*S® drives control the exact positioning of telescoping boarding ramps for weatherproof direct access between aircraft and terminal.

Reeves mechanical variable speed drives control the movement of handling systems for fast loading and retrieval of passenger baggage.

Dodge couplings, torque-arm speed reducers, bearings, and pulleys on conveyors from cargo holds to carousels help deplaning passengers make connections on the ground.

Reliance Electric is more than 20,000 people interacting around the world, including industry managers concerned with the needs of the transportation and communications industries. They offer industrial and commercial automation components, systems, and services that no other

company can match. And they're backed by distribution and service centers to maintain the equipment they supply.

For fiscal 1974, our interaction policy paid off with sales of $580 million and record earnings of $2.10 per share, fully diluted. Sales to the commercial, industrial, service, and international markets in the first half of 1975 were $326,564,000, and fully diluted earnings were a record $1.23 per share, compared to $.96 per share for the same period in 1974. This multinational interaction is outlined in our corporate profile. For a copy, write B. C. Ames, President, Reliance Electric Company, 29325 Chagrin Blvd., P.O. Box 22280, Cleveland OH 44122.

**Successful businesses interacting.**

**RELIANCE ELECTRIC** ☈

*Source:* Reliance Electric Co.

control. Many advertising and promotion managers will react defensively to this criticism by showing that their overall budget is broken down into detailed expenditures for different activities and programs so that each component part can be controlled. In most cases they are correct. The detail does in fact exist, and they in fact manage the component pieces of their advertising and promotion budget closely. However, it is still a budget and not a plan. You can control actual expenditures within the budget and still not know whether the money was worth spending. For example, what were the budgeted expenditures designed to do in terms of achieving added volume, or gaining new feature recognition or new account interest? When were these accomplishments to occur? What profit impact was anticipated, and how does it relate to the advertising and promotion costs? These are the kinds of questions that need to be answered as part of the advertising and promotion plan to justify budgeted expenditures and provide the basis for determining whether the funds were well spent.

Many of those involved in advertising and promotion activities will argue that you can't define what you are trying to accomplish with advertising and promotion dollars in such precise terms. They claim the dollars budgeted or spent should be regarded as an investment that will somehow pay off in terms of a better image for the company or a better reputation for a product. Those who take this point of view are asking management to accept a lot on faith—which simply does not make sense when so much money is involved.

## The Policy Statement

To be effective, planning and control must begin with an outline of a policy that defines broadly when and how advertising and promotion dollars should be spent. Ideally, the president of the company should take on this task, since he or she is in a better position than anyone else to provide a statement that will set the tone for the way these activities are managed throughout the organization. The responsibility may be delegated to a division general manager or even a product or market manager as long as they have direct responsibility for profit and loss in the area where the dollars will be spent. The president of one industrial company clearly established the parameters for advertising and promotion spending with the following memorandum:

January 15, 1981

To: All General Managers

Subject: Advertising and Promotion Expenditures

I was appalled to find that we spent $3.7 million, or nearly 1 percent of sales, for various types of advertising and promotion last year. Moreover, expenditures for these activities have grown at better than a 15 percent rate each year for the last five years. I don't know how all of this money was spent, but I do know that a lot of it is wasted on repetitive type product ads in various trade journals, giveaway pen and pencil sets, golf balls, and calendars, uncontrolled attendance at trade shows, corporate promotional brochures, etc.

The main reason these expenditures have gotten out of control is that they have been managed at the corporate level and no one with a direct profit responsibility has felt the burden of responsibility for them. Effective February 1, the corporate advertising and promotion function will be disbanded and each division manager will be responsible for the advertising and promotion required in his operation. While each division will be responsible for their own advertising and promotion budget, all budgets should be developed around the following ground rules:

1. No more giveaway items that don't have a direct tie to our business;
2. No more loosely controlled participation in trade shows;
3. No media advertising unless it is specifically designed to:
   a. introduce a new product or new product features;
   b. introduce an existing product to a new market;
   c. introduce the company to some user or customer group or some important part of the financial community that does not know us.
4. No expenditures for any advertising and promotion activities that are not backed by a solid plan that can be used as a vehicle for measurement and control.

As a result of this memorandum, the company's advertising and promotion expenditures were reduced by 60 percent without any loss of market position or selling effectiveness. The approach outlined by the president in this case may be too tough and not applicable in every situation, but it is the kind of a starting point that is essential to ensure proper planning and control.

## The Plan

Once this kind of direction has been provided, the next step is to make sure that a comprehensive advertising and promotion plan is developed to support all proposed expenditures. When completed, the promotional plan should become part of the overall marketing and business plan for presentation to senior management. No special format or approach is required as long as the promotional plan includes the following:

1. A brief statement that defines the objectives of advertising and promotion in meaningful terms, with emphasis on the word "meaningful." For example, a broad statement claiming that advertising and promotion will be used to promote product recognition and the corporate image is not worth saying, since it doesn't mean anything. A statement like the following expresses a serious intent to manage these activities in a businesslike way that provides the best possible chance of generating a return for the dollars spent:

   All our advertising and promotion activities are designed to help sell our company and its products. We expect to work closely with sales and marketing management to ensure that every dollar we spend *supports* their efforts and will ultimately contribute to profit results. We will always ensure that our activities are integrated into sales and marketing plans and that every spending proposal is accompanied by a specific set of goals that will provide the basis for measurement. We will never commit or spend any advertising or promotion dollars on the basis of vague hopes or objectives or without the approval of the line manager responsible for profits.

2. A summary of the budgeted costs for each project or program and a brief written description of the specific marketing and business objectives to be accomplished. Most objectives should be stated in quantifiable terms so that performance can be measured.

3. A measurement program to determine whether approved advertising and promotion goals have been achieved as defined and whether expenditures for these activities were cost effective.

4. A schedule of advertising and promotion events designed in such a way that spending can be cut back without destroying the entire program if the business runs into a difficult period.

Following an approach like this is not easy, but it is well worth the effort. It imposes a discipline on the advertising and promotion management team that helps them function as business partners to support sales and marketing management. It forces an objective analysis of individual projects or programs and expenditures, highlights weaknesses in the overall communications program, and allows selective pruning of nonessential items. And most important, it provides a solid basis for review and control.

## Review and Control

Assuming the advertising and promotion plan has been developed along the lines described above, the final step for management is to ensure that satisfactory results are achieved. This can be done through a full marketing review, or it can be done separately if management chooses. However it is done, a formal review should be conducted at least quarterly and those responsible should be required to explain any variance from planned objectives, timetables, spending levels, or results. If management fails to conduct such a review on a regular basis, you can be sure that the planning process will deteriorate and that a lot of dollars will be wasted on ill-conceived activities that contribute very little to market performance or profits.

As in any business situation, the key to effective review and control is the quality of the plan. There is simply no way to effectively review performance unless you know what it is you want to do in the first place. This is why the detailed planning described earlier is so important.

Many people in the advertising and promotion world will argue that you can't be as specific as we have suggested. Don't buy this argument. If those making the advertising and promotion proposals can't define specific economic benefits they intend to achieve with the expenditures they propose, the money would be better spent if given to charity. When the advertising and promotion budget is based on a sufficiently detailed plan, the review sessions can focus on planned accomplishments and adjustments can be made to ensure objectives are achieved. Alternatively, if it is clear that the objectives cannot be achieved for whatever reasons, spending for advertising and promotion activities can be scaled back or stopped so that more profit flows to the bottom line.

## SUMMARY

Advertising and promotion activities are useful tools for any company: they can build recognition and volume, introduce a new product or service, explain cost benefits to a wide potential customer base, and turn up sales prospects. The key, however, is planning and control so that the dollars spent on this activity have some chance of bringing the company the return it wants. A lot of money is involved, and a lot of it is often wasted because it is difficult to construct the proper mix of activities and to quantify the results.

Business-to-business advertising has special requirements if it is to be successful, and it is up to the marketing organization to get the type of advertising that will work. Most important is planning and control; an advertising budget is not a plan, and occasional checks on how the budget is being spent is not an effective review and control program. The budget must be related to a detailed plan that is formally reviewed on a regular basis to see that the company gets its money's worth from its advertising and promotion effort.

## REVIEW QUESTIONS

1. In what ways can industrial advertising and promotion support a product-market plan?
2. Why are a lot of industrial advertising expenditures wasted or poorly directed?
3. When should the industrial firm not advertise a product?
4. How is industrial advertising different in importance and content from consumer advertising?
5. Why are planning and control essential for all industrial advertising and promotion decisions?

# IV

# DEVELOPING AND EVALUATING PLANS

# 13

# Developing Strategies and Plans

Why Planning Is Important
Some Planning Pitfalls
  Matching Concept and
  Context
  Confusing Various Types
  of Planning
  Overemphasizing the
  System
  Lack of Alternatives
Some Successful Practices
  Good Direction
  Planning Based on
  Cold, Hard Facts
  Superior Programming
Summary
Review Questions

In the fall of 1978 Joe Cohen, a two-year associate with a well-known international consulting firm, was assigned to a study project for a large pump and valve manufacturing company. The study was designed to help the company strengthen its approach to planning so that it could be more responsive to changing market conditions. The company's management believed that outside assistance was necessary to integrate the best features of the planning process that had been developed in its individual subsidiaries, which had been brought together through acquisition.

Each of the four consultants on the study team was assigned to different areas of the business. Joe's assignment was to work with the electronic valve division of the company to define its planning requirements and to recommend a planning approach for the division that would tie in with the planning requirements of the other divisions and the whole corporation. Joe had worked as a product manager for a large food products company and had been very involved in designing and implementing a planning process for that operation. Because of his strong sales and marketing background, he spent a good deal of time with sales and marketing management in the division. After several weeks, he thought he knew enough about the client company's requirements to develop a schematic drawing of the planning and control process that should be followed. As you might expect, he drew heavily on the successful experience he had had with his former employer.

Joe reviewed his work with two division product managers as well as the marketing vice president of the client operation and found that they were generally supportive and enthusiastic. So he was very surprised when the partner in charge of the consulting assignment reacted very negatively to Joe's efforts during the study team review meeting. The partner was blunt: "You have developed an approach for marketing planning and control that may make sense in a package goods business, but is not at all applicable here. You are getting paid to think deeply about the particular planning requirements of our client's operation. If you can't do a better job of discerning these, you can't be a very effective consultant."

When the review meeting ended, Joe sat there. He looked over the schematic he had prepared. Where had he gone wrong? What was so different about the planning requirements of this industrial company?

What are probable differences between this company and Joe's former employer?

Why would a business plan for an industrial firm require a different approach from one for a packaged goods company?

What should be Joe's first step in rethinking his plan?

**C**orporate life would be a lot easier if management could forget or wish away the whole idea of formal business planning, for no one yet has been able to figure out how to get business plans into written form without a lot of hard work. But planning is likely to become a more important management tool in the future as companies face increasingly more complex and difficult situations and continue to scramble to add new products and markets to their base.

## WHY PLANNING IS IMPORTANT

Formal planning, which means committing plans to writing, has been accepted as a way of business life for the past 20 years. The discipline helps managers avoid the mistakes that are bound to occur when they try to ad lib their way through a complex situation. Planning has taken on added importance in recent years as the world has been caught up in a maelstrom of change that has greatly increased the risks and chances of failure for any business venture. Of course, there is really nothing new about change, especially in business. What is different is the velocity with which change is occurring and the sudden impact such change can have on almost any business. Businesspeople all around the world continue to reel from a series of events that are clear evidence of the increasing velocity of change: exploding technology, rapidly increasing foreign competition, the energy crisis, and changing interest rates and currency values. Beyond these, a number of fundamental social changes, like declining birth rates, fewer marriage and family formations, and more two-worker households, have far-reaching implications for most industrial activities. They have caused and will cause real growth to decline in certain markets and to explode in others. They have made or will make dinosaurs out of some products and processes that have historically been mainstays of the American economy. They have caused or will cause other products or processes that have been considered uneconomic in the past to become much more attractive in the future.

Many people tend to view these developments as unusual dislocations that will become less disruptive over time. We don't believe this is the case at all; we believe these developments will have greater impact on industrial operations of all types in the years ahead, and that others like them are going to occur with greater severity and frequency. Many people also argue that it is impossible to plan in an environment characterized by so much change and uncertainty. Actually, these conditions make planning more important. It is essential, not helpful, for management in general and marketing management in particular to devote much more time to thinking about: (1) the direction of these trends and developments; (2) what impact they are likely to have on various businesses; (3) what can be done to minimize the risks or capitalize on the opportunities likely to occur as a result of these changes; and (4) what to do if things turn out differently than expected. Developing answers to these questions and finding responses to a number of scenarios are essential for survival in a period of accelerating change and increasing uncertainty.

Despite the need for and inherent logic of formal business planning, very few companies are really satisfied with the results they achieve for all the time and effort involved.

The comment of one vice president typifies the frustration and disappointment of many executives:

> We knock ourselves out every year with a major time commitment and massive paper flow to put together a strategic plan for the business that is heavily based on marketing input. But we can't really point to any substantive benefits that are directly traceable to all the extra effort. As I see it, our marketing group has not done the job it should in thinking through a strategy. If it had, we'd have a lot stronger edge in the marketplace. At this point I am not sure whether it is something important that we ought to do better or whether it is just a fad that we ought to get rid of.

Why should his reaction be the rule rather than the exception? What are the pitfalls that cause planning results to fall short of expectations? Most important, what lessons can be learned from the experience of those few industrial companies that can honestly point to concrete results from their planning efforts?

# SOME PLANNING PITFALLS

Ignorance of planning theory or mechanics is not the cause of the disappointments so many companies are experiencing. Most industrial managers in both line and staff positions are well aware that effective planning depends on market and economic facts, results in detailed operating programs (not just budgets), and provides the best basis for measurement and control. Few executives are unfamiliar with the concept of formal planning. Various approaches to formal planning have received their share of emphasis in the business literature and the academic world over the past several years, and apparently most executives have tried them. Yet major problems crop up in many companies when they set about putting some kind of a formal planning approach into practice. These problems fall into four categories:

1. Failure to fit the concept to the industrial context
2. Confusion over types of planning
3. Overemphasis on the system at the expense of content
4. Lack of alternative strategies

Let's examine each of the problem categories a bit more closely before moving on to see what steps have been taken by companies that have successfully integrated an effective approach to business planning.

## Matching Concept and Context

Planners often run into trouble when they try to use, without change, concepts developed for planning in consumer goods companies. To a large extent, the disappointing results encountered by industrial companies reflect their failure to recognize two distinguishing characteristics of most industrial companies that dictate a need for a particular planning approach.

The first is the multiplicity of markets and channels discussed in Chapter 2. This diversity of market and channel combinations requires discrete marketing strategies. A consumer goods company typically markets its several brands through one or two channels to a common consumer group. A multiproduct industrial manufacturer is likely to sell in a wide range of different markets through a variety of channels. For example, it would not be uncommon for a manufacturer of electrical components to sell its major product lines in as many as 30 distinct markets through several different channels and face different competitors in different markets. As you can appreciate, anyone who tried to cover this complex network of markets and channels with a single marketing plan would be doomed to failure. What is actually needed is a number of discrete plans, one for each combination of products and markets that can be managed as a discrete entity (often called a product-market business).

Juggling a large number of markets and channels is not the only problem facing planners in industrial marketing. They must also plan around and with the other functions of the business, since marketing simply does not control factors like engineering or manufacturing that typically make or break performance in the marketplace. As we have stated, marketing success in the industrial world depends largely on the activities of functions like engineering, manufacturing, and technical service. This means that changes in marketing strategy are likely to be based on product design, manufacturing cost, or service innovations, rather than on advertising, promotion, and merchandising—the core elements of the consumer goods marketing plan. Because the success of marketing plans depends to a large extent on activities in other functional areas and on the share of total company resources each product-market business receives, it is unrealistic to expect product managers, market managers, or even the head of marketing to handle the job without the full participation of operating managers. The role of the marketing planner in an industrial company is to analyze and interpret market requirements and determine what operating managers in all functional areas of the business must do to meet these requirements. The planner draws together ideas for an assigned product or market, but the resulting plan is a total business plan, not just a marketing plan.

Obvious as this point might seem, it is frequently overlooked in industrial companies. Having embraced formal planning as a sophisticated way of running the business, many executives try to turn the entire job over to marketing or sales management. After a couple of years of frustration, they are ready to write off the whole effort as a monumental waste of time. The real cause of their disappointment lies not in the concept, however, but in the way it has been applied (see the box). Unfortunately, this has been the experience of a great many otherwise well-managed companies. Far too much planning is carried on as a parallel activity that gets plenty of lip service, but little real attention from the line decision makers.

## Confusing Various Types of Planning

Confusion over the distinctions among strategic planning, long-range planning, operational planning, corporate strategy, and product-market strategy also leads to major diffi-

---

## PLANNING ISN'T WORTH THE EFFORT

A major chemical company added a group of six managers to its marketing organization, gave them a planning format to follow, and told them to develop a written plan for achieving a stronger and more profitable position in their assigned markets. All six managers, eager to earn their spurs, embarked on a massive fact-gathering and writing effort. After several months, hundreds of pages of plans and supporting documentation had been written, but no one in top management was much impressed. The president put it this way:

> I'm being generous when I say the end products are only slightly better than useless. Admittedly, we have some better market facts now, but the plans are based on a lot of ideas for product and market development that just aren't in line with my idea of the direction this business should take. On top of that, they've left out a lot of technical and capital considerations that really count. I've concluded that our market managers are simply too far out of the mainstream of the business to do an intelligent job of planning for us.

Not surprisingly, the market managers felt they too had good cause for complaint. As one of them put it:

> The first month of effort was worthwhile. We were putting a fact base together that is essential for intelligent planning. But after that we were flying blind. We never had any idea from top management on the kind of business the company wanted or didn't want, the minimal return it expected, or the kind of support it would be willing to throw into various markets. Worse still, we had no cooperation from the development group, the plants, or even the sales force, where decisions that really influence the business are made. The planning we did was bound to be a bust.

---

culties in accomplishing the planning job. These are all distinctly different types of planning, and the terms cannot be used interchangeably without creating confusion. To start with, it is useful to point out the differences and the relationships between strategic and operational planning.

STRATEGIC PLANNING VERSUS OPERATIONAL PLANNING.  *Strategic* planning defines the basic direction of the business and provides the basis for allocating and committing resources, both labor and capital, to a course of action designed to achieve corporate objectives. The distinguishing feature of strategic plans or decisions is that they typically involve a commitment of resources to a particular course of action. And once these resources are committed, it is difficult to change directions. This is not to say a commitment to a strategic course of action is irrevocable, but a penalty is incurred if directions are changed once a company starts to implement a strategic decision. For example, there is no way to reverse a decision on an acquisition once it has been made or to retract funding commitments for new product or market development once the project is underway without suffering some kind of a time and cost penalty.

The time frame involved is another distinguishing characteristic of strategic planning. Generally, strategic planning covers a period of several years. Three to five years is a reasonable period in industrial manufacturing companies, since most strategic decisions or actions (such as building a new manufacturing facility, developing new products or a position in new markets, or completing acquisition or divestiture programs) can be implemented within this period. Heavy manufacturing or resource companies may need to plan over an even longer period to allow sufficient time for completion of the huge capital projects often required to add new capacity or to develop natural resources.

*Operational* planning, on the other hand, is typically done annually, and operating plans should be designed to implement strategic business decisions. They also provide management with an annual budget for controlling performance year to year, quarter to quarter, or even month to month. Many of the cost and time commitments reflected in the operating plan are the result of strategic decisions to develop new products, build new plant facilities, strengthen positions in new markets, or make an acquisition effort in one direction or another. Since the operating plan is a vehicle to help implement the strategic plan, it is obvious that the two types of plans must be directly linked. In effect, the first year of a strategic plan serves as the foundation for next year's operating plan.

HOW SALES FORECASTS TIE IN: THE HEAD NUMBERS.     The pivotal factor in any operating plan is the sales forecast. Manufacturing levels as well as expense budgets are related to the sales forecast when the operating plan is put together. The sales forecast is also the most variable and least controllable set of numbers in any business plan. Manufacturing costs are far more predictable since there is generally an experience base from which manufacturing costs at various volume levels can be predicted with a fair degree of accuracy. Also, expense levels for most sales, general, and administrative activities or programs are known from prior experience and are therefore more predictable. Sales results on the other hand are dependent on a host of uncontrollable factors like the economy, competitor actions, industry or user developments, and so on.

There are a variety of techniques for making sales forecasts that range from simple trend line extrapolations to sophisticated statistical and computer based projections developed around relevant market and economic indicators, as we've shown in Chapter 6. Regardless of how the sales forecast is made, however, it is still a guess about future events and has all the uncertainty of any prognostication. In most manufacturing companies, multiple forecasts are prepared by different individuals or groups within the organization, and it is general management's job to sort out these forecasts and ensure that they are properly used to plan, manage, and control the business. Let's examine the different types of forecasts that are likely to be made in any industrial concern.

First, most salespeople are asked to make a "grass roots" sales forecast for their accounts and territories. The aggregate of individual sales forecasts typically reflects the optimistic view of an enthusiastic sales force and is generally an unrealistic set of numbers for making operating or financial commitments. Recognizing this point, sales management usually scales back the salespeople's forecast and recommends a lower set of numbers for planning purposes. If product managers are involved in the organization, they will make sales forecasts for their assigned product line, based on their best estimates of market conditions and the competitive situation. The aggregate of the product forecasts is a good cross-check against the forecast made by sales management, but also may be on the high side since it is unlikely that everything will turn out the way all the product managers expect. Many companies also have additional sales forecasts made by independent market or economic research groups to get still another picture of sales expectations. Finally, it is not unusual for manufacturing management to "second guess" any of these forecasts and make a forecast of its own to schedule its manufacturing operations. A manufacturing manager for a bearing company put it this way: "The sales guys always have a 'pie in the sky' forecast that they never make, and I am not going to build product to a forecast like that."

It is general management's job to make certain that everyone in the organization has a clear understanding of what forecast is going to be used for what purposes. Probably the best approach is to use one of the more optimistic forecasts as a basis for setting sales quotas, establishing incentive programs, and evaluating individual sales performance. This avoids the need to set sales goals that are lower than the salespeople think they can achieve and hopefully will stretch the sales force toward better performance. A second, more conservative forecast, however, should be used to make operating and financial plans and commitments. It is always much easier to adjust these plans and commitments upward if higher sales are achieved than it is to scale them back if actual sales results fall below forecast. Following this approach will help management avoid the embarrassment of having to explain that profits suffered because sales were lower than forecast and that operating and expense ratios got out of line.

PRODUCT-MARKET STRATEGY VERSUS CORPORATE STRATEGY. Beyond the distinction between strategic and operational planning, a distinction needs to be made between the two categories of strategic planning that should be carried out in any multibusiness company.

The first category of strategic planning is product-market strategy. We noted earlier that a separate strategy is needed for each identified product-market business. A well-defined product-market strategy should show where the business is heading and what kind of growth and profits can be expected. Division marketing and general management have the major responsibility for developing product-market strategy by helping to determine answers to questions like these:

1. Is the basic cost and profit structure of the business competitive? If not, what does it take to get marginal operations on a competitive footing?
2. Is the business focused on the right market segments? If not, how should the focus be shifted?
3. What external factors are likely to affect growth and profit potential favorably or unfavorably?
4. Is the operation's technology even with, ahead of, or behind major competitors?
5. Should investments be made in engineering, marketing, or manufacturing to enlarge or improve the business?
6. Should investments be made to integrate forward to strengthen market position or backward to improve the profit structure and/or ensure a stable source of supply?

7. Is plant capacity available to handle increased volume expectations? If not, when will new capacity be needed, and how much?
8. How much new capital is required for what projects, and what payoff is expected?
9. What is the sales, profit, and cash flow outlook for the business, and what is the probability of achieving these results?

Once product-market strategies are developed for each business unit, corporate management has the basis for deciding what strategic moves, if any, are required at the corporate level. This leads to the second type of strategic planning typically done by corporate management, which is designed to answer two fundamental questions:

1. Does the outlook for all the company's strategic business units, in the aggregate, meet corporate growth and profit goals?
2. If not, how big is the gap, and what are the ways to close it?

Exhibit 13-1 shows how a gap can be calculated by aggregating the planned performance of all business units and comparing the result with corporate goals. As you can see, the company's operating divisions have projected earnings well below the corporate objective of 15 percent compounded growth each year, and an earnings gap of $1.20 per share is expected. If we assume there are 5 million shares outstanding, the company needs to pick up $6 million of after-tax earnings over the next five years to close the gap. In this kind of situation, corporate management has three alternatives:

1. Change the corporate earnings target.
2. Restructure division plans to close the gap.
3. Redeploy capital into new businesses with sufficient earnings power to close the gap.

Obviously, some combination of these alternatives is also a choice, and probably the most prudent approach to follow when a strategic planning gap occurs. Whatever the decision, it is likely to change the structure or even the basic direction of the company.

It is strategic planning gaps like these that cause companies to expand certain businesses, sell off others, make acquisitions, and take other actions that reshape the basic character and earnings stream of the business. When you read that some company has sold one of its business units or diversified into a completely new area, you may be seeing the actual results of a shift in corporate strategy. Corporate management has decided that the current structure of its business is not satisfactory to achieve its goals and has carried out a strategic decision to change that structure.

Warner-Lambert and Diamond Shamrock are two companies that have undergone a major restructuring of their businesses. Warner-Lambert sold off its Entenmann's bakery products unit and used the proceeds to buy Imed, a west coast manufacturer of sophisticated medical electronics equipment. These moves were designed to take the company deeper into the medical equipment field. Diamond Shamrock sold off certain of its chemical and plastic units and acquired Sigmore and Natomos to further its objective to become an energy resource company.

**EXHIBIT
13-1**

## CALCULATING THE AGGREGATE OUTLOOK

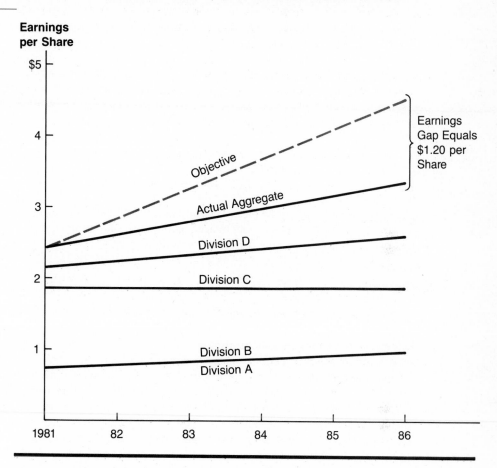

## Overemphasizing the System

Many companies have developed comprehensive planning systems that define formats and procedures in great detail. Although some of this structure is necessary, in too many cases the system is so detailed and so rigid that it is a hindrance rather than a help to the planning process. In effect, the system becomes the end product rather than the means to an end, and management is deluded into thinking that it is doing a good job of planning when in fact it is not. Of all the roadblocks, the problem of structure is the most frustrating to managers charged with the responsibility for planning. They recognize that good planning is hard work and cannot be done without a certain amount of pencil pushing. But they bitterly resent demands for excessive written material or filled-in forms that serve no practical business purpose. A product manager for an electronic equipment manufacturer voiced this complaint:

> As part of my planning responsibility, I have to follow a format prescribed by the corporate planning group that calls for a point-by-point discussion of history and a laundry list of problems and opportunities. I'm "gigged" if I don't cover every point in the format, and there's no way to do it in less than ten pages of text. That takes a lot of time—mostly wasted time. All the product managers are sore about it. Much of what we have to write is a rehash of the same old things year after year. In effect, we're being discouraged from concentrating on the issues of the business that are really critical. What they want to see, apparently, is a nice, neat set of plans that all look alike. It just doesn't make sense.

Unfortunately, situations like this are not unusual. Some overzealous staff person or corporate group designs a series of forms that are completely out of phase with the realities of the business. The resulting paperwork chews up great blocks of precious time without producing anything more than a lot of accounting schedules and some kind of written description of what would have been done anyway.

## Lack of Alternatives

Given the dynamics of most business situations, it is surprising to find that many planners have tunnel vision in thinking about how the business should be run. Many plans are nothing more than repetitions of prior programs, and hardly worth the paper they are written on. This is the reason so many industrial companies are chronically behind the competition and plagued with poor results. The tendency to base current plans on past practice was forced into the open in one company when each planner was asked by top management to outline alternative strategies for developing his or her assigned market area and to summarize the commitments required (financial, staff, facilities) and the payoff expected (sales, profits, ROI). The request drew a complete blank. The planners were so locked into their accustomed way of thinking about selling their products that they could not conceive of a different approach that made any commercial sense at all.

This planning problem stems from a deficiency that has plagued industrial businesses seemingly forever. Far too many managers have let their businesses "die on the vine" or missed major opportunities because they thought only about selling and promoting their products and technologies instead of serving the marketplace. Levitt called this failing "Marketing Myopia" in his classic *Harvard Business Review* article.[1] It is exceedingly difficult to think about abandoning traditional products, technologies, and basic business beliefs to preserve or secure a stronger position in markets. However, the tendency to concentrate on existing products and technologies without sufficient regard for what is going on in the marketplace is a critical weakness. William Brickner, the CEO of Diamond Shamrock, put the importance of this point into focus when he responded to a question about the loss of vitality in American industry with this comment:

[1] Theodore Levitt, "Marketing Myopia," *Harvard Business Review*, July–August 1960, p. 176.

To my mind, one central reason is this—our strategies have become too rigid. In trying to make our companies more manageable, we've constructed formula after formula which tells us how to run our businesses, and too often we get so tied up in the formula, we forget the real world. We're like a football team that sticks to its game plan late in the fourth quarter—even though it's losing 21–0.

Insufficient or less-than-candid analysis is a prime cause of unimaginative planning. Many planners either misjudge or fail to understand the underlying economics of the business or the changes in the marketplace (competitive moves, shifts in usage or demand patterns) that call for new strategies. Many planners also appear reluctant to face up to unpleasant truths about their competitive situation, such as high price, low product quality, or poor service, that place the company in an untenable position. Without a thorough, candid appraisal of the business climate, the need for fresh ways of running the business goes unrecognized. Thus, instead of getting a choice among alternatives, top management all too frequently has to settle for a single recommendation that usually calls for the continuation of the same old strategies.

## SOME SUCCESSFUL PRACTICES

Despite the pitfalls in the path of formal planning, many companies have successfully built formal planning into their management process. Without exception, these companies concentrate on developing market-driven plans that are part and parcel of the management process of each product-market business. They have reached this level of sophistication primarily because of three factors:

1. Better direction from the top
2. Planning based on cold, hard facts
3. Superior programming for implementation

Let's examine each of these vital factors in some detail to see how they can lead to better ways of doing things.

### Good Direction

The business planning done in leader companies produces results because it is carried out with full recognition of the multiplicity of products, markets, and channels, and of the need for a total business rather than a sales or merchandising orientation. The president of an automotive parts company demonstrated the importance of this point with the following comment:

It took me three years to realize that our marketing people couldn't come up with the kind of plans I wanted for our products and markets unless I worked closely with them. They have always been able to develop a picture of where our markets are heading, identify the opportunities that exist, and interpret what we have to do to build the business. But so many considerations and options require a general management perspective that marketing can't be expected to come up with recommendations that make sense from my point of view. Unless I set the basic direction and targets for our business, specify who is to plan what, see to it that engineering, manufacturing, and sales really work with marketing to provide what is needed, and then challenge and contribute any ideas I can on how our business can be developed, the whole planning effort is nothing more than a paperwork exercise.

This comment underscores several ways in which top management must participate in the planning process to make it pay off. It must define objectives and guidelines, as well as planning units; follow a practical approach; define expected content; ensure coordination; and contribute ideas.

CORPORATE OBJECTIVES AND GUIDELINES.   "If only top management would tell me what they want!" is a common complaint among division and middle managers with major planning responsibilities. Perhaps some of them expect too much. Perhaps some would like top management to spell everything out for them in detail. But they are right in asking for guidelines that spell out the rules of the game. It is unquestionably a necessity for anyone who holds a key planning responsibility to know in specific terms how fast top management wants the business to grow, what products and markets should be emphasized, what kinds of businesses should be avoided, and what profit returns are acceptable.

Guidelines like these are essential to provide a directional framework for managers actually doing the planning in the various business units. The key here is to make sure that the criteria are rational and in line with the realities of the business. Guidelines should provide focus and direction without putting anyone in a strait jacket (see the box). Continuing emphasis on guidelines and targets tends to force the strategic thinking and planning in each business unit into areas of business that have the potential to accomplish corporate objectives and out of areas where this possibility does not exist.

PLANNING UNITS.   As we have said, it is usually unrealistic to develop plans for an industrial division or product business as a whole. It makes more sense to find a way of segmenting the business according to some combination of product, market, customer, supplier, or application. These segments should be the building blocks for planning rather than the large operating units that are typically shown on corporate organization charts. The slogan "small is beautiful" is a most appropriate reminder to business planners. It is much easier to develop strategies for discrete product-market segments than for some big organization unit that houses multiple product-market businesses with quite different customers, competitors, and product requirements.

Sometimes these planning units cross organizational boundaries, as when products in several divisions combine to serve a particular market. A multinational company in the electrical products field combined the utility products produced in three separate divisions into one strategic planning unit so that a comprehensive plan could be developed for achieving a larger position in the power utility market. It is not unusual for companies that are successful at strategic planning to break five or six major organization units

## GIVING DIRECTION THE RIGHT WAY

This letter from the president of a machine tool manufacturer to the company's division managers set the stage for effective planning:

As you know, our fundamental purpose is to earn a return for our shareholders that is more attractive than they could expect from other investments with similar risks. To do this means we must consistently compound our earnings at a rate that is 5 to 7 percent higher than inflation and achieve a return on stockholder equity in excess of 22 percent. For the corporation to achieve this kind of performance means that each operating unit must compound its earnings growth at the same rate and achieve an after-tax return on assets of at least 20 percent. In most cases we will need to improve our after-tax return on sales to 7 percent or better to achieve the target return on net assets.

Sustained performance at these levels will place our company in the upper quartile of all *Fortune* 500 companies, which is what we need to do to generate attractive gains for our shareholders. These goals are mathematically compatible given our capital structure, debt limitations, and dividend requirements. Even more important, they are achievable. In fact, the leader companies in our industry have done better over the past several years.

It should be obvious that we need to refocus several parts of our business to achieve the profit goals outlined in the second paragraph. As you commence your planning assignments, be sure to keep the following ground rules in mind.

1. We want to reduce our dependence on the automotive industry specifically and capital goods spending in general so that we can achieve a more stable earnings pattern.
2. We want to shift our focus from building and selling traditional products to serving selected markets (e.g., aerospace, oil field, electronics, office equipment), which we believe have more attractive growth prospects than the economy overall.
3. We want to grow our business in these target markets at the expense of our position in our traditional businesses and we want to recover capital that is marginally employed in any of our current operations.
4. We want to set up all of our service and repair operations as discrete profit centers and grow these businesses faster than our total business; we will enter new service and repair areas to do so.
5. We want to operate an increasing percentage of our business in a nonunion environment and we will incur the cost penalties and supply the capital required to do so.
6. We don't want to put new capital into any product-market business that does not offer the possibility of achieving our profit goals within the next two to three years.
7. We will accept a negative cash flow to support growth as long as earnings projections grow faster than 20 percent each year and there are no shortfalls from plan.

down into 50 or more discrete chunks for strategic planning purposes. Reliance Electric is a case in point. Although the company is managed around five major organization units (electrical products, mechanical products, Toledo scale, telecommunications, and Federal Pacific), the business is planned and controlled around more than 100 separate product centers, each with its own plan.

PRACTICAL APPROACHES.    To avoid overemphasis on form or systems, top management should insist on a straightforward planning approach. Although any approach to planning obviously needs to be tailored to the particular characteristics and requirements of the situation, it is essential to keep several fundamental points in mind:

1. In most mature industrial operations, past trends are the most likely predictors of the future. Following this line of reasoning, the planning for each product-market business should start with a straight-line extrapolation of sales and profit trends over five years. In most cases, this projection will provide a realistic picture of what future results are likely to be, assuming no change in the business cycle or direction of the business. If the results of this first projection appear to be satisfactory, the whole purpose of planning should be to ensure that they are achieved. If the results are unsatisfactory, the focus should shift to doing whatever is necessary to improve them.
2. Only four factors can cause future results to depart from the projection of past trends: (a) a change in the rate of growth of the total market, (b) a change in the definition or scope of the market served, (c) a change in market share position, and (d) a change in the cost or profit structure of the business. The extent to which management intends to cause improvements in any one or a combination of these factors so that planned results depart from the initial trend projection can and should be quantified. It is essential to know how much change is required in any of these areas as a basis for thinking through the programs, actions, and decisions that serve as the foundation for the plan.
3. The great bulk of the planning effort should revolve around cross-functional discussions covering such points as (a) how the business has performed to date; (b) what forces are at work that will affect its future; (c) what kinds of improvements in market growth, market share, or the basic cost-profit structure can realistically be achieved; and (d) what requirements and commitments are needed from each functional group to make the right things happen. This give-and-take cross-functional discussion should be the heart of the planning process. It promotes a team effort, ensures that problems and alternatives are considered in light of overall business needs, and provides the basis for making commitments that will lead to successful implementation.
4. The agreed-upon programs, actions, and decisions that will lead to improved results, as well as the rationale for assuming success, should be defined in a few convincing sentences. Anything more generally means that the planners are trying to get by with verbiage instead of good ideas.
5. Facts, not emotions, should control all decisions. No "sacred cows" should be allowed, and everyone should understand there is no single way to run the business. If overall growth and profit targets cannot be achieved in a reasonable time frame with the current business structure, the focus should be on how it can be changed. If the

business cannot be restructured to achieve growth and profit targets, management should focus its efforts on the best way to recover the capital employed.

There is nothing sophisticated about these points, but keeping them in mind prevents devoting a lot of time and effort to generating a massive flow of paperwork and a lot of useless "pie in the sky" plans.

EXPECTED CONTENT. In companies with many divisions or business units, the chances are great for a wide variety of interpretations if top management does not provide direction as to the end products expected. The trick is to provide direction without locking anyone into a straitjacket. The following memorandum sent to all operating managers by the president of a multidivision company serving the oil field industry illustrates how direction can be provided without getting everyone strapped into an elaborate set of forms and procedures.

As we move toward our plan review dates, it is important to agree on what your end products should look like. I think you can summarize everything I want to see on a few slides.

1. Define in a paragraph or two what it is your division is seeking to do in a way that provides the rationale for the growth and profit goals you have set. In other words, state the business mission you have defined for your division and the strengths you intend to build on to accelerate profit growth.
2. Show a five year history of sales, market share, earnings before taxes, return on sales, return on net assets and cash flow and compare with our corporate targets. Do this for your division overall and for each product-market segment for which you have prepared a strategic plan.
3. Show three year projections of sales, market share, earnings before taxes, return on sales, return on net assets and cash flow for your division overall and for each product-market segment.
4. List the key strategic decisions, commitments and programs required for your division and for each product-market business. If major capital or expense commitments are required, be sure to highlight these and indicate the probable timing. Also, be sure to comment on your priorities in the event that corporate resources cannot fund everything you want to do.
5. Describe what strategic alternatives you could pursue to accelerate your profit growth, assuming no constraints on capital or short-term profit requirements.

Be sure to have the backup detail to respond to questions that are sure to be raised during your presentation. You will undoubtedly want to have your whole management team with you so that questions can be directed to those most directly responsible.

In another successful company, top management chose to be even more definitive and provided the form shown in Exhibit 13-2, which was to be completed for each product-market business. As you can see, it covers many of the same points outlined in the president's letter to his operating managers. The choice of a form or a letter is a matter of

# PLANNING SUMMARY FORM

**EXHIBIT 13-2**

STRATEGIC SUMMARY

1. Product and/or Service

2. Customers

3. End Use

4. Rank | Direct Competitors | Yr. before Last Market Share | Last Year (CY ___) Sales, This Market | Market Share

1.
2.
3.
4.
5.
6.
7.
8.
9.

Total Direct Market    100% $ _____ K _____ 100%

5. Competitive Advantages

VERSUS LARGEST COMPETITOR

6. Competitive Disadvantages

VERSUS LARGEST COMPETITOR

7. Market Alternatives (Competing Techniques)

8. Factors Affecting Future Market Growth

9. Summary of Strategy

SIMPLE DECLARATIVE STATEMENTS OF WHAT IS TO BE DONE AND HOW IT WILL BE DONE, THEN AMPLIFY AS NECESSARY, INDICATING KEY IMPLEMENTATIONAL EMPHASIS AND ACTIONS.

TYPE:
Build
Hold
Harvest
Withdraw
Explore

DIRECTION:
Base
Market Seg.
Output Diff.
Mark't Devel.
Outp't Devel.

POSTURE:
Leader
Me Too
Performance
Value
Price
Economy
Prestige

10. History/Forecast

Market
Share of Market, %
Sales
Operating Profit, % to Sales
Date

*Source:* Regency Electronics Co.

style, as long as the content required is appropriately defined. The end products required may vary from company to company, but the objective should always be to avoid a lot of details, forms, and schedules and concentrate instead on content that brings the strategic issues and options into sharper focus.

COORDINATION.   Even the most carefully conceived marketing organization structure will fail unless marketing planners work effectively with the other functions that influence performance in the marketplace. To do this, they must command the respect of their functional counterparts. And all concerned must have a clear understanding of how they are expected to work together.

A manufacturer in the building products field learned this lesson the hard way. The company set up a product management group in its marketing organization to spearhead business planning for each product area. During the first two years of the group's existence, the plans developed fell far short of everyone's expectations, and there was much friction between the product management group and other functional managers. One of the product managers put his finger on the problem when he pointed out the many functions other than marketing and sales he had to work with to do a good planning job. Much of the difficulty he encountered, he said, stemmed from misunderstanding on the part of many functional managers about the role product managers should play in the planning process. Even the product managers themselves, he added, were unsure about their responsibilities.

Recognizing the need to put the product group on a stronger footing for dealing with functions outside marketing, the president took three steps. He decided first to replace four of the product managers, who were basically sales-oriented, with people who had stronger technical backgrounds and a better grasp of the business as a whole. He then eliminated the position of group product manager and moved the product managers up to a level on an organizational par with their major contacts in other functional areas, thus enabling them to communicate more effectively. Even more important, since the product managers reported directly to the marketing vice president, they could stay in close touch with top management. Third, he held a series of meetings with the executives of all major functions to explain what the product managers were trying to accomplish and how the different functions should work with them. At these meetings, the president made it clear that he was looking to the product managers to play a lead role in developing plans geared to the characteristics and requirements of the marketplace. He also left no doubt that he expected all functions to cooperate with them. This no-nonsense statement on their role cleared away any misconceptions blocking effective interaction between the product managers and other functions and paved the way for a much more productive planning effort.

IDEAS AND ALTERNATIVES.   If top management truly wants to find ways of improving profits and growth, it must actively participate in the development of strategies by challenging their underlying assumptions and by contributing alternative ideas. Most strategic decisions, particularly those that involve a change in direction, require the experience, perspective, and "feel" of top management—not just its blessing. To be sure, many top executives try to do this; but the way they do it often stifles rather than encourages new ideas. They must take pains to avoid the atmosphere of an inquisition and instead encourage an open exchange of ideas and opinions. In such an environment one idea leads to another, and the management team soon finds itself exploring new and imaginative ways of developing the business.

An interfunctional give-and-take discussion of this sort led one heavy machinery manufacturer to adopt a new marketing strategy that gave its parts operation a chance for survival. In this company, as in many others, parts sales had traditionally been a major source of profits. Now management was concerned because "parts pirates" (local parts producers) were cutting sharply into its business. Asked to develop a marketing strategy that would reverse the trend, the parts manager first came up with a plan that called for adding three salespeople and cutting prices on a large number of parts. As he acknowledged, the plan was essentially no more than a holding action. During the planning review session, in which all functions took part, the company president encouraged everyone to take an entrepreneurial look at the parts business and to try to think of ways to preserve or even enlarge it. Predictably, fresh ideas were hard to come by in a business that had been run the same way for years. But eventually three ideas emerged that were considered worthwhile: (1) build a service organization and sell contracts for maintenance service instead of just parts; (2) decentralize the parts business and set up local parts and repair shops to compete head to head with local competitors; and (3) start to buy and sell parts for other manufacturers' equipment in order to spread overhead costs. The parts manager was naturally somewhat reluctant to do any of these things, since they would revolutionize his end of the business. But with top management backing and encouragement and a knowledge of the business, he did the required analytical work and came back with two possible strategies based on the first two ideas that offered a much more attractive outlook.

This process does not always lead to a viable strategy, since it is not always possible to overcome the scarcity of fresh ideas characteristic of a business that has been run the same way for years. Moreover, alternative strategies are not always visible on a first pass. But the more successful companies insist that all plans include alternative strategies and avoid getting locked into a self-defeating "business as usual" pattern of thinking. Free generation of ideas among marketing, top management, and other functions is really the heart of the planning process, for it is during these discussions that marketing presents the requirements of the marketplace and the other functions discuss feasible ways of responding to them. A discussion to generate strategies must be driven by an intimate knowledge of trends in the business brought about by changing customer requirements, competitive actions, and emerging technologies. With all the opportunities and constraints out in the open, top management has a good basis for deciding how to allocate corporate resources. Once the best combination of ideas is agreed on, the various functions are in a position to make commitments on the timing and costs of the actions that underlie the marketing plan. Leading company executives insist this is the best vehicle for triggering fresh ideas and ensuring interfunctional coordination.

## Planning Based on Cold, Hard Facts

Companies that excel in strategic planning never let emotions or wishful thinking influence their plans and decisions. Their managements are well aware of several truisms that greatly influence the outlook for most industrial companies.

To begin with, strategic thinking must always start with the market. This is particularly true now, when market growth is no longer an automatic "given" in most industrial situations. In the 1960s and early 1970s, it was not unrealistic to think in terms of 4 to 5 percent real growth for most businesses, since GNP was growing close to that rate in real terms. Since 1973, however, the rate of real growth and GNP has declined significantly. Most economists are now projecting a prolonged phase of lower economic growth. Multinational competition has increased, and an increasing number of industrial markets are likely to be stagnant or slow growing. This does not mean that growth is impossible or should be forgotten as an objective in the industrial world. It does mean that product-market strategies must be realistically geared to four "facts of life":

1. Rapid growth for any industrial product tends to be short term because new products and new competitors will generally find their way into attractive growth markets. A "boom market" can mislead management in its strategic thinking and planning. The importance of market share is often overlooked because sales are growing rapidly with the market. The need for fully competitive costs and products is often obscured because a growth market will absorb marginal producers and products. But the euphoria of a growth market will not continue forever, and marginal producers and products will fail as the market moves into a mature stage.

2. Rapid growth usually does not return to a mature industry; although it is possible for a mature or declining market to experience short growth spurts, strategy should be guided by the market's long-term prospects. There are exceptions to this generalization, however. When rapid growth does return to a mature industry, it is because of some structural change in the underlying technology or economy. For example, from 1950 to the mid-1960s the industrial scale market was essentially saturated and showed very limited unit growth. In the mid-1960s, however, the technology shifted from mechanical to electronic. The significant advantages of electronic scales motivated many customers to replace mechanical scales that were still perfectly usable. The combination of a large number of replacement sales plus higher unit volume triggered a growth rate in the market that was significant for the next ten years. Similarly, the market for automatic screw machines has been flat to declining for the past ten years. However, automatic screw machines are the most efficient means known to produce small arms munitions. If a major war should break out (God forbid), the market demand for these machines would grow dramatically.

3. Competition tends to be more intense in low-growth markets because a company in a high-growth environment can increase its sales without taking market share from its competitors. When a market is flat or declining, however, growth occurs only at the expense of others. For this reason, a division in a stagnant market can be a greater managerial challenge than one in a high-growth market.

4. Changes in products, technology, and distribution continue to occur in stagnant industries. For example, the technology for producing steel and automobiles has improved dramatically during the past decade despite greatly increased competition and unfavorable market trends. Stagnant demand, therefore, does not mean stagnant technology.

Given these "facts of life," the key to developing a successful product-market strategy is to ensure that it is developed around some genuine competitive advantage gained by a distinctive approach, such as offering products with distinctive performance or cost characteristics, using alternative sales and distribution channels and/or manufacturing processing, offering superior postsale service, or achieving an advantageous cost structure. Whatever the approach, the objective is always to establish a clear and favorable differentiation from competitors. Without such an advantage, it is unlikely that any strategy will provide the basis for generating above-average profit growth over the long term. Product performance, price, and service are the basics of any industrial business, and a disadvantage in any one of these areas simply cannot be offset by hard work or brilliant management. This means that in situations where disadvantages in any of these areas exist, the product-market strategy must focus on ways to correct or overcome them.

Companies that compete most successfully in the industrial world develop their strategies around three approaches, all designed to achieve and sustain a competitive advantage.

1. They concentrate on growth segments within the markets they serve. Even the most stagnant markets generally offer a segment—a particular customer group, product characteristic, or type of distribution—capable of supporting better than average rates of growth. For example, electronic test, medical, and office equipment markets have sustained attractive growth rates during the current recessionary period.
2. They emphasize high quality and product innovation. Innovations, especially those that are proprietary, are difficult and expensive for competitors to imitate. They keep a product from becoming a commodity and thus allow the company to compete on a basis other than price. Toledo Scale took the lead in moving the very mature and slow-growing weighing industry into electronics and picked up significant market share and profits by introducing sophisticated computing scales for parts counting and other industrial applications.
3. They continuously strive for operating efficiencies by specializing and automating to reduce unit costs, by consolidating products and facilities if demand increases to take advantage of scale, and by seeking broader and more efficient distribution to lower costs. In short, they recognize the need to drive toward the lowest possible cost base to be an effective competitor over the long term.

Many managers talk a good game about making a factual assessment of the performance, competitive standing, and outlook for their business, but few really do it in a tough-minded way. Instead, too much emphasis is generally placed on verbal explanations of why sales have not materialized, why profit returns are low, or why competitors seem to have an edge. The objective should be to strip away all the rhetoric and rationalizations and simply look at the cold, hard facts. There are several ways to make this factual assessment: flow charts, life cycle analysis, and historical pattern analysis.

FLOW CHARTS.    A flow chart should show the major steps involved in serving the customer, from sourcing the raw material to providing postpurchase service. Once this flow chart is developed, it is much easier to pinpoint competitive strengths and weaknesses. Exhibit 13-3 shows how this was done for a manufacturer of industrial scales and weighing systems.

As you can see, these flow charts present a much sharper picture of the company's

**EXHIBIT
13-3**

## FLOW CHART ANALYSIS OF STRENGTHS AND WEAKNESSES

A. Identifying points of leverage

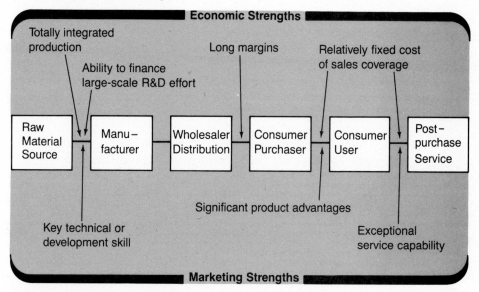

B. Identifying points of vulnerability

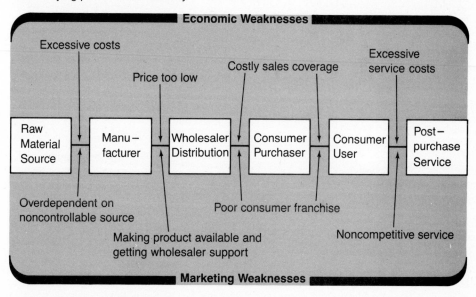

*Source:* B. C. Ames, "Marketing Planning," *Harvard Business Review,* September–October 1968, p. 107.

competitive strengths and weaknesses than a simple listing of the same points. They can also be used to gain management understanding and agreement on how the business flows, where major assets are committed, and how the company is positioned in the market against its competitors so that better questions can be raised about the real advantages of perceived strengths and the seriousness of perceived weaknesses.

LIFE CYCLE ANALYSIS.   Another useful way to look at the facts is to relate the current competitive position of each product-market business to its position on a life cycle curve. Understanding this relationship is crucial, since it enables management to see which businesses offer real growth potential and which do not. Exhibit 13-4 shows how a manufacturer of machine tools made such an analysis of its major product lines. As you can see, this chart suggests that the company has the strongest competitive position in its mature product lines and very little strength in product lines with attractive growth prospects. The picture can be made even clearer by positioning competitor products on the same chart. There are obviously a number of additional factors that need to be considered before conclusions can be drawn; however, this chart alone provides a useful foundation for thinking through the strategic alternatives open to management.

**EXHIBIT
13-4**

## *LIFE CYCLE PORTFOLIO ANALYSIS*

**Competitive
Position**

| | EMERGENCE | GROWTH | MATURITY-1 | MATURITY-2 | DECLINE |
|---|---|---|---|---|---|
| Excellent | | | | Automatic screw machines | |
| Good | | | | Dedicated transfer lines | |
| Average | | | | Standard drill press | |
| Poor | Computer controls | Robotics factory automation | | | |

**Industry Life Cycle Stage
(Prospects)**

*Source:* Framework developed by H. Igor Ansoff in personal discussions.

HISTORICAL PATTERNS.   Still a third way to look at the facts is to simply plot historical growth and profit patterns for each product or market business on a grid developed around corporate growth and profit targets. Plotting average performance over some period of time or even last year's results shows how well each product-market segment has performed against corporate targets and how much improvement is required to bring the business up to par. Exhibit 13-5 shows such a grid. In this example, the two axes of the grid reflect the company's return on assets and compounded growth rate targets (17.5 percent return on average net assets and 14 percent growth). As you can see, the grid is divided into four quadrants: high profit–low growth, high profit–high growth, low profit–low growth, and low profit–high growth. The ultimate aim, of course, should be to move all the product-market businesses into the upper righthand quadrant – the high profit–high growth category. Businesses in the lower left quadrant – low profit–low growth – would obviously be under pressure for significant improvement as strategic plans are developed. Arrows can be used, as shown, to indicate the direction management intends to go with any particular product.


A SUCCESSFUL EXAMPLE.   These analyses, or any others like them, are only useful if they contribute to management's understanding of the business and ability to make intelligent strategic decisions or plans. Let's look at how one outstanding company, which we will call company A, built a marketing strategy for its major product line on just this sort of understanding.

After a thorough analysis of demand and share trends, the planners in this company recognized that they were operating in a slow-growth business, offering a commodity product for which demand was highly inelastic. They therefore concluded that (a) it would not make sense to sacrifice short-term profits to build a larger share position, since the value of a share point would not increase enough to pay off such an investment, and (b) although price is an important consideration in market share, it would not influence total demand. They also uncovered an important trend: Company A was losing market position to the strong second-place factor in the industry, company B. Since no other important shifts in market share had occurred, company A concluded that its marketing strategy should be aimed first and foremost at reversing its losses to company B. Next, the planners at company A compared their own profit structure with that of company B to find the weaknesses and strengths of the two companies. Their analysis produced the information shown in Table 13.1.

Admittedly, obtaining information of this sort about competitors is tough. No one is going to hand it to you, and it is not likely to be available in published material. But, as discussed in Chapter 4, bits of data on competitor sales and capacity levels can be pieced together from annual reports, newspaper articles, and trade and government publications. By combining such data with one's own experience, conservative assumptions can be made about competitor costs and efficiency to complete the picture.

By the time the planners in company A had completed this comparative analysis, they were in a position to predict what company B's strategy was likely to be. Assuming that B knew its own market and economic position, they thought it would seek further share gains by competing on price. Specifically, they expected B to:

**EXHIBIT
13-5**

# BUSINESS SEGMENT PROFIT/GROWTH GRID
## (ROANA* and NSB‡ Growth)

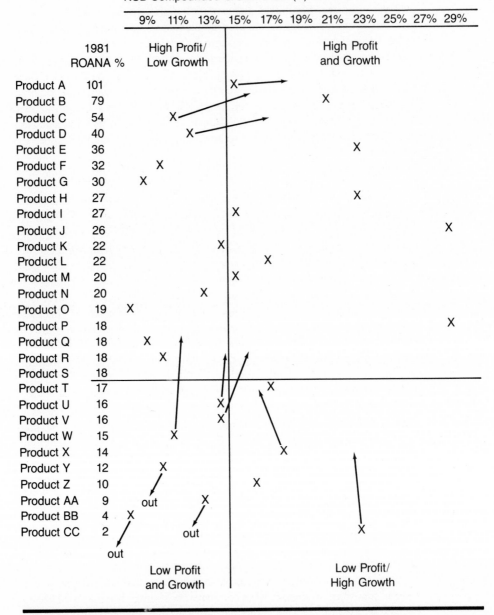

NSB Compounded Growth Rate (X) 1977–81

|  | 1981 ROANA % | High Profit/ Low Growth | | High Profit and Growth |
|---|---|---|---|---|
| Product A | 101 | | | |
| Product B | 79 | | | |
| Product C | 54 | | | |
| Product D | 40 | | | |
| Product E | 36 | | | |
| Product F | 32 | | | |
| Product G | 30 | | | |
| Product H | 27 | | | |
| Product I | 27 | | | |
| Product J | 26 | | | |
| Product K | 22 | | | |
| Product L | 22 | | | |
| Product M | 20 | | | |
| Product N | 20 | | | |
| Product O | 19 | | | |
| Product P | 18 | | | |
| Product Q | 18 | | | |
| Product R | 18 | | | |
| Product S | 18 | | | |
| Product T | 17 | | | |
| Product U | 16 | | | |
| Product V | 16 | | | |
| Product W | 15 | | | |
| Product X | 14 | | | |
| Product Y | 12 | | | |
| Product Z | 10 | | | |
| Product AA | 9 | | | |
| Product BB | 4 | | | |
| Product CC | 2 | | | |

Low Profit and Growth

Low Profit/ High Growth

*ROANA = Return on Average Net Assets
‡NSB = Net Sales Billed

| TABLE 13.1 | PROFIT STRUCTURE ANALYSIS | | |
|---|---|---|---|

| Economic Indicators | Companies | | Conclusions |
|---|---|---|---|
| | A | B | |
| Current dollar sales | $403 | $146 | A's sales volume is roughly twice B's. |
| Breakeven point | $217 | $121 | B's breakeven point is lower, but B is operating much closer to breakeven than A. |
| Contribution margin rate (sales dollars less variable costs) | 48% | 45% | Contribution margin rates are about the same. |
| Contribution loss from 5 percentage point drop in unit margin | $20 | $7.3 | However, because of differences in dollar volume, company A stands to lose far more marginal income than B by lowering unit margin. |
| Volume gain to offset 5 percentage point drop in unit margin | $46.5 | $18.2 | Thus, the volume needed to offset a 5 percentage point drop in unit margin would be much greater for company A. |
| Equivalent share point gain | 7.0 | 2.8 | |

Cut prices on the products competitive with company A's highest volume products to upset price stability and to force company A to retaliate or give up volume.

Add new industrial distributors by giving larger discounts, and go after company A's distributors in prime markets.

Emphasize development of lower-cost products, thereby gaining more flexibility to compete on a price basis.

Given these assumptions, the planners in company A decided that their counterstrategy should be to avoid going for volume through pricing or by adding to unit costs. The key points of the strategy were to:

Hold a firm price line with distributors, even at the risk of losing share in the most price-sensitive markets.

Build the marketing program around activities (services) whose costs do not vary with volume, such as upgrading and enlarging the sales force, strengthening distributor programs, and improving the physical distribution and warehousing network.

A superficial review of the situation would undoubtedly have led the planners to come up with quite a different strategy. In view of the high contribution rate and apparent profit leverage on volume, the most obvious strategy would have been to cut price to counteract any aggressive pricing actions by company B. Instead, company A planners decided to avoid price concessions or any actions that would raise unit costs. They recommended concentrating on marketing programs with costs that could be amortized over their much larger unit volume and on other programs that would reduce their cost base. Management agreed, reasoning that this strategy would enable the company to lead from strength rather than play into the hands of its major competitor.

The details of company A's strategy may be open to dispute. In themselves, however, they are not important. The purpose of the example is to show how a penetrating analysis of market and economic facts can provide a reasoned basis for strategy development. This is the process by which sophisticated planners gain significant advantages over competitors, and it is easy to see the three reasons why:

1. Planners can help focus management attention on actions that really count in the marketplace and make sure that these are based on facts and judgment, not hunch or opinion.
2. They can adopt an aggressive posture instead of having to rely on retaliation or defensive maneuvers.
3. They can minimize the impact of surprise competitive moves by developing contingency plans.

## Superior Programming

There is no single best strategy that is exactly right for a situation or that will guarantee success. Properly executed, quite different strategies for the same product-market business can be equally successful. What this says is that execution is a crucial ingredient in the success of any strategy. "Weak leadership can wreck the soundest strategy; forceful execution of even a poor plan can often bring victory." So wrote the Chinese general and philosopher Sun Zi in 514 B.C. Today, 25 centuries later, that axiom still holds in business.

Successful execution depends on programming, which simply means identifying the sequence of steps and events that must occur to achieve planned objectives and then following through to ensure that these steps and events take place on schedule. Everybody goes through the motions of programming, but leader companies follow three ground rules that enable them to do a superior job of strategy implementation.

1. Management will approve no major program or project that is not inextricably linked to a product-market strategy. This approach may sound a little narrow-minded, but it makes eminent good sense, for the linkage keeps the functional areas of a business working together for a common purpose and prevents them from being sidetracked to functionally interesting activities that lack commercial relevance. There is really no way to evaluate a program's usefulness without the background of a product-market strategy.

2. Management makes some sort of organizational provision for follow-through on major programs, particularly those that cut across functional lines. In some cases, managements have enlarged the role of product managers. In others, they have set up a task

force with responsibility for following a program to completion. One industrial controls producer took the first approach to implement a complete redesign of the product line to improve performance characteristics and to lower cost. Even though the bulk of the actual work had to be done by engineering and manufacturing, the president pulled the responsible product manager out of the marketing department and made him fully accountable for coordinating and pushing the program through. As the president told us:

> This program can make or break us in the marketplace. It's so vital to us I'd watch over it myself if I could let some other things slip. Since I can't, I want someone to do it for me, and the product manager is the logical one to do it. I know I'm stretching his role somewhat in giving him this assignment, and I know some noses are going to be out of joint in engineering and manufacturing, but the job is too important not to have a full-time program manager.

Whatever the approach, the objective is always to ensure interfunctional coordination for all major programs and to overcome any obstacles to successful completion.

3. Leader companies see to it that the detailed steps involved in major programs are mapped out in such a way that performance can be measured against these individual steps. For some time, companies in the aerospace, military electronics, construction, and other industries have been using network scheduling techniques to control large and complex projects. Well-managed industrial companies apply similar techniques to ensure interfunctional coordination on a wide variety of programs that affect market performance, since they permit managers to flag potential problem areas and initiate corrective action before the program slips or gets off track.

In one company, the program for introducing a new line of flow meters was broken down into 25 steps over an 18-month time span. The first step was a kick-off meeting with R&D, engineering, manufacturing, and marketing to define performance and cost requirements. Subsequent steps tracked the new product idea through development, manufacture, and market launching. Each week, management received a report showing whether scheduled steps had been completed and if not, where the bottleneck was. This feedback made it much easier to trace problems to their source for collective action. Said the president: "The program is too important to us to rely for control on typical accounting reports. They simply tell us after the fact whether we won or lost. They're no help when it comes to making sure the program doesn't collapse." It would be absurd to structure every program in so much detail. But detailed planning is essential for effective control over major programs that involve many functions and require tight scheduling and careful adherence in order to achieve profit and market objectives.

## SUMMARY

Formal business planning can help managers cope with the complexity and velocity of change in today's business world. Yet few companies are completely satisfied with their results, especially when considering the time and effort involved in drafting a comprehensive business plan.

When planning fails to produce satisfactory

results, the problem can usually be traced to (1) failing to fit the concept to the industrial context, (2) confusing the various types of planning, (3) overemphasizing the system at the expense of content, and (4) failing to develop alternative strategies. Companies that have built formal planning into the management process have succeeded because of better management from the top, planning based on hard facts, and superior programming for implementing the plan.

Formal business planning can undoubtedly make a real contribution to the performance of any industrial company, just as it has in consumer goods companies. But if it is to have a real impact, it has to be adapted to the particular requirements of the business. The focus must be on achieving substantive improvements in thinking and actions through tough-minded analysis, continual interchange between marketing and technical executives, and top management inputs.

## REVIEW QUESTIONS

1. Why is it increasingly more important to plan overall product-market strategies?
2. Why has a lot of industrial business planning been an exercise in number pushing that results in "death in the drawer" plans?
3. What factors make industrial market planning different from consumer goods market planning?
4. Why *must* industrial market planners work closely with other functions that influence the performance of the business?
5. Distinguish among strategic planning, product-market strategy, and operational planning.
6. What is the role of top management in industrial business planning?
7. In an industrial product-market, how would one identify the points of vulnerability and the points of leverage?
8. What are the links between a product-market strategy and programs and follow-through responsibility?

# 14

# Evaluating Strategies and Plans

Structural Considerations
  Strategy Statement
  Recommended
  Programs and Control
  Summary Projections
  Structure Overview
Credibility Issues
  Fact Base
  Sales, Cost, Profit
  Projections
  Key Performance Ratios
  Risk-Reward Ratio
  Allowances for
  Contingencies
Management Approach
and Attitude
  Functional Integration
  Management
  Commitment
Summary
Review Questions

Fred Cook was brimming with confidence as he began his presentation to the corporate president and his staff. He had been appointed product manager for the company's line of programmable controllers last fall and had worked hard for six months to put a plan together. He was especially pleased because the general manager of the division had expressed confidence in the plan and had asked him to make the presentation.

During his first month as product manager, Fred had seen that previous sales and marketing efforts had been badly misdirected. Not nearly enough emphasis had been given to several large target accounts, and the export market had been completely neglected. It didn't take him long to work out an aggressive plan that would increase sales volume by 40 percent the first year and at least 25 percent a year for each of the following four years. As he enthusiastically explained the plan for improving the export business, he noted that the corporate president was frowning and obviously not following the presentation. Fred was explaining why growth potential in the export market was so significant when the president suddenly interrupted: "I haven't any interest in wasting more time reviewing a lot of optimistic sales projections. This business has lost money each of the last four years and more volume is not the answer. The cost structure is way out of line, and my guess is we will have to write off a couple of million dollars' worth of obsolete inventory at the end of this year. The only thing I want to see is a total business plan that will help us decide whether we should stay in this business or get out."

After a few seconds of stunned silence, Fred's general manager said he could get together the kind of plan the president wanted, but he would need help from the corporate controller and the director of corporate planning. They would have to start all over again, thought Fred; and six months of hard work had gone down the drain.

What is wrong with Fred's plan?

What should a total business plan encompass?

Is it wise to try to salvage Fred's plan by incorporating it into a larger plan? Why or why not?

n the previous chapter we talked about the importance of planning in the industrial world and emphasized the need to develop business strategies and plans that commit all key operating functions to courses of action that will effectively serve the market. We also discussed the need for an integrated business plan for industrial products, since success or failure in the market generally depends more on how functions like manufacturing, engineering, and distribution perform than on what goes on within the marketing department itself. For this reason, the industrial company's planning should encompass the full range of business activities. The marketing function should take the lead in drawing the plan together, but the end product should be a total business plan rather than a stand-alone marketing plan like those found in the consumer products world.

Most industrial companies recognize the importance of planning and prepare both longer-term strategic plans and annual operating plans. But despite all the time and effort that goes into planning, there are wide variations in the quality of the end products. Some are very useful instruments that provide the basis for directing and controlling the business. Unfortunately, many others lack the substance to be a useful management tool. Of course, no one can guarantee the success of any plan, and there is no readymade checklist that will show absolutely whether a plan is good or bad. There are, however, several good articles that outline in some detail what the content of a plan should be and what considerations should be covered.[1,2] More important, there is a logical thought process to be followed that will greatly assist management in deciding whether a plan is a solid vehicle for moving the business ahead or just a lot of words and numbers without real substance. This chapter describes how to use this thought process to decide whether proposed plans are soundly conceived and worth the commitment of resources to carry them out, or whether they should go back to the drawing board for more work. There is nothing sophisticated about this thought process. It is based on common sense and a basic understanding of the requirements for business success in industrial markets. We have organized our discussion of this thought process under three broad questions:

1. Is the plan structured correctly?
2. Is there anything about the plan that detracts from its credibility?
3. Is management's attitude and approach to planning sound?

Although these broad questions may be obvious, the answers are often obscure, and it frequently takes a lot of digging and detailed questioning to bring them into focus.

## STRUCTURAL CONSIDERATIONS

To start with, the plan should be a complete and self-explanatory document. This means that even without prior knowledge of the business, anyone should be able to read the plan

[1]B. C. Ames, "Keys to Successful Product Planning," *Business Horizons,* Summer 1960, p. 49.
[2]E. Raymond Corey, "Key Options in Market Selection and Product Planning," *Harvard Business Review,* September–October 1975, p. 12.

and decide whether it makes sense. That is, they would understand the direction management has in mind for the business, why this direction was selected, and how the company intends to pursue this route. A plan that is understandable and reads well is not necessarily sound, but unless it has these attributes, it simply isn't worth further review. Far too much time will be wasted trying to figure out what the plan really means, what management intends to do, and whether proposed actions are worthwhile.

## Strategy Statement

To provide this understanding, the plan should be prefaced by a brief strategy statement that explains in one or two paragraphs what management is trying to do with the business and the basis for believing that the plan can be accomplished. Here is an example of a well-worded statement taken from a plan to build a business in the telecommunications equipment market:

> Our continuing objective is to build a $300 million business in the telecommunications equipment market within the next three years. We intend to concentrate our efforts on the equipment area involved in the "subscriber loop" where we have a significant technical base. We do not intend to get into switching or toll transmission, nor do we intend to get into the interconnect business. We will sell only through commonly accepted channels to Bell System and independent companies.
>
> We will achieve this objective by introducing several new products with significant cost and/or performance advantages that will help telephone operating companies hold down or cut back their labor costs and prolong the useful life of their existing plant and equipment. These new products will account for 50 percent of our volume growth each year through 1987. We will also have to acquire several new products and pools of technology that we do not now have to serve this market.
>
> Accomplishing this plan will enable us to sustain a real growth rate of better than 10 percent a year, bring our after-tax ROS to 10 percent and our after-tax ROA to 25 percent.

A clear directional statement like this is the hallmark of any good business plan. It states a precise objective and a time frame for reaching it. It defines the market segments the business has targeted and explains the competitive basis for believing the business can be enlarged. It defines the focus of management attention—both what will be done and what will not be done. It states the type of action management intends to take, and it states the expected financial results. In short, it provides an initial perspective on whether those responsible for the plan have a concept for running the business that makes sense.

One point about defining a concept for the business is worth emphasizing. It is equally important to define what you do *not* want to do as it is to define what you *do* want to do. Defining what you do not want to do is like getting a "no" answer in "20 Questions." Even though a "no" answer is negative information, it provides an insight to the ultimate solution. Similarly, a statement defining what you do not want to do in a business helps bring the strategic direction you do want to take into sharper focus. Note how the telecommunication strategy statement achieved precision by naming the business in which the company would not engage.

A statement like the following is in direct contrast to the statement we just examined:

> We intend to grow our business in motor controls at the fastest possible rate and maximize profits. We intend to broaden our customer base and gain market share. This will require competitive products and an especially strong selling effort.

As you can see, this statement doesn't really describe any kind of business concept or focus. It doesn't establish any parameters on the size or scope of the overriding business objective; it makes no attempt to define a strategy for accomplishing this objective; and it says nothing about the financial implications. The lack of thought in this statement is highlighted by stating the converse—a test frequently used to determine whether a politician has said something of substance or simply spewed out a lot of rhetoric. If a statement does not make sense when the converse is stated, it probably isn't worth saying. Does it make sense to think in terms of growing the business at the "slowest possible rate," to make "minimum profits," or offer "noncompetitive products" supported with a "very weak selling effort"? The words "fastest rate," "maximum profits," "competitive products," and "strong selling effort" don't mean much more.

## Recommended Programs and Control

The body of the plan should outline a series of actions and programs linked to the business concept or objective. Given the strategy statement for telecommunications, you would expect to see recommended actions and programs designed to develop new or improved products for the "subscriber loop" market and thus improve profit margins to the 10 percent level. If planned actions and programs do not fit this pattern, the logic has to be faulty and something is fundamentally wrong with the plan.

All the recommended actions and programs should be defined in sufficient detail to provide the basis for effective management control. For example, do the key programs proposed to improve performance in one area or another show the major steps to be taken, the costs involved, the timetable for accomplishment, and who is responsible for each step, so that appropriate corrective action can be taken if something slips? Are there any parts of the plan where actual performance cannot be measured so there is no basis for control? For example, many companies are saddled with information systems that do not provide the basis for tracking costs and profits for individual products or markets. There may be other gaps like this in the company's information system. If this is the case, plans to improve sales and profits for these individual product or market segments—or for anything else where actual results cannot be determined—cannot be controlled. Since it doesn't make sense to plan something you can't control, any part of a plan that falls into this category should be discounted. Ensuring sufficient detail to provide control is crucial. If the characteristics essential for control do not exist, the plan does not have much value as a practical management tool and will more than likely end up simply gathering dust in someone's drawer.

## Summary Projections

Finally, the plan should be summarized in a series of cost and profit projections that are also consistent with the business strategy or concept statement. In the case of the telecommunications plan, these projections should reflect a growth pattern that heads toward a $300 million business in three years. Profit results should show 10 percent after-tax ROS and 25 percent after the ROA. If the projections show a different picture, something needs to be corrected before the plan is subjected to detailed review.

## Structure Overview

Step one in reviewing any industrial marketing or business plan should be to examine the plan document for completeness and logic. Is it understandable, and does it make sense? Is there a brief summary statement that explains clearly what management is trying to do with the business? Does this statement sound reasonable, and is it supported by recommended actions and programs that will move the company closer to its goal? Are recommended actions and programs sufficiently detailed? Do sales, cost, and profit projections make sense in light of what management wants to do and the actions and programs that are proposed?

This first step in the review process does not entail any kind of in-depth questioning or analysis. It shouldn't. There is no use wasting time getting into detail if the basics are not right. Any plan that cannot pass this superficial examination of its structure and content should be reworked before more management time is wasted reviewing a document that is inherently unsound.

# CREDIBILITY ISSUES

Assuming the plan is structurally sound, the next step should be to look for weaknesses or inconsistencies that detract from the plan's credibility. A lot of things can detract from credibility. The best way to make sure all the bases have been covered is to follow five lines of questioning: (1) Is the fact base sound? (2) Do the sales, cost, and profit projections make sense? (3) Are key physical ratios reasonable? (4) Does the risk-reward ratio make sense? (5) Has adequate allowance been made for contingencies?

## Fact Base

A solid fact base is crucial to good business planning. It is the foundation for management's evaluation of the product, market, and competition, as well as cost and profit projections. Few will disagree with the importance of solid facts in good planning, but it is essential to understand that what are often presented as facts are not really facts at all. When the truth comes out, many of these statements of fact turn out to be:[3]

---

[3] These comments on facts are based largely on a memo written by Hal Geneen when he was CEO of ITT.

1. "Apparent facts"     that have grown up with the business and never really been challenged. For example, "our product costs more, but it performs better," or "our distributors will revolt if we attempt to sell direct." Are these really facts, or simply folklore that may not hold up under objective scrutiny?

2. "Assumed facts"      that are necessary assumptions about the future, but not facts— for example, GNP will grow or inflation will run at a certain rate, costs will increase by a certain amount, competitors will react in a certain way. Statements of this kind should be clearly labeled as assumptions and not presented as facts.

3. "Reported facts"     that tend to be given unwarranted validity simply because they have been published by some association or industry "expert." Published data should never be accepted as fact until the source and method of collecting the data has been identified and found to be satisfactory.

4. "Hoped for facts"    that represent situations management would like to believe but do not reflect an accurate picture of the situation. "We are the most profitable company," or "we have the best sales force" are typical examples of "hoped for facts."

5. "Half true facts"    that have a certain element of validity but not the certainty of an incontrovertible fact. "The market has grown at an average rate of 10 percent a year over the past five years" may be a true statement. But it is misleading if five years ago the market had dipped to an unusually low level and much of the 10 percent growth was simply a catchup to where the market should have been.

In many situations, these distinctions between facts that are real and facts that are not real may not be too important. But in business planning, the distinctions are vital. The whole plan is worthless if it is based on anything except real facts. And there is no way to make sure that proposed actions and programs are based on nothing but incontrovertible facts except through hard-nosed questioning that challenges some of the facts and places the burden of proof on those presenting the plan.

## Sales, Cost, Profit Projections

How do you tell whether the sales, cost, or profit projections in a plan are sound? What do you look for in making this kind of evaluation? You do not have to be a financial wizard, but you do have to have a solid understanding of cost and margin relationships and how they change or should change as volume moves up or down. Exhibit 14-1 shows several red flag indicators of weakness in the sales, cost, and profit projections that management should look for whenever a plan is being evaluated.

1. Watch out for sales projections that call for a faster rate of market growth than historical patterns show or that require a significant gain in market share. Market growth

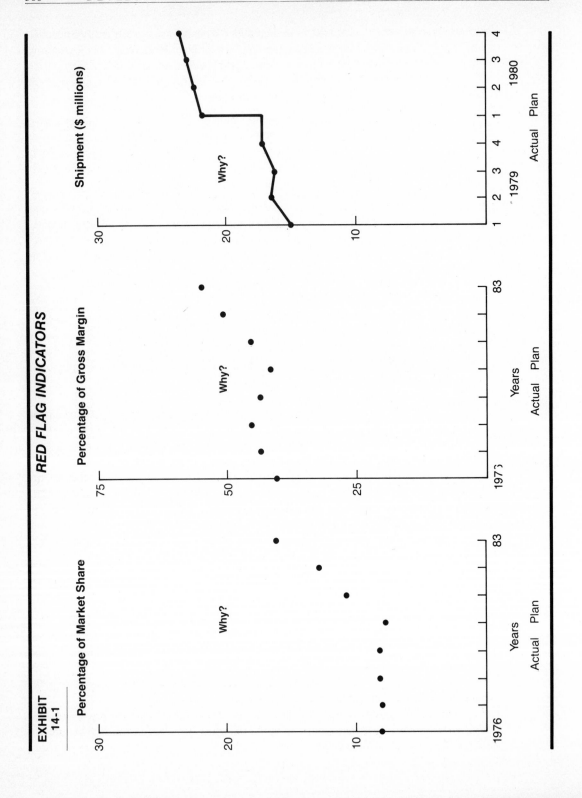

**EXHIBIT**
**14-1**

*RED FLAG INDICATORS*

rates or share positions may increase in the industrial world, but not easily and generally not quickly. Every perceived opportunity for market gain is usually accompanied by some risk or threat that could cause a decline. In most cases, vulnerabilities or threats are overlooked and only opportunities are emphasized. When the success of a plan depends on accelerated sales growth, especially with market share improvement, it is essential to dig into the reasons why the change is projected and ensure that they are valid. It is generally much safer to bet on a business plan geared to a conservative sales forecast—and then "scramble" to exceed the plan if the market opportunity develops—than it is to bet on a plan with a higher sales forecast that requires a cutback in costs and operations if the market opportunity does not occur.

2. If cost and profit projections show sharp improvement from past patterns, look for the reasons for this change. Cost and profit patterns do not typically improve unless someone does something to make it happen. Who is going to do what? When? What is the evidence that it can be done and will yield the desired result? Watch out for long-term "hockey-stick" projections (three to five years out) that are much more favorable than projections for next year. It is difficult to hold anyone accountable for long-term improvements, and they usually represent wishful thinking rather than any concrete plan.

3. Be wary of an abrupt change in the operating rate that causes profits to improve sharply over a prior period. Planners frequently overlook the practical problems involved in stepping up production and jump the business from one operating level to another without allowing sufficient time for manufacturing to gear its operations to a higher level. This oversight shows up most frequently when a much higher operating level for the year is planned and then spread evenly over the 12-month period. As a result, first-quarter profit projections tend to be overstated.

4. Be sure that gross margins are adequate to cover all related expenses and generate satisfactory profit margin. Of course, gross margins vary widely across businesses, but it pays to be suspicious of the profit potential of any industrial business with a gross margin that is much less than 50 percent. Gross margin equals sales dollars less all manufacturing costs to cover the product from raw material to finished stock. It does not include costs of distribution, product development, corporate charges, or sales and administration. In some cases, particularly where the business is based on the sale of a relatively few high-ticket products or systems, sales, marketing, and administrative expenses are sufficiently low to permit a satisfactory profit level with a lower gross margin. Nevertheless, a gross margin under 50 percent should be viewed as a "red flag." It is essential to find out why gross margin is lower and whether it makes sense.

5. Check to see that anticipated cost increases for labor and materials are adequately reflected in economic projections. In today's inflationary climate, it is all too easy to underestimate cost increases for these items in a way that leads to unrealistic profit projections. The only way to avoid this possibility is to ask very specific questions about the allowances for cost increases that have been factored into profit projections. For example, ask purchasing what price increase is expected on steel, castings, bearings, or other important items, and when. Ask employee relations management what kind of wage or benefit increases are anticipated for both hourly and salaried workers, and when. Ask insurance management how much allowance has been made for increasing costs of medical, disability, and liability insurance, and why. Then ask the controller if all these allowances have been correctly factored into the plan.

6. Examine expense levels for key areas to ensure that they are correct in light of prior spending patterns and the job that needs to be done. In some cases, planned expenses may be too low. Some managers may cut back on expenditures that should be made in critical areas such as new product or market development in a way that makes their current profit look good but is harmful to the long-term health of the business. In other cases, planned expense levels may be too high. Sloppy planning habits lead many managers to increase their budgets automatically for advertising, promotion, sales, and other areas that can move up or down very easily, without regard for what is really required to support the plan.

Industry comparisons that will help determine whether a particular expense level is too low or too high are generally available through competitor reports, trade association data, or industry publications. If sales, advertising, or product development expense is out of line with published industry data, it is important to ask why. An easy and frequent answer to this question is that the comparisons are not valid ("apples and oranges" is a common claim). Don't settle for this answer. There may well be differences in what different companies include in various expense categories, but if the ratios are significantly different there is a good chance something is fundamentally wrong.

7. Be sure that profit on incremental volume is satisfactory. In any business that has a sound economic structure, higher volume should generate higher profit margins and hence significantly higher earnings, since it should be possible to achieve leverage on the fixed cost component. Unfortunately, most costs tend to be far too variable as volume increases and far too fixed when volume declines. As a result, the profit gain from added volume does not vary as directly with volume as it should. It is not unfair in most industrial companies to look for something like a 30 percent increment in profit on incremental volume and to insist on a clear explanation whenever this is not projected. Conversely, if volume should decline, it is not unfair to ask why the same profit margins cannot be maintained and why profit dollars should be any lower than they were when the business grew through this volume to a higher level.

## Key Performance Ratios

Three performance ratios deserve examination in the evaluation of any industrial plan, since they are indicators of how efficiently the business is being managed. These ratios may vary in importance, depending on the situation, but it is doubtful that any business can be healthy if they are out of line with industry standards or key competitors.

PRODUCTIVITY.   The first ratio to consider is some measure of productivity. This is simply some measure of output versus input that can be tracked over time and compared with other businesses. With labor costs increasing in most situations, this ratio is especially important because improved productivity is essential to maintain or improve profit margins. There is no single measure of productivity that applies in every situation, but ratios like sales, shipments, or production units per employee, value added per employee (sales minus direct material cost), or total labor cost per unit shipped will indicate the direction of the trend. Obviously, any of these ratios have to be adjusted for inflation and different degrees of vertical integration to ensure meaningful comparisons. If productivity gains are not shown in the plan and supported by concrete actions and pro-

## PRODUCTIVITY MEASURES AT TRW

TRW has developed what is probably the most sophisticated approach to productivity measurement. It actually evaluates its key operations against these six productivity performance measures:

1. Sales per employee (constant dollars)
2. Sales divided by total deflated employee compensation costs
3. Value added—sales minus direct material costs—per employee
4. Sales divided by deflated materials cost
5. Sales per unit of energy consumed
6. Sales divided by plant and equipment replacement costs, less depreciation

grams to achieve improvement, there is good reason to challenge the cost and profit structure.

Many well-managed companies are currently devoting much more management time and attention to productivity improvement in an effort to become more competitive. A recent article in *Business Week*[4] outlined many sophisticated measures of productivity that are employed by such companies as General Electric, Westinghouse, United Technologies, and TRW (see the box).

CAPITAL USE.   The second performance indicator has to do with how efficiently working capital is being used. In today's inflationary environment, enormous amounts of capital can be tied up very inefficiently if these ratios are out of line, and profit performance can suffer greatly as a result. Moreover, it is easy to develop a plan for increased sales that may do the company more harm than good if the costs of added working capital requirements are not adequately considered. These ratios also vary widely from business to business, but comparisons can be made with industry and competitive data. There is also a cross check against these ratios that applies in most industrial manufacturing companies. In most manufacturing industries, the investment in inventories and receivables should not exceed 35 cents for each dollar of sales. This rule of thumb may not always be applicable, but questions should be raised about the working capital investment when this figure is exceeded.

PRODUCERS TO SUPPORTERS.   A third indicator to examine is the ratio of what might be called "results producers" to "supporters" in the organization. This ratio does not reflect a traditional way of looking at a business, nor does it tie in with common definitions of work assignments. It is, nevertheless, a useful indicator of any operation's cost structure and profit-making capability. Anyone that contributes directly to results should be included in the category of "results producers." This would include all direct hourly workers, all sales personnel with specific sales assignments, all engineers involved in designing products or responding to customer requests for special features, service technicians that install and/or maintain the equipment, and anyone else who performs a function directly linked to a company's design, manufacture, sales, and service capabilities. All

[4]"The New Broader Gauges of Productivity," *Business Week,* April 19, 1982.

other personnel in the organization fall into the category of "supporters." They provide support services to the "results producers." This group includes all full-time managers, all staff personnel, all secretarial and clerical help, and anyone else in the organization who does not actually design, make, sell, or service the company's products.

As a general rule, the ratio of "supporters" to "results producers" should be something close to 1 to 3. Whenever the ratio gets close to or exceeds 1 to 1, it is very difficult for any organization involved in traditional industrial manufacturing and sales activities to generate a satisfactory profit. Not enough people are producing, and support costs are too high. Obviously, this ratio does not hold in process or highly automated businesses where large capital investments supplant many direct workers and a large number of highly skilled manufacturing or process engineers are required to operate and maintain the equipment. With this exception, however, it is a good indicator to check whenever a marketing or business plan continues to show marginal profits on a growing sales base.

These ratios, of course, vary widely with different businesses, and what are correct ratios for one situation may not be correct for another. Moreover, there will always be arguments over definitions and the appropriateness of a particular ratio in a given situation. Despite these difficulties, ratios can be developed for any situation, and they can help determine whether or not the cost-profit structure is sound. It should not take long to determine what is a fair measure of performance for any particular situation. And certainly the value of each increment of improvement (each day's reduction in receivables, each added thousand dollars of sales per employee) can be calculated to determine whether profit improvements can or should be made and whether enough emphasis has been placed on these improvements in the plan.

## Risk-Reward Ratio

Some wise person has been quoted as saying, "Risk and opportunity always go hand in hand." This point is important to keep in mind in reviewing any business plan. It should be obvious that every plan involves some degree of risk, since no one can predict future events with absolute certainty. However, the degree of risk varies widely from plan to plan, and it is essential to ensure that the opportunity for reward is commensurate with the degree of risk involved. Let's examine the contents of some different plans to see how the degree of risk varies and what some of the factors are that cause these differences.

EXAMPLE A.   In the spring of the planning year, marketing management for a manufacturer of electronic communication equipment submitted a plan to double sales volume for one of its new and high-growth product lines. Doing so required a plant addition involving a $2 million investment and an equal investment for added working capital. The company's sales of this product had doubled during the previous four years, and the total market was projected to more than double during the next five years. This total market projection was not out of line with past growth trends and was supported by a growing customer base that perceived real economic advantages in the company's product. Product cost estimates had proved valid, and projected profit returns on sales and investment were well in excess of the company's accepted hurdle rates. Payback on the new plant addition was planned in 2.4 years.

EXAMPLE B.   The marketing and sales executives in a machine tool company presented a plan to take the company into robotics. The plan emphasized the growing interest in robotics in both foreign and domestic markets and projected a dramatic increase in sales during the next decade. The company's product development group had developed a modular concept for a line of robots that appeared to offer opportunities for major cost savings in the manufacturing process. Product development also claimed that the line would have better speed, range, and load-carrying capability than any other competitive offering. Pictures of a design or "breadboard" prototype were presented to prove the feasibility of product development claims. Continuation of the program required additional funding of $2.7 million for further product development activities and a joint venture with another independent research firm to ensure the control capability that would be necessary. Management of the product development group was committed to having a prototype for the machine tool show in the fall of the following year, and marketing expected to capitalize on the introduction of the new robot with an integrated sales and promotion program to major potential users. The company had available manufacturing capacity to meet projected sales requirements, and no immediate investment was required for new plant or equipment. Total costs of pursuing the plan were about $5 million, with product development and market development expenses accounting for the great bulk of this sum. A payback period of 4.5 years was projected; profits beyond that point were expected to grow at a much faster rate than anything the company had ever experienced.

IMPLICATIONS.   It doesn't take much insight to see that the potential risk-reward ratio in example A is much more attractive than that in example B. Both situations are based on a set of exciting market characteristics and appear to offer attractive growth opportunities. However, the plan in example A is based on a proved product with an attractive sales and profit history; the plan in example B is based solely on claims of what the product development group can do against a formidable array of competitors already in the market. Moreover, the payback period in example A is much shorter term, and the company's exposure to potential loss is much less.

All these points are relatively easy to see when the examples are succinctly described on paper. They are not nearly as easy to see in a real life situation, especially when the plan is presented by enthusiastic and articulate marketing and engineering managers who have the utmost confidence in their own abilities. For this reason, it is always worthwhile to ask two specific questions: (1) "What is the risk-reward ratio?" and (2) "What happens if customers or competitors react differently than anticipated?"

Obviously, the degree of acceptable risk, irrespective of potential rewards, varies from company to company, depending on its size and financial condition. However, an attractive risk-reward ratio is an important ingredient to check out in any business plan. In a high-risk situation, the potential reward should be several times (6 to 10) the dollars placed at risk in a relatively short time frame. In situations where the risk is less, the company can settle for reduced reward opportunities because of the greater certainty of achieving planned results. In any event, a plan should never be approved unless those proposing it can respond to questions about the risk-reward ratio in a way that demonstrates they have given it serious consideration as their plan was developed.

## Allowances for Contingencies

Many explanations of business planning compare the plan to a roadmap, and for the most part this analogy is correct. Like a roadmap, the plan shows where you want to go and how you should get there. However, you can be a great deal surer you will get where you want to go when you are following a roadmap than when you follow a business plan, no matter how brilliantly the plan may have been conceived and prepared. Unexpected road construction or detours might thwart the driver's plan to follow exactly the route planned. But these difficulties are minor compared to the roadblocks any business plan is likely to encounter. Unforeseen changes in the economic climate, competitor actions, customer or user requirements, or internal performance or capabilities all represent uncertainties that are an order of magnitude more severe than those facing a driver following a map.

Unless adequate allowances are made for these contingencies when the plan is developed, it is almost certain to be too optimistic. It is not prudent to accept any business plan when successful execution requires all the pieces to fall into place exactly as planned. There must be some margin for error. How much depends on the penalties involved if the plan is not successful. When the penalties are very severe, the plan should not be accepted unless there is a high probability of success even if Murphy's law prevails. (Murphy's law holds that everything that can possibly go wrong will go wrong.) In most cases, it is not necessary to be quite so pessimistic as long as reasonable allowances for contingencies have been factored into the plan.

The best way to make this determination is to ask a series of "what if" questions. What happens to planned results if:

Sales volume is 5, 10, or 20 percent below forecast?

Critical costs are above estimates by some significant number?

Deadlines for important project completions are missed?

Material shortages or unusually slow deliveries occur?

Competitors cut prices by a significant amount?

Naturally, the questions will vary with each situation, but the technique is always the same. Simply look for the key variables and ask what happens if any of them go wrong. Inadequate answers probably indicate that insufficient thought was given to the possibility of things going wrong as the plan was developed.

# MANAGEMENT APPROACH AND ATTITUDE

Two final points must be considered to complete the evaluation. First, it is important to determine whether the plan is integrated and truly reflects the thinking and requirements of all key areas of the business, or whether it is simply a sales and marketing proposal that none of the other business functions know anything about. It is equally important to determine that the entire management team really believes in and is committed to achieving plan results.

## Functional Integration

One of the most common and serious deficiencies of industrial marketing plans is that they are just that—marketing plans. They have been drawn together by sales and marketing management and have not been properly integrated with the plans of other key functional departments. This is the key reason so many so-called industrial marketing plans have so little meaning and make so little contribution to the management and decision-making process. When marketing plans are developed in a vacuum, sales forecasts are discounted or "second guessed" by manufacturing, and inventory levels inevitably get out of line. Product development activities tend to be far too technically directed and thus out of phase with market trends. The sales force operates with an unhealthy emphasis on volume, and too little thought is given to focusing on selected customers or market segments that could make the business stronger and more profitable.

It is not difficult to determine whether a plan is really an integrated instrument to help manage the business. The first clue is what the plan is called. If it is called a "marketing plan," it probably is just that, and it probably has all the shortcomings identified above. The second clue is how it is presented. If it is written and presented solely by marketing management, it is a fair bet that other functional departments have not been adequately involved. Another way of checking is to ensure that all functional departments are represented when the plan is presented and by asking some objective questions. For example, ask manufacturing people if they agree with the sales forecast and if their inventory and production plans are actually geared to it. Ask if the planned mix of sales is compatible with existing production capabilities or if this factor was even considered when the sales plan was developed. Ask the controller if his or her department has determined the relative profitability of alternative sales strategies and if this information was considered as sales plans were drawn together. Ask engineering people to identify their planned project priorities and show how engineering time will be allocated to these projects. Then ask marketing people to explain how these priorities and allocations tie into their assessment of marketing needs and opportunities.

The answers to these kinds of questions will clearly and quickly indicate if the plan is based on a true team effort with cross-functional input. If it is not, it is not worth much and should be rejected.

## Management Commitment

Management commitment to a plan is a difficult concept to define and probably the most difficult area to probe. At the same time, it is in many respects the most important area to know about. A deep-rooted sense of commitment is the reason some managers or groups overcome all the things that go wrong and still achieve planned results. It is the same ingredient that enables a team to win against tough competition even though the best players are injured or all the breaks in the game go against them.

Without attempting to be a psychologist, there are several things you can look for to determine whether this sense of commitment exists. What has been the track record of those submitting the plan? It is a positive sign if they have a history of fulfilling commitments. Conversely, if the group has not met its commitments in the past, it is essential to find out what has changed that makes their commitment to the current plan any more meaningful. Is there evidence that individuals understand how a failure to meet their personal or functional commitments would jeopardize the ability of the whole group to accomplish the plan? Is there any indication that anyone in the group feels that any function has overcommitted or that they have been pressured into making commitments that are unrealistic?

It is unlikely that people will admit they are not committed to a plan they developed and recommend. But questions directed to each functional area about the certainty or difficulty of achieving its part of the plan help everyone see what must be done to accomplish the plan. Such questioning helps to establish the importance of each individual's personal commitments not only to the plan, but to the rest of the organization. In a sense, it helps to develop a form of peer pressure, which is just as important in the execution of the business plan as it is in other walks of life. No one enjoys being in the position of having let teammates down.

None of the questions raised in this discussion should be difficult to answer if the plan has been properly put together and coordinated across all key functions of the business. Management should be able to answer crisply and directly. Excessively long, vague, or indirect answers are a good indication that the plan is not solid and should not be approved.

## SUMMARY

After reading this chapter, some product or marketing managers may conclude that many of the points discussed have little to do with their marketing planning responsibilities. They may argue that the marketing function should not be concerned with such things as inventory turns, productivity measures, or expense levels in other functional areas. Those who think this way are wrong. Industrial marketing managers have a broad responsibility for making sure the total business is geared to meet market requirements and achieve maximum profit growth. This means they must be aware of and concerned about any activity in any functional area of the business that impacts the company's cost-profit structure and ability to compete. To do their job properly, they must be aware of and concerned about the total dynamics of the business and ensure that all the points covered here —structural issues, credibility issues, and management's attitude—have been properly considered in the evaluation of their plans. Otherwise, they will not provide the business leadership they should for their assigned product or market areas. Brilliant management or marketing skills alone are never sufficient to offset fundamental deficiencies in the cost-profit structure of a business, and any such deficiency must be challenged in a business plan review.

## REVIEW QUESTIONS

1. How does management determine whether a plan will advance corporate goals?
2. What are the five lines of questioning to follow when testing a business plan's credibility?
3. How do you tell whether sales, cost, or profit projections in a plan are sound?
4. What are the key performance ratios that indicate how efficiently a business is being managed?
5. What is the risk-reward ratio?
6. What is the most common and serious deficiency of industrial marketing plans?

# V

# STRUCTURING AND MANAGING THE ORGANIZATION

# 15

# Organization Alternatives

Alternative Structures
  The Four Basic
  Structures
International Marketing
Selecting an Alternative
  Requirements for
  Competitive Success
  Marketing Strategies and
  Plans
  Realities of the Present
  Situation
  Management Philosophy
  Principles of Organization
When to Make a Change
Summary
Review Questions

David Foster, vice president of sales and marketing for Newtown Tool Company, was nervous as he walked toward the headquarters conference room for his first staff meeting with the company's new president. The new president, who had a reputation for being a tough-minded executive, had been brought in by the board of directors to provide stronger marketing leadership.

Newtown Tool had been in business for over 70 years and was widely recognized as the market leader, with the most complete line of cutting tools in American industry. David had started with the company as a new sales engineer 24 years earlier and progressed through a number of sales management assignments before being promoted to his present position in 1976. He was recognized as the top sales executive in the company and was frequently called upon to negotiate large orders with both key distributors and direct accounts.

The staff meeting got underway. The president expressed himself as enthusiastic about the company's opportunities for achieving further profit growth if management did the right marketing job. He then asked for a brief report from the head of each functional department. The manufacturing vice president described the company's three plant facilities and pointed out the need for additional capacity, probably within the next two years. The technical director explained several projects underway to develop new products. David was explaining the attractive sales gains made by the company over the past five years and describing the strong position the company enjoyed with many of its major accounts when the president interrupted:

"You sound more like a sales manager than my vice president of marketing. What I want to know from you is: (1) How the market is segmented by end users and the relative profitability of each of these segments. (2) What the cost and profit structure looks like for our major product lines and which line is the most profitable. (3) How much money we make on direct sales versus sales through distributors and the volume trends for these two channels over the past five years."

David hesitated; he did not have the information to answer the questions then and there. The new president's response did not reflect a lot of sympathy:

"Let me make a couple of points just to set the record straight and to make sure all of you understand my point of view. First, the questions I've asked you are questions that any good marketing executive should be able to answer without batting an eye. Second, I don't expect you to personally develop and maintain all the knowledge required to answer these questions. However, you need to think through the kind of organization assistance you need to ensure that this information is always at your fingertips, since I don't want to spend a lot of time deciphering vague or general answers."

After the meeting, the new president apologized for being so abrupt, and said he would be glad to talk with David anytime about organization alternatives.

What factors in the company should determine the approach used to structure the organization?

What should be the objective of organizational structure?

What problems could conceivably result from overstructuring?

T his chapter discusses alternative ways to organize the marketing function within a company. Organization alternatives is an important subject to consider, but it is also one that must be kept in proper perspective. Management in many companies tends to devote too much time and emphasis on alternative ways to perfect or strengthen the organization, and the danger of overorganizing or overstructuring is very real. As we stressed in Chapter 1, structure is one of the trappings of marketing frequently pointed to by management as an indicator of its commitment to marketing. However, by itself an organization structure is nothing more than lines and boxes on a chart; it does not in any sense ensure solid marketing performance or leadership. It is all too easy for managers to delude themselves into thinking they have an outstanding marketing company because they have a large or highly structured marketing organization.

Organizations, particularly those that are highly structured, are anathema. One could easily argue that the whole world would be a much better place if the need for large-scale organizations, with their layers of staff and formal procedures for almost everything, did not exist. They make it easy for groups to "syndicate the risk" so that no one can be held accountable for anything. They cover up incompetence and enable those at higher levels to pass the blame for anything that goes wrong down the line. They lead to rigidity and a lack of sensitivity and response to changed or changing conditions that often determine whether the organization succeeds or fails. In short, they are breeding grounds for bureaucracy that tend to interfere with or even thwart the achievement of the organization's very reason for being.

Here is a quote from a recent article in *The Atlantic Monthly* that clearly illustrates how overemphasis on organization and structure has placed much of American industry at a competitive disadvantage.[1]

The sudden proliferation of staff positions within American firms is particularly striking by comparison with firms in other nations. In the typical Japanese factory, for example, foremen report directly to plant managers. The foreman in the typical American factory must report through three additional layers of management. Until very recently, Ford Motor Company had five more levels of managers between the factory worker and the company chairman than did Toyota.

Bureaucratic layering of this sort is costly, and not only because of the extra salaries and benefits that must be paid. Layers of staff also make the firm more rigid, less able to make quick decisions or adjust rapidly to new opportunities and problems. In the traditional scientifically managed, high-volume enterprise, novel situations are regarded as exceptions, requiring new rules and procedures and the judgments of senior managers. But novel situations are a continuing feature of the new competitive environment in which American companies now find themselves.

The typical sequence now runs something like this: A salesman hears from a customer that the firm's latest bench drill cannot accommodate bits for drilling a recently developed hard plastic. The customer suggests a modified coupling adapter

[1]Robert B. Reich, "The Last American Frontier," *The Atlantic Monthly,* March 1983.

and an additional speed setting. The salesman thinks the customer's suggestion makes sense, but he has no authority to pursue it directly. Following procedures, the salesman passes the idea on to the sales manager, who finds it promising and drafts a memo to the marketing vice president. The marketing vice president also likes the idea, so he raises it in an executive meeting of all the vice presidents. The executive committee agrees to modify the drill. The senior product manager then asks the head of the research department to form a task force to evaluate the product opportunity and design a new coupling and variable-speed mechanism.

The task force consists of representatives from sales, marketing, accounting, and engineering. The engineers are interested in the elegance of the design. The manufacturing department insists on modifications requiring only minor retooling. The salespeople want a drill that will do what customers need it to do. The finance people worry about the costs of producing it. The marketing people want a design that can be advertised and distributed efficiently, and sold at a competitive price. The meetings are difficult, because each task force member wants to claim credit for future success but avoid blame for any possible failure. After months of meetings, the research manager presents the group's findings to the executive committee. The committee approves the new design. Each department then works out a detailed plan for its role in bringing out the new product, and the modified drill goes into production.

If there are no production problems, the customer receives word that he can order a drill for working hard plastics two years after he first discussed it with the salesman. In the meantime, a Japanese or West German firm with a more flexible, teamlike approach has already designed, produced, and delivered a hard-plastics drill.

All this is not to suggest that organizations are unnecessary institutions or that the business world can do without them. A carefully thought through organization structure is the only logical vehicle for directing and coordinating the diverse but related activities of large numbers of people toward common goals. Moreover, with increasing emphasis on expanding products and markets all around the world, it is clear that the need for organizations that work effectively is not likely to decline. What we are suggesting, however, is that management must recognize how easy it is for any organization to become bureaucratic, particularly as it grows larger. While bureaucracy is a problem for any organization, it is devastating to sales and marketing activities where crisp, responsive decisions and actions are crucial to meet customer and market needs. Recognizing bureaucratic symptoms, such as those in the example just described, is a continuing management responsibility. Even more important is the need to assess constantly how the organization is functioning and to think through alternative ways the organization and decision-making process can be streamlined to avoid the development of bureaucracy.

Given this perspective on organization structures, let's examine alternative ways of organizing marketing activities and the considerations that would lead to the selection of one alternative over another.

# ALTERNATIVE STRUCTURES

The correct structure for any business function or operating unit is always a lively subject for discussion since there are so many different approaches that could be followed and so many different "expert" ideas of what is right or wrong. Looked at in fundamental terms, the organization structure for any business unit is simply a framework for carrying out the key activities essential to the success of the operation. Designing this framework requires careful thought, since there is always a variety of ways it can be structured, and major penalties to be paid if it is designed incorrectly. It is probably unrealistic to think in terms of a perfect solution to any organization question, since there is not likely to be a perfect match between people's skills and capabilities and job requirements. For this reason, compromises and tradeoffs are almost always involved in developing any organization plan. The objective should be to seek the right balance between an organization approach that theoretically makes the most sense and one that is practically possible given the realities of the situation—existing skills and capabilities, time or cost constraints, or profit pressures.

There are probably more inherent difficulties in organizing the marketing department effectively than there are in organizing most other functional areas. To start with, all marketing activities must be structured in a way that will ensure leadership and direction to all the other functional disciplines, the very essence of the marketing concept. In other words, there is very little chance of having a successful marketing effort if the functions outside marketing go their own way without looking to the marketing organization for leadership. Also, a large number and wide variety of activities may be a part of the marketing department, including both headquarters marketing (market research, market planning and development, sales planning) and direct sales activities performed in many remote locations. This means the strategy, plans, and programs developed in the marketing support groups must be translated into action in widely separated geographic areas and frequently through diverse channels to distinct market segments and customer groups. Finally, many people in the marketing group have highly specialized skills that contribute significantly to the company's success. Since these skills are not easy to find and hold on to, management must take care not to drive them off or put them into a position where they cannot contribute. Given these conditions, it is clear that careful thinking and analysis is required to determine how the organization can be structured to overcome these difficulties and meet marketing requirements.[2]

## The Four Basic Structures

Although it is unlikely that you can find any two marketing organizations in the industrial world that are exactly alike, there are really only four basic alternatives to consider. The marketing organization can be structured around:

[2]These points were outlined by Arnold Corbin in "Organization for Marketing," *Handbook of Modern Marketing* (New York: McGraw-Hill, 1970).

The key marketing *functions* (sales, sales order entry, market research, advertising, distributor development)

Major *product lines* or product groups (A-C motors, D-C motors, drive systems, controls)

Primary or *target markets* (end use, industry, geographic)

Some combination of these three approaches.

As a general rule, there are several alternative structures to choose from within each of these four basic alternatives.

Exhibit 15-1 illustrates a traditional marketing organization structured around the key marketing functions. It is commonly used in single-product, single-market companies where all marketing efforts are directed toward strengthening the sales, market, and product position of the product. There is nothing very complicated about this structure, and not a lot of choices to make once the key marketing functions are defined. All are simply grouped under the marketing department head. In addition to the advantage of simplicity, it probably provides the best basis for control, since decision making can be centralized. However, it has proved to be an awkward approach for managing the complexities of the marketing function when multiple products or markets are involved.

When companies add new product lines or move into new markets, organizational problems become far more difficult because the potential for conflict between products or markets exists (e.g., which product or market gets priority for capital, sales effort, manufacturing capacity, etc.). This means the organization must be structured to ensure that each important product or market segment gets its fair share of time and attention from each of the key activities that affect that segment. There are several ways this can be accomplished, but the most common approach generally involves some form of organization developed around individual products or markets. Exhibit 15-2 shows one example of how an industrial marketing organization might be structured completely around products or markets. This type of structure may be useful when a company has several different product businesses and management wants to centralize the overall marketing responsibility. Several multibusiness companies have followed this approach with varying degrees of success. There is always some question about the ability of one marketing executive to provide effective marketing leadership for a group of diverse businesses with quite different requirements. More important, the structure tends to be top-heavy with managers and too costly, since each of the key functional marketing activities is set up separately for each product or market division.

Exhibit 15-3 shows an arrangement that provides sales specialization by product, which is usually a more cost-effective structure. Here, the headquarters market support functions are centralized and responsible for work on all products. The selling organization, on the other hand, is structured around separate product sales groups responsible for sales of a single product line. There are two weaknesses in this arrangement. First, the responsibility for planning for all products falls on the shoulders of the department head. In this case, a marketing planning manager is shown to help share the burden. But it is difficult and unfair to hold this position accountable for much of anything, since the

EXHIBIT
15-1

## SIMPLE FUNCTIONAL ORGANIZATION

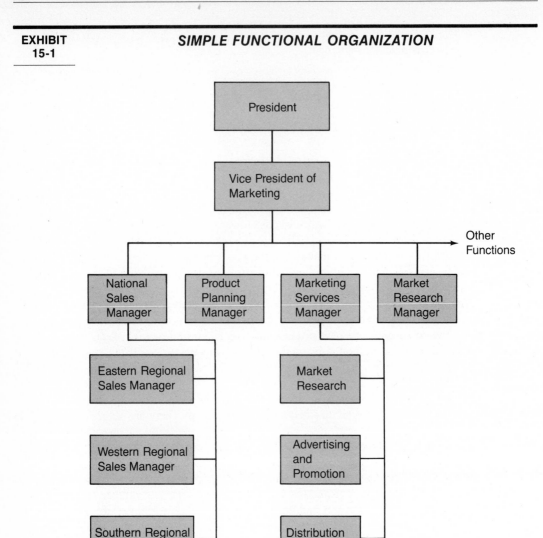

planner typically has nothing to do with implementation. Also, there is no provision made for easy interaction and coordination with manufacturing, engineering, and other functions that affect product performance in the marketplace.

Exhibit 15-4 shows another marketing organization structured around product or market managers. This approach is usually followed when different but related products are

**EXHIBIT
15-2**

## PURE PRODUCT OR MARKET ORGANIZATION

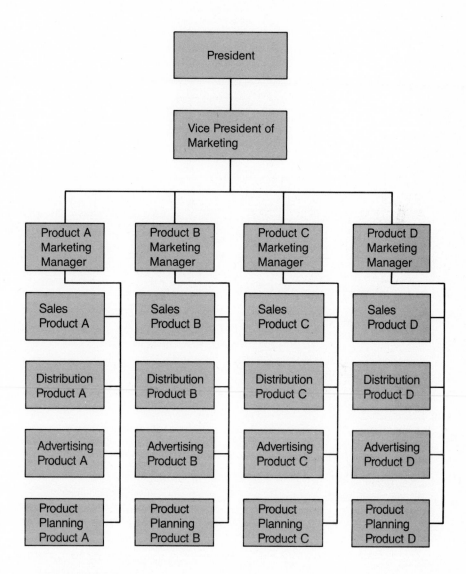

Note: Structure would be
developed around
marketing as well.

**EXHIBIT 15-3**    *PRODUCT OR MARKET SALES ORGANIZATION*

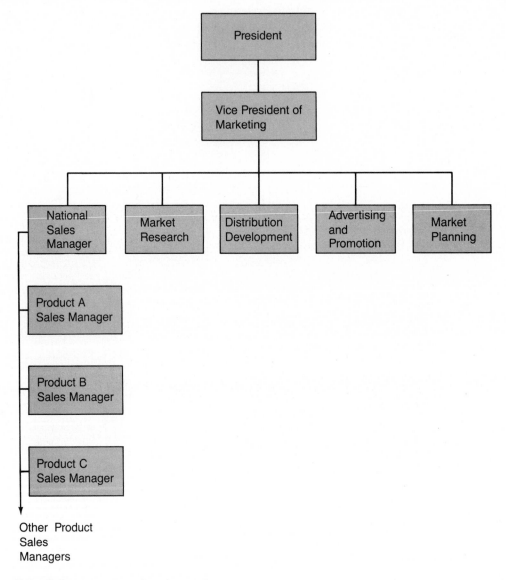

Note: Sales management assignments
could be set up around markets
as well.

**EXHIBIT
15-4**

## TYPICAL PRODUCT OR MARKET ORGANIZATION

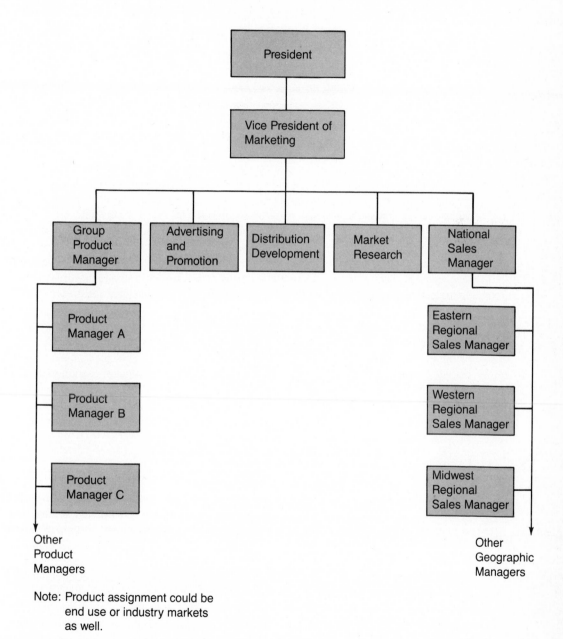

Note: Product assignment could be
      end use or industry markets
      as well.

sold to a common set of customers that can be served by a single sales organization. Manufacturing and engineering activities tend to be scrambled, not separated for each product area. It is an approach used successfully by a growing number of multiproduct industrial companies to achieve stronger management for each product-market business. The product manager serves as the marketing head for a product and makes sure it gets a fair share of attention from sales, manufacturing, engineering, and all other functions that affect the product.

The selling organization is generally structured around geographic areas, with sales-people handling all products. Product sales specialists can be assigned to different areas if more specialized product knowledge is required. Obviously, the same approach could be used to structure around markets if a company had a single line of products flowing into multiple markets and wanted the planning emphasis on markets rather than products. Because of the importance of this organization concept, we will discuss it in much greater detail in the next chapter.

As you look at Exhibit 15-4, note that it shows the product (or market managers) reporting to a group product manager, who in turn reports to the head of the marketing organization. This is the arrangement you see in most industrial companies, but it is not necessarily correct. The product manager function tends to be downgraded when it reports through a group product manager. Moreover, a strong case can be made for positioning product or market managers in the organization so they report directly to general management. The reasoning behind this arrangement contains a good measure of logic. To be effective in the industrial world, product or market managers must extend their thinking, planning, and influence across all functions of the business. In carrying out this role, product or market managers in effect serve as extensions of general management, performing many of the tasks general management would perform if it had the time. This being so, it is advantageous for them to report directly to general management rather than to the head of marketing. The relationship between the product or market managers and general management is clearer and not filtered by a third party. And working relationships with functions other than marketing tend to be much smoother when product or market managers have a direct reporting link to general management.

## INTERNATIONAL MARKETING

Additional organization issues are raised when a company moves into the international arena. If a company simply exports into foreign markets, sales, shipping, billing, and collection arrangements are typically handled by an export department. Although export opportunities are significant in many industrial companies and involve a lot of specialized work because of the problems inherent in doing business with many different countries, the organization issues are not that difficult. Generally, export activities are best handled under the leadership of an export manager. The key questions are what activities need to be covered, and where the export group should be positioned in the company's overall structure. Many industrial companies have assigned responsibility for export to the marketing department, with the export manager reporting directly to the head of marketing. This arrangement works out well, since it places the responsibility for balancing priorities and requirements between domestic and foreign markets with one individual and provides for a close association between domestic and export sales efforts.

In recent years, many companies have found that import restrictions and other barriers designed to enhance nationalistic interests make it difficult to rely solely on export activities to achieve their growth and profit objectives. For this reason, they have taken various steps to secure an ownership position in operations set up to manufacture, assemble, sell, and service their products within these countries. When an industrial company takes this step and establishes an operation to manufacture and sell in foreign countries, the complexity of organizational considerations is greatly increased. One or some combination of the basic organization alternatives discussed above (structuring around functions, products, or markets) will more than likely be an appropriate framework for setting up the marketing department. However, now the whole question of how to support, control, and coordinate product line businesses in foreign countries where market requirements, competitors, and the rules and methods of doing business are quite different becomes a very important consideration.

The question of support is crucial, particularly as it relates to marketing. Many foreign subsidiaries of highly successful companies fail to meet expectations or even "die on the vine" because they do not receive sufficient technical and marketing support from the domestic organization. There is simply no way to be competitive in most markets around the world without top-flight technology and marketing, and the organization arrangement must ensure that these capabilities are available. Product control and coordination are also important, especially when the company manufactures and sells in different countries. Here, it is essential to ensure adherence to such things as quality standards, design features, and pricing strategy so that the product line does not drift out of control. This is particularly important in today's environment, when there are frequently economic reasons for sourcing parts or products in one country to sell in another. Moreover, many major customers frequently have operations in different countries and want to be sure that the product and service they buy from the same suppliers in these countries are priced and perform the same as in the home market.

Two basic approaches can be followed in structuring international operations. One approach, which many companies have employed, is to set up separate international units at the corporate level that parallel the structure used to manage domestic operations. Exhibit 15-5 shows how this arrangement looks. This approach works best when the foreign operations are sufficiently large to be relatively independent and do not require much support from their domestic counterparts. However, if foreign operations are dependent on the domestic home base for product and marketing assistance, control and coordination problems can occur because there is no provision, on paper at least, for integration until you get to the very top of the organization chart. To overcome this problem, some companies have assigned worldwide responsibility for each product business to the domestic operation. If there is only one or possibly two product businesses with operations abroad, this approach could well be the best choice, since international activities are relatively self-contained.

The problem becomes more difficult in multibusiness companies with several operations in various countries. Here, considerations of whether and how to provide centralized financial management, purchasing, legal services, and industrial relations and how

EXHIBIT
15-5

### ONE APPROACH TO INTERNATIONAL MANAGEMENT

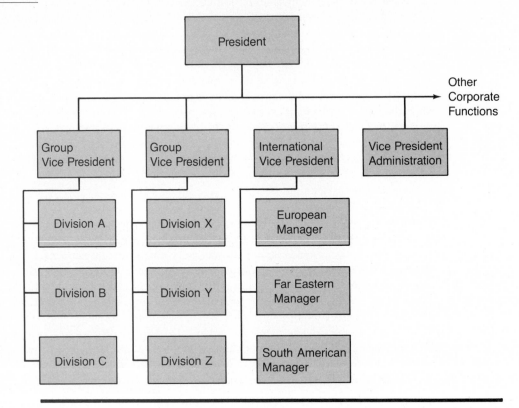

to ensure administrative consistency across all operations in the same country add to the complexity of setting up an appropriate organization. Exhibit 15-6 shows how a large electrical products company employed a matrix approach to ensure that the company's foreign operations received the proper support from domestic divisions and that division operations within various countries were managed in a way that ensured administrative consistency and achievement of total corporate growth and profit objectives.

Under this concept, domestic division management is held accountable for total product profit performance on a worldwide basis and has direct responsibility for approving growth and profit plans, product market strategy, product development, and acquisition proposals from its counterpart operation in each foreign country. The general manager of each foreign operation is held responsible for developing operating plans, for achieving operating results, and for market evaluation and development that will lead to additional profit growth in that country. Finally, a country management group is established and assigned responsibility for the total growth and profitability of all operations in the country and for providing financial management and other staff support to all operating units in a

**EXHIBIT 15-6**

## A MATRIX APPROACH TO INTERNATIONAL MANAGEMENT

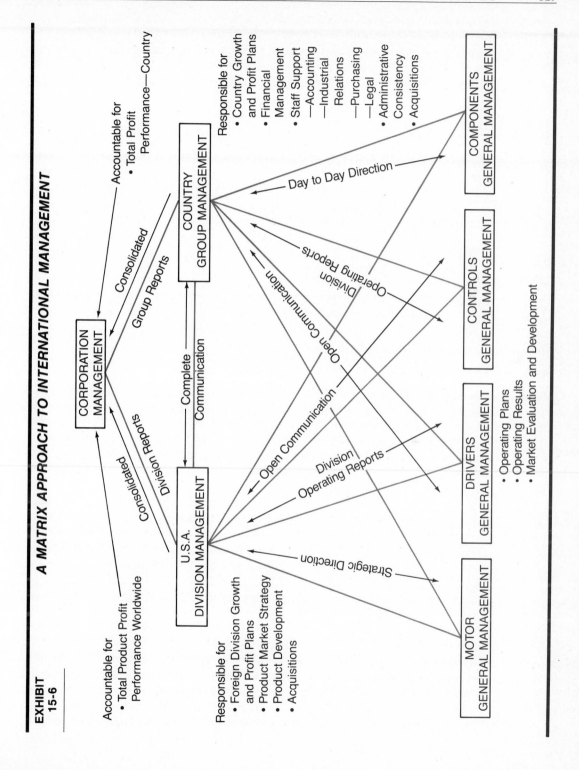

Accountable for
• Total Product Profit Performance Worldwide

Accountable for
• Total Profit Performance—Country

CORPORATION MANAGEMENT

COUNTRY GROUP MANAGEMENT

U.S.A. DIVISION MANAGEMENT

Consolidated Group Reports

Consolidated Division Reports

Complete Communication

Responsible for
• Country Growth and Profit Plans
• Financial Management
• Staff Support
  —Accounting
  —Industrial Relations
  —Purchasing
  —Legal
  —Administrative Consistency
• Acquisitions

Responsible for
• Foreign Division Growth and Profit Plans
• Product Market Strategy
• Product Development
• Acquisitions

Day to Day Direction

Division Operating Reports

Open Communication

Division Operating Reports

Strategic Direction

COMPONENTS GENERAL MANAGEMENT

CONTROLS GENERAL MANAGEMENT

DRIVERS GENERAL MANAGEMENT

MOTOR GENERAL MANAGEMENT

• Operating Plans
• Operating Results
• Market Evaluation and Development

way that will ensure administrative consistency. The foreign division manager reports on a matrix basis to both the domestic general manager and the country manager. And both domestic division management and the country manager report directly to corporate management so that conflict situations can be resolved as required.

# SELECTING AN ALTERNATIVE

The final choice of an organization approach should be influenced by several key considerations:[3]

1. The requirements for competitive success
2. Basic marketing plans and strategies
3. Realities of the present situation
4. Management philosophy
5. Principles of organization

Let's examine each of these points separately and see how they influence the ultimate choice of a marketing organization.

## Requirements for Competitive Success

Every company has a wide range of requirements it must meet to participate successfully in a particular business. Certain manufacturing facilities are required, certain staff skills are important, certain technical skills are essential, certain financial measurements must be met, and so on. However, some requirements are central to the success of any business. For example, styling and distribution are central requirements in the automobile industry; cost control and selling a mix of products are central requirements in any chemical operation; and price, distribution, and product performance are central requirements in the electronic component business.

How does an understanding of these requirements relate to the marketing organization plan? The answer is clear if you think about it. Understanding these requirements helps to point up the range of activities that must be carried on in a successful marketing organization and how the marketing department should interact with other key functions of the business unit. More important, it should indicate which of these activities are pivotal so they can be given proper emphasis, and it should provide insights into what arrangement would be most appropriate to ensure that they are carried out effectively.

## Marketing Strategies and Plans

Common sense suggests that anticipation of the future should be an important input in evaluating organization alternatives. Plans for the strategic selection of certain products or markets for emphasis can affect the selection of an organization approach. For exam-

[3]The discussion of these points is taken from material developed by D. Ronald Daniel, a director of McKinsey and Company, Inc.

ple, a company with major expansion plans in certain products or markets probably has a need to shift from a functional marketing organization that covers all products and markets to separate product or market groups for each priority area. This kind of a shift is essential to ensure the focus and emphasis required for each target product or market business. Conversely, when the market softens or business in target industries turns down, it may be appropriate to shift away from separate product or market groups to a more centralized arrangement as a means of achieving tighter control and cutting back costs.

## Realities of the Present Situation

Two practical considerations are most important in deciding on the merits of one organization alternative versus another. The first is existing staff resources, which is always a consideration since it is generally impractical to think in terms of staffing any organization with a completely new group of people. And it would not make sense to adopt an organization approach completely unsuited to the background and experience of the people in the existing marketing group. So most organizations must be tailored somewhat to the capability of the people that will make them work. More than one company has had a disastrous experience trying to make some appealing organization concept work that was far too sophisticated for its existing group of people.

On the other hand, it doesn't make sense to turn away from an attractive organization alternative simply because people are not available. The best approach is probably to develop a target structure and then move toward it as new people are hired. Doing this may take two to three years, but it can be done effectively as long as everyone knows what the target structure is and interim changes are designed to move the organization in a consistent direction.

The second important practical consideration relates to cost and affordability. There are a lot of organization approaches that would be nice to have, but they simply are not affordable. For example, it would be nice to have sales specialists for every product line or product and market managers for every conceivable product or segment of the business. However, the cost-benefit relationship is simply not attractive. That does not mean management should never be willing to invest in an organization and people to build for the future. Nevertheless, the bottom line for business is profit, and the cost of one organization alternative versus another must always be considered.

## Management Philosophy

Whenever organization alternatives are weighed, attention must be given to the philosophy that reflects top management's thoughts, values, and attitudes on how the organization should be managed. You simply cannot make a structure work if it requires a different management style or philosophy than actually exists. Management philosophy, which always emanates from the top, determines whether the organization will be run as a "tight ship" or whether a "free wheeling" approach will be followed. It defines the degree of toughness or paternalism that will characterize the organization. It indicates the level at which key decisions will be made and the degree of authority that will be granted.

Many managers have different ideas on these points, and there is no one set of ideas that is absolutely correct. As you can appreciate, all these factors have an important bearing on organization planning. It is essential to understand how management thinks and to understand how and why an organization functions as it does. For example, it would be difficult to use any kind of a decentralized organization approach around products or markets if top management insisted on maintaining a tight rein on all decision-making authority.

## Principles of Organization

Finally, some time-honored principles of organization should be considered. All kinds of principles have been developed over the years. Although some are valid, many are too rigid to be useful in today's complex business environment. Nevertheless, it is useful to understand what points were important to some of the early experts on organization theory. The boxes on page 333 present two examples from the literature that have stood the test of time.

Principles like these are frequently used by senior managers in real life situations to guide organization thinking in their operations. Here is a memo from a company president to his staff that makes it very clear he wants all the parts of the company to be structured according to his principles:

To: All Operating Managers

From: President

I have a strong belief that each of our three large operating units has way too many salaried and management people in their overhead structure. I believe that many of these people are marginal performers and that many of them are way overpaid for what they do. I would much rather see us have a far more streamlined organization with fewer people earning a lot more money. Please be prepared to address this point during your next organization review. In addressing this point, remember a few principles that make sense to me in structuring and staffing any organization.

- No assistants or assistants to: there is no room for "gophers" anywhere.
- No one-over-one, one-over-two, or one-over-three situations in any organization. If a manager isn't managing at least five people his job isn't structured right.
- No marginal performers at any level.
- No unnecessary duplication of division staff in plant operations (i.e., division controller–plant controller, division engineer–plant engineer).
- No more than five layers between division managers and production workers.
- No secretaries supporting less than 3 to 4 managers.
- Everyone in the organization accountable for some measurable result.

Please be prepared to discuss any exceptions to these principles that exist in your organization during our next review session.

There are many different ideas on how these principles should be used in organization planning. Some experts believe that any organization should be rigidly structured around

## PRINCIPLES OF ORGANIZATION

### James O. McKinsey

1. In every business there should be centralized control accompanied by proper delegation of authority.
2. Responsibility and authority should go hand in hand.
3. Activities should be classified so that specialists will be developed.
4. The number of subordinates reporting to each executive should be limited.
5. Proper means should be provided for effective coordination of activities.
6. The distinction between line and functional control should be recognized.
7. The personal element must be recognized.

*Source:* McKinsey and Company, Inc.

## PRINCIPLES OF ORGANIZATION

### Harold Stieglitz

*Objectives*
1. The objectives of the enterprise and its component elements should be clearly defined and stated in writing. The organization should be kept simple and flexible.

*Activities and Grouping of Activities*
2. The responsibilities assigned to a position should be confined as far as possible to the performance of a single leading function.
3. Functions should be assigned to organizational units on the basis of homogeneity of objective to achieve most efficient and economic operation.

*Authority*
4. There should be clear lines of authority running from the top to the bottom of the organization and accountability from bottom to top.
5. The responsibility and authority of each position should be clearly defined in writing.
6. Accountability should always be coupled with corresponding authority.
7. Authority to take or initiate action should be delegated as close to the scene of action as possible.
8. The number of levels of authority should be kept to a minimum.

*Relationships*
9. There is a limit to the number of positions that can be effectively supervised by a single individual.
10. Everyone in the organization should report to only one supervisor.
11. The accountability of higher authority for the acts of its subordinates is absolute.

*Source: Organizational Planning* (New York: National Industrial Conference Board, 1962).

them. Certainly the company president expressed a strong point of view. Probably the most balanced approach is to use them as a checklist to ensure that a particular organization has not been inadvertently structured in a way that flies in the face of what those with experience regard as good practice. On the other hand, there may be very good reasons for departing from some of these principles, and the structure should not be modified or discarded simply to comply.

In other words, the principles should be used as guidelines, not controlling considerations in any organization plan. By definition guidelines are just that, and they can be violated if it makes sense to do so. For example, the old saw that authority should be consistent with responsibility does not hold true in the case of a traditional product management arrangement in which the product manager has all kinds of responsibility without commensurate authority. Also, some quantitative limit on the span of control, such as 4, 5, or 7 people reporting to a superior, is not a rule that should be followed rigidly. There are plenty of industrial sales and service organizations that have as many as 15 or even 20 individuals reporting to a supervisor who carries the responsibility very effectively. The number of individuals reporting to a superior depends entirely on what is required in the way of supervision, not solely on some principle of organization.

# WHEN TO MAKE A CHANGE

The need to change or restructure the marketing organization depends on two factors. First, how effectively the current organization operates. Second, how adequately it provides the focus necessary to capitalize on future product and market opportunities. Deciding that the market organization is or is not functioning effectively right now is obviously a judgment call, but there are several questions you can ask to help make this judgment.

1. Is the organization responsive to customer needs, competitive actions, and/or shifting market requirements? Is it easy for customers to do business with the organization? Are quoted delivery dates met? Are customer inquiries or requests for quotes on special items handled promptly?

2. Does the organization produce creative business strategies and solid business plans that result in a competitive advantage for each of its priority products and markets?

3. Does the organization fulfill its role as the lead function of the business and ensure that all key functions are properly geared to serve the company's target markets? Are the communication links with manufacturing, engineering, and finance clearly defined?

4. Does the organization provide the necessary focus or emphasis on priority product-market segments? If the marketing strategy is focused on products or markets A, B, and C, is the organization structured to facilitate the same focus?

5. Does the organization achieve planned market performance and profit objectives? Are prompt corrective actions taken when actual performance falls behind plan? Is it clear who is accountable for results in each segment of the business and for each major program?

If the answer to any of these questions is negative, some kind of change is required. It may well be that a structural change in the organization to provide for better planning, closer coordination with other functions, stronger sales management, or some other such improvement is the answer. However, it is also essential to determine whether the problem really stems from a fault in the structure or in the people involved. Performance evaluation is especially important. No organization structure will ever work effectively with inadequate performers. Nor are inadequate performers likely to work any more effectively under a new or changed alternative structure. A lot of time can be wasted shuffling boxes on a chart or putting names in different boxes if management does not face up to fundamental weaknesses in the people involved.

Looking to the future, the key questions to ask are these: What are the product-market areas selected for emphasis? How do we ensure the strong management and entrepreneurial drive to capture the business in these areas? If major opportunity areas are not specifically assigned in a way that brings these skills to the forefront, some organization change is in order. The change may be as simple as giving some individuals dual role assignments (such as, continue as regional sales manager and also be responsible for planning growth in the marine market). Conversely, the change may require a major restructuring of the organization to provide stronger product or market management. Although different approaches may be used to achieve proper product-market assignments, the objective should always be the same: to ensure that someone feels the burden of responsibility for profit growth in each product-market area. Otherwise, these areas will be fun and interesting to talk about, but nothing much will happen to advance the company's position.

One final caveat on organization can be best illustrated with a quote from history:

> We trained hard—but it seemed that every time we were beginning to form up into teams, we would be reorganized. I was to learn later in life that we tend to meet any new situation by reorganizing. And what a wonderful method it can be for creating the illusion of progress while producing confusion, inefficiency and demoralization.[4]

What was true in A.D. 66 holds true today. A change in the organization structure, by itself, is never the answer to more effective marketing. Unfortunately, in far too many cases managements tend to tinker with the organization whenever they run into trouble in the marketplace instead of searching for and facing the causes of problems. It is unquestionably important to think through how the marketing organization should be structured in light of market requirements and what jobs have to be done. It is also true that periodic adjustments are necessary to keep the structure geared to the changing requirements of the marketplace. But organization changes by themselves will not make a significant difference in marketing performance.

In the next chapter, we'll dig deeper into the problems and considerations that come into play as we move from the straightforward functional approach to marketing organization toward a product or market management structure.

---

[4]From *Petronii Arbitri Satyricon,* A.D. 66, attributed to Gaius Petronius.

## SUMMARY

Certain organization alternatives and considerations are important as a backdrop for reviewing, planning, or altering any marketing organization. The four basic ways of organizing marketing are by key marketing function, by major product lines or groups, by primary or target market, or some combination of these three. When a company moves into the international arena, the alternatives are to set up parallel international units at the corporate level or to assign worldwide responsibility for each product business to the domestic organization. Which structure is selected depends on the company's requirements, plans for the future, and present situation.

## REVIEW QUESTIONS

1. What are the four basic organization alternatives for the industrial marketing organization?
2. How does the strategic emphasis of certain products or markets affect the selection of an organization approach?
3. What are the two basic alternatives in structuring international operations?
4. What two factors determine whether to change or restructure the marketing organization?
5. How are individual responsibilities and performance often at the root of an "organizational" problem?

# 16

# Product-Market Management

When Should the Concept
Be Employed?
Making the Concept Work
  Clear Responsibilities
  Proper Position in the
  Organization
  The Right Qualifications
  Adequate Training and
  Orientation
  Appropriate Performance
  Measures
When Both Product and
Market Managers Are
Required
  Examples
  Who Does What
  System Changes
Summary
Review Questions

After several discussions with his vice president of marketing, Al Waters, president of Electronic Systems, Inc., decided that the company should restructure its marketing organization around product managers. The business was growing very rapidly, and he was concerned about things slipping "between the cracks." Electronic's major competitor appeared to be gaining market share, and he had heard the vice president of marketing for that company describe in glowing terms how its product managers worked. He knew his people were not enthusiastic about product managers, but he pushed ahead anyway and actually hired two people from the competitor to fill product management positions. Two other product managers were appointed from the company's sales force. Waters had agreed to review periodically with his staff how the product manager idea was working, and a meeting had been scheduled for this purpose. Unfortunately, Waters could not attend the meeting because of prior commitments, and asked one of his administrative assistants to substitute for him.

Jack Sanford, vice president of manufacturing, and Robert Dixon, vice president of engineering, were the most negative in their reactions to the product management group. They had the same basic complaint: They were convinced the product managers were interfering with their ability to do their jobs. Although four product managers had been appointed to manage the company's four major product lines, the two who had been brought in from the outside were the ones who had received the most notice. Jack claimed, "They don't really know anything about our company's business and yet they try to tell me how and in what quantities to manufacture." Bob Dixon was "damned sick and tired" of having young "hot-shot" MBAs telling him how much should be spent for development projects and which projects should get top priority.

It didn't take long for a heated argument to start. The two new product managers reacted defensively, claiming that they had to be involved in setting priorities in both the manufacturing and engineering areas or they couldn't do their jobs. One of the product managers made the point that he had been told by the president of the company to think and act like a general manager. The two critics responded with the same words: "Your job is to plan and coordinate, not to be a general manager. We get along fine with the other product managers, but you two will wreck our whole operation if you keep trying to tell people what to do."

Is Waters' rationale for restructuring around product managers sound?

What mistakes did Waters make in introducing product managers into the company?

Is it possible to manage a product line without participating in manufacturing and engineering decisions? How much authority does a product manager need?

The product or market management concept is not a new organization alternative. It has been employed successfully in many large, complex multiproduct corporations to achieve the vigorous product or market leadership that top executives of smaller, more tightly knit companies provide through a centralized organization. Both positions have been used successfully throughout industry to provide the necessary market orientation and to ensure sound planning for various product-market segments. And the purpose of both has always been the same: to safeguard the commercial health of the business by ensuring that the necessary plans, decisions, and commitments made throughout the company effectively meet the changing needs of the marketplace.

Product managers are most appropriate when a company has multiple products flowing into a common market through the same channels and to the same customer groups. Market managers get the nod in the reverse situation—when the company needs to develop different markets for its products and the focus is on developing the market rather than on taking the product to market. In the discussion and examples that follow, any of the comments we make or examples we cite about product managers apply to market managers, and vice versa.

Despite its widespread application, the product or market management concept is not an easy one to make work, and many companies have been disappointed with the results. For example, a marketing vice president in a basic metals company complained: "We moved to a product management setup because we thought we could improve our profits if we had product managers with full-time responsibility for planning to improve the overall mix of products moving through our plants. But it's beginning to look as though we were kidding ourselves. Our product management group costs us $500,000 a year, but I can't honestly say our product mix is any more profitable today than it was before they were around. Our product managers have put all kinds of plans together, but not one of them has really done the job we wanted." Assuming the concept is sound, why is the record so mixed? Our analysis of the experience of a wide range of companies suggests that product or market management pays off only under very special circumstances and only when very specific organizational requirements are met (see the box, page 346). In this chapter we discuss who should use product and/or market managers and how they can be used most effectively.

## WHEN SHOULD THE CONCEPT BE EMPLOYED?

The job of product or market manager was created to fill a critical need in large, multiproduct companies where manufacturing, engineering, and sales had responsibility for all products. In these situations, the task of managing all the factors bearing on the success of each of many products had proved too much for any one executive to handle. And it was unrealistic to expect functional department heads to balance and coordinate the interests of many products in the best interests of the company. It was to fill this void that the product or market manager form of organization was created.

## HOW THE CONCEPT WORKS

The experience of a leading electronics manufacturer shows how a strong product manager can positively affect a business.

For years, this company had dabbled in the nuclear instrumentation field with little success. Its sales growth had lagged behind the competition, and profits were too slim to support the development effort needed to keep pace with the field. Understandably, management had its doubts about this business, but problems in other product areas were always more important. For some time, the instrumentation business was allowed to drift. Many managers had an interest in it, but no one had specific responsibility for results. Eventually, under pressure of mounting problems, management decided to reorganize its marketing department along product management lines. One product manager was assigned full-time to the company's nuclear instrumentation line. The charter: to develop a plan for getting some market momentum behind the line—or a plan for withdrawing from the business.

Within three months, the product manager was convinced that the potential of the nuclear instrumentation line alone was too limited to justify the company's continued interest. But he had also identified a real opportunity to expand into the much broader and more attractive controls field. Accordingly, the plan he submitted called for adding technical staff and acquiring a small foreign manufacturer to obtain the broader base of products the company would need to compete in the controls area. His plan was adopted, and today his product line is the fastest-growing and most promising segment of the company's entire business.

It doesn't follow, however, that just because a company has multiple products and many product problems, product or market management is the answer. In companies where each product-market group really represents a distinct business large enough—or potentially large enough—to support its own production and marketing operations, it may make more sense to divisionalize the company and set up separate and self-sustaining units for each major product or market group. In other companies, it may be better to set up separate marketing groups for each product and/or market and keep the manufacturing operations centralized. This makes more organizational sense when complete divisionalization is not feasible, but sales, distribution, and marketing requirements are significantly different for each product. In still other companies it may be advantageous to have separate sales operations for each product-market group, with marketing and manufacturing activities maintained centrally. This is a more logical approach when separate customer groups must be served, when the business of each product is too small for divisionalization, or when the only place product specialization is important or practical is in the sales area.

The product or market manager concept should be used only when these alternatives are impractical or undesirable. Usually this situation exists when the product businesses involved are small, when functional activities (manufacturing, engineering, sales) are common or scrambled for all products, and when divisionalization or separate marketing groups do not make economic sense. Likewise, when there is a common set of customers for all products, setting up separate product-market sales forces is usually costly and awkward; it is more sensible to have a single sales manager representing all the company's products to this common customer group. In short, only in multiproduct companies where physically separated operating divisions, marketing groups, or sales units are not practical is product or market management the preferred organizational alternative. In these cases, the product or market manager provides a means of ensuring individual attention for all major products or markets without separating off any part of the line operations.

The only difference between the product manager and the market manager is the marketing circumstances that make one approach more effective than the other. The product manager approach is more appropriate for companies with a number of different products that have to be produced and marketed through the same manufacturing, marketing, or sales divisions. If a company has an essentially homogeneous, or at least closely related, line of products that appeal to different segments of the market, the market manager approach may make more sense, since it may put appropriate focus on each of the marketing opportunities.

## MAKING THE CONCEPT WORK

Because the product or market manager concept is an organization anomaly (that is, responsibility is not matched with authority), it is a difficult one to make work. Special management care and attention is required for successful implementation. Let's examine some of the problems encountered when the concept is employed and how these problems can be avoided.

Often the product–market manager concept never gets off the ground in a company because managers are simply appointed and their jobs set up on the basis of what someone has heard about what some other company has done. No one takes the time to think through the specific requirements for the company involved.

The frustrating experience of a large electronics company dramatically illustrates the importance of careful attention to organizational needs. Four product managers were appointed; no other organizational changes or staff additions were made. They were expected to resolve an Augean stable load of problems that had plagued the company for a long period of time. For example, inventories and manufacturing costs were way out of line; there was serious slippage on engineering projects; and the sales organization had let the backlog drop below the safety level. These were all difficult problems, rooted deep in the line operations of the company. To think that the new product managers, by themselves, could solve these problems was totally unrealistic.

Not only did top management place superhuman requirements on the new product managers, it also failed to provide the kind of training that might have helped them grow in their jobs. The experience of these managers had been, for the most part, in sales. It was understandably difficult for them to flag potential problems in manufacturing and engineering, and next to impossible for them to develop appropriate programs of action or to persuade line executives to respect their recommendations. Instead of helping and supporting the new product managers, management blamed them for everything that went wrong. This, in turn, weakened the one weapon they had—the respect of line executives for their competence. Consequently, the product managers were unable to begin to develop the cooperative relationships they needed with the various functional executives.

The product managers unenthusiastically compared their position to "walking blindfolded on a treadmill." They recognized that it was impossible to handle all the problems management expected them to deal with. They lived in jittery anticipation that management might blame them for almost anything that went wrong. Within a short time, three of the four were replaced, and there was a general feeling of dissatisfaction with the whole idea.

A closer look at the experience of this company suggests the organizational requirements that must be met if the product or market manager is to have a chance at success. It becomes apparent that all concerned must clearly understand the role and responsibilities of the product or market manager, that the managers must have access to line management, that the managers themselves must be chosen carefully, that they must receive adequate training and orientation, and that appropriate standards of performance must be applied when judging their success.

## Clear Responsibilities

There are many different points of view on what the product or market manager's role really is. Some say the activity should be limited to product or market planning. Others argue that this is far too restrictive, since many other factors contribute to the success of a product. Many say the product or market manager should have full profit responsibility and final authority over many important decisions—for example, pricing, inventory levels, and product improvements. An equal number contend that he or she should not have final decision-making responsibility in any of these areas, since these are properly line decisions. Obviously, the product or market manager's responsibilities differ from one company to another and should be tailored to the particular needs of each product at a particular point in time. However, the biggest risk in all situations is that the responsibilities are defined in a way that blocks the manager from fulfilling a business management role. As a general rule, therefore, the manager's responsibilities should be defined as broadly as possible even though he or she lacks the line authority to carry out these responsibilities alone.

Because the job can vary so from company to company—and because the scope is potentially so broad—the objectives, responsibilities, and working relationships should be committed to writing as a basis for gaining agreement and understanding. Exhibit 16-1 is an example of a product manager's position statement that shows the kind of detail required. Note that in addition to describing the product manager's responsibilities in specific and "how to" terms, this position description defines his or her relationships with other key functions in substantial detail. This emphasis on relationships is key, since the product manager does not have line control over any of these functions, yet his or her success depends on how effectively he or she works with and through them to achieve business objectives.

When management is reluctant to give its product managers enough responsibility or appropriate status in the organization, the job frequently degenerates into a low-level

| EXHIBIT 16-1 | *A PRODUCT MANAGER'S STATEMENT* |
|---|---|

## GENERAL POSITION DESCRIPTION FOR PRODUCT-MARKET MANAGER

Any position description for a manager handling an assignment for a single or a group of products or markets should be specific for that particular assignment at that particular time. Therefore, this position description outlines only the general objectives, responsibilities, and relationships of our product managers. Specific objectives and priorities should be defined each year (or more frequently if necessary) for each product management assignment.

### General Objectives

All product-market managers share a common objective to generate maximum profit growth and return on the assets employed in their assigned area of the business. To achieve this objective each product-market manager is expected to think, plan, and operate like an overall business manager, even though he or she does not have commensurate authority. This means he or she must:

1. Quickly develop a clear understanding of the business economics for his or her product-market. As a minimum he or she should know: (1) the value of assets committed to the product-market business and where they are employed, (2) which costs vary how much with volume, (3) what the major cost and expense elements are and (4) what actions have the greatest impact on costs and profits, and how these economics compare with competitors. To get this basic economic understanding of the business, the product-market manager should feel free to discuss any aspect of the business with executives at any level in any functional area—and he or she should challenge any statement that doesn't seem to make sense.
2. Always be sure the cost-profit structure for each product-market or added increment of volume or market share is sound and never be misled by so-called full line, volume, or market share benefits.
3. Avoid being misled by standard or accepted accounting procedures or pricing formulas that may produce wrong information, leading to incorrect operating or economic decisions.
4. Insist on having a monthly net profitability analysis (including all allocations for each product-market segment) and make certain that allocation assignments are reasonable.
5. Pinpoint the poor profit performers with low gross margins (i.e., 40 percent or lower), and, after making sure that the financial data and results are really correct, initiate action to:
   a. Raise the selling price.
   b. Improve the cost structure (both direct and indirect costs; short and longer term actions).

*Source:* Much of this position description was developed for use at Reliance Electric by E. G. Orahood, executive vice president.

EXHIBIT
16-1

*(cont'd)*

   c. Withdraw from the market. *Note:* In some cases a large price increase can be the first step to withdrawal or it can be the means of achieving a satisfactory profit on a lower level of volume.

   d. Come up with other possible solutions.

6. Pinpoint the good profit performers with high gross margins (i.e., 50 percent or better), and, after checking to make sure the numbers are accurate, initiate action to:

   a. Make certain that competitors do not undermine the present market share position with a lower price strategy.

   b. Increase selling and promotional emphasis to gain immediate market share while maintaining high profit margins, and step up development activities to ensure a continued strong market and profit position for the longer term. *Note:* Opportunities often exist in geographic markets or channels where market share is below average.

7. Plan and control new product development activities and initiate improvements to maintain competitive leadership. All major investment recommendations for new or redesigned products must be supported with a marketing and total business plan. Detailed budgets including engineering hours, expenses, and capital must be established for these plans so they can be tracked and charged against the correct products.

8. Develop both an annual business plan and an updated five year plan for his or her assigned product area. To be meaningful and realistic, these plans must consider the limits of resources available. Typical resources (all of which have limits) are:

   a. Plant, machinery, workforce (additional capacity available by increasing the workforce or shift supervision).

   b. Engineering hours.

   c. Engineering talent and capability.

   d. Sales hours.

   e. Sales talent and specialization.

   f. Expense dollars.

### *Responsibility and Authority*

Given the objectives described above, it is clear that the product-market manager is charged with the same (or part of the same) basic responsibility of the general manager. The product-market manager has direct responsibility for pricing and for the level of finished goods inventory (at factory and distribution locations) for his or her products. Although the product manager does not have direct line control over many of the people influencing the profit results, he or she must cover all areas and initiate action when he or she is not getting the proper results or responses from other disciplines. This includes taking conflicts that cannot be resolved to general management for resolution.

**EXHIBIT
16-1**

*(cont'd)*

### Relationships

The product-market manager must work closely with the following departments to achieve desired results:

1. *Sales:* To implement specific product sales programs, to ensure proper sales emphasis on assigned products, to obtain continuous and meaningful feedback from the marketplace, i.e.: (1) Competitive activity: e.g., product, price, strategies, capacity, economic structure. To ensure an adequate "Profit Return" on all expense dollars charged against his or her product by sales (for direct sales, activities, order entry, etc.). To work with Sales Managers to: (1) Evaluate distributor performance. (2) Establish target accounts. (3) Ensure that competent salespeople are assigned on all key accounts. (4) Achieve market penetration in specific channels, locations, or accounts.

2. *Engineering and Development:* To ensure market input in setting priorities, to evaluate and plan new product development alternatives, to improve costs or performance of existing products, to correct defects in existing products.

3. *Financial:* To ensure understanding of business economics, to obtain current and meaningful reports on the cost structure and profitability of his or her assigned products, to ensure allocations made against his or her assigned products are reasonable and fair, to obtain reports on total assets assigned to his or her particular products, to monitor results achieved on new product development or redesign and check against predicted return.

4. *Advertising and Sales Promotion:* To develop a specific promotional plan for the upcoming fiscal year and determine the budget dollars to be charged against the products, to define clearly the objectives of such a plan and the return expected, to monitor results and to take quick action to cancel continuing promotional efforts if results are not being achieved. *Note:* Industrial advertising and promotion can be a "sink hole." Spending proposals often follow historical precedent without concrete plans to achieve specific results on dollars expended. For this reason, the product manager is directly responsible for ensuring that he or she obtains definite measurable results for his or her dollars.

5. *Marketing Research:* To obtain realistic potentials for his or her products by trading areas, channels, and sales locations, to obtain feedback data to indicate degree of market penetration by sales location and by individual salesperson, to obtain regular reports showing status on each specific product.

6. *Manufacturing:* To understand plant capacities and manufacturing costs for each product, to understand specific economics (for his or her own operations and competitors) of: (a) standards versus specials; (b) different lot sizes; (c) spare parts manufacturing.

7. *Order entry and sales service:* To monitor and obtain continuous feedback from the field for the following functions: (a) ensure prompt and correct entry of order; (b) ensure correct and factual scheduling of order to meet customers' needs; (c) ensure that schedules are met and that correct items are shipped.

clerical assignment. The contrasting experiences of two market managers from competing companies illustrate this dramatically. In the one case, the market manager played a very strong role in planning for and managing the company's business in her assigned market. She constantly analyzed market conditions and requirements and made sure that programs were developed and implemented to capitalize on major market opportunities. She pinpointed selected areas for distribution-building programs and obtained approval to increase warehouse stocks for faster delivery. To keep costs down, she got the manufacturing and development departments to program a 10 percent cost reduction in a line of distributor products. Once a year she worked up and presented a written business plan for enlarging the company's position in her market to top management. As soon as this was approved, she began working with all departments to ensure that their plans were tied into the overall plan for her market. She then followed up with appropriate line executives to see that programs and decisions affecting her market were implemented and carried out effectively.

She was, in fact, the business manager for her market area. By contrast, her counterpart's job was structured so that he was a combination fact-gatherer for higher-level management and correspondence clerk for his assigned market area. He collected information, which he passed on to line executives so they could make plans or decisions. He was not expected and made no effort to draw together an overall plan for his market. He spent much time dealing with routine sales correspondence that should have been handled in the field. And he never followed up on programs that affected his market business to see that they were carried out properly. As a result, both management and market manager rapidly became disillusioned with the whole idea.

## Proper Position in the Organization

As we have emphasized, the concept of product or market managers is an organizational anomaly in that it violates a longstanding organization principle; that is, responsibility should always be matched by equivalent authority. The product or market manager is not a line executive in the classic sense, for he or she has little or no actual authority. Nor is he or she staff in the traditional sense, since his or her responsibilities usually go far beyond analysis and recommendations. He or she usually has the unqualified responsibility for seeing that everything related to the product or market gets done well and on time and that satisfactory profit growth is achieved.

The manager's success depends largely on how well he or she is able to develop and maintain a host of complex working relationships with other executives throughout the organization. It is extremely important, therefore, to keep the channels as clear as possible. It is even more important to recognize that each product manager's assignment must be tailored to enable him or her to focus on the particular activities that are vital to the product's growth and profitability, regardless of what they are or where they fit in the organization. In effect, the product manager serves as a hub or nerve center to ensure interfunctional coordination with all the functions and activities that affect the product business (see Exhibit 16-2). In this position, the product manager must ensure that the communication flow between functions is clear and accurate and that all the various efforts for the product line are synchronized.

**EXHIBIT
16-2**

## *THE PRODUCT MANAGER AS HUB*

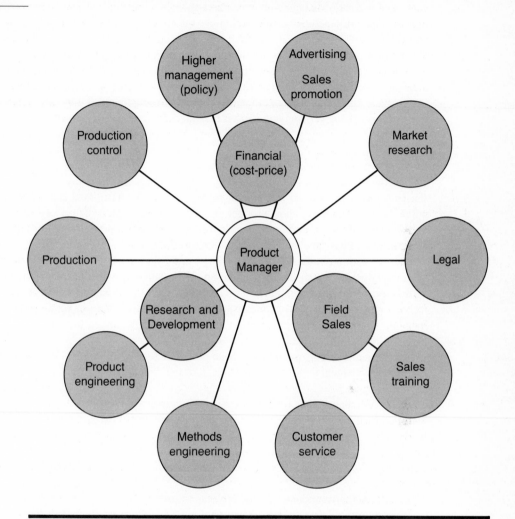

*Source:* Karl H. Tietjen, "The Industrial Product Manager," *Handbook of Modern Marketing* (New York: McGraw-Hill, 1970).

A product manager in the plastics field found the organizational barriers in his company crippling. In sharp contrast to the hub concept, he was organizationally cut off from direct contact with product scheduling or product development. Top management, applying a generalized concept of the job, had restricted the product manager's assignment to the marketing area. Yet the profit for his product depended heavily on maintaining uninterrupted production, even at a sacrifice in unit margins. And product improvements were the major weapon for entering new markets and capturing the new business that would strengthen his competitive position. He rightfully complained: "These activities are the heart of this business. Unless I get into these areas with both feet, my role as product manager is a joke." Management must make sure its product and market managers are positioned in the organization structure to have the status and access to key decision makers required to carry out their assignments. It is essential to avoid burying them beneath layers of organizational levels if they are to function effectively. In fact, many companies have moved their product and/or market managers out of the marketing department to a position reporting directly to the general manager so that they are not restricted by organizational lines. Although this is not the most common arrangement, it underscores the importance of positioning product and market managers as high in the organization as practical.

## The Right Qualifications

The product-market manager concept simply will not work with anything less than outstanding people on the job. Product or market managers, more than anyone else, should influence the destinies of their product or market. All the line executives in the company have functional responsibilities that span all products or markets; product or market managers are the only ones with a full-time commitment to a particular product or market. Moreover, with no authority to order things done, they must convince line executives to act on the programs and ideas they develop. They can do this only if they are the most informed people in the company about the product, how it is manufactured, its underlying technology, and the needs of the marketplace. They must have imaginative yet practical ideas for meeting these market needs that are practically linked to the dynamics of the business, plus the personal skills to get their ideas accepted.

Managements often lose sight of these points in setting up or making product-market manager assignments and make mistakes like the following:

> In one company, four of the five incumbents were made product managers after they failed to make the grade in the field selling force.

> In another company, the market manager's compensation range was locked into the salary structure at such a low level that it was impossible to attract the caliber of person needed to do the job.

> In still another company, the pattern was to use the product manager position as a training ground for promising younger people to groom them for district sales management assignments.

The results were the same in all these cases: Those appointed to product or market manager positions did not have sufficient experience and business skills to do the job. In such situations, there is little justification for blaming the concept.

On the other hand, the difficulty of finding qualified people to fill product or market positions cannot be passed over lightly. One president put this problem in perspective when he said: "I have no doubt about the usefulness of the product manager concept. However, I do have doubts about our ability to find the paragons who can effectively fill these jobs. We have a hard enough time finding good general managers; now we must uncover people with comparable ability or potential at a starting salary level we can afford to pay." Actually, this overstates the case. A good product or market manager does not have to be an expert in everything that relates to the product. To start with, he or she has to have a solid appreciation of the product and how it is manufactured, what is important for success in the marketplace, and good business sense. The rest can be mastered as part of on-the-job training. Many companies have found that product or market manager jobs are the best possible proving ground for general management assignments. Every product or market manager is not going to graduate to general manager, but he or she has to have many of the requisite capabilities.

In short, then, those companies that have achieved outstanding results from their product or market managers have succeeded largely because they staffed the job with qualified people. A definition of "qualified" includes multiple abilities. The product or market manager must have—or must develop--superior product or market knowledge, management skills, and planning abilities. Even more important are other skills that are frequently overlooked. A demonstrated sense of business judgment, the personal skills to operate effectively on a staff basis, the faculty to deal effectively with a full range of business problems, and the verbal ability to articulate a point of view and persuade others to see it are also requisites for any product or market manager.

One company in the electronics industry recently achieved a major turnaround in its business chiefly as a result of settling for nothing less than recognized leaders in their fields for each of its product manager positions. This required changing the salary structure so that these managers were paid on a par with the number two person in the marketing department, and in certain cases even providing stock options to attract the very best people for these jobs. This increased costs, but management today is convinced that the company's markedly improved performance is attributable to this action and that it has been well worth the added investment. In another company, concerned about lagging growth in its major market, management drafted the person generally considered to be "the best commercial brain in the company" for the market manager position. This move made good sense, because the market area contributed nearly 50 percent of the company's profits.

Often, the established compensation range is not adequate to attract the caliber of manager needed. Consequently, there is an understandable tendency to settle for second best. But the odds are heavy against any company that does not stick to the standards established here. For effective product management depends, more than on anything else, on the skills of the individuals appointed to the jobs.

## Adequate Training and Orientation

It should be obvious that the role of product or market manager is unique, and few come to it fully experienced. As a result, management must be prepared to provide for the thorough orientation and training of people appointed to product or market management positions. Those companies that have taken the time and effort to indoctrinate and train their product and market managers properly have received a real payoff in improved performance.

One such company has a three-part program for new product and market managers. In the first part of the program, the new product or market manager is given a list of specific first steps to be taken when beginning the assignment. The following six tasks (excerpted from the company's written program) illustrate the kind of startup activities the much longer list covers:

1. Study carefully all available descriptive literature about your position. Pay particular attention to the position description, especially that part which defines the role and relationships. It is up to you to become thoroughly familiar with the major responsibilities of the position. Obtain a clear understanding of your working relationships with other executives in the company. Use the "role and relationships" description as a basis for discussions with other executives to ensure complete understanding and agreement on the way you will work together.

2. Talk to the vice president of marketing about how you should manage your assigned product line. Since your role is an extension of the role of the vice president of marketing, you should become familiar with his ideas on: major problems related to the product line, significant opportunities for strengthening market position, overall marketing strategy, and internal strengths and weaknesses affecting the marketing of the product line.

3. Talk to the vice presidents of manufacturing, engineering, and finance about your product business. Be sure you establish a communication link with all these departments. Also, be sure you get a picture of their ideas for strengthening your product business. Finally, listen to any caveats they might have about things to avoid as you take on your new assignment.

4. Become familiar with the company's marketing planning and control process. Study the principles, elements, and steps in planning described in the planning guide (see description of second part of the company's program). Discuss with the planning director the technique, format, and timing involved in developing a product marketing plan.

5. Take steps to ensure that you will have adequate information available to you and that you know how to use it. Read the memorandum "Interpreting Control Reports to Pinpoint Trouble Spots" (see description of third part of the company's program), using it as a guide to discuss your needs with market research and the controller.

6. Develop a first-cut business plan for your product or market area. Review it with and obtain the endorsement of the vice president of marketing. Discuss it also with other key executives to ensure their understanding of the plan as the standard of executing programs and measuring performance during the ensuing period.

The new product or market manager who has a series of specific task assignments, beginning the first day of the job, stands a much better chance of getting the right start than the person who is left on his or her own to figure out how to get underway.

In the second part of the program, each product or market manager is coached in the fundamentals of planning. Here special emphasis is put on showing the manager:

What constitutes a plan, and what areas deserve major attention

How it should be developed and tied together with other departments' plans

How it relates to budgeting and other operating procedures

How it fits into the management process, including how it should be used once it is completed and approved

When and how it should be modified

In the third and final part of the program, a working guide aimed at helping the product or market manager carry out the role is developed and continuously updated. This guide focuses on the "how to" aspects of the product or market manager's job and covers explanations of such basic activities as these:

Developing the product strategy and plans

Recommending capital appropriations

Keeping abreast of the economics of the product's business

Working with engineering and manufacturing to interpret market requirements and develop the cost impact of manufacturing on product design alternatives

Interpreting sales and financial reports to pinpoint trouble spots and areas where attention is needed

Such a guide serves as a useful reference document for new and experienced product or market managers alike. As new ideas or improved procedures are developed, the manager is given the extracurricular assignment of developing a new guideline. The objective is to develop a handbook that will give the product or market manager a running start in mastering most of the knotty tasks within his or her sphere of responsibility.

Properly done, any one of the three parts to this program unquestionably requires some time and effort. And it would be wrong to think that every company should have a program this extensive. However, the example shatters the idea that training a product or market manager is impossible. Many companies could achieve a much higher level of performance by taking a cue from this program.

## Appropriate Performance Measures

Because of the wide variations that exist in product or market manager assignments, it is difficult to agree on standards of performance that will provide a basis for evaluating how well the job is being carried out. Although product profitability and share of market performance are indicators that cannot be overlooked indefinitely (since, after all, the primary role of the product or market manager is to provide the specialized attention needed to improve these), it is not fair to hold product or market managers accountable for these factors on a short-term basis. Too many influences beyond their control contribute to profit and market share changes.

The following criteria are a fairer and much more realistic basis for evaluating how a product manager is performing over the short term:

1. Is he or she on top of varying market conditions and requirements so that he or she is able to interpret accurately the changing needs of the product or market business?
2. Does he or she draw together complete and imaginative plans for the product or market assignment that are acceptable to top management?
3. Do his or her plans include concrete programs for effecting required improvement in the product or market business?
4. Does he or she follow up and, if necessary, modify approved plans to see that product or market objectives are achieved?
5. Is he or she generally regarded by other functional executives as the most knowledgeable about product or market requirements for the area, and do they look to him or her for ideas on what they should do to meet product or market needs?

Ultimately, however, it is results that count. If results are not satisfactory after a product or market manager has been on the job for two years or more, the person probably should be replaced. The ability to plan, communicate, and follow up are certainly attributes. But in the final analysis profit growth is the hallmark of successful product or market management, and the product or market manager has to be measured against this standard.

## WHEN BOTH PRODUCT AND MARKET MANAGERS ARE REQUIRED

As long as a company has a series of products that funnel into one market or a single product line that flows out into several markets, a single product manager or market manager can handle this responsibility. As Exhibit 16-3 shows, it is relatively easy to carve out a discrete area of responsibility for such a manager under these fairly simple product or market conditions. But because product and market proliferation have increased greatly in a large and growing number of industrial companies, many find themselves selling multiple products in multiple markets, with no neat product-market match. Rather, they have to cope with a crisscross of products and markets, which dramatically increases the complexity of the planning and management job to be done, as Exhibit 16-3 shows.

Under these circumstances, planning from only one perspective—product or market—tends to be self-defeating. Neither one nor the other can be downgraded or disregarded in the planning process without severe penalty. If product managers are chosen, each one is likely to concentrate on selling his or her assigned products, rather than on determining what it takes to serve the markets more effectively. In so doing, the managers will probably miss important opportunities in related products and services. Even more important, without sufficient focus on the market, the chances are good that the product lines will lag behind competitive offerings or even become obsolete, as the managers find themselves unable to keep up with changing user needs. If market managers are selected, each will tend to focus on meeting the requirements of his or her assigned market without regard for the impact that these actions or recommendations may have on the company's ability to meet the needs of other market areas with the same product line. Thus, if a company has exceptionally strong or persuasive managers covering one or two market

# EXHIBIT 16-3

## THREE PRODUCT-MARKET BUSINESS SITUATIONS

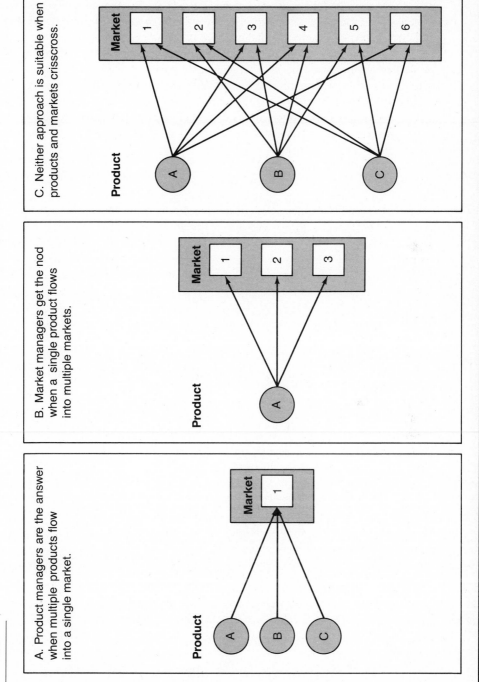

A. Product managers are the answer when multiple products flow into a single market.

Product

Market

B. Market managers get the nod when a single product flows into multiple markets.

Product

Market

C. Neither approach is suitable when products and markets crisscross.

Product

Market

*Source:* B. Charles Ames, "Payoff from Product Management," *Harvard Business Review*, November–December 1963.

areas, it can very easily end up with product plans or actions in these markets that seriously jeopardize the company's position in other market areas.

How does a company ensure the right planning emphasis and balance in this kind of situation? A growing number of industrial companies have found that the only solution to this dilemma is to stop trying to decide between product or market managers and instead to use them both. Under this dual arrangement, market managers have an external focus toward the market and are responsible for determining what the company should do to be more responsive to market needs. The product manager's job is to seek a balanced response to the needs and opportunities in certain markets without jeopardizing the company's position in others and without placing an unfair burden on manufacturing and engineering.

This dual approach positions the center of gravity for a particular product or market business between these two managers. In so doing, it provides the basis for achieving (a) the market orientation that is so essential to competitive success in any business and (b) a system of checks and balances to ensure that unbridled enthusiasm for market response does not wreak havoc within the business. It is clear that a matrix management approach conceived this way offers a means of coping with the complex product-market situation that exists in many large-scale companies. However, when product and market managers are set up to work parallel with each other, the potential for conflict is automatically created. After all, the fundamental purpose of either of these two jobs is to fight for time and attention from engineering, manufacturing, and sales for their assigned products or markets. The potential for conflict is brought out sharply when both product managers and market managers are present in an organization. Let us look at the inner workings of this conflict more closely.

Since the market managers' primary responsibility is to identify and meet their market's needs, they will quite naturally seek modifications in the existing product or service package without regard for any other market or the functional difficulties they may create. And since the product managers are responsible for keeping their product lines responsive to the needs of all the company's markets in terms of costs, design or performance characteristics, pricing policy, service and warranty arrangements, and so on, they cannot bend indiscriminately to the requirements any one market manager perceives. But although it is inevitable, the conflict arising from the interaction of product managers and market managers should not be viewed as negative. In fact, this kind of conflict is specifically what the dual management concept is designed to produce, and it should be regarded as a positive force. If it is properly managed, the conflict should help uncover a multiplicity of market opportunities that would otherwise go unnoticed, and at the same time provide a mechanism for sorting through these opportunities so that the company's overall interests are best served.

## Examples

Here are two examples of how this dual management approach has been employed.

THE ENGINE MANUFACTURER.    An engine manufacturer found that its three product lines were losing ground in terms of both market and profit growth after a period of rapid expansion. Management saw the need for market managers because the products were sold in three separate markets, each with its own distinct characteristics and requirements. At the same time, there was a clear need for greater management attention to key products.

After a lot of give-and-take discussion, the president concluded that both product and market managers were necessary. Within a few months, the market managers had developed a host of ideas for modifications in the existing product and service packages as well as several promising ideas for new product entries. The product managers then screened these ideas, and the two groups, working together, were able to help the company develop a stronger product-market strategy that nearly doubled volume and earnings per share.

THE TEXTILE COMPANY.   A textile fibers company, confronted with a similar situation, actually made the shift from product managers to market managers as the key planning unit. This company sold three basic fibers in several end-use markets with different characteristics and requirements, and management reasoned that a market focus on planning was more appropriate than a product focus. A chaotic situation arose, however, when plant and development managers discovered they could not possibly respond to all the requests coming to them from the market managers. As one plant manager put it: "Our production costs on product X have gone up by 12 percent because of all the short-term requests for additional stocking requirements. Also, we are running out of capacity for one of our most profitable products, and no plans are being formulated to add new capacity. It is a fine thing to be responsive to market needs, but someone had better watch out for product costs and capacity, or we will have a plant full of unprofitable business and will lose the chance to sell more of our profitable items."

Management then reinstated a product management group to work with the market managers. The product managers quickly took hold of the product planning problems that had led to the chaotic situation in plant and development operations. At the same time, the market managers provided the end-user orientation so essential to success in the marketplace. As a result of product and market manager cooperation, the company struck a better balance between control of its manufacturing process and market response and achieved a short-term profit pickup of several hundred thousand dollars and a much stronger market share position.

## Who Does What

If management decides that this dual approach is appropriate, the next step is to decide how the roles of the two types of managers should be defined and how they should work together. By and large, product managers should be held accountable for all aspects of product line management, including long-term profitability. Market managers, on the other hand, should be held accountable for the long-term growth and profitability of their assigned markets. More specifically, the two roles can be defined as follows.

Market managers should concentrate on:

> Developing a comprehensive understanding of customer and end-user operations and economics and specifying ways that the existing product or service package can be improved to provide a competitive edge.

Identifying related products and/or services that represent attractive opportunities for profitably enlarging the company's participation in the market through either internal development or acquisition.

Drawing together at regular intervals an organized summary of the most attractive opportunities in the marketplace, specifying what must be done internally to capitalize on them, and recommending a first-cut strategy for the business.

Developing a reputation for industry expertise among key customer and end-user groups and bringing this know-how to bear on the negotiation of major orders and on the training and development of field personnel.

Product managers should focus on:

Protecting the pricing integrity of their product—that is, seeing to it that the pricing policies and practices in one market do not jeopardize the company's position or profit structure in another.

Maintaining product leadership by making certain that product design, cost, and performance characteristics not only are broadly responsive to customer needs in all markets, but also are not inadvertently altered to meet the needs of one market at the expense of the company's position in another.

Ensuring that the product is responsive to market needs while at the same time avoiding changes that will clutter the engineering and production process with a proliferation of small-lot, custom, or special orders; in effect, they temper market managers' enthusiastic customer orientation with sober judgments on operating capability and economics.

Ensuring that production scheduling and capacity are intelligently planned to meet profitably the current and anticipated aggregate demand of various markets.

Providing the in-depth technical and/or product knowledge required to support selling efforts on major and complex applications.

The broad activities just cited are always the core of the job for both market and product managers. However, the makeup and importance of the company's various products and markets should determine exactly how the jobs are structured. Product managers invariably function on a full-time basis but may, of course, be given responsibility for more than one product. There is little latitude in structuring this position. The market manager's job, however, is quite a different matter. It may be structured in three different ways, depending on the number, importance, and geographic spread of the markets involved.

1. Most companies assign the market manager a full-time staff role, dividing the product and market planning job into two parts and setting up the two groups—product managers and market managers—in parallel, as shown in Exhibit 16-4(a). This first approach is popular because it is a natural evolution from either product or market managers and is the easiest to introduce. This is the approach when all the markets are equally important

to the company and the number to be covered is relatively small—say, four to eight. Under these circumstances, it is practical to have a full-time staff planner for each one.

2. Some companies give the market manager line sales responsibility as well as the staff planning assignment, as shown in Exhibit 16-4(b). This means that the market manager has direct responsibility for a group of salespeople who specialize in selling to the accounts that make up that market. Theoretically this second approach is best, since it gives one person combined responsibility for both planning and execution within each market area and thus makes it possible to hold him or her fairly accountable for results. It also ensures that he or she has firsthand knowledge of customer and market requirements and helps avoid ivory tower planning. But practically, its application is limited because it is often difficult to justify the degree of sales specialization inherent in this kind of arrangement. Although most companies can point to a cluster of accounts in certain geographic areas for which they could economically justify a specialist salesperson, to get national coverage they must inevitably turn to the general sales representative who sells all products to all markets. Accordingly, in most cases it simply is not feasible to work out an arrangement where the sales force can be divided neatly under several market managers.

3. Still other companies have used the market manager as a part-time planner. These companies add market planning assignments to the responsibility of senior salespeople, sales managers, or application engineers who have some expertise in a given end-use market. This compromise approach is normally followed by companies that deal in such a large number of markets they simply cannot afford to provide full-time market manager coverage for each one. For example, one company identified over 30 markets that needed to be brought into focus. Even after considering various ways these markets might be combined into planning assignments, the number of full-time market managers required could not be justified. Consequently, the company gave market planning assignments to selected salespeople who had special experience or a concentration of accounts in key markets.

Although these approaches to the market manager's job are described separately, they can be combined as necessary to meet the needs and structure of the marketplace. For example, one company was able to give two of its market managers line sales responsibility because there were groups of specialist salespeople that could logically be assigned to them. The company could also justify two additional part-time market manager assignments with the thought in mind that these positions could be upgraded to full-time assignments if the markets developed to any great extent.

## System Changes

Management must change the information and planning systems to reflect the existence and needs of both managers. Product managers need detailed operating information (engineering standards, production schedules, and cost breakdowns) to perform their jobs effectively. Market managers must have access to cost information for all products sold in their markets and to detailed market and customer information. Ultimately, both managers should have profit and loss statements for their respective areas as a benchmark for evaluating performance.

**EXHIBIT
16-4**    **TWO APPROACHES TO MEET THE NEEDS OF THE MARKETPLACE**

A. Market manager in staff capacity only . . .

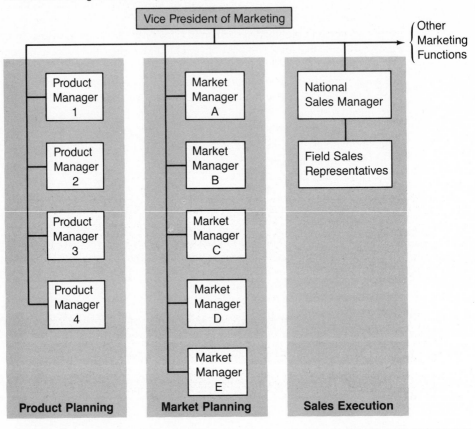

Product Planning    Market Planning    Sales Execution

*Source: Harvard Business Review,* March–April 1971.

In many cases, the kind of cost, operating, and market information required for intelligent product and market planning either is not available or is in a form that is unusable. Correcting this situation may require a major effort (special research projects, restructuring of accounting information). Even with a modified information system, product and market managers also need a close working relationship with engineering, manufacturing, and finance so that they can secure the assistance necessary to interpret much of this information in the correct manner. Regardless of the effort involved, the information and assistance must be provided, or the concept does not stand a chance of getting off the ground.

On the planning side, two changes are necessary. One is a change in the way strategic plans are developed. Market managers should be given the responsibility for developing

B. ... and with combined line and staff responsibility

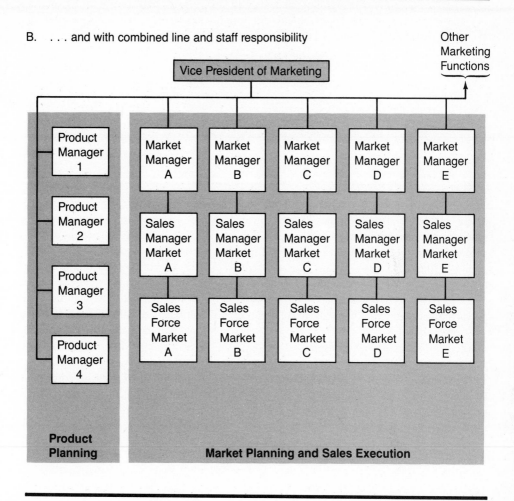

an overview of their market and a no-holds-barred set of recommendations for capitalizing on the opportunities they see. They should then review their ideas with the product managers concerned with their markets to determine what is feasible and what is not, as well as to gain agreement on a point of view that can be presented to other functional managers. From this point on, the process follows a normal planning pattern, with all functional managers collaborating to come up with a final recommendation for top management. The other change in planning has to do with the way top management reviews and responds to strategic recommendations. Basically, the planning system must be adjusted to cope with increased planning inputs. If the dual approach is successful, it should generate a vastly increased number of options and recommendations for building the business in various product and market segments.

One company generated some 20 different strategic options for building just one product-market business with different levels of resource commitment and payoff expectations. To cope with this avalanche of ideas, top managers had to draw extensively on their central planning staff and set aside substantial blocks of their own time to decide which options to accept and which to reject. This may be a unique situation, but bear in mind that the fundamental purpose of this dual management approach is to generate more ideas and recommendations for accelerating growth and profits. Top management must properly evaluate and respond to this flow of ideas to avoid frustration and discouragement in the product and market groups that could cripple the concept.

## SUMMARY

There are no ready-made rules to guarantee effective product or market management, but certain specific steps can be taken to avoid the common pitfalls. First, weigh the concept against other organization alternatives to make sure that it offers the best means of fulfilling the needs of the operation. Above all, make certain it is not being installed simply because it has worked for a competitor or some other company. After the pros and cons of each alternative have been considered, the case for product management may not be as clear-cut as it seemed at first glance. And since it is a difficult concept to make work, it should be chosen only when it is demonstrably the best alternative.

Even in those situations where all conditions are favorable, whether or not a product or market manager is successful depends largely on whether or not top management creates the proper environment. In the last analysis, all this requires is attention to fundamentals: starting with the right people, carefully defining their planning responsibilities, structuring their jobs properly, providing the necessary guidance and direction, and applying appropriate performance measures.

Using both product and market managers provides a basis for achieving the kind of product and market planning necessary in most multibusiness companies. The concept unquestionably means added staff, added expense, and greater complexity in the management process. And making the concept work will probably add problems for most companies. But if a company with a crisscross of products and markets balks at attempting this organization approach simply because it sounds too complex or because it will add to marketing overhead, it is missing a real bet. For it has been the experience of those who have tried it that this concept can provide a significant payoff in increased market opportunities, stronger competitive actions, and profits that far outweigh either the added costs involved or the difficulties of making it work.

## REVIEW QUESTIONS

1. When should product managers be used?
2. What are some reasons why the product management concept often breaks down?
3. What are some steps that will help to make the product management concept more effective?
4. When is it useful to add market managers?

5. Why is a smaller one-line company sometimes an ideal "product management" system?
6. What is the dilemma in product and/or market management?
7. When should the dual product and market management approach be used?
8. What are the inevitable areas of conflict that product and market management creates?

9. How might the roles of product and market managers be defined to have the dual approach work better?
10. What qualifications should be considered when selecting candidates for either product or market manager positions?

# 17

## Guidelines for Effective Implementation

Planning and
Implementation
Organization and Staffing
People Development
Summary
Review Questions

Frank Wilson had just finished two years as division vice president of marketing. During this time, he and selected members of his management team had attended several management development courses and read numerous books and articles on the broad subject of management. Despite these efforts to improve their management skills, their performance had been less than satisfactory. The following deficiencies had been emphasized in Frank's latest management review.

Sales were close to plan, but profits were far from expectations.

New product introductions were lagging.

Costs and expenses were over budget.

The organization did not seem to have either the managerial capabilities or sense of urgency to correct these problems.

Frank was particularly concerned about one comment made by the boss during the review meeting:

One problem you have, Frank, is that you haven't focused on the substance of what it takes to be a good manager and get things done. My advice to you is to stop going to so many management seminars and start to work on the fundamental management problems that exist in your organization. You've allowed politics to come into the picture, you've too many mediocre people in key jobs, and too many people spend too much time in committees that never seem to get anything done.

Later he sought advice from John McSweeney, who had retired from the company but had been a very successful marketing executive when the company had performed at its peak. After listening to Frank, John made the following comment:

Frank, I'm afraid you and your management team have gotten too enamored with a lot of management trappings and have failed to do the hard work required to be effective. Being a good manager is a tough job and requires many tough decisions. It sounds to me like you have listened to a lot of people tell you about good management methods, but you haven't made the effort to make sure they are followed in your organization.

What *does* it take to be a good manager?

How can Frank keep politics from disrupting the organization?

If Frank is to replace his "mediocre" people, what qualities should he seek in job candidates?

What personal qualities suggest that an employee is worth developing for the future?

**I**ndustrial marketing has little chance for success without effective management throughout the organization. To some extent, this point applies to consumer marketing as well. Consumer marketing, however, is more of a discrete function that can often succeed despite weak management, if enough creative genius and money are poured into the key marketing activities. Conversely, marketing in the industrial world is more of a philosophy designed to guide the way the business is managed. This in turn dictates the need for very strong management at all levels, since this marketing philosophy must permeate the entire organization if it is to serve as the cutting edge of the business.

Business reference libraries are full of good articles and books about management theory, techniques, and requirements; management seminars and management programs abound in universities and graduate schools. We do not in any sense intend to duplicate or compete with these efforts in this book. We do believe, however, that many of the management principles emphasized in the literature and in management programs seem to be too easily forgotten. In fact, we submit that many of the problems facing American business today are the direct result of ineffective management that has strayed from some basic principles that should be the very foundation of the management process in any organization.

The purpose of this chapter is to reaffirm briefly these principles without attempting to review all the points one could make about what it takes to be an effective manager. To do this, we have attempted to distill from the literature and our own experience a number of practical guidelines we believe any manager must follow to be effective. As far as we know, these guidelines have never been explicitly defined in other books or articles. At least we have never seen them. Nor do we believe they have been taught or covered explicitly in any school for managers. We believe firmly that real understanding of, and commitment to, these guidelines must be chiseled into one's makeup through real life experience in management situations until they become as deeply ingrained as any other fundamental beliefs that affect the way we intuitively think and act.

For purposes of organization, we have divided the ground rules into three groups that we believe represent the core responsibilities of every manager's job:

1. *Planning and implementation.* Determining specifically what needs to be done and how it will be accomplished and then following up to ensure that everyone understands his or her role and does his or her part to accomplish results.
2. *Organization and staffing.* Determining the number and kinds of people needed to accomplish the objectives of the organization and dividing the tasks among them.
3. *People development.* Determining and carrying out the actions necessary to ensure a continuous upgrading of skills within the organization and an infusion of new people required to continually strengthen the organization's capabilities.

Obviously, a variety of activities can fall under these core responsibilities, and the activities undoubtedly vary in importance from situation to situation. In our judgment, however, these three core responsibilities are always the heart of any manager's job whenever and wherever the management of people and tasks to accomplish certain objectives is required. Let's look first at some important ground rules that underlie the manager's planning and implementation responsibilities.

## PLANNING AND IMPLEMENTATION

### Ground Rule 1

Good planning is the key to successful results for any business operation. Operating without a plan is like flying blind or playing Russian roulette; far too much is left to chance. To be of any value, the business plan must be down on paper. If it is not in writing, it is fair to assume that a quality plan simply does not exist, no matter how enthusiastically a proposition might be described. The discipline of committing a plan to writing is the only way to eliminate the holes and vagaries that are virtually certain to be present when a plan is "ad libbed." Although management should insist on written plans, it is essential to avoid becoming so enamored of flowery prose or format that substance is lost. Any plan, regardless of its complexity, can be put down in a few paragraphs. Good planning requires good thinking and substance; eloquence and form are not substitutes.

It is also essential to understand that planning alone never accomplished anything; somebody has to do something to get results. The danger of becoming so enamored with planning that nothing gets done is very real. As a general rule, most of the benefits from planning typically accrue from the first 30 to 50 percent of the effort. The remaining time and effort devoted to planning simply make people more comfortable and enable them to avoid getting on with what really needs to be done. Failure to achieve planned results means that the plan was no good to begin with, or that execution was bad. Either way, it is the manager's responsibility. Although it is unrealistic to expect that every plan will be achieved, the organization's success depends ultimately on its ability to achieve planned results. Any manager who repeatedly fails to create good plans or fails to overcome the difficulties that stand in the way must be moved aside so that someone who has these abilities can be given a chance.

A key point to remember is that the management task is much more difficult when the responsibility for planning and execution is divided between two people or groups. If planned results are not achieved, the person or group responsible for execution can argue that they did a good job but the plan was not sound. Conversely, the person or group responsible for planning will ultimately argue that the plan was sound but execution was weak. The manager in this case is caught in the middle, and assuming both parties or groups report to the manager, he or she is the person who will be held accountable. For this reason, the smart manager always tries to assign a combined responsibility for planning and execution to an individual or group and also seeks to push this responsibility as far down in the organization as possible.

## Ground Rule 2

Every manager must be tough-minded in identifying issues, and evaluating problems or proposals. A manager should approach an evaluation of any situation with an open mind, but always maintain a questioning or challenging point of view. Pat solutions or easy answers are seldom correct. And solutions or answers based solely on experience or "gut feel" are most often wrong.

For this reason, management should insist that all complex issues, analyses, and recommendations be committed to writing and supported by hard facts. This doesn't mean that every idea spawned by the organization has to be committed to writing; there is no need for a paper avalanche. However, as stated earlier, committing one's thoughts to writing is the only way to ensure good thinking. It helps to avoid the faulty thinking that so often occurs when someone "fires from the hip." Anyone who cannot get his or her thoughts into writing in a way that makes sense to the reader hasn't really thought through what he or she wants to say or do.

## Ground Rule 3

Once a plan is approved, it is the manager's job to ensure that everyone in the organization has a deep-rooted sense of commitment to achieve results. This is a crucial point, since the failure of some to meet their commitments is the chief reasons so many plans are unsuccessful. Most commitments are broken because of an attitude of always finding an excuse or a rationale for not doing something that was supposed to be done. For this reason, management should insist that all commitments be met once they are made and be critical of anyone who does not meet them. These people must understand that they have fallen down on their jobs and damaged the entire group's credibility and ability to perform. It makes no difference whether the commitment seems trivial (to return a telephone call or pass on certain information by a certain time) or crucial (to meet a project completion or delivery date). Once made, the commitment must be met.

Unless management rigorously enforces this attitude, commitments will be broken, planned results will not be achieved, and the organization's credibility will suffer. Credibility is a precious asset, both for the manager and the organization. Without it, neither the manager nor the organization can be effective (see the box).

## Ground Rule 4

One of the most difficult tasks of any manager is to keep priorities straight. It is very easy for managers to duck current problems or issues that are often unpleasant to face by shifting their thoughts to longer-range problems or new opportunities. Falling into this trap is a mistake that is certain to lead any manager into major difficulties. To avoid it, managers should always follow these priorities:

1. Stay on top of day-to-day activities to minimize surprises that can wreck the business, and keep senior management informed of all developments, good or bad.

## HOW IS COMMITMENT LIKE HAM AND EGGS?

In the business world the word *commitment* is not one to take lightly. The truth of this point was driven home in the following situation:

The president of a U.S. based telecommunications company had reached an agreement with a bank in England to buy a company—from an estate for which the bank was a trustee—for a price based on planned earnings for the year. The president and his team spent the better part of two days visiting top mangement of the English company and touring the operation. The products, facilities, manufacturing methods, and technology all seemed to be satisfactory. Sales and profit, however, were about 10 percent below plan for the year to date, and since there were only four months remaining in the year, the president naturally was concerned whether earnings to justify the sale price would be achieved. Management of the English concern assured the president that they could make up the gap that now existed, but he was not entirely satisfied.

At a final meeting between both management groups, the president continued to have nagging doubts about the English firm's ability to achieve its planned earnings. Because the matter was so important, he asked the same question several times at different times during the meeting. "Are you guys really committed to actually achieving your sales and earnings plan?" Each time he emphasized the word *commitment,* and each time he was assured that the plan would be achieved. After he repeated the question for the fourth time, one of the English managers said, "You are obviously driving at something with your repeated question about our commitment. I know what the word *commitment* means, but I am not sure I understand what you mean when you use that term in the context you are using it." Before he could respond, another English manager spoke up. "Actually it's quite simple and analogous to 'ham and eggs.'" Noting that his analogy had brought a quizzical look to everyone's face, he then went on to say, "In the case of ham and eggs the chicken is involved but the pig is committed. Isn't that the way you are using the word *commitment* in your question to us?" The president responded quickly, "That is a perfect analogy. It reflects exactly what I mean."

2. Achieve planned results that have been approved by management.
3. Then, and only then, start to plan for longer-term growth and development.

Every manager typically has more things to do than he or she can possibly get done. Slotting tasks under these priorities is the only way to put "first things first."

## Ground Rule 5

Every manager must keep the surprises out of the operation. Most business surprises are a reflection of not knowing or anticipating what is going on, and this gap simply cannot be tolerated in today's dynamic business environment. To avoid surprises, a manager must be active, not reactive. An active manager seeks to make things happen rather than getting caught off base and then scrambling to salvage a situation that could have been avoided if he or she had stayed on top of the operation. Active managers never drift into decisions or actions or permit them to be taken by default. They know what is going on and what they are doing at all times.

To be an active manager, a person must know the details of the operation. The greatest threat to the business is past success that tends to breed complacency. For this reason, active managers continually ask hard, probing questions even when the business is doing well. They also cut across or through organization lines to get the information they need. In doing this they must be careful not to interfere with lines of authority or the decision-making process. However, they communicate freely and openly with everyone in the organization and encourage everyone to communicate with them. They know this is the only way they will really know what is going on. Any manager who tries to get by without knowing the details of the operation is bound to be superficial and can only be reactive because he or she doesn't know enough to take any kind of action until a crisis develops. There is no way this kind of manager can succeed. One crisis will lead to another, and the whole operation will ultimately drift out of control.

## Ground Rule 6

No individual manager should ever seek or accept the credit for good results. Good results flow from a successful team effort, and the whole team deserves the credit. Conversely, however, every manager must shoulder the responsibility when the organization fails to perform. Poor results occur when the manager has not done a good job of planning, staffing, organizing, and following up, which we have stressed are inescapable core responsibilities.

Now let's look at some basic ground rules that affect organization and staffing.

# ORGANIZATION AND STAFFING

## Ground Rule 1

It is essential to recognize that it is the quality and capabilities of people, not the genius of the structure, that makes any organization work or fail. Blindly following organization concepts or principles simply because they are theoretically correct or because they have proved successful elsewhere is a sure route to wasted talents and efforts and inadequate results. Capable people who are fair minded and dedicated can make almost any organization structure work. Conversely, self-centered, politically motivated people or marginal performers will not be effective under any arrangement. There is nothing more useless or damaging to morale and results than shuffling the same names among different boxes and titles if the people involved do not have the necessary skills or personal attributes. It accomplishes nothing, and everyone in the organization generally knows it. Even more damaging, it deludes management into thinking it has taken positive action when in fact it has not really faced up to the problems.

This does not mean that organization changes should never be made. Of course, they are necessary to better utilize talents, streamline the decision-making process, achieve better planning and control, reduce costs, and so on. But the effective managers ensure that they do not fall into the common trap of tinkering with the organization as a means of escaping or putting off fundamental personnel problems that are difficult or uncomfortable to face.

## Ground Rule 2

The management pyramid in any organization narrows quickly and limits the opportunities available to test and nurture fresh talent. This means that a sufficient number of lower-level management positions must be preserved as a proving ground to test and provide experience for high-potential individuals who appear to have capacity for growth. Turnover should not be considered a problem in these positions unless it is excessively high or too low. Clogging all the lower rungs on the management ladder with men or women who are not going any further undermines the whole organization. It creates a pool of mediocrity that is the logical source for meeting organization needs. More important, it causes good people to become frustrated because they are blocked from upward movement. Unless this frustration is relieved, they will ultimately leave because they are not given an opportunity to take on added responsibility in a time frame that is reasonable to them.

## Ground Rule 3

Every manager should have a backup person who is potentially better qualified for the job than he or she is. If a manager concludes that he or she does not have anyone in the organization who has the necessary potential, he or she must give top priority to bringing in someone who does. This does not mean that the staff should automatically be enlarged. In most cases, it means that one or two individuals within the organization who do not have the necessary qualifications or potential should be replaced by someone of this caliber. Ensuring this kind of backup is crucial. No manager has a right to feel he or she has done a good job if a logical successor is not clearly visible or if a succession plan is not clear.

## Ground Rule 4

Everyone in the organization should always know what is expected of him or her, how his or her assignment fits into the whole, and how his or her performance will be measured. This means that each individual should have a set of specific results that he or she agrees to accomplish within a certain time frame so that there is no confusion about what he or she is supposed to do. To be meaningful, these objectives should be defined in measurable terms so that there can be no misunderstanding or argument about what was accomplished and what was not. Accomplishment of these objectives should then serve as the standard of performance to determine how well the individual performs.

The organization's whole system of rewards and penalties should reinforce this management by objective (MBO) concept. Payoff should always be for achieving planned results and not for effort alone. In other words, those who achieve results should receive significant recognition and reward; those who fall short must expect more limited rewards.

## Ground Rule 5

As many individuals advance in age, they reach a point where their job responsibilities tend to move beyond their energy level or capabilities. This is a natural development and should be expected. Unless someone figures out a way to halt or reverse our life process, it will happen to most of us. Senior management and the organization have an obligation to men and women who have served loyally and now encounter this situation. They should be treated fairly and be given assignments where they have an opportunity to make a continuing contribution. But if they can no longer pull their own weight on mainstream assignments, they must be moved aside. It is not fair to the organization to allow them to continue as weak links, and it certainly is not fair to the incumbents who must struggle to keep up.

Conversely, advancing age alone should not be regarded as a reason for excluding anyone from consideration for added responsibility. There is nothing more wasteful than pushing an experienced man or woman to the sidelines simply because the calendar has advanced, when he or she still has the energy and capability to succeed.

## Ground Rule 6

Managers must always be alert for misfits who are almost certain to creep into the organization, no matter how carefully people are screened or evaluated, and move quickly and decisively to weed them out. We have used the term "misfits" purposely, because these people often represent a destructive force in the organization. They should not be confused with individuals who depart from the norm to create healthy organizational improvements. Rather, they are the "rotten apples" in the barrel that destroy the whole. Three types of misfits are especially damaging to any organization:

1. Anyone who does not have the integrity or intellectual honesty necessary to command absolute trust.
2. "Politicians" who always have their fingers in the air to see which way the wind blows and are more interested in making the right move than in doing or saying what is right.
3. Organization bullies who are bastards to their subordinates and sycophants to their superiors.

Not moving quickly on anyone who fits any of these descriptions detracts from the manager's credibility. Most people in the organization know who the "misfits" are and think less of the manager's capability or integrity if he or she permits them to remain.

## Ground Rule 7

Although widely used in many organizations, most committees and committee assignments are a complete waste of time. They may be an ideal vehicle for government and other bureaucratic organizations that are most interested in the appearance of getting something done and in syndicating the risk on tough decisions and issues. However, no committee ever made a decision, accepted a commitment, or developed a program for which it could really be held accountable. And committee members almost inevitably find a way to avoid criticism of their specific role by pointing to what other committee members did or said.

For these reasons, a committee may be an appropriate vehicle for brainstorming sessions to spark new ideas, to ensure cross-functional coordination on major projects, or where an oversight function is required and it is unfair to assign the responsibility to an individual (such as an audit committee of a board). However, in the mainstream of business management, where accountability for actions and decisions is essential, committees should play a very limited role.

These are the ground rules to keep in mind as organization and staffing considerations are weighed. Now let's look at some ground rules to ensure a continuing stream of talent for the organization.

# PEOPLE DEVELOPMENT

## *Ground Rule 1*

A primary task of every manager is to create an attractive work environment for the people in the organization so they can perform, develop, and fulfill their aspirations. This doesn't mean that the manager should try to make everyone happy or to make all the tasks easier. Rather, the manager seeks to develop a work environment that has these characteristics:

1. Everyone speaks and acts with absolute honesty and integrity at all times. It is not easy to ensure that these principles are always followed, particularly in larger companies where effective communication is often difficult and where the chance for different interpretations of policies and situations is very great. It is management's job to ensure everyone understands that honesty and integrity are full-time principles that cannot be turned on and off to suit one's desires and needs of the moment. Management must make it clear that sticking to these principles comes first, even if it means sacrificing some things (such as new business, added sales, increased earnings) that are obviously to the company's advantage. There is no way management can compromise on these principles and still create and maintain an outstanding work environment.
2. There is open communication up, down, and across the organization. Everyone recognizes both the right and necessity to be open and constructively critical of things that can be improved. No "sacred cows" are tolerated. Superiors are willing to really listen to the other points of view, and are willing to say "I'm wrong" if facts and logic show that this is the case.
3. There is a genuine interest in getting problems out on the table and correcting them, rather than pinpointing blame or scurrying to keep one's "shirttails" clean. Everyone knows his or her individual assignments, but works hard and effectively as a team member. Since team results are the goals, no one tries to be a hero or make a grandstand play.

There is always an air of excitement in the organization that one can sense when he or she is on a winning team, and it is the manager's responsibility to create this excitement. Unless this kind of environment exists, good people will leave and only the mediocre will remain. And any organization staffed with the mediocre is certain to lose.

## Ground Rule 2

Managers should recognize that the most frequent and insidious personnel mistake they can make is to live too long with marginal or poor performers. Most managers delude themselves into thinking that they are being fair by allowing these individuals to continue and that somehow time will correct the situation. Nothing could be farther from the truth. Basic personality flaws or skill deficiencies generally do not get corrected with time. It is totally unfair to the individual and a reflection of weak management to reach an agonizing conclusion that someone cannot do the job after he or she has been on it for several years.

As a general rule, it should not take more than six months to a year to determine whether someone can perform on a given assignment. The capable manager is tough-minded in performance evaluations, "ruthless" in decisions on who can perform and who cannot, and then eminently fair and decisive in the way he or she carries these decisions out.

## Ground Rule 3

No individual in the organization should ever be damned simply because he or she is "too ambitious," "too aggressive," "too impatient," or "too demanding," as long as he or she is a good thinker and fair and straightforward in his or her dealings and actions. Although people described in these terms are typically cast in an unfavorable light by personnel appraisal systems, they actually represent the kind of people that should be advanced or developed. They may be more difficult to manage, but they will make things happen for the better and enhance the organization's chances for success.

It is those who are too easygoing, too willing to compromise principles to avoid conflict, or more interested in being liked than getting things done who should come under fire. They are the weak links in an organization that makes it impossible to develop a strong team or achieve outstanding results.

## Ground Rule 4

Every manager should ensure that all people in the organization know exactly where they stand and what their career outlook is at all times, even if it hurts. This doesn't mean that people should expect to have their career path mapped out for them, or to be promised future promotions if they do this or do that. It does mean, however, that people should know whether they are performing well or poorly in their current assignment and whether they are regarded as having the potential for future growth.

There is nothing kind about glossing over weaknesses an individual could correct if he or she were made aware of them. Nor is there anything kind about allowing someone to think that he or she is doing better than he or she really is or has a greater opportunity in

## EVALUATING HONESTLY: IT'S ONLY FAIR

When managers are reluctant to be as frank or honest as they should in their discussions with employees about performance and opportunities for personal growth, situations like the following can easily develop.

The new president of a large electrical products manufacturer decided to travel and work with a half dozen of the company's sales engineers to develop a better understanding of the company's customers and selling requirements. He was particularly impressed with one of the younger sales engineers who had graduated from Lehigh University and had been with the company for three and a half years. This young man had an outstanding academic and extracurricular record, was very personable, and obviously very interested in moving into a sales management position. He told the president that he enjoyed his work with the company very much and that his only disappointment so far was that he had not been given a district manager's position that had opened up. That position had been given to another salesman who had been with the company for about five years. Although disappointed, he was still enthusiastic about his future with the company. He explained, "My regional manager assured me that I would be a very eligible candidate when the next opening occurred."

That evening the president had dinner with the regional manager to discuss the events of the day. Among other things, he complimented the regional manager on the quality of the sales engineers he had met and noted that he was particularly impressed with the young man from Lehigh University. He went on to say how enthused this young man was about the company and the opportunity he saw to become a district manager in the near term. The president was more than a little surprised at the regional manager's response. "Frankly, I don't see him as a near term candidate. He has too much to learn. Moreover, there is some question in my mind whether he is not better off in a career selling position." Since this didn't square with what the sales engineer had said, the president made it a point to get the young salesman together with the regional manager the next morning. During this discussion, it was obvious that the regional manager did not want to tell the sales engineer about his limitations as directly as he had told the president. After the regional manager made several vague comments about the salesman's performance and potential, the president brought the matter to a head by stating in very blunt terms the way he understood the regional manager's position and asked if that was correct. The regional manager responded "yes" and a look of disappointment was apparent on the young sales engineer's face.

The young sales engineer subsequently resigned from the company and later became associated with another major equipment manufacturer where he is now the senior sales officer of the company. While the experience with the regional manager and the president may have been painful for the sales engineer, it helped him on to a career path that was ultimately more successful for him.

the organization than is actually the case. There is no reason to be rude or inconsiderate in explaining where deficiencies exist, but the explanation must be clear and straightforward. Failing to be clear or completely honest can easily hurt someone's chances to become an effective contributor and may even jeopardize that person's career. No manager has the right to do that (see the box).

## Ground Rule 5

Finally, every manager must understand that inherited characteristics or background have nothing whatsoever to do with an individual's effectiveness. Managers cannot be influenced or even notice whether an individual is black or white, young or old, Christian or Jewish, male or female, an Ivy Leaguer or someone from the ghetto. Rather, managers must concentrate an evaluation on the things that really count:

1. Who has faced the problems squarely? Who has the guts to tell it like it is? Who does not?
2. Who is an effective contributing team member? Who is not?
3. Who has and can articulate good ideas? Who cannot?
4. Who produces results? Who gets the job done? Who does not?

Managers who concentrate on personal characteristics and do not give sufficient consideration to the things that really count are going to lose. Competition and the whole world will pass them by, led by those who know what it takes to succeed.

## SUMMARY

There is nothing new or particularly sophisticated about any of the points covered in this chapter. They have been recognized and followed by good managers for years. They are based directly on common sense, logic, and a sense of fair play, which we believe are the underpinnings of effective management in any situation.

None of these ground rules is hard to accept; the difficulty develops in trying to follow them. Doing so requires managers to dig deeper into problems, to stay on top of more details, to make more difficult decisions, and to take more uncomfortable actions than many people care to do. We don't claim that following these ground rules alone is any guarantee of management or marketing success. A host of other factors weigh heavily in each situation. We do submit, however, that any manager's chances for success are greatly reduced if he or she does not follow these guidelines and that there is virtually no chance of a successful marketing effort if they are not broadly followed throughout the organization.

## REVIEW QUESTIONS

1. Why are the people more important than the organizational structure?
2. What is the difference between efforts and results when selecting, developing, and promoting people?
3. What is the relationship between sound plans, commitments, and results?
4. How does a good manager reduce the number of surprises in the business?
5. Why should ambitious, aggressive, or demanding people be tolerated?

# VI

# CASE STUDIES

# WRT, Inc.: Engineered Products Division

## Creating a Market - Driven Orientation

## COMPANY BACKGROUND

WRT, Inc., was established in 1894 as a railroad car manufacturing company in western Pennsylvania. The company has grown steadily over the years and has 19 operating divisions in eight states, Canada, Germany, and New Zealand. WRT is engaged in the industrial manufacture of several hundred different products in more than 50 plants and has a total corporate sales volume of approximately $1.5 billion (1983). The company strategy is based on several autonomous divisions and relatively small plants, most of which are located in small to middle-sized communities. WRT stresses product quality and is known for its excellence in engineering and research.

The Engineered Products (EP) Division, the largest plant of the Electronics Group, is located in Indiana. The plant began operations in 1950 as a research facility for vacuum power tubes. A few years later, EP received a contract to design and develop a battery to launch and guide a classified U.S. Army weapon. Over the next few years, EP won several more military and space contracts. Since 1966, almost all of EP's sales have been related to military and space batteries and battery components. Today, EP employs 526 people and is recognized around the free world by the military and space battery industry as the leader in terms of dollar sales volume, product diversification, and technical expertise.

Through the years, the EP Division has participated in an extensive number of projects, and this involvement resulted in the development of a large number of battery-related products, most of which disappeared immediately after the expiration of the contract that generated them. The division had an engineering-driven philosophy. Few marketing efforts were made. However, its sales continued growing at a satisfactory pace, with an average pretax return on sales of about 8 percent (see Exhibit 1).

This case was modified from one originally developed by Professors Joseph W. Leonard, Miami University, and John Thanopoulous, the University of Akron.

| EXHIBIT 1 | ENGINEERED PRODUCTS DIVISION |
|:---:|:---:|
| | Sales Volume (in $000) |

| Customer (End User) | 1972 | 1974 | 1976 | 1978 | 1980 |
|---|---|---|---|---|---|
| U.S. Army | $2721 | $2685 | $ 2340 | $ 2046 | $ 3048 |
| U.S. Navy | 860 | 704 | 660 | 2960 | 3641 |
| U.S. Air Force | 2142 | 2899 | 3509 | 3214 | 4684 |
| Dept. of Energy* | 820 | 1490 | 2631 | 3140 | 3966 |
| NASA | 1421 | 1656 | 2124 | 2291 | 1744 |
| U.S. Marine Corps | 160 | 179 | 130 | 64 | 0 |
| Commercial | 0 | 0 | 0 | 416 | 0 |
| Foreign | 0 | 36 | 424 | 622 | 941 |
| Unknown/other | 0 | 1 | 71 | 83 | 20 |
| Total | 8124 | 9650 | 11889 | 14836 | 18044 |

*Formerly the Atomic Energy Commission and then the Energy Research Development Agency.

# EP ORGANIZATION

At the end of the 1960s, EP spent significant amounts of capital to expand existing facilities, remodel the old ones, and update its equipment. This resulted in an era of overdependence on long-term loans. The long-term debt was necessary if the EP Division was going to continue to compete successfully for military and space projects. But it was catastrophic for Wes Cooper, the division's controller who had initiated the change. Cooper resigned in 1973, having failed to justify the overreliance on loans and the subsequent high interest payments. Then, WRT provided some funds and a new controller, David Levine. Levine quickly proved to be extremely competent. He simplified processes, increased control, and pioneered a planning and scheduling system. Subsequently, he gained for himself the title of senior vice president of WRT with strategic planning responsibilities and designated his head accountant, Andy Parker, as the new controller.

Andy had joined EP in 1977 and almost immediately had started a friendship with Bruce Jacobs, EP's newly recruited contract manager, who also held a Ph.D. in economics. Parker had worked for 18 years as financial planner for Singer (especially associated with the B-52 plane). The organizational chart for the division is shown in Exhibit 2.

One-third of the EP Division workers were classified as white-collar employees; among them almost 80 percent had an engineering background. Only 30 people out of the 526 employees were in administration, purchasing, accounting, controlling, personnel, and security of the facilities, leaving the main part of EP engineering and production oriented (see Exhibit 3 for top executive profiles).

EXHIBIT
2

## ORGANIZATIONAL CHART

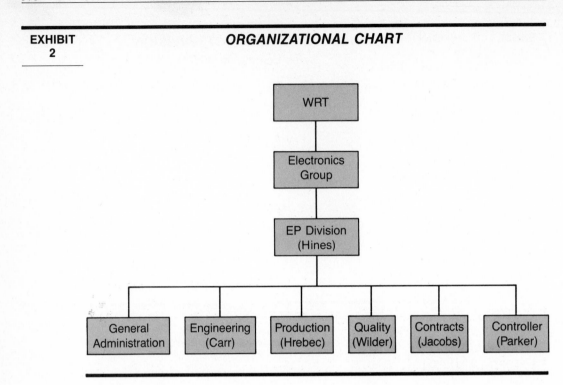

# A NEW PROJECT

On May 29, 1980, a land developer and light manufacturer in Arizona contacted the EP Division to seek information and subsequently ordered 660 lithium battery systems at a price of $1,205.50 per unit for delivery in 1981. Fun City Enterprises, Inc., the ordering firm, was in the land developing business for retirement communities and recently had extended operations into the production of goods that potentially would have been sold exclusively through its own captive markets. Fun City was operating five retirement communities with a permanent population of more than 6,000 residents. The latest addition was going to be the development of an electric golf cart, oversized and with roadworthy specifications, which was planned to be marketed even outside its markets. This cart, which was designed to be used as a second family car, was fast (up to 39 miles per hour) and able to travel 75 miles on a single charge. The only reliable power unit Fun City was able to find was the Li24N (lithium battery) system, patented and produced by the EP Division.

Bruce Jacobs handled the sale with extreme care. He realized the potential of commercial sales[1] from the very beginning, but he also realized that "rocking the boat is dangerous." "The life of a marketer in an engineering firm is pitiful," he said during the last days

---

[1]EP considers all nongovernment end user sales to be commercial. Therefore, commercial sales would include what would normally be classified as industrial products.

of January [1981] to Parker. "First of all, you do not understand their [engineers'] language; then, they want to produce whatever toys fancy their minds; and finally, they want *you* to sell them. Now, I must say that they have ideas. . . . This Li24N, for example, was a very good one . . . but it applies basically to military and space programs. It is much more than what they need in a golf cart."

"But this is what Fun City asked for, and they pay good money, too!" interrupted Parker.

"Well, that's the point," continued Bruce, "golf carts do not need a space battery. They need a less demanding and a cheaper one. We must study the marketplace. The suppliers must understand the marketplace—if the buyers cannot see it. Otherwise, somebody from the competition will give Fun City a cheaper replacement battery next year. Then, this nice door to commercial sales will close for us."

General Manager Hinds walked in and heard the last part of the conversation. He did not say a word but he registered one further thought—to expand Jacobs' job description from contracts to the title of marketing. He suggested to Bruce Jacobs, "Why don't we re-title your job 'Manager of Contracts and Marketing'?"

Bruce responded, "Sure, that will help."

The General Manager, Hinds, liked the golf cart project because he was also an avid golfer. Hinds felt extremely secure about his division and was respected for his technical and production knowledge. He had excellent engineers, high-level technology, good production facilities, competent product assurance and control systems, and an impressive backlog of military orders (see Exhibit 4). But he wanted the nongovernment inquiries to get more serious attention. Hinds also realized that profit margins were declining and that the only reason he could afford to pay interest payments was that Cooper had done all this modernization when interest rates were low (relative to 1981). What if competition were to start hitting lower? New markets had to be found.

| EXHIBIT 3 | TOP EXECUTIVE PROFILES | | | |
|---|---|---|---|---|

| Name | Title | Age/Years with EP | | Education |
|---|---|---|---|---|
| Joe Hinds | General manager | 54 | 21 | B.S.E.E. |
| Jim Carr | Engineering manager | 51 | 16 | B.S.M.E. |
| Herb Gailey | Asst. engr. manager | 46 | 16 | B.S. (physics) |
| Ed Duff | Asst. engr. manager | 42 | 16 | B.S.C.E. |
| Jeff Wilson | Asst. engr. manager | 49 | 27 | B.S.C.E. |
| Bruce Jacobs | Contract manager | 38 | 3 | Ph.D. (economics) |
| Dennis Hrebec | Production manager | 62 | 11 | B.S. (tech.) |
| Ronald Wilder | Quality control manager | 57 | 4 | B.A. (history) |
| George Hill | Purchasing manager | 64 | 47 | High school |
| Andy Parker | Controller | 43 | 3 | M.B.A., CPA |
| Tony Tolbs | Production specialist | 58 | 21 | B.S., M.E. |

| EXHIBIT 4 | CURRENT BACKLOG (in $000) As of April 1, 1983 | | | |
|---|---|---|---|---|

| | | | | |
|---|---|---|---|---|
| Thermal | 4451 | | U.S. Army | 2281 |
| Ordnance (fuse) | 182 | | U.S. Navy | 127 |
| Silver zinc | 2417 | | U.S. Air Force | 3821 |
| Nickel cadmium (sealed) | 64 | | Dept. of Energy | 1458 |
| Nickel hydrogen | 675 | | NASA | 1041 |
| Lithium | 1943 | | Foreign | 696 |
| | | | Commercial | 308 |
| Total | 9732 | | Total | 9732 |

*Note:* April 1, 1982, backlog was 11,640.

The whole EP Division was thrilled with the new application of the Li24N. Further, one of those golf carts was given as a present to Jacobs to use for within-plant transportation. When the cart was not used, it was parked at the front entrance of the division with a sign: "The sky is the limit for the use of our products." Jacobs had also done an excellent job of creating contests within the division to create a brand name for the golf cart battery. After nearly two months of these activities, the general manager, Hinds, wrote the following memo to Bruce Jacobs:

This division is beginning to look and feel like a county fair with banners, prizes, and gimmicks. If we are to generate more nongovernment sales, I don't believe this circus can continue. We need orders and contracts for nongovernment uses of our batteries. Please see me at your earliest convenience.

Bruce Jacobs stormed into the general manager's office and stated: "I've been working my ass off on the assignment to explore other uses for our batteries. I assigned Tony Tolbs the task of collecting potential leads for future commercial customers. Tony has a thorough knowledge of most of the batteries we have produced since 1973. He presented me on Monday with an extensive report of our potential customers with commercial applications. I spent two days with him summarizing the information" (see Exhibit 5). "Furthermore, we have been sending people to marketing seminars at well-known universities so we can really be market-focused. We have also considered contracting with a West Coast firm to teach aggressive selling skills to many of our people." The general manager replied:

Bruce, I like you. But some of our good old customers are even beginning to complain. For example, Jerry Day, the Boeing program manager on the air-launched cruise missile, was upset because of all the hype he saw here with the golf cart battery. In a similar vein, when a high-level army procurement officer called last week from Washington, D.C., our key guy was out visiting hog farmers in Iowa about using our batteries to power their windmills. And finally, all the five people who went off to the university-sponsored marketing programs were disappointed. Jeff Wilson said all that was covered was how to market pantyhose and jello. Jim Bartlett said one professor spent an hour explaining how he measured pupil dilation when housewives read food advertisements. Tom Treeger said that the pretty coeds walking on campus were the only thing that got his attention during the five-day course. Bruce, on October 1, a little over one month from now, I want a plan from you on how we will move some of our battery technology to nongovernment or commercial applications. I will then present that plan to corporate, and we will measure you by that plan.

**EXHIBIT 5**

# POTENTIAL COMMERCIAL APPLICATION INFORMATION

### Appliances and tools

Rockwell Intl., Pittsburgh, PA
Desa Industries, Inc., Park Forrest, IL
Widder Corp., Naugatuck, CT
National-Detroit, Inc., Rockford, IL
RE: Very good potential markets, appears to be price sensitive.

a future contacts
c Ni-Cad, Lithium
g $30,000

### Ballooning

Raven Industries, Inc., Sioux Falls, SD
RE: Limited opportunities.

a future contacts
c Ni-Cad, others

### Buoys/beacons

Tideland Signal Corp., Houston, TX
Enviromarine Systems, Inc., Houston, TX
Carliste & Finch Co., Crystal Lake, IL
RE: Fair potential, many other possible customers.

a MS has "no bid" in past
c Nickel-Zinc and others
f $35 to $750
g $100,000

### Calculator batteries

Texas Instruments, Dallas, TX
RE: TI will add MS to its potential supplier's list and will solicit quotations; excellent opportunities.

a Jacobs letter, 4-10-81
c Ni-Cad, Lithium
e $1 to $10
g unlimited

### Diving equipment

Desco Corp., Milwaukee, WI
Dacor Corp., Northfield, FL
RE: Limited opportunities.

a MS had "no bid" in past
c Ni-Cad (?)

### Electric timers

Rhodes, Inc., Avon, CT
RE: Limited opportunities.

a telecon inquiry 8-80
b 600
c Ni-Cad, 1 a-hr
e ASAP

### Emergency railroad car braking

Briggs & Turivas, Inc., Dennison, OH
RE: Potential for sales up to $150,000 per year.

a quoted 10-80
b 500
c Thermal, CAP-694
d 8-81
e 120 days
f $84.50
g $42,250

### Emergency/stand-by lights

Emergency Lighting, Inc., Cohasset, MA

a quoted 4-81
b 1,000
c Ni-Cad, 3 a-hr
d 9-81
e ASAP
f $12
g $12,000

Cooper Electronics, Inc., Farmingdale, NY
RE: Outstanding potential; used in schools, plants, motels, restaurants, stores, mines, etc.

a future contact
c Ni-Cad

### Fire alarms

Borg-Warner Corp., Cedar Knolls, NJ
RE: Good follow-on potential; good custom (larger size, increased power) design possibilities.

a telecon inquiry, 3-30-81
b 400, 800
c Li6Sp
d 6-81
f $125
g $50 to $100,000

Charter Security Alarm Corp., Southpark Circle, SC
RE: Unknown potential.

a future contact
c Lithium

### Fish locators

Lowrance Electronics, Inc., Tulsa, OK
*RE:* Limited (?) opportunities.

a "no bid," 12–80
b 1,000
c Lithium
d 3–81
e 60 days

### Forklifts

Lektro, Inc., Warrenton, OR
*RE:* Conventional lead acids have life, reliability, and maintenance problems.

a convention, 9–80
b 100 up
c Li12n
d 1–82
e $1,600
f $160,000

### Hearing aids

Maico Hearing Instruments, Inc., Minneapolis, MN
Telex Communications, Inc., Minneapolis, MN
Audiotone Div., Royal Industries, Phoenix, AZ
*RE:* Potential up to $150,000 per year.

a future contacts
c Lithium

### Human electric limbs

Larkotex Co., Texarkana, TX
P. W. Hanicke Mfg. Co., Kansas City, MO
*RE:* Unknown potential.

a future contacts

### Liferafts

Air Cruisers Co., Belmar, NJ
*RE:* Fair potential, not price sensitive.

a future contact
c modified Thermal

### Marine searchlights

Rowe Co., Woburn, MA
*RE:* Limited potential.

a future contact
c Ni-Cad, others

### Mini-motor bikes

Doerr Electric Corp., Cedarburg, WI
Fidelity Electric Co., Inc., Lancaster, PA
*RE:* Excellent growth potentials; international opportunities.

a future contacts
c Ni-Cad, Lithium
f $60 to $225

### Mining vehicles

Elreco Corp., Cincinnati, OH
The Jepsen Company, Cleveland, OH
*RE:* Unknown potential.

a future contacts

### Model airplanes

Kraft Systems, Inc., Vista, CA
*RE:* Limited potential.

a future contact

### Outdoor camping equipment

Coleman Co., Inc., Wichita, KS
*RE:* No response from Coleman, unknown potential.

a Jacobs' letter, 4–29–81
c Ni-Cad

Suntek Solar Products, Ltd., San Marcos, CA
*RE:* Unknown potential.

a future contact

### Pacemakers (cardiac)

Hewlett-Packard Co., Palo Alto, CA
Medcor, Inc., Hollywood, FL
Photon Sources, Inc., Livonia, MI
Cardiac Data Corp., Inc., Philadelphia, PA
*RE:* Limited potential.

a future contacts
c Lithium

### Personnel carriers

Taylor-Dunn Electric Vehicles, Anaheim, CA
*RE:* Limited potential.

a future contact
c Lithium, Ni-Cad

*Codes:* a Request    c Battery type or model number    e Estimated delivery date    g Estimated total sales
b Quantity (in units)    d Estimated receipt of order date    f Estimated unit price    RE Remarks
*Notes:* When a code letter is omitted, no information is available. There is no necessary connection between the company name quoted and the respective product information.

*(continued)*

**EXHIBIT 5**

*(continued)*

### Photographic equipment

TBD
RE: Very good potential, but competitive.

a future contacts
c Ni-Cad, Lithium

### Radios/receivers

Motorola, Inc., Schamburg, IL
Fisher Corp., Chatsworth, CA
E-Systems, St. Petersburg, FL
Zenith Radio Corp., Glenview, IL
RE: Virtually unlimited potential, but competitive.

a future contacts
c Ni-Cad
f $1 to $25
g to $500,000

### Remote water & oil pumps

Gould, Inc., Electric Motor Div., St. Louis, MO
RE: MS will be asked to quote on future requirements.

a letter request, 12–80
b 440
c Ni-Cad, 1.5 a-hr
d lost to GE
f $60

Sargent Industries, Odessa, TX
RE: Fair potential (?).

a future contact

### Respirators

Thompson Respiration Products, Inc., Boulder, CO
American Hospital Supply Corp., McGaw Park, IL
RE: Unknown potential.

a future contacts

### Robotized applications

Smithfield Industries, Inc., Clarksville, TN
Vim Systems, Inc., Syracuse, NY
Novatek, Inc., Burlington, MA
RE: Unknown potential, international possibilities.

a future contacts

### Sailboats

Whittaker Corp., Los Angeles, CA
RE: MS's quote was "in the ballpark."

a letter request, 9–80
b 4,800
c Ni-Cad
d mid-82
e 120 days
f $172
g $825,000

### Smoke alarms

Molydenun Corp., Pompano Beach, FL
RE: Excellent growth potential, but price competitive.

a future contacts
c Ni-Cad
e $2 to $10

### Solar energy storage

Solar Power Corp., Woburn, MA
RE: Limited follow-on potential.

a contacted 3–81
b 36
c Ni-Cad, Lithium, Nickel-Zinc
d 10–81
e ASAP
f $110
g $3,960

Energy Control Systems, Mountainview, CA
RE: Unknown potential.

a contacted 5–81
b 60
c Nickel-Zinc
d 10–81
e 6–82
f $800
g $48,000

Solar Usage Now, Inc., Gascom, OH
TBD
RE: Many good possibilities.

a future contacts

### Trolling (fishing) motors

Eska Co., Dubuque, IA
Minn-Kota, Inc., Mankato, MN
Palmer Industries, Inc., Endicott, NY
RE: Unknown potential.

a future contacts
c Li12n

### Tugboats

Diamone Manufacturing Co., Inc., Savannah, GA
RE: Limited potential.

a future contact

### Weather warning alarms

Tulsa Communications & Electronics Co., Tulsa, OK
RE: Good potential; primarily for municipality uses, perhaps some institutions (schools, hospital).

a future contact
c Ni-Cad, Lithium

### Wheelchairs

Everest & Jennings, Inc., Los Angeles, CA
Rosenthal Manufacturing Co., Chicago, IL
American Stair-Glide Corp., Grandview, MO
RE: Unknown potential.

a future contacts

### Windmills

Aeromotor Windmills & Pumps, Inc., Denver, CO
RE: Good follow-on potential.

a letter, by 6–81
c Lithium
d 9–81
e ASAP
g $10,000

Energy Conserving Products, Inc., Kansas City, MO
RE: Fair potential.

a letter, by 7–81
c Nickel-Zinc, Lithium
g $25,000

### Wristwatches

Hamilton Watch Co., Inc., Lancaster, PA
RE: Fair potential for "super-thin" battery for expensive watch market.

a telecon inquiry, 4–81
c Lithium
d 12–81
e mid-82
f $75
g to $50,000

Codes: a Request    c Battery type or model number    e Estimated delivery date    g Estimated total sales
b Quantity (in units)    d Estimated receipt of order date    f Estimated unit price    RE Remarks
Notes: When a code letter is omitted, no information is available. There is no necessary connection between the company name quoted and the respective product information.

# 2

# Warwick Company

## Developing a New Electronic Component

Following the development of a new type of electronic circuit capacitor, executives of the Warwick Company were faced with the problem of timing the introduction of this new product. The development of the new capacitor had been undertaken by Warwick in response to a request from the Cavalier Company, a large manufacturer of television and radio sets and an important customer of Warwick. In February, Cavalier executives were forced to postpone plans for use of the new capacitor eight months, from April to November. Warwick personnel were thus faced with the question of whether they should introduce the capacitor immediately to other radio and television manufacturers or wait until Cavalier was able to make use of the capacitor.

## DEVELOPMENT OF THE WARWICK CAPACITOR

In September of the previous year, executives of Cavalier had asked Warwick to attempt the development of a new circuit capacitor designed especially for use in printed wire chassis boards.[1] They wanted a capacitor that could be seated in the board more easily than capacitors then in use to reduce the costs of television and radio manufacture. Cavalier executives made only a general request and offered no specific ideas for developing a new capacitor, nor did they offer to supply funds for its development.

Warwick personnel agreed to attempt the development of a capacitor that would satisfy the needs of the Cavalier Company. Engineers at Warwick believed it would be possible to develop a capacitor made from a ceramic compound, which would meet Cavalier

---

[1] A printed wire chassis board is composed of a thin, rigid sheet of dielectric (nonconducting) material which has component mounting holes in the proper locations. These holes are connected by copper conductors which are bonded to the dielectric sheet.

specifications. They had considerable experience working with the ceramic materials used in the manufacture of various Warwick products. In late October, samples of a new ceramic capacitor were supplied to Cavalier for testing and evaluation. Cavalier engineers had attended and taken active part in several meetings held by Warwick engineers where the shape, size, and strength of the new capacitor had been discussed.

By mid-December, Cavalier engineers reported that the capacitors had performed "exceedingly well" in tests that had been conducted. Cavalier executives then requested that production quantities of the capacitor be delivered prior to March 19. If quantities could be delivered on or before that date, Cavalier production executives believed they could include the capacitor in a television chassis scheduled to go into production.

The manufacturing and engineering departments of the Warwick Company, however, reported that it would be impossible to meet this request because of the problems of acquiring the machinery and manpower necessary to begin full-scale production of the capacitors. Thus, by mutual agreement, the target date was reset for April 30. On this date, Cavalier was planning to begin the production of a second television chassis design.

In early February, however, Cavalier executives reported that technical difficulties in readying the television receiver for production had been encountered and that it would be impossible to include the new capacitor in the set scheduled to go into production on April 30. The earliest date the new capacitor could be utilized in a Cavalier television chassis would be November.

Cavalier executives made it clear they were quite anxious to be the first to use the new capacitor. They pointed out that since they had come to Warwick with the request for a better capacitor, they had, in effect, given Warwick the idea that had led to the creation of the new capacitor. Thus they felt justified in asking Warwick to wait until after Cavalier's November model had made its appearance before introducing this new component to other manufacturers of radio and television receivers.

It may be noted that there were approximately 30 large potential users manufacturing radios, television sets, and automobile radios. Another 40 or more small firms were also considered to be potential customers. Warwick engineers were currently working with several large television chassis manufacturers on the design of printed wire circuit boards for new television sets. By introducing the new capacitor at this time, Warwick engineers would be able to incorporate the new product in their design work and could take orders for the new capacitors.

# THE PRODUCT

A capacitor is a device designed primarily to store electricity in a static form. It consists essentially of two conducting terminals or plates, separated by a dielectric. The capacitor developed by Warwick engineers for use in radio and television receivers consisted of a tiny piece of ceramic coated on both sides with a silver material. The silvered surfaces were conducting terminals or plates, and the ceramic mass the dielectric material. The unique features of the Warwick capacitor were its tapered shape and dimensional stability.

The Warwick capacitor was designed to replace the conventional disc capacitor offered by competitors. Executives pointed out that the new capacitor would not affect the performance characteristics of the television or radio set in which it was used. The principal advantage of the new capacitor was that its use made possible various manufacturing savings. Executives indicated that by using the Warwick ceramic capacitor, a radio or television set manufacturer would be able to reduce the nonproductive preparation time required by the use of a disc capacitor.[2] Further, since the capacitors had dimensional stability, it would now be possible to package these components for magazine feeding and thus enable manufacturers to replace what was a manual operation with one that would be automatic.

Finally, they pointed out that the Warwick capacitor could be purchased for $18 per thousand as compared to $27 per thousand for comparable disc capacitors. (As many as 35 capacitors were used in a conventional television chassis.) In spite of their own enthusiasm about the capacitor, however, Warwick's management realized that television and radio set manufacturers might be unwilling to design the capacitor into their sets[3] until they had performed tests on the product and assured themselves of its acceptability.

The new capacitor had a patent pending. Some executives, however, anticipated a legal snarl in any patent litigation involving the patentability of the unit as a whole. The patentable features of the capacitors, they believed, were in the techniques of production, and they doubted whether the capacitor itself was unique except for its simplicity of construction.

# WARWICK COMPANY

The Warwick Company was a manufacturer of specialty electronic components. Printed wire chassis boards, resistor capacitor networks, delay cables, television tuners, and electronic components were sold direct to manufacturers in the radio, television, and electronics industry by Warwick's small sales force. Sales of the company's products were expected to approximate $21 million in the current year. Through a program of basic research on materials and active applications assistance to manufacturers of radio, television, and electronic products, the Warwick Company had succeeded in establishing a good industry reputation.

# CAVALIER COMPANY

The Cavalier Company was one of several large manufacturers of radio and television sets as well as other consumer-type electrical appliances. The company was believed to

---

[2]Lead wires of the disc capacitor frequently became bent and tangled in packing, shipping, and storing and required straightening or forming and spacing before placement in a wire board. Furthermore, once the disc capacitor was soldered in the printed wire boards, the excess length of lead wire had to be trimmed off.
[3]Warwick engineers believed that only minor printed circuit board redesign would be required to enable present boards to incorporate the new capacitor.

have a 15 percent share of the total television receiver market. Cavalier had long been a good customer of Warwick and was expected to account for approximately 10 percent of Warwick's total sales in the current year. Cavalier bought approximately 30 percent of Warwick's printed circuit board production, and the sale of printed circuit boards constituted approximately 15 percent of Warwick's total sales.

# Jones & Jones, Counselors at Law

## Procurement of Word Processing Equipment

Shortly after he was hired in January 1979, Richard Stuart, the new administrative manager, met with the executive committee of the senior partners of Jones & Jones, a well-established law firm in a small-sized northwestern city. The purpose of the meeting was to discuss the developing problem of slow output and turnaround time for document preparation by the firm's 16 attorneys. The committee chairman stated: "Although we have not carefully examined the issue, we have a feeling that we're losing too much time and money with our present equipment. Some of our secretaries claim that if we could have more up-to-date word processing (WP) equipment, we could effect considerable savings in our input, recording, and editing time. This WP equipment would probably replace our current IBM Mag Card[1] machines."

Stuart promised the committee that he would be looking into the word processing problem over the coming months. The committee agreed with him that the best course of action was to "make haste slowly." Obtaining this new equipment would represent a relatively large capital outlay for the firm, would certainly entail major changes in work flow, and might even affect the composition of the secretarial work force.

## BACKGROUND OF THE NEW ADMINISTRATIVE MANAGER

Stuart, an attorney, had had several years of experience in law practice administrative management. As part of his continuing management training, he had attended a seminar in spring 1978 on the new field of word processing. At that seminar, he had learned about the unique problems of WP: equipment procurement, operating procedures, and personnel considerations. He had learned about the many information sources available

[1]For this and other word processing and data communications terms, see Appendix A.

This case is reproduced with the permission of Dr. Stuart U. Rich, professor of marketing and director, Forest Industries Management Center, College of Business Administration, University of Oregon, Eugene, Oregon. Copyright © 1982.

in the field, such as professional word processing organizations and publications. He also followed informative articles on the subject that appeared regularly in magazines like *The Office*.

Stuart was involved in several long-range projects for the firm. Among them were whether or not to obtain a computer, and if so, whether to buy or lease. Another major decision concerned updating the firm's word processing equipment. If the firm were to get a computer, should it be used only for bookkeeping, timekeeping, and billing, or should it be put to other uses, such as word processing? Stuart decided that a decision on WP, as well as a definitive search for word processing equipment, had to be suspended until a decision could be made about the computer.

In March 1979, Stuart decided that a small "preliminary production survey" should be conducted of the type and amount of document preparation work being done in his firm. Therefore, he asked Susan Norman, the busiest Mag Card operator, to keep a month-long log of all the types of wills, pleadings, and documents she produced on her machine and for whom they were produced. She also kept track of the amount of overtime she incurred and special scheduling problems.

## INVESTIGATION OF EQUIPMENT AVAILABILITY AND THE OMICRON PROPOSAL

In the meantime, Stuart investigated the available equipment on the market. He attended a local office equipment show, gathered brochures, spoke to sales representatives, and went to see machinery demonstrations. Most of the new equipment, both stand-alone and shared logic, had the following features: changeable type, keyboard error corrector, half spacing, visual display (through cathode ray tube or CRTs), auxiliary output, minimum 250,000 character storage capacity, minimum 350 words per minute (wpm) output, and magnetic or floppy disk storage media. Most of the eight systems he investigated seriously had automatic underlining, justification, and line counters.

According to information in the brochures he picked up and conversations he had with equipment sales reps at the office equipment show, costs were comparable. The Tau Type, for instance, was $17,990, and the Tau Text (a simpler model) was $11,990. The Wang 20 sold for $18,700. The Alpha 80 was priced between $16,000 and $18,000, depending on the auxiliary equipment included. Vydec's two models were $17,400 and $18,700. Lanier's models ranged from $17,400 to $18,900. Omicron's was $16,125. In fact, upon Stuart's request for further information, the Omicron representative submitted a proposal on March 28, 1979. The proposal for the Omicron X cited the price of $16,125 to include hardware, software, and the operator training program. There would be extra charges for freight ranging from $250 to $750, depending on which mode was chosen. The Omicron X had interface with the Omicron computer as well as with the IBM computer. The floppy disks would cost $4 to $6, depending on the quantity purchased. Leasing arrangements for 36, 60, and 66 months were also available.

Several of the WP vendors provided user lists of their equipment. Stuart checked the Alpha 80 with five law offices around the state. He interviewed two local law firms and two large government agency users of the Tau Type. He also spoke to two local Omicron users. None of the users he consulted had anything negative to say about the equipment they were using. Some had uncomplimentary comments about other equipment, however. Stuart also investigated the many published information sources on WP equipment. He gathered brochures and information from manufacturers and sales reps and started a large file. Among the information sources he relied on were the equipment specification reports and industry application articles put out by the independent DataPro Research Corporation of New Jersey. One DataPro article (dated June 1977), "Word Processing and Law Firms," mentioned several of the needs and advantages of the new word processing equipment in a law practice. It noted: "The primary output of any law office is . . . paper—legal documents which must be perfect. This need for error-free documentation . . . requires many revisions and draft cycles. . . . Personnel is the largest expense area for a law firm. . . . [Word processing can allow a firm] to gradually decrease its secretarial staff . . . [or] free up attorney time, allowing the firm to increase its caseload and its profits. . . . [WP can also] release space needed for secretaries and files."

Stuart also consulted a chapter in a recent book on law office management, which described the recent growth of the word processing market and the many new products competing in that market. The booklet mentioned that the Alpha Company was growing rapidly. The booklet urged that if stand-alone WP equipment were to be used, a firm should "stick with industry leaders such as Lanier or Tau." It mentioned that good shared-logic machines were Omicron and Wang. The booklet urged the reader to look for text editing equipment that was expandable, programmable, and communicating. One of the most helpful information sources was a 60-page booklet by Kline D. Strong, *Word Processing Equipment*, published by the American Bar Association in 1979. This booklet reviewed the evolution of word processing equipment over the last 15 years. It also told the reader how to acquire, evaluate, and select WP equipment. The booklet included a glossary, special notes, and illustrations of current types of equipment and features.

By September 1980, Stuart had investigated the computer question enough to decide that, if it were obtained, it would be an IBM System 34 or an Omicron. Now the question was what interface potential there should be between the computer (either IBM or Omicron) and the type of WP equipment the company would buy. For $250, a software package could be purchased that would allow the firm to use an IBM floppy disk with an Alpha 80. Stuart also understood that it was possible to hardwire the Alpha 80 to the IBM System 34.

## PRODUCTION SURVEY AND WORD PROCESSING EQUIPMENT FEATURES

Stuart decided that he had enough background information to ask for a full-scale production survey of all secretaries in the firm. This study was undertaken in October and completed in November. It proved that the firm could benefit from two stand-alone processing stations.

A reprint of a November/December 1979 *Legal Economics* article called "An Evaluation of the Odyssey 2001," by Richard Loftin, was very informative. This article described the "perfect" WP for a law firm and described all the features of such a machine. The local Tau sales representative had sent this reprint to Stuart not long after his last visit because a chart showed Tau Type to have most of the features mentioned in the article. Stuart noted that the Omicron and Alpha equipment had essentially the same features as the Tau Type. These three companies appeared to be among the leaders in offering the desired WP equipment features. Stuart then sent the article to Lois Groves and Susan Norman, the two Mag Card operators, with a request for their review and comment.

Lois Groves listed the features mentioned in the article that she thought she could use all the time: print speed, automatic carriage return, automatic underscore, automatic centering, insert, background printing, search, delete, automatic page ending, temporary margin and variable line spacing, free-floating cursor, and stored phrases. She said that the features she probably would not use as much were disk capacity, dual disks, repagination, and footnote tie-in. (Most of these listed features were present in the equipment of all three companies under consideration.) Susan Norman wrote that of the features mentioned in the article, the following would be helpful to her: stored phrases, disk capacity, document index, stored formats, dual disks, software-based logic, print speed, multi-line display, temporary margin and variable line spacing, automatic underscore, automatic centering, insert, move, page turning and random access, search, background printing, repagination, delete, automatic page ending, global search and replace, automatic carriage return, and a free-floating cursor. She said she probably would not use the search or footnote tie-in features very often.

In the final production survey, monthly figures were reported. Susan Norman reported that she had over 3,629 mag cards to be converted, 989 of which were master cards (boiler plate forms, will masters, etc.). Lois Groves reported that she had 900 cards. Stuart discovered that the Alpha 80 would take 10 seconds to convert each card. It would take 30 seconds to convert each card for the Omicron, and 2 minutes, 30 seconds for the Tau. The Alpha 80 and Omicron X conversions were included in the price of the machines. Tau would charge $0.25 per card. Alpha and Tau could convert the cards locally. Omicron had to send the cards away to be converted.

# MEMORANDUM ON EQUIPMENT NEEDS

Based on the reports of Norman and Groves, as well as on the equipment information he had secured to date, Stuart sent a memorandum to all the firm's partners outlining problems in the WP area. First he recommended that the firm acquire a dual station standalone WP machine to replace one mag card machine now on rental. In 1981 another dual station machine should replace the remaining mag card and possibly be supplemented by a limited-memory display typewriter. He then outlined the firm's present equipment costs and capabilities:

The Mag Card 6240 (which has the heaviest use) has a monthly rent of $412. The Mag Card A (which has the second heaviest use) rents for $300 per month. The Mag Card II, which the firm is in the process of purchasing, has a $44 per month maintenance charge. The Mag Card 6240 prints 550 wpm. It is one of the best "blind," or nondisplay, machines around. The Mag Card II and Mag Card A print 150 wpm. Our standard IBM Selectric II produces an average of 70–80 wpm.

The advantages of new WP equipment are: (1) video screens (the operator can see what is typed and make immediate corrections before ordering the machine to print); (2) simultaneous playback (background printing—the operator can work on another project while the first project is being played out); (3) line, word insert, delete, move commands (the operator can insert, delete, or move words, lines, and entire paragraphs); and (4) global search and replace (with one instruction the machine can go through the entire document to replace or correct a word that is repeated).

The result of these functions is to double production. One other large local firm did a before-and-after production survey with machines and found that (a) total lines produced doubled for each operator, and (b) average turnaround time per project decreased 40 percent, from five hours to three.

Presently available equipment uses disks or diskettes (somewhat like 45 rpm phonograph records), and falls into three basic categories:

1. Stand-alone equipment—single station equipment, consisting of processor, video screen or display, keyboard, and separate printer. Usually, second stations can be added at reduced cost.
2. Shared logic and distributive logic equipment, where several stations (display plus keyboard) share a central processing unit (full-scale computer) and one or more printers. A memory is located at each input terminal.
3. Limited-memory typewriters—single-station stand-alone equipment whose memories will hold one or more pages of typing.

My conclusions:

1. Technology is passing us by.
2. We need to upgrade our equipment at a low cost.
3. Our immediate need is to increase production at minimum cost.
   a. Shared logic systems are computer-based systems and are the most expensive.
   b. Limited-memory typewriters with on-line displays would improve individual productivity, but should only be used as a supplement to WP machines.
   c. Our least expensive alternative would be to replace one existing machine with stand-alone equipment. Increased cost would be $480 per month. We can add a second station sharing the same printer for $210 per month, depending on the type of equipment selected. Shipping and installation charges would be approximately $300.
4. In view of rising personnel costs and increasing equipment capability, we should add more equipment rather than more secretaries.
5. A major question is whether we will want to integrate WP and data processing (DP).

The decision criteria to use for procuring this equipment would be:

Features of equipment

Ease of operation and training

Software (ease and cost of upgrading)

Promptness of service and maintenance

Cost

Ease of conversion from present equipment

Strength of manufacturer

Potential for communication with other WP equipment or computer

Integration with DP equipment

## TAU AND ALPHA PROPOSALS

On March 12, 1980, the local Tau representative submitted a proposal. The proposal quoted the system at $14,900, plus $300 for delivery, installation, and training. The system would include a printer at no extra charge. A sheet feeder would be $1,500 extra. The proposed lease terms would be $437 per month for five years, and $773 per month for three years. There would be a 10 percent purchase option at the end of 60 months. Finally, the Tau representative stated that the Tau Type should be able to have communication interface with the IBM System 34 in about one month's time at no extra charge.

On March 14, the Alpha representative submitted a proposal. Each separate Alpha 80 console would cost $11,000, and each separate printer would cost $4,700. The sheet feeder was $1,895. An interface cable cost $139 whether it was used for one machine or two. This cable would provide communication interface with the IBM System 34. A five-year lease would cost $643 per month for one machine and $1,099 per month for two. A three-year lease would cost $883 per month for one machine and $1,505 per month for two. The proposal also stated that there was ability to link up with telephone lines to Westlaw (a legal research data base). Operator training would be included with the equipment purchase.

## FINAL EVALUATION OF PROPOSALS

On March 19, Stuart wrote to Norman and Groves to tell them he had narrowed the selection of WPs down to the Alpha 80, the Tau Type, and the Omicron X. A decision had to be made by mid-April so that the equipment could arrive in mid-May and be operating at a reasonable level by July 1. He asked them to lend assistance on evaluation of the following:

Features: What do you like? What would you like to use? How frequently? What don't you like?

Ease of operation: What can be most quickly learned?

Ease of conversion: What would have to be converted from card to disk, and how long would it take?

On March 20, Stuart sent a follow-up memo asking the following questions:

How many phrases can be stored? How is hyphenation handled? Do you lose what's on the screen or on the disk in case of power outages? Can you single and double space on the screen? What about readout? If you hit a key and accidentally erase the lines or page, can you call back what was on the screen? How? Is there a disk drive in satellite stations? How difficult is it to change the ribbon? Are there limits to the number of characters per document in indexing?

On March 20, Groves reported her impressions of the Tau Type. She had spent two hours at a machine demonstration and was very enthusiastic about several of the features, including the Protect feature (an auxiliary battery that keeps the machine going so that it does not erase what was recently typed in, in case of a power outage). She also liked the three different hyphenation codes, the automatic indexing program, and the phrase storage capacity. On March 26, Groves reported on the Omicron X demonstration. She was convinced after watching the machine work that she did not want to work on it.

On March 27, Norman reported on the machines she had seen. She did not like the Omicron. The controls were hard to reach, and the disks were in an awkward position. She did not like the underscore, hyphenation, screen print, or correction key mechanism features. She said she liked both the Alpha 80 and the Tau Type, and carefully outlined the advantages of each. She saw only a few minor disadvantages about the Tau and could not see anything about the Alpha that she did not like.

On March 27, Groves wrote an evaluation of the Alpha 80 and said she liked this machine even more than the Tau Type. She liked the full-page screen, which showed black on white. She also liked the disk capacity and the hyphenation and centering features. "This machine is the only one," she reported, "that shows single *or* double space on the screen." She liked the short training time required—only two days versus four days for Tau. Power outages would eliminate only the page being inputed into the Alpha 80; outages would not erase a prerecording or a master. "ALPHA 80 IS *THE* ONE," Groves concluded.

All three bidding vendors seemed to offer good equipment service. Alpha had a contract with a local service company, the Repair Shop. The firm already had a service contract with this company for repairing and maintaining the mag card machines. The Repair Shop had a good reputation for efficient service.

Stuart had originally preferred the Omicron. He thought it was important that he, and perhaps some of the other professional staff, could operate the WP equipment. He rated the Omicron X highest on ease of use. On the other hand, he trusted Groves' and Norman's judgments of the machines they had seen demonstrated. Moreover, they were good operators and had worked for the firm for several years. Good word processing operators were hard to find, and he did not want to risk alienating them. It would probably be an uphill battle to convince them that the Omicron was the best machine.

## CONCLUSION _____

On April 2, 1980, Stuart wrote the executive committee. He made the following comments on his preliminary analysis of WP options:

| | |
|---|---|
| Alpha 80 strengths: | Full-page screen master station; page shown on screen as is; ease of conversion; strength of manufacturer; potential for communications; delivery time. |
| Alpha 80 weaknesses: | Print speed; only ½ screen on satellite station; eyestrain from black print on white screen; lack of cues (ease of operation). |
| Tau Type strengths: | High-speed printing; all latest features. |
| Tau Type weaknesses: | ⅔ page screen; more expensive and difficult conversion; manufacturer strength; communications feature. |
| Omicron strengths: | Full-page screen in both stations; high-speed printing; better operating cues. |
| Omicron weaknesses: | More difficult and expensive conversion; uncertainty on communications ability; operators don't like it. |

Stuart had to give his final recommendation to the executive committee and to the other partners of the firm no later than April 15, 1980. The partners had to give final approval on an expenditure item of this magnitude. They would, however, listen carefully to his advice on the type of equipment to be obtained.

# APPENDIX A

## Glossary of Word Processing Terms*

*Cathode Ray Tube (CRT).* A television-like picture tube used in visual display terminals.

*Cursor.* A lighted indicator that marks the current working position on a display.

*Diskette (Floppy Disk).* A portable unit of magnetic storage.

*Hardwired.* A type of word processing system control unit design in which all editing control is wired (soldered) into the system.

*Hyphenation.* The division of a word (between syllables) at the end of a line of text by inserting a hyphen and moving the remainder of the word to the next line. Hyphenation is used in order to make the line lengths more consistent. Most word processing systems will check line lengths, and where required, will prompt the operator for hyphenation decision. Some systems have special software or dictionaries to permit automatic hyphenation decisions.

*Justification.* The ability of a word processing or text editing system to adjust all typed lines so that they are the same length (i.e., all lines begin exactly at the left margin and end exactly at the right margin).

*Magnetic Card (Mag Card).* Tab-size card coated with magnetic material, holding about 50 to 100 lines (about 100 characters each) of text and codes.

*Memory Typewriter.* A typewriter capable of storing keyboarded material and playing it back automatically.

*Most of these definitions of terms found in the case are from DataPro Research Corporation, *DataPro Reports on Word Processing,* McGraw-Hill, 1981; and John Zarrello, *Word Processing and Text Editing,* Microcomputer Applications, 1980.

*On-Line.* A word or data processing operation that is performed on a local system connected to and sharing the facilities of a remote central processor.

*Software.* A term coined to contrast computer programs with the hardware of a computer system. Software is a stored set of instructions, which govern the operation of a computer system and make the hardware run.

*Software-based.* A word processor system design whereby word processing (or other) software is "loaded" or read into the system's random access memory via a form of media upon system startup.

*Stand-Alone Word Processing System.* The classic, single-station word processor such as a mag keyboard or video display system that does not have the processing power of a central computer.

*Shared-Logic Word Processing System.* A multiterminal (operator console) system where each terminal shares the word processing power, storage, and peripherals of a central computer.

# CASE

# 4

# Gulfcoast Chemical, Inc.

## Managing Supply Sources and Finished Goods Inventories

In January 1974, James Varner, manager of procurement at Gulfcoast Chemical, was faced with several problems in managing the supply of one of the company's primary products, Antalex, a selective herbicide. He had few options in his decisions in dealing with two single source suppliers, one that supplied the primary ingredient in Antalex, and the other the converter that produced the end product. Reportedly, Antalex had been surpassing all sales expectations, but Gulfcoast was faced with depleted inventories at the start of the buying season for 1974. The converter, Rand Chemical, was presenting unreasonable contract demands, and its people were insulting and abusive to Gulfcoast managers. Further, Rand's price for the upcoming year was 45 percent above that of the previous contract. Hendrix Chemical, the supplier of the principal ingredient in Antalex, had increased its price by nearly 50 percent and had been making very erratic deliveries.

## CONTRACT NEGOTIATIONS

Varner felt he had no alternative with Rand but to accept the contract offered, but to do so under protest. The price was to be $2.75 per pound, as Rand had demanded. The quantity was revised to 2.4 million pounds from the previous estimate of 3.9 million pounds for 1974–75 production. Rand also negotiated for and won a right of first refusal, which meant that should Gulfcoast get any quotations from another source, Rand had the right to match the quotation, thus preventing Gulfcoast from developing a second source unless Rand could not meet the other quotation item by item. Further, Rand held out for and won a five-year contract, and all contract provisions pertained to that period of time.

This case was written by Professor Ronald L. Schill. Copyright © 1979 by the Graduate School of Management, Brigham Young University.

In effect, Gulfcoast was prevented from developing another source of supply if Rand chose to match any quote obtained from another source.

The Rand contract contained price escalators to increase the price above $2.75 in future periods. Varner had been unable to negotiate a lower price, even though his market volume forecasts were considerably above original estimates because of the strong demand for Antalex. Varner had taken a risk in revising the quantity to 2.4 million pounds, but he did not want to be in a position of having to pay high penalty charges for the additional 1.5 million pounds (3.9 million original less 2.4 million revised) should Hendrix fail to make deliveries. Under the new contract, volume increases would have no effect on price.

Rand had been very firm in the contract sent to Gulfcoast and had refused to negotiate any of the terms. If Gulfcoast was to get delivery in the spring of 1974, it was to be under Rand's terms and conditions. Varner reported:

> It was a constant gut-wrenching situation in production scheduling as well during the rest of the marketing season in 1974. I lived on the edge of my chair. We began looking for other suppliers as an option to Hendrix. I sent numerous expediters to Hendrix, but we still had severe delivery and quality problems through the spring. They just couldn't seem to make the plant run. A lot of things kept popping up. Orthochlorobenzene is all organic in production, and this caused all kinds of problems. Toluene was short in supply, and the starting material for DCBTF, tetrahydrofuran, a solvent used in conversion at Rand, was short. In the latter part of the year we finally got into such a situation with isobuteraldehyde that we had to import it from Germany. Hendrix had severe shortages of it as well as parachlorotoluene. At one point we actually bought parachlorotoluene from Carlson and furnished it to Hendrix. Ethyl alcohol became short, and we bought corn futures to try to get a handle on the price of alcohol made from corn and to guarantee the supply of alcohol. In importing isobuteraldehyde from Germany, we had difficulties in getting a port to let it in, since its flash point (rapid burning) is so low. We talked with the Coast Guard and Port Authority in Texas City to bring it in there, but finally had to bring it to the Danton Chemical Company factory in Tennessee, where they converted it to what we needed and then sent it to us. We just couldn't get it into the country in its volatile form.

## MARKETING PROBLEMS BEGIN

In 1974 marketing problems began to show up. Gulfcoast failed to meet projected sales in the Midwest, the corn area of the United States. Sales were down by 75 percent in the spring of 1974. Marketing began getting concerned over sales in mid-spring, but by that time Gulfcoast was in the process of buying 2.4 million pounds of Antalex. Expected sales in 1974 were 1.2 million pounds, and it seemed that only 300,000 pounds would be sold during the planting season. This caused grave concern about whether or not the 2.4 million pounds being produced for shipment to distributors during 1974 would be needed for the revised sales forecast of 2.4 million pounds in 1975. There was a lag effect in sales; distributors bought in advance of sales to dealers. Dealers, in turn, also bought in advance of actual sales to farmers. Although Gulfcoast had been told by its distributors that the 1.09 million pounds produced in 1973 had cleared their inventories, distributors ordered very little in the spring of 1974.

In June 1974, with the selling season to farmers over, actual sales to distributors amounted to only 650,000 pounds for the previous six months. It seemed doubtful there would be further sales in the remaining months of that year. Marketing personnel checked into the problem and found that although Gulfcoast had been shipping large quantities to the distributors, the product had been bottlenecked at the dealer level and was not getting on the ground. Dealers had bought heavily in anticipation of shortages and had stockpiled inventories. This, in turn, had led to inaccurate reporting of actual sales to farmers by distributors. When the result finally affected dealers, and when stocks were built up to what they wanted, they stopped orders from the distributors, who in turn cut orders from Gulfcoast.

At an August 1974 Gulfcoast sales meeting it was reported that dealers still had huge inventories of Antalex, which had not been put on the ground. Dealers had demanded a buy-back from distributors when shortages did not materialize as they expected and when sales of Antalex did not come up to their expectations. Such buy-backs were typical in the industry. The distributors, in turn, pressed Gulfcoast for buy-backs. Not only was Varner concerned over what had happened, he also wondered *why* it had happened. Why had the marketing personnel at Gulfcoast not kept closer check on actual sales to farmers and applications in the field? Why had marketing put so much pressure on making deliveries, without understanding the impact of shortage perception on accurate demand estimation? Had marketing personnel been completely unaware of the hoarding in the channel?

At the meeting it was also announced that a major reason for the sales decline at the farmer level was a rumor regarding the adverse effects of Antalex in certain applications. Actual field tests had shown that Antalex was not as superior a product as had initially been believed in terms of range of weeds and lack of need for a second herbicide. Another equally damaging rumor pertained to the effect of Antalex on yield. In two isolated cases, Antalex had been shown to be phytotoxic to corn: It stunted corn plants and reduced yields per acre. Marketing managers had found that in these two instances, if Antalex was not applied exactly as it should be, in certain soil conditions—cold and wet —where soils were heavy clay in composition, there would be stunting. The problem, however, was limited to these conditions, as far as management could determine. However, the rumor that Antalex caused stunting and reduced yield had evidently spread like wildfire.

Although Varner was very concerned over the marketing operation, his greater concern was what, if anything, he could do about the suppliers of Antalex components. He knew that Rand in particular would be very unsympathetic to the news that dealers had stockpiled excess quantities of Antalex in late 1973 in anticipation of the shortage.

# Raytronics Corporation

## Surveying Customers' Requirements

The Raytronics Corporation was a $115 million manufacturer of electronic components with headquarters in San Jose, California. After a three-year joint R&D venture with a major West Coast university's electrical engineering department, an extremely efficient high-RPM, low-horsepower motor was developed. The small motor had a significantly longer life than competitive products and consumed approximately 40 percent less energy. The Raytronics motor was designed to last 50 percent longer than competitive motors and had a registered trademark called the Responder. Before making a final decision on product development and a pilot production facility in Phoenix, Arizona, Raytronics wanted to know more about customer requirements, market size, and the growth prospects of applications for the Responder.

Approximately 70 percent of Raytronics' sales was to large original equipment manufacturers. The remaining 30 percent represented sales to small manufacturers and electronic distributors. The electronic distributors sold to small OEMs and the repair aftermarket. Being primarily an OEM supplier with a narrow customer base, Raytronics always worked closely with customers. Market surveys were usually not conducted. However, the Responder was believed to have potential in a wide range of applications that were primarily outside Raytronics' existing customer base. The Responder project manager, Jim Bartlett, wanted the following information:

1. Who is involved in specifying and/or purchasing high-speed motors?
2. How many units or what dollar value do they purchase each year?
3. What is the size of each end-use segment?
4. What are the more popular high-speed sizes?
5. Where and from whom do they currently buy this item?
6. Who are the major competitive manufacturers?
7. How do end users learn about new electrical or electronic products?

| EXHIBIT 1 | **PROSPECTS FOR SMALL, HIGH-SPEED ELECTRONIC MOTOR** |
|---|---|

| *SIC Categories* | *Products Manufactured* |
|---|---|
| 3572 | Typewriters |
| 3573 | Electronic computing equipment |
| 3579 | Office machines |
| 3586 | Measuring and dispensing pumps |
| 3636 | Industrial sewing machines |
| 3728 | Aircraft auxiliary equipment |
| 3824 | Fluid meters and counting devices |

Bartlett went to a nearby public library to examine the Standard Industrial Classification Manual (SIC). He identified seven four-digit SIC categories as prospects for the small high-speed electronic motor (see Exhibit 1). Two of the categories (3573 and 3579) were codes that contained firms to which Raytronics was selling its other products. To the best of Bartlett's knowledge, Raytronics did not sell to firms in the remaining five SIC groupings.

Raytronics' internal customer lists and contacts provided one source for surveying prospects in the 3573 and 3579 SIC groups. Bartlett was considering the purchase of lists for the other SIC groups from Dun and Bradstreet's Market Identification Service, Standard & Poor's, Thomas's *Register,* or trade associations and trade magazines. After learning how many business organizations existed in each of the SIC categories, Bartlett could then select a sample. In some SIC groups, he believed he might be able to do 100 percent "sampling." Since he was primarily interested in understanding the requirements and market potential of the largest prospective customers, he would have to consider the time and cost involved in his choice of a sample.

Bartlett believed his secretary or another Raytronics employee could do the interviewing if the information were gathered by telephone. A mail survey was another possibility. Bartlett had never designed or conducted a market survey. Exhibit 2 is the first draft of the questionnaire he developed. He circulated the questionnaire to his associates at Raytronics for comments and suggestions concerning his choice of SIC categories, sampling approach, interviewing method, and questionnaire content. At the same time, Bartlett asked an outside marketing research firm to provide suggestions and submit a proposal to conduct the project.

EXHIBIT
2

# OEM CUSTOMER MARKET SURVEY

| Company Name | SIC Code |

| City | State |

| Individual Interviewed | Title |

Good _____ , I'm _____ ,
calling for Raytronics Corporation in San Jose, California. We are conducting a survey among
knowledgeable executives like yourself about small high-speed motors, and I'd appreciate your
cooperation. I'll be as brief as possible.

1. To what extent are you involved in the _____ specifying or _____ purchase of small,
   high-speed electric motors? (Check which ones.)
   _____ Very involved
   _____ Somewhat involved
   _____ Not involved (Ask to speak to person most involved in that location and start
   interview again.)
             _____ Terminate
             _____ Refused

2. What is the primary use of the high-speed motors you buy? _____

3. What volume of small, high-speed motors would you normally purchase over a year's time?
   _____ Current purchases    _____ Peak    _____ Purchase activity next year

| _Units_ | _Yearly Dollar Value_ |
|---|---|
| _____ Less than 100 | _____ Less than $5,000 |
| _____ 100–300 | _____ $5,000–$150,000 |
| _____ 300–500 | _____ $15,000–$250,000 |
| _____ Over 500 | _____ Over $250,000 |

4. What price do you usually pay? _____

5. What size (fractional horsepower) high-speed electric motors do you mostly purchase?
   _____

6. What RPMs do you require? _____

7. What is the average life of the small, high-speed motors you build into your original
   equipment? _____

**EXHIBIT
2**

*(cont'd)*   8.   Where do you usually buy your small, high-speed motors? (Prefer names and locations if possible.)

| | *Name* | *Location* |
|---|---|---|
| From a distributor | | |
| Direct from the | | |
| factory | | |

9.   What is the primary reason you would select one supplier over another?

_____ Competitive pricing          _____ Technical capability
_____ Response time to quotes      _____ Fabrication capability
_____ Inventory availability       _____ Location
_____ Other (quality, service, delivery) _____

10.  Do you usually buy your high-speed motors packaged with other components, or do you buy only the motor?

_____ Package          _____ Motor          _____ Both

11.  In making your purchasing or recommendation decision for high-speed motors, please describe how important the following are (check the appropriate items):

| | No Importance | | Somewhat Important | | Very Important |
|---|---|---|---|---|---|
| *Factor* | *1* | *2* | *3* | *4* | *5* |
| Manufacturer's reputation | | | | | |
| Distributor reputation | | | | | |
| Availability | | | | | |
| Service after the sale | | | | | |
| Price | | | | | |
| Warranty | | | | | |

12.  Which of the following is most important? (Check one.)

_____ Manufacturer's reputation
_____ Distributor reputation
_____ Availability
_____ Service after the sale
_____ Price
_____ Warranty

13.  How do you receive information on the products you consider? (May check more than one, but not more than three.)

_____ Mailings from manufacturers
_____ Mailings from distributor
_____ Trade publications

**EXHIBIT
2**

*(cont'd)*

_____ Salespeople – distributor
_____ Salespeople – manufacturer
_____ Word of mouth
_____ Other _____

14.  How would you prefer to receive information on new products? (Check no more than three.)
_____ Mailings from manufacturers
_____ Mailings from distributors
_____ Trade publications
_____ Salesperson – distributor
_____ Salesperson – manufacturer
_____ Word of mouth
_____ Other _____

15.  For purposes of classification, how many employees are at this location? _____

16.  What is the approximate age of your manufacturing facility at this location? (in years)
_____

# Industrial Consolidated Corporation

## Identifying and Evaluating Applications for a New Material Product

## COMPANY BACKGROUND

Industrial Consolidated Incorporated (ICI) was a privately held industrial products company whose products were sold primarily into the OEM and replacement sectors of the U.S. transportation market. This company had the reputation of being a well-run, profitable business. Before being spun off from Global Incorporated in 1981, the business had the following sales and profitability picture (see Table 1). The recession of 1981–82 had shown ICI's vulnerability in the marketplace. This recession was particularly hard on the transportation sectors, where the bulk of the company's products was sold. Consequently, the company sought to diversify its market exposure with its existing technical and production capabilities. Part of this strategy was to be implemented by the company's Materials Research Center, where an Advanced Concept Group was formed.

| TABLE 1 | PERFORMANCE OF ICI AS AN OPERATING GROUP OF GLOBAL, INC. | | |
|---|---|---|---|
| | *1980* | *1979* | *1978* |
| Net sales | 559.9 | 524.9 | 439.9 |
| Pretax earnings | 63.7 | 81.5 | 73.5 |

*Source:* Global, Inc., Annual Report, year ended December 31. All figures in millions of dollars.

*Source:* This case is adapted from a case study prepared by Professor Timothy L. Wilson.

## Advanced Concept Group

The Advanced Concept Group reported directly to the Industrial Consolidated vice president of technology and had the responsibility of identifying higher-technology business opportunities for the corporation. The concept implied that key individuals were to be given access to corporate capabilities in a project management organization. That is, project leaders were not to be limited to laboratory personnel in developing embryo businesses, but could draw temporarily on any corporate personnel. Projects were to be funded on an individual basis and have the support of operating management. Two caveats were associated with project selection:

1. Any business developed as a consequence of successful project completion had to have a connection with the present business in production or engineering.
2. Any technology identified for development had to be market-driven. That is, a prevailing need had to be identified before a project could be formally initiated.

One of the first opportunities considered for exploration was an electro-deposited (ED) iron foil technology. Essentially the technology made it possible to deposit a continuous web of pure iron foil in thickness of about one mil (0.001 inches) and in widths up to 72 inches. In metallurgical terms, a foil is a very thin coat or sheet of material applied to another surface. Rights to this technology were offered by Great Britain's Electricity Council, and several engineers within the laboratory were familiar with features of this technology.

The possibilities inherent in pursuing this business opportunity were not totally strange to ICI personnel. One of the operating divisions of Global produced a copper foil by a similar technology for manufacturers of printed circuits. Although profit and loss statements of individual divisions were confidential within both firms, individuals within the ICI organization recognized that Global's Foil Division returns exceeded ICI returns. Furthermore, the present chairman of ICI had once been the general manager of Global's Foil Division.

One problem that existed for iron foil was that it lacked the well-defined market niche that copper foil possessed. A study was thus initiated to seek the niche(s) or applications that an iron foil might serve. Unsuccessful earlier attempts had been made in the past to market an iron foil. U.S. Steel made a concerted effort to market a rolled foil in the late 1960s and early 1970s before withdrawing from the market "due to a lack of sufficient volume by their internal guidelines." Two British firms tried to commercialize an ED foil in the mid-1970s based on Electricity Council technology. These firms also withdrew from commercialization efforts. Global caused a flurry of interest in the technology in 1979 when it won an IR-100[1] technical award for developing the ED foil. Toyo Kohan, a Japanese firm, had been "offering" an ED foil since January 1981.[2] Igenta Sheet Steel, also of Japan, offered a "steel paper" that was undoubtedly a rolled product. Therefore,

---

[1]The Industrial Research Institute recognizes the top 100 technical innovations in the United States each year.
[2]Offering is placed in quotes here because it was not uncommon for the Japanese to conduct "market studies" by offering a product for sale with intent to sell only if adequate business developed for the new product.

although a study was to be made on a product concept, prospective interviewees had had an opportunity to be acquainted with previous marketing efforts for iron foil.

# IDENTIFYING PRODUCT PROPERTIES

Although samples of materials existed, a commercial process did not exist for producing the material, nor was it clear what the end product would actually be like. The management at the Advanced Concept Group concluded a study would help define the end product.

The concept of an electro-deposited iron foil suggested that the end product would have certain inherent properties or characteristics. One set of characteristics was derived from the fact that it was a "pure iron." Thus, strength, ductility, thermal expansion, electrical conductivity, and magnetic permeability would be similar to pure iron. A second set of characteristics derived from the fact that the material was electro-deposited, which meant a deposit could be formed on it by an electrode or by electrolysis. Thus, the product had certain characteristics of electro-deposited copper, for instance. These characteristics included purity, thinness range, width, ability to be coated and laminated, and reasonable production cost.

Iron foil could be manufactured in ⅓ to 3 mil thicknesses in widths to 72 inches, with 1 to 2 mils being the thickness of production preference. Because the material was electrolytically deposited from aqueous electrolytes, it could subsequently be coated with protective surface layers in a continuous fashion. Tin, zinc, nickel, copper, and chromium had been deposited in this fashion in pilot runs with ED foil. Although the technology had not been specifically developed for the purpose, it was likely that the material could be treated to give better adhesion to circuit board material. Further, if desired, the material could be photo-treated and etched, as was commonly done for printed circuit applications.

Neither production costs nor a selling price has yet been set for this material. Various analyses, however, had established the following guides for pricing response to any inquiries:

| Thickness (mils) | Price ($/sq ft) |
|---|---|
| 1 | 0.10–0.11 |
| 2 | 0.20–0.22 |
| 3 | 0.30–0.33 |

Cost for coatings, either electro-deposited or lacquered, would, of course, be in addition to the above, as would slitting or adhesive bonding services.

These sets of circumstances, or possible end-use benefits, helped to establish some guidelines in finding niches or applications for this material. Economic considerations indicated the material would not easily substitute for aluminum foils or even rolled iron foils of identical thickness. Applications needed to be found that were associated with the

ED material's thinness, purity, width, ability to be bonded, or ability to be coated. The most attractive applications would therefore be found where greatest value added was provided to the end product.

## COMPETITIVE MATERIALS

Iron foil would enter a market presently supplied by a number of materials with a variety of properties. These materials vary from an electro-deposited (ED) foil virtually identical to the foil being considered by ICI to such different materials as specialty papers and vinyls. Overall, a demand of several billion square feet per year was being satisfied by these materials. A portion of this market could be penetrable by an iron foil, depending on the foil's competitive position. A synopsis of the materials that were found in the field by an internal market research team is given in this section, and a summary of their observations is shown in Table 2.

JAPANESE STEEL.    The Japanese were exporting steel foil to the United States, and the steel was being used primarily in the construction segment. At that time, the use was fairly small and was estimated to be about 5MM square feet per year. Purchasers were not particularly willing to talk about details of this material, perhaps because of the U.S. steel industry's problems with imports. The availability of the product in narrow widths (27 inches) suggests that the material was probably a rolled material. One company, however, (Toyo Kohan) had been offering to sell an ED foil.

In addition to the foil sold directly as a material, Japanese material was imported in the form of shadow masks for TV sets. Both Dai Nippon Printing and Dai Nippon Screen Manufacturing exported screens to the United States and supplied about one-half of the domestic screen market. These two companies reportedly had enough capacity to supply the world's demand for picture tubes.

U.S. THIN GAUGE.    Teledyne Rodney was the principal domestic supplier of thin-gauge material. They supplied plain carbon alloys in a variety of thicknesses and widths to 42 inches. Selected stainlesses were supplied as well. Price, of course, depended on composition, thickness, width, and temper. They offered a minimum order ($50) of 24-inch wide, 2 mil, 1010, full-hard material for $0.23 per square foot. This price would be discounted to $0.21 per square foot for a 100-pound order and prices of $0.09 to $0.06 per square foot might be possible for larger orders. From purchasers, a lot of Rodney's plain carbon and aluminum-killed (AK) material was sold at about $0.30 per square foot for 6 mil, partially hard foil.

CANSTOCK.    The U.S. can industry had been responsible for making a 1008 to 1010 carbon, 6 mil, black-plated material available at very reasonable prices for other applications, particularly cable wrapping. Bethlehem Steel, in particular, was singled out as a source of this material. Distribution was through regional distributors who also slit this product to 3/8- to 3/4-inch widths, except for larger customers, who did their own slitting.

The base price of this material was about $0.23 per square foot with additional costs for slitting and small order quantities.

HEAVIER GAUGE. The building materials (panels, doors) and novelty (magnetic boards, games) sectors did not use a foil material to any extent. About the thinnest material these segments used was a 28-gauge material (15 mil), frequently galvanized. Most of the major integrated steel firms supplied this material either directly to customers for orders over 40,000 pounds (at approximately $0.20 per square foot) or through distributors for smaller orders (at approximately $0.35 per square foot). About $0.01 to $0.02 was added for galvanized material. It might be noted that although significant price competition existed on the supply side, this market tended to be rather price insensitive because of the value added by the purchaser. Manufactured prices of doors, for instance, were approximately $2.50 per square foot. Thus, if an ED foil was suitable for this application, it would be the competition with other suppliers and not price sensitivity of the customer that would have a major impact on price.

ALUMINUM FOIL. Mention of "foil" in the marketplace frequently invited comparison with aluminum foil. Although a market of approximately a billion square feet existed for this material, it appeared unlikely that much of it would be penetrable by an iron foil. Commodity aluminum foil traded for approximately $0.01 to $0.02 per square foot; one could buy branded wraps at the retail level for $0.04 per square foot. Some segments of this business were so competitive that major suppliers abandoned them. There was a segment of demand for 3 mil aluminum foil, however (heating elements, carrier for ED copper), at $0.06–$0.10 per square foot that was close to being penetrable.

ED COPPER. The commercial material most similar to an ED iron from a production standpoint was ED copper. Global and Square D were the major suppliers of this material, which was used primarily in printed circuit board fabrication. This material carried a premium price both because of its ability to be bonded directly to many substrates and because the end application itself was rather price insensitive. Material was distributed directly in the U.S. market to the actual end user or through circuit board fabricators, who in turn sold finished components to end users.

SS/Cu CLAD. Texas Instruments had evidently attempted to extend its cladding technology to other markets. This material offered strength, EM, and magnetic shielding in one package for cable wrapping. It did, however, carry a price premium ($0.70 per square foot estimate) that would limit it to about 1 percent of the largest applications.

PAPER. Generally, no comparisons existed between paper and foil, either in properties or cost. The popular box material, single corrugated cardboard, for instance, sold for $0.05 per square foot. For one application, however, a comparison was in order. One firm was purchasing a treated paper that was used as the inner liner on a steel sheet/urethane foam external commercial wall construction. This construction had replaced wall materials in Britain, but could not be used in the United States because the paper-covered urethane constituted an "exposed" urethane foam. The paper cost $0.20 per square foot. It

## TABLE 2    COMPETITIVE SITUATION FOR ELECTRO-DEPOSITED IRON FOIL

| Competitor | Product Description | User Segments | Manufacturers | Method of Distribution | Price per Square Foot | Estimated Volume in Use in U.S. Market (MM sq ft/yr) | Comments |
|---|---|---|---|---|---|---|---|
| Japanese steel | Both ED foil and rolled foil 1–2 mil, 27″ wide. | Construction (roofing underlay to obtain Class B fire retarding). | Toho Kohan et al. | Direct to large U.S. distributor. Trading companies' direct market development. | $0.15–$0.20 to final distributor. $0.06–$0.10 to larger user. | 5 | Believed to be material sold by Koppers and Masonite. Offered to RCA et al. |
| U.S. thin gauge | Rolled foil, 24–42″ wide, 2–5 mil, var. tempers. Also a low-carbon AK material and 1002 material. | Construction (Honeycomb), TV masks and shields. | Teledyne Rodney | Four regional service centers. | $0.04–$0.40 depending on temper, volume, thickness. | 30 | Sold on per pound basis— much activity in 6 mil at $0.25 sq ft. |
| Canstock | 1008–1010 6 mil material slit to 3/8–3/4″ wide for special applications. Black annealed. | Cable wrapping. | Bethlehem et al. | Regional distributors. Also source for Teledyne Rodney. Direct to large users who slit in-house. | Base $0.25 per sq ft, with additions for slitting; small lots may double price. | 225 | Treated as by-product or co-product of Canstock businesses. |
| Heavier gauge | 20–28 gauge (15–36 mil), frequently galvanized. Up to 48″ wide. | Construction (composite panels, doors); novelty. | Major steel mills | Direct for volumes greater than 40,000 lb. AM Castle, Ryerson, etc., for smaller lots. | $0.19 direct, $0.37 through distributor. $0.01–$0.02 for galvanized (28 gauge 15 mil). | 1000 | Major competition on supply side. Significant value added (10×) by fabricators. |
| Aluminum foil | .03–.02 mil commodity foil. | Packaging, cable wraps, construction (moisture barrier). | Alcoa, Reynolds | Primarily direct. | $0.01–$0.02, depending on thickness, volume. $0.06–$0.10 for thicker quality foils. | 1000 | Commodity business for which some firms are no longer supplying. |

| | | | | | | |
|---|---|---|---|---|---|---|
| ED copper | .0005–.003 PC foil. | PC electronics, some construction (panels, doors). | Global, Square D | Primarily direct—either to end user or laminator. | $0.20–$1, depending on thickness, volume. | 400 | Significant value added in fabrication (10–100×). |
| SS/Cu clad | EMI shielding/strength wrapping for cable. | Cable wrapping. | Texas Instruments | Direct—intro stage. | $0.70 (est.). | 1 | Product offering to cable manufacturers to incorporate strength, EM shielding, magnetic shielding in one package. |
| Paper | Treated paper that serves as interior surface on steel-foam-paper composite. | Construction. | ? | Direct. : | $0.20 | 10 | Incorporated into HH Robertson's British equivalent of Forma-wall. Not used in U.S. because constitutes "exposed" urethane. |
| Vinyl | 2 mil, adhesive backed. | International packaging. | 3M, Avery International | Direct to container manufacturer. | $0.50 | 50 | Finds use because flexible, strong, printable. |
| Conductive coatings | Material applied to plastic cabinets to reduce EMI emissions. | Digital processing equipment—computer, word processor, electronic games manufacturers. | Udylite, Lundy | Direct to cabinet manufacturer. | $0.20–$2 | 5 | Would grow to 200MM sq ft if all plastic were coated. 10/83 regulation. |

was thought that an ED iron foil was evaluated for this application. Further trials would be in Britain because of processing capabilities; none presently existed in the United States.

VINYL.    A 2 mil, adhesive-backed vinyl was produced by a number of firms (3M, Avery International) that had found application in a variety of markets. One application was for international packaging in piggy-back trucks. The film provided protection, strength, and a printing surface for advertisement and instruction. This material was sold directly to container manufacturers (as opposed to paper manufacturers) and carried a cost of about $0.40 to $0.55 per square foot.

CONDUCTIVE COATING.    The anticipated market for EMI shielding of plastic cabinets had generated information on a number of coatings suitable for this shielding. Included among these coatings were electroless deposits, conductive paints, and conductive glass mats. Price ranges were $0.20–$2 per square foot, depending on the type of coating.

## POTENTIAL MARKETS

Because an ED foil had not existed as a commercial product, it was very difficult to determine the potential market size for the product. It was known, however, that when U.S. Steel was producing a 2–5 mil rolled foil, they sold 900 tons in 1970 at $0.25–$0.60 per pound. The single largest market they had at that time was for TV masks, although packaging promised to be their largest growth area. With respect to the latter, it should be mentioned that this segment was also the most price sensitive; it was in this area that U.S. Steel was competing head-on with aluminum.

Of course, there was a large price discrepancy between the $0.25–$0.60 per pound for the U.S. Steel products and the $2–$2.50 per pound (the equivalent of $0.10/sq ft/mil thickness) commanded by an ED foil. Without knowing the price elasticity of demand, however, present demand could not be projected from the U.S. Steel information. Nevertheless, at one time another firm reportedly determined a long-term sales potential of 600 tons for an ED foil in the U.S. market at $2–$2.50 per pound. This firm's projections were much more targeted than the earlier U.S. Steel sales. Potentials at the higher prices were primarily in the building material laminates and printed circuit board market segments.

The director of this project in the Advanced Concept Group was Dr. John Donahue. Dr. Donahue was now faced with the task of conducting a comprehensive market study. The study was to determine the attractiveness of electro-deposited iron foil properties in various end-use market segments. Based upon the market facts, he was then to consider the development of a market-entry business plan for the new product.

Since John Donahue had a technical Ph.D. from an Eastern university, he felt quite capable of evaluating the properties of the new product in different end uses and up against various other materials. Due to the many technical parameters in each application, he strongly believed he and only very qualified members of the Advanced Concept

Group should be directly involved in all field visits and interviewing. However, he was not at all confident of his ability to determine the market potentials, pricing, and competitive strategies. Furthermore, since John Donahue had never designed a market study, he sought assistance in conducting such a study.

After analyzing the information in Table 2, reading the past three years of correspondence on this project, and talking to many people within ICI, Donahue concluded that at least five broad markets for ED iron foil existed: as a construction and building material, for use in packaging, as an electronic material, for electrical applications, and in novelty advertising applications. These five market groupings are shown in Table 3. After being advised to go through an SIC manual, Donahue was able to identify 18 more specific segments within the five broad groupings. But he then did not know how to proceed to evaluate the potential for iron foil in some or all of these segments.

**TABLE 3**

## POTENTIAL MARKET SEGMENTS FOR ELECTRO-DEPOSITED IRON FOIL
### (Numbers are SIC codes for the segment)

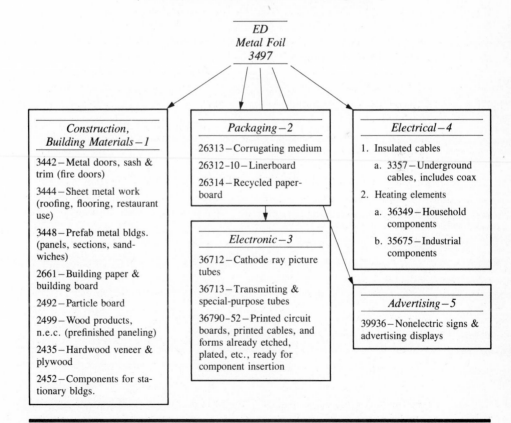

*ED Metal Foil 3497*

*Construction, Building Materials — 1*

3442 — Metal doors, sash & trim (fire doors)

3444 — Sheet metal work (roofing, flooring, restaurant use)

3448 — Prefab metal bldgs. (panels, sections, sandwiches)

2661 — Building paper & building board

2492 — Particle board

2499 — Wood products, n.e.c. (prefinished paneling)

2435 — Hardwood veneer & plywood

2452 — Components for stationary bldgs.

*Packaging — 2*

26313 — Corrugating medium

26312‑10 — Linerboard

26314 — Recycled paperboard

*Electronic — 3*

36712 — Cathode ray picture tubes

36713 — Transmitting & special‑purpose tubes

36790‑52 — Printed circuit boards, printed cables, and forms already etched, plated, etc., ready for component insertion

*Electrical — 4*

1. Insulated cables
   a. 3357 — Underground cables, includes coax
2. Heating elements
   a. 36349 — Household components
   b. 35675 — Industrial components

*Advertising — 5*

39936 — Nonelectric signs & advertising displays

# Trus Joist Corporation

## Developing a New Market for an Established Product

Mr. Mike Kalish, salesman for the Micro=Lam® division of Trus Joist Corporation, had just received another moderate order for Micro=Lam laminated veneer lumber; however, the order held particular interest for him. The unique feature was that Micro=Lam was to be used as a truck-trailer bedding material. This represented the second largest order ever processed for that function.

Earlier in the fall of 1978, Kalish spent some time contacting prospective customers for truck-trailer flooring in the Northwest and Midwest; however, the response from manufacturers had been disappointing. Despite this reception, smaller local builders of truck trailers were interested and placed several small orders for Micro=Lam laminated veneer lumber. The order Kalish had just received was from one of the Midwestern companies he had earlier contacted, renewing his belief that the trailer manufacturing industry held great potential for Micro=Lam as a flooring material.

## COMPANY BACKGROUND

The Trus Joist Corporation, headquartered in Boise, Idaho, is a manufacturer of structural wood products with plants located in the Pacific Northwest, Midwest, Southeast, and Southwest. Annual sales, which totaled over $78 million in 1978, were broken down into three major product categories: the Micro=Lam division, contributing 7 percent of sales (the majority of Micro=Lam sales were internal); the commercial divisions, with 82 percent of sales; and residential sales, with 11 percent of total sales.

In the late 1950s, Art Troutner and Harold Thomas developed a unique concept in joist design, implemented a manufacturing process for the design, and then founded the Trus

This case is reproduced with the permission of Dr. Stuart U. Rich, professor of marketing and director, Forest Industries Management Center, College of Business Administration, University of Oregon, Eugene, Oregon. Copyright © 1980.

Joist Corporation. By 1978, the company employed over 1,000 people, of whom about 180 were sales personnel. The majority of salespeople were assigned to the regional commercial division sales offices; four outside salespeople were assigned to the Micro=Lam division. The functions of selling and manufacturing were performed at each of the five geographically organized commercial divisions; therefore, the salespeople concentrated on geographic selling. The Micro=Lam division was more centralized in nature, conducting all nationwide sales and manufacturing activities from Eugene, Oregon.

In 1971, Trus Joist introduced and patented Micro=Lam laminated veneer lumber. The product is made of thin 1/10-inch or ⅛-inch thick veneer sheets of Douglas fir glued together by a waterproof phenol formaldehyde adhesive. Under exact and specified conditions, the glued sheets are heated and pressed together. The Micro=Lam lumber, or billet,[1] is "extruded" from specially-made equipment in 80-foot lengths and 24-foot widths. The billets can be cut to any customer-desired length or width within those limiting dimensions. The billets come in several thicknesses ranging from ¾ inch to 2½ inches; however, 1½ inches and 1¾ inches are the two sizes produced regularly in volume.

## MARKETING MICRO = LAM

When Micro=Lam was first introduced, Trus Joist executives asked an independent research group to perform a study indicating possible industrial applications for the product. The first application for Micro=Lam was to replace high-quality solid sawn-lumber 2″ × 4″ truss chords[2] in open-web joist designs, and solid sawn-lumber flanges[3] on wooden I-beam joists (TJI). Into the fall of 1978, this still represented the majority of Micro=Lam production. The findings of the research report suggested Micro=Lam could be used as scaffold planking, mobile home truss chords, and housing components. These products accounted for about 25 percent of Micro=Lam production. Kalish had also begun to develop new markets for Micro=Lam, including ladder rails and framing material for office partitions. When marketing Micro=Lam to potential customers, Trus Joist emphasized the superior structural qualities of the product over conventional lumber. Micro=Lam did not possess the undesirable characteristics of warping, checking, and twisting; it showed greater bending strength and more structural stability. In some applications, Micro=Lam offered distinct price advantages over competing wood alternatives, and this factor always proved to be a good selling point. Manufacturers were often concerned about the lead and delivery time involved with ordering Micro=Lam. Trus Joist promised to deliver within one to three weeks of an order, which was often a full two weeks to two months ahead of other wood manufacturers.

[1]Micro=Lam is manufactured in units called *billets*, and the basic unit is one billet foot. The actual dimensions of a billet foot are 1′ × 2′ × 1½″, and one billet is 80′ × 24′ × 1½′.
[2]Truss chords are the top and bottom components in an open-web truss incorporating wood chords and tubular steel webs. A *truss* is an assemblage of wooden members that forms a rigid framework to support a roof or other part of a building.
[3]Flanges are the top and bottom components in an all-wood I-beam. For more detail on these and other technical terms in this case, see William Dean and David S. Evans, eds., *Terms of the Trade: A Handbook for the Forest Products Industry,* Random Lengths Publications, Inc.

| EXHIBIT 1 | MECHANICAL PROPERTIES OF WOOD USED FOR TRAILER DECKING |

| Common Name of Species | Specific Gravity (% moisture content) | Modulus of Elasticity (million PSI) | Compression Parallel to Grain and Fiber Strength Max. Crush Strength (PSI) |
|---|---|---|---|
| Apitong | .59 | 2.35 | 8540 |
| Douglas fir | .48 | 1.95 | 7240 |
| Alaska yellow cedar | .42 | 1.59 | 6640 |
| White oak | .68 | 1.78 | 7440 |
| Northern red oak | .63 | 1.82 | 6760 |
| Micro=Lam* | .55 | 2.20 | 8200 |

*Micro=Lam using Douglas fir as the veneer faces of the lumber.
Notes: Modulus of elasticity is a measure of stiffness of a piece of lumber under load. Compression parallel to grain indicates the loading that might be applied to the end of a short post, such as a stud, or compression member in a truss, where the loading force acts parallel to the grain. PSI means pounds per square inch.
Source: U.S.D.A. Handbook No. 72, Wood Handbook: Wood as an Engineering Material, rev. ed., 1974, U.S. Forest Products Laboratory.

The industrial application report had also suggested using Micro=Lam as a decking material for truck trailers. This use became a reality when Sherman Brothers Trucking, a local firm that frequently transported Micro=Lam, made a request for Micro=Lam to redeck some of its worn-out trailers. To increase the durability of the flooring surface, the manufacturing department of Trus Joist replaced the top two veneer sheets of Douglas fir with Apitong. Apitong was a Southeast Asian wood known for its strength, durability, and high specific gravity. This foreign hardwood had been used in the United States for several years because of the diminishing supplies of domestic hardwoods (see Exhibit 1).

The pioneer advertisement for Micro=Lam as a trailer deck material had consisted of one ad in a national trade journal and had depicted the Micro=Lam cut so that the edges were used as the top surface. The response from this ad had been dismal and had resulted in only one or two orders. The latest generation of advertisement depicting Micro=Lam as it was currently being used (with Apitong as the top veneer layers) had had better results. This ad, sent to every major truck or trailer manufacturing journal as a news release on a new product, resulted in 30 to 50 inquiries that turned into 10 to 15 orders. Approximately 15 decks were sold as a result of the promotion.

Everyone at Trus Joist believed the current price on Micro=Lam was the absolute rock bottom. In fact, most people believed Micro=Lam was underpriced. The current price of Micro=Lam included a gross margin of 20 percent. The price of 1¼-inch thick and 1½-inch thick Micro=Lam was based on the costs of a 1½-inch billet. The total variable costs of 1½-inch material were multiplied by 5/6 to estimate the same costs of 1¼-inch material. There had recently been some discussion over the appropriateness of this ratio. Some of the marketing personnel believed a more appropriate estimate of the variable costs for the 1¼-inch Micro=Lam would be the ratio of the number of veneers in a 1¼-inch billet to the number of veneers in a 1½-inch billet, or 14/16. At the present time, the costs of veneer represented 55 percent of the selling price. Glue cost was approximately $0.13 per square foot; fixed overhead represented $0.14 per square foot; and other variable costs amounted to approximately $0.125 per square foot. The total variable cost was divided by .80 to cover all selling and administrative expenses and to secure a profit.[4]

In 1977, truck trailer manufacturers ordered and used 46 million square feet of decking for installation in new truck-trailer construction. This figure was understated because re-decking or replacement of worn-out floors of trailers had not been incorporated, and there was little organized information to determine what this potential could be. As of 1975, 236 truck-trailer manufacturers produced $646.7 million worth of trailers (see Exhibits 2 and 3).

The problem Kalish saw with this aggregate data was that it was not broken down into the various segments of trailer builders. For example, not all of the 236 manufacturers produced trailers with wooden floors. Among those not using wooden floors, for example, were tankers and logging trailers. Kalish believed the real key to selling Micro=Lam in this industry would be to determine on what segment of the trailer industry he should concentrate his selling effort. Kalish also knew he somehow had to determine trailer manufacturers' requirements for trailer decking. The Eugene–Portland, Oregon, area offered what he thought to be a good cross-section of the type of trailer manufacturers that might be interested in Micro=Lam. He had already contacted some of those firms about buying Micro=Lam.

## GENERAL TRAILER COMPANY

Jim Walline had been the purchasing agent for General Trailer Company of Springfield, Oregon, for the past two and one-half years. He stated: "The engineering department makes the decisions on what materials to buy. I place the orders after the requisition has been placed on my desk."

General Trailer was a manufacturer of several different types of trailers: low-boys, chip trailers, log trailers, and flatbeds. In 1977, General manufactured five flatbeds and redecked five flatbeds. General did most of its business with the local timber industry; however, in 1977 it sold three flatbeds to local firms in the steel industry.

The flatbeds General Trailer manufactured were 40 to 45 feet long and approximately 7 feet wide. Log trailers were approximately 20 to 25 feet long. General Trailer manufactured trailers primarily for the West Coast market, although it had sold a few trailers to users in Alaska. On the West Coast, General's major competitors were Peerless, Fruehauf, and Trailmobile, all large-scale manufacturers of truck trailers. Even though General was comparatively small in size, it did not feel threatened because "We build a top-quality trailer, which is not mass produced," as Mr. Walline put it.

General had been using Apitong as a decking material until customers complained of

[4]All cost figures have been disguised.

## EXHIBIT 2

# TRUCK-TRAILER SHIPMENTS AND DOLLAR VALUE
(by calendar year)

|  | 1975 | 1974 | 1973 | 1972 | 1971 |
|---|---|---|---|---|---|
| Complete trailers and chassis | 67,888 | 191,262 | 167,201 | 141,143 | 103,784 |
| Value | $613,702,000 | $1,198,520,000 | $ 956,708,000 | $795,500,000 | $585,264,000 |
| Containers | 4,183* | 10,108* | 18,626 | 18,166 | 8,734 |
| Value | $ 18,071,000 | $ 27,343,000 | $ 60,159,000 | $ 51,527,000 | $ 26,514,000 |
| Container chassis | 2,936 | 12,883 | 12,790 | 15,498 | 9,775 |
| Value | $ 14,898,000 | $ 42,076,000 | $ 33,143,000 | $ 39,028,000 | $ 24,999,000 |
| Total units | 75,007 | 214,253 | 198,617 | 174,807 | 122,293 |
| Value | $646,671,000 | $1,267,939,000 | $1,050,010,000 | $886,055,000 | $636,777,000 |

*Containers not reported June–October 1974 and January–March 1975.
Source: Ward's Automotive Yearbook, 1978, p. 91.

# TRUCK-TRAILER MANUFACTURERS

Allentown Brake & Wheel Service, Inc., Allentown, Pa.
Allied Products Corp., Chicago, Ill.
Aluminum Body Corp., Montebello, Cal.
American Body & Equipment Co., Grand Prairie, Texas
American Trailers Inc., Oklahoma City, Okla.
Anthony Co., Streator, Ill.
Atlantic International Corp., Baltimore, Md.
Atlantic International Marketing Corp., Baltimore, Md.
Atlantic Manufacturing Corp., Baltimore, Md.
Atlantic Mobile Corporation, Cockeysville, Md.
Atlas Hoist & Body, Inc., Montreal, Que., Can.
Bartlett Trailer Corp., Chicago, Ill.
Bethlehem Fabricators, Inc., Bethlehem, Pa.
Adam Black & Sons, Inc., Jersey City, N.J.
Black Diamond Enterprises, Inc., Bristol, Va.
Herman Born & Sons, Inc., Baltimore, Md.
Budd Co., Troy, Mich.
Centennial Industries Division, Columbus, Ga.
Copco Trailer Division, South Bend, Ind.
Custom Trailers, Inc., Springfield, Mo.
Delta Truck Trailer Co., Inc., Camden, Ark.
Distribution International Corp., Ft. Washington, Pa.
Dorsey Corp., Chattanooga, Tenn.
Dorsey Trailers, Inc., Elba, Ala.
Dura Corp., Southfield, Mich.
Durobilt Mfg. Co., El Monte, Cal.
Eight Point Trailer Corp., Los Angeles, Cal.
Essick Mfg. Co., Los Angeles, Cal.
Evans Products Co., Portland, Ore.
Expediter Systems, Inc., Birmingham, Ala.
Firmers Lumber & Supply Co., Sioux City, Iowa
Ford Motor Co., Dearborn, Mich.
Ford Motor Co. of Canada Limited, Oakville, Ont., Can.
Fruehauf Corp., Detroit, Mich.
Fruehauf Trailer Co. of Canada Ltd., Dixie, Ont., Can.
General Body Mfg. Co., Inc., Kansas City, Mo.
Gerstenslager Co., Inc., Wooster, Ohio
Great Dane Trailers, Inc., Savannah, Ga.
Hawker Siddeley Canada Ltd., Toronto, Can.
Hendrickson Mfg. Co., Lyons, Ill.
Hercules Mfg. Co., Henderson, Ky.

Hesse Corp., Kansas City, Mo.
Highway Trailers of Canada Ltd., Cooksville, Ont., Can.
Hobbs Trailers, Fort Worth, Texas
Hyster Co., Portland, Ore.
Leland Equipment Co., Tulsa, Okla.
Lodestar Corp., Niles, Ohio
McCade-Powers Body Co., St. Louis, Mo.
McQuerry Trailer Co., Fort Worth, Texas
Meyers Industries, Inc., Tecumseh, Mich.
Mindustrial Corp., Ltd., Toronto, Ont., Can.
Mitsubishi Electric Corp., Chiyoda-ku, Tokyo, 100, Japan
Moline Body Co., Moline, Ill.
Montone Mfg. Co., Hazelton, Pa.
Nabors Trailers, Inc., West Palm Beach, Fla.
Noble Division (Waterloo Plant), Waterloo, Iowa
OMC-Lincoln, Lincoln, Neb.
Ohio Body Mfg. Co., New London, Ohio
Olson Trailer & Body Builders Co., Green Bay, Wis.
Pike Trailer Co., Los Angeles, Cal.
Pointer Truck Co., Renton, Wash.
Polar Manufacturing Co., Holdingford, Minn.
Pullman Incorporated, Chicago, Ill.
Pullman Trailmobile, Chicago, Ill.
Ravens-Metal Products, North Parkersburg, W. Va.
Reliance Trailer Manufacturing, Cotati, Cal.
Remke, Inc., Roseville, Mich.
Rogers Bros. Corp., Albion, Pa.
Shetky Equipment Corp., Portland, Ore.
Southwest Truck Body Company, St. Louis, Mo.
Starcraft Corp., Goshen, Ind.
Sterling Precision Corp., West Palm Beach, Fla.
Thiele, Inc., Windber, Pa.
Timpte Inc., Denver, Colo.
Timpte Industries, Inc., Denver, Colo.
Trailco, Hummels Wharf, Pa.
Transport Trailers, Cedar Rapids, Iowa
Troyler Corp., Scranton, Pa.
Utility Tool & Body Co., Clintonville, Wis.
Valley Tow-Rite, Lodi, Cal.
Peter Wendel & Sons, Inc., Irvington, N.J.
Whitehead & Kales Co., River Rouge, Mich.
Williamsen Truck Equipment Corp., Salt Lake City, Utah

*Source: Standard & Poor's Register*

the weight and expansion-contraction characteristics when exposed to weather. At that time, Mr. Schmidt, the general manager and head of the engineering department, made the decision to switch from Apitong to laminated fir.

Laminated fir (consisting of solid sawn-lumber strips glued together) was currently being used as the material for decking flatbeds, and Pacific Laminated of Vancouver, Washington, supplied all of General's fir decking. General would order material only when a customer bought a new trailer or needed a trailer redecked. Walline was disappointed with the two- to three-week delivery time, since it often meant that much more time before the customer's trailer was ready. Laminated fir in 40-foot lengths, 11¾-inch widths, and 1¼-inch thickness was used. General paid approximately $2–$3 per square foot for this decking. Even though Pacific Laminated could provide customer-cut and edged pieces with no additional lead time, General preferred ship-lapped fir in the previously noted dimensions, with the top two layers treated with a waterproof coating. The different types of trailers General manufactured required different decking materials. Lowboys required 2¼-inch thick material, and General used 3″ × 12″ rough-cut fir lumber. Chip trailers required MDO (medium density overlay) plywood with a thickness of 5 to 8 inches, and with a slick surface.

Walline said it had used Micro=Lam on one trailer; however, the customer had not been expecting it and was very displeased with the job.[5] Therefore, the current policy was to use only laminated fir for the local market, unless a customer specifically ordered a different decking material. Trailers headed for Alaska were decked with laminated oak supplied by a vendor other than Pacific Laminated. Walline said that if he wanted to make a recommendation to change decking materials, he would need to know price advantages, lead times, moisture content, availability, and industry experience with the material.

## MAYFLOWER MOVING AND STORAGE

"We already use Micro=Lam on our trailers," was the response of Mr. Sherman, president of Mayflower Moving and Storage Company, when asked about trailer decking material. He went on to say, "In fact, we had hauled several shipments for Trus Joist when we initiated a call to them asking if they could make a decking material for us."

Mayflower Moving and Storage owned 60 trailers (flatbeds) which it used to haul heavy equipment and machinery. It had been in a dilemma for eight years with the type of materials used to replace the original decks. Nothing seemed to be satisfactory. Solid Apitong was tough, but it was too heavy and did not weather very well. Plywood did not provide adequate weight distribution and had too many joints. Often the small wheels of the forklifts would break through the decking, or heavy equipment with steel legs would punch a hole through the decks. Laminated fir was too expensive. Mayflower Moving and Storage was currently redecking a trailer per week. It usually patched the decks until

---

[5]After purchasing Micro=Lam, General Trailer modified the material by ripping the billets into 1½-inch widths and then relaminating these strips back into 12-inch or 24-inch wide pieces of lumber. This remanufacturing added substantial costs. Also, the laminations were now directly exposed to the weather. Moisture could more easily seep into cracks or voids, causing swells and buckling.

the whole bed fell apart; then the trailer would sit in the yard waiting for a major over-haul. The trailers by this time needed cross beams repaired and new bearings, besides a new deck.

Sherman went on to say: "The shop mechanic just loves Micro=Lam. This is because it used to take the mechanic and one other employee two days to redeck a trailer, and now it just takes the shop mechanic one day to do the same job." Advantages (over ply-wood and Apitong) of the Micro=Lam pieces were ease of installation, excellent weight distribution due to the reduced number of seams, and reduced total weight of the bed. Sherman explained that they usually purchased four or five decks at a time and ware-housed some of the materials until a trailer needed redecking.

Sherman thought the original decking on flatbeds was some type of hardwood, prob-ably oak, which could last up to five years; however, a similar decking material had not been found for a reasonable price. The plywood and fir decks used in the past eight to ten years had lasted anywhere from one to two years, and some had worn out in as little as six months. After using Micro=Lam for six months, Mr. Sherman expected the decking to last up to three to five years.

When asked about the type of flooring used in moving vans, Sherman emphasized the top care those floors received. "We sand, buff and wax them just like a household floor; in fact, we take such good care of these floors they will occasionally outlast the trailer." The original floors in moving vans were made of laminated oak and had to be kept extremely smooth to allow freight to slide freely without the possibility of damaging items. The local company purchased all its moving vans through Mayflower. The only problem with floors in moving vans was that jointed floors would occasionally buckle because of swelling.

The fact that Micro=Lam protruded ⅛ inch above the metal lip that edged the flatbed trailers posed no problem for Sherman. "All we had to do was plane the edge at 45°. In fact, the best fit will have the decking protrude a hair above the metal edge," Sherman said. Just prior to this, Sherman had recounted an experience with the first shipment of Micro=Lam. Because the deck was too thick, Mayflower Moving and Storage had about ⅛ inch planed from one side of the decking material. However, the company shaved off the Apitong veneer, exposing the fir. Sherman said that he laughs about it now, but at the time he wasn't too pleased.

## PEERLESS TRUCKING COMPANY

"Sure, I've heard of Micro=Lam. They [Trus Joist salespeople] have been in here . . . but we don't need that good a material." This was the response of Mel Rogers, head of the Peerless Purchasing Department, Tualatin, Oregon, when asked about the use of Micro=Lam as a truck decking material. Rogers, a 30-year veteran of the trailer manu-facturing industry, seemed skeptical of all laminated decking materials.

The primary products manufactured by Peerless (in Tualatin) required bedding mate-rials very different from Micro=Lam. Chip trailers and rail car dumpers required metal beds to facilitate unloading. Low-boys required a heavy decking material (usually 2″ × 12″ or 3″ × 12″ rough planking), as Caterpillar tractors were frequently driven on them. Logging trailers had no beds.

Approximately 60 decks per year were required by Peerless in the manufacture of flat-beds and in redecking jobs. Micro=Lam could have been used in these applications, but fir planking was used exclusively except for some special overseas jobs. Fir planking was available in full trailer lengths, requiring eight man-hours to install on new equipment. Usually, five or six decks were stocked at a time. The estimated life of a new deck was two to three years.

Fir planking had been selected for decking applications on the basis of price and durability. Peerless purchased fir planking for $1,000 per MBF. Decking material thickness was critical, according to Rogers, because any deviation from the industry standard of 1⅜ inches required extensive retooling. Any new decking materials for use in original equipment manufacture had to be approved by the Peerless engineering department. Alternative decking materials could have been used locally if specified by the customer.

## FRUEHAUF TRUCKING COMPANY

"I'd be very happy if someone would come up with a durable [trailer] deck at a reasonable price," was the response of Wayne Peterson when asked about Fruehauf's experience with decking materials. Peterson was service manager for Fruehauf's factory branch in Milwaukie, Oregon. Fruehauf Corporation, with principal manufacturing facilities in Detroit, was one of the nation's largest manufacturers of truck trailers.

The facilities in Milwaukie produced 40-ton low-beds as well as assembled truck bodies manufactured in Detroit. The low-beds were subjected to heavy use, often with forklifts, which required a decking material of extreme strength and durability. Laminated decking materials then available were therefore excluded from this application. The decking materials used in the truck bodies were specified by the sales department in Detroit, based on customer input. Generally, Apitong or laminated oak was installed at the factory. Any new product to be used in original equipment manufacture had to be approved by Fruehauf's factory engineering department.

The Milwaukie operation did about 15 redecking jobs per year. The decking material was specified by the customer on the basis of price and weathering characteristics. The materials used were laminated oak (11½″ W × 40′), Apitong (7″ × 1⅜″−random lengths), Alaska yellow cedar (2″ × 6″ T&G), fir planking (2″ × 6″ T&G), and laminated fir (24″ W × 40′). Alaska yellow cedar was priced below all other decking materials, followed (in order) by fir planking, laminated fir, laminated oak, and Apitong.

Fruehauf's suppliers of decking materials were as follows: laminated fir−Pacific Laminating, Vancouver, Washington; Alaska yellow cedar−Al Disdero Lumber Company, Portland, Oregon; and Apitong−Builterials, Portland, Oregon. There were no specific suppliers for the other materials.

A minimum inventory of decking materials was kept on hand to allow for immediate repair needs. Orders were placed for complete decks as needed. A redecking job typically required 30 man-hours per 7′ × 40′ trailer, including the removal of the old deck and installation of the new one. Decking materials available in full trailer lengths were preferred because they greatly reduced installation time as well as improved weight distribution, and had fewer joints along which failure could occur. Use of alternative products, such as composition flooring of wood and aluminum, were not under consideration. Alaska yellow cedar and fir planking had the best weathering characteristics, whereas Apitong and laminated oak weathered poorly. Oak and Apitong did, however, have a hard, nonscratching surface that was desirable in enclosed use. When asked about the weathering characteristics of laminated flooring in general, Peterson responded: "It's all right for the dry states, but not around here."

## COMPETITION

There were a large number of materials with which Micro=Lam competed in the trailer flooring market, ranging from fir plywood to aluminum floors. Trus Joist felt that the greatest obstacles to Micro=Lam's success would be from the old standard products like laminated fir and oak, which had a great deal of industry respect. For years, oak had been the premier flooring material; recently, however, supplies were short, delivery times long (two months in some cases), and prices were becoming prohibitive (see Exhibit 4).

Kalish had found that in the Northwest, Pacific Laminated was one of the major flooring suppliers to local manufacturers. Pacific Laminated produced a Douglas fir laminated product that was very popular; however, like oak, it was relatively high-priced. Despite the price, Pacific Laminated could cut the product in dimensions up to 2 feet wide and 40 feet long. Delivery time was excellent, even with special milling for shiplapped or tongue and groove edges and manufacturing to user thicknesses.

---

**EXHIBIT 4**     **DECKING MATERIAL PRICES, NOVEMBER 1978**

| Product | Price | Form |
|---|---|---|
| Alaska yellow cedar | $650/MBF | 2″ × 6″ T&G 15′ lengths |
| Apitong | $1.30–$2.00/ lineal foot* | 1⅜″ × 7″ random lengths |
| Fir planking | $1.00/bd ft | 2″ × 6″ T&G random lengths |
| Fir laminated | $2.50/sq ft | 1¼″ × 11¾″ × 40′ |
| Micro=Lam | $1.30/sq ft $1.50/sq ft | 1¼″ × 24″ × 40′ 1½″ × 24″ × 40′ |
| Oak laminated | $2.20/sq ft | 1⅜″ × 1½′ × 40′ |

*Lineal foot = price per unit length of the product.
*Sources:* Al Disdero Lumber Company, Portland, Oregon; Builterials, Portland, Oregon.

# CONCLUSION _____

Although Kalish had had limited success marketing Micro=Lam to truck-trailer manufacturers, he was concerned with the marketing program for his product. Several trailer
manufacturers had raised important questions concerning the price and durability of
Micro=Lam compared to alternative decking materials. He knew Micro=Lam had
some strong attributes, yet he was hesitant to expand beyond the local market. Kalish
was also wondering about what action he should eventually take to determine the additional information he would need to introduce Micro=Lam nationally as a trailer decking material. One thought that crossed his mind was the use of a survey questionnaire.
He knew that he would also be expected to define the company's marketing strategy for
this product. Meanwhile, small orders continued to trickle in.

# Cantro Corporation

## Marketing and Pricing Strategies for Multiple Product Lines

Late in November, Mr. John Williams, marketing manager of the industrial valve division of the Cantro Corporation, was reviewing the pricing policy for his division's products: lubricated plug valves and eccentric plug valves. His recommendations concerning factory prices were to be submitted to the division general manager later that week.

Cantro was a highly diversified, multidivision corporation with sales volume in excess of $770 million. The industrial valve division was formed as a separate Cantro division about 20 years ago. Its product line was sold to the industrial and construction market by a salaried sales force which handled the product lines of several other Cantro divisions. The division's income statement for the fiscal year ending September 30 is shown below.

|  | Eccentric Plug Valves (000) | Lubricated Plug Valves (000) | Division Total (000) |
|---|---|---|---|
| Factory sales | $34,380 | $25,738 | $60,118 |
| Variable costs | 7,426 | 10,167 | 17,593 |
| Mfg. overhead* | 8,911 | 12,200 | 21,111 |
| Gross margin | 18,043 | 3,371 | 21,414 |
| Division marketing‡ |  |  | 7,316 |
| Division overhead |  |  | 4,465 |
| Division profit |  |  | 9,633 |
| Corporate overhead |  |  | 3,009 |
| Profit before tax |  |  | 6,624 |

*Allocated at 120% of variable cost.
‡Includes sales force cost billed by Cantro to the division at 10% of factory sales.

This case was made possible through the cooperation of a firm which prefers to remain anonymous. It was prepared by Professor Derek A. Newton. Copyright 1970 by the Graduate Business School Sponsors, University of Virginia.

# PRODUCT AND MARKET CHARACTERISTICS

Lubricated plug and eccentric plug valves were used in a wide variety of gas and fluid control applications. Major customers of the division's products were to be found in the chemical, construction, oil and gas, public works, and utilities industries. These valves were used also by original equipment manufacturers (OEM) of such items as pumps, compressors, steam turbines, engines, steam condensers, and plumbing, refrigeration and air conditioning machinery.

Lubricated plug valves were used in installations requiring "on" or "off" transmission of gases or fluids. These valves were made in steel, semi-steel, or in a wide variety of alloys depending on user requirements as to temperature, pressure, impurities, corrosion and other operating conditions affecting the use of the valves. They were generally available with port sizes from ½ inch to 24 inches; straightaway, three-way or four-way flow control; and could handle up to 200 pounds per square inch (psi) cold working pressure. They were manufactured with very close tolerances between the plug and body sealing surface. The plug was generally seated on low-friction surfaces for ease of turning and to prevent sticking. Each valve's lubricating system was designed to provide sufficient pressure to force the lubricant over all seating surfaces without contaminating the contents of the line. In one typical installation, 33 lubricated plug valves, ranging in sizes from 8 inches to 16 inches, handled the monthly flow of 2 million barrels of gasoline, diesel oil, and stove oil in a marine terminal of a major oil company.

Eccentric plug valves were used in installations requiring control over the amount of flow or rate of transmission of gases or fluid. These valves came with port sizes from ½ inch to 24 inches and were generally cast in nickel iron. Flow control was straightaway or three-way. These valves could handle up to 400 psi cold working pressure. The advantage of predetermined amount of flow, not simply "on" or "off," was achieved by using a ball plug with one flat side, which was rotated within the valve. All surfaces were coated with a substance such as neoprene which assured minimum torque for turning ease, a perfect seal, no lubrication, and no contamination of the contents of the line. In one typical installation 10 eccentric plug valves, ranging in size from 2 inches to 6 inches, handled the raw and digested sludge in a sewage treatment plant in a medium-sized city.

Of the approximately 1,000 independent industrial distributors in the domestic United States who sold these classes of product, Cantro had franchised about 150 of them to sell its valves. The division's valves were also sold through Cantro's network of 35 corporate-owned distributors, which handled a variety of Cantro products. The division's coverage was national, with distributors in all key areas. They usually received a 20 percent margin on list prices.

Among the division's competitors, the Howe Company was considered by Williams to be the most influential in pricing practices. He believed Howe obtained 60 percent to 70 percent of its business through independent distributors upon whom it exercised strong price discipline by means of its experienced sales force. In the past Howe had preferred to lose business before changing its prices. Along with the Dumas Valve Company, Howe enjoyed a major share of the lubricated plug valve business accounted for by the petroleum industry. Williams further estimated that Howe's profit margins were comparable to those of the industrial valve division and to Dumas.

The Dumas Valve Company, although comparable to Howe in size and scope, was more responsive to industry price moves. Williams believed that Dumas enjoyed strong product distribution through independent distributors.

The Nagel Corporation was a large diversified company with a valve division that operated similarly to Cantro's. Williams believed, however, that Nagel had a stronger independent distribution system than Cantro.

NFC, Inc., was the only major competitor that tended to undersell the market (at prices 5 percent to 10 percent below the industry level). Williams believed that NFC pricing actions bore on Howe's reluctance to increase prices. He judged NFC's distribution system weak compared to other major competitors.

The Kindley Company was similar to NFC in size and scope of operations except that it rarely deviated from industry pricing practices. Williams believed its product distribution was relatively weak, but for its sales volume, it was an "aggressive advertiser."

All six major competitors offered similar service functions and were, according to Williams, held in equally high regard in the industry as dependable suppliers. Williams judged Howe to have the best sales force, with Dumas, Cantro, and Nagel "in a close tie for second."

The division spent less on advertising than did most of its key competitors. Williams believed that its advertising expenditures had been adequate, however, because the division benefited from Cantro's corporate institutional advertising. Williams also believed that the division's advertising—as measured by readership surveys—had been more effective than that of competitors. Measured media expenditures in the industry were as follows:

| Howe Co. | $825,000 |
| Dumas Valve Co. | 352,000 |
| Kindley Co. | 257,000 |
| Cantro | 196,000 |
| Nagel Corp. | 185,000 |
| NFC, Inc. | 65,000 |

Recent industry brand preference studies indicated that the division ranked about the same level in preference as it did in market share. This relationship was particularly valid with purchasing agents. The division had consistently ranked higher among consulting engineers than with either contractors or plant operating personnel because the Cantro sales force tended to concentrate on the former. Howe and Dumas, in contrast, concentrated their sales force calls on contractors and plant personnel, and consequently ranked higher in brand preference studies with the latter. All six competitors directed heavy sales effort toward OEM and utility purchasing agents.

# ECCENTRIC PLUG VALVE PRICING

Eccentric plug valves were the division's original product line, and although its share of the market had declined in the last five years, the division was still the major factor in this industry segment. The table below gives market share estimates prepared by Williams.

|  | Current Share | Share Five Years Ago |
|---|---|---|
| Cantro | 36.0% | 46.4% |
| Dumas Valve Co. | 22.9 | 12.5 |
| Nagel Corp. | 19.0 | 14.5 |
| NFC, Inc. | 7.5 | 5.0 |
| Howe Co. | 7.0 | 15.0 |
| Kindley Co. | 4.0 | 4.0 |
| Balance of market | 3.6 | 2.6 |
|  | 100.0% | 100.0% |

The market for eccentric plug valves had increased 70 percent in the last five years, but Williams believed that this rate of growth had recently tapered off to about 4 percent to 5 percent a year. Until ten years ago, the division supplied two competitors, Nagel and Dumas, and enjoyed a 70 percent market share. The decision of these two competitors to self-manufacture eccentric plug valves not only eliminated those sales, but provided more competition for Cantro with other customers. Currently, the division sold about 60 percent of its eccentric plug valve volume to direct accounts, for example, hydraulic and pneumatic systems manufacturers, other OEMs' contractors, and end users such as chemical plants, utilities, and government installations; about 20 percent to competitor-customers; and about 10 percent each to independent and Cantro-owned distributors. List prices ranged from $10 to $3,500 per unit.

Williams believed that brand image and features were more important to the eccentric plug valve purchaser than were price and availability. Because of the division's leadership in the development of eccentric plug valves with high reliability at rated temperatures and pressures, this product line commanded a 5 percent to 10 percent price premium above competitors who invariably followed Cantro's price moves while maintaining this differential. Williams believed that the division had cost advantages over competitive eccentric plug valves due to higher volume production, which, when combined with a higher average realized price, led to a higher rate of profit. Williams was concerned, however, about product maturation. He believed that competitive products were beginning to approach the quality and reliability level of the division's eccentric plug valves and the advantages of certain key product features once held by the division had all but disappeared. Williams was doubtful that the division's research and development personnel, or anyone else's for that matter, could keep eccentric plug valves from becoming a commodity. According to Williams, direct accounts were becoming harder to sell on the idea of paying a premium for Cantro eccentric plug valves, particularly on large orders. Fortunately for Cantro, valve-port sizes and other technical specifications tended to vary among valve manufacturers, which led purchasing agents, consulting engineers, contractors, and plant-operating people to order from catalogues rather than ask for competitive bids. Williams added, "If people ever go in for competitive bidding in a big way, that will be the end of our premium price."

Williams had held several discussions with the division's controller, the Cantro field sales manager, and the two division product managers. The controller stated that, after considering the expected effects of increases in variable costs of 5 percent, a 2½ percent price increase was necessary on eccentric plug valves to achieve the division profit target (before corporate overhead) of 15 percent of sales for the coming fiscal year. From the controller's standpoint, the 2½ percent price increase was the bare minimum, since it was below the rate of general inflation and below the 4.5 percent and 5.0 percent price increases realized in each of the past two years.

The Cantro field sales manager was in favor of holding existing price levels on eccentric plug valves and increasing sales and promotional expenses as a means of stopping the erosion of the division's market share. He maintained that higher prices would increase the incentive for competitor-customers to manufacture their own valves. He also wanted to improve brand acceptance with the contractors and plant personnel. Sooner or later, he claimed, the price differential over key competitors would have to be narrowed.

The eccentric plug valve product manager believed that a modest price decrease would probably be followed by others in the industry and would preclude further losses from competitor-customers who might decide to self-manufacture. Although the product quality and features justified a price premium over competition, he claimed maintaining high price levels was "asking for trouble."

## LUBRICATED PLUG VALVE PRICING

Although there had been occasional short-term declines, the market for lubricated plug valves had shown consistent growth during the past 20 years. During the past five years, industry sales volume had doubled, but Williams anticipated that for the next five years the growth rate would stabilize at about 5 percent a year. This recent accelerated growth was due primarily to the petroleum industry, a segment of the market that accounted for about 25 percent of the lubricated plug valve business, which the division had been unable to penetrate. Williams estimated market share data as follows:

|  | Current Share | Share Five Years Ago |
|---|---|---|
| Howe Co. | 33.7% | 23.0% |
| Dumas Valve Co. | 21.2 | 17.0 |
| Nagel Corp. | 11.2 | 12.0 |
| Kindley Co. | 11.2 | 10.0 |
| Cantro | 9.6 | 9.8 |
| NFC, Inc. | 7.0 | 6.0 |
| Balance of market | 6.1 | 22.2 |
|  | 100.0% | 100.0% |

The division's lubricated plug valve sales volume was split as follows: 50 percent to direct accounts, 15 percent to independent distribution, and 35 percent to Cantro-owned distributors.

Williams viewed lubricated plug valves as "pretty much a commodity item" with little product differentiation. Almost all plants and industrial concerns were prospects for this class of equipment, but a larger volume of sales was accounted for by industrial distributors for replacement purposes. Factory unit prices of lubricated plug valves ranged from $20 to $5,000. Williams believed that purchasers were more interested in price and availability than they were in brand image and features. Again, however, purchasing from catalogues was still common practice. Williams estimated that less than 10 percent of the industry's volume was placed on competitive bids.

Four years ago, the division followed the lead of some other manufacturers and increased prices by 3 percent. The increase was kept in effect for seven months, but since the Howe Company did not increase its prices, the other manufacturers rescinded their increases and the division was forced to rescind its increase also. A year later the division attempted to take the lead by announcing and placing into effect a 5 percent increase. After two months, it was forced to retract the increase when Howe refused to move even though other competitors had followed the division's lead. Williams estimated that this abortive attempt had cost the division about $250,000 in lost orders. Last year, Dumas had attempted to lead the industry in an increase, but called back its new price lists before the increased prices were to take effect.

In discussing the lubricated plug valve pricing situation with the controller, sales manager, and lubricated plug valve product manager, Williams discovered a strong consensus for "letting well enough alone," despite the expected 5 percent increase in variable costs.

## CONCLUSION

In thinking about his pricing recommendations to the division general manager, Williams focused on the latter's key criteria:

1. Maintain and increase market share.
2. Improve profits.
3. Maintain a posture of leadership through stable and responsible pricing practices.

# Hartman Elevator Corporation

## Competitive Bidding for a Parts-Service Contract

## BACKGROUND

The Hartman Elevator Corporation was founded in Chicago in 1867. It was one of the first manufacturers of hoists, winches, and the steel cable used in elevator equipment. As a natural progression from hoists, winches, and steel cables, the company began building and installing "lifts" for commercial use in retail stores and warehouses. These lifts were the forerunners of modern-day elevators. The Hartman Elevator Corporation was also a pioneer in what were first called moving stairs and later became known as escalators. But Hartman had always concentrated on the installation and servicing of elevators. In 1983, it was one of the four major elevator manufacturers in the United States, with 22,000 employees and annual sales nearing $200 million.

There are a number of basic components in an elevator. First, there is the car or cab that carries passengers and freight. To enter the elevator, there are doors at each floor it serves. The cab travels on rails or tracks. The cab is powered by a hydraulic shaft in the bottom or by an overhead cable and electrical motor system in the hoistway. Lower buildings, up to five stories, are often powered from the bottom by a hydraulic elevator that has a pump, motor, and valve. Virtually all high-rise buildings requiring high speed cab operation are powered by overhead electrical motor and electronic switching equipment.

Hartman has three separate businesses or divisions within the company. All three are separate profit centers. The first is called the Manufacturing and Fabrication Division, which produces elevator parts and assembled and fabricated elevators. This manufacturing business sells some parts and subassemblies to independent service firms that repair and maintain elevators. The second business is called the New Construction Division. This division bids on new construction projects that require the installation of elevators. The division works closely with architects who develop building specifications. Once a contract bid is awarded, the division works with the developer or the general contractor. The third business is the servicing and repairing of existing or "in-place" elevators. Elevator maintenance consists of periodic inspections, the repair of defective or worn parts, and a 24-hour on-call service for breakdown repairs. The repair or service business is generally conducted on a contract basis for a one-, three-, or five-year period.

The demand for elevators and the subsequent repair service is strongest where new construction and renovation are growing. Office buildings, which are usually multiple-story, are a major growth market. Universities were a major growth market in the 1960s and 1970s, but with demographic shifts, there has been little new university construction. Hospitals continue to be a major growth market for new elevator installations. Renovation of high rises and inner-city apartment buildings has also been a stable growth market. Hartman tends to concentrate on the medium-height buildings (under 15 stories) where less high-speed electronic equipment is needed. The over-20-story buildings require very fast equipment to move passengers rapidly. The older buildings, requiring more frequent elevator repair, are generally under 20 stories.

## Regulated Inspections and Safety

State, county, or city ordinances throughout the United States mandate periodic safety inspections of passenger and freight elevators. This fact keeps the in-place elevator repair business less cyclical than new construction-related elevator installations. The government-regulated inspections and safety checks, like state auto inspections, create a continuous demand for parts and repair service.

Safety is a major concern of passengers and owners of buildings. Commercial and rental tenants expect an elevator that works safely 24 hours a day. Safety and product liability are therefore of great concern to the producers of elevator systems and parts. Hartman spends $3 million annually on insurance premiums to cover any claims. About 40 percent of the cost of an elevator is for safety devices. The training of Hartman service people constantly stresses safety in all inspections and repair procedures.

## New Construction Installations

The new elevator (OEM) business is very different from the aftermarket repair parts and service business. The new elevator buyer provides more technical performance guidelines for manufacturers. New installations nearly always involve multiple decision makers before and after the bid is awarded. The architect, general contractor, subcontractor, and possibly the owner or developer are involved in the purchase and installation of a new elevator. These buying influences frequently have a list of three or four approved elevator manufacturers. Usually two or three or these are invited to bid on a specific building's elevator requirements. Sometimes the new construction specs are written to favor one manufacturer's product. For example, if the performance requirements state that the elevator must travel at 1,400 feet per minute in a 30-story building, usually only one or two manufacturers' products can meet those requirements.

It typically takes one or two people two to three weeks to prepare a bid on a new construction installation. Architectural changes can cause the potential bidder to resubmit the bid. A large, new construction requiring elevator installation can take one to two years to complete. Escalation clauses are built into most new construction elevator contracts to pass on labor and material cost increases. Construction delays add a major element of risk to the installers of new elevator systems. The pricing terms of the contract typically require the customer to make progress payments as materials are delivered to the site and as installation progresses. The progress payments help the supplier's cash flow for the 6 to 24 months a new installation requires.

## Profit and Product Mix

Elevator manufacturing, despite the massive product involved, becomes predominantly a service business. Ten-million-dollar elevator banks in high-rise complexes have been virtually sold at cost. Service contracts are where the profit is, and this business is much less cyclical than the new installation part of the industry. Hartman Elevator was at one time heavily dependent on new installations. However, by 1983 the company goal of 60–40 sales (service to new installations) was achieved, and profit also emphasized the service side in a 70–30 percent contribution. Sales in 1983 were nearly $155 million, with about $93 million from service contracts. The combined profits from new installations and service contracts have met the corporate profit target of a 15 percent compounded return on assets.

# CHANGING BUYER-SUPPLIER PRACTICES

The OEM elevator builder historically would buy into an account by charging a price that was intentionally marginal, breakeven, or a loss situation. This approach allowed the elevator builder to secure the lucrative 20- to 30-year aftermarket inspection, service, repair, and parts business. But as the number of in-place elevators increased, more independent service firms entered the market. Before the entrance of the independents, there was an industry understanding that those who installed the elevator would also continue the servicing and maintenance. No firm repaired another manufacturer's elevators.

It was very easy to enter the elevator repair business. In 1974, about 400 independent elevator service companies existed in the United States. In 1983 there were nearly 1,500 service firms, many employing only one or two people. In the recessions of 1974–76 and 1982–83 many unemployed technicians went into the elevator service business. Since more younger skilled technicians were laid off in the older, large cities, a prize opportunity existed for those people. The older and larger cities had more elevators in place to service, and the OEMs, with high overheads, had high prices. Ease of entry and low overhead led entrepreneurs to make deep inroads into the major elevator manufacturers' repair businesses.

Today, if one of the four major U.S. elevator manufacturers does a new installation, there is no guarantee that it will receive the service contract. The service contract is usually a separate agreement. However, many customers will prefer to have the installer do the service for the first three to five years. A small number of customers, perhaps 15 to 18 percent, continue to renew the service contract with the original installer. Large multiple-building property owners, like the major insurance companies and major *Fortune* 100 firms, tend to prefer to place the service business with the larger elevator service firms, including the larger independents. These customers also tend to put the business out to three or four local firms to bid on.

The producers and many larger independent service firms have in-house emergency capabilities to do rework and renovation projects. Projects of this type, which frequently lead to at least a one-year service contract, are rarely done by the one- or two-person service firm. In the last four to six years, there has been an increasing trend toward obtaining bids from other elevator firms before renewing a service contract. This comparison shopping was more common at the large account ($3,000–$5,000 per month charge) where there were multiple elevators at the location. There were two major reasons for changing elevator service suppliers. They were poor service, price, or a combination of the two. Poor service could be seen in slow response time, long repair periods, or frequent shutdowns. Poor service could also result from incompetent or careless repair personnel, or infrequent inspections for preventive maintenance. A poor service situation often led a customer to cancel one contract and sign another with a different service firm. However, even with satisfactory service, a service firm could lose an account due to a lower bid price from a competitor.

## Services Provided

Bob Lowe, president of Hartman Elevator Corporation, stated:

> An elevator service or maintenance agreement should be viewed as a health insurance policy that provides coverage for your body and its parts. The customer pays a monthly fee, or health insurance premium, to have periodic checkups or examinations. The preventive maintenance service agreement is like the practice of preventive medicine with an HMO [Health Maintenance Organization], where for a flat known monthly fee a certain level of service is provided for all the customer's family or active elevator units. The customer does not receive any surprise bills for repairs.

A typical elevator maintenance agreement states the extent of coverage, as shown in the sample agreement in Exhibit 1. The elevator service firm periodically inspects (usually every two weeks), adjusts, and lubricates each unit. The service person also determines which parts—motor, cables, brake shoes, and so on—should be repaired or replaced and when. Whatever is replaced or repaired is part of the fixed monthly service fee. No additional costs are added to the contracted agreement. However, sometimes before a service firm will provide full coverage on an older elevator, it will require up-front repair work, possibly costing $3,000–$20,000, to be done before it will enter into a monthly full-service agreement. A preproposal inspection visit helps to determine if an elevator needs to be brought up to a certain level of operation before a service proposal is written and a contract signed. The specific items covered in the maintenance agreement are listed in Exhibit 1 under "Extent of Coverage." As is shown in the agreement, the company is not responsible for repairs caused by negligence, vandalism, or misuse.

EXHIBIT
1

# HARTMAN ELEVATOR CORPORATION

## Proposal for Elevator Maintenance

We propose to furnish Hartman Maintenance Service on the following described elevators in your building located at

Lackawanna, New York 14239
Bethlehem Steel Lackawanna Works
Main Office Building

## Extent of Coverage

Under the terms and conditions of this agreement subsequently set forth we will maintain the entire elevator equipment as herein described, using skilled elevator personnel directly employed and supervised by us.

We will systematically and regularly examine, adjust, lubricate as required, and if conditions warrant, repair or replace the following:

Elevator machine
Elevator motor
Generator
Controller parts
Gears
Worms
Bearings
Rotating elements
Thrusts
Brake magnet coils
Brake magnet stators
Brake shoes and linings
Commutators and brushes
Windings and coils
Contacts and magnet frames
Resistance for motor and oper. circuits

We Also Agree To:

Examine all safety devices and governors periodically.

Check and equalize tension of all hoisting ropes.

Renew all ropes when necessary to insure adequate factor of safety.

Repair or renew conductor cables when necessary.

Renew guide shoes gibs or rollers as necessary to insure smooth and quiet operation.

Lubricate all guide rails properly except when roller guides are used.

Furnish special Hartman Lubricants compounded to our specifications.

Maintain all accessory equipment except such items as are hereinafter excluded.

## Responsibility for Repairs or Renewals

We shall not be required to make repairs or renewals necessitated because of negligence or misuse of the machinery, equipment, or car, or due to any other cause beyond our control except ordinary wear.

We shall not be required to make safety tests or to install new attachments or devices on the equipment as directed or recommended by insurance companies or by governmental authorities.

The following items of equipment are not included in this agreement: refinishing, replacing, or repairing of elevator car enclosures, car door panels, hoistway enclosures, hoistway door panels, frame, and sills.

## Hours of Work

All work is to be performed during regular working hours of the regular working day of the elevator trade.

**EXHIBIT**
**1**

*(cont'd)*

Overtime emergency adjustment call-back service only is included, at no additional charge. If overtime examinations or repairs are requested, you are to pay us, at our regular billing rates, for the bonus (overtime) hours only.

## Insurance Coverage

Hartman Elevator Corporation is insured at all locations where it undertakes business operations for the types of insurance and limits of liability as follows:

A. Comprehensive Liability—Up to One Million Dollars ($1,000,000) single limit per occurrence including:

1. Bodily Injury Liability—All sums which the Company shall become legally obligated to pay as damages because of bodily injury, sickness or disease, including death at any time resulting therefrom, sustained by any person other than its employees and caused by occurrence.
2. Property Damage Liability—All sums which the Company shall become legally obligated to pay as damages because of injury to or destruction of property, caused by occurrence.

Automobile Liability—
3. Bodily Injury Liability—All sums which the Company shall become legally obligated to pay as damages because of bodily injury, sickness or disease, including death at any time resulting therefrom, sustained by any person other than its employees, caused by occurrence and arising out of the ownership, maintenance, or use of any automobile.
4. Property Damage Liability—All sums which the Company shall become legally obligated to pay as damages because of injury to or destruction of property, caused by occurrence and arising out of the ownership, maintenance, or use of any automobile.

The cost of the above, our standard insurance coverage, is included in this quotation or contract.

## Price Adjustment Provision

The contract price shall be adjusted at the end of each year of the Agreement. The adjusted price shall be effective for the forthcoming year and shall be calculated as follows:

Twenty percent (20%) of the total contract price shall be adjusted by the percentage of increase or decrease in the "Wholesale Commodity Price Index for Metals and Metal Products" published by the U.S. Department of Labor, Bureau of Statistics. The index used in establishing the initial price of this contract was _305.4_ for the month of _May_ 19_83_.

Eighty percent (80%) of the total contract price shall be adjusted by the percentage of increase or decrease in the straight time hourly labor cost for the elevator mechanic in the area in which the equipment is maintained, in effect on the adjustment date as compared to the hourly labor cost used in establishing the prior year's price. The hourly labor cost used in establishing the initial price of this contract was $ _21.70_ .

For the purpose of the Agreement and subsequent adjustments, the "straight time hourly labor cost" shall be the actual hourly rate paid to the mechanics, plus union negotiated fringe benefits and labor related statutory taxes. Union negotiated fringe benefits include, but are not limited to pensions, vacations, paid holidays, group life insurance, sickness and accident insurance, and hospitalization insurance. Labor related statutory taxes include, but are not limited to, F.I.C.A., Federal and State unemployment taxes.

**EXHIBIT
1**

*(cont'd)*    Special Conditions

### Terms

This agreement will be effective on ___July 1, 1983___ and will continue until terminated as provided herein. Either party may terminate this agreement at the end of the first five-year period or at the end of any subsequent five-year period by giving the other party ninety (90) days prior written notice.

PRICE ___Twenty-six Hundred___ ($__2,600.00__) DOLLARS Net per month, payable monthly, receipt of invoice.

At the termination of each one-year period in which this agreement is in force, this price is to be subject to adjustment in accordance with the Price Adjustment Provision as set forth on Page 2 of this agreement.

Purchaser shall pay as an addition to the price stated, a sum equal to the amount of any taxes in whatever form the same may now or hereafter be exacted from the seller on account hereof.

Hartman Elevator Corporation reserves the right to discontinue this contract at any time by notification in writing should invoices rendered for the maintenance or repair of the equipment described under the terms of this agreement not be paid within thirty (30) days from date of invoices.

It is understood and agreed that this proposal and your acceptance thereof shall constitute, exclusively and entirely, the agreement for the service herein described; that all other prior representations or agreements, whether written or verbal, shall be deemed.to be merged herein and that no other changes in or additions to this agreement shall be recognized unless made in writing and signed by both parties, and that this agreement is not binding upon Hartman Elevator Corporation until approved by one of its executive officers at Chicago, Ill.

Respectfully submitted,

HARTMAN ELEVATOR CORPORATION

By _____

Approved _____

Date _____

ACCEPTANCE IN DUPLICATE

Date _____

Firm Name _____

By _____ Title _____

## Contract Prices and Terms

Service contracts for elevators are usually for one, three, or five years. The price quoted in a proposal, which when signed becomes the contract agreement, is firm for the duration of the contract. If a service firm bids too low and is unable to earn a satisfactory profit from the account, legally it must still honor the contract for the specified period.

Most elevator service contracts provide for automatic "price adjustment" in the monthly fee at the end of each 12-month period. The price adjustments are escalator clauses (see Exhibit 1) for increases in material and labor. These escalator cost increases are passed on to the customer in the form of a higher monthly service fee. Both supplier and customer are legally bound to the escalator clauses and pricing terms detailed in the signed agreement. In some instances, especially with larger customers, there is occasionally a renegotiation of the terms and escalators in the existing contract.

## Service People

The major cost of inspecting and repairing an elevator is the labor cost of the service person. For most service agreements, the labor is 70 to 80 percent of the total cost of the annual contract. The remaining 20 to 30 percent of the cost is for parts and materials. There are wide variations in the cost of skilled technicians across the United States. A highly skilled master elevator repair person in San Francisco is billed at $27 an hour, $21.70 an hour in Buffalo, and $9 an hour in a small North Carolina town. A technician's helper in San Francisco is paid more than a master technician in North Carolina. As new elevators become less electromechanical and more electronic, the repairperson will be a highly skilled electronic technician. Hartman has repairpeople on an incentive system to locate new elevator accounts that are having service problems. The service person has a lot of continuous contact with customers. His or her performance is seen as having a strong impact on how satisfied the customer is. Service people are also the first to know when a customer is going to cancel or put the business out for serious bidding. Nationwide, Hartman has approximately 610 service personnel.

## Service Network

Hartman has 96 service centers in the United States. Each is a separate profit center. In larger cities like Houston, there might be two or three service centers. Each service center has from 4 to 15 service people who make inspections and repairs at each service account. All the service centers carry an inventory of parts for the more common items. In large cities like Philadelphia, a service center will have $100,000 or more in parts inventory. The average Hartman service center has from $30,000 to $40,000 in repair parts. Nationwide, Hartman has over $4 million in parts inventory at all the service centers. Parts are frequently shipped between service centers to meet customers' needs. The parts of the major manufacturers are often not interchangeable. Parts "pirates" make many of the short life and higher margin aftermarket replacement parts. Independent elevator service firms can buy replacement parts from the producer's local service centers or from the pirates.

## National Service Training Center

Hartman maintains the most extensive service training center of any competitor at its corporate headquarters in Chicago. The training center has model elevators to teach employees how to repair "foreign" or non-Hartman models. The company's training center is a major selling tool. It allows potential customers to see how strongly safety factors are emphasized and how extensively service people are trained in troubleshooting. All competitive manufacturers' manuals and service instructions are kept in a guarded, brick-lined, fireproof room. Service personnel are trained from all these manuals. Copies of the manuals are also shipped to branch service centers if they obtain a contract on a model for which they do not have the technical repair information.

## Traffic Studies

Service personnel are taught to conduct elevator traffic studies at the training center. A traffic study is a procedure using electronic equipment to study passenger patterns and elevator performance. A one- to two-week traffic analysis can help determine if more or less elevator capacity is needed, how long people wait for elevators, and travel times. The analysis helps tell the owner how well the existing elevators are serving the needs of building occupants. The smaller independent service firms do not do traffic studies.

## Service Salespeople

Hartman has approximately 125 salespeople in the United States. They report to 16 regional managers, who in turn report to a national sales manager in Chicago. The salespeople are paid on a straight salary plus bonus basis. The bonus is not calibrated to a yearly sales volume. Rather, the annual performance review for each person considers the number of new accounts signed and the duration of each service contract. Also important in the evaluation is the number of canceled accounts in each sales territory. The number of conversions from annual to 3- to 5-year periods is also considered in the salesperson's annual performance review.

## The Buffalo Sales-Service Office

The Buffalo, New York, service center has two salespeople, eight servicepeople, and a secretary-bookkeeper. The annual sales volume of the branch was about $1 million in 1982 in service contracts. In actual amount of service provided, the branch reached a peak in 1978 and has since reduced its service staff from 11 to 8 technicians. Escalator price adjustments and new contracts have kept the billed dollar volume nearly flat for the last three years. The Buffalo office covers a radius of approximately 75 miles north to the Canadian border, east toward Rochester, and west and south to the Pennsylvania state line.

The Buffalo area has experienced a continuous decline for the last decade, with very little new construction requiring elevators. By 1983 many existing establishments with elevators in place were shrinking or closing down. High unemployment of skilled younger workers was chronic. Many unemployed and aggressive skilled technicians started independent elevator repair firms in the Buffalo metropolitan area. In 1983 there were 14 elevator service firms listed in the Buffalo Yellow Pages. This included four of the major elevator manufacturers' service centers. Nearby Rochester, though slightly smaller in population than Buffalo, had only seven elevator firms. Three were major national producers and four were independents. With the combined effects of a declining commercial base and many small competitors in the Buffalo market, the competition was intense. The Hartman sales manager in Buffalo, Peter Van Dyke, described the competition as "cutthroat." He also said: "The competitive situation in Buffalo makes it difficult to retain customers and even more difficult to obtain replacement accounts for the lost business."

## The Bethlehem Steel Account

In 1968, Hartman finished installing four new elevators in the offices of Bethlehem Steel's Lackawanna works near Buffalo. For the next 15 years, the purchasing department at the Lackawanna works renewed the five-year service agreement with Hartman. The Bethlehem account was one of the Buffalo office's larger accounts. Most of the office's service contracts were $1,000 to $2,000 per month. The long-time Bethlehem account was contracted at $2,600 per month.

In 1982 the Bethlehem Corporation had a large loss. The high-cost Lackawanna works had been in the red for the past few years. In an attempt to reduce costs, the Lackawanna senior purchasing officer called Peter Van Dyke and said: "Peter, we have to put this elevator contract out to bid. I've got strict orders from the corporate purchasing office in Bethlehem, Pa., to ask for bid proposals for all our elevator service contracts. Hartman has always given us A-1 service, but this is a new corporate policy."

Peter Van Dyke had already submitted Hartman's bid, as shown in Exhibit 2. After visiting with his long-time purchasing agent friend at the Lackawanna works, he learned that Bethlehem had already had two bids from smaller independent service firms, as shown in Exhibit 2. The purchasing agent advised Van Dyke that if Hartman's bid was not close to or lower than the other two, Hartman would probably not get the contract.

| EXHIBIT 2 | COMPETITIVE BIDS AT BETHLEHEM* | | | |
|---|---|---|---|---|
| | *Per Month* | *Annual* | *Three-Year* | *Five-Year* |
| Hartman† | $2,600 | $31,200 | $93,600 | $156,000 |
| Independent A | 2,010 | 24,120 | 72,360 | 120,600 |
| Independent B | 1,820 | 21,840 | 65,620 | 109,200 |

*All bids had escalator clauses for local labor and material increases each year.
†Existing five-year contract renewable at Bethlehem Steel.

Van Dyke knew that the Hartman Elevator corporate office in Chicago bought most of its yearly steel requirements for elevators from Bethlehem's various mills. Peter called the metals purchasing manager at the corporate office and learned that Hartman bought approximately 150,000 tons of sheet and bar steel from Bethlehem every year. The second source, U.S. Steel, supplied only about 15 percent of Hartman's annual metal requirements. Van Dyke then visited with the purchasing agent in Lackawanna to explain the fact that Hartman was a major Bethlehem customer and always provided good elevator service. He also cautioned the purchasing agent about the possible poor service and repair work of the smaller independents. The purchasing agent replied: "Peter, we've done business together for the last 15 years. Our kids all grew up together, and you're a good friend. But I've already sent everything about the elevator contract to our corporate purchasing people down in Bethlehem, Pa. They will make a final decision on a vendor in the next month, and I believe they will make it solely on the basis of price."

Van Dyke went back to the office and called his regional manager, Bob Pease, in Montclair, New Jersey, to explain the problem. Bob Pease said: "I was aware of the problem when I worked in your Buffalo office. We have similar problems in other areas of the northeastern United States. I'll back you up in any attempt to keep the account. Since you are in need of a bid price that is far below our corporate target, it will require approval from corporate in Chicago before you can submit a revised bid proposal. Also, since corporate does buy an awful lot of steel from Bethlehem every year, we need to leverage that pressure point. The quickest and best way to solve this is to call Bob Lowe, our president, and have him apply some pressure and help you submit a competitive bid." Van Dyke immediately put in a call to the president, Bob Lowe. Two days later, Lowe returned the call.

VAN DYKE:  Bob Pease said I should call you for help. We have a real problem in Buffalo. If we don't submit a more competitive price on a five-year piece of elevator service business at Bethlehem Steel in Lackawanna, we'll lose $156,000 worth of business. The corporate purchasing agent in Pennsylvania put it out to competitive bid after 15 years of satisfied service from us. Our past price is now way out of line with the two independent bids. Furthermore, as you know, our corporation buys 150,000 tons of steel from Bethlehem's mills every year. Bob Pease thought maybe you could call the corporate P.A. at Bethlehem and help us.

LOWE:  How much lower are the competitive bids?

VAN DYKE:  One is 30 percent below us, and the other is more than 25 percent below ours.

LOWE:  If we do a quality job and sell our excellent service capabilities and technical know-how, we don't have to go around cutting prices and getting locked into unprofitable business.

VAN DYKE:  But this is not the Chicago or Dallas market. This situation is more competitive. If you saw the lost business report last quarter on the largest hospital in Buffalo, you would see we just are not competitive.

LOWE:        What happened at that large hospital account?

VAN DYKE:    Our long-time sponsor, the hospital purchasing agent, was no longer involved with the decision. The new hospital administrator there was very removed from the good service we provide, and he just bought on the basis of price and kicked us out. All the hospitals here are really looking at their costs. Our $5,300 monthly charge for all the elevators in that hospital was far above the $4,100 a month they went with. They signed a three-year contract for $147,000. Our price was $190,800. Even though the hospital P.A. was on our side in a lukewarm way, the hospital director and board, who had to approve the appropriation, went with the cheapest bid.

LOWE:        Sounds to me like the purchasing decision in the hospital and now at the Bethlehem situation is moving up in the organization. Maybe we have to tell our quality story higher up in the organization.

VAN DYKE:    When it moves to that level, they just buy on initial price. They don't care about our rapid response time, technical testing, or Chicago training center.

LOWE:        I'll call the corporate P.A. at Bethlehem, Pennsylvania.

Lowe then called the corporate purchasing agent at Bethlehem Steel. Lowe mentioned that Hartman was a large customer of Bethlehem and bought direct from their mills. The Bethlehem purchasing agent said, "We are not unhappy with your service, but we are just making every kind of cost reduction that we possibly can. We will make our decision in the next three to four weeks on the best value, aside from any consequences to our sales department. I'm responsible for purchasing of maintenance and repair items. Sales is another department, and I don't get evaluated on sales dollars." Lowe then called Van Dyke in Buffalo:

LOWE:        I don't think that P.A. was moved at all. In the short run we might lose the account. But I bet if they get shoddy service and have elevator shutdowns, they will come back to us in the longer term. Furthermore, I wonder how much quality elevator service business we can have with these steel firms. Some are dinosaurs looking at a tar pit. We are buying more and more foreign-source steel every year.

VAN DYKE:    But we're losing a lot of business because of price. We have a lot of account turnover that results in a high cancellation rate. Last year this Northeastern region had a 38 percent cancellation rate.

LOWE:        Yes, and a lot of those were marginal contracts. We don't want another situation like what happened at West Virginia University. They kept wanting to renegotiate the contract every year to where the margin shrunk to peanuts. We have a corporate minimum gross margin guideline of 35 percent, and we will not change that except in very special situations. We must enforce that discipline. If we give anyone a special price deal, it may take years, if ever, to get it to an acceptable profit level.

VAN DYKE: This Buffalo situation is very special. When we are 10 to 12 percent above the independents, we can still get the business. I can then compete with our quality, that we've been in business a long time compared to the fly-by-night independents. In that price range differential, our national training center, and traffic analysis also help bring in and retain customers. But when we are 20 to 30 percent more than a competitor, they'll give us the shaft every time. At worst, I need a three- to five-year fixed price contract with no escalators and a going-in price that is 15 percent above the lowest bidder. We'll renegotiate later on to get the margin up. We should also give them a little discount if they sign a three- or five-year contract.

LOWE: It's Friday morning now, and I have a meeting the rest of the day about the Japanese company Fujitec, which is building a parts manufacturing facility in a vacant tire factory in Akron, Ohio. Let me think about this Bethlehem bidding situation and get back to you at the first of next week.

# CASE

# 10

# Pape Bros., Inc.

## Introducing a New Hydraulic Log Loader

## INTRODUCING A NEW HYDRAULIC LOG LOADER

"He's gone too far this time!" barked Bill Gould, startling his secretary, who was just setting a cup of coffee on his desk. Bill Gould, general sales manager at Pape Bros., Inc., was referring to the November 1973 sales report he was reading and specifically to actions taken by salesman Bob Moore.

## THE COMPANY

Pape was a medium-sized heavy equipment dealer with headquarters in Eugene, Oregon, and five other retail outlets located in Oregon at Coos Bay, Klamath Falls, Medford, Redmond, and Roseburg. For the past 15 years, Pape had been the exclusive Caterpillar dealer throughout central and southern Oregon, offering Caterpillar equipment, warranty, and the well-known Caterpillar "Cat Plus" parts and service programs.

Pape had experienced good sales throughout 1973 with total sales expected to reach $40 million by year's end. Although 40 percent of company sales were to industrial end users in construction, earth moving, and materials handling, at least 60 percent were to end users in the lumber industry.

Most of the company's sales in the lumber industry had been to gypos (small contract loggers) and to lumber and plywood mills. The gypos used Caterpillar skidders and dozers for yarding (hauling logs from the cutting area to the "landing," or loading area) and for building roads. The mills used Caterpillar forklift trucks and wheel loaders for moving logs, lumber, and plywood in or around the mill.

Caterpillar Corporation, with sales of over $3 billion, offered a broad line of heavy diesel-powered equipment, yet offered only one product, the skidder, specifically designed for use in the timber industry. The timber industry, however, had been changing rapidly since World War II, and the demand for more specialized equipment had hurt Pape sales in the forest industries, due to the fact that Caterpillar did not, and most probably would not, get into this specialized market. It was too small to interest a major international corporation.

To compensate for Caterpillar's lack of interest in forest industry products, Pape had attempted to sell other brands of equipment to complement the Caterpillar line in the logging and wood products manufacturing markets. Unfortunately, Pape had found that the good major brands of equipment had already been taken by other distributors, and the equipment that was available to Pape was usually unsuitable.

The absence of a Caterpillar hydraulic log loader was an example of the problem that plagued Pape at the time.

# HYDRAULIC LOG LOADERS

After logs were yarded to a landing and piled, they were placed on trucks by some type of loading equipment. In the past, almost all logs had been loaded by large mechanical-cable loaders. These loaders resembled a crane on a tractor carriage, with large grapples and a steel cable mechanism for opening, closing, raising, and lowering the grapples. In the past few years, these giants had begun to be replaced by smaller hydraulic units.

## Pros and Cons of Hydraulic Log Loaders

The hydraulic units offered several advantages over the mechanical cable loaders. First, all the hydraulic units were more positive and easier to maneuver than the cable loaders. The hydraulic loaders eliminated the swinging of the logs that occurred with cable units and slowed the loading time. This also made the hydraulic unit easier to learn to use, thus making loader operators easier to train and easier to find. The hydraulic unit was more maneuverable and often eliminated the need for a "second loader." A "second loader" was an individual who stood by the log truck and signaled the truck driver to pull forward or back up so that the logs could be lowered onto the truck in the proper manner. The hydraulic units could extend the boom and grapples forward and backward, thus eliminating the need for the truck to move and at the same time saving a logging outfit a "second loader's" wages.

The ability of the hydraulic loading unit to reach out and down had other cost-saving implications for a logging firm. The hydraulic units could creep along a logging road and pick up logs that had fallen near the road and within reach of the loader. These were very "cheap" logs to a logging firm, since the step of yarding was eliminated.

Two major disadvantages had slowed the entry of hydraulic loaders into the log loading field. The hydraulic units were not nearly as powerful as the mechanical-cable units and therefore not able to "pick" as big a log. The second disadvantage, at least in the minds of logging firms, was the possibility of a hydraulic failure due to a broken line in the hydraulic system. Logging was rough work, and loggers demanded tough equipment. Although most contractors could see the savings involved, they were also concerned by the enormous costs of loader breakdown.

## Important Trends

Two major trends seemed to point toward a growing market for hydraulic log loaders. The use of smaller logs and more emphasis on environmental protection were expected to increase demand for the smaller and more versatile hydraulic units. The hydraulic loaders were capable of handling logs with up to 6-foot diameters and required less landing space to operate. The hydraulic loaders were also being used extensively in thinning operations in managed forests.

## Barko

Gould knew that Pape needed to get into the hydraulic loader market, but he was not sure how to go about doing it. Pape had gotten a dealership for the Barko hydraulic log loader at the beginning of the year. Pape had soon realized that the Barko was too small and light for the larger trees in the West.

Sales of the Barko had been slow so far in 1973, with only four sold and no further sales expected that year. Each machine sold for $110,000. Pape figured after service and warranty work that it would make a before-tax profit of 2.5 percent. Reports from salespeople indicated that the Barko loader was not highly regarded by most logging firms, and for this reason Gould did not expect sales to increase for the Barko in the coming year.

# CATERPILLAR CONVERSIONS

Sitting in his office now, sipping coffee, Gould was contemplating the low sales of the Barko and what one of his best salespeople, Bob Moore, had done.

Moore was one of the 10 salespeople whose territory covered the West Lane and South Benton County areas. Moore had joined Pape right out of college and had proved an excellent salesman by quadrupling sales in his territory in less than a year. Besides his ability to sell, Moore had already impressed Gould in another way. Last year he had come up with the idea to convert Caterpillar's 992 Wheel-Loader to a wheel log loader capable of unloading a log truck at a mill in one pass. The conversion was accomplished by replacing the shovel bucket with large log forks built to specification by the Medford Corporation.

Moore had come upon the idea when a mill operator complained to him that Caterpillar produced no wheeled log loader. After checking with Jim Carter, service manager for Pape who had an engineering background, Moore found out that the conversion could be fairly easily accomplished. Moore had then actually forced Pape to go ahead with the conversion by selling four converted machines before they even existed. Gould had gone along with the idea, and the conversion had been successful; sales of the converted Caterpillar wheel loader had been growing steadily now for over a year.

## The 235 Hydraulic Excavator

What concerned Gould now, however, was the fact that Moore had sold Skirvin & Sons (a logging firm in Philomath, Oregon) a Caterpillar 235 Hydraulic Excavator converted to a hydraulic log loader. This piece of equipment did not exist, and Gould had strong doubts about whether the conversion would be possible.

Moore had come on the excavator conversion in response to seeing four hydraulic log loaders delivered into his sales territory during the year. Currently five hydraulic loaders, including the Barko, were produced in the East and Midwest and sold in Oregon. Within Pape's Caterpillar dealership, Lorane hyraulic log loaders currently sold to 60 percent of the market. The Lorane loaders were sold by Skagit Corporation in Eugene, which specialized in new and used logging equipment. Not only was Skagit an aggressive dealership, but its Lorane loader had proved to be a solid and dependable machine. The other 40 percent of the hydraulic loader market was fairly evenly divided among the Barko, the American, the P&H, and the Bucyrus-Eric loaders.

Although conversion of the 992 wheel loader to a log loader had been a relatively straightforward mating of log forks to Caterpillar hydraulics, conversion of the 235 Excavator to a log loader had proved to be much more complicated and costly. One difficulty immediately apparent was the problem of what to do with the backhoe portion of the excavator. This section would be replaced by a long, specially manufactured logging boom and grapples. Caterpillar had sold Pape the 992 wheel loader without the standard bucket, but the 235 excavator had to be purchased complete with backhoe. The backhoe, it was hoped, could be sold to an outside buyer or else as a package along with the log loader. There was also a good chance that if Pape began ordering quite a few 235s for conversion, Caterpillar would come around and sell the machine without the backhoe.

The loading of logs with the converted excavator would call for different balance characteristics than those of the excavator. Extra pounds of fabricated counterweights would need to be added to the existing 12,000-pound weight that came standard on each Caterpillar 235 hydraulic excavator. The excavator would also need to have guarding added to protect the operator and the fuel and hydraulic tanks from the possibility of injury or damage if a log was dropped during loading. The boom and grapple for the loader could be manufactured by Pierce Corporation or Young Iron Works. The Pierce setup was lower in cost than the Young boom and grapple, yet did not offer the maneuverability and reach available with Young's product.

## Cost Estimates for Conversion

Cost estimates for the 235 conversion were drawn up by Jim Carter:

| | |
|---|---|
| Cost of Caterpillar 235 hydraulic excavator (less backhoe) | $ 85,000 |
| Young boom and grapples | 8,333 |
| Extra weight | 1,000 |
| Extra guarding | 4,000 |
| Labor and other conversion expenses | 10,000 |
| Variable cost per loader with Young setup | $108,333 |

Cost of the machine with the Pierce boom and grapple was $3,000 less per machine.

Allocation of overhead to this conversion process was estimated at $250 a day, which was arrived at by assuming 5 percent of the service department's fixed daily overhead of $5,000 a day. The service department would carry out the conversion of the excavator as it currently did with the 992 wheel loader conversion. Converting the 235 was expected to take eight days' work on each machine, working on only one machine at a time. Although some parts and materials were expected to increase in cost over the coming year, Jim Carter felt these costs would be mostly offset by a decrease in labor and conversion expenses as the process became more familiar. If Pape decided to go ahead with the conversion, it would drop the Barko line and concentrate on the Caterpillar-based hydraulic loader exclusively.

### Conversion Problems

The idea of converting the Caterpillar 235 to a hydraulic log loader had first been considered three months earlier, and since that time Moore and Carter had been busy trying to work out the details. Unfortunately, Pape had only a smaller Caterpillar 225 hydraulic excavator available to work with. Using this converted 225 on an alder logging operation at the coast near Reedsport, the men had experienced hydraulic pressure difficulties and generally poor performance in lifting and loading these small logs. Gould had spoken with Carter just last week, and the conversation had gone like this:

GOULD:    How are you and Bob coming along with the conversion, Jim?

CARTER:   Well, I think we've gotten the bugs out of the hydraulics system and the weighting and guard specifications are all worked out too.

GOULD:    Which boom and grapples do you feel we should go with?

CARTER:   The Young setup is by far the better performer. It may raise the price some to go with Young, but I think we'll have a better machine and a better seller. Bob Moore claims that Lorane loader owners sure wish they had the Young boom and grapples on their machines.

GOULD:    Is the conversion going to work, Jim, or do you know yet?

CARTER:   I'll be honest with you, Bill, I'm not sure yet. Bob Moore is fairly convinced we have it whipped, and he may be right. The 235 is a lot more machine than the 225, and it should pick a 6-foot diameter log. You know as well as I do, Bill, that if it does handle that size log, we've got a winner. Right now I would say we have a 50-50 chance of the machine working like it should.

## SALE OF A HYDRAULIC LOG LOADER ──────────────

Now Gould was looking at the sales order for a Pape 235 hydraulic log loader, which Moore had submitted along with his monthly sales report. Moore had quoted Skirvin &

Sons a price of $120,000, and had promised the full six-month Caterpillar warranty. This warranty basically amounted to Pape buying back the machine if Skirvin were not satisfied. If the machine did not perform correctly and Pape were forced to buy it back, Pape could stand to lose up to $17,000 on the transaction. On the other hand, Moore had also submitted an impressive sales forecast for the loader; if it did work, it could mean big sales for Pape.

## Market Potential for the Pape Hydraulic Loader

The sales forecast was a compilation of the 10 territory salespeople's opinions concerning future sales of the new loader with the Young boom and grapples. All salespeople agreed with Moore that the potential sales of the loader were very good. They felt they could sell four log loaders in each territory the next year, but they felt that the price of the loader would directly affect the number of sales they could make. Every salesperson felt sure he or she could sell to those four buyers if the price of the Pape loader were as low as $100,000. This would mean that the Pape loader would be priced $10,000 below the price of the Barko. At the price of the Barko, each salesperson believed he could sell at least two machines, or half the hydraulic loader market. At $120,000 per loader, which was the price of the Lorane, the estimated sales per territory had dropped to one Pape loader. Above this price, only a handful of salespeople could realistically predict a sale. Four salespeople still felt they could sell one machine at a top figure of $135,000. In fact, one salesman strongly believed that with a Young setup and a Caterpillar warranty, he could sell one Pape loader in his territory for as high as $150,000. He admitted it would be hard work to get that price, but he felt there were customers who would pay a healthy premium for Caterpillar quality and service. "Hell," he said, "when you sell the Cadillac of heavy equipment, you can ask a Cadillac price." A summary of price and expected sales is shown below.

| Price of Loader | Expected Sales |
|---|---|
| $100,000 | 40 |
| 110,000 | 20 |
| 120,000 | 10 |
| 135,000 | 4 |
| 150,000 | 1 |

## Graph Results

From this information, Moore had plotted the five points on graph paper and had immediately noticed that a smooth curve would connect the points (Exhibit 1). From this curve, he had composed this more complete table:

| Price of Loader | Expected Sales |
|---|---|
| $100,000 | 40 |
| 105,000 | 28 |
| 110,000 | 20 |
| 115,000 | 14 |
| 120,000 | 10 |
| 125,000 | 7 |
| 130,000 | 5 |
| 135,000 | 4 |
| 140,000 | 3 |
| 150,000 | 1 |

**EXHIBIT 1**

## MARKET POTENTIAL
### Pape Hydraulic Loader (Young boom and grapples)

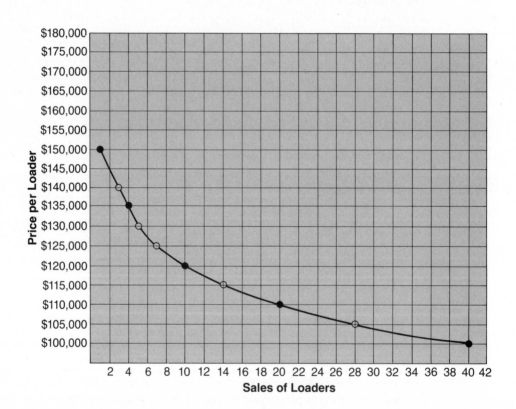

Looking at these figures, and the graph in front of him, Gould wondered whether it was time for him to shorten the reins on his salespeople. Even though Pape company policy had always allowed salespeople a free hand in managing territory sales, Gould pondered just how wise this policy was. For example, Moore was a super salesman, and his wheel loader conversion had proved both timely and profitable; even so, he was beginning to doubt whether this idea would be successful. He also was uncertain about how valid the sales forecast was because it was based solely on salespeople's opinions. He wondered whether the shape of the curve he had in front of him was realistic. He was thinking that this type of activity might be better carried out by the Pape promotion department.

Gould had the sales order in front of him. He could sign it and send it along or disapprove it and stop things before they got too far along. He wondered if there were some way he could untangle things and base a course of action on some type of decision tree that would incorporate the probability of the conversion being successful. If he stopped the project now, Pape was certain to lose $10,000, which Carter and Moore had sunk so far into investigating the feasibility of the conversion. Another question he knew he must deal with was the price Moore had given Skirvin & Sons. Was this a price Pape could live with for future sales? It seemed to him that some particular price might optimize profits from loader sales. If this were so, Pape would most certainly not want to price below this figure, or would it? Finally, Gould wondered whether Pape should stay with standard Caterpillar products and forget any modifications altogether.

# S. C. Johnson and Son, Ltd.

## Marketing Direct and with Distributors

Four months ago, in November 1980, George Styan had been appointed division manager of INNOCHEM, at S. C. Johnson and Son, Limited (SCJ),[1] a Canadian subsidiary of S. C. Johnson & Son, Inc. INNOCHEM's sole product line consisted of industrial cleaning chemicals for use by business, institutions, and government. George was concerned by the division's poor market share, particularly in Montreal and Toronto. Together, these two cities represented approximately 35 percent of Canadian demand for industrial cleaning chemicals, but less than 10 percent of INNOCHEM sales. It appeared that SCJ distributors could not match the aggressive discounting practiced by direct selling manufacturers in metropolitan markets.

Recently, George had received a rebate proposal from his staff designed to increase the distributor's ability to cut end-user prices by "sharing" part of the total margin with SCJ when competitive conditions demanded discounts of 30 percent or more off the list price to end users. George had to decide if the rebate plan was the best way to penetrate price-sensitive markets. Moreover, he wondered about the plan's ultimate impact on divisional profit performance. George had to develop an implementation plan for the rebate plan, or draft an alternative proposal to unveil at the 1981 Distributors' Annual Spring Convention, three weeks away.

## THE CANADIAN MARKET FOR INDUSTRIAL CLEANING CHEMICALS

In 1980, the Canadian market for industrial cleaning chemicals was approximately $100 million at end-user prices. Growth was stable at an overall rate of approximately 3 percent per year.

[1]Popularly known as "Canadian Johnson Wax."
Copyright © 1982, The University of Western Ontario, by Professor Roger More.

"Industrial cleaning chemicals" included all chemical products designed to clean, disinfect, sanitize or protect industrial, commercial, and institutional buildings and equipment. The label was broadly applied to general purpose cleaners, floor maintenance products (strippers, sealers, finishes, and detergents), carpet cleaners and deodorizers, disinfectants, air fresheners, and a host of specialty chemicals such as insecticides, pesticides, drain cleaners, oven cleansers, and sweeping compounds.

Industrial cleaning chemicals were distinct from equivalent consumer products typically sold through grocery stores. Heavy-duty industrial products were packaged in larger containers and bulk and marketed directly by the cleaning chemical manufacturers or sold through distributors to a variety of end users. Exhibit 1 includes market segmentation by primary end-user categories, including janitorial service contractors and the in-house maintenance departments of government, institutions, and companies.

## Building Maintenance Contractors

In Canada, maintenance contractors purchased 17 percent of the industrial cleaning chemicals sold during 1980 (end-user price). The segment was growing at approximately 10 to 15 percent a year, chiefly at the expense of other end-user categories. *Canadian Business* reported: "Contract cleaners have made sweeping inroads into the traditional preserve of in-house janitorial staffs, selling themselves on the strength of cost efficiency. . . ."[2] Maintenance contract billings reached an estimated $1 billion in 1980.

Frequently, demand for building maintenance services was highly price sensitive, and since barriers to entry were low (small capitalization, simple technology), competition squeezed contractor gross margins below 6 percent (before tax). Variable cost control was a matter of survival, and only products bringing compensatory labor savings could command a premium price in this segment of the cleaning chemical market.

A handful of contract cleaners did specialize in higher-margin services to prestige office complexes, luxury apartments, art museums, and other "quality-conscious" customers. However, even contractors serving this select clientele did not necessarily buy premium cleaning supplies.

## In-House Maintenance Departments

GOVERNMENT.   In 1980, cleaning chemical sales to various government offices (federal, provincial, and local) approached $2 million. Typically, a government body solicited bids from appropriate sources by formally advertising for quotations for given quantities of particular cleaning chemicals. Although bid requests often named specific brands, suppliers were permitted to offer "equivalent substitutes." Separate competitions were held for each item and normally covered 12 months' supply, with provision for delivery "as required." Contracts were frequently awarded solely on the basis of price.

[2]"Contract Cleaners Want to Whisk Away Ring-Around-the-Office," *Canadian Business*, 1981, 22.

EXHIBIT
1

## SEGMENTATION OF THE CANADIAN MARKET FOR INDUSTRIAL CLEANING CHEMICALS

### By End User Category

| End User Category | Percentage of Total Canadian Market for Industrial Cleaning Chemicals (end user value) |
|---|---|
| Retail outlets | 25% |
| Contractors | 17 |
| Hospitals | 15 |
| Industrial and office | 13 |
| Schools, colleges | 8 |
| Hotels, motels | 6 |
| Nursing homes | 5 |
| Recreation | 3 |
| Government | 3 |
| Fast food | 2 |
| Full-service restaurants | 2 |
| All others | 1 |
| Total | 100% = $95 million |

### By Product Category

| Product Category | Percentage of Total Canadian Market for Industrial Cleaning Chemicals |
|---|---|
| Floor care products | 40% |
| General purpose cleaners | 16 |
| Disinfectants | 12 |
| Carpet care products | 8 |
| Odor control products | 5 |
| Glass cleaners | 4 |
| All others | 15 |
| Total | 100% = $95 million |

INSTITUTIONS.   Like government bodies, most institutions were price sensitive owing to restrictive budgets and limited ability to "pass on" expenses to users. Educational institutions and hospitals were the largest consumers of cleaning chemicals in this segment. School boards used an open bid system patterned on the government model. Heavy sales time requirements and demands for frequent delivery of small shipments to as many as 100 locations were characteristic.

Colleges and universities tended to be operated somewhat differently. Dan Stalport, one of the purchasing agents responsible for maintenance supplies at The University of Western Ontario, offered the following comments:

> Sales reps come to UWO year 'round. If one of us (in the buying group) talks to a salesman who seems to have something to say – say, a labor-saving feature – we get a sample and test it. . . . Testing can take up to a year. Floor covering, for example, has to be exposed to seasonal changes in weather and traffic.
>
> If we're having problems with a particular item, we'll compare the performance and price of three or four competitors. There are usually plenty of products that do the job. Basically, we want value – acceptable performance at the lowest available price.

Hospitals accounted for 15 percent of cleaning chemical sales. Procurement policies at University Hospital (UH), a medium-sized (450-bed) facility in London, Ontario, were typical. UH distinguished between "critical" and "noncritical" products. Critical cleaning chemicals (i.e., those significantly affecting patient health, such as phenolic germicide), could be bought only on approval of the staff microbiologist, who tested the "kill factor." This measure of effectiveness was regularly retested, and any downgrading of product performance could void a supplier's contract. In contrast, noncritical supplies, such as general purpose cleaners, floor finishes, and the like, were the exclusive province of Bob Chandler, purchasing agent attached to the Housekeeping Department. Bob explained that performance of noncritical cleaning chemicals was informally judged and monitored by the housekeeping staff:

> Just last year, for example, the cleaners found the floor polish was streaking badly. We [the Housekeeping Department] tested and compared five or six brands – all in the ballpark pricewise – and chose the best.

BUSINESS. The corporate segment was highly diverse, embracing both service and manufacturing industries. Large-volume users tended to be price sensitive, particularly when profits were low. Often, however, cleaning products represented such a small percentage of the total operating budget that the cost of searching for the lowest-cost supplier would be expected to exceed any realizable saving. Under such conditions, the typical industrial customer sought efficiencies in the purchasing process itself; for example, by dealing with the supplier offering the broadest mix of janitorial products (chemical, paper supplies, equipment, etc.). Guy Breton, purchasing agent for Securitech, a Montreal-based security systems manufacturer, commented on the time-economies of "one-stop shopping."

> With cleaning chemicals, it simply isn't worth the trouble to shop around and stage elaborate product performance tests . . . I buy all our chemicals, brushes, dusters, towelling – the works – from one or two suppliers. . . . buying reputable brands from familiar suppliers saves hassles – backorders are rare and Maintenance seldom complains.

# DISTRIBUTION CHANNELS FOR INDUSTRIAL CLEANING CHEMICALS

The Canadian market for industrial cleaning chemicals was supplied through three main channels, each characterized by a distinctive set of strengths and weaknesses:

1. Distributor sales of national brands.
2. Distributor sales of private label products.
3. Direct sale by manufacturers.

   Direct sellers held a 61 percent share of the Canadian market for industrial cleaning chemicals, while the distributors of national brands and private label products held shares of 25 and 14 percent, respectively. Relative market shares varied geographically, however. In Montreal and Toronto, for example, the direct marketers' share rose to 70 percent and private labelers' to 18 percent, reducing the national brand share to 12 percent. The pattern, shown in Exhibit 2, reflected an interplay of two areas of channel differentiation: discount capability at the end-user level, and the cost of serving distant, geographically dispersed customers.

## Distributor Sales of National-Brand Cleaning Chemicals ,

National-brand manufacturers, such as S. C. Johnson and Son, Airkem, and National Labs, produced a relatively limited range of "high-quality" janitorial products, including many special purpose formulations of narrow market interest. Incomplete product range,

---

| EXHIBIT 2 | EFFECT OF GEOGRAPHY ON MARKET SHARE OF DIFFERENT DISTRIBUTION CHANNELS | | |
|---|---|---|---|

| Supplier Type | Share Nationwide | Share in Montreal and Toronto |
|---|---|---|
| Direct marketers | 61%* | 70% |
| Private-label distributors | 14 | 18 |
| National-brands distributors | 25† | 12 |

| *Dustbane | 17% |
|---|---|
| G. H. Wood | 13 |
| All others | 31 |
| Total | 61% |

| †SCJ | 8% |
|---|---|
| N/L | 4 |
| Airkem | 3 |
| All others | 10 |
| Total | 25% |

combined with shortage of manpower and limited warehousing, made direct distribution not feasible in most cases. Normally, a national brand company would negotiate with distributors that handled a broad array of complementary products (equipment, tools, and supplies) by different manufacturers. "Bundling" of goods brought the distributors' cost efficiencies in selling, warehousing, and delivery by spreading fixed costs over a large sales volume. Distributors were therefore better able to absorb the costs of after-hour emergency service, frequent routine sales and service calls to many potential buyers, and shipments of small quantities of cleaning chemicals to multiple destinations. As a rule, the greater the geographic dispersion of customers, and the smaller the average order, the greater the relative economies of distributor marketing.

Comparatively high gross margins (approximately 50 percent of wholesale price) enabled national-brand manufacturers to offer distributors strong marketing support and sales training along with liberal terms of payment and freight plus low minimum order requirements. Distributors readily agreed to handle national-brand chemicals, and in metropolitan markets, each brand was sold through several distributors. By the same token, most distributors carried several directly competitive product lines. George suspected that some distributor salesmen only used national brands to "lead" with and tended to offer private labels whenever a customer proved price sensitive, or a competitor handled the same national brand(s). Using an industry rule of thumb, George estimated that most distributors needed at least 20 percent gross margin on retail sales to cover their salesmen's commission of 10 percent on retail sales, plus delivery and inventory expenses.

## Distributor Sales of Private-Label Cleaning Chemicals

Direct selling manufacturers were dominating urban markets by aggressively discounting end-user prices—sometimes below the wholesale price national-brand manufacturers charged their distributors. To compete against the direct seller, increasing numbers of distributors were adding low-cost private-label cleaning chemicals to their product lines. Private labeling also helped differentiate a particular distributor from others carrying the same national brand(s).

Sizable minimum order requirements restricted the private-label strategy to the largest distributors. Private-label manufacturers produced to order, formulating to meet low prices specified by distributors. The relatively narrow margins (30 to 35 percent of wholesale price) associated with private-label manufacture precluded the extensive marketing and sales support national-brand manufacturers characteristically provided to distributors. Private-label producers pared their expenses further by requiring distributors to bear the cost of inventory and accept rigid terms of payment as well as delivery (net 30 days, FOB plant).

In addition to absorbing selling expenses normally assumed by the manufacturer, distributors paid their salesmen higher commission on private-label sales (15 percent of resale) than national brands (10 percent of resale). However, the incremental administration and selling expenses associated with private-label business were more than offset by the differential savings on private-label wholesale goods. By pricing private-label chemicals at competitive parity with national brands, the distributor could enjoy approximately a 50 percent gross margin at resale list, while preserving considerable resale discount capability.

Private-label products were seldom sold outside the metropolitan areas where most were manufactured. First, the high costs of moving bulky, low-value freight diminished the relative cost advantage of private-label chemicals. Second, generally speaking, it was only in metro areas where distributors dealt in volumes great enough to satisfy the private labeler's minimum order requirement. Finally, outside the city distributors were less likely to be in direct local competition with others handling the same national brand, reducing the value of the private label as a source of supplier differentiation.

For some very large distributors, backward integration into chemical production was a logical extension of the private labeling strategy. Recently, several distributors had become direct marketers through acquisition of captive manufacturers.

## Direct Sale by Manufacturers of Industrial Cleaning Chemicals

Manufacturers dealing directly with the end user increased their gross margins to 60 to 70 percent of retail list price. Greater margins increased their ability to discount end-user price—a distinct advantage in the price-competitive urban marketplace. Overall, direct marketers averaged a gross margin of 50 percent.

Many manufacturers of industrial cleaning chemicals attempted some direct selling, but relatively few relied on this channel exclusively. Satisfactory adoption of a full-time direct selling strategy required the manufacturer to match distributors' sales and delivery capabilities without sacrificing overall profitability. These conflicting demands had been resolved successfully by two types of company, large-scale powder chemical manufacturers and full-line janitorial products manufacturers.

LARGE-SCALE POWDER CHEMICAL MANUFACTURERS.   Economies of large-scale production plus experience in the capital-intensive manufacture of powder chemicals enabled a few established firms, such as Diversey-Wyandotte, to dominate the market for powder warewash and vehicle cleansers. Selling through distributors offered these producers few advantages. Direct selling expense was almost entirely commission (i.e., variable). Moreover, powder concentrates were characterized by comparatively high value-to-bulk ratios, and so could absorb delivery costs even where demand was geographically dispersed. Thus, any marginal benefits from using middlemen were more than offset by the higher margins (and associated discount capability) possible through direct distribution. Among these firms, competition was not limited to price. The provision of dispensing and metering equipment was important, as was 24-hour servicing.

FULL-LINE JANITORIAL PRODUCTS MANUFACTURERS.   These manufacturers offered a complete range of maintenance products, including paper supplies, janitorial chemicals, tools, and mechanical equipment. Although high margins greatly enhanced retail price flexibility, overall profitability depended on securing a balance of high- and low-margin business, as well as controlling selling and distribution expenses. This was accomplished in several ways, including:

Centering on market areas of concentrated demand to minimize costs of warehousing, sales travel, and the like.

Increasing average order size either by adding product lines which could be sold to existing customers, or by seeking new large-volume customers.

Tying sales commission to profitability to motivate sales personnel to sell volume, without unnecessary discounting of end-user price.

Direct marketers of maintenance products varied in scale from established nationwide companies to hundreds of regional operators. The two largest direct marketers, G. H. Wood and Dustbane, together supplied almost a third of Canadian demand for industrial cleaning chemicals.

# S. C. JOHNSON AND SON, LTD.

S. C. Johnson and Son, Ltd. (SCJ) was one of 42 foreign subsidiaries owned by the U.S.-based multinational, S. C. Johnson and Son, Inc. It was ranked globally as one of the largest privately held companies. SCJ contributed substantially to worldwide sales and profits and was based in Brantford, Ontario, close to the Canadian urban markets of Hamilton, Kitchener, Toronto, London, and Niagara Falls. About 300 people worked at the head office and plant; another 100 were employed in field sales.

## INNOCHEM Division

INNOCHEM (Innovative Chemicals for Professional Use) was a special division established to serve corporate, institutional, and government customers of SCJ. The division manufactured an extensive line of industrial cleaning chemicals, including general purpose cleansers, waxes, polishes, and disinfectants, plus a number of specialty products of limited application, as shown in Exhibit 3. In 1980, INNOCHEM sold $4.5 million of industrial cleaning chemicals through distributors and $0.2 million direct to end users. Financial statements for INNOCHEM are shown in Exhibit 4.

## INNOCHEM Marketing Strategy

Divisional strategy hinged on reliable product performance, product innovation, active promotion, and mixed channel distribution. Steve Remen, market development manager, maintained that "customers know our products are of excellent quality. They know that the products will always perform as expected."

At SCJ, performance requirements were detailed and tolerances precisely defined. The Department of Quality Control routinely inspected and tested raw materials, work in process, packaging and finished goods. At any phase during the manufacturing cycle, Quality Control was empowered to halt the process and quarantine suspect product or materials. SCJ maintained that nothing left the plant "without approval from Quality Control."

**EXHIBIT 3**

## *INNOCHEM PRODUCT LINE*

*For all floors except unsealed wood and unsealed cork*

Stripper: **Step-Off** — powerful, fast action
Finish: **Pronto** — fast drying, good gloss, minimum maintenance

Spray-Buff
Solution: **The Shiner Liquid Spray Cleaner**
or
**The Shiner Aerosol Spray Finish**
Maintainer: **Forward** — cleans, disinfects, deodorizes, sanitizes

*For all floors except unsealed wood and unsealed cork*

Stripper: **Step-Off** — powerful, fast stripper
Finish: **Carefree** — tough, beauty, durable, minimum maintenance
Maintainer: **Forward** — cleans, disinfects, deodorizes, sanitizes

*For all floors except unsealed wood and unsealed cork*

Stripper: **Step-Off** — for selective stripping
Sealer: **Over & Under-Plus** — undercoater-sealer
Finish: **Scrubbable Step-Ahead** — brilliant, scrubbable
Maintainer: **Forward** — cleans, disinfects, sanitizes, deodorizes

*For all floors except unsealed wood and cork*

Stripper: **Step-Off** — powerful, fast stripper
Finish: **Easy Street** — high solids, high gloss, spray buffs to a "wet look" appearance
Maintainer: **Forward** — cleans, disinfects, deodorizes
**Expose** — phenolic cleaner disinfectant

*For all floors except unsealed wood and unsealed cork*

Stripper: **Step-Off** — for selective stripping
Sealer: **Over & Under-Plus** — undercoater-sealer
Finishes: **Traffic Grade** — heavy-duty, floor wax
**Waxtral** — extra tough, high solids
Maintainer: **Forward** — cleans, disinfects, sanitizes, deodorizes

*For all floors except asphalt, mastic and rubber tile.* Use sealer and wax finishes on wood, cork and cured concrete; sealer-finish on terrazzo, marble, clay and ceramic tile; wax finish only on vinyl, linoleum and magnesite.

Sealer: **Johnson Gym Finish** — sealer and top-coater cleans as it waxes
Wax Finishes: **Traffic Wax Paste** — heavy-duty buffing wax
**Beautiflor Traffic Wax** — liquid buffing wax
Maintainers: **Forward** — cleans, disinfects, sanitizes, deodorizes
**Conq-r-Dust** — mop treatment

Stripper: **Step-Off** — stripper for sealer and finish
Sealer: **Secure** — fast-bonding, smooth, long-lasting
Finish: **Traffic Grade** — heavy-duty floor wax
Maintainer: **Forward**, or **Big Bare**

Sealer-Finish: **Johnson Gym Finish** — seal and top-coater
Maintainer: **Conq-r-Dust** — mop treatment

General
Cleaning: **Break-Up** — cleans soap and body scum fast
**Forward** — cleans, disinfects, sanitizes, deodorizes
**Bon Ami** — instant cleaner, pressurized, or pump, disinfects
Toilet-Urinals: **Go-Getter** — "Working Foam" cleaner
Glass: **Bon Ami** — spray-on foam or liquid cleaner
Disinfectant
Spray: **End-Bac II** — controls bacteria, odors
Air Freshener: **Glade** — dewy-fresh fragrances
Spot
Cleaning: **Johnson's Pledge** — cleans, waxes, polishes
**Johnson's Lemon Pledge** — refreshing scent
**Bon Ami Stainless Steel Cleaner** — cleans, polishes, protects

All-Purpose
Cleaners: **Forward** — cleans, disinfects, sanitizes, deodorizes
**Break-Up** — degreaser for animal and vegetable fats.
**Big Bare** — heavy-duty industrial cleaner
Carpets: **Rugbee Powder & Liquid Extraction Cleaner**
**Rugbee Soil Release Concentrate** — for pre-spraying and bonnet buffing.
**Rugbee Shampoo** — for power shampoo machines
**Rugbee Spotter** — spot remover
Furniture: **Johnson's Pledge** — cleans, waxes, polishes
**Johnson's Lemon Pledge** — refreshing scent
**Shine-Up Liquid** — general purpose cleaning
Disinfectant
Spray: **End-Bac II** — controls bacteria, odors
Air Freshener: **Glade** — dewy-fresh fragrances
Glass: **Bon Ami** — spray-on foam or liquid cleaner

Cleaning: **Break-Up** — special degreaser designed to remove animal and vegetable fats
Equipment: **Break-Up Foamer** — special generator designed to dispense Break-Up Cleaner

General
Cleaning: **Forward** — fast-working germicidal cleaner for floors, walls — all washable surfaces
**Expose** — phenolic disinfectant cleaner
Sanitizing: **J80 Sanitizer** — liquid for total environmental control of bacteria. No rinse necessary if used as directed
Disinfectant
Spray: **End-Bac II Spray** — controls bacteria, odors

**Flying insects:** Bolt Liquid Airborne, or Pressurized Airborne, P3610 through E10 dispenser
**Crawling insects:** Bolt Liquid Residual or Pressurized Residual, P3610 through E10 dispenser
Bolt Roach Bait
**Rodents:** Bolt Rodenticide — for effective control of rats and mice, use with Bolt Bait Box

| EXHIBIT 4 | PROFIT STATEMENT OF THE DIVISION<br>($ thousands) | |
|---|---|---|
| | Gross Sales | $4,682 |
| | Returns | 46 |
| | Allowances | 1 |
| | Cash discounts | 18 |
| | Net sales | 4,617 |
| | Cost of sales | 2,314 |
| | Gross profit | $2,303 |
| | Advertising | 75 |
| | Promotions | 144 |
| | Deals | – |
| | External marketing services | 2 |
| | Sales freight | 292 |
| | Other distribution expenses | 176 |
| | Service fees | 184* |
| | Total direct expenses | $   873 |
| | Sales force | 592 |
| | Marketing administration | 147 |
| | Provision for bad debts | – |
| | Research and development | 30† |
| | Financial | 68 |
| | Information resource management | 47 |
| | Administration management | 56 |
| | Total functional expenses | $  940 |
| | Total operating expenses | 1,813 |
| | Operating profit | $  490 |

*Fees paid to SCJ (corporate) for corporate services.
†A portion of a research chemist's cost to conduct R&D specifically for industrial products.

"Keeping the new product shelf well stocked" was central to divisional strategy, as the name INNOCHEM implies. Products launched over the past three years represented 33 percent of divisional gross sales, 40 percent of gross profits, and 100 percent of growth.

INNOCHEM had a sales force of 10 that sold and serviced the distributor accounts. These salespeople were paid almost all salary, with some bonus potential up to 10 percent for exceptional sales volume increases. The company had also recently committed one salesperson to work with large direct accounts. The advertising budget of $75,000 was primarily allocated to trade magazines and direct mail advertisements directed at large segments of end users such as maintenance contractors. Sales promotions, by contrast, were directed mainly at distributors, and consisted largely of special pricing and packaging deals to get distributors to bid Johnson products more aggressively in offers to end users.

## Mixed Distribution Strategy

INNOCHEM used a mixed distribution system in an attempt to broaden market coverage. Eighty-seven percent of divisional sales were handled by a force of 200 distributor salesmen and serviced from 50 distributor warehouses representing 35 distributors. The indirect channel was particularly effective outside Ontario and Quebec. In part, the tendency for SCJ market penetration to increase with distances from Montreal and Toronto reflected Canadian demographics and the general economics of distribution. Outside the two production centers, demand was dispersed and delivery distances long.

Distributor salesmen were virtually all paid a straight commission on sales, and were responsible for selling a wide variety of products in addition to Johnson's. Several of the distributors had sales levels much higher than INNOCHEM.

For INNOCHEM, the impact of geography was compounded by a significant freight cost advantage: piggybacking industrial cleaning chemicals with SCJ consumer goods. In Toronto, for example, the cost of SCJ to a distributor was 30 percent above private label, while the differential in British Columbia was only 8 percent. On lower value products, the "freight effect" was even more pronounced.

SCJ had neither the salesmen nor the delivery capabilities to reach large-volume end users who demanded heavy selling effort or frequent shipments of small quantities. Furthermore, it was unlikely that SCJ could develop the necessary selling and distribution strength economically, given the narrowness of the division's range of janitorial products (industrial cleaning chemicals only).

## The Rebate Plan

The key strategic problem facing INNOCHEM was how best to challenge the direct marketer (and private-label distributor) for large-volume, price-sensitive customers with heavy service requirements, particularly in markets where SCJ had no freight advantage. In this connection, George had observed:

> Our gravest weakness is our inability to manage the total margin between the manufactured cost and end-user price in a way that is equitable and sufficiently profitable to support the investment and expenses of both the distributors and ourselves.
>
> Our prime competition across Canada is from direct selling national and regional manufacturers. These companies control both the manufacturing and distribution gross margins. Under our pricing system, the distributor's margin at end-user list on sales is 43 percent. Our margin (the manufacturing margin) is 50 percent on sales. When these margins are combined, as in the case of direct selling manufacturers, the margin becomes 70 percent at list. This long margin provides significant price flexibility in a price-competitive marketplace. We must find a way to attack the direct marketer's 61 percent market share.

The rebate plan George was now evaluating had been devised to meet the competition head-on. "Profitable partnership" between INNOCHEM and the distributors was the underlying philosophy of the plan. Rebates offered a means to "share fairly the margins available between factory cost and consumer price." Whenever competitive conditions required a distributor to discount the resale list price by 30 percent or more, SCJ would give a certain percentage of the wholesale price back to the distributor. SCJ would sacrifice part of its margin to help offset a heavy end-user discount. Rebate percentages would vary with the rate of discount, following a set schedule. Different schedules were to be established for each product type and size. Exhibits 5, 6, and 7 outline the effect of rebates on both the unit gross margins of SCJ and individual distributors for a specific product example.

The rebate plan was designed to be applicable to new incremental business only, not for existing accounts of the distributor. Distributors would be required to seek SCJ approval for end-user discounts of over 30 percent or more of resale list. The maximum allowable end-user discount would rarely exceed 50 percent. To request rebate payments, distributors would send SCJ a copy of the resale invoice along with a written claim. The rebate would then be paid within 60 days. Proponents of the plan maintained that the resulting resale price flexibility would not only enhance INNOCHEM competitiveness among end users, but would also diminish distributor attraction to private labels. As he studied the plan, George questioned whether all the implications were fully understood and wondered what other strategies, if any, might increase urban market penetration. Any plan he devised would have to be sold to distributors as well as to corporate management. George had only three weeks to develop an appropriate action plan.

**EXHIBIT 5**

# DISTRIBUTORS' REBATE PRICING SCHEDULE
## An Example Using Pronto Floor Wax

| Code 04055 | Product Description Pronto Fast Dry Fin | Size 209 Lit | Pack 1 |
|---|---|---|---|

*Eff. date: 03-31-81*
*Resale List Price 71   613.750*
*Distributor Price List 74   349.837*
*Percent Markup on Cost with Carload & Rebate*

| Discount (%) (1) | Quote (FST) (incl) (2) | Rebate (%) (3) | $ (4) | 2% | | 3% | | 4% | | 5% | |
|---|---|---|---|---|---|---|---|---|---|---|---|
| | | | | Net (5) | MU % (6) | Net | MU % | Net | MU % | Net | MU % |
| 30.0 | 429.63 | 8.0 | 27.99 | 314.85 | 36 | 311.35 | 38 | 307.86 | 40 | 304.36 | 41 |
| 35.0 | 398.94 | 12.0 | 41.98 | 300.86 | 33 | 297.36 | 34 | 293.86 | 36 | 290.36 | 37 |
| 40.0 | 368.25 | 17.0 | 59.47 | 283.37 | 30 | 279.87 | 32 | 276.37 | 33 | 272.87 | 35 |
| 41.0 | 362.11 | 17.5 | 61.22 | 281.62 | 29 | 278.12 | 30 | 274.62 | 32 | 271.12 | 34 |
| 42.0 | 355.98 | 18.0 | 62.97 | 279.87 | 27 | 276.37 | 29 | 272.87 | 30 | 269.37 | 32 |
| 43.0 | 349.84 | 18.5 | 64.72 | 278.12 | 26 | 274.62 | 27 | 271.12 | 29 | 267.63 | 31 |
| 44.0 | 343.70 | 19.0 | 66.47 | 276.37 | 24 | 272.87 | 26 | 269.37 | 28 | 265.88 | 29 |
| 45.0 | 337.56 | 20.0 | 69.97 | 272.87 | 24 | 269.37 | 25 | 265.88 | 27 | 262.38 | 29 |
| 46.0 | 331.43 | 20.5 | 71.72 | 271.12 | 22 | 267.63 | 24 | 264.13 | 25 | 260.63 | 27 |
| 47.0 | 325.29 | 21.0 | 73.47 | 269.37 | 21 | 265.88 | 22 | 262.38 | 24 | 258.88 | 26 |
| 48.0 | 319.15 | 21.5 | 75.21 | 267.63 | 19 | 264.13 | 21 | 260.63 | 22 | 257.13 | 24 |
| 49.0 | 313.01 | 22.0 | 76.96 | 265.88 | 18 | 262.38 | 19 | 258.88 | 21 | 255.38 | 23 |
| 50.0 | 306.88 | 23.0 | 80.46 | 262.38 | 17 | 258.88 | 19 | 255.38 | 20 | 251.88 | 22 |
| 51.0 | 300.74 | 24.0 | 83.96 | 258.88 | 16 | 255.38 | 18 | 251.88 | 19 | 248.38 | 21 |
| 52.0 | 294.60 | 25.0 | 87.46 | 255.38 | 15 | 251.88 | 17 | 248.38 | 19 | 244.89 | 20 |
| 53.0 | 288.46 | 26.0 | 90.96 | 251.88 | 15 | 248.38 | 16 | 244.89 | 18 | 241.39 | 19 |
| 54.0 | 282.33 | 28.0 | 97.95 | 244.89 | 15 | 241.39 | 17 | 237.89 | 19 | 234.39 | 20 |
| 55.0 | 276.19 | 30.0 | 104.95 | 237.89 | 16 | 234.39 | 18 | 230.89 | 20 | 227.39 | 21 |

(1) Discount extended to end user on resale list price.
(2) Resale price at given discount level (includes federal sales tax).
(3) Percentage of distributor's price ($613.75) rebated by SCJ.
(4) Actual dollar amount of rebate by SCJ.
(5) Actual net cost to distributor after deduction of rebate and "carload" (quantity) discount.
(6) Effective rate of distributor markup.

**EXHIBIT**
**6**

### EFFECT OF REBATE PLAN ON MANUFACTURER AND DISTRIBUTOR MARGINS
#### The Example of One 209-Liter Pack of Pronto Floor Finish Retailed at 40% below Resale List Price

*Under Present Arrangements*

| | |
|---|---:|
| Base price to distributor | $349.84 |
| Price to distributor, assuming 2% carload discount* | 342.84 |
| SCJ cost | 174.92 |
| SCJ margin | $167.92 |
| Resale list price | 613.75 |
| Resale list price minus 40% discount | 368.25 |
| Distributor price, assuming 2% carload discount | 342.84 |
| Distributor's margin | $ 25.41 |

*Under Rebate Plan*

| | |
|---|---:|
| Rebate to distributor giving 40% discount off resale price amounted to 17% distributor's base price | $ 59.47 |
| SCJ margin (minus rebate) | 108.45 |
| Distributor margin (plus rebate) | 84.88 |

*Competitive Prices*

For this example, George estimated that a distributor could buy a private-branded "comparable" product for approximately $244.

*A form of quantity discount which, in this case, drops the price the distributor pays to SCJ from $349.84 to $342.84.

EXHIBIT
7
## EFFECT OF END-USER DISCOUNT LEVEL ON MANUFACTURER AND DISTRIBUTOR MARGINS UNDER PROPOSED REBATE PLAN
### The Example of One 209-Liter Pack of Pronto Fast Dry Finish*

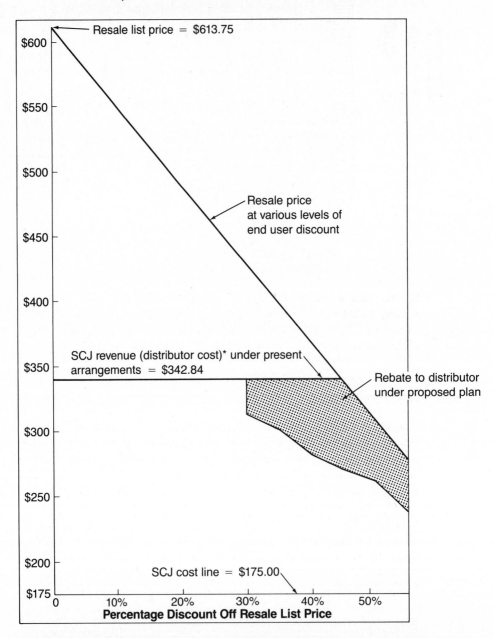

*Assuming 2% quantity ("carload") discount off price to distributor.

ing in order to obtain approval for market entry. The initial product was to be a computer-controlled electronic PBX with capacity to handle from 100 to 800 telephone extensions. This market entry would bring ROLM into direct competition with AT&T, ITT, Northern Electric, Philips, Nippon Electric, and many others.

## THE COMPANY

ROLM corporation had been founded in 1969 by four electrical engineers: Mr. Richeson, Mr. Oshman, Mr. Loewenstern, and Mr. Maxfield. In fact, the name of the corporation was an acronym based on the first letters of their names. All were in their late twenties to early thirties at the time of the founding and all were, or had been, employed by electronic or computer firms in the San Francisco Bay Area. As Bob Maxfield recalled: "The company was the result of four guys deciding they wanted to go into business for themselves and having a couple of ideas about the kinds of products they might offer." Their original ideas were basically commercial applications of systems developed originally for the military and included a system for police departments to keep track automatically of the location of every police vehicle. Another idea was a system that would allow toll bridges to monitor regular users of the bridge automatically by means of

This case was prepared by Professor Adrian B. Ryans of the University of Western Ontario. Reprinted from *Stanford Business Cases 1979* with permission of the publishers, Stanford University Graduate School of Business, copyright © 1979 by the Board of Trustees of the Leland Stanford Junior University.

a transponder attached to each vehicle, thus permitting bills to be issued to each regular user at the end of the month. A business plan was developed around these ideas and was presented to venture capitalists, but it did not arouse much enthusiasm among potential suppliers of capital.

In the fall of 1968, Bob Maxfield and Gene Richeson attended the Fall Joint Computer Conference. This particular show in many respects heralded the coming minicomputer boom. Data General, subsequently to become a major factor in the minicomputer industry, and a dozen other new manufacturers announced their first products at this show. A few months later, while the four of them were sitting around "blue-skying" about potential business, Gene Richeson suggested that what the world really needed was a low-cost off-the-shelf military minicomputer.

No standard computer could withstand the severe environmental conditions encountered in military missions. At that time, the major manufacturers of militarized computers ("mil-spec") were IBM and Sperry Univac, who manufactured the computers on a custom basis, resulting in long lead times and high cost—often $150,000 for a system. The Data General commercial NOVA minicomputer, on the other hand, cost about $10,000 and Gene Richeson, based on his knowledge of the requirements of the various military applications, felt that such a computer would have sufficient power for most of these applications. Bob Maxfield, who had the most experience with computers, felt that a militarized version of the Data General computer could be manufactured to sell for less than $30,000. As they discussed the possibilities further, they decided that it would be ideal from the customer's viewpoint if a militarized computer could be made software compatible and input–output compatible with an existing commercial minicomputer. This would allow the user to do the development work and system testing on the lower cost commercial machine in a laboratory environment, only using the "mil-spec" computer when the system was actually deployed in the military equipment.

The next question they addressed was which commercial minicomputer they should choose. They selected the Data General NOVA computer for two reasons. First, Data General was a start-up company and thus might be interested in licensing the design and software to ROLM: and, given its small size, the decision would probably be made quickly. The second reason was the Data General machine used the latest technology, which required a smaller number of components than competitive minicomputers. This was an important factor in designing a reliable machine for military applications. They phoned Edson de Castro, president of Data General, and told him they were thinking of starting up a company to manufacture "mil-spec" computers and asked him if he would be interested in licensing hardware and software designs to them. De Castro was interested, so they flew to Data General's home office in Boston and negotiated an agreement with him.

On the basis of their data, they developed a business plan and were successful in getting sufficient money to start the business. ROLM began operation on June 1, 1969, and a working model was displayed at the Fall Joint Computer Conference in 1969. The first production unit was shipped in March 1970. In the first quarter of fiscal year 1971, which began in July 1970, ROLM showed a profit and remained profitable thereafter. Subsequent computers were based on ROLM's own designs.

The ROLM "mil-spec" computers typically were purchased by contractors of the U.S. Department of Defense, the Defense Department itself, and certain industrial customers who required computers that could operate in severe environments. The computers were generally used in research, development, and testing applications. Individual purchase orders were usually for small quantities. The company generally provided a central processing unit (CPU), a main memory, a chassis, a power supply and a variety of input–output equipment, peripheral equipment (terminals, printers, magnetic discs, and tapes), and software. Customers could thus configure a system to meet their own needs. The company employed a direct sales organization which totaled about eight people in 1973. Kenneth Oshman, besides being president of ROLM, also acted as head of the marketing organization.

## The Decision to Diversify

By fiscal 1973, sales had reached $3.6 million. An income statement and balance sheet for ROLM are included in Exhibit 1. Early in 1973, top management of ROLM became concerned about the potential size of the segment of the military computer market in which ROLM competed. There was a strong feeling among ROLM's top management that their market segment would be saturated by the time their annual sales reached $10 million to $20 million. Given that they had an objective to build a major company, they began to look for areas of diversification that would allow ROLM to continue its growth. They felt that any diversification should build on their main technological expertise in computers, so they investigated other computer-related businesses that they might enter. The PBX market was an obvious candidate. As Oshman pointed out, "The computer-based PBX is very much a computer system, and we already had 80 percent of the technology; we figured we could get the other 20 percent easier than the telephone companies could get the computer technology." The idea was initially abandoned when they realized that the cost of setting up a national sales and service organization would be beyond ROLM's resources. Nevertheless, the proposal kept resurfacing during the following months. As Bob Maxfield recalled: "We all felt it would be fun to develop a computer-controlled telephone system, so we decided to look at it more carefully in March 1973." Once the decision had been made to look at the PBX business more closely, it was decided to set up a separate organization to do the product development and market analysis. They felt either the "mil-spec" computer business or the proposed PBX business would receive second-class treatment if personnel attempted to work in both areas simultaneously.

To head the product development side of the project, Maxfield was successful in recruiting Jim Kasson from Hewlett-Packard. Kasson, whom Maxfield had known socially for a number of years, had a background in data acquisition and control systems and was very knowledgeable about computers. He also brought with him from Hewlett-Packard another very good engineer. Together with ROLM's top computer software specialist they became, in June 1973, the three-person ROLM PBX technical feasibility team. In August 1973, Dick Moley, a marketing manager in Hewlett-Packard's computer division, joined ROLM to do the market analysis for the PBX.

| EXHIBIT 1 | ROLM CORPORATION FINANCIAL DATA |

### Income Statement for Fiscal Year Ending June 29, 1973

| | |
|---|---|
| Net sales | $3,637,000 |
| Costs and expenses | |
| Cost of goods sold | 1,572,000 |
| Product development | 455,000 |
| Marketing, administrative, and general | 964,000 |
| Interest | 14,000 |
| Total costs and expenses | 3,005,000 |
| Income before taxes | 632,000 |
| Provision for income taxes | 311,000 |
| Net income | 321,000 |

### Balance Sheet for Quarter Ending September 28, 1973

| | | | | |
|---|---|---|---|---|
| *Current Assets:* | | | *Current Liabilities:* | |
| Cash | $ 202,000 | | Accounts payable and accrued payroll | $ 306,700 |
| Receivables | 442,000 | | Income tax payable | 139,400 |
| Inventories | 994,600 | | Other current liabilities | 31,900 |
| Other current assets | 43,100 | | Notes payable | 24,400 |
| Total current assets | 1,681,700 | | Total current liabilities | 502,400 |
| | | | | |
| *Other Assets:* | | | Lease Contracts Payable – Long Term | 97,500 |
| Capital equipment | $ 440,700 | | *Stockholders' Equity:* | |
| Accumulated depreciation | 228,300 | | Capital stock | 170,800 |
| Net capital equipment | 212,400 | | Paid in surplus, net | 610,800 |
| Other assets | 24,100 | | Retained earnings | 536,700 |
| Total other assets | 236,500 | | Total equity | 1,318,300 |
| *Total Assets* | 1,918,200 | | *Total Liabilities and Equity* | 1,918,200 |

*Source:* Company records

# TELECOMMUNICATIONS INDUSTRY IN THE UNITED STATES

The telecommunications system in the United States was operated by American Telephone and Telegraph (AT&T) and some 1960 independent telephone companies. AT&T was split into five major operations:

1. The General Department, which provided staff assistance in advertising, finance, engineering, legal, and marketing to the rest of the corporation.

2. Western Electric, which manufactured telephone equipment for the Bell System operating companies. Under the terms of a 1956 consent decree with the Justice Department, Western Electric sold its products exclusively to the Bell System operating companies and to the U.S. Government. In 1972, Western Electric's total sales were greater than $7 billion.

3. The Bell Telephone Laboratories, which conducted basic research and designed equipment for manufacture by Western Electric.

4. The Long Lines Department, which installed and operated the interstate long distance network and handled all international calls. It received revenues from both the Bell System operating companies and the independent telephone companies for providing these services.

5. The 24 Bell System operating companies which provided and operated the telephone system at a local level. They covered about 85 percent of the telephones in the United States. Sixteen of the operating companies were wholly owned by AT&T, and it owned a majority interest in six of the others.

In 1972, AT&T had telephone operating revenues of $21.4 billion and had 109 million phones in service, of which some 14 million were business phones connected to PBX, or functionally similar, systems.

The 1960 independent telephone companies provided local telephone service in areas not served by AT&T. These companies, as well as the Bell System operating companies, were regulated by state public utility commissions. They varied greatly in size from very small rural telephone companies to major corporations such as General Telephone which had operating revenues in the United States of almost $2 billion. The 10 largest independent telephone companies are shown in Exhibit 2.

## The Emergence of the Telephone Interconnect Industry

Prior to 1968, all telephone company tariffs in the United States had contained a blanket prohibition against the attachment of customer-provided terminal equipment (such as telephones, answering machines and PBXs) to the telecommunications network. The historic 1968 Carterfone decision of the Federal Communications Commission (FCC) held that these blanket prohibitions were unreasonable, discriminatory, and unlawful, and the FCC required that the telephone companies file new tariffs that did not contain such blanket prohibitions. This decision opened up the vast market for terminal equipment to a variety of new competitors.

The Carterfone decision did allow the telephone companies to take reasonable steps to protect the telephone system from any harmful effects of interconnected equipment. New tariffs filed in early 1969 by the telephone companies required that protective connecting arrangements be installed on each line to protect and insulate the public network. In the next few years these connecting arrangements became a major bone of contention between the suppliers of customer interconnect equipment and the telephone companies. Interconnect equipment suppliers charged that the connection arrangements sometimes caused technical problems, that the telephone companies used delaying tactics in installing them, and that they unnecessarily raised costs (an average charge by the telephone

EXHIBIT
2

## TEN LARGEST INDEPENDENT TELEPHONE COMPANIES

| Names and Addresses | Telephones | Percentage of Total Independent Telephone Industry | Total Operating Revenues |
|---|---|---|---|
| General Telephone & Electrics Corp. (U.S. only), New York, New York | 10,622,000 | 45.81 | $1,881,000,000 |
| United Telecommunications, Inc., Kansas City, Missouri | 2,642,300 | 11.40 | 448,684,000 |
| Continental Telephone Corporation (U.S. only), Chantilly, Virginia | 1,774,200 | 7.65 | 299,536,000 |
| Central Telephone & Utilities Corporation, Lincoln, Nebraska | 1,059,600 | 4.57 | 194,055,000 |
| Mid-Continent Telephone Corporation, Hudson, Ohio | 593,500 | 2.56 | 82,842,000 |
| Rochester Telephone Corporation, Rochester, New York | 535,100 | 2.31 | 89,502,000 |
| Puerto Rico Telephone Company, San Juan, Puerto Rico | 357,400 | 1.54 | 64,277,000 |
| Lincoln Telephone & Telegraph Company, Lincoln, Nebraska | 239,800 | 1.03 | 37,176,000 |
| Commonwealth Telephone Company, Dallas, Pennsylvania | 154,900 | .67 | 18,857,000 |
| Florida Telephone Corporation, Ocala, Florida | 143,600 | .62 | 29,068,000 |

companies of $7 to $10 per line per month) for the users of the interconnect equipment. The telephone companies responded to these charges by pointing out that they had rapidly developed a large number of protective connecting arrangements for different types of terminal equipment and had installed several hundred thousand of them by 1974.

# PBXs AND KEY SYSTEMS

Interconnect equipment was any equipment attached to where incoming telephone company lines terminated on a customer's premises. Although such equipment took a wide variety of forms, including answering and recording devices, in the business market most of the sales volume was in two product classes: private branch exchanges (PBX) and key telephone systems.

A PBX is a local telephone switch system within a company which handles incoming, outgoing, and intraoffice calls.[1] As shown schematically in Exhibit 3, a PBX consists of four major parts:

[1] Some companies distinguished between PBX, a manually switched private branch exchange, and PABX, an automatic PBX, where all switching was done without operator intervention. Here PBX will be used to cover both types of equpiment.

**EXHIBIT 3**

## PBX SYSTEM INCLUDING KEY SYSTEM

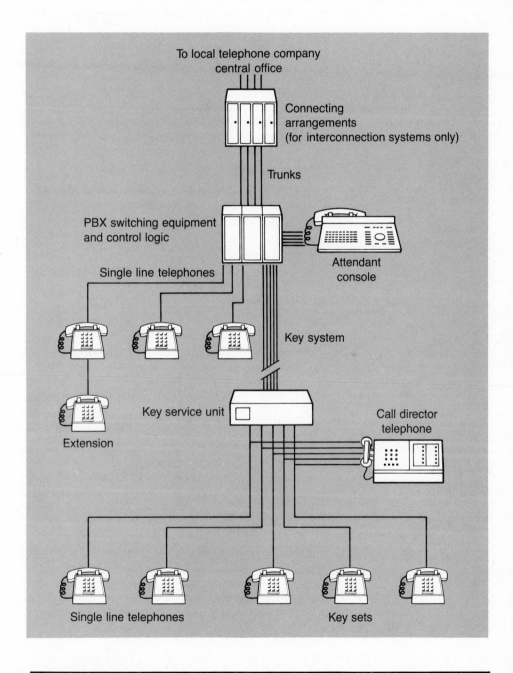

To local telephone company central office

Connecting arrangements (for interconnection systems only)

Trunks

PBX switching equipment and control logic

Attendant console

Single line telephones

Key system

Extension

Key service unit

Call director telephone

Single line telephones

Key sets

*Source:* SRI Long-Range Planning Service

1. Switching equipment and control systems. The switching system is the electro-mechanical or electronic equipment that connects the various internal (telephone extensions) and external lines in the system and provides ringing, busy signals, dial tone, and intercom services. The control system is the system that actuates the switching functions.
2. Trunk circuits. These are lines connecting the PBX to the public switched network.
3. Attendant console. This is the equipment used by an inside operator to complete or transfer calls, to determine which lines are busy, and to handle a variety of other tasks such as taking messages and paging.
4. Telephone station equipment. These are the individual telephones and key systems (a telephone that allows a person access to several lines with a single illuminated push-button set) located throughout the building or organization.

While key systems were commonly part of the PBX telephone system in large companies, stand-alone key systems were commonly used in smaller organizations (typically those with 40 or fewer telephones) as the sole system. Here they connected the outside lines directly to the user's extension telephone. Usually one pushbutton on each telephone was connected to a common line providing an intercom capability. The technology involved in automatic PBXs had evolved in recent years — from electromechanical step-by-step systems, to electromechanical crossbar systems, to electronic systems.[2]

*Step-by-step systems* were first offered at the beginning of the century and were the primary PBX product of the telephone companies for many years. These electromechanical systems could be expanded indefinitely as long as the customer had space for the very bulky equipment. If maintained well, they provided economical and reliable service, but offered very limited features. They were also expensive in terms of installation labor and maintenance and generated a large amount of "noise," making them unsuitable for data communications.

*Crossbar systems* were the next step in PBX evolution. These were again electromechanical switches, and variations of them had been available for years. These systems were much more compact than the step-by-step systems, being housed in cabinets, and had lower labor and maintenance costs. Once they were set up and adjusted, they provided very reliable service but were costly to expand beyond the capacity of the original installation. Modern cross-bar systems offered the user a number of features, such as:

*Selective toll restriction.* The system could be set up so that only certain individuals could dial long distance calls.

*Station transfer.* The user could transfer an incoming call from outside the company to another extension within the system without going to the switchboard operator.

*Consultation hold.* An incoming call could be held while the person dialed another number to secure information for the caller. This procedure did not require the telephone to be a key telephone equipped with a hold button.

---

[2]A brief description of the switching and control systems technology can be found in Appendixes A and B.

*Add-on conference.* A third person could be dialed so that a three-way conference could be held. Again, a key telephone was not required.

*Electronic telephone switching systems* were the most recent technological development. The original work on electronic switching systems had been done at Bell Laboratories in the mid-1950s and the first commercial electronic central office (i.e., a switching system within the Bell system) was opened in 1965. Electronic switching technology only began to be used in the PBX market in the early 1970s and by 1974 there were about 20 electronic PBX models on the market. Most of these electronic systems used space division multiplexing (SDM)[3]. Electronic systems with time division multiplexing (TDM), which allowed several signals and calls to go over one pair of wires, promised to significantly simplify and reduce the costs of cabling a building for the PBX system. Electronic systems contained both memory and logic capabilities. The control logic—that is, how the appropriate circuits were interconnected during use—was implemented in two basic ways. The method greatly affected the flexibility of the equipment. The two ways were:

1. *Wired logic.* Here the logic was stored on printed circuit cards and control actions were predetermined by the wiring connections on the cards. This limited the flexibility of the system and the ease with which it could be modified.
2. *Stored program logic* (computer controlled). Here all logic was stored either in exchangeable memory or by programming. Changes in the control logic could be readily made by changing the program.

Stored program logic gave a PBX great flexibility and the potential to meet future demands that wired logic systems could not match. Besides providing the normal control (connection) functions and a range of features to aid the telephone user, a computer-controlled electronic PBX could be used to record details of all toll calls (call detail recording), could monitor usage of the system, and could even perform self-diagnostic functions if there were problems with the equipment. In addition, if a company placed Tie Lines and WATS (Wide Area Telephone Service) lines on direct access (i.e., no operator was needed), the electronic switch could be programmed to seek the least costly route for a long-distance call. With additional memory, a wide range of features could be made available on an electronic PBX, including all of those available on a crossbar system. Thus, in an electronic PBX, the systems features were in the central switching unit rather than the particular telephone or key unit. The user could make use of a particular feature either by dialing a code or pressing a couple of buttons on the telephone. Some of the features that could be offered on electronic systems included:

*Classes of service.* Each telephone station could be given access to only those services necessary for the person to perform his or her job. For example, some telephones could only be allowed to call certain long-distance area codes.

[3]See Appendix A for explanation of technology.

*Automatic dialing and speed calling.* Each user could store frequently called numbers in the system. The switch dialed the number when the user dialed a code. The stored numbers could easily be changed by the user.

*Call forwarding.* A code instructed the switch to forward any incoming call to a specified number.

*Station number changes.* When the user was relocated and wished to retain his or her current number, this change could easily be entered into the system. No telephone moving charges would be incurred as long as a telephone existed at the user's new location.

*Automatic call distribution.* A number could be set up for a particular department and any incoming calls to that number were distributed by the switch to any free department telephone.

Electronic systems could therefore provide a range of useful features to the user. While basic electronic systems were more costly than similar electromechanical systems, the marginal cost of adding features after installation was much lower. They promised to be more reliable than electromechanical systems although experience with electronic systems was not yet large enough to provide a convincing maintenance and reliability record. Electronic systems, particularly those based on the TDM technology, were also more suitable for tying into data communication terminals. This was expected to become an increasingly important consideration by the late 1970s when many more users were expected to be using their telecommunications systems for both voice and data transmission.

# COMPETITION IN THE PBX AND KEY SYSTEMS MARKET _____

After 1968 a customer could purchase a PBX or key system from one of two basic types of suppliers: (1) the telephone company providing service in that area, or (2) an interconnect company. As Exhibit 4 suggests, the structure of the interconnect market was quite complex. In some cases companies manufactured the equipment and distributed it through one or more suppliers who installed and serviced the equipment. In other cases, the manufacturer might be a manufacturer-supplier selling directly to the end user or through a separate supplier subsidiary. These subsidiaries often would distribute the products of other manufacturers also.

## Manufacturers of PBX and Key Systems

The manufacturers of PBX equipment were a pretty diverse group. Western Electric, the supplier of the Bell System, Northern Telecom, the U.S. subsidiary of Northern Electric, the Bell Canada manufacturing arm, and the major suppliers to the independent telephone companies, such as GTE-Automatic Electric, North Electric, and Stromberg-Carlson, were all well-established in the North American market—having supplied equipment to the various telephone companies since prior to the 1968 Carterfone decision. The PBX equipment manufactured by these suppliers for the independent telephone companies

**EXHIBIT
4**

## *STRUCTURE OF THE MARKET FOR PBXs AND KEY SYSTEMS*

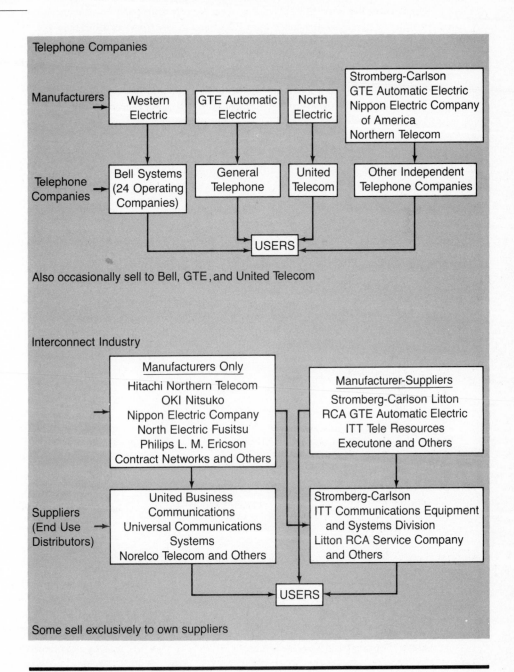

Telephone Companies

Manufacturers → Western Electric | GTE Automatic Electric | North Electric | Stromberg-Carlson / GTE Automatic Electric / Nippon Electric Company of America / Northern Telecom

Telephone Companies → Bell Systems (24 Operating Companies) | General Telephone | United Telecom | Other Independent Telephone Companies

USERS

Also occasionally sell to Bell, GTE, and United Telecom

Interconnect Industry

Manufacturers Only
Hitachi Northern Telecom
OKI Nitsuko
Nippon Electric Company
North Electric Fusitsu
Philips L. M. Ericson
Contract Networks and Others

Manufacturer-Suppliers
Stromberg-Carlson Litton
RCA GTE Automatic Electric
ITT Tele Resources
Executone and Others

Suppliers (End Use Distributors) →
United Business Communications
Universal Communications Systems
Norelco Telecom and Others

Stromberg-Carlson
ITT Communications Equipment and Systems Division
Litton RCA Service Company and Others

USERS

Some sell exclusively to own suppliers

*Source:* LSI Long-Range Planning Service

was, in 1968, generally similar to Western Electric's and offered only traditional features. The Carterfone decision provided an opportunity for another group of manufacturers to enter the U.S. market. These were largely European and Japanese manufacturers who had extensive experience with PBXs and key systems in other markets. With the encouragement of the interconnect suppliers (i.e., the companies selling to the end users), they modified their equipment and were able to offer end users features previously unavailable in the United States. By the early 1970s the Japanese and European companies had captured about 75 percent of the U.S. PBX and key system interconnect market.[4] The major companies in this group were OKI, Nippon Electric, Hitachi, and Nitsuko (all Japanese), and L. M. Ericsson (Swedish). International Telephone and Telegraph (ITT) also entered the U.S. market after the Carterfone decision and by 1973, some industry observers felt it had the best line of PBX equipment available in the United States. A list of the major manufacturers ranked in terms of their estimated 1973 sales to U.S. interconnect suppliers is shown in Exhibit 5. As Exhibit 4 also suggests, some of these com-

| EXHIBIT 5 | MAJOR MANUFACTURERS OF INTERCONNECT EQUIPMENT RANKED IN ORDER OF ESTIMATED 1973 SALES TO U.S. INTERCONNECT COMPANIES |
|---|---|

| Company | Manufacturing Locations |
|---|---|
| OKI Electronics of America/OKI Electric of Japan | Japan and U.S. |
| Nippon Electric Company | Japan and U.S. |
| Hitachi | Japan and U.S. |
| Nitsuko* | Japan |
| International Telephone and Telegraph (ITT) | U.S. and Spain |
| L. M. Ericsson | Sweden |
| Northern Telecom (subsidiary of Northern Electric of Canada) | Canada and U.S. |
| Stromberg–Carlson | U.S. |
| North Electric (subsidiary of United Telecommunications | U.S. |
| Fujitsu | Japan |
| General Telephone and Electronics (GTE)— Automatic Electric | U.S. |
| North American Philips—Norelco | Netherlands and U.S. |
| CIT/TELIC | France and U.S. |
| Iwatsu* | Japan |
| Meisei | Japan |
| Siemens | Germany |
| Lynch | U.S. |
| Toshiba* | Japan |

*Key systems only.
*Source:* SRI Long-Range Planning Service

[4]That is, 75 percent of PBX and key system market which was not serviced by the AT&T operating companies or the independent telephone companies.

panies had also been quite successful in selling their products to some of the telephone operating companies. This resulted, in some cases, in end users being able to obtain identical equipment from either the telephone operating company or an interconnect supplier. The opening of the interconnect market had also brought a number of new U.S. manufacturers into the market. Wescom, Tele/Resources and Philco Ford had all developed electronic PBXs and were supplying them to the independent telephone companies or to interconnect suppliers. Litton and RCA, which had entered the market as national interconnect companies, were buying PBXs from others and were both rumored to be developing electronic PBXs. Other large manufacturers, active in foreign markets, were also believed to be ready to enter the market. IBM was also viewed as a possible entrant, since it had developed a very strong position in the European PBX market with two expensive electronic PBXs. The major manufacturers of electronic PBXs and a brief description of their equipment and market position is contained in Exhibit 6.

Notable in their absence from the list of manufacturers in Exhibit 6 were the Japanese and European manufacturers. The major Japanese manufacturers (Nippon, Hitachi, Fujitsu, and OKI) and the leading European manufacturer, L. M. Ericsson, produced high-quality electromechanical PBX equipment. Until the devaluation of the dollar in 1973, the Japanese PBX equipment had been very competitively priced. Ericsson had always sold its equipment at premium prices in the United States. Both the major Japanese manufacturers and Ericsson were rumored to be developing electronic PBXs.

## Interconnect Companies

The number of interconnect companies had grown rapidly since 1968, and by 1973 there were thought to be about 300 of them in the United States. These interconnect companies analyzed customer needs for PBXs and key systems, designed and recommended a system, installed it, and serviced it. Interconnect companies could be divided into two basic groups, national suppliers and small regional or local suppliers. Estimated sales for the major interconnect suppliers in 1973 are shown in Exhibit 7.

The four largest national companies—Litton, Stromberg–Carlson, ITT, and United Business Communications—had offices throughout the United States and were divisions of much larger corporations. In 1973, ITT was the only one of the four that had a wholly owned manufacturing subsidiary. Stromberg–Carlson Communications was the result of the acquisition by General Dynamics, in June 1973, of Arcata Communications, Inc., and Arcata Leasing from Arcata National. The two Arcata National units had offices in 20 major metropolitan areas across the United States, and had generated losses of close to $4 million after taxes on sales of $25 million in the final year before General Dynamics acquired them. Eventually, as the acquired interconnect supplier was integrated with the Stromberg–Carlson manufacturing unit, Stromberg–Carlson would, like ITT, have an integrated manufacturing and distribution organization.

There were also three other companies that were national in scope. Universal Communications Systems, a subsidiary of American Motor Inns, and Teleci, a subsidiary of Holiday Inn, both specialized in the hotel/motel segment of the market, and RCA Service Company specialized in hospitals and universities. Industry observers believed these companies were profitable. The hotel/motel segment of the market had some fairly unique characteristics that made it a good candidate for specialization. It required only a voice

| EXHIBIT 6 | **ELECTRONIC PBX MANUFACTURERS AND THEIR PRODUCT OFFERINGS IN 1973** |
|-----------|------------------------------------------------------------------------|

| | | Technologies Used* | |
|---|---|---|---|
| Manufacturer | Model | Control | Switching |
| Western Electric | 801A | Electronic-wired logic | Space division (SDM)– reed relay† |
| | 812A | Electronic-wired logic | SDM-crossbar |
| | 101 ESS (3A) | Electronic-computer | Time division (TDM) electronic (PCM)‡ |
| | 101 ESS (4A) | Electronic-computer | TDM-electronic (PCM) |
| ITT | TD-100 | Electronic-wired logic | TDM-electronic (PAM)** |
| | TE-400A | Electronic-wired logic | SDM-electronic |
| | TE-400G | Electronic-wired logic | SDM-electronic |
| | TCS-2 | Electronic-computer | SDM-electronic |
| Stromberg–Carlson | 400A | Electronic-wired logic | SDM-reed relay |
| | 800A | Electronic-wired logic | SDM-reed relay |
| Wescom | 501 | Electronic-wired logic | SDM-electronic |
| Tele/Resources | TR-32 | Electronic-wired logic | TDM-electronic (PAM) |
| Philco Ford | PC-192 | Electronic-computer | SDM-electronic |
| | PC-512 | Electronic-computer | SDM-electronic |
| IBM | 2750 | Electronic-computer | SDM-electronic |
| | 3750 | Electronic-computer | SDM-electronic |
| Northern Telecom | SG-1 | Electronic-wired logic | TDM-electronic (PAM) |
| | SG-2 | Electronic-wired logic | TDM-electronic (PAM) |
| ROLM | Proposed | Electronic-computer | TDM-electronic (PCM) |

*See Appendix A for a brief discussion of the technological issues.
†Reed relay was an evolutionary switching approach that bridged the gap between electromechanical crossbar and fully electronic switching.
‡PCM – pulse code modulation. Here all signals that are transmitted are digital signals.
**PAM – pulse amplitude modulation. Here all signals that are transmitted are analogue signals.

communications system, phones were not moved, key sets were rarely used, most calls were ingoing or outgoing, and a record of all outgoing calls had to be made for billing purposes. Universal Communications Systems and Teleci chose to meet the needs of this segment by importing Japanese electromechanical PBXs that could meet these requirements at low costs.

The regional interconnect suppliers were generally small companies which typically served a geographical area within a 50- or 100-mile radius of their home office. Many

**EXHIBIT 6**

*(cont'd)*

| Number of lines PBX can handle | Comments |
|---|---|
| 46–270 | Western Electric produced a very broad line of PBXs, most of which were still electromechanical. The 801A and 812A were both semielectronic. In the 101 |
| 400–2000 | systems all switching was actually done in a Bell System central office, not on |
| 400–800 | the customer's premises. An electronic central office was needed for the ESS. Only a small proportion of Bell central offices was electronic. |
| 2000–4000 | |
| 40–100 | ITT's fully electronic PBXs covered all line sizes. Many observers felt it had the best line of PBXs on the market in 1973. Shipment of the TD-100 PBX was |
| 100–400 | expected to begin in early 1974. |
| 400–800 | |
| 600–6000 | |
| 100–400 | Both were semielectronic PBXs. |
| 400–800 | |
| 40–120 | This PBX was being sold to independent telephone companies. Shipments were expected to begin in early 1974. |
| 40–164 | This PBX required unique and expensive phones and was sold only to interconnect suppliers. There were large order backlogs in late 1973. |
| 64–192 | The PC-512 was introduced in 1972 and was marketed to independent tele- |
| 128–512 | phone companies. It was very expensive relative to competitive offerings and was not believed to be selling well. |
| 256–756 | IBM had been successfully selling these very expensive PBXs in Europe. They |
| 256–2264 | were really only feasible for installations requiring more than 500 telephones. |
| 40–80 | The SG-1 was introduced in 1972 and had been selling very well in the U.S. |
| 80–120 | and Canada. The SG-2 was not yet in production. |
| 100–800 | |

had originally been in the sound and/or communications equipment business and had simply diversified into the interconnect market. Some of the major regional interconnect suppliers were Tele/Resources (New York), The Other Telephone Company (Minnesota), Fisk Electric (Texas), and Scott Buttner Communications (California). Most of the interconnect companies were very small, with telecommunications sales generally being less than $2 million—Tele/Resources, believed to be the largest of these companies, had sales of about $4 million. Industry observers believed that these companies, unlike many of the national suppliers, were profitable. This was probably the result of lower overheads, knowledge of local requirements, and the flexibility of small companies. Many of these companies were seriously undercapitalized.

| | EXHIBIT 7 | ESTIMATED SALES BY INTERCONNECT COMPANIES IN 1973 |

| Company | Sales (Millions of dollars) |
| --- | --- |
| Litton Business Telephone Systems | 25 |
| Stromberg–Carlson Communications* (subsidiary of General Dynamics) | 25 |
| ITT – Communications Equipment and Systems Division | 18 |
| United Business Communications (subsidiary of United Telecommunications) | 14 |
| Universal Communications Systems (subsidiary of American Motor Inns) | 9 |
| RCA Service Company | 8 |
| Norelco Communications* (subsidiary of North American Philips) | 5 |
| GTE – Automatic Electric* | 7 |
| Teleci (subsidiary of Holiday Inns) | 3 |
| Tele/Resources | 4 |
| ITT – Terryphone† | 4 |
| Others (about 300, mostly local) | 60 |
| Total | 182 |

*Excluding sales to local suppliers, figures for which are included under "Others."
†Key system sales only.
*Source:* SRI Long Range Planning Service

Some industry observers felt that the interconnect suppliers had been unable to fully exploit what they believed to be the major weaknesses of the telephone companies, namely, their fairly obsolete product line and their inability to respond quickly to the changing market and technology. Much of the Japanese and other PBX equipment the interconnect suppliers were handling was only marginally superior in terms of features to the equipment manufactured by Western Electric. Thus they were forced to compete largely on the basis of lower price, more flexible pricing arrangements, and greater installation flexibility. Even the Tele/Resources PBX, while fully electronic and easy to install, was not a great deal more flexible than conventional PBX equipment and, in addition, required expensive special phones. Also, it was said to be difficult to maintain. Nevertheless, the first two years of production of this PBX was sold out within a few months of its being introduced.

Interconnect companies, both regional and national, stocked spare parts for their customers' PBXs so that they could rapidly get a customer's malfunctioning telephone system operating again. The faulty parts were then returned to the manufacturer for repair. Since this could take weeks—even months—the interconnect companies generally carried substantial inventories of spare parts.

## The Response of the Telephone Companies

The AT&T operating companies and the independent telephone companies were vigorously resisting the encroachment of the interconnect suppliers into the PBX and key systems market. In 1970, AT&T had established a huge task force with people from Bell Labs, Western Electric and AT&T marketing and engineering at a new facility in Denver, Colorado, to develop a new, more competitive PBX product line. This resulted in four new competitively priced electronic or semielectronic PBXs (shown in Exhibit 6) being introduced between 1971 and 1973. But even this progress was not rapid enough for some of the AT&T operating companies and they began to buy PBXs from outside suppliers. General Telephone had also taken similar steps to remain competitive.

The telephone operating companies also modified their pricing structures to improve their competitive position. Traditionally, telephone companies only leased equipment to users; thus the user paid an installation charge and a monthly rental/service fee (which could, of course, be increased from time to time) that continued as long as the customer had the equipment. By 1973, some of the telephone companies were giving their customers the option of paying for the use of the equipment with a "two-tier" pricing arrangement. With a "two-tier" pricing scheme, the customer signed a lease for the equipment for a specified number of years (usually between 5 years and 10 years). Then the cost of the equipment was split into two portions—the "capital" cost of the equipment, which could be paid off immediately, and the maintenance/administrative charge, which was paid over the life of the lease and which could be increased during this period.

# CURRENT STATUS OF THE INTERCONNECT MARKET AND FUTURE PROSPECTS

In a proprietary report published by the Long Range Planning Service of SRI International, it was estimated that sales by interconnect suppliers had grown from virtually zero in 1968 to $182 million (at end-user prices) in 1973. Manufacturers' selling prices were approximately 50 percent of the end-user prices, and given that there was a substantial amount of inventory at the supplier level, manufacturers' shipments were expected to total $120 million in 1973.

The $182 million sales estimate was broken into three categories:

1. $130 million in PBX sales. This included 3300 PBXs with 248,000 telephones. This was estimated to be 12.4 percent of the dollar value of all new and replacement PBX installations in 1973.
2. $47 million in key systems sales. This included 6000 key systems with 72,000 telephones. This was estimated to be 6.7 percent of the dollar value of all new and replacement key system installations in 1973.
3. $5 million in service and maintenance revenues which included charges for telephones added to the original system and moving telephones within an office.

SRI also attempted to project the market growth through 1985. Given the uncertainties surrounding the interconnect market, both conservative and optimistic projections were made. These projections took into account probable shakeouts in the industry, stronger competition from the telephone companies, regulatory factors, and a shortening life cycle (hence more frequent replacement) for this type of equipment.

On the basis of SRI's assumptions, total interconnect supplier sales were expected to be in the range of $1.1 to $1.7 billion by 1985; this was expected to give interconnect suppliers an installed base penetration of 21 percent to 30 percent for PBXs and 15 percent to 21 percent for key systems. During this period SRI expected rapid technological development to continue with computer-controlled or stored-logic electronic switching systems being standard in PBX and key systems by 1980.

## PBX AND KEY SYSTEMS CUSTOMERS

One of the first things Dick Moley had done after joining ROLM in August 1973 was to talk to several large companies about their communication problems. Commenting on these interviews Moley said: "What they came up with was very interesting—because what they said their problems were, were problems that were not being addressed by the interconnect equipment or the Bell System equipment at the time, and that is where we saw our opportunity. What they said was that the largest portion of their bill, frequently 70 to 80 percent, is toll expenses. If you are a large electronics company, for example, you have Foreign Exchange lines, Tie lines and WATS lines. Trying to get people to use these—to get them to go to the proper tables and look up how to call a number in a particular city, say Los Angeles—to dial 76 for Los Angeles, then dial 9 for an outside line, then dial the telephone number—is very difficult. Even if a person does all this, the line frequently will be busy. Similarly, to gain access to a WATS line, the caller may have to call a special operator and wait for a line to become available. So what happens in many companies, of course, is that many people make many long-distance calls without bothering to use these expensive facilities. Furthermore, many companies wish to keep track of who was calling which numbers, both to control abuse and to bill departments for their real use of facilities, rather than simply making an arbitrary allocation. Many people also felt restrictions on toll calling on a telephone-by-telephone basis and automated queuing for WATS lines seemed to be needed features. The equipment available in 1973 simply did not address these needs, and the Bell System obviously didn't have a great incentive to optimize the use of toll calling facilities, since it would negatively impact its revenues."

A second major area of concern that surfaced in these interviews was the cost of making, and the time required to make, changes in the telephone system when people were relocated. This was particularly true in firms that used a project type of organization or in organizations that were experiencing rapid growth, where the average times between moves of a phone could be as short as six months. Every time personnel changes were made and people were relocated, the telephone company had to be called in to change wires and relocate the phones and sometimes the companies had to wait quite a long time for these changes to be made. Furthermore, the Bell System and independent telephone company tariffs to make these changes varied across the country. In some areas it cost about $15 to move a phone, whereas in other areas, such as New York, it might cost $75 for the same service. ROLM estimated on average the real cost of performing this service was about $50. Many large companies operating in several parts of the country were aware of these differences and realized that under pressure from the Public Utility Commissions for the telephone companies to stop "subsidizing business," these charges would probably rise in areas where they were low. One very large firm of consultants operating in San Francisco, where the cost of moving a phone was only about $20, was already spending over $400,000 per year on these moves and changes.

"Another area that was an absolute nightmare was key phone systems," commented Dick Moley. "We saw that in our own offices that year when Ken Oshman's office had to be relocated, two men spent a whole day recabling 125-pair cables to the new location for the key phone system. The cost was nominal, but it clearly cost the telephone company a lot of money to make these changes. We then asked ourselves why are key systems so difficult to move? The reason is that each light on the call director's pushbutton set takes six wires to activate, so you may need a very thick (1 inch in diameter) 125-pair cable from the switching equipment to the call director telephone with 20 or so lines, and you clearly can't afford to run such a cable all over the building. So essentially the wiring is customized for the key system. That seemed to us to be totally insane with the available electronics. So we said we can do it differently. What we can do is use a key phone with a three-pair cable—one pair for voice, one pair to power the electronics and the third pair to digitally signal which button is depressed and to indicate which button to light. Thus, if we standardize the building wiring completely on three-pair cables which connect to wall sockets much like electrical wiring, the user will not have to rewire the building if some phone is moved. They might have to plug in a special box and make an arrangement back in the switching equipment to make sure it was connected to a switch to drive a key phone rather than a single line phone, but no rewiring will be necessary."

Large customers would be critical to ROLM's success in the marketplace, since the computer-controlled PBX system that they were developing was designed to handle 100 to 800 lines. This line range had been chosen because cost-effective computer-controlled models that would provide the kind of benefits customers desired could not yet be cost competitive for installations of less than 100-line capacity. In 1973 only a very small number of Fortune 500 companies were buying from interconnect suppliers. Most of the sales by the interconnect companies had been made to smaller organizations; in fact, about 75 percent of the interconnect equipment was sold to hotels and motels, wholesalers and retailers, stockbrokers, insurance agencies, hospitals and clinics, attorneys, banks, stockbrokers, manufacturers, and service industries. Few of the installations made by the interconnect companies had more than 100 lines.

For these reasons, a final issue Dick Moley raised in his interviews with the large companies was why they had not bought equipment from interconnect suppliers. A major reason the companies cited was that they saw few economic benefits from buying from interconnect suppliers. The main benefit was that they could purchase the equipment and hence freeze their equipment cost (since they would be unaffected by telephone company rental rate increases). But equipment was usually only 20 to 30 percent of their costs, and when a discounted cash flow analysis of the purchase versus rental choice was made, the savings often turned out to be minor. Meanwhile, if the equipment was purchased, the company was locked into equipment that might soon become obsolete. It seemed that smaller companies were much less likely to do a discounted cash flow analysis and seemed to be largely attracted to the interconnect PBXs by their marginally better features and the belief they would get better service from these companies than they would from the telephone operating companies. An additional factor that might help explain the failure of the interconnect companies to penetrate larger companies was that few of the interconnect suppliers appeared to have sales organizations that were capable of conducting a multi-level sales campaign at several levels of decision making in prospective large companies.

From his discussions with the large companies Moley also gained a better appreciation of the decision-making process for PBXs and key systems. Voice communication decision makers were generally low-level office managers or communication managers. These decisions had historically been made at a low level because the decisions to be made with respect to telecommunications equipment were generally of a minor nature. Until 1968, the Bell System operating company or the independent telephone company was a monopoly supplier and hence there was no choice of vendor. The office or communications manager often relied greatly on the recommendations of the telephone company salesperson and, in fact, frequently the manager was a former Bell System employee. The main responsibilities of the manager were largely those of placing orders with the telephone company and coordinating installation and service activities. When alternative suppliers to the telephone companies became available, they were very cautious about recommending them, since the risks of poor service and the possibility of the interconnect supplier going out of business were not inconsequential. Furthermore, since switching to an interconnect supplier typically required that the equipment be purchased rather than leased, they usually lacked the authority to make the decision themselves, and the capital expenditure had often to be approved at very high levels in the organization — sometimes even at the board of directors level. The communication manager was not usually accustomed to preparing these types of proposals and doing the necessary internal selling to get the proposals approved.

The results of the customer interviews made ROLM management very enthusiastic about their potential entry into the telecommunications market. As Moley remarked, "Out of our discussions I and the others in ROLM management became really enthusiastic, because clearly here is a vast market where we potentially have the capability to solve meaningful customer problems and save companies large amounts of money. Computer technology was the key to solving these problems — we could optimize call routings, handle toll restrictions, too. If there are telephones in place, handling moves and changes becomes simply a matter of remotely reprogramming the switching equipment — nobody needs to visit physically the customer's office or plant."

## THE ROLM PBX

By October 1973, Jim Kasson and his two associates had made considerable progress on the technical aspects of the ROLM product. The conventional wisdom in the telephone industry trade magazines at the time was that time division multiplexing (TDM) with pulse code modulation (PCM) switching technology and stored logic (computer control)

control technology would not be viable, cost-effective technologies until the late 1970s or early 1980s. Jim Kasson was now convinced it was a viable technology in 1973. As a result of some clever circuit work and ROLM's knowledge of minicomputers, software, and PCM technology, they were convinced their approach would work and would be cost-effective. They had already "bread-boarded" (i.e., laid out the electronic circuitry in a crude way) key technology elements that were new to ROLM and they even had a couple of telephones in the laboratory working with their switching circuitry. In effect, the technological advances they were taking advantage of promised to change the nature of PBX manufacture from a labor- and capital-intensive operation to a technology-intensive electronic assembly operation which would require the manufacturer to have minicomputer, software, and solid-state switching expertise. These were all technologies in which ROLM management felt their company had significant strengths.

The management of ROLM was convinced that the flexibility of a computer-controlled PBX built on a TDM technology would change the economics of a business communication system's installation, maintenance, and operation, besides providing excellent user convenience. For example, with their PBX it would be possible to prewire a building with standard three-pair cable connected to wall outlets. Then all that was necessary to install a complete system was to connect the cables to the PBX, plug the standard telephone sets into the sockets, and enter into the computer the locations and extension numbers of the telephones. In the case of a multiline key set, the information entered into the PBX would include information on all the extensions which are to be routed to the set. Moves and changes of extensions would be a straightforward matter of entering the new configuration information into the computer. No longer would it be necessary to have the wiring tailored to the specific configuration and have ancillary keyset switching equipment located remote from the PBX. The features, both standard and optional, that they proposed to offer on the ROLM PBX are listed in Exhibit 8.

Thus their proposed product was a minicomputer-controlled TDM system which could handle both voice and data communications. In essence it had all the capabilities of the successful IBM computer-controlled PBXs, plus the additional capability of handling key telephones without requiring large cables and key service units. Furthermore, unlike the IBM PBXs, which cost from two to three times as much as conventional systems, the ROLM PBX was expected to be price competitive in the range of 100 to 500 extensions, a range which, they estimated, accounted for 60 percent of the dollar value of all PBX systems.

# DECISIONS FACING ROLM IN OCTOBER 1973 _____

Although many of the technical uncertainties with respect to the product had been resolved, there were several dark clouds on the horizon. The Bell System was aggressively attempting to stop the competitive erosion by moves on both the regulatory front and by improving equipment and developing new pricing schemes. In June 1973, at the urging of the telephone companies, the North Carolina Utility Commission had proposed banning all interconnect equipment from the state. Although in January the Federal Communications Commission ruled that its own ruling preempted state regulation of interconnect

**EXHIBIT 8**

## FEATURES AND SERVICES TO BE OFFERED ON THE PROPOSED ROLM PBX

### Station Features—Standard

| | |
|---|---|
| Direct outward dialing | Lockout with secrecy |
| Station-to-station dialing | One-way splitting |
| Nonconsecutive station hunting | Outgoing trunk camp-on |
| Programmable class of service | Processor-controlled changes—Type A |
| Consultation hold—all calls | Trunk answer from any station |
| Call forwarding, unlimited | Tie trunks |
| Flexible station, controlled conference | Toll restriction |
| Group call | Trunk-to-trunk connections station—Type B |
| Indication of camp-on to station | Trunk-to-trunk consultation |
| Individual transfer—all calls | |

### Station Features—Optional

| | |
|---|---|
| Alternate routing (toll call optimization) | Redundancy |
| Automatic redial | Off premises extension |
| CCSA access | Private lines |
| Dictation access and control | Music on hold—attendant |
| Direct inward dialing | Music on hold—system |
| Direct inward system access | Music on camp-on |
| Discriminating ringing | Reserve power—inverter |
| Plug-in station (with keyset adapter) | Speed calling |
| Secretarial intercept | Area code restriction |
| Station DTMF to rotary dial conversion | Traffic measurement |
| Tenant service | Paging interface |
| Automatic identification of outward dialing | |

### Attendant Features—Standard

| | |
|---|---|
| Attendant camp-on | Switched loop trunk selection |
| Attendant conference | Switched loop station selection |
| Attendant console | Flexible intercept |
| Attendant transfer of incoming call | System alarm indications |
| Attendant transfer—outgoing | Multiple trunk groups—unlimited |
| Attendant trunk busy lamp field | |

### Attendant Features—Optional
Busy lamp field
Busy verification of stations

---

equipment, the issue was still in the courts. ROLM management was also concerned about other regulatory actions the Bell System might take. On the pricing front, the Bell System and the independent telephone companies had made their pricing structures more competitive and had the potential to make further moves in that direction. Furthermore, the Bell System's intensified product development efforts were likely to result in products that were technically much more competitive with the proposed ROLM offering than was the current product line, although ROLM would probably have a year or so lead time. Other interconnect manufacturers would probably be into the market with more competitive offerings even earlier than the Bell System.

ROLM's board of directors, in preliminary discussions of the proposed entry, were not totally convinced of the wisdom of ROLM, a $4 million company, moving against such formidable competitors and openly questioned whether this was the best area in which to invest the company's limited resources. Investment bankers also raised similar concerns. Even within the top ranks of ROLM management there were executives who were quite unsure about whether a move into the telecommunications market was in ROLM's best interest. The treasurer and the director of manufacturing had both formerly worked for Arcata Communications and had seen at first hand the problems of the interconnect business. They were among those expressing concern.

From a manufacturing cost viewpoint, ROLM management was not concerned about the disparity in size between ROLM and its competitors, whose manufacturing experience base for the most part was built on electromechanical equipment (which was labor- and capital-intensive), whereas ROLM's equipment was largely electronic. In their view, this made it feasible for ROLM to compete with the likes of Western Electric.

## Pricing the PBX

Kasson and his team had concluded that with a further investment of $500,000 in engineering and manufacturing, they could get the product into production. If given the go-ahead, they expected to have a prototype working in the laboratory by mid-1974 and to begin shipping systems in early 1975.

Detailed estimates of manufacturing costs had been developed by Kasson and others on the PBX team. With a sales price based on two and one half times manufacturing cost (direct materials, direct labor, and overhead based on direct labor cost), the ROLM PBX promised to be cost competitive with the most closely competitive models available in the United States. They anticipated that volume discounts would be given to customers ordering multiple PBXs, if they decided to market the product through telephone companies or interconnect companies. Since the ROLM PBX made heavy use of electronic components (e.g., the minicomputer, the computer memory and integrated circuits), the cost of the PBX was expected to decline over time as the cost of electronic components continued their decline. Electromechanical PBXs, and even electronic PBXs based on analogue technologies, were expected to experience a much more static cost future.

## Channels of Distribution for the PBX

In many respects ROLM's management felt the most crucial decision facing them in 1973 was the choice of channels of distribution for their PBX system. Dick Moley felt they had several alternatives open to them:

SELL TO THE BELL SYSTEM.   The operating companies of the Bell System had traditionally relied exclusively on Western Electric for all their equipment. However, the competitive pressures from the interconnect companies had resulted in several of the operating companies, including the largest one, Pacific Telephone, buying equipment from other suppliers. Pacific Telephone had bought electromechanical PBX systems from Japanese suppliers and more recently it had bought Northern Telecom's fully electronic PBX, which handled up to 120 lines. The former move was not a very radical one, since the Japanese designs were similar to Western Electric designs and could be installed and maintained by their field service force without any extensive retraining. The Northern Telecom purchase was more significant since this did require retraining the field service force. Since the Bell operating companies were still believed to control some 80 percent of the installed PBX base, even a small share of this market would represent a huge sales volume to ROLM.

SELL TO THE INDEPENDENT TELEPHONE COMPANIES, SUCH AS GENERAL TELEPHONE.   While the independent telephone companies covered about 15 percent of the phones in the United States, they were more concentrated in rural areas and were growing about 50 percent more rapidly than AT&T. This reflected the movement of industry and population away from major metropolitan areas. Since larger companies still tended to concentrate in major metropolitan areas, the independent telephone companies' share of the large PBX (greater than 100 lines) market was much less than 15 percent. Their captive manufacturing subsidiaries were not as strong as Western Electric, and the independent telephone companies had never relied on them as much. But even taking into account that the independent telephone companies were a much smaller factor in the market than the Bell System, they still represented a large, burgeoning market—with companies like Stromberg–Carlson and several Japanese and European manufacturers very active in it.

SELL TO THE INTERCONNECT COMPANIES.   These were concentrated in the larger metropolitan areas. Here ROLM had two alternatives: *(a)* The national companies such as Litton Business Systems, ITT, RCA Service Company, United Business Communications and Stromberg–Carlson Communications or *(b)* the regional companies such as Tele/Resources, Fisk Telephone Systems and Scott-Buttner Communications.

Many of the national suppliers were in trouble due to the lack of experienced managers, higher than anticipated investments, heavier than anticipated installation and maintenance expenses, too rapid geographic expansion resulting in loss of control, and the difficulty of providing quick and adequate service capability on a nationwide basis. These problems were exacerbated by the fiercely competitive nature of the markets, the heavy legal expenses, and the drain on management time necessary to challenge some of the telephone companies' new pricing schemes before the regulatory commissions. These chaotic market conditions had resulted in some companies getting into difficulties and being forced to merge with others.

Some of the regional interconnect companies were doing quite well in their local markets. They bought their equipment from a variety of manufacturers, including Nippon, Stromberg–Carlson and Tele/Resources. Generally the manufacturers required them to handle the equipment on a nonexclusive basis, so that two or more interconnect companies in the same market area might carry the same PBX line. The regional companies typically were undercapitalized and sold small systems. It was very seldom that one handled a PBX with a capacity larger than 100 lines. Most of the equipment they were handling was still electromechanical. While marketing through regional interconnect companies had some advantages, particularly from a servicing perspective, there was a real question of whether large companies with multiple locations would want to deal with multiple interconnect companies. Some of the other manufacturers, including Northern Telecom, handled large sales directly, and simply subcontracted with the regional interconnect companies for installation and maintenance services.

SELL DIRECT. This would require ROLM to recruit and train their own field sales force. This approach had some obvious sales advantages, especially when it came to dealing with large accounts with multiple locations around the country.

## Dick Moley's Task

Dick Moley had to make decisions with respect to channels of distribution and pricing and also with respect to such closely related issues as the amount and nature of advertising and sales promotion to be directed at end users. By the November 1973 board meeting he hoped to have selected and laid out in some detail the marketing plan for the ROLM PBX. He hoped he would be able to present a convincing case for ROLM's entry into the PBX market.

## APPENDIX A

### PBX and Key Systems Technology

Much of the technological change in PBX systems was occurring in the switching and control systems. The technological alternatives in both the switching and control systems are shown in Appendix B. With respect to the switching system, two major alternatives were possible: space division multiplexing (SDM) and time division multiplexing (TDM). An SDM system was one in which separate individual transmission paths were set up for the duration of the call. A TDM system was one in which the speech on each active line was sampled at a very high rate, so that no information was lost, and the samples were assigned to unique time slots on a common transmission line. The original signal could be reconstructed from these samples when needed. The ability to handle many calls on one line promised to lower costs. In a TDM system the samples could be trans-

mitted as either an analogue (pulse amplitude modulation [PAM]) signal or a digital (pulse code modulation [PCM]) signal. If pulse code modulation was used, then all signals were digital—making such a system ideal for transmitting data as well as voice. This was expected to be an increasingly valuable feature by the late 1970s, as more and more companies wished to transmit both data and voice over the same telecommunications system. Furthermore, if a digital signal was sent over a reliable transmission line, there was no cross-talk or distortion, which one could get if an analogue system were used. ROLM engineers believed that a PBX with a TDM analogue system could not (with the technology then available) be designed to handle more than 120 lines without excessive cross-talk. Partly for this reason, TDM with pulse code modulation was carrying an increasing share of the Bell System's long-distance traffic. Nevertheless, many observers in the early 1970s did not expect that the pulse code modulation technology would be cost-effective in PBXs until the late 1970s.

The control system could be either distributed control or common control. A distributed control system was one in which the control logic was distributed throughout the PBX system (e.g., if key phones were used, some of the control logic was in the key phone unit), whereas a common control system was one in which all the control functions were centralized in one set of logic. With a common control system, the control equipment was only tied up during the time the connection was made and not during the conversation. A wired logic common control system basically did with electronic components what was otherwise done by electro-mechanical relays. On the other hand, a computer-controlled common control system added a new dimension to the PBX. New circuits had to be added to a wired logic system in order to alter its properties and capabilities, but a computer-controlled system's functions could be altered by changing its program. This gave a computer-controlled system great flexibility and the potential to meet future demands that wired logic systems could not match.

# APPENDIX B

PBX Technological Alternatives

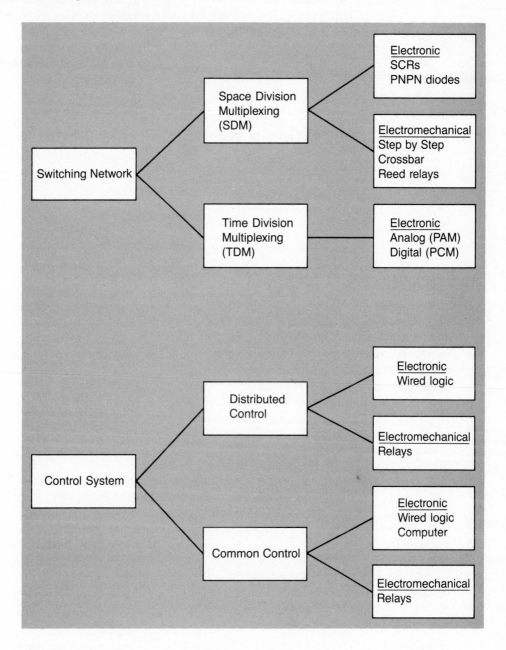

# Judson Industries, Inc.

## Evaluating a Market Reentry Situation

## BACKGROUND

Easy Drive is a registered trademark for a motor-driven power tool used for installing mobile home anchors into the earth. The anchors are widely used to secure mobile homes in place to help protect against wind and storm damage. The product is manufactured by Judson Industries, a manufacturer of a wide variety of industrial products. Judson Industries determined that a simpler, easier way of installing mobile home anchors was needed because existing methods required hand twisting, truck/tractor auger devices, and heavy and cumbersome hand-held power tools. Easy Drive worked fast because it turned at 18 RPM when anchoring a full-rated load. It was a powerful tool that developed more torque than any existing hand-held model. Easy Drive was lightweight; it weighed only 30 pounds. The top management of Judson Industries believed there was a definite market for this new product.

Easy Drive was first introduced into the market in early 1980. One hundred and sixty-four units were sold in the first year with virtually no advertising. In 1981, sales increased to 312 units. However, late in 1981 a small oil leak was discovered around the main gear. Fortunately, the oil leak did not affect the performance of Easy Drive. Soon after the leak problem was corrected, gears started breaking. Easy Drive soon developed an image of shoddy workmanship and poor quality. The demand for replacement parts far exceeded the normal inventory, which caused severe delays in the service and repair of defective Easy Drives. A new senior engineer took over the project, redesigned the gear system, and improved the oil seal. By late 1982, the product ran well and had no serious performance problems. However, the image of poor quality and slow service still plagued Easy Drive in the marketplace. A total of 151 new units were sold in 1982. The

Names of the corporation and its executives are disguised. This case is to serve as a basis for class discussion rather than to illustrate effective or ineffective decision making. This case was modified from one originally prepared by Professor A. H. Kizilbash.

senior engineer, Philip Voss, Jr., now in charge of Easy Drive, believed sales should have been three to four times that number.

# COMPETITION

Jones Anchor, Inc., was a company founded by former Judson Industries employees. In 1982, management noticed a major void in the market and developed a tool to compete with Easy Drive. This machine was less powerful, turned at only 6 RPM, and was considerably more cumbersome than Easy Drive. By being thoroughly familiar with the Easy Drive product problems, Jones Anchor was able to capitalize on Judson Industries' weaknesses. Jones Anchor's product was sold at a much lower price, carried a one-year warranty, and was delivered faster. The promotional slogan for the Jones product was "safe slow speed," implying that faster-turning tools were not as safe to use because, if the worker slipped, he or she could be injured. It also claimed that less soil was disturbed when the anchor was driven slowly and that it made a better and more permanent installation.

# PREVIOUS MARKETING OF EASY DRIVE

SERVICE/WARRANTY.   As a matter of policy, Judson Industries performed all repair and warranty service at the plant in Lincoln, Nebraska. In order to compete with Jones Anchor, Judson extended its warranty from three to six months.

TARGET MARKET.   The primary target market for Easy Drive was the mobile home installer who places the home on the site and secures it. The installer may be an independent or associated with one or more mobile home parks. Other markets for Easy Drive included anchoring of (1) playground equipment, (2) rental equipment (light construction equipment), and (3) transformers and other devices for public utilities. The utility market was thought to be particularly large and promising. However, Easy Drive was probably not well suited for this use, as the job required a more powerful anchoring device.

DISTRIBUTION.   Judson is a well-established firm in the electrical, construction, and maintenance markets. The firm employs 110 salespersons who call on approximately 4,000 franchised distributors across the nation. None of these distributors, however, sells to the mobile home installation market. Judson salespersons did not have experience in selling to the mobile home and related markets. Judson's line consisted of over 3,000 items, and it was unrealistic to expect that existing salespersons and agents would give Easy Drive much importance.

Philip Voss's first goal was to establish a network of distributors for Easy Drive. He felt that the best distributors would be those who sold anchors and other items required in the installation of mobile homes, such as skirting, awnings, steps. Thirty-five distributors of this type were recruited. Most distributors sold Easy Drive directly to the installers, but some dealers also operated in this market. The dealers would buy from the distributor and resell to the end user. In many instances, it was discovered that the dealer would allow the free use of Easy Drive to buyers who would purchase their anchors from him. Goods were shipped to distributors on 2/10, net 30 terms. From the beginning, many of these distributors were slow in paying, and when product difficulties developed, some did not pay at all. The mobile home market was growing slowly, and the high cost of money forced some Easy Drive distributors into bankruptcy.

PRICE.    At the time of introduction, Easy Drive was priced at a target level to provide a suitable rate of return for Judson. Drop shipments were permitted without any penalty, so many distributors simply took orders and had Judson ship the units directly to customers. This allowed the distributors to enjoy a 25 percent margin without ever taking physical possession of the goods. Judson introduced a new price structure to promote stocking of Easy Drive by distributors. Under the new policy, a 30 percent margin was allowed for an order of three or more units, and a 20 percent margin was given for one or two units shipped to a distributor for stock. A 7.5 percent markup was allowed for any quantity drop-shipped. The 1982 pricing schedule is shown in Exhibit 1.

Early in 1982 it was discovered that the cost of manufacturing Easy Drive had risen drastically, partly because of reduced demand that caused smaller production runs. The costs of materials and parts had also risen significantly. Judson's profit margin had dipped to approximately 7 percent below the corporate minimum objective of 15 percent before taxes. It was felt by management that Easy Drive could become a profitable product and surpass corporate profit goals if at least 250 units per year could be sold without having to raise the price.

PROMOTION.    Up to this point in time, only one effort was made to advertise the product. Three advertisements were placed in the only national publication aimed at the target market. This ad stressed speed, power, time saved, and compact size. It was run for the three prime months of the anchoring season, and a moderate number of inquiries were generated. Voss was not sure how many inquiries were converted to actual sales.

Judson Industries also rented a small booth each year at the National Mobile Home Exhibition. The show is attended by park operators and mobile home installers. Easy Drive was mounted on a display stand where it could be operated by interested persons. Representatives of Judson Industries and Voss were present at the booth to give out literature and answer questions. No records were kept of the inquiries, leads, and actual sales that resulted from the trade show. Voss also considered having a booth at two or three regional mobile home trade shows. .

FUTURE SITUATION.    Judson has not conducted any market research or gathered any data on the total size of the anchor market. Judson's past and present share of the market is therefore unknown. There is agreement among management personnel that three specific markets should be catered to: (1) placement of new mobile homes, (2) nonanchored existing mobile homes, and (3) replacement of worn-out anchors in presently anchored homes. Projected sales for the remainder of 1982 will bring the year's total sales to only about 40 percent of the forecasted goal. At a profit margin of 7 percent below the minimum

**EXHIBIT 1**

## EASY DRIVE DISTRIBUTOR PRICE SHEET

Effective June 7, 1982

| Cat. No. | Description | Ship Wt. (lb) | List | Dealer | Drop Shipped Any Quantity | Distributor 1-2 Units for Your Stock | Distributor 3 or More Units for Your Stock | Distributor 12 or More Units for Your Stock |
|---|---|---|---|---|---|---|---|---|
| 211-40 | Easy Drive, 120 V., 0–60 Hz. | 40 | $760.40 | $581.50 | $541.90 | $487.30 | $435.69 | $410.64 |
| | *Anchor adapters\** | | | | | | *Any Quantity* | |
| 46-00 | 1" square (hollow) | 1½ | 12.65 | 9.00 | 8.40 | | 6.60 | |
| 31-00 | ¾" square solid drive | 2½ | 19.75 | 14.55 | 12.60 | | 9.80 | |
| 42-96 | 1¼" hex upset drive | 1½ | 21.00 | 17.00 | 14.90 | | 12.50 | |
| 54-77 | Ovaleye & Clevis styles | 3 | 36.35 | 28.00 | 25.15 | | 19.75 | |
| 22-11 | 1" hex upset style | 1½ | 16.35 | 12.00 | 10.25 | | 8.50 | |

*Adapters were also manufactured and sold by Judson Industries. The adapters were "heads" that attached to Easy Drive for the various sizes of anchors.

acceptable to Judson Industries, Easy Drive was a candidate for elimination. Voss had been transferred to another Judson production facility as an expediter.

# PROPOSED NEW MARKETING PLAN

In the summer of 1982 a young salesman, Dave Francis, was recruited by Judson. He had experience selling to the mobile home market for a manufacturer of complementary products. As the new product manager, Francis was to be responsible for Easy Drive. After looking at the available information, Francis proposed the following marketing plan for Easy Drive.

## Objectives

1. Increase sales of Easy Drive to an acceptable level (first-year goal, 250 units).
2. Reestablish Easy Drive in the marketplace as a high-quality, reliable tool.
3. Position Judson Industries in the market as the "expert" in the field of anchoring.
4. Provide customer service equal to or better than competition.
5. Develop a reliable channel of distribution.

## Conduct Research in the Following Areas

1. The mobile home industry to determine the number of mobile homes being shipped per year, how many are forecast for the future, and to what geographic locations they are being shipped.
2. The anchor/tie-down industry to find the volume of mobile home anchors and/or tie-down systems being sold, and what the characteristics are of each (Should we offer more adaptors?).
3. Mandatory tie-down areas to document what states require tie-downs, what HUD requirements might apply, and which insurance companies insist upon tie-downs.
4. Mobile home installers to determine what "makes them tick," what their buying motives are, etc. This, of course, would demand face-to-face interviews as well as secondary research.
5. Calculation of Judson's market share.

## Distribution

The next phase requires establishing a reliable channel of distribution. New distributors must be selected (and be willing to participate) on the following basis:

1. Must have satisfactory credit rating; credit reports to be obtained prior to first contact.
2. Must enter a qualifying stocking order of $2,500, based on dealer price, for tools.
3. Reorders for tools and accessories subject to regular sheet prices.

4. Will report warranty to our center; will be factory trained; will keep a "perpetual inventory" of repair parts; will be paid for warranty work according to a labor hour chart; will receive discount on all parts used for out-of-warranty repairs; parts will be returnable at cost if franchise dissolved; and must maintain records of sales and repairs and report monthly to Judson.
5. Must have active outside sales force.
6. Geographically separated from other selected distributors.
7. Selection to begin August 16, 1982: (a) Cooperative personal calls with agent and product manager and/or national sales manager; (b) obtain initial order and sign franchise agreement.

## Promotion

Advertising is to be done in national and regional publications emphasizing the product benefits to the user and also the "new" faster service at authorized service centers. Cooperative advertising with distributors is a possibility in regional publications.

Advertising is to begin in January 1983 with the special National Mobile Home Exhibition issue of *Mobile Home Merchandiser* (nationally distributed), and again in February, March, and April issues. These are buying months for installers in preparation for the upcoming anchoring season. In warmer climates where seasonality is not a factor, advertising can begin in October and November.

Judson's salespeople will participate in Counter Days where they will first hold a sales meeting with distributor sales personnel to be certain they are educated and "up to date" on the product. Counter Days are an ongoing promotional tool and should be used periodically throughout the year to keep potential customers informed. They are also cooperative affairs in that the cost is shared by Judson and the distributor. A movie of the Easy Drive in action will be developed to assist in demonstrating the product, and this is expected to be available October 1, 1982.

Judson will participate in at least one trade show (national) with the potential of entering others as determined during the September planning meeting. The movie will be made available to distributors wishing to exhibit at regional shows.

Anchoring seminars are to be developed by Judson salespeople along with a distributor sales rep who will conduct a seminar for a group of installers and park operators. Although these seminars are to be informative sessions on proper installation techniques, etc., their main purpose is to get an order! An incentive should be offered to the purchaser, distributor salesperson, and Judson salesperson for orders written at the seminar. The purchaser should receive a free adaptor, and the latter two cash bonuses.

# Gould, Inc.–Graphics Division

## Selecting a Product-Market Strategy

In August 1969, Mr. Willard C. Koepf, national sales manager of the Graphics Division of Gould, Inc., was asked by corporate headquarters to review the marketing possibilities for the electrostatic printer Gould 4800 and to formulate a marketing plan for the beginning fiscal year. The printer, which was the division's only product, had been introduced with high expectations at the Spring Joint Computer Conference in Boston in May 1969. "Our feelings ranged from the belief that customers would break down our door to take the device from our hands to the opinion of the engineers that the product was almost too good to be put on the market," Koepf commented.

So far, no orders for the printer had been received. During the computer show, however, potential end users had examined the product with interest, and the printer had been given extensive coverage in the trade press. Leading original-equipment manufacturers (OEMs) such as IBM, Honeywell, Burroughs, and Univac had been equally interested in the product, but none of them had made a commitment to push it to end users and to provide the necessary interfacing and software support. As he was thinking about the most suitable marketing approach for the printer, Koepf wondered particularly whether he should concentrate his marketing efforts on the OEMs or whether the Graphics Division should try to sell the product directly to end users.

## COMPANY BACKGROUND

The Graphics Division in Cleveland, Ohio, was one of 26 quasi-independent operating divisions of Gould, Inc., a diversified concern resulting from a merger, effective July 31, 1969, of Gould National Battery, Inc., and the Clevite Corporation.

Prior to the merger, the Graphics Division had been a department of Brush Instruments Division of the former Clevite Corporation. Clevite, an old, well-established company, was manufacturing and marketing such diverse products as copper foil for printed circuits; engine bearings and bushings; hearing aids; torpedoes; as well as a wide array of high-precision data display instruments for scientific, industrial, and aerospace applications, such as oscillographs, biomedical recorders, and plotters.

In its chosen fields, and more especially in the instruments sector, Clevite had enjoyed a solid reputation as a high-quality/high-price supplier. Selling the company's products required highly specialized technical sales teams as well as a close relation with customers. Its favorable acceptance in well-known markets had enabled the company to concentrate on the task of engineering and producing premium goods. Clevite did not undertake systematic market research, and its corporate marketing staff had been kept very small.

The merger of Clevite and Gould National Battery, Inc., had been initiated by Gould's president, Mr. William T. Ylvisaker. He had been appointed chief executive of Gould National Battery late in 1967. Gould National Battery, founded in 1905, had relied mainly on the manufacturing and marketing of automotive and industrial batteries, with a minor part of its revenues coming from the sale of engine parts and air/oil/fuel filters to machinery manufacturers and the automotive aftermarket. In 1967, the company was generally considered as an ailing member of a stagnant industry, facing a declining market share and a fall in earnings of 25 percent between 1962 and 1967.

To turn the company around, Ylvisaker looked for opportunities to broaden the base of Gould through a strategy of planned acquisitions of compatible businesses and emphasis on new-product development. "We sat down and asked ourselves, 'What is this company?'" one company officer said.

> The definition we came up with was not one of products or markets; we define our business in terms of technology. We thought that if we defined our business in terms of markets or products, we might finally find ourselves in a lot of unrelated technologies and be unable to stay in a leadership position. Since technology is usually the basis for new products, this could be most serious. I think it is harder to develop good technology than to revise a distribution system and a marketing organization. If you define your business in terms of technologies, you have a sounder basis for growth.
>
> This is really why the Clevite Corporation was attractive for us. While there was some similarity in terms of markets served and products produced between Gould and Clevite, they were not serious direct competitors and were really different. But Gould National Battery has know-how in electrochemistry, electromechanics, and electronics from the battery business, as well as in metallurgy from the engine-parts business. Similarly, Clevite was dealing with electrochemistry in their production of electroplated foil and bearings, with electromechanics and electronics in their Brush Division, and also with metallurgy. So the merger was consistent with our concept of the business.
>
> We want excellence in a few selected technologies. I don't mean necessarily high technology – we are not breaking down new or fundamental barriers. We don't do basic research, but good application research. We want to be in the leading edge of existing technology, we want to be innovative in terms of products and processes.

We are all committed to building a business on a good, sound, solid basis. Our financial goals are to maintain a 15 percent growth in earnings per share over the next ten to fifteen years. To reach this goal requires two key things. (1) You must be willing to invest at that rate in new products and engineering, fixed assets and working capital. We are willing and able to do this. (2) You must be in markets that are growing at a rate of 15 percent a year. But we aren't yet and we must be. Our major thrust, therefore, will most likely be in the electronics field in order to get that growth. Statistically, we stand a better chance if we emphasize the electronics business. Certainly, one of the problems is to get into these growing markets.

The new electrostatic printer was seen by Gould's management as a way to enter the rapidly growing computer peripheral market. Gould envisaged the development of a complete line of computer peripheral devices and was prepared to invest up to $10 million in developing this line. Management was prepared to forego immediate profits on new investments but expected that such investments should become profitable within at least five years.

The organization of Gould, Inc., after the merger of Gould National Battery and Clevite, was based on the principal technologies used by the companies. Exhibit 1 shows an organization chart. Exhibit 2 gives a breakdown of sales by product and major customer groups for fiscal year 1969.

# THE ELECTROSTATIC PRINTER

The Gould 4800, a machine about the size of a teletype console, was a nonimpact printer using the technology of electrostatic printing. It was designed as an output-printing device for data from computers, magnetic tape, punched-card readers, cathode-ray-tube (CRT) memories, or telecommunication lines. It could print both alphanumeric characters and graphs at a speed of 4,800 86-character lines per minute, or the equivalent of one 8½ × 11 inch page per second. Here is the list of features as presented in Gould's sales catalogue:

| | |
|---|---|
| 4800 lines per minute | electrostatic printing – silent operation |
| alphanumerics and graphics | high-contrast, smudge-proof hard copy |
| versatility of application | programmed control of output forms |
| built-in character generator-controller | minimum maintenance |
| built-in control lines | reliable low-voltage operation |

The printer was a "by-product" of the Brush Division's activity in the field of data display instruments. In the course of the development of high-speed oscillographs, Brush engineers had gotten the idea that the oscillograph technology they were working on could be used in the creation of a high-speed printer for which, they thought, a wide market would exist in view of the fact that the existing computer printing devices were working at a much lower speed than the data-processing units to which they were connected.

EXHIBIT
1

## *PARTIAL ORGANIZATION CHART OF GOULD, INC.*

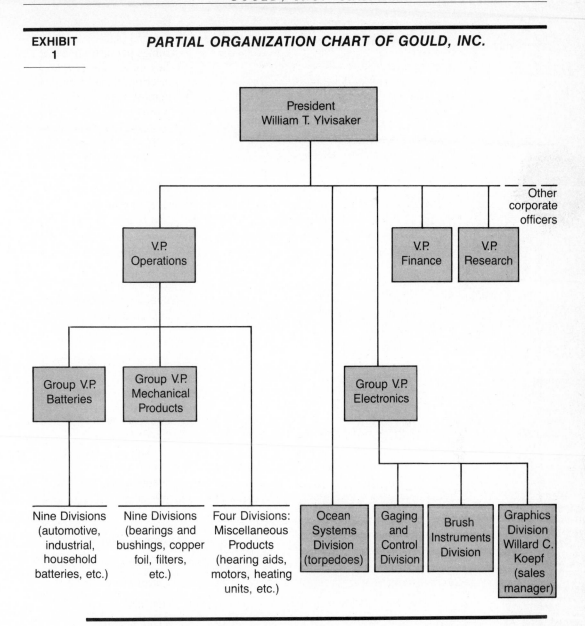

Indeed, one of the most widely discussed problems in the computer industry was the relative slowness of printout equipment compared to the speed of computers themselves.

Development work on the electrostatic printer was started in 1963. Initially, two engineers were engaged in it full time; in 1966, the development group was enlarged to four engineers. No formal budget had been established for development. Management's attitude, as one executive described it, had been, "Just work on it and see what can be done."

## EXHIBIT 2    COMBINED SALES OF GOULD NATIONAL AND CLEVITE BY PRODUCTS GROUPS AND MAJOR CUSTOMER GROUPS FOR FISCAL YEAR ENDED JUNE 30, 1969

*Percentage of Product Group Sales by Major Customer Groups*

| Products Groups | Machinery Manu-facturers | Trans-portation | Heavy Ind. Eng. Mfrs. | Auto Mfrs. | Automotive After-market | Con-sumer | Govern-ment | Metal/ Plastics Mfrs. | Medical/ R&D Labs | Community Utilities | Electro. Mfrs. |
|---|---|---|---|---|---|---|---|---|---|---|---|
| *Batteries* Sales (in millions): $140.4 % of total sales: 42.8% | 14.2% | 3.6% | –% | 1.1% | 42.4% | 10.3% | 4.4% | 9.4% | 0.3% | 7.5% | 2.2% |
| *Mechanical products* Sales (in millions): $111.8 % of total sales: 34.0% | 10.5 | 19.7 | 9.3 | 30.1 | 23.9 | – | 1.4 | 1.7 | – | 0.2 | 2.5 |
| *Electronic products* (including misc. products and torpedoes) Sales (in millions): $76.2 % of total sales: 23.2% | 2.4 | 2.1 | 0.5 | 1.4 | 0.1 | 6.3 | 38.3 | 1.9 | 1.9 | 1.8 | 43.2 |

*Source:* Company records

Total development costs, up to the market introduction in May 1969, amounted to roughly $500,000.

In 1968, a prototype of the printer had become ready, and shortly afterward, the development group was separated from the Brush Division to form the Graphics Division, headed by a general manager, Mr. Koeblitz, who had been engineering manager of the Brush Division for approximately 12 years. A national sales manager, Mr. Koepf, was hired. He had worked in computer-related industries for approximately four years.

With its printing speed of 4,800 lines per minute, the Gould 4800 was at least four times faster than conventional line printers used for computer output. In contrast to these conventional line printers, the Gould 4800 could also print any kind of graphic output, such as charts, graphs, line drawings, curves, and vectors. Graphic output for engineering and scientific purposes was typically produced on high-precision, high-price XY plotters like the Brush 1000. The Gould 4800 printed graphic output 200 to 400 times faster than these plotters.

The major elements in the printing process of the Gould 4800 were an electromagnetic printing head and specially coated paper. Gould had applied for patents for both, but management of the Graphics Division thought the process was not so unique that the patents could not be circumvented by competitors with similar technologies in less than two years.

The printing head contained a row of 600 styluses that could be selectively charged to 300 volts. As a web of the special paper passed beneath the styluses, the coating acquired an opposite electrical charge beneath each charged stylus. The charge then attracted a dark toner in a liquid suspension to form the characters as an array of black dots. The liquid evaporated and the printed output came out dry. Since there were few moving parts and no printing hammers as in a conventional line printer, the Gould 4800 operated noiselessly and presented relatively fewer maintenance problems.

Like all nonimpact printers, the Gould 4800 produced only single copies at a time. Since specially coated paper had to be used, the output could not be printed on preprinted forms. The copies from Gould's printer were brilliant white with a high-gloss surface, like the paper used in oscillographs and Brush analog recorders. They had the standard letter size of 8½ × 11 inches, which the design engineers believed to be the most acceptable format. The cost of the paper to users was set at 4.2¢ per 8½ × 11 inch page. This compared to the 0.14¢ per page of plain one-ply tab paper used in conventional impact printers.

The paper supply for the Gould 4800 was from a 300-foot roll. The paper-feeding mechanism moved the paper at a continuous speed of 10 inches per second on the average. The dominant form of paper supplied in conventional line printers came packaged "fanfolded"—that is, in accordion fashion, with each sheet easily torn from every other sheet at the perforated creases that connected them.

The paper used in the Gould 4800 was unperforated, and so far engineers had not developed a paper-output collecting, folding, or cutting device.

For use of the printer on-line with a computer, a translating or interface device was necessary which brought the data output of the computer into the format or arrangement desired by the user. The commercial utilization of the Gould 4800, therefore, required the creation of appropriate interfaces for computers of many manufacturers. It could also become necessary to create interfaces for different computer languages within each computer manufacturer's equipment. In addition, an extensive programming effort was required to develop software or application packages for various industry users. The prevailing experience in the computer industry had been that the end users of a particular piece of peripheral equipment like a printer or a card puncher were usually not willing to develop the necessary software or interfacing themselves. They expected this to be included in the "package." In addition, they were not favorably disposed to making modifications in existing programs to be able to run with a particular new peripheral device.

Production of the Gould 4800 was primarily an assembly operation and required the same technology as used in the Brush Instruments Division. Brush had free capacity available for up to 200 units per year, which enabled the Graphics Division to utilize the manufacturing department of Brush Instruments for the initial production. Direct manufacturing costs amounted to roughly $4,500 per unit.

The paper used in the Gould 4800 was regarded as equally important to the printing process as the hardware. Management therefore regarded it as desirable to control the production of the paper to insure reliability. A pilot paper coater had been built, but management had already started ordering items for a paper coater with a capacity of 50,000 rolls per shift. Completion of the facility, requiring an investment of roughly $450,000, was planned for February 1970. The present paper costs to users of 4.2¢ per sheet reflected the Graphics Division's own manufacturing costs. With the larger paper coater, management expected to reduce manufacturing costs to 3¢ per sheet.

# THE MARKET FOR COMPUTER PERIPHERAL EQUIPMENT ___

The computer peripheral market which the Graphics Division was about to enter had grown faster than the computer mainframe market in recent years, and although forecasts differed widely, the market was expected to continue its growth for some time to come.

The market was characterized by intense competition and rapid technological development. The major computer manufacturers, notably IBM, Honeywell, RCA, CDC, and NCR, were selling their own peripheral devices, competing against each other, against a number of smaller manufacturers, such as Mohawk Data Sciences and Digitronics, and against special-purpose terminal houses like Sanders Associates and Bunker-Ramo. Many new companies had recently been attracted to the peripheral-equipment field.

Compatibility of the peripheral device with the communicating computer was a necessity and had been a major stumbling block to many of the smaller companies. In order to overcome this difficulty, a number of smaller companies with limited resources—for example, Mohawk—had found it desirable to sell through one of the mainframe computer manufacturers. This approach relieved the peripheral company of the maintenance and marketing burden and enabled it to rely on the well-established customer relations of the computer manufacturer. It was realized, though, that total reliance on the marketing effort of the mainframe manufacturer might make it difficult for the peripheral company to establish an identity of its own in the market.

Peripheral-equipment purchase decisions among end users were normally in the province of the data processing department manager or an executive with similar functions.

The orientation of this group, according to a recent study, was strongly toward their traditional suppliers, the computer manufacturers, among which IBM held the dominant position. Reluctance to "experiment" was widespread, notably with regard to devices that might present compatibility problems. A survey among 1,600 computer users, conducted by The Diebold Group,[1] revealed a decided preference for a single vendor of both the computer and peripheral equipment for 31 percent of the respondents. But 19 percent mentioned multivendor preference and 50 percent remained uncommitted. As stated in the survey report, however, in cases where the mainframe manufacturer had all the desired peripheral equipment available, the user's expression of preference to use multiple vendors had to be taken with some caution. Still, the rate of development of useful new peripheral products by new or non-mainframe manufacturers was so great that computer users generally felt it necessary to give serious consideration to these sources of products.

# THE MARKET FOR ELECTROSTATIC PRINTERS

Little market research had been undertaken prior to or during the development work for the Gould 4800. "The engineers relied more on their own feelings," one executive observed. "Maybe they talked to some of the Burroughs[2] people who service our own computer; but on the whole, contacts with the computer industry have been minimal."

Even after the prototype had become ready, very little market information was gathered before the printer was introduced in 1969. Koepf explained:

> We are a very small division. From the very beginning, we were running the division almost like our own little business. We don't have the time and the money to do much research. There is no planning group, no research group like in some of the larger divisions of Gould. All the planning and budgeting work splits essentially between Bill Koeblitz, our general manager, and myself. In early 1968, The Diebold Group made a study for us on the printer market. They had data on conventional printers, but when it came to electrostatic printers, they had to guess. Electrostatic printing is entirely new. Ours is not a "me-too" product. So, it's very difficult to say anything really firm about the market. But everybody knows that existing printers are much too slow.

The Diebold Group had undertaken to estimate the market potential for high-speed nonimpact printers for the period 1968 to 1972. Their estimate, which was based on extensive industry surveys, amounted to a total of 14,000 units for the 1968–1972 time period and included thermographic, electrostatic, and electrographic equipment. Direct ink printers were not included because of their low speed. This forecast posed the question of what portion of the potential market for high-speed nonimpact printers could be expected for electrostatic devices. As noted by the consultants, the factor that was most likely to affect this determination was the degree of support that major OEMs would give to the electrostatic printing technology. In the judgment of The Diebold Group, OEM

[1] A major consulting company in the computer field.
[2] A manufacturer of EDP equipment.

support was necessary for electrostatic printers to capture a significant portion of the anticipated market for high-speed nonimpact printers. The consultants were confident that at least one major OEM would complement its product line with an electrostatic printer, and on the basis of this belief, they predicted that at least one-half of the forecasted 14,000-unit market potential for high-speed nonimpact printers would be for electrostatic printers. The consultants assumed that 50 percent of the electrostatic market would subsequently go to this innovating OEM and thought it reasonable for Gould to obtain about 20 percent of the remaining market with an aggressive marketing policy.

So far, the Graphics Division had only one direct competitor, Varian Data Products, a smaller but well-known company manufacturing an electrostatic printer which was very similar in all its functional features to the Gould 4800. Varian had introduced its product in 1968 and tried to market it at prices between $15,000 and $18,000 direct to end users, with discounts of 30 to 40 percent offered to OEMs. Koepf thought that manufacturing costs for the Varian printer were higher than those for the Gould 4800. Paper costs to users were identical, i.e., 4.2¢ per 8½ × 11 inch page. Koepf believed that Varian was not an important factor in the market and that its product had serious operational problems. No exact sales figures were available, but Koepf thought that Varian had sold only a few units.

The Graphics Division saw the Gould 4800 as a potential entrant into five basic functional areas of the information-terminal market and into one broad area of miscellaneous new applications not yet served by other devices: (1) computer line printer; (2) hard-copy printer of cathode-ray-tube (CRT) displays; (3) proof-copy or hard-copy printer for computer-output-to-microfilm (COM) systems; (4) high-speed communications printer, replacing teletype machines; (5) quick plotter from a computer plotting program; and (6) in the miscellaneous area, servicing a multiplicity of scientific, medical, military, and commercial applications (like proofreading for computerized typesetters). Little information existed on the particular requirements for this last-mentioned market segment.

## Line-Printer Market

The line-printer market represented by far the largest market segment under consideration. The Graphics Division estimated that about 8,000 line printers had been installed during fiscal year 1969, equivalent to a shipment value of $160 million, and that the market was growing at a rate of 10 to 15 percent per year.

Virtually every traditional computer installation used a line printer as its main printout device, and all the OEMs carried such printers as part of their product line. The purchase price of these machines ranged from $11,500 (Mohawk, 750 lines per minute) to $64,000 (Mohawk, 1,250 lines per minute). They could be rented for a monthly fee, including full maintenance, ranging from $315 to $1,020; IBM, for example, charged $875 per month for its 1403/3 model (1,100 LPM).

The existing printers were usually capable of printing up to six copies simultaneously on ordinary tab paper. They could also easily accommodate special-purpose preprinted forms of different sizes and thicknesses. The most common paper width used was 14⅞ inches. Most users of line printers required multiple copies of their output, and for cost reasons these had to be simultaneously produced, rather than serially or off-line on copying machines. Preprinted forms were used extensively, especially by organizations such as banks, insurance companies, credit card companies, and magazine publishers. Programming a printer to produce forms was generally not regarded as an alternative to the use of preprinted forms.

The speed of all existing line printers was many times slower than the rate at which the computer processor could generate data. Multiprogramming techniques had been developed, however, permitting the processor to activate more than one printer at a time and thus reducing the user problems with jobs previously limited by printer speed.

## CRT Hard-Copy Market

The market for the Gould 4800 as a device for printing permanent copies of data displayed on CRT screens was regarded as one of the fastest-growing segments, with an estimated annual growth of 30 to 40 percent. Shipments of CRT hard-copy printers in fiscal year 1969 were estimated at 700 units or $5 million. Among the users of CRT hard-copy printers were banks, stockbrokers, and insurance companies, as well as high-technology companies like aerospace firms that used CRTs for engineering purposes. In management's view, the almost perfectly silent operation of the Gould 4800, allowing its use in an office environment where the noise level had to be kept at a minimum, and the high printing speed, constrained only by the CRT or the telephone line, made the Gould 4800 well suited for the application as a CRT hard-copy printer.

A number of CRT hard-copy printers were currently marketed by mainframe manufacturers and some of the larger computer peripheral manufacturers (IBM, 3M, Litton Industries, Beta Instruments Corporation). These machines used a thermographic or photographic process and were selling at user prices from $6,000 (3M) and $12,600 (Litton/Datalog) to $33,000 for a high-precision IBM machine. printing costs of these devices were considerable, since specially coated paper had to be used; they ranged from roughly 12¢ (3M) to about 18¢ (IBM, Litton/Datalog) per copy. The machines currently being marketed generally gave a higher resolution[3] than the Gould 4800, a fact of particular interest in engineering applications.

## CRT Microfilm Market

The market for CRT microfilm printers was still a small segment of the computer peripheral market, but growing at a rate of 30 to 40 percent annually. In fiscal year 1969, about 100 units had been shipped, representing a value of roughly $15 million. Manufacturers of these machines were Kodak, 3M, and Datagraphics. The Gould 4800 was not a substitute for these devices, but rather a supplement for high-speed paper output. Some of the CRT microfilm machines were also equipped for paper output, which they printed at the same or at an even higher speed than the Gould 4800.

## Communications-Printer Market

The market for communications printers was dominated by the familiar teletypes, manufactured by a sizable number of specialized companies. More recently, the traditional

---

[3]Dots per inch, determining clarity and accuracy of output.

teletype had been supplemented by the "Inktronic," using direct ink printing technology. In fiscal year 1969, an estimated 30,000 teletypes had been shipped, representing a value of about $35 million. Management expected this market to grow by 10 to 15 percent annually.

Impact teletypes reaching a speed of 10 characters per second were selling for roughly $1,000 to users. There was at least one faster unit available, operating at 37 characters per second, which was priced at $3,600. Direct ink printers had a speed of 250 characters per second and ranged between $5,000 and $7,000 in price. Both impact teletypes and direct ink printers printed on ordinary paper, with an average cost per page to users of 0.5¢ for impact printers and 0.8¢ for the "Inktronic." The impact teletype could also be equipped for multiple copies.

Theoretically, the Gould 4800 could print several thousand characters per second as a communications printer. Printing at such a speed required, however, that a communications line be available which could transmit data at such a speed. So far, no equipment existed, either from a private company or from the Bell system, for transmitting faster than 2,000 bits per second, that is, 250 characters per second, on dial-up lines. The smallest telephone charge for a dial-up line was for three minutes; thus, at printing speeds of 250 characters per second, the telephone charges for one and ten pages (60 lines with 80 characters each) were the same, since both did not take more than three minutes (e.g., $0.65 for transmission between New York and Philadelphia at a rate of $0.65 for the first three minutes and $0.15 for each additional minute). An increase in the speed of transmission for dial-up lines to 3,600 bits per second (450 characters) by the end of 1969 and to 4,800 bits per second (600 characters) in 1971 was expected.

Privately leased transmission lines were available for transmitting up to 9,600 bits per second (1,200 characters). The cost of a private line was proportional to the length of the line and was a fixed monthly fee independent of usage. For example, the cost for a private line from New York to Philadelphia was about $350 per month.

PLOTTER MARKET.   The sales volume of plotters in fiscal year 1969 had been estimated by management at $10 million, equivalent to shipments of roughly 500 units. It was expected that this segment would show an annual growth of 30 to 40 percent. In the judgment of Koepf, the Gould 4800 offered a number of advantages over the conventional digital XY plotters, such as higher speed, more versatility because of symbol-plotting and character-printing ability, and less service requirements, since no ink and no moving pens were used. The Gould 4800, however, did not offer the precision of conventional plotters: The smallest plotting increment possible with the Gould 4800 was 12.5 milli-inches, compared to 0.01 milli-inches obtainable from conventional plotters. Many users of plotters also required a wider paper web than 8½ inches and the possibility to use different plotting surfaces—e.g., translucent paper.

Users of plotters fell into two broad categories: (1) scientific and engineering users and (2) nonscientific, or commercial, users.

Scientific and engineering users were the most important group requiring computer graphics and plotting techniques. Companies and institutions in this group included automobile companies, aircraft and aerospace manufacturers, universities, and scientific laboratories. Computer-aided plottings were required in the generation of high-accuracy engineering designs or in the solution of complex problems such as the plotting of missile trajectories. Most of these users had considerable computer experience and close contact with computer mainframe manufacturers. They required high accuracy and extensive software support for the plotter to meet these frequently changing, sophisticated plotting needs. The initial purchase price of the plotter was a less important consideration for them than accuracy, versatility, and an extensive software library. A number of large companies were currently serving this user group with digital XY plotters, among them IBM marketing plotters, manufactured by California Computer Products, Inc., as part of IBM's full line of computers and peripheral devices.

The group of nonscientific, commercial users included companies and organizations requiring a plotter for fairly simple graphical representations of mathematical functions or time series (e.g., histograms, weekly or monthly sales and profit curves, line fitting). Minute accuracy was of less concern to this group of users. Their plotting needs appeared to be relatively stable over time and of limited sophistication. Consequently, it was expected that only a modest software library would be necessary. In the judgment of The Diebold Group, graphic output among commercial users of data-processing equipment was still in its very infancy, amounting to less than 1 percent of total printed output. Commercial users seemed to be largely unaware of the potential applications for a plotting device. The Diebold Group expected, however, an increasing popularity in graphic data output, primarily due to the emergence on the market of graphic CRT terminals.

## INITIAL MARKETING PLANS

Management of the Graphics Division believed that most printing and plotting would ultimately be nonimpact to meet "instant information" requirements, to keep down sound pollution, and to provide absolute reliability. The Gould 4800, in management's view, met these needs completely, and it was expected that the design would receive rapid technical acceptance in its first year of exposure.

Management's sales forecast provided for a total volume of $800,000 in fiscal year 1970, $2.5 million in fiscal year 1971, and $5 million in fiscal year 1972. Exhibit 3 shows a breakdown of sales expectations in 1970 by market segments. It was expected that fiscal year 1970 would end with a loss, but management anticipated breaking even during fiscal year 1971.

The price to end users for the Gould 4800 had been set at $15,000, plus $4,000 for a character generator, which was required to prevent excessive burdening of expensive computer memory space with output-format instructions. Manufacturing costs of the character generator amounted to roughly $750. The price to OEMs was $9,900 for 1 to 9 units of the Gould 4800, plus $3,200 for the character generator. Quantity discounts were available to OEMs, as shown in Exhibit 4. Koepf explained:

> When we initially priced the product, we didn't really know what to charge and what the market would bear. We thought that a larger spread between the users' price and the OEM price than was usually available for peripheral equipment would get us the interest of the OEMs for the product.

So far, no rental arrangements had been considered for the Gould 4800.

EXHIBIT
3

## SALES FORECAST FOR FISCAL YEAR 1970
## BY MARKET SEGMENT

| Segments or Application | Sales Volume Dollars | Units |
|---|---|---|
| Line printer | $420,000* | 34 |
| CRT hard copy | 45,000 | 5 |
| CRT microfilm | 0 | 0 |
| Teletype | 40,000 | 4 |
| Plotter | 180,000 | 20 |
| Miscellaneous | 115,000† | 10 |
| Total | $800,000 | 73 |

*Includes 34-character generators.
†Includes paper and supplies.
*Source:* Company records

One of the major issues facing management was whether to concentrate sales effort for the Gould 4800 on end users or on OEMs. The Diebold Group had prepared estimates for the required annual marketing expenditures for both approaches. A summary of their calculations is given in Exhibits 5 and 6. Based on the assumption that for direct selling to end users, a total sales force of 20 salespeople would be needed, and that the Graphics Division would do all its programming, interfacing, and equipment maintenance itself, the consultants arrived at a figure of $1.19 million as total annual marketing and support costs for selling direct to end users. For the approach of selling through OEMs and systems

EXHIBIT
4

## OEM PRICE LIST

| Printer: Yearly Unit Quantity Regularly Scheduled | Unit Price |
|---|---|
| 1–9 | $9,900 |
| 10–19 | 9,158 |
| 20–34 | 8,910 |
| 35–49 | 8,663 |
| 50–99 | 8,415 |
| 100–499 | 8,168 |
| 500–999 | 7,920 |
| 1,000 up | 7,670 |
| Character generator | 3,200 |

| EXHIBIT 5 | CONSULTANTS' ESTIMATE OF AVERAGE ANNUAL MARKETING AND SUPPORT COSTS, SELLING DIRECT TO END-USER MARKET |
|---|---|

*Sales Considerations:*

| | | |
|---|---|---|
| Salespeople's salaries (20 reps) (excluding commissions) | $200,000 | |
| Employee benefits | 50,000 | |
| Overhead | 150,000 | |
| Travel and business expenses | 120,000 | |
| Recruiting costs (including relocation) | 18,000 | |
| Training program | 20,000 | |
| Trade shows | 80,000 | |
| Advertising | 50,000 | |
| Total average annual sales considerations | | $688,000 |

*Support Considerations:*

*Programming:*

| | | |
|---|---|---|
| Programmers' salaries | $145,000 | |
| Employee benefits | 36,000 | |
| Overhead | 109,000 | |
| Recruiting costs (including relocation) | 13,000 | |
| Total average annual programming considerations* | | $303,000 |

*Maintenance:*

| | | |
|---|---|---|
| Maintenance engineers' salaries | $108,000 | |
| Employee benefits | 27,000 | |
| Overhead | 81,000 | |
| Recruiting costs (including relocation) | 4,000 | |
| Training program | 4,000 | |
| Travel and business expenses | 43,000 | |
| Revenue from maintenance contracts | (70,000) | |
| Total average annual maintenance considerations | | $199,000 |
| Total average annual marketing and support costs | | $1,190,000 |

*Cost of computer time required to test and "debug" program not included.
*Source:* The Diebold Group

houses, they came up with a figure of $254,000 as average annual marketing and support costs. This estimate was based on the assumption that a sales force of five would be sufficient and that the OEMs would shoulder a large part of the programming, interfacing, and maintenance burden. The consultants concluded that it would be advisable for the Graphics Division to concentrate its marketing effort on the OEMs and systems houses.

Management's initial thinking essentially followed this recommendation. Koepf explained:

EXHIBIT
6

## CONSULTANTS' ESTIMATE OF AVERAGE ANNUAL MARKETING AND SUPPORT COSTS, SELLING TO OEMs AND SYSTEM HOUSES

*Sales Considerations:*

| | |
|---|---|
| Salespeople's salaries (5 reps),* employee benefits, overhead, travel and business expenses, recruiting costs (including relocation), training program | $140,000 |

*Programming Considerations:‡*

| | |
|---|---|
| Salaries, benefits, overhead, and recruiting costs | $ 60,000 |

*Maintenance Considerations:***

| | |
|---|---|
| Salaries, employee benefits, overhead, recruiting costs, training program, and travel | $ 54,000 |

| | |
|---|---|
| Total average annual marketing and support costs | $245,000 |

*Based on the assumption that five salespeople would incur about 20 percent of costs shown in Exhibit 5.
‡Based on 20 percent of programmers' expenses in Exhibit 5.
**Based on 20 percent of maintenance engineers' expenses (excluding revenue from maintenance contracts) in Exhibit 5.
*Source:* The Diebold Group

We just wanted to sell the machine; if you go directly to end users, you must have all the answers on programming, cost, and interfacing. We aren't quite ready for this. We thought that our product is so good that the OEMs would take it and run with it. We wanted them to do our homework for us; that is, provide users with interfacing, software, and maintenance.

Initial market response has been slower than expected. End users, in spite of a high expressed interest, had remained hesitant, and first discussions with OEMs had shown some signs of reluctance to push the product before end-user pull had built up. Koepf commented:

The OEMs told us, "Great, this is a wonderful machine; when you get some of our users interested to buy, come back and see us." But people just don't like to be the first ones to try a new product.

# APPENDIX A

## Diagram of Printing Technologies

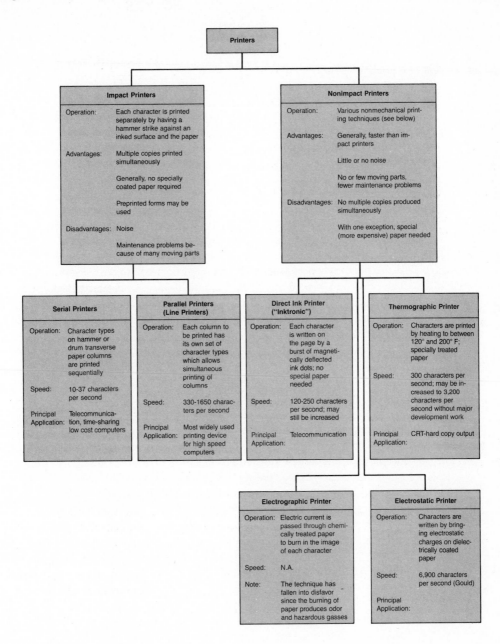

The Eagle Pump Company was founded in 1945 in Dallas, Texas, by Fred Eagleton, a mechanical engineer. Eagle initially manufactured specialty tools for the oil and gas industry. The specialty tools provided capital for Fred Eagleton to design and manufacture a quality high-pressure patented pump. By the mid-1950s, the patented Eagle pump enjoyed a reputation as the best high-pressure injection pump available. The pump was particularly well suited to the requirements of secondary oil and gas recovery with steam injection. Eagle's location in Dallas, Texas, helped it capture a dominant market position in the oil and gas industry. After Eagleton's death in 1964, his son Frederick, Jr., was in charge of the rapidly growing company. However, his son had interests in car racing and sold the company in 1965 to a group of eight investors. The company's growth and high profits continued, and its pump was still considered the best quality high-pressure pump in 1968, when the company was sold for the second time to a major coal company. In 1971, the coal company was losing money and needed the cash Eagle Pump was generating. In 1973, the coal company sold Eagle for 2.5 times what it had paid for it in 1968. The buyer was one of the largest steel companies in the United States. Eagle Pump was again sold in 1982 at the peak of the energy boom to a large integrated oil company. Division sales for 1979–1982 are shown in Exhibit 1.

Eagle's pumps were regarded as the "standard of oil patch high-pressure injection pumps." The pumps were widely recognized as the best engineered for high pressure steam injection and corrosion problems in the oil fields. The company was managed by leading engineers. In the energy boom of the 1970s, Eagle's plant operated six days a week, with three full shifts. The plant manager said: "We had railroad cars of metal coming in at one end of the plant and tractor trailers loading finished pumps at the other end." The energy bust in 1982 had a dramatic effect on Eagle. By late 1982, orders fell by 31 percent from the previous record year and new bookings were down by over 50 percent. In early 1983, Eagle had to reduce its work force by 58 percent. Commenting about this situation, the plant manager said:

| EXHIBIT 1 | DIVISIONAL SALES BY TYPE OF ACCOUNT *(in millions)* | | | |
|---|---|---|---|---|
| | *1979* | *1980* | *1981* | *1982* |
| 1. Stocking distributor | $10.1 | $11.9 | $14.5 | $13.4 |
| 2. Nonstocking distributor | 4.1 | 5.2 | 7.3 | 4.1 |
| 3. Direct sales | 9.9 | 13.7 | 18.7 | 9.7 |
| 4. International | 5.1 | 7.1 | 10.6 | 5.1 |
| 5. Interdivisional | 1.1 | 1.0 | 1.4 | 2.3 |
| 6. Reverse osmosis | 0.6 | 0.9 | 1.2 | 2.4 |
| | $30.9 | $39.8 | $53.7 | $37.0 |

*Note:* Stocking and nonstocking distributors sold both pumps and parts. The remaining types of accounts were nearly all pump unit sales.

This was boom to bust in four months. It will take us another seven to ten months to reduce these material inventories. I've been in this business at Eagle since 1958, and all we've ever shown were higher sales each year since we started making these pumps. Shrinking and down-sizing have never been a way of doing things in this company or in the oil and gas industry.

The frequent buying and divesting of Eagle Pump had many negative effects on the business. Initially, the division was primarily bought as a financial "cash cow," which meant it was milked for cash, with little reinvestment. Much of the company's manufacturing was inefficient, and Eagle was believed to be a high-cost producer. The new owners knew little about the high-pressure injection pump business, which had no technical, manufacturing, or marketing unity with their other operations. Relationships with customers and distributors were neglected, especially when the energy boom allowed Eagle to ride the growth curve and sell all it could produce.

With a sharp decline in new orders and a rapidly diminishing backlog, the oil company parent saw the need for a new management team. In 1982 it hired a bright and aggressive 39-year-old general manager, Mike Crown, from another company to build up the existing business and to find new uses for Eagle pumps. Crown was the first nonengineer to head the division. He had had 15 years of experience selling specialty piping to oil and gas companies. The organizational chart is shown in Exhibit 2. As soon as Crown obtained an understanding of the company, he was going to take a hard look to see if it was properly organized around market opportunities. One of the first personnel changes Crown made was to dismiss the marketing manager and hire Billie Williams, a man he had worked with three years earlier.

# PRODUCT LINES

Eagle was the largest manufacturer of high-pressure injection pumps. The pumps and parts had been made at the original location since 1958. As the company grew, adjacent

**EXHIBIT
2**

*EAGLE PUMP DIVISION ORGANIZATION*

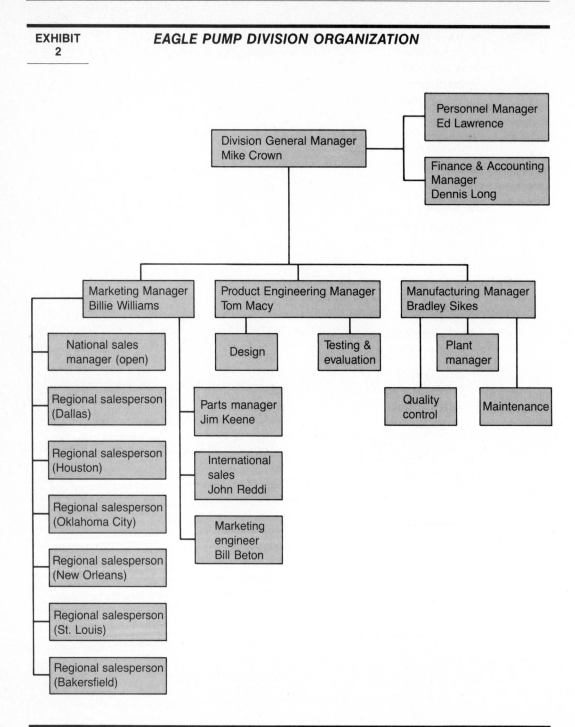

land was acquired and extensions added to the original building. A small new facility was being constructed on the Texas-Mexico border and was scheduled to begin pilot production in late 1983.

A centrifugal pump line Eagle manufactured was usually selected for applications that require high pressure. Eagle's pumps had a high volumetric efficiency and consumed less energy than other types of pumps. The rated or recommended speed of pumps is important when a design engineer selects a pump to go into a new installation. Most pump manufacturers use the term "rated" speed interchangeably with "recommended" speed. The customer's design engineer selects a rated speed that will provide sufficient suction and discharge performance in moving the material. The recommended speeds of the Eagle lines of pumps are shown in Exhibit 3.

Because Eagle pumps were well engineered, they were often operated at much higher RPMs than competitive pumps, which would fail or need parts more frequently. Eagle pumps were the only ones that held up in the severe operating conditions of the South African gold mines. The head of engineering stated:

> Our pumps can be run at the highest RPMs with no problems. We use the highest-quality Timken bearings and have the strongest crankshafts. A helicopter literally drop-shipped one of our pumps into an oil-gathering field in Odessa, Texas, with no damage whatsoever. Our 100 percent inspection is another check to make sure no defects leave our shipping dock.

Eagle had 16 product lines or series, as shown in Exhibit 4. Within each of the 16 series there were two or three different models, for a total of 48 different pumps. Exhibit 4 also shows the quarterly shipments of all pumps for the 1980–1982 period. One Eagle oil field distributor described Eagle's product line as

> . . . the best and broadest in the industry. But at $4,000 to $35,000 per pump, depending on the size, I can't stock many of them. Some of them are hot items and others rarely ever fit a customer's steam injection pumping requirements.

| EXHIBIT 3 | RECOMMENDED SPEEDS OF EAGLE PUMPS |
|---|---|

| Pump Series | Stroke | Recommended Speed | Maximum Speed |
|---|---|---|---|
| E-10, E-50, E-100, E-200 | 2 3/16" | 400 RPM | 500 RPM |
| E-330, E-300 | 3 1/8" | 400 RPM | 500 RPM |
| E-125 | 3 1/2" | 400 RPM | 500 RPM |
| E-100 | 4 1/2" | 400 RPM | 500 RPM |
| E-165 | 4 1/2" | 360 RPM | 400 RPM |
| E-160 | 6 1/8" | 324 RPM | 360 RPM |
| E-250, E-360, E-600 | 7 1/8" | 324 RPM | 360 RPM |

## EXHIBIT 4

## 1980–1983 QUARTERLY PUMP UNIT SHIPMENTS

| Pump Series | 1980 | | | | | 1981 | | | | | 1982 | | | | | 1983 |
|---|---|---|---|---|---|---|---|---|---|---|---|---|---|---|---|---|
| | 1st | 2nd | 3rd | 4th | Total | 1st | 2nd | 3rd | 4th | Total | 1st | 2nd | 3rd | 4th | Total | 1st |
| E-10/E-15 | 58 | 26 | 39 | 76 | 199 | 84 | 107 | 37 | 36 | 264 | 3 | 13 | 9 | 30 | 55 | 41 |
| E-50 series | 79 | 28 | 67 | 77 | 251 | 73 | 58 | 56 | 41 | 228 | 31 | 20 | 9 | 10 | 70 | 7 |
| E-100 series | 42 | 42 | 79 | 59 | 222 | 70 | 97 | 75 | 57 | 299 | 36 | 14 | 8 | 8 | 66 | 20 |
| E-200 series | 36 | 27 | 14 | 19 | 96 | 23 | 50 | 21 | 41 | 135 | 41 | 33 | 15 | 22 | 111 | 26 |
| SE-200 series | 118 | 97 | 69 | 75 | 359 | 112 | 115 | 95 | 114 | 436 | 84 | 53 | 53 | 54 | 244 | 76 |
| E-300 series | 11 | 6 | 10 | 17 | 44 | 18 | 19 | 38 | 32 | 107 | 176 | 101 | 26 | 33 | 347 | 34 |
| SE-300 series | | | 5 | 9 | 14 | 13 | 29 | 41 | 40 | 123 | 4 | 2 | 2 | 3 | 11 | 2 |
| 6X-100 series | | | | | | | | | | | | | | | | |
| 6X-125 series | 52 | 37 | 89 | 59 | 237 | 58 | 65 | 50 | 69 | 242 | 32 | 16 | 8 | 11 | 67 | 7 |
| 6X-160 series | 12 | 3 | 2 | 5 | 22 | 12 | 16 | 11 | 15 | 54 | 49 | 16 | 25 | 8 | 98 | 9 |
| 6X-165 series | | | 1 | 3 | 4 | 6 | 8 | 18 | 28 | 60 | 14 | 8 | 5 | | 27 | |
| 6X-250 series | | 2 | 1 | 2 | 5 | 7 | 1 | 8 | 4 | 20 | 30 | 9 | 4 | 6 | 49 | 2 |
| 6X-300 series | | | | | | | | | 25 | 25 | 7 | 5 | | | 12 | 1 |
| 6X-360 series | | | | | | | | | | | 3 | 2 | 3 | 1 | 9 | 2 |
| 6X-600 series | 1 | 3 | 3 | | 7 | 1 | 1 | 1 | 5 | 8 | 1 | | 8 | 3 | 12 | |
| 3L-450/5L-750 | | | | | | | | | | | 1 | | 2 | | 3 | |
| | | | | | | 1 | | 3 | 1 | 5 | 1 | 1 | | 1 | 3 | |
| Total | 409 | 271 | 380 | 401 | 1461 | 478 | 566 | 454 | 508 | 2006 | 513 | 293 | 177 | 200 | 1184 | 227 |

*Note:* The major difference among these lines is the size of the basic design. The E-10 is the smallest model, and the 3L is the largest.

## Competition

In addition to Eagle, four other companies produced high-pressure injection pumps. Two were divisions of major U.S. steel companies that also owned large chains of oil field supply stores. The third competitor, Oilflo, was the only one that carried a full line which competed with Eagle across the board. Oilflo was founded in the mid-1960s by ex-Eagle employees. Located in Dallas, Texas, it was a privately held firm with sales believed to be about 35 percent less than Eagle's. The fourth competitor was a manufacturer of industrial pumps that recently began selling in the oil field market.

Many more competitors produced parts for high-pressure oil field pumps. In addition to the four producers of pumps that also produced parts, there were 18 to 20 pump parts suppliers. Most of these were small two- to five-person firms. However, four of the parts firms were believed to be $20 to $30 million businesses. These suppliers were called "parts pirates." The parts suppliers did little or no repair or service work, but were essentially small machine shops that made standard parts for the more popular models of high-pressure injection pumps.

## New Technology

In 1976, the first vertical turbine generator injection pumps were introduced to the oil fields. The new technology was very different from the high-pressure injection pumps produced by Eagle and its competitors. A new vertical turbine generator pump system cost about $60,000, compared to $100,000 for an older Eagle type pumping and steam-generating system. The vertical turbine generator pumps also had fewer parts to wear out and be replaced. However, compared to the conventional Eagle pumping and steam injection system, the turbine pumps consumed significantly more electrical energy, which resulted in higher operating costs. As energy costs increased, their cost of operation increased accordingly. The turbine pumps were less tolerant of pressure differentials than the conventional injection pumps, and every 8 to 12 months the turbine pumps would wear out a $2,500 mechanical seal. When the turbine pumps were first introduced for secondary recovery, they had many breakdowns. Furthermore, since the turbine pumps reduced much of the maintenance work the conventional injection pumps required, there were many instances of worker sabotage. The generally conservative nature of the oil field production business resulted in slower adoption of new systems. This was in contrast to the more rapid adoption of new systems by the oil and gas exploration companies. However, over the last three years, the vertical turbine generator pumping system was making stronger inroads in the OEM market. Worthington, Gould, and Byron-Jackson were the major producers of vertical turbine generator pumps.

## Product Warranty and Guarantee

All Eagle pumps are guaranteed for one year from the date the end user received the product. The pumps are repaired or replaced free of charge within the one-year period. All Eagle pumps are sold with a warranty card. Often the warranty card was filled out by the distributor and contained only the distributor's name. The distributor usually did not

---

**EXHIBIT
5**
### EAGLE PUMP WARRANTY ACTIVATION

Pump Figure No. _____ Serial No. _____

Distributor _____

Address _____

End user _____

Location _____

Date shipped from factory _____

Date shipped from distributor _____

Date pump installed on location _____

If pump was altered in any manner from the way it was shipped from the factory, please describe alterations below:

_____

_____

_____

---

identify the end user by name or location because of concern that the customer and Eagle might do business directly and bypass the distributor. Even if the end user did complete the warranty card, the customer sometimes bought the pump as a spare for one or two years and did not immediately place it in service. This situation caused Eagle to have a problem enforcing its one-year warranty. Exhibit 5 shows the reverse side of a prepaid postcard that was intended to activate the warranty and provide end-user information to Eagle. There was no warranty on parts due to the lack of a serial number and the errors caused by independent repairpeople in the field.

Since Eagle pumps were engineered to perform above the recommended speeds, there were few warranty claims. But since most of the warranty cards were inaccurately or not completed, Eagle had little knowledge of where its pumps were operating and what material was being pumped at each location.

# END USERS _____

## Oil and Gas Systems

The largest current use of Eagle pumps was in the oil and gas industry. In Bakersfield, California, Eagle estimated they had 2,000 to 2,500 of their pumps in operation. Steam flooding was a specific oil market technique for which most Eagle pumps were used in Bakersfield. Steam flooding is a method of secondary oil recovery where steam is pumped down and forces more oil out of the well. Steam flooding injection oil recovery systems always require a high-pressure pump. Natural gas plants treat gas by taking the hydrogen sulfide and water out of the gas. High-pressure injection pumps are used for this purpose. Natural gas by-products like LPG are then injected into a pipeline, and high-pressure injection pumps are also used to perform this task. With the energy boom ending in 1982, relatively few new oil or gas installations were being constructed. The oil pump injection business was then more concentrated in the replacement population of existing pumps and pump parts. This situation created a lot of excess production capacity at Eagle's large production facility in Dallas.

## Car Wash Systems

Automated high-pressure car wash systems need high-pressure pumps. Two of the largest automated car wash builders were located near Eagle in Texas and Oklahoma. In the early 1970s, Eagle pumps were designed into many of the original car wash equipment systems. Eagle was a major factor in the car wash pump market. But as the automatic car wash business became more cost-sensitive, Eagle lost most of the OEM business to lower-priced pumps and was subsequently "designed out" of most new systems. The average car wash system needs water pumped at 700 to 800 PSI, whereas Eagle pumps operated at 2000 PSI. Eagle's engineering manager, Tom Macy, stated:

> We could have built low-pressure pumps for car washes, but we were more interested in the high-pressure needs of oil and gas. We once had a committee to rethink this market. We never had anyone do a study or take responsibility for the car wash market. The pump we sold to car washes was the same one that went to the oil and gas folks. We never had the car wash replacement pump or parts business. Once in a while we'd get a phone call here in Dallas from one of the car wash people, but we didn't have distributors to serve that replacement market. They do a lot of car washing in the snow and frost belt, where people take salt off their cars. Those aren't the same areas or distributors as where there are oil fields. Furthermore, after we'd sell the OEM car wash builders a pump, we had no idea where in the U.S. they were shipping and installing the finished system, which might later need parts or a replacement pump.

## Reverse Osmosis Market

Eagle had had an interest in the reverse osmosis market for the last 15 years. Reverse osmosis (RO) is a process in which salt or brackish water is pumped with high pressure against a membrane filter. The fresh water migrates to one side of the membrane, and the salt water stays on the other side. The company that developed the membrane came to Eagle for the first pumps used to test the membranes. When the membrane producer's design engineers wrote technical papers in this area, they referred to the Eagle pumps. That helped establish Eagle's name in the RO market, where high pressure was necessary. Some Eagle pump sales had been going to RO systems builders for the last five years, as shown in Exhibit 1. Since this was also a different market for Eagle, it did not have distributors that repaired pumps or supplied parts. A few replacement unit and part orders were received by telephone. About 90 percent of the RO sales were direct, and not through distributors. The size and growth prospects of the commercial RO market were not known to Eagle. The U.S. military appeared to be a more immediate customer for the RO process and Eagle pumps. Eagle was the only RO pump specified by the U.S.

Navy for turbine-driven ships that required 3,000 gallons of volume per hour. The Navy had recently placed an order for 10 pumps for $95,000, but did not request shipment for 11 months. The U.S. Army adopted the Navy RO specifications that qualified only Eagle to supply the item. The Army planned to use RO systems for making fresh water from brackish water for troops in the field. The military customers preferred products that were overengineered to ensure more fail-safe use. All military customers were sold direct by Eagle salespeople.

## Additional End Users

Over the years, a few Eagle pumps had been sold as sewer cleaning pumps in municipal waste systems. This was believed to be a very price-sensitive market. A long-time Eagle engineer stated:

> We have received inquiries for a lot of strange applications that are foreign to us. That's how the car wash systems business came in, over the transom. Since the pumping of oil and gas is what we know best, other applications took a low priority.

The marketing manager, Billie Williams, walked into the room and heard the last part of the conversation and added:

> Heck, we don't even have good market data on the oil and gas market we are supposed to know. I just wish we had market shares by geographic oil and gas regions. Since we sell to distributors who build systems for oil and gas end users, we don't have enough contact and feedback from our ultimate customers. Our distributors don't know where many of the customers are either, especially if they didn't sell them the original pump, and we are really in the dark about the location and size of the parts market for high-pressure injection pumps.

## Oil and Gas OEM Installations

The large oil companies have engineering departments that write specifications and sometimes specify a brand to the pump distributor that builds the OEM system. The high-pressure injection oil field pumping system typically consists of a pump, a diesel or electric motor, and a V-belt chain drive all mounted on a "skid." The specifying of the type and size of pump is guided by what is being pumped, how much per day, and at what pressure. The OEM system builder uses the end user's technical performance parameters to select the pump brand. The pump manufacturer had to call on both the end user and the OEM builder to sell the system.

# THE AFTERMARKET

The repair and replacement pump purchase was somewhat less formal and planned than the OEM buying decision. However, the larger oil company maintenance departments would frequently specify the general type of pump and quantity desired and then put the

**EXHIBIT**
**6**

### *LEADING INDICATORS OF NEW OIL AND GAS CONSTRUCTION*

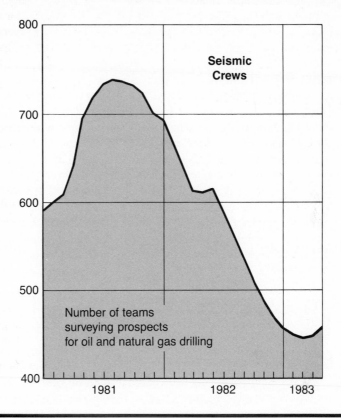

*Sources:* Energy Department and Society of Exploration Geophysicists. *The Wall Street Journal,* July 5, 1983, p. 21.

business out to bid for quotes. If a large end user had 20 pumps of one brand in an oil field, the 21st would most likely be the same brand to reduce repair problems and the number of parts needed. The smaller independent company maintenance departments usually bought one pump at a time from the pump distributor they had bought from before. Normally they did not ask for quotes from multiple distributors. They also did not plan the purchase and usually waited until the last minute to repair or replace a pump. During the oil boom years, customers did not have the time to conduct preventive maintenance on their high-pressure injection pumping systems. They waited until the pressure fell or visible leaks occurred. A few large oil companies were now beginning to conduct preventive maintenance on all their equipment.

When a high-pressure system breaks down, the oil company needs a replacement pump or part immediately because the cost of downtime could be between $2,000 to $5,000 per hour in a secondary recovery well. Either the oil company's maintenance personnel or an independent pump service firm did the repair work. Approximately 70 percent of the repair work was done by independent repair firms. Since competitive high-pressure units and parts were interchangeable, the repair person did not have to specify original equipment and part brand names.

## OEM Pump Demand

The number of OEM oil pump installations is a function of the price of oil and the resulting amount of exploration activity. The number of geophysical survey teams prospecting for oil and gas is an early leading indicator of new oil and gas construction. Exhibit 6 shows the dramatic decrease in active seismic teams between 1981 and 1983. The oil and gas equipment repair or aftermarket, however, is more dependent on the number of in-place and operating pumping jacks and offshore platforms. The demand for aftermarket replacement equipment material and parts is considerably less cyclical than it is for items going into oil and gas OEM equipment. When an independent repair firm inspected a faulty high-pressure injection pump in the field, it usually informed the oil firm of the cost of the needed repairs. As the cost of repairs approached the cost of a new pump, the repair firm suggested that a new pump be installed. A pump repair was an oil firm maintenance expense item, but a new pump was usually categorized as a capital equipment appropriation.

## Pump and Component Parts Aftermarket

The size of the pump and component parts aftermarket depends on the in-place pump population and age of each unit. Since Eagle had the largest oil field population of any manufacturer of high-pressure injection pumps, there was considerable potential for replacement pumps and parts. Due to the incomplete warranty card information, Eagle did not have information on the location or age distribution of in-place units. To help Eagle's planning, the engineering department had attempted to determine the average life of a pump and the wear-out life for parts. But due to wide variances caused by differences in viscosity, the chemical content of the crude oil, suction pressures, and the RPMs at which the oil firm operated the machine, it was very difficult to identify "average life" and recommend repair and replacement schedules. However, it was common for Eagle's high-pressure injection pumps to be in continuous operation for 20 to 35 years.

High-pressure injection pumps had wear-out parts in the fluid and power drive ends of the pump. Major wear parts in the fluid end included the packing, plungers, valves, valve seats, and sometimes the fluid end. Eagle manufactured and sold all these parts. The major wear parts in the power end of the pump included the main bearings, the connecting rod bearings, the wrist pins and bushings, the oil seals, and the crankcase packing. Pumping speeds, suction conditions, and nature of the fluid being pumped determined the life of these parts. Eagle produced nearly 800 parts, many of which were different sizes of the same basic design. Eagle's wide product line created the need for a larger number of parts. Most of the parts made by the five competitors were interchangeable. This interchangeability also created an attractive opportunity for parts pirates and allowed distributors to sell products to the parts pirates.

The fluid end parts were the major part of a pump repair bill. In a typical repair situation, 20 to 30 percent of the cost was labor, with possibly some machine shop time, and the remaining 70 to 80 percent was for parts, usually always at the fluid end. For example, a purchase price of $6,000 for a new high-pressure injection pump would require yearly fluid end parts costing between $600 and $1,400. The plungers would cost $150 to $200 each, and a pump would have three or five of them. Valves for the pump would cost approximately $30 each, times three or five per pump. Packing was $50 to $60 for the pump. Every two or three years, a major overhaul was usually needed. Over a conservative 20-year pump life, it was common for the parts cost to be two or three times the initial purchase cost.

Historically, all the major manufacturers of high-pressure injection pumps neglected the parts market. As one Eagle pump distributor stated:

> The previous management at Eagle was more interested in selling pumps or metal tonnage rather than pursuing parts. Some producers saw the pump parts business as a nuisance, and therefore let in the parts pirates. I never understood why they all favored the higher dollar volume but lower profit margin pump business over the higher margin parts business.

Eagle employed a man by the name of Jim Keene to manage the aftermarket parts business. He was 59 years old and had been an Eagle salesman for 29 years before taking this position. Keene was also independently wealthy from the sale of his Eagle stock in 1965 to the group of investors.

## Parts Pirates

The higher profit margin, large pump population needing parts, and neglect by the major pump producers attracted a large number of parts pirates to the injection pump business. Many pirates were previously employed in the machine shops or sales areas of the pump sales and service distributors. It was easy to enter the parts market, since it only required a machining tool, usually a used one, and a small inventory of metal stock from which to machine parts. Most were located in the center of major oil field areas in simple structures with two or three employees. In the Bakersfield, California, oil-producing area, there were eight known parts pirates doing business. In the state of California, there were believed to be about 20 such businesses. One Bakersfield pump distributor described the parts pirates:

> These bootleggers are everywhere. Most were once pump repair service people who saw the prices, profit, and potential in the parts side of this business. They also know where all the pumps are in the area. They sell to anyone. They literally have little over their heads; often there is only an old barn or open shed with a roof to shelter them from the sun. They play havoc with parts prices. We can't buy parts from Eagle at the prices the parts pirates sell them for and still make an attractive profit.

Four very large parts pirates were located in Texas and California. The Houston parts pirate was believed to be even larger than some of the pump producers. The large parts pirates had modern and economical machining centers to make economical shorter runs for the lower-volume parts. The four major pirates also sold a significant amount of their production to the five high-pressure injection pump manufacturers. Eagle bought approximately 30 percent of its pump parts from these low-cost suppliers. To be more competitive with parts pirates, Eagle was building a new parts plant along the Texas-Mexico border. This plant was nearing completion.

The parts pirates were in many cases producing at 50 to 60 percent below Eagle's current costs, and an increasing number of their parts were of excellent quality. A small number of the parts pirates in the oil fields were beginning to do pump repair work, often working through the night or the entire weekend to put a pump back in operation for an oil producer.

Since the independent parts suppliers were low-cost producers, they sold most of their output to distributors at prices that were 30 to 50 percent below the prices distributors paid the five major producers. The pirates published parts substitution sheets to make it easy for distributor counter people to substitute their products for the manufacturers' items. This situation encouraged many Eagle distributors to stock the lower-priced parts as well. The pump producers often "shared the shelf" with competitive parts producers. Eagle had no policy or position on this common occurrence.

The independent parts producers sold to three types of accounts. The bulk of their production was sold to the same specialty pump distributors Eagle sold its pumps through. The parts producers also sold a significant amount of their output to the five injection pressure pump manufacturers. Finally, a small but increasing amount of the high-volume parts were sold by the independents to the oil field supply houses. The oil field supply houses were considered general stores in the oil production field, selling a wide range of maintenance and supply items. They did little repair work and were essentially similar to a "walk-in auto supply distributor." Pump salespeople referred to the supply houses as "Rope, dope, and soap stores." Eagle did not sell parts directly to the supply houses, but rather sold to its distributors, who in turn were supposed to resell the high-volume items to the supply houses. Some Eagle distributors sold parts to supply houses on a consignment basis. When Billie Williams asked one Eagle distributor why he sold parts to supply houses on consignment, the distributor stated:

> It's nice to have samples of what you're selling. They only have our more popular parts. They usually sell the samples and then we ship them more. This is no different than what your nonstocking distributors do when they repeatedly sell the pump demos you give them on consignment.

The Eagle distributors had relatively few parts sales to the supply houses. Since the Eagle distributors did not separately report pump and parts sales by account to Eagle, the precise amount of distributor sales of parts to supply houses was unknown.

On April 30, 1983, the Eagle Pump Company parts manager, Jim Keene, was called into Mike Crown's office to discuss the reasons why the Eagle parts business had declined for the last three quarters. Keene said he would prepare a memo on the situation within a week. Exhibit 7 shows Keene's response, dated May 5, 1983.

| EXHIBIT 7 | PARTS BUSINESS MEMO |
|---|---|

May 5, 1983

To:     Mike Crown, Division GM

From:   Jim Keene, Parts Manager

Subject: Reasons for and Possible Solutions to our Parts Decline

## Reasons for Parts Decline

1. *Parts Pirates*

   Like Eagle's pumps business, the parts pirates' business has tapered off. To counter this lower level business situation, the pirates have put on a concentrated effort to penetrate distributors, supply stores, and service shops.

2. *Eagle Parts Suppliers*

   Some of the same suppliers that sell us OEM parts are making very strong efforts at penetrating our markets (i.e., setting up master distributors and contacting our distributors in an effort to sell to them). The discounts given to their master distributors are approximately the same given to us and other OEMs.

3. *Lack of Distributor Inventory*

   The distributor, in most cases, does not have the proper inventory mix of parts in stock to sell what the customer wants.

4. *Distributors Not Selling to Supply Stores*

   This is the situation with a majority of our distributors. They feel they cannot sell to supply stores at a 20 percent discount. Therefore, the parts pirates are getting this business.

5. *Lack of Distributor Training*

   Many distributors lack technical pump knowledge and therefore miss sales opportunities.

6. *Lack of Eagle and Distributor Salespeople in the Field*

   Companies and distributors that have salespeople in the field are making the contacts. This includes both old and new contacts.

## Possible Solutions to Parts Sales Decline

1. Sell direct to supply stores, giving them a 20 percent discount off list.
2. Take a stronger stand with distributors regarding the carrying and selling of parts made by parts pirates.
3. Sell parts on consignment to distributors and/or supply stores. This would be a fixed amount.
4. Hold a meeting with the Distributor Council to discuss their problems and possible solutions.
5. Redesign parts for lower costs and improve performance.
6. Have more sales concentration in the areas of our large pump population—Odessa, Oklahoma City, southern Texas, western Texas, and especially Bakersfield; use both Eagle and distributor sales personnel.
7. Have distributors hire separate outside sales parts personnel.
8. Conduct an in-depth analysis of each of our distributors and determine who needs help, who should be dropped, and where we need to add new ones.

# DISTRIBUTION

## *Eagle Sales Force*

Eagle Pump had six salespeople who were responsible for both pumps and parts sales in their territories. The six were based in Dallas, New Orleans, Houston, Oklahoma City, Bakersfield, and St. Louis. They were also responsible for sales through distributors and sales served direct by Eagle's factory. The salespeople spent most of their time calling on the direct accounts. They sometimes helped Eagle's pump distributors call on end-use customers. Eagle did not have an established policy regarding which accounts should be sold direct or through a distributor. If a distributor located a customer whose technical problems it was not able to solve or one geographically outside its area, Eagle did not compensate the distributor for the lead. Eagle's Houston salesman said:

> It really hacks off the distributors when we sell any account direct or don't pay them for a sale outside their geographic area. It causes some distributors to play down our line and not pass on leads to us when they are not in their territory. However, Eagle does not have a history of taking a distributor account and selling it direct. But an OEM, regardless of its annual purchase, can approach Eagle and usually be sold direct. There is no set rule.

It took about seven to ten months for a new salesperson to learn the Eagle line and trouble-shooting expertise in oil and gas applications. The Eagle salespeople were considered good trouble-shooters and were known for conducting excellent technical seminars for design engineers and maintenance personnel. During the energy boom years, four of Eagle's salespeople were paid over $90,000. Each salesperson was given a car, full automobile expenses, and a substantial expense account. The salespeople were paid on a combined base and commission schedule for pump sales. The sale of parts was not in the quota or compensation plan. Their quotas were set every year on aggregate pump sales, whether they were sold through distributors or direct. Eagle's salespeople were paid a commission on what the distributor bought. Some distributors believed this compensation method encouraged the salespeople to overload distributors with pump inventories. With the sudden energy bust in 1982, most of Eagle's stocking distributors had large inventories. In early 1983, the Eagle salesman in Oklahoma City resigned to join a competitive distributor's sales force. The lower-performing salespeople in St. Louis and Denver were laid off. As of June 1, 1983, Eagle had three full-time salespeople. However, the marketing manager, division general manager, and marketing engineer each spent 15 to 20 percent of his time in the field working with customers and distributors.

Eagle salespeople received a base salary of $3,200 to $4,300 a month. Sales quotas were added to that and were based on market potentials. For example, in 1982, the Houston salesperson had a base quota of $2 million in pump sales and a quota tied to commission of $0.5 million. Due to the industry decline in 1982, none of the salespeople met their quotas and therefore they received no commission in 1982. After high commissions in 1981 and no commissions in 1982, morale was low. The Dallas salesperson said: "I'm working twice as hard for half the pay—it's not the most exciting situation I've been in." Some of the salespeople were entrepreneurs and had parallel business activities in real estate development, mobile trailer sales, and used oil field equipment sales.

The Eagle salespeople spent most of their time with direct OEM accounts. The marketing manager, Billie Williams, believed there was a need for a sales incentive system for both pumps and parts, but he was not sure what the percentage should be between the two. Williams stated:

> I like to keep carrots in front of our salespeople at all times, but they also need to know they have a barn to come back to. I'm also thinking about an incentive in the form of money or vacations that goes directly to the distributor salespeople who push our products. Such incentive money or so-called spiffs work in other industries outside of oil and gas.

## Pump Distributors

Williams described the typical Eagle distributor as follows:

> Since Eagle makes a high-quality technical pump, we need very specialized distributors. These guys are both systems fabricators and component and parts distributors. They provide engineering, fabrication, parts, replacement units, and repair service for oil and gas operators. They can build a system for the customer or sell the components to end users. They put the pumps, torque converters, clutches, couplings, drive unit and controls on a platform or skid. They also sell compressors, diesel and electric engines, and all that is needed to build the system. Our pump distributors have engineers who go in and evaluate an end user's requirements and specifications before submitting a price quotation. The fabricators, engineers, and draftsmen work closely with the customer in all stages of a job. Every situation is carefully analyzed to assure that the proper components are on the skid. The fabricators' engineers prepare a schematic flow and bills of material for each job. On more complex projects, in-depth conferences are held between the client's engineering personnel and the fabricator's engineers. The distributors usually have testing facilities to test and break in the completed system.

The specialty distributors usually had one to three outside salespeople and an inside salesperson. All had a parts counter for walk-in business. The Houston distributor, Penn Industries, described its business as follows:

> We are a very technical distributor that performs a lot of value-added. We are not just order takers or inside salesclerks. We have graduate engineers who design a system from a concept or a customer's specs. We then fabricate the appropriate package, install it, and service it until it's running to the customer's satisfaction. We have a counter, but we are not an auto parts store that does everything across a counter with catalogs.

All of Eagle's stocking distributors are shown in Exhibit 8 along with their annual purchases from Eagle (1980–1982), the year-end dollar value of their Eagle pumps and parts, inventory, and the number of branch locations. Where there are multiple or branch

EXHIBIT
8

## EAGLE PUMP STOCKING DISTRIBUTORS
### Pumps and Parts

| Distributor's Main Location | Sales | | | Inventory | Number of Locations (December 30, 1982) |
| --- | --- | --- | --- | --- | --- |
| | 1980 | 1981 | 1982 | | |
| 1. Oil and Gas Equipment Broken Arrow, OK | $  – | $  – | $  349,700 | $215,700 | 1 |
| 2. Bakersfield Pump Co. Bakersfield, CA | – | – | 161,100 | 5,400 | 1 |
| 3. Farley Pump & Supply Denver, CO | 324,540 | 851,329 | 817,210 | 46,210 | 4 |
| 4. Cook Industries Tulsa, OK | 2,082,100 | 3,315,900 | 2,504,400 | 934,530 | 7 |
| 5. United Industries Grand Rapids, MI | 178,710 | 132,201 | 205,604 | 36,370 | 2 |
| 6. Croton Equipment Carbondale, IL | 215,901 | 355,216 | 423,404 | 66,410 | 1 |
| 7. James Pump & Supply Lafayette, LA | 344,770 | 489,276 | 1,778,701 | 469,270 | 1 |
| 8. Miller Engine & Equipment, Wichita Falls, TX | 379,110 | 697,117 | 1,551,501 | 83,090 | 1 |
| 9. Oil Service Kansas City, KS | | 188,624 | 1,243,060 | 154,156 | 1 |
| 10. Western Equipment Denver, CO | 455,333 | 657,845 | 645,761 | 205,650 | 9 |
| 11. Flow Equipment Bakersfield, CA | 486,650 | 716,100 | 740,799 | 115,110 | 3 |
| 12. LaPine Equipment Longview, TX | 74,203 | 277,701 | 1,340,234 | 67,515 | 1 |
| 13. Penn Industries Houston, TX | 815,090 | 1,374,267 | 1,715,100 | 569,450 | 6 |
| 14. Gulf States Supply Houston, TX (added in 1981) | – | 1,397,401 | 2,375,400 | 835,170 | 6 |
| 15. Fluid Pumps Bakersfield, CA | 115,217 | 287,171 | 1,077,191 | 172,660 | 1 |
| 16. Rucker Engine & Pump Oklahoma City, OK | 374,104 | 360,991 | 413,876 | 148,420 | 1 |

locations for one distributor, they are usually in different cities or states. The 16 distributors in Exhibit 8 account for the majority of Eagle distributor sales. The average stocking Eagle distributor had annual total sales (systems, components, parts) of between $6 and $40 million. The remainder of Eagle's distributor sales were through nonstocking distributors.

Many of the Eagle distributors stocked nothing and sold very little each year. The nonstocking distributors had all the Eagle catalogs and literature. Eagle had no distributor stocking policy for pump units or parts. If a nonstocking distributor got an order, it would still collect the 20 percent standard commission on Eagle pumps. When the marketing manager asked one distributor in Texas why he didn't stock Eagle products, the distributor replied:

> We must know the business is out there before we'll put anything in stock. Plus, Eagle has many dead lines and parts that never sell. That really impacts a distributor who lives on inventory turnover. Without knowing the market potential for their product lines, they can't tell us what and how much to inventory.

The Gulf States Supply distributor, with six branches and headquarters in Houston, commented:

> I wish Eagle was able to have the oil field maintenance people come in and demand Eagle pumps and parts. As it is now, they usually come in, say what their pumping requirements are, and our counter people can sell them whatever they think will do the job. Eagle provides very little direction to its distributors and does even less for end users. Just call Eagle in Dallas for technical help sometime. If Bill Beton is not around, no one calls back for days. Eagle comes around and makes promises, but nothing happens. They have not set policies for distributors. Some of the manufacturers of rotary and low-pressure pumps we carry have very clear rules on how to work with and help distributors.

## Distributor Territory Coverage

In the 1960s and early 1970s, Eagle rarely had more than one distributor in larger geographic areas. But as oil and gas drilling expanded and the older in-place pumps needed more repair and parts, and as more distributors wanted to represent Eagle, additional distributors were signed up. Exhibit 9 shows the geographic locations of Eagle's entire distributor network. Williams described the distributor territory coverage:

> In many geographic areas, we now have double or overlapping coverage and in some areas little or none. But I like dual coverage because if we drop one or he drops us, we still have a guy there carrying our lines. In 1981 we signed up a new distributor to carry our lines, Gulf States Supply in Houston, which had six branches in the Gulf states. He is a real hustler who really woke up the other Eagle distributors in the areas where he had branches that competed with them.

Eagle recently gained the Gulf States distributor in Houston and his six branches because an Eagle competitor, Oilflo, would not allow Gulf States to carry its pump line in all locations because of conflicts with existing distributors in the designated territories. Eagle had no mechanism for resolving the inevitable conflict that occurs when one Eagle distributor opens or acquires a branch where another Eagle distributor already has a branch. Eagle did not provide any distributor with protection or assurance that there would be no other distributor nearby. None of its distributors had specific territories or designated areas of geographic responsibility.

EXHIBIT
9

## LOCATIONS OF EACH EAGLE DISTRIBUTOR, BY STATE AND CITY

**ALABAMA**
Birmingham

**ARKANSAS**
El Dorado

**CALIFORNIA**
Anaheim
Bakersfield (4)
Irvine
Los Angeles
Santa Barbara

**COLORADO**
Denver (2)
Grand Junction (2)

**CONNECTICUT**
Hartford

**FLORIDA**
Miami
West Palm Beach

**GEORGIA**
Atlanta

**IDAHO**
Boise

**ILLINOIS**
Arlington Heights
Carbondale
Chicago

**KANSAS**
Chanute
Liberal
Plainville
Wichita (2)

**LOUISIANA**
Baton Rouge
Lafayette (2)
New Orleans (2)
Shreveport

**MASSACHUSETTS**
Bedford

**MICHIGAN**
Detroit
Grand Rapids
Traverse City

**MINNESOTA**
Duluth
Minneapolis

**MISSISSIPPI**
Biloxi

**MISSOURI**
Kansas City

**MONTANA**
Billings

**NORTH DAKOTA**
Fargo
Willston (2)

**NEW MEXICO**
Farmington
Hurbs

**NEW YORK**
Buffalo
Syracuse

**NORTH CAROLINA**
Charlotte

**OHIO**
Cleveland
Columbus
Mansfield
Monroe
Newark
Wooster

**OKLAHOMA**
Broken Arrow
Oklahoma City (2)
Tulsa

**OREGON**
Eugene
Portland

**PENNSYLVANIA**
Pittsburgh (2)

**TEXAS**
Corpus Christi (2)
Dallas (2)
Ft. Worth
Houston (5)
Longview (2)
Odessa (2)
Wichita Falls

**UTAH**
Salt Lake City

**VIRGINIA**
Richmond

**WASHINGTON**
Seattle
Spokane

**WEST VIRGINIA**
Charleston
Wheeling

**WISCONSIN**
Milwaukee

**WYOMING**
Casper (2)
Evanston
Rock Springs

Williams asked many Eagle distributors two questions: How large a geographic radius can you travel to effectively and profitably service? How far does the typical walk-in customer drive to buy from you? The answer to the first question was usually stated in terms of driving times. Based on the distributor responses, it appeared that a 60- to 70-mile radius was about the maximum for a one-day service job. The drive there would take about 1½ hours, work on the pump would take 3 to 5 hours, and a return trip was another 1½ hours. Longer distances were inefficient for the pump service distributor and increased the downtime cost of a problem oil well. The maximum driving time and radius for walk-in customers was about 50 miles.

Most of Eagle's larger distributors, especially those with multiple locations, believed Eagle had too many distributors in many markets that were now competing for a smaller total amount of business. This was less of a problem in boom times, when every distributor had a lot of business. A Denver distributor stated:

> The greatest problem for Eagle is that for any given specialty pump item, there is overdistribution causing competition among Eagle distributors. They need fewer but stronger distributors. Eagle should cancel some, restrict the area of others, and add more where needed.

### Distributor Relationship

Williams was aware he had serious problems with distributors. He decided to spend the next week in the field traveling with the three Eagle salespeople. The Houston salesperson stated:

> We are lucky these distributors stay with us. Some are good ole boys, but many would bolt if they had another product line with Eagle's quality image and customer franchise.

Williams traveled with the California salesman for a day, and at dinner that evening the rep summarized to Williams how he thought distributors in his territory viewed Eagle:

> The distributors in California see all the end users as their private customers, rather than as our common customer. Many of the distributors out here don't like me to call on end users in their territory. Even though we don't have a history of taking distributor accounts direct, most will not show me "their" customer or mailing lists. However, when there is a technical problem at an end user, then it's an Eagle problem and not theirs. The better distributors are just beginning to see us as partners.

In June 1983, Williams decided to call a distributors' meeting, which all Eagle salespeople would also attend. Eagle had not held a distributor council meeting for many years. Williams called the meeting to get to know the distributors better and to get feedback from them. All but one stocking distributor attended the meeting. A summary of the meeting was put into the Distributor Council minutes (Exhibit 10).

## PRICING AND PROFIT MIX

Eagle had a company target of 30 to 40 percent gross margin on pumps; the floor was a 30 percent gross margin. Specialty pump orders were to be priced at a 65 percent gross margin. There were no quantity discounts for OEM or distributor sales. For parts, Eagle had a 70 percent gross margin pricing objective and was the highest priced parts

EXHIBIT
10

## MINUTES: DISTRIBUTOR COUNCIL MEETING
### June 16–18, 1983, Dallas, Texas

1. Eagle should clean up its distribution situation.
2. What is Eagle's policy on selling to nonstocking distributors?
3. Eagle's distribution policy appears ruthless and arbitrary.
4. Distributors need direction from Eagle to expand market applications for existing pumps, i.e., sewage, mining, reverse osmosis.
5. New application case histories that solve common application problems in expanding markets need to be written and shared with distributors.
6. Need a clear written definition of what an OEM is, along with an OEM policy statement.
7. A quarterly distributor newsletter might be published by Eagle, including:
   a. Case histories.
   b. Competitive information.
   c. Distributor personnel changes.
   d. Eagle personnel changes.
   e. New distributor appointments.
   f. Service tips.
   g. Application photos and stories.
8. The council thought there should be a limited number of OEMs and that:
   a. Before signing on an OEM, current distributors need to be given a chance to see if they can meet the OEM's needs.
   b. If Eagle decides to sign on an OEM even if the local distributor can meet its needs, the distributor needs to receive some type of compensation.
9. If a particular distributor is not doing the job expected, it should be canceled with sufficient notice. Eagle should not just surround an existing distributor with more distributors to get the coverage needed. Eagle should be careful not to oversaturate an area with distributors.
10. What is Eagle's intention for the reverse osmosis market? Will this be a direct market or a distributor market?
11. *Media Advertising*
    a. Direction should be toward testimonials/applications, with reprints available for distributors to use.
    b. Co-op advertising programs in regional and local publications were suggested.
    c. When Bingo card responses are received from ads, all distributors in that particular geographic area should be sent two copies of the request for information.
    d. The Council did not feel that Yellow Pages advertising was particularly effective in selling

---

supplier. Recent competitive action by parts pirates had caused Eagle to price all parts at a 60 percent gross margin. Historically, 40 percent of Eagle sales were from parts, but 60 percent of profits. In 1983, Eagle believed parts would be about 60 percent of sales and 80 percent or more of profits. OEMs that were sold direct by Eagle were given discounts of 20 percent for both parts and pumps.

Eagle's pump distributors received a discount of 35 percent on parts and 20 percent on

**EXHIBIT
10**

*(cont'd)*

pumps, although for parts there is some feeling it is effective. A study of effectiveness should be undertaken.

    e. Direct mail was thought to be very effective and could possibly be used in a cooperative program, too.

    f. Would like to have Eagle personnel attend trade shows on a regional basis; possibly part of a co-op, too.

12. *Catalogs and Literature*

    a. The catalogs are not up to industry standards. They are lacking in the following areas:

        1. Incomplete engineering and technical information.

        2. Need a separate engineering section.

        3. Need a system for keeping catalogs complete and up to date.

        4. Each distributor salesperson needs a catalog.

    b. All literature needs a place for a distributor to put its name and address.

    c. The gallons per minute curve charts are more easily read than when the same information is put in statistical columns.

13. *Training*

    a. A list of all training aids available should be sent to all distributors.

    b. All training schools and display models should be announced.

    c. Eagle should develop a mailing list for the distributors to complete, so the right person would get the direct mail. The list should be updated twice a year.

    d. Eagle product training was noted as being excellent.

14. *Pricing*

    a. A 20 percent discount on pumps is a small discount. Distributor profits were primarily made on parts.

    b. What is the monthly escalation of pump prices based on? Should it be matched with some economic measurement? It seems to be out of range with the current inflation rate.

    c. Most distributors were stunned by the recent price on application (POA) pricing program, since many now wonder what their purchased inventory is worth.

    d. If parts prices are competitive with those of parts pirates, distributors will build more inventories and increase sales effort. If there are significant differences between the parts pirates' and Eagle's prices, those differences should be highlighted.

    e. Is there a possibility for a 5 percent cash discount for pumps?

    f. Since a cash-rich major oil company has now purchased Eagle, distributors are wondering whether the company will consider floor planning some distributors' inventory on a consignment basis.

---

pumps. A typical pump unit sale by a distributor in 1982 sold at a suggested list price of $6,500. Many distributors believed their 20 percent discount from list price on pumps was insufficient. The typical pump distributor's total profit was approximately 40 percent from parts, and 30 to 40 percent from parts and service work. The remaining 20 to 30 percent came from pump unit sales. Billie Williams and Mike Crown, the division general manager, were considering installing a quantity discount of 5 percent for distributors that placed a combined pump and parts order of $200,000 or more. Williams was concerned that the quantity discounts might encourage distributors to hold back orders until they had accumulated enough for the discount.

The Eagle suggested resale price for distributor parts to the supply houses was 20 percent off list. That left the distributor with 15 percent from the 35 percent discount. Many distributors believed it would be costly for them to sell to supply houses from their stock. To solve this concern, Williams was considering shipping direct to the supply houses and then providing the distributor with 10 percent for doing the paperwork. However, due to the parts pirates' low prices, it was doubtful that Eagle's prices could be at all competitive with the no-brand parts. The supply houses generally did not stress a brand, for which Eagle could receive a premium. The supply houses were often disloyal buyers that sold fast-turnover pump parts on a generic basis. Some pirates were selling private label parts to the supply houses at 50 percent below Eagle's supply house list price. If Eagle sold parts direct to the supply houses, it was concerned about receiving more complaints from distributors, since the Eagle parts were very profitable for the distributors.

## Price on Application Program (POA)

To be more competitive, Eagle announced a new distributor pricing program on May 1, 1983, which was already bringing many complaints from distributors. As part of the POA program, if a distributor had a prospect for a new pump, it could call the factory in Dallas to see what price Eagle would allow to be competitive. For example, if a competitor submitted a $6,100 price for a pump that normally sold at list for $7,500, Eagle would usually meet or match it and give the distributor a 15 percent commission on the sale price. The stocking distributors complained that the program was reducing the value of their inventory, and many now wanted rebates. Many of the POA prices to the end user were less than the cost of the pump to the distributor. The POA program temporarily stopped the use of all pump price sheets.

On July 12, 1983, Williams met with Crown to discuss the POA program and other marketing issues. Williams first commented:

> We aren't really managing our sales and distribution. Many of the distributors are managing us and acting more like reps than distributors. In fact, in some territories we have competition between our distributors; if they sell someone else parts, we are competing with our own distributors. We need to agree on firm policies and put them into a new distribution agreement. This means we will have to evaluate, cancel, restrict, and add new distributors. There will be a lot of hot tempers and bad-mouthing because we've kept so many on for decades. We will also have inventory return problems. Fire sales will anger our better distributors. But if they don't give us the coverage, penetration, and customer service, why mess with them?

Crown:

> Our sales and distribution emphasis should follow our product-market strategy. We must get this sorted out fast because this morning I got bad news from Brad Sikes, our accountant. This last quarter the first red ink in Eagle's history appeared on the

books. The $80,000 loss isn't as bad as it looks, because most of it is due to depreciation charges. The fact that they paid two times book value for this business caused management to write up the assets and now write off large depreciation expenses. But our cash flow is still not healthy. We are extending payables from 30 to 60 days. We really can't lay off any more people. The burden is on you to improve our top line so we can show a better bottom line.

Williams:

I will start by analyzing the California oil patch market because it is so important to us. Our sales reps there just sent me a distributor territory report (Exhibit 11) on all the present and potential distributors in California.

---

**EXHIBIT 11**    *CALIFORNIA DISTRIBUTOR REPORT*

1. J. D. Pump Sales and Service (present distributor)
   Santa Barbara, California
   About 50% of the business is pumps.
   Territory covered: Santa Barbara & Ventura areas, onshore and offshore.

   *Manufacturers' lines:*
   Eagle—mostly parts, few pumps.
   Viking and FMC (noncompetitive lines).
   Parts from pirates.

   *Facilities and capabilities:*
   6 service trucks on the road.
   Rebuild pumps and do light fabrication.
   Small rented facility.

   *Personnel:*
   Owner/president is the only salesman.
   1 salesman let go recently due to industry slump.

   *Overall:*
   An aggressive firm, but don't know if they'll survive the industry shakeout.

2. Flow Equipment (present distributor)
   Bakersfield, California—largest location
   About 40% of the business is pumps.
   Stocking Eagle distributor.
   About $100,000 in Eagle inventory.
   Territory covered: Branch locations—Bakersfield, Anaheim, Concord.

   *Manufacturers' lines:*
   Eagle.
   Ingersol Rand (noncompetitive).
   Toyo—new Japanese line.

**EXHIBIT
11**

*(cont'd)*

*Bakersfield location:*
    About 80% of this store's sales are pumps.
    Eagle pump & parts inventory.
    Do fabrication of pump skids.
    Only 2 field service trucks.
    1 outside salesman.

*Anaheim location:*
    No Eagle pumps or parts stocked.
    No service and few sales here.
    Appears to be office for Flow Equipment's owner to conduct other business.

*Concord location:*
    Small inventory of Eagle parts.
    1 service truck.

*Overall:*
    Is really a one-location operation (Bakersfield) and not gaining much penetration in other areas.

3. Fluid Pumps (present distributor)
   Bakersfield, California
   95% of business is pumps for oil fields.
   Stocking Eagle distributor.
   About $105,000 in Eagle inventory (mostly pumps); high sales-to-inventory ratio.
   Only location.

*Manufacturers' lines:*
    Eagle.
    Viking (noncompetitive).
    Crane-Deming (noncompetitive).
    FMC (noncompetitive).

*Facilities and capabilities:*
    12 service trucks.
    Does a lot of rebuilding.
    Large machine shop—makes many pump parts—is actually a parts pirate, who also sells parts he makes. Last year probably sold $400,000–$500,000 of parts he made.

*Personnel:*
    Jim Walker runs a one-man show. He's in late sixties and without him, the long-time loyal customers would leave.
    Business is for sale; he wants $2 million for it. No successor.
    Many other distribution people learned the pump business from Jim.
    A legend in the California oil patch.
    2 full-time salesmen.

*Overall:*
    Might consider buying this as a company store. If we cancel him, he'll say a lot of bad things about us. However, I doubt if he will grow with our business, and he doesn't want to expand the business. A very independent guy who's been an Eagle distributor for 28 years.

**EXHIBIT
11**

*(cont'd)*   4. Western Pump Supply (potential new distributor)
Bakersfield, California (headquarters)
95% of the business is for pumps in the oil fields and for irrigation.

*Manufacturers' lines:*
Oilflo—competitive, whole line.
Worthington (noncompetitive).
Meyers (noncompetitive).
Blackmen (noncompetitive).
Roper (noncompetitive).

*Branch locations:*
Bakersfield
Santa Barbara
Ventura
Long Beach
Fresno

*Facilities and capabilities:*
12–13 service trucks.
All locations have machine shop facilities.
Can machine or manufacture parts for any pumps.
Total of 21 salesmen—6 inside and 15 outside.
Computer network between all branches.
Modern structures at all locations.
Has an 8,000-name direct mail list continually updated.

*Overall:*
Is one of our largest competitors carrying the Oilflo line.
Sales manager and two other salesmen are ex-Eagle factory salesmen. They know our line.
Willing to change to our line because most high-pressure pumps in California are Eagle's.
However, they want an exclusive for all of California, Arizona, and Nevada.

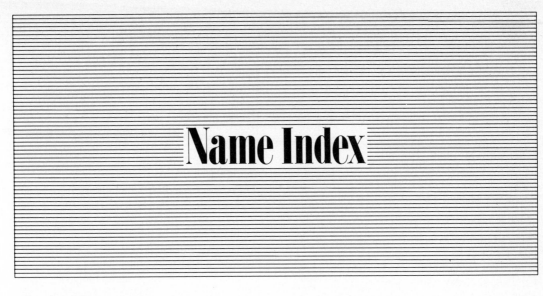

# Name Index

Acme-Cleveland, 232–234
Addressograph-Multigraph Corporation, 207
Adlee, Lee, 167*n*
Airbus Industrie, 192
Air Products and Chemicals, 200
Alcan Aluminum Ltd., 81
Allied Corporation, 200, 247
Altos Computer, 8
American Association of Mechanical Engineers, 47
American Digital Data Systems, 52
American Iron & Steel Institute, 38
American Telephone and Telegraph (AT&T), 472–473, 485
Anderson, William, 86
Ansoff, H. Igor, 292
ARMCO, 38
Asbudnick, Fred, 43*n*
AT&T (American Telephone and Telegraph), 472–485

Balsley, Howard L., 124*n*
Bell System, 473, 478, 486, 488–492, 494, 512
Bell Telephone Laboratories, 473, 485
Bendix Corporation, 200, 247
Bethlehem Steel Corporation, 410, 442–444
Black & Decker, 145
Blondo, John J., 167*n*
Boeing Aircraft Corporation, 21, 190, 191, 196
Bonoma, Thomas, 248*n*
Booz, Allen & Hamilton Inc., 142, 143
Brickner, William, 280

Brown, Rex, 193*n*
Buckner, Hugh P., 36*n*
Bundesbank, 57
Burroughs (firm), 8, 92, 502, 509

Cannon, J. W., 41*n*
Canon U.S.A., 92
Caterpillar Tractor Company, 21, 55, 60–61, 75, 77, 164, 223, 229, 238, 446–451, 453
CDC (Control Data Corporation), 8, 92, 508
Clark Industrial Truck, 76
Cleveland Twist Drill, 177
Clover, Vernon T., 124*n*
Control Data Corporation (CDC), 8, 92, 508
Convergent Technologies, 8
Coppett, John, 254
Corbin, Arnold, 320*n*
Corey, E. Raymond, 93, 199*n*, 301*n*, 386*n*
Crawford Fitting Company, 257, 260
Crisp, Richard D., 127*n*
Cummins Engine, 167
Cyert, Richard M., 50*n*

Dana (firm), 41
Daniel, D. Ronald, 330*n*
Data General, 470
Datagraphics, 511
Dean, William, 417*n*
Delta Airlines, 196
Demosthenes, 92
Diamond Shamrock, 278, 280

Diebold Group, 509–510, 513, 514
Dilworth, James B., 40*n*
Doboy Packaging Machinery, 57
Douey, Brian H., 167*n*
Drucker, Peter, 68
DuPont de Nemours & Company, E. I., 24, 107–108, 148

Ericssen, L. M. (firm), 480, 481
Esley, James A., 121*n*
Evans, David S., 417*n*
Exxon Corporation, 49

Fairbanks Morse (firm), 146
Faris, Charles W., 37*n*
Fisk Electric, 483
Ford Motor Company, 41, 45, 47, 418
Foremost-McKesson (firm), 146
*Fortune* 100 companies, 18, 91
*Fortune* 500 companies, 283, 487
Frieden (firm), 146
Fruehauf Trucking Company, 419, 424–425

Garda, Robert A., 101*n*, 102, 104, 106
GE (General Electric Company), 20, 21, 51, 81, 92, 144, 148, 165, 196, 257–259, 309
Geneen, Hal, 304*n*
General Dynamics Corporation, 480
General Electric Company (GE), 20, 21, 51, 81, 92, 144, 148, 165, 196, 257–259, 309
General Motors Corporation (GM), 19–21, 25, 38, 81, 198, 235
General Telephone & Electronics (GTE), 149, 155, 247, 473, 485
General Telephone & Electronics (GTE)–Automatic Electric, 478
Gilbreth International, 58
GM (General Motors Corporation), 19–21, 25, 38, 81, 198, 235
Goodrich Company, B. F., 39, 254
Goodyear Tire & Rubber Company, The, 191
Grace & Company, W. R., 247
Grimm, Richard, 161
GTE (General Telephone & Electronics), 149, 155, 247, 473, 485
GTE (General Telephone & Electronics)–Automatic Electric, 478

Harris (firm), 167
Hart, Norman A., 248*n*, 251*n*

Hershy, Robert, 86*n*
Hewlett-Packard, 164, 190, 471
Hinds, Joe (case study), 379, 380
Hitachi, 480
Hofman, Philip B., 150
Holiday Inn, 481
Honeywell Inc., 92, 502, 508
Howe Richardson (firm), 146
Hurst, T. R., 200*n*

IBM (International Business Machines Corporation), 8, 41, 70, 71, 93, 144, 146, 148, 163, 164, 188, 190, 191, 199, 223, 470, 489, 502, 508, 509, 511, 513
Ingersoll-Rand (firm), 235
Industrial Research Institute, 408*n*
Integrated Circuit Engineering Corporation, 53
International Business Machines Corporation (IBM), 8, 41, 70, 71, 92, 93, 144, 146, 148, 190, 191, 199, 223, 470, 489, 502, 508, 509, 511, 513
International Harvester Inc., 92
International Standards Association, 47
International Telephone and Telegraph (ITT), 247, 480, 481, 492

John Deere (firm), 24, 92, 96
Johnson & Johnson Company (J&J), 50, 58, 150, 161

Kaiser Aluminum, 81
Kami, Michael, 92*n*
Kawasaki (firm), 48
Kizilbach, A. H., 496*n*
Kodak (firm), 107, 511
Kotler, Philip, 126*n*

Leonard, Joseph W., 376*n*
Levitt, Theodore, 13*n*, 280
Litton Business Systems, 492
Litton Industries, 481, 511
Lockheed Aircraft Corporation, 21
Lotshaw, Elmer, 121*n*
LTV (firm), 247

McCuistion, Tommy, 227*n*, 257
McDonnell-Douglas Aircraft Corporation, 21, 196
MacEwen, Edward, 247–248
McGraw-Hill Research, 255
McKinsey, James O., 333

Mackintosh Consultants, 27
Magee, John F., 193n
Makridatis, Spyros, 127n
Market Research Corporation of America, 29
Martin Marietta (firm), 200
Mead Paper (firm), 223
Merck Pharmaceutical Company, 131
Mohawk Data Sciences and Digitronics, 508, 510
Monsanto Corporation, 24, 247
More, Robert, 454n
Motorola (firm), 167

NAMCO Controls Division (of Acme-Cleveland),
    232–234
Narus, James A., 225n
National Bureau of Standards, 47
NCR Corporation, 8, 35, 51, 52, 86, 92, 146, 508
Newton, Derek A., 427n
Nielsen Company, A. C., 29, 217
Nippon Electric Company, 35, 480
Nitsuko (firm), 48
Northern Telecom, 478, 492

Orahood, E. G., 234, 343

Paccar (firm), 256
Parker Hannifin Corporation, 29, 235, 254, 257
Peters, Thomas J., 41n, 190
Petre, Peter D., 188n
Petronius, Gaius, 335n
Pfizer (firm), 223
Philco Ford (firm), 481
Pitney Bowes Corporation, 70
Platten, John H., Jr., 36n
Proctor and Gamble, 58

Radio Corporation of America (RCA), 92, 508
Radio Corporation of America (RCA) Service Com-
    pany, 481, 492
Raytheon (firm), 167
Regau, Lawrence G., 191n
Regency Electronics Company, 286
Reich, Robert B., 318n
Reliance Electric, 35, 87, 151, 183–184, 234, 241,
    261–264, 284, 343
Reynolds Aluminum, 81
Rich, Stuart A., 390n, 416n, 446n
Robinson, Patrick J., 37n
Rodger, Leslie W., 247

Rolls Royce, 21, 56–57, 200
Rosenn, K. S., 200n
Ross, Joel, 92n
Ruter, Vincent G., 47n
Ryans, Adrian B., 469n

Salomon Brothers, 8
SAMI, 217
Schill, Ronald I., 399n
Schonberger, Richard V., 41n, 48n, 56n
Sheth, Jagdish, 37n
Shill, Ronald L., 63n
Sigmore and Natomos, 278
Simon, Herbert A., 50n
Singer (firm), 146
Slaybaugh, John, 234
Smith, Paul L., 191n
Smith Kline Corporation, 131
Snyder, Ray, 241
Society of Automotive Engineers, 47
Sperry (firm), 8
Sperry UNIVAC, 163, 470, 503
SRI International, 484, 485
Stieglitz, Harold, 333
Strauss, George, 39n
Stromberg-Carlson Communications, 478, 481, 492
Sultan, R. G. M., 196n
Sundstrand Corporation, 167
Sun Zi, 296

Technicare, 161
Teleci (firm), 481; 482
Tele/Resources, 481, 483, 484, 492
Tenneco Chemical Company, 52, 200
Terborgh, George, 176n
Texas Instruments, 410
Thanopoulos, John, 376n
3M, 57, 223, 247, 254, 511
Tietjen, Karl H., 347
Toledo Scale, 146, 290
Trow, Donald B., 50n
TRW, 309

UAW (United Automobile Workers), 81
Ulvia, Jacob W., 193n
Underwriters Laboratory, 47
Union Carbide, 24
United Automobile Workers (UAW), 81
United Electrical and Radio Machine Workers Union,
    91

United States (U.S.) Steel Corporation, 247, 414
United Technologies, 21, 309
UNIVAC, 163, 470, 502

Voorhees, Ray, 254

Warner-Lambert (firm), 278
Waterman, Robert H., 41*n*, 190
Webster, Frederick E., 37*n*
Weigand, Robert E., 191*n*
Western Electric, 144, 473, 478, 480, 484, 485, 491, 492

Westinghouse, 196, 309
Wheelwright, Steven C., 127*n*
Williams, Vearl A., 54*n*
Wind, Yoram, 37*n*
Wolfe, Harry D., 127*n*
Woodside, Arch, 37*n*

Xerox Corporation, 36, 45, 92, 131, 164, 223

Zarrello, John, 397*n*
Zenz, Gary, 42*n*, 45*n*

# Subject Index

Account size, market segmentation based on, 103
Acquisition (merger), access to new technology by, 167
Acquisition programs
  of DOD, 62–63
  *see also* procurement
Administration
  of pricing policy, 177–178, 180–182
  *see also* management
Advancement (career opportunity), 372, 373
Advertising and promotion, 245–268
  basis of effective, 89, 256–261
  control of, 255, 261, 265–267
  expenditures for, 248–251, 261, 265
  planning of, 261, 265–267
  and promotional mix, 253–256
  special problems of, 250–252
Aftermarket, *see* MRO market
Alternative(s), planning, 280–281, 287–288
Alternative organization, 320–334
  selecting, 330–334
  *see also* product-market management; product-market managers
Analysis
  competitive, 82–84
  economic, key sales based on, 206–209
  insufficient, and unimaginative planning, 281
  internal sales, 113–118
  life cycle, 292
  of past bids, 190–191, 201
  planning and flow chart, 290–292

product line, 153–154
profit structure, 295
*see also* assessment of markets; evaluation; value analysis
Applicability of product-market management, 339–341
Assessment of markets, 110–137
  by conducting market studies, *see* market studies
  of current market position, 112–119
  of market potential, 119–123
  market segmentation evaluation based on, 134–136
  project proposals for, 131–134
*Atlantic Monthly, The* (magazine), 318
Attitudinal shift, effective marketing requiring, 4–5

Bidding, competitive, *see* competitive bidding
Bid-history analysis, 190–191, 201
Broadening of customer base, 21
Budgets, *see* spending
Bureaucracy, *see* organization
Business strategy, *see* strategy
*Business Week* (magazine), 309
Buying
  industrial-consumer differences in, 22–23
  market segmentation based on common buying factors, 102, 104
  rational, 22
  *see also* customer(s); procurement
Buying center (decision-making unit), 37
Buying committee, role of, 39–40
Buy situations, *see* make-buy customers

Capital
  planning and evaluating use of, 309
  *see also* return on investments
Career opportunity (advancement), 372, 373
Case studies, 375–543
  Cantro Corporation, 427–432
  Eagle Pump Company, 518–543
  Gould, Inc., 502–517
  Gulfcoast Chemical, 399–401
  Hartman Elevator Company, 433–445
  Industrial Consolidated Incorporated, 407–415
  Jones & Jones, 390–398
  Judson Industries, Inc., 496–501
  Pape Bros., Inc., 446–453
  Raytronics Corporation, 402–406
  ROLM Corporation, 469–495
  S. S. Johnson and Son, Ltd., 454–468
  Trus Joist Corporation, 416–426
  Warwick Company, 386–389
  WRT, Inc., 376–385
Catalogs, promotional, 253–254
*Census of Manufacturers,* 124
Channels of distribution, 29
  *see also* distribution network management; distributors
Charts, use of flow, in planning, 290–292
Classification of customers by annual sales, 94, 95
Commerce, Department of, 47
*Commerce Business Daily* (newspaper), 64
Commissions, 214, 216
Commitment
  to action, 6–10
  to implementation, 366, 367
  to plans, 313–314
Common buying factors, market segmentation by, 102, 104
Communication, implementation and open, 371
Compensation plan, sales, 214–217
Competition
  cost reduction programs and, 182–184
  economics of, 80–81
  effects of foreign, 205
  and market entry success factors, 81–87
  planning and, 289
  pricing and, 173, 182, 183. *See also* pricing
  product development and, 88, 192
  and selection of alternative organization, 330
  steps in conduct of competitive analysis, 82–84

structure of, 79–80
  understanding, 87–89, 173
Competitive bidding, 186–202
  analysis of past bids and, 190–191, 201
  customer's requirements and, 189–190, 200
  guidelines for, 200–201
  long- and short-term, 191–194
  negotiations in, 197–198
  pricing terms in, 195–196, 198–199
  proposal for, 196–197
  as source of competitive intelligence, 85
  supply contract obligations in, 199–200
Competitive intelligence, gathering, 84–87
Complexity of products, effects of, on sales, 205
Component products (subassemblies), 96
  estimating market potential for, 122
Conflicting demands made on first-line sales supervisors, 211–212
Consumer market, industrial versus, *see* industrial market–consumer market differences
Consumer spending, effects of changes in, 20
Context of planning, matching concept of planning with, 273–274
Contingencies, making allowances for, in planning, 312
Contract obligations, 199–200
Control
  of advertising and promotion, 255, 261, 265–267
  of planning, 303
Conversion factors in market potential estimation, 123–124
Cooperation
  functional, and commitment to action, 7–8
  implementation and team membership, 371–372
Coordination of planning, 287
Corporate objectives, *see* objective(s)
Corporate strategy, product-market strategy versus, 277–279
Cost
  achieving low, as strategy, 163
  allocation of indirect, 180
  and competitive bidding, 193
  to customers, need to understand, 70–75
  factors affecting, 176, 177
  information on, need by market managers, 357
  labor, reducing, 80, 81
  of new product, 150–152, 159–164, 174
  of new technology, 159–161
  pricing and relationship between profit and, 173

product line, 179–180
programs to reduce, 182–184
projection of, in planning, 304–308
total selling, 206
value analysis of, 43, 45, 46
*see also* pricing
Cost-benefit to customers, 75–79
Cost-plus bids, 195–196
Councils of distributors, 236–237
*County Business Patterns* (journal), 101, 124
Credibility of plans, 304–312
Current market position, assessing, 112–119
Current profits, matching product development expenditures with, 159–164
Customer(s)
  basis for segmentation of, 23. *See also* market segmentation
  classified by annual sales, 94, 95
  competitive bidding and requirements of, 189–190, 200
  competitive intelligence as source of, 86
  cost-benefits to, 75–79
  costs to, need to understand, 70–75
  differences between industrial market and consumer market, 28–29
  distribution selling decision and potential for, 228
  follow-on sales and training employees of, 192
  group of, selected for emphasis, 6
  identifying requirements of, 8
  large, competitive bidding and, 197–198
  operations and products of, 68–70
  understanding, 87–89
  *see also specific types of customers, for example,* end-users
Customer base, industrial market–consumer market differences in, 21

Decentralization, competition and, 80
Decision-making unit (buying center), 37
Defense, Department of (DOD), 62–63
Delivery
  ability to compete and shorter cycles of, 182
  analysis of delivery performance system, 58–59
  distribution selling and need for rapid, 227
Demand
  derived, *see* derived demand
  measuring industry capacity against, 173
  Derived demand, 20–21
  market potential estimation based on, 123

Design of product, *see* product design
Desk research (secondary market study), 124–125
Development
  of distributors, 237–238
  *see also* training and orientation
Direct-mail promotion, 254
Direct sales calls, 255–256
Distribution channels
  multiplicity of, 29
  *see also* distribution network management; distributors
Distribution network management
  developing policies for, 231–234
  factors affecting distribution selling decision and, 227–229
  recognizing market differences in, 228–229
Distributors, 221–244
  councils of, 236–237
  development of, 237–238
  evaluating performance of, 238–241
  group, 242–243
  matching, to market segments, 229–230
  multidivisional, 242–243
  relationship between producers and, 225–227
  selecting new, 242
  territories assigned to, 230–231
  training and support of, 232–233, 235
  turnover by, and yearly ROI of, 235–236
Divisionalization, product-market management versus, 340
DMI (Dunn's Market Identifiers), 98
DOD (Department of Defense), 62–63
*Drill Doctor's Book* (Ingersoll-Rand), 235
Dunn's Market Identifiers (DMI), 98

Economic analysis
  sales decisions based on, 206–209
  *see also specific elements of economic analysis*
Economic-based procurement, 41–42
Economic order quantity (EOQ), 37
Economics
  of competition, 80–81
  pricing and inadequate understanding of, 172–173
Economy, U.S., categories of, 99
EEO (Office of Equal Employment Opportunity), 57
Elasticity of demand, pricing and understanding, 173
Employees
  career opportunity for, 372, 373
  customer's, follow-on sales and training of, 192

implementation and need for qualified, 11–12
*see also* sales force; staffing; workforce
*Encyclopedia of Associations,* 124
End-users
  cost-benefit to, 75–79
  industrial market–consumer market differences in information needed by, 29–30
  market segmentation by, 88, 101–103
  sales focusing on, 217–218
Enforcement of pricing policy, 180–182
Engineering
  influence of, on procurement, 39
  reverse, 45–47, 192
  shifting orientation from, to marketing, 7–8
  *see also* product development
Engineering (technical) bids, 188
Engineering in the field (technical service), 223, 224
EOQ (economic order quantity), 37
Environmental Protection Agency (EPA), 57
Equal Employment Opportunity, Office of (EEO), 57
Equipment and machinery products, 96, 97
Errors
  in market segmentation, 93–96
  in product development, cost of, 159, 161
Escalators, fixed-priced bids with, 195
Estimation
  of market potential, 119–123. *See also* market studies
  *see also* projections, planning
Ethics of gathering competitive intelligence, 87
Evaluation
  of management approach to planning, 312–314. *See also* planning
  of market segments, 134–136
  of suppliers, 37, 57–59
  *see also* analysis; assessment of markets; performance evaluation; planning evaluation
Existing organizational structure, selecting alternative to, 331
Existing product lines, pruning, 152–155
Expenditures, *see* spending
Experience (learning) curve, 81, 174, 175
Expert opinion, seeking, in primary market studies, 126
Exporters, leading U.S., 24, 25

Facts
  as basis of successful planning, 288–296
  making plans credible, 304–305

Failures and deficiencies, 4–5
  commitment to action and facing up to, 9–10
Federal Communications Commission (FCC), 473, 489–490
First-line sales supervisors, 210–214
Fixed-price bids, 195
Fixed-priced bids with escalators, 195
Flow charts, analysis of, in planning, 290–292
Focus group interviews, 126
Follow the leader strategy, 163
Follow-on sales, 192–194
Follow-up sales, 201
  *see also* MRO market
Forecasting, 127, 128
  sales, 276–277, 305–308
  *see also* estimation; projections, planning
Foreign competition, 205
Formal planning, *see* planning
*Fortune* (magazine), 24, 25, 38, 71
Four-digit Standard Industrial Classification (SIC), 98, 100, 101, 103
Functional cooperation, commitment to action and, 7–8
Functional integration of plans, 313
Functional organization, 321, 322

General management, *see* management
Geographic considerations in market segmentation, 103, 104, 106
Goals, *see* objective(s)
Government-funded research, 167
Government procurement, 62–64, 229
Government spending, 20
Gross National Product (GNP), uselessness of, in estimating market potential, 121–122
Gross profit margin, planning and, 307
Group distributors, 242–243
Growth
  rate of, as consideration in planning, 289, 290
  targets for, pricing and, 178–179

Handbooks, problem-solving, 257, 259
*Harvard Business Review* (journal), 280
Historical data and patterns
  market potential estimation with, 119–122
  planning based on, 293

Implementation, 10–15, 362–374
  organization and staffing and, 368–371
  people development and, 371–374

planning and, 365–368
of product-market management, 341–352
Indirect costs, allocation of, 180
Industrial focus group interviews, 126
Industrial market–consumer market differences, 17–32
  in buying, 22–23
  in customer base, 21
  in end-user information, 29–30
  in importance of technology, 23
  in interdepartmental dependence, 24, 28
  in multinational markets, 23–24
  in multiplicity of markets and distribution channels, 29
  in nature of demand, 20–21
  in product management, 30
Industry, defined, 26
Inflation
  impact of, on pricing, 174, 176, 182
  planning and, 307
Information
  end-user, industrial market–consumer market differences in, 29–30
  needed in market studies, 124. See also market studies
  product-market management and changed system of, 357–360
  reliable, implementation and, 12–14
  see also facts; historical data and patterns
Initial pricing, follow-on versus, 192–194
Initial purchase cost to customer, 71
Innovation, see product development
Installation cost to customer, 71
Integration of plans, 313
Intelligence, gathering of competitive, 84–87
Interdepartmental dependence, industrial market–consumer market differences in, 24, 248
Internal sales analysis, 113–118
International markets, see multinational markets
Interviewers, qualities required of, 129–130
Interviews, 125–127
  focus group, 126
  mail and telephone, 127
Inventions, see product development
Investments, see return on investments
Issue identification, implementation and, 365

Joint ventures, as sources of new technology, 167

Justice, Department of, 93
Just-in-time (JIT; kanban) system, 41, 59

Kanban (just-in-time system), 41, 59

Labor costs, competition and reduction of, 80, 81
Large customers, competitive bidding and, 197–198
Learning (manufacturing experience) curve, 81, 174, 175
Licensing agreements, new technology obtained with, 167
Life cycle
  of technology, 154, 159, 160
  see also product life cycle
Long-term bids, 191–194
Long-term corporate strategy, marketing strategy as part of, 31
Long-term goals, commitment to action and, 8–9
Lost bids, analysis of, 191
Low-cost strategy, 163

Machinery and equipment products, 96, 97
Mail interviews in primary market studies, 127
Mail promotion, 254
Maintenance, repair, and overhaul market, see MRO market
Make-buy customers
  selling to, 54–55
  sourcing decisions by, 50–52
Management
  alternative organizational structure and philosophy of, 331–332
  distribution network, see distribution network management
  evaluating approach of, to planning, 312–314. See also planning
  marketing as responsibility of top, 5–6
  product development, 164–166
  purchasing, influence of, 37–38. See also procurement
  of R&D activities, 164–166. See also product development
  sales, marketing role for, 218–219
  sales compensation plan as tool of, 214–217
  shortcomings of, in pricing, 171–178
  solutions of, to pricing, 178–184
  see also product-market management; product-market managers; and specific aspects of management, for example: evaluation; implementation

Management by objectives (MBO), 369
Manufacturing
  competition and efficiency in, 81. *See also* competition
  effects of different approaches to, on cost, 177. *See also* cost
  shifting orientation from, to marketing, 7–8
  SIC subdivisions in, 99, 100
  *see also* original equipment manufacturers
Manufacturing experience (learning) curve, 174, 175
Market(s)
  defined, 94, 119
  planning and multiplicity of, 274. *See also* planning
  pricing and inadequate understanding of, 172–173. *See also* pricing
  and product development, 158. *See also* product development
  *see also* industrial market–consumer market differences; *and specific types of markets*
Market entry, success factors in, 81–87
Marketing
  defined, 5
  key dimensions of, 5–6
Marketing focus, sales focus versus, 30
Market managers
  differences between product managers and, 341
  *see also* product-market management; product-market managers
Market organization, 321–330
  international, 326–330
Market potential, 119–123
Market segmentation, 91–109
  by account size, 103, 104
  based on geographic considerations, 103, 104, 106
  combining levels of, 103–105
  by common buying factors, 102, 104
  by end-use application, 88, 101–103
  errors in, 93–96
  evaluation of, based on market assessment, 134–136
  as foundation of strategy, 92–93
  matching distributorship with, 229–230
  and number of segments, 104–105
  by OEMs, users, and aftermarkets, 96–98, 101, 103
  planning based on growth rate of segments, 290
  pricing and, 172. *See also* pricing
  and resegmentation, 107–108
  responsibility for, 108

by SIC codes, 98–101, 103
  summary of approaches to, 107
  validating, 105–107
Market share, pricing and overemphasis on, 174
Market studies, 123–131
  information needed for, 124
  for new product, 130–131
  primary, 125–130
  secondary, 124–125
Materials (products), 97
Materials requirement planning (MRP), 40–41
Matrix approach to international marketing organization, 328–330
MBO (management by objectives), 360
Media advertising, 254–259, 261–264
*Merck Manual*, 235
Mergers, new technology acquisition and, 167
*Metalworking Directory* (directory), 98
Monitoring techniques for intelligence gathering, 85
MRO (maintenance, repair, and overhaul) market (aftermarket)
  competitive bidding and, 191–194
  customer base in, 21
  distributors for, 223, 229–230
  estimating potential in, 122
  market segmentation by, 96–98, 101, 103
Multidivisional distributors, 242–243
Multinational markets
  industrial market–consumer market differences in, 23–24
  organization of, 326–330
  profit targets for, 179
Multiple sourcing, 55–56
Murphy's law, 312

Negotiations, bidding, 197–198
Net profitability statements, 180
New distributors, selecting, 242
New product
  cost of, 150–152, 159–164, 174
  market studies for, 130–131
  profit and, 143
  *see also* product development
New technology
  cost of, 159–161
  outside sources of, 166–167
  product development and, 145–149. *See also* product development

News clipping services as sources of competitive intelligence, 86
Noninterchangeable parts, follow-on sales and, 192

Objective(s)
  growth, 178–179
  long-term, and commitment to action, 8–9
  management by, 367
  planning and, 282. *See also* planning
  profit improvement as, 5, 6
Occupational and Safety Health Administration (OSHA), 57, 70
OEMs, *see* original equipment manufacturers
Open communication, implementation and, 371
Operating costs of customers, 72–73
Operation(s), customer's, need to understand, 68–70
Operational planning, strategic versus, 275–276
Opinion
  of experts in primary market studies, 126
  of sales force in primary market studies, 130
Organization, 316–336
  alternative, *see* alternative organization
  decentralized, competition and, 80
  implementation and, 368–371
  market, *see* market organization
  position of product managers in, 346–348
  when to change, 334–335
Orientation, *see* training and orientation
Original equipment manufacturers (OEMs), 29, 49, 62, 78
  competitive bidding by, 188, 198
  customer base of, 21
  distributorships for, 229, 231, 235
  as market potential, 122
  segmentation by, 96–98, 101, 103
*O-Ring Handbook* (Parker Hannifin Corporation), 235, 237
OSHA (Occupational and Safety Health Administration), 57, 70
Outside research, 166–167
Overhaul market, *see* MRO market
Overhead costs, allocation of, 180

Paperwork of first-line sales supervisors, 213–214
Parts
  distribution selling decision and stockable, 228
  follow-on sales and noninterchangeable, 192
Past bids, analysis of, 190–191, 201
Patent(s), follow-on sales and, 192

Patent dockets as source of competitive intelligence, 85
People development, *see* training and orientation
Performance, *see* performance evaluation; performance ratios; product performance
Performance evaluation
  of delivery system, 58–59
  of distributors, 238–241
  implementation and, 372–374
  of product-market managers, 351–352, 357
Performance ratios, plan evaluation and, 308–310
Personal characteristics, performance evaluation based on, 374
Personnel, *see* employees; sales force; staffing; workforce
PETS (price in effect at time of shipment), 196
Pioneer innovator strategy, 163
Planning (and plans), 270–298
  advertising, 261, 265–267
  alternatives in, 280–281, 287–288
  based on facts, 288–296
  competitive bid proposal as total plan, 196–197
  implementation and, 365–368
  importance of, 272–273
  matching context and concept of, 273–274
  materials requirement, 40–41
  overemphasis on, 279–280
  product development and, 155–156, 290
  product-market management and changes in, 357–360
  programs for, 296–297, 303
  providing direction for, 281–288
  of sales analysis, 118–119
  and selection of alternative organizational structure, 330–331
  strategic, *see* strategic planning
  types of, 274–279
Planning evaluation, 299–314
  of management approach toward plan, 312–314
  of plan credibility, 304–312
  structural considerations in, 301–304
Planning units, 282, 284
Policy statement on advertising and promotion, 265–266
Population trends, demand and, 20–21
Position, organizational, of product managers, 346–348
Position description of product managers, 343–345
Practical approach to planning, 284–285

Premium pricing, 177
Pressure point (rate of change) curves, 115–120
Price in effect at time of shipment (PETS), 196
Pricing, 88–89, 169–185
  and competitive bidding, 195–196, 198–199
  initial, follow-on versus, 192–194
  management deficiencies in, 171–178
  management solutions to, 178–184
  and price as buying factor, 102
  profit and, 173, 177–180
  relationship between distributor turnover and price, 236
  value analysis of prices, 43, 45
Primary (target) market organization, 321
Primary market studies, 125–130
Principles of organization and selection of alternative organizational structure, 332–334
Priorities, implementation and determining, 366–367
Problem-solving handbooks, promotion with, 257, 259
Procurement, 33–64
  economic-based, 41–42
  effects of, on sales, 205
  government, 62–64, 229
  influences on, 36–40
  maintaining relationship with suppliers and, 59–60
  materials requirement planning and, 40–41
  sourcing decisions and, 50–59
  standards and specifications and, 47–50
  value analysis in, 42–47
Producer-distributor relationship, 225–227
Producer-to-supporter ratio in planning evaluation, 309–310
Product(s)
  quality of, see quality of product
  sales affected by complexity of, 205
  understanding customer's, 68–70
  see also new product; and specific types of products
Product design, 6
  customers and, 88
  effects of, on cost, 177
Product development, 140–168
  and ability to compete, 88, 182
  cost of, 150–152, 159–164, 174
  customers and, 88
  defining product-market focus for, 150
  following disciplined process in, 156–158
  management of, 164–166

  matching current profits to spending for, 159–164
  outside research and, 166–167
  planning and, 155–156, 290
  product life cycle and, 142–149, 154
  product performance and, 150–152
  pruning of existing product lines and, 152–155
  value analysis as guide to, 45
Production capacity
  competitive bidding and, 201
  demand measured against, 173
Productivity, competition and, 80
Productivity ratio in planning evaluation, 308–309
Product life cycle
  analysis of, in planning, 292
  cost of, to customer, 74–76
  product development and, 142–149, 154
Product line
  determining cost of, and profit from, 179–180
  pruning existing, 152–155
Product management, industrial market–consumer market differences in, 30
Product-market focus, defining, for product development, 150
Product-market management, 341–352
  applicability of, 339–341
  implementation of, 341–352
  workings of, 340
Product-market managers, 342–360
  and need for both product and market managers, 352–360
  performance measures for, 351–352
  qualifications needed by, 348–349
  responsibilities of, 342–346
  training and orientation of, 349–351
Product-market strategy, corporate versus, 277–279
Product organization, 321–326
Product performance
  as buying factor, 102
  product development and, 151–152
Profit
  competitive bidding and, 192–193, 201
  effects of inflation on, 174, 176
  estimation of, in selection of market segment, 134, 136
  from existing product lines, 155
  improving, as goal, 5, 6
  internal analysis of, 113–119
  matching current, with spending in product development, 159–164

new product contributions to, 143
paid distributors, 224
planning and projections of, 304–308
pricing and, 173, 177–180
in soft market conditions, 184
statement of loss and, product-market managers'
performance evaluation with, 357
structure of, 295
volume and, 174, 176, 183, 184, 308
see also return on investments
Projections, planning, 304–308
summary of, 304
Project proposal for market assessment, 131–134
Promotion, see advertising and promotion
Promotional mix, 253–256
Proposals
bid, 196–197
project, for market assessment, 131–134
Proprietary products, follow-on sales and, 192
Public relations publicity, 254
Public sector, see entries beginning with term: government
Purchase cost, initial, 71
Purchasing managers
influence of, 37–38
see also procurement

Qualifications
and concept implementation with qualified personnel, 11–12
of interviewers, 129–130
of product-market managers, 348–349
Quality assurance programs, ability to compete and, 182
Quality of product
as buying factor, 102
as factor in planning, 290
Questionnaires, primary market studies using, 127, 129

Rate of change (pressure point) curves, 115–120
R&D (research and development), see product development
Real costs to customers, 75, 77
Repair market, see MRO market
Replacement aftermarket, see MRO market
Request for a quote (RFQ), 189
Research and development (R&D), see product development

Resegmentation, 107–108
Result producer-to-supporter ratio in planning evaluation, 309–310
Return on investments (ROI)
competitive bidding and, 192, 193
distribution and yearly, 235–236
inflation and, 176
internal analysis of, 115
see also profit
Reverse engineering, 45–47, 192
Review of advertising and promotion, 267
RFQ (request for a quote), 189
Risk
in competitive bidding, 188
in product development, 156–158
Risk-reward ratio in planning evaluation, 310–311
ROI, see return on investments

SAC (Strategic Air Command), 63
Sales, 203–220
customer classification by annual, 94, 95
end-user focus and, 217–218
follow-on, 192–194
follow-up, 201. See also MRO market
forecasting, 276–277, 305–308
internal analysis of, 113–119
key decision of, based on economic analysis, 206–209
to make-buy customers, 54–55
and selling costs, 206
steps for successful, 209–210
volume of, see volume
see also customer(s); distribution network management; distributors
Sales calls, direct, 255–256
Sales compensation plan as management tool, 214–217
Sales focus, marketing focus versus, 30
Sales force
compensation plan for, 214–217
first-line supervision of, 210–214
gathering of competitive intelligence by, 85
opinions of, in primary market studies, 130
pricing policy and, 178, 179
training of, 89
see also employees; staffing; workforce
Sales management, marketing role for, 218–219
Sales supervisors, first-line, 210–214
Sample selection for primary market studies, 125

Secondary market studies (desk research), 124–125

Segmentation, *see* market segmentation

Selling, *see* sales

Seminars, promotion with, 254

Seniority, compensation based on, 216

Service
  as buying factor, 102
  rapid, distribution and, 227
  technical, 223, 224
  *see also* MRO market

Short-term bids, 191–194

SIC (Standard Industrial Classification) codes, 98–101, 103

Sister divisions as sources of competitive intelligence, 85–86

Soft market conditions, 182–184

Sole sourcing, 55–56

Sourcing decisions, 50–59

*Special Report on Buying and Selling Techniques Used in the British Engineering Industry* (McGraw-Hill), 251

Specifications, *see* standards and specifications

Spending
  on advertising, 248–251, 261, 265
  consumer, public and private, 20
  product development, 159–164

Staffing
  implementation and, 368–371
  *see also* employees; sales force; workforce

Stages of product development, 156–157

Standard Industrial Classification (SIC) codes, 98–101, 103

Standards and specifications
  aftermarket and, 192, 201
  procurement and, 47–50

Start-up costs, 71

Stockable parts, distribution selling decision and, 228

Strategic Air Command (SAC), 63

Strategic planning
  concept implementation and, 13, 15
  operational versus, 275–276

Strategy
  corporate versus product-market, 277–279
  implications of understanding competition and customers for, 87–89
  market segmentation as foundation of, 92–93. *See also* market segmentation
  pricing, 88–89, 177

product development, 163
statement of, preceding plans, 302–303. *See also* planning

Structural considerations in plan evaluation, 301–304

Subassemblies, *see* component products

Subsidiaries as sources of competitive intelligence, 85–86

Supervision, first-line sales, 210–214

Suppliers
  evaluation of, 37, 57–59
  maintaining relationship with, 59–60
  as source of competitive intelligence, 85
  *see also* procurement

Supply contract obligations, 199–200

Support of distributors, 232–233, 235

*Survey of Industrial Purchasing Power,* 98

Surveys, primary market studies with, 125–126

Switching costs to customers, 72, 74

Target market (primary) organization, 321

Team membership, implementation and development of, 371–372

Technical (engineering) bids, 188

Technical considerations in product development, 158

Technical service (engineering in the field), 223, 224

Technology Assessment, Office of, 160

Technology
  industrial market–consumer market differences in importance of, 23
  life cycle of, 154, 159, 160
  planning and changes in, 289
  *see also* new technology; product development

Telephone interviews in primary market studies, 127

Territory assignment to distributors, 230–231

*Thomas's Register of American Manufacturers,* 98, 124

Top management, *see* management

Total selling costs, 206

Trade associations
  and secondary market studies, 124
  using, in estimation of market potential, 123, 124

Trade shows
  promotion with, 254, 257
  as sources of competitive intelligence, 86

Training and orientation
  of customer's employees, follow-on sales and, 192
  of distributors, 232–233, 235
  of first-line sales supervisors, 212–213

implementation and, 371–374
of product-market managers, 349–351
role of, in advertising, 254
of sales force, 89
Turnover by distributors, 235–236

United Nations (UN), 47
United States Air Force, 63
United States Coast Guard, 229
United States economy, categories of, 99
United States exporters, leading, 24, 25
University research, 166–167
Users
  segmentation by, 96–98, 101, 103
  *see also* end-users

Validation of market segments, 105–107
Value analysis, 37
  in procurement, 42–47

Volume
  as factor in distribution selling decision, 228
  pricing and, 174, 177
  pricing and, in soft market conditions, 182–184
  profit and, 174, 176, 184, 308

*Wall Street Journal* (newspaper), 247, 261
*Wall Street Transcript* (newspaper), 86
Waste in advertising and promotion, 247–252
Wired bids, 192, 201
Workforce
  size of, as conversion factor for market potential
    estimation, 123
  *see also* employees; sales force; staffing
Writing of specifications, 48–50

Yearly return on investments (ROI), distribution and,
  235–236

# About the Authors

*B. Charles Ames* joined Acme-Cleveland Corporation as President and Chief Executive Officer in 1981 and was named Chairman in 1983. Before joining Acme-Cleveland, Mr. Ames served as President and Chief Executive Officer of Reliance Electric Company during that company's most dynamic period of profit growth. His other prior positions include Director and Managing Director, Cleveland office, McKinsey and Company, Inc., an international management consulting firm, and Director of Marketing for General Telephone & Electronics Corp.

Mr. Ames received his M.B.A. from the Harvard Graduate School of Business Administration. While at McKinsey, Mr. Ames served as the firm's practice leader in industrial marketing and developed a special interest in product-market and corporate growth strategies. He has spoken and written extensively and has authored five articles for *The Harvard Business Review.* Two of his articles were included as chapters in *The Art of Top Management* and *A Handbook of Modern Marketing,* both published by McGraw-Hill. One of his articles is included in *Harvard Business Review on Management,* a book by Harper & Row containing a selection of the best articles published in the *Review* over the past 25 years. He serves on the Board of Directors of Diamond Shamrock Corp., Hanna Mining Company, Warner-Lambert Company, and The Progressive Corporation.

*James D. Hlavacek* is a Professor of Business Administration in the Weatherhead School of Management at Case Western Reserve University in Cleveland, Ohio, where he also serves as head of the Marketing Division. Before coming to Case Western, Professor Hlavacek was a faculty member at Rutgers University Graduate School of Business. He received a Ph.D. in business from the University of Illinois. Dr. Hlavacek's interests have resulted in many articles, which have appeared in such publications as *The Harvard Business Review, Journal of Marketing, California Management Review, The Academy of Management Journal,* and the *Journal of Marketing Research,* and he has authored the book, *Joint Ventures for Product Innovation.*

Professor Hlavacek is Vice President and Director of the American Marketing Association, a previous Director of the European Association for Industrial Marketing, and serves as Editor-in-Chief of the quarterly *Journal of Industrial Marketing Management.* He also teaches in university executive development programs and in many in-house corporate programs. Dr. Hlavacek has developed product-market executive development training programs for many well-known technical based manufacturing businesses in the United States, Canada, and Europe. He is a principal in Industry Marketing, Inc., a firm specializing in developing and leading in-house marketing management executive programs for technical manufacturing corporations.